ACCA

PAPER P1

GOVERNANCE, RISK AND ETHICS

P
R
A
C
T
I
C
E

&

R
E
V
I
S
I
O
N

K
I
T

> BPP Learning Media is an **ACCA Approved Content Provider** for the ACCA qualification. This means we work closely with ACCA to ensure our products fully prepare you for your ACCA exams.
>
> In this Practice and Revision Kit, which has been reviewed by the ACCA examination team, we:
>
> - Discuss the **best strategies** for revising and taking your ACCA exams
> - Ensure you are well **prepared** for your exam
> - Provide you with **lots of great guidance** on tackling questions
> - Provide you with **three** mock exams
> - Provide the **ACCA exam answers** as well as our own for selected questions
>
> Our **Passcards** also support this paper.

FOR EXAMS IN SEPTEMBER 2017, DECEMBER 2017, MARCH 2018
AND JUNE 2018

BPP
LEARNING MEDIA

First edition 2007
Eleventh edition February 2017

ISBN 9781 5097 0861 1

(previous ISBN 9781 4727 4442 5)

e-ISBN 9781 5097 0999 1

British Library Cataloguing-in-Publication Data
A catalogue record for this book
is available from the British Library

Published by

BPP Learning Media Ltd
BPP House, Aldine Place
London W12 8AA

www.bpp.com/learningmedia

Printed in the United Kingdom

Your learning materials, published by BPP Learning Media Ltd, are
printed on paper obtained from traceable, sustainable sources.

Contents

Question index

The headings in this checklist/index indicate the main topics of questions, but questions are expected to cover several different topics.

Mock exam 1

Mock exam 2

Mock exam 3 (September/December 2016 Exam)

Topic index

Listed below are the key Paper P1 syllabus topics and the numbers of the questions in this Kit covering those topics.

If you need to concentrate your practice and revision on certain topics or if you want to attempt all available questions that refer to a particular subject, you will find this index useful.

Syllabus topic	Question numbers
Risk correlation	20(c), 61(a)
Risk culture	20(d), 25, Mock 2 Q4
Risk management	10(b), 46, 58(c), 60(b), 62, 65, Mock 1 Q3, Mock 1 Q4
Risk manager	19(a)
Risk monitoring	Mock 1 Q4, Mock 3 Q3
Risk perception	58(c)
Rules-based approaches	4(a), 9(a), 12(b), 13, 26(a)
Sarbanes-Oxley	4(a), 44
Social issues	55(d), 60(a)
Social responsibility	14, 39, 46, 52(c), 65, Mock 1 Q1, Mock 2 Q4(d)
Stakeholders	41, 51-53, 55(a), 59(d), 64, 66, Mock 1 Q1(a)
Strategic risks	31, 37(c), 52(b), 60(d), Mock 2 Q1(c)
Sustainability	37(a), 51(d), 62, Mock 1 Q1(c)
Technological risk	46
Teleological approach	33(c), 48, 61(d), Mock 2 Q3(c)
Trade unions	55(b)
Transparency	8(b), 52(c), 61(d)
Tucker's 5 question model	41(a), 52(a)
Whistleblowing	44

Helping you with your revision

BPP Learning Media – Approved Content Provider

As an ACCA **Approved Content Provider**, BPP Learning Media gives you the **opportunity** to use revision materials reviewed by the ACCA examination team. By incorporating the examination team's comments and suggestions regarding the depth and breadth of syllabus coverage, the BPP Learning Media Practice & Revision Kit provides excellent, **ACCA-approved** support for your revision.

Tackling revision and the exam

Using feedback obtained from the ACCA examination team review:

- We look at the dos and don'ts of revising for, and taking, ACCA exams

- We focus on Paper P1; we discuss revising the syllabus, what to do (and what not to do) in the exam, how to approach different types of question and ways of obtaining easy marks

Selecting questions

We provide signposts to help you plan your revision:

- A full **question index**

- A **topic index** listing all the questions that cover key topics, so that you can locate the questions that provide practice on these topics, and see the different ways in which they might be examined

Making the most of question practice

At BPP Learning Media we realise that you need more than just questions and model answers to get the most from your question practice.

- Our **Top tips** included for certain questions provide essential advice on tackling questions, presenting answers and the key points that answers need to include.

- We show you how you can pick up **Easy marks** on some questions, as we know that picking up all readily available marks often can make the difference between passing and failing.

- We include **marking guides** to show you what the examiner rewards.

- We include **comments from the examiners** to show you where students struggled or performed well in the actual exam.

- We refer to the **BPP Study Text** for exams in September 2017, December 2017, March 2018 and June 2018 for detailed coverage of the topics covered in questions.

Attempting mock exams

There are three mock exams that provide practice at coping with the pressures of the exam day. We strongly recommend that you attempt them under exam conditions. **Mock exams 1 and 2** reflect the question styles and syllabus coverage of the exam; **Mock exam 3** is the ACCA September/December 2016 exam paper.

This exam is compiled from questions selected by the examination team from the September 2016 and December 2016 exams. They do not reflect the entire September or December exams but contain questions most appropriate for students to practise.

Revising P1

Firstly we must emphasise that you will need a good knowledge of the whole syllabus. Any part of the syllabus could be tested within compulsory Question 1. Having to choose two out of three optional questions does not really represent much choice if there are areas of the syllabus you are keen to avoid. Although (like all syllabuses) this syllabus may have seemed a lot when you were studying, we actually believe that it is not as large as some of the syllabuses you have previously studied.

That said, there are certain topics that are stressed in the syllabus and by the examination team, and therefore are core:

- Concepts underpinning corporate governance, in particular integrity, accountability and transparency
- Stakeholders in organisations and in decisions
- The agency problem
- Features of, and arguments for and against, principles vs rules based approaches
- Sarbanes-Oxley
- Corporate governance best practice in relation to the board, board committees, remuneration and reporting
- Elements of control environment
- The main control procedures
- Risk assessment framework
- The main strategies for dealing with risks
- The key ethical positions
- Kohlberg's framework
- Methods of ethical decision-making
- Gray, Owen, Adams seven positions on corporate social responsibility
- Meaning of sustainability

Your knowledge of other topic areas needs to demonstrate breadth. You need to have a good idea of:

- The different types of risks (not just financial) that it can face
- The elements of control and risk management systems
- The impact of culture
- The main elements of corporate and professional codes
- The main areas discussed in corporate social responsibility debates

Reading articles

The examination team has stressed the importance of reading the technical articles published in *Student Accountant* that relate to P1. Articles relating to P1 are available on ACCA's website. Some of the articles are written by the examination team and all are reviewed by him.

It's also useful to keep reading the business pages during your revision period and not just narrowly focus on the syllabus. Remember that the examination team has stressed that this paper is about how organisations respond to real-world issues, so the more you read, the more practical examples you will have of how organisations have tackled real-life situations.

Question practice

You should use the Passcards and any brief notes you have to revise these topics, but you mustn't spend all your revision time passively reading. **Question practice is vital**; doing as many questions as you can in full will help develop your ability to analyse scenarios and produce relevant discussion and recommendations.

Make sure you leave enough time in your revision schedule to practise the longer Section A questions, as such questions are compulsory in the exam. The scenarios and requirements of Section A questions are more complex and will integrate several parts of the syllabus, therefore practice is essential. Also ensure that you attempt all three mock exams under exam conditions.

Passing the P1 exam

Displaying the right qualities

The examination team will expect you to display the following qualities.

Qualities required	
Fulfilling the higher level question requirements	This means that when you are asked to show higher level skills such as **assessment or evaluation**, you will only score well if you demonstrate them. Merely describing something when you are asked to evaluate it will not earn you the marks you need.
Identifying the most important features of the organisation and its environment	You must use your **technical knowledge and business awareness** to identify the key features of the scenario.
Sorting the information in the scenario	You will get a lot of information, particularly in the Section A scenario, and will be expected to **evaluate how useful** it is and **use it** to support answers such as comparisons and discussions. Over 50% of marks in most questions are likely to be available for direct application of knowledge to the scenario.
Selecting relevant real-life examples	You may gain credit for using **good examples**, providing you use the examples to illustrate your understanding of the points in the scenario.
Using the governance and ethical frameworks	Remember that the examination team has emphasised the importance of accountants showing awareness of their responsibilities. You may be expected to **apply the frameworks** to determine what the problem is (for example which stakeholders should be considered) and to identify appropriate solutions.
Criticising the approaches you use	You may be expected not only to **apply** guidance such as **corporate governance codes** or **principles-based ethical guidance**, but also criticise the approaches you use.
Arguing well	You may be expected to discuss both sides of a case, or present an argument in favour or against something. You will gain marks for the **quality** and **logical flow of your arguments**.
Making reasonable recommendations	The measures you recommend must be **appropriate** for the organisation; you may need to discuss their strengths and weaknesses, as there may be costs of adopting them. The recommendations should clearly state what has to be done.

Avoiding weaknesses

Our experience of, and examination team feedback from, other higher level exams enables us to predict a number of weaknesses that are likely to occur in many students' answers. You will enhance your chances significantly if you ensure you avoid these mistakes:

- **Failing to provide what the question verbs require** (discussion, evaluation, recommendation) or to write about the topics specified in the question requirements

- **Repeating the same material** in different parts of answers

- **Stating theories and concepts** rather than applying them

- **Quoting chunks of detail** from the question that don't add any value

- **Forcing irrelevancies into answers**, for example irrelevant definitions or theories, or examples that don't relate to the scenario

- **Giving long lists or writing down all that's known** about a broad subject area, and not caring whether it's relevant or not

- **Focusing too narrowly on one area** – for example only covering financial risks when other risks are also important

- **Letting your personal views prevent you from answering the question** – the question may require you to construct an argument with which you personally don't agree

- **Unrealistic or impractical recommendations**

- **Vague recommendations** – instead of just saying improve risk management procedures, you should discuss precisely **how** you would improve them

- **Failing to answer sufficient questions**, or all parts of a question, because of poor time management

Choosing which questions to answer first

We recommend that you spend time at the beginning of your exam carefully reading through all of the questions in the paper, and each of their requirements. Once you feel familiar with your exam paper, we then recommend that you attempt the compulsory Section A question first, ensuring that you spend adequate time reading and planning before you begin to write up your answer. Comments from examination teams of other syllabuses that have similar exam formats suggest that students appear less time-pressured if they do the big compulsory questions first.

During the second half of the exam, you can put Section A aside and concentrate on the two Section B questions you've chosen.

However our recommendations are not inflexible. If you really think the Section A question looks a lot harder than the Section B questions you've chosen, then do those first, but **DON'T run over time on them**. You must leave yourself at least 1 hour and 37 minutes to tackle the Section A question. When you come back to it, once you have had time to reflect, you should be able to generate more ideas and find the question is not as bad as it looks.

Remember also that small overruns of time during the first half of the exam can add up to leave you very short of time towards the end.

Tackling questions

Scenario questions

You'll improve your chances by following a step-by-step approach to Section A scenarios along the following lines.

Step 1   **Read the background**

Usually the first couple of paragraphs will give some background on the company and what it is aiming to achieve. By reading this carefully you will be better equipped to relate your answers to the company as much as possible.

Step 2   **Read the requirements**

There is no point reading the detailed information in the question until you know what it is going to be used for. Don't panic if some of the requirements look challenging – identify the elements you are able to do and look for links between requirements, as well as possible indications of the syllabus areas the question is covering.

Step 3   **Identify the action verbs**

These convey the level of skill you need to exhibit and also the structure your answer should have. A lower level verb such as define will require a more descriptive answer; a higher level verb such as evaluate will require a more applied, critical answer. It should be stressed that **higher level requirements and verbs** are likely to be most significant in this paper.

Action verbs that are likely to be frequently used in this exam are listed below, together with their intellectual levels and guidance on their meaning.

Intellectual level		
1	Define	Give the meaning of
1	Explain	Make clear
1	Identify	Recognise or select
1	Describe	Give the key features
2	Distinguish	Define two different terms, viewpoints or concepts on the basis of the differences between them
2	Compare and contrast	Explain the similarities and differences between two different terms, viewpoints or concepts
2	Contrast	Explain the differences between two different terms, viewpoints or concepts
2	Analyse	Give reasons for the current situation or what has happened
3	Assess	Determine the strengths/weaknesses/ importance/ significance/ability to contribute
3	Examine	Critically review in detail
3	Discuss	Examine by using arguments for and against
3	Explore	Examine or discuss in a wide-ranging manner
3	Criticise	Present the weaknesses of/problems with the actions taken or viewpoint expressed, supported by evidence
3	Evaluate/critically evaluate	Determine the value of in the light of the arguments for and against (critically evaluate means weighting the answer towards criticisms/arguments against).
3	Construct the case	Present the arguments in favour or against, supported by evidence
3	Recommend	Advise the appropriate actions to pursue in terms the recipient will understand

Also make sure you identify all the action verbs; some question parts may have more than one.

Step 4   **Identify what each part of the question requires**

Think about what frameworks or theories you could choose if the question doesn't specify which one to use.

When planning, you will need to make sure that you aren't reproducing the same material in more than one part of the question.

Also you're likely to come across part questions with two requirements that may be at different levels; a part question may for example ask you to explain X and discuss Y. You must ensure that you

fulfill both requirements and that your discussion of Y shows greater depth than your explanation of X (for example by identifying problems with Y or putting the case for and against Y).

Step 5   **Check the mark allocation to each part**

This shows you the depth anticipated and helps allocate time.

Step 6   **Read the whole scenario through, highlighting key data**

Put points under headings related to requirements (eg by noting in the margin to what part of the question the scenario detail relates).

Step 7   **Consider the consequences of the points you've identified**

Remember that you will often have to provide recommendations based on the information you've been given. Consider that you may have to criticise the code, framework or model that you've been told to use. You may also have to bring in wider issues or viewpoints, for example the views of different stakeholders.

Step 8   **Write a brief plan**

Your plans should be produced within your answer book.

Make sure you identify all the requirements of the question in your plan – each requirement may have sub-requirements that must also be addressed. If there are professional marks available, highlight in your plan where these may be gained (such as preparing a report).

Step 9   **Write the answer**

Make every effort to present your answer clearly. The pilot paper and exam papers so far indicate that the examination team will be looking for you to make a number of clear points. The best way to demonstrate what you're doing is to put points into separate paragraphs with clear headers.

Discussion questions

Remember that **depth of discussion** will be important. Discussions will often consist of paragraphs containing two to three sentences. Each paragraph should:

- **Make a point**
- **Explain the point** (you must demonstrate why the point is important)
- **Illustrate the point** (with material or analysis from the scenario, perhaps an example from real-life)

In this exam a number of requirement verbs will expect you to express a viewpoint or opinion, for example construct an argument, criticise, evaluate. When expressing an opinion, you need to provide:

- **What the question wants**. For instance, if you are asked to criticise something, don't spend time discussing its advantages. In addition if a scenario provides a lot of information about a situation, and you are (say) asked to assess that situation in the light of good practice, your assessment is unlikely to be favourable.

- **Evidence** from theory or the scenario – again we stress that the majority of marks in most questions will be given for applying your knowledge to the scenario.

Gaining the easy marks

Knowledge of the core topics that we list under topics to revise should present you with some easy marks. The pilot paper suggests that there will be some marks available on certain part questions for definitions, explanations or descriptions that don't have to be related to the scenario. However don't assume that you can ignore all the scenarios and still pass!

As P1 is a Professional level paper, 4 or 5 **professional level marks** will be awarded in the compulsory question. Some of these should be easy to obtain. The examination team has stated that some marks may be available for presenting your answer in the form of formal business letters, briefing notes, memos, presentations, press releases, narratives in an annual report and so on. You may also be able to obtain marks for the format, layout, logical flow and persuasiveness of your answer.

What you write should always sound professional, and you will be awarded marks for good introductions and conclusions. You must use the format the question requires. You must also lay your answer out so that somebody could actually read it and use it. A good way to end all documents is to invite further communication.

How you make the document persuasive will depend on who you are and who the recipients are. If you are writing to shareholders you should consider how much information you need to provide. If you are trying to convince the reader that a decision is right, you should focus on the benefits. If you are apologising for something that has gone wrong, you need to reassure the reader and ensure they are happy with the information you provide.

Reports

A report should have the following formal elements at the top:

- Title
- Report writer
- Report recipient
- Date

It should include:

- An introduction summarising its scope, terms of reference and the information used
- Findings/points made, in sections with headings. The points should be specific and factual
- Recommendations/conclusions at the end

It should be written in the first person (I).

Memorandum

A memorandum should have the same formal elements at the top as a report. Its recipient should be referred to as you. A memo should finish with a conclusion or recommendation – you should not end it with yours faithfully.

Letter

A letter should include:

- The address of the sender
- The date it is written
- If to a single recipient, the recipient's name and address at the top.

It should have:

- An introductory paragraph, setting out the reasons why the letter is written

- A clear and logical flow of content

- A personal element, using the first person (I, our company) and referring to the recipients and their interests

- A concluding paragraph, re-emphasising the purpose of the letter and, if appropriate, inviting further action by the recipient(s) (eg please get in touch if you would like further information)

If it is a business letter, addressed formally (Dear Sir), it should be signed Yours faithfully. If the addressee is named, it should be signed Yours sincerely.

Speech or statement at meeting

A speech should:

- Be easy to read out. If you answer any questions requiring speeches **during your revision** you should read your answer to yourself to see whether you say it easily. (Do **NOT** however, read your answer aloud in the actual exam!)

- Begin with a formal introduction, for example Welcome Ladies and Gentlemen
- Provide an overview of what will be covered
- Connect each section with narrative designed to make the speech sound convincing, logical and persuasive
- **Not** contain bullet points (how would you deliver them)
- End with an invitation to respond: 'Thank you for listening. I now open the floor to questions'.

Briefing notes

These may be required for use at a board meeting or to inform external stakeholders such as institutional shareholders. They should:

- Start with the key points, with background information later on or in appendices
- Be written in the third person, referring to the directors or the company

Press or website statement

The statement should have:

- A first paragraph that emphasises the key points
- Background information later in the statement or in appendices
- A third person narrator

Management narratives in annual report

The narrative should have:

- A first paragraph that clearly introduces the purpose of the statement
- A narrative that clearly supports this purpose
- A clear structure, with separate points being distinguished
- A third person narrator

Article in newspaper or magazine

The article should be clearly focussed on the issues to be discussed and designed to attract the reader's attention by the use of paragraph 'headlines'. The article must be tailored to the readership of the publication, explaining (or maybe better not using) terms they are unlikely to know. Generally articles should have short sentences and avoid the use of the passive. The article may not necessarily be unbiased. The question requirements may ask you to use the article to promote an argument or viewpoint, and the article would then have to be slanted in that direction.

Exam information

Format of the exam

		Number of marks
Section A:	1 compulsory case study	50
Section B:	Choice of 2 from 3 questions (25 marks each)	50
		100

Time allowed: 3 hours and 15 minutes. The pass mark is 50%.

Section A will be a compulsory case study question with typically four or five sub-requirements relating to the same scenario information. The question will usually assess and link a range of subject areas across the syllabus. It will require students to demonstrate high-level capabilities to understand the complexities of the case and evaluate, relate and apply the information in the case study to the requirements.

The examination team has stressed the importance of reading the case in detail, taking notes as appropriate and getting a feel for what the issues are. Scenarios may be drawn from any situation involving aspects of governance; this is likely to be, but need not be, in an organisational setting.

Professional marks will be available in Section A for presentation, logical flow of argument and quality of argument.

Section B questions are more likely to assess a range of discrete subject areas from the main syllabus section headings; they may require evaluation and synthesis of information contained within short scenarios and application of this information to the question requirements.

Although one subject area is likely to be emphasised in each Section B question, students should not assume that questions will be solely about content from that area. Each question will be based on a shorter case scenario to contextualise the question.

The paper will have a global focus.

Analysis of past papers

The table below provides details of when each element of the syllabus has been examined in the ten most recent sittings and the question number and section in which each element was examined.

Since September 2016, ACCA have been issuing two 'hybrid' exams each year, after the December and June exam sessions. These exams are compiled from questions selected from the two preceding sessions eg in December 2016, the hybrid exam questions were compiled from September 2016 and December 2016 exams.

Covered in Text chapter		Sep/Dec 16	Mar/Jun 16	Sept/Dec 2015	J15	D14	J14	D13	J13	D12	J12
	GOVERNANCE AND RESPONSIBILITY										
1	Scope of governance		1d	1a	2c	1a	1a 1c		1d	2a, c 4b, c	1d, 2a
1	Agency		1a, 2b	1a	2a	1d		2b	3b		1d
3	Board of directors	1a	3a		1b, 1d	2b 3a 3b 4c		3b, 4a	4c		3c, 4b, c
3, 5, 8	Board committees			3a	3a, 3b, 3c			3a	2b		2b
3	Directors' remuneration	1b		1b				1c	4b,c		
2	Different approaches to governance				1a	2b 2c		2a, c	4a	2b	4a
2, 11	Corporate social responsibility				1c, 2a	2b		3c			
3	Reporting and disclosure						2c 4c				
2	Public sector governance		1d				2a 2b				
	INTERNAL CONTROL AND REVIEW										
4, 5, 7, 8	Management control systems						4b		1c	1d	1c
4, 7, 8, 10	Internal control, audit and compliance	1c		1d			4a	1d	2a	3a, b	
7, 8	Internal control and reporting	2a		1d				2b	2c		
8	Management information	2b								3c	
	IDENTIFYING AND ASSESSING RISK										
5, 7	Risk and the risk management process		4a	3a	1d		2a				1a
6	Risk categories	3a			1c	1c	2b		3c	1d	
5, 7, 8	Risk identification, measurement and assessment	3b					1d	4b	1a, 3a		
	CONTROLLING AND MANAGING RISK										
5, 8	Risk targeting and monitoring			3b, 3c							2b, c
5, 7, 8	Risk reduction and control					4c		1b	3c	1b	2c
5, 7	Risk, avoidance, retention and modelling							1b			
	PROFESSIONAL VALUES, ETHICS AND SOCIAL RESPONSIBILTY										
9	Ethical theories	2c	3b	4a, 4b	4a		4a		1d	4a	1b
9, 11	Different approaches to ethics and social responsibility	4c		2b	2b	1d	4b				

Covered in Text chapter		Sep/ Dec 16	Mar/ Jun 16	Sept/ Dec 2015	J15	D14	J14	D13	J13	D12	J12
10	Professions and the public interest		1b, 1c				3c				
10	Professional practice and codes of ethics	4b	3c	1c			1b	4c			3b
10	Conflicts of interest and consequences of unethical behaviour	1d, 4a	2a	4b		1b, 3c	3a			1c	3a
9, 10	Ethical characteristics of professionalism		2c					4c			
11	Integrated reporting and sustainability	1c, 3c	4b, 4c	2b, 2c	4b	1d	3b	1a	1b	1a	

IMPORTANT!

The table above gives a broad idea of how frequently major topics in the syllabus are examined. It should not be used to question spot and predict for example that Topic X will not be examined because it came up two sittings ago. The examiner's reports indicate that the examiner is well aware some students try to question spot. Examiners avoid predictable patterns and may, for example, examine the same topic two sittings in a row.

BPP LEARNING MEDIA

Useful websites

The websites below provide additional sources of information of relevance to your studies for *Governance, Risk and Ethics*.

- www.accaglobal.com

  ACCA's website. The students' section of the website is invaluable for detailed information about the qualification, past issues of *Student Accountant* (including technical articles) and a free downloadable Student Planner App.

- www.bpp.com

  Our website provides information about BPP products and services, with a link to ACCA's website.

- www.ft.com

  This website provides information about current international business. You can search for information and articles on specific industry groups as well as individual companies.

- www.economist.com

  Here you can search for business information on a week-by-week basis, search articles by business subject and use the resources of the Economist Intelligence Unit to research sectors, companies or countries.

- www.investmentweek.co.uk

  This site carries business news and articles on markets from *Investment Week* and *International Investment*.

- www.pwc.com

  The PricewaterhouseCoopers website includes UK Economic Outlook.

- www.cfo.com

  Good website for financial officers.

- www.bankofengland.co.uk

  This website is useful for sourcing Bank of England publications.

Questions

GOVERNANCE AND RESPONSIBILITY

Questions 1 to 18 cover governance and responsibility, the subject of Part A of the BPP Study Text for Paper P1.

1 Sentosa House (Examiner question)   49 mins

Sonia Tan, a fund manager at institutional investor Sentosa House, was reviewing the annual report of one of the major companies in her portfolio. The company, Eastern Products, had recently undergone a number of board changes as a result of a lack of confidence in its management from its major institutional investors of which Sentosa House was one. The problems started two years ago when a new chairman at Eastern Products (Thomas Hoo) started to pursue what the institutional investors regarded as very risky strategies whilst at the same time failing to comply with a stock market requirement on the number of non-executive directors on the board.

Sonia rang Eastern's investor relations department to ask why it still was not in compliance with the requirements relating to non-executive directors. She was told that because Eastern was listed in a principles-based jurisdiction, the requirement was not compulsory. It was simply that Eastern chose not to comply with that particular requirement. When Sonia asked how its board committees could be made up with an insufficient number of non-executive directors, the investor relations manager said he didn't know and that Sonia should contact the chairman directly. She was also told that there was no longer a risk committee because the chairman saw no need for one.

Sonia telephoned Thomas Hoo, the chairman of Eastern Products. She began by reminding him that Sentosa House was one of Eastern's main shareholders and currently owned 13% of the company. She went on to explain that she had concerns over the governance of Eastern Products and that she would like Thomas to explain his non-compliance with some of the stock market's requirements and also why he was pursuing strategies viewed by many investors as very risky. Thomas reminded Sonia that Eastern had outperformed its sector in terms of earnings per share in both years since he had become chairman and that rather than question him, she should trust him to run the company as he saw fit. He thanked Sentosa House for its support and hung up the phone.

Required

(a)   Explain what an 'agency cost' is and discuss the problems that might increase agency costs for Sentosa House in the case of Eastern Products.   **(7 marks)**

(b)   Describe, with reference to the case, the conditions under which it might be appropriate for an institutional investor to intervene in a company whose shares it holds.   **(10 marks)**

(c)   Evaluate the contribution that a risk committee made up of non-executive directors could make to Sonia's confidence in the management of Eastern Products.   **(4 marks)**

(d)   Assess the opinion given to Sonia that because Eastern Products was listed in a principles-based jurisdiction, compliance with the stock market's rules was 'not compulsory'.   **(4 marks)**

(Total = 25 marks)

2 Frank Finn (Pilot paper)   49 mins

In a recent case, it emerged that Frank Finn, a sales director at ABC Co, had been awarded a substantial over-inflation annual basic pay award with no apparent link to performance. When a major institutional shareholder, Swanland Investments, looked into the issue, it emerged that Mr Finn had a cross directorship with Joe Ng, an executive director of DEF Co. Mr Ng was a non-executive director of ABC and chairman of its remuneration committee. Swanland Investments argued at the annual general meeting that there was 'a problem with the independence' of Mr Ng and further, that Mr Finn's remuneration package as a sales director was considered to be poorly aligned to Swanland's interests because it was too much weighted by basic pay and contained inadequate levels of incentive.

Swanland Investments proposed that the composition of Mr Finn's remuneration package be reconsidered by the remuneration committee and that Mr Ng should not be present during the discussion. Another of the larger institutional shareholders, Hanoi House, objected to this, proposing instead that Mr Ng and Mr Finn both resign from their respective non-executive directorships as there was 'clear evidence of malpractice'. Swanland considered this too radical a step, as Mr Ng's input was, in its opinion, valuable on ABC's board.

Required

(a) Explain **four** roles of a remuneration committee and how the cross directorship undermines these roles at ABC Co. **(12 marks)**

(b) Swanland Investments believed Mr Finn's remuneration package to be 'poorly aligned' to its interests. With reference to the different components of a director's remuneration package, explain how Mr Finn's remuneration might be more aligned to shareholders' interests at ABC Co. **(8 marks)**

(c) Evaluate the proposal from Hanoi House that both Mr Ng and Mr Finn be required to resign from their respective non-executive positions. **(5 marks)**

(Total = 25 marks)

3 Seamus O'Brien (12/07)   49 mins

At a recent international meeting of business leaders, Seamus O'Brien said that multi-jurisdictional attempts to regulate corporate governance were futile because of differences in national culture. He drew particular attention to the Organisation for Economic Co-operation and Development (OECD) and International Corporate Governance Network (ICGN) codes, saying that they were, 'silly attempts to harmonise practice'. He said that in some countries, for example, there were 'family reasons' for making the chairman and chief executive the same person. In other countries, he said, the separation of these roles seemed to work. Another delegate, Alliya Yongvanich, said that the roles of chief executive and chairman should always be separated because of what she called 'accountability to shareholders'.

One delegate, Vincent Viola, said that the right approach was to allow each country to set up its own corporate governance provisions. He said that it was suitable for some countries to produce and abide by their own 'very structured' corporate governance provisions, but in some other parts of the world, the local culture was to allow what he called, 'local interpretation of the rules'. He said that some cultures valued highly structured governance systems while others do not care as much.

Required

(a) Explain the roles of the chairman in corporate governance. **(5 marks)**

(b) Assess the benefits of the separation of the roles of chief executive and chairman that Alliya Yongvanich argued for and explain her belief that 'accountability to shareholders' is increased by the separation of these roles. **(12 marks)**

(c) Critically evaluate Vincent Viola's view that corporate governance provisions should vary by country. **(8 marks)**

(Total = 25 marks)

4 West vs Leroi (6/08)   49 mins

At an academic conference, a debate took place on the implementation of corporate governance practices in developing countries. Professor James West from North America argued that one of the key needs for developing countries was to implement rigorous systems of corporate governance to underpin investor confidence in businesses in those countries. If they did not, he warned, there would be no lasting economic growth as potential foreign inward investors would be discouraged from investing.

In reply, Professor Amy Leroi, herself from a developing country, reported that many developing countries are discussing these issues at governmental level. One issue, she said, was about whether to adopt a rules-based or a principles-based approach. She pointed to evidence highlighting a reduced number of small and medium sized initial public offerings in New York compared to significant growth in London. She suggested that this change could be attributed to the costs of complying with Sarbanes-Oxley in the United States and that over-regulation would be the last thing that a developing country would need. She concluded that a principles-based approach, such as in the United Kingdom, was preferable for developing countries.

Professor Leroi drew attention to an important section of the Sarbanes-Oxley Act to illustrate her point. The key requirement of that section was to externally report on – and have attested (verified) – internal controls. This was, she argued, far too ambitious for small and medium companies that tended to dominate the economies of developing countries.

Professor West countered by saying that whilst Sarbanes-Oxley may have had some problems, it remained the case that it regulated corporate governance in the 'largest and most successful economy in the world'. He said that rules will sometimes be hard to follow but that is no reason to abandon them in favour of what he referred to as 'softer' approaches.

Required

(a)   There are arguments for both rules and principles-based approaches to corporate governance.

    (i)   Describe the essential features of a rules-based approach to corporate governance.   **(3 marks)**

    (ii)   Construct the argument against Professor West's opinion, and in favour of Professor Leroi's opinion that a principles-based approach would be preferable in developing countries. Your answer should consider the particular situations of developing countries.   **(10 marks)**

The Sarbanes-Oxley Act contains provisions for the attestation (verification) and reporting to shareholders of internal controls over financial reporting.

Required

(b)   Describe the typical contents of an external report on internal controls.   **(8 marks)**

(c)   Construct the arguments in favour of Professor Leroi's remark that external reporting requirements on internal controls were 'too ambitious' for small and medium companies.   **(4 marks)**

(Total = 25 marks)

5 TQ (6/09)   49 mins

TQ Company, a listed company, recently went into administration (it had become insolvent and was being managed by a firm of insolvency practitioners). A group of shareholders expressed the belief that it was the chairman, Miss Heike Hoiku, who was primarily to blame. Although the company's management had made a number of strategic errors that brought about the company failure, the shareholders blamed the chairman for failing to hold senior management to account. In particular, they were angry that Miss Hoiku had not challenged chief executive Rupert Smith who was regarded by some as arrogant and domineering. Some said that Miss Hoiku was scared of him.

Some shareholders wrote a letter to Miss Hoiku last year demanding that she hold Mr Smith to account for a number of previous strategic errors. They also asked her to explain why she had not warned of the strategic problems in her chairman's statement in the annual report earlier in the year. In particular, they asked if she could remove Mr Smith from office for incompetence. Miss Hoiku replied saying that whilst she understood their concerns, it was difficult to remove a serving chief executive from office.

Some of the shareholders believed that Mr Smith may have performed better in his role had his reward package been better designed in the first place. There was previously a remuneration committee at TQ but when two of its four non-executive members left the company, they were not replaced and so the committee effectively collapsed. Mr Smith was then able to propose his own remuneration package and Miss Hoiku did not feel able to refuse him. He massively increased the proportion of the package that was basic salary and also awarded himself a new and much more expensive company car. Some shareholders regarded the car as 'excessively' expensive. In addition, suspecting that the company's performance might deteriorate this year, he exercised his entire share options last year and immediately sold all of his shares in TQ Company.

It was noted that Mr Smith spent long periods of time travelling away on company business whilst less experienced directors struggled with implementing strategy at the company headquarters. This meant that operational procedures were often uncoordinated and this was one of the causes of the eventual strategic failure.

Required

(a)   (i)   Explain the ways in which a company director can leave the service of a board.   **(4 marks)**

    (ii)   Discuss Miss Hoiku's statement that it is difficult to remove a serving chief executive from a board.   **(4 marks)**

(b) Assess, in the context of the case, the importance of the chairman's statement to shareholders in TQ Company's annual report.

(5 marks)

(c) Criticise the structure of the reward package that Mr Smith awarded himself.

(4 marks)

(d) Criticise Miss Hoiku's performance as chairman of TQ Company.

(8 marks)

(Total = 25 marks)

6 Tomato Bank (6/10)   49 mins

Five years ago, George Woof was appointed chief executive officer (CEO) of Tomato Bank, one of the largest global banks. Mr Woof had a successful track record in senior management in America and his appointment was considered very fortunate for the company. Analysts rated him as one of the world's best bankers and the other directors of Tomato Bank looked forward to his appointment and a significant strengthening of the business.

One of the factors needed to secure Mr Woof's services was his reward package. Prior to his acceptance of the position, Tomato Bank's remuneration committee (comprised entirely of non-executives) received a letter from Mr Woof saying that because his track record was so strong, they could be assured of many years of sustained growth under his leadership. In discussions concerning his pension, however, he asked for a generous non-performance related pension settlement to be written into his contract so that it would be payable whenever he decided to leave the company (subject to a minimum term of two years) and regardless of his performance as CEO. Such was the euphoria about his appointment that his request was approved. Furthermore in the hasty manner in which Mr Woof's reward package was agreed, the split of his package between basic and performance-related components was not carefully scrutinised. Everybody on the remuneration committee was so certain that he would bring success to Tomato Bank that the individual details of his reward package were not considered important.

In addition, the remuneration committee received several letters from Tomato Bank's finance director, John Temba, saying, in direct terms, that they should offer Mr Woof 'whatever he wants' to ensure that he joins the company and that the balance of benefits was not important as long as he joined. Two of the non-executive directors on the remuneration committee were former colleagues of Mr Woof and told the finance director they would take his advice and make sure they put a package together that would ensure Mr Woof joined the company.

Once in post, Mr Woof led an excessively aggressive strategy that involved high growth in the loan and mortgage books financed from a range of sources, some of which proved unreliable. In the fifth year of his appointment, the failure of some of the sources of funds upon which the growth of the bank was based led to severe financing difficulties at Tomato Bank. Shareholders voted to replace George Woof as CEO. They said he had been reckless in exposing the company to so much risk in growing the loan book without adequately covering it with reliable sources of funds.

When he left, the press reported that despite his failure in the job, he would be leaving with what the newspapers referred to as an 'obscenely large' pension. Some shareholders were angry and said that Mr Woof was being 'rewarded for failure'. When Mr Woof was asked if he might voluntarily forgo some of his pension in recognition of his failure in the job, he refused, saying that he was contractually entitled to it and so would be keeping it all.

Required

(a) Criticise the performance of Tomato Bank's remuneration committee in agreeing Mr Woof's reward package.

(10 marks)

(b) Describe the components of an appropriately designed executive reward package and explain why a more balanced package of benefits should have been used to reward Mr Woof.

(10 marks)

(c) Construct an ethical case for Mr Woof to voluntarily accept a reduction in his pension value in recognition of his failure as chief executive of Tomato Bank.

(5 marks)

(Total = 25 marks)

7 KK (12/10)

KK is a large listed company. When a non-executive directorship of KK Limited became available, John Soria was nominated to fill the vacancy. John is the brother-in-law of KK's chief executive Ken Kava. John is also the CEO of Soria Supplies Ltd, KK's largest single supplier and is, therefore, very familiar with KK and its industry. He has sold goods to KK for over 20 years and is on friendly terms with all of the senior officers in the company. In fact last year, Soria Supplies appointed KK's finance director, Susan Schwab, to a non-executive directorship on its board. The executive directors of KK all know and like John and so plan to ask the nominations committee to appoint him before the next AGM.

KK has recently undergone a period of rapid growth and has recently entered several new overseas markets, some of which, according to the finance director, are riskier than the domestic market. Ken Kava, being the dominant person on the KK board, has increased the risk exposure of the company according to some investors. They say that because most of the executive directors are less experienced, they rarely question his overseas expansion strategy. This expansion has also created a growth in employee numbers and an increase in the number of executive directors, mainly to manage the increasingly complex operations of the company. It was thought by some that the company lacked experience and knowledge of international markets as it expanded and that this increased the risk of the strategy's failure. Some shareholders believed that the aggressive strategy, led by Ken Kava, has been careless as it has exposed KK Limited to some losses on overseas direct investments made before all necessary information on the investment was obtained.

As a large listed company, the governance of KK is important to its shareholders. Fin Brun is one of KK's largest shareholders and holds a large portfolio of shares including 8% of the shares in KK. At the last AGM he complained to KK's chief executive, Ken Kava, that he needed more information on directors' performance. Fin said that he didn't know how to vote on board reappointments because he had no information on how they had performed in their jobs. Mr Kava said that the board intended to include a corporate governance section in future annual reports to address this and to provide other information that shareholders had asked for. He added, however, that he would not be able to publish information on the performance of individual executive directors as this was too complicated and actually not the concern of shareholders. It was, he said, the performance of the board as a whole that was important and he (Mr Kava) would manage the performance targets of individual directors.

Required

(a) Explain the term 'conflict of interest' in the context of non-executive directors and discuss the potential conflicts of interest relating to KK and Soria Supplies if John Soria were to become a non-executive director of KK Limited. **(8 marks)**

(b) Assess the advantages of appointing experienced and effective non-executive directors to the KK board during the period in which the company was growing rapidly. **(7 marks)**

(c) Explain the typical contents of a 'best practice' corporate governance report within an annual report and how its contents could help meet the information needs of Fin Brun. **(10 marks)**

(Total = 25 marks)

8 HHO (6/11)

In the country of Laland, aid organisations registered as charities are not subject to the same financial reporting requirements as limited companies (this is not the case in many other countries where they are treated equally in law). One person to take advantage of this is Horace Hoi who has led his vigorous campaign in favour of animal protection for the past 25 years. As a highly competent self-publicist for his charity and an engaging media performer, he has raised the public profile of his charity substantially. He can and does raise large amounts of money for his charity through his personal charm and passionate appeals on television and in large meetings of supporters. His charity is called the 'Horace Hoi Organisation' (HHO) and its stated aim is to 'stop animals suffering'. Mr Hoi has recently become the subject of criticism by the media because of allegations that he lived a lavish lifestyle and personally owned a large mansion and a number of classic cars. The HHO recently bought a private jet to support Mr Hoi in his travels around the world for speaking engagements and for his work for the HHO charity. One journalist reported that most of the donors to HHO are well-meaning individuals, mainly of modest means, who care greatly about animal suffering and who would be 'horrified' if they knew of the luxury in which Mr Hoi lived.

Despite the fact that Mr Hoi had claimed that he personally takes only a modest salary from the organisation for his work, a journalist recently estimated Mr Hoi's personal wealth, thought to be gained from the HHO, to be around $10 million. When challenged to disclose the financial details of the HHO and Mr Hoi's own personal earnings, a HHO spokesman simply replied that this was not required under the law in Laland and that the HHO was therefore fully compliant with the law. The HHO has refused to join a group of other charities that have undertaken to make full financial disclosures despite it not being mandatory in law. The HHO says that although it does produce financial information for the charity and tax authorities, it has no intention of making this information public. The HHO also makes no disclosures about its governance structures and was once criticised as being 'intentionally opaque in order to hide bad practice'.

In yielding to the media pressure to provide some information on its financial affairs, HHO eventually published a pie chart on its website saying that its expenditure was divided between animal shelters (57%), field work helping animals (32%), administration (6%) and other causes (5%). This was the totality of its public financial disclosure.

Required

(a)   Discuss the ways in which charities differ from public listed companies and explain how these differences affect their respective governance structures.   **(9 marks)**

(b)   Define 'transparency' and construct the case for greater transparency in the governance of the Horace Hoi Organisation.   **(8 marks)**

Audit committees can have a role in reviewing internal controls and addressing areas of deficiency.

Required

(c)   Explain how an audit committee might assist in addressing the apparent internal control deficiencies at HHO.

                                                                                                                  (8 marks)

                                                                                                         (Total = 25 marks)

9 Geeland (12/11)   49 mins

There has been a debate in the country of Geeland for some years about the most appropriate way to regulate corporate governance. Several years ago, there were a number of major corporate failures and 'scandals' caused in part by a number of single powerful individuals dominating their boards. Business leaders and policy-makers were sceptical about a rules-based approach, and this led the Geeland stock exchange to issue guidance in the 'Geeland Code' as follows.

> 'Good corporate governance is not just a matter of prescribing particular corporate structures and complying with a number of rules. There is a need for broad principles. All stakeholders should then apply these flexibly to the varying circumstances of individual companies.'

Given the causes of the Geeland corporate governance failures, there was a debate about whether the separation of the roles of chairman and chief executive should be made a legal requirement. This resulted in the stock exchange issuing guidance that whilst a rules-based or 'box ticking' approach would specify that 'the roles of chairman and chief executive officer should never be combined … We do not think that there are universally valid answers on such points.'

One company to take advantage of the flexibility in Geeland's principles-based approach was Anson Company. In July 2010, Anson Company announced that it had combined its roles of chairman and chief executive in a single role carried out by one individual. In accordance with the Geeland listing rules, it made the following 'comply or explain' statement in its 2011 annual report.

> 'Throughout the year the company complied with all Geeland Code provisions with the exception that from 1 July 2010 the roles of chairman and chief executive have been exercised by the same individual, William Klunker. We recognise that this has been out of line with best practice. We understand the concerns of shareholders but believe that we have maintained robust governance while at the same time benefiting from having Mr Klunker in control. On 31 July 2012 Mr Klunker will step down as executive chairman, remaining as chairman until we conclude our search for a non-executive chairman to succeed him, no later than March 2013.'

Required

(a) Briefly distinguish between rules and principles-based approaches to corporate governance. Critically evaluate the Geeland stock exchange's guidance that 'all stakeholders should then apply these flexibly to the varying circumstances of individual companies.' **(12 marks)**

(b) Explain why a separation of the roles of chairman and chief executive is considered best practice in most jurisdictions. **(8 marks)**

(c) Assess the 'comply or explain' statement made by Anson Company in its 2011 annual report. **(5 marks)**

(Total = 25 marks)

10 Dale Gas (12/11)   49 mins

After the government of Haitchland decided to privatise its monopoly gas supplier (transferring it from government control to private ownership by issuing and selling shares), there was a period of transition as the new board took shape. A great deal of internal reorganisation and culture change was deemed necessary as the company moved to the private sector. The new company, called Dale Gas, set up a committee structure in readiness to comply with stock exchange listing rules. During this transitional period, some directors left and new ones, more familiar with operating in listed companies but unfamiliar with the gas industry, joined the board.

It was unanimously agreed by the new board that the previous chief executive, Helen Evans, should continue in her role after the privatisation. Tom Nwede, a fund manager at XY Investments, one of the company's major new institutional shareholders, said that the company would be exposed to higher market risk if she were to leave the company, so it was very important that she stayed on. She was seen as a highly competent CEO with excellent strategic and communication skills. She commanded the confidence and trust of the employees and also the new institutional investors.

One of the first actions of the new remuneration committee was to propose a doubling of Mrs Evans's salary. The committee said that she had been underpaid when the company was state-controlled because of government constraints on the salaries of public servants. The committee said that she now needed to receive a salary commensurate with the importance of the job and in line with other public listed companies of similar size. This proposal was widely publicised. Some criticised it on the basis that if her previous salary was considered sufficient then, why was it now felt necessary to double her rewards after privatisation?

Her new salary was put to the vote at the company's first annual general meeting after privatisation. Although many small shareholders (some protesting at the AGM itself) voted against her salary increase, it was easily passed by the proxy votes of the large institutional shareholders who did not attend the meeting in person. Tom Nwede, the XY Investments fund manager, said that the votes of the institutional shareholders were crucial in ensuring that Mrs Evans was retained, thereby mitigating market risk.

Required

(a) Explain the purposes of a chief executive's reward package and review the factors that might influence the level of reward for Mrs Evans after the privatisation. **(10 marks)**

(b) Define 'market risk' and justify, giving reasons, Tom Nwede's belief that retaining Mrs Evans was crucial in mitigating market risk. **(10 marks)**

(c) Define, and explain the advantages of, 'proxy voting' in the context of the case. **(5 marks)**

(Total = 25 marks)

11 Lum (6/12)   49 mins

Lum Co is a family business that has been wholly-owned and controlled by the Lum family since 1920. The current chief executive, Mr Gustav Lum, is the great grandson of the company's founder and has himself been in post as CEO since 1998. Because the Lum family wanted to maintain a high degree of control, they operated a two-tier board structure: four members of the Lum family comprised the supervisory board and the other eight non-family directors comprised the operating board.

Despite being quite a large company with 5,000 employees, Lum Co never had any non-executive directors because they were not required in privately-owned companies in the country in which Lum Co was situated.

The four members of the Lum family valued the control of the supervisory board to ensure that the full Lum family's wishes (being the only shareholders) were carried out. This also enabled decisions to be made quickly, without the need to take everything before a meeting of the full board.

Starting in 2008, the two tiers of the board met in joint sessions to discuss a flotation (issuing public shares on the stock market) of 80% of the company. The issue of the family losing control was raised by the CEO's brother, Mr Crispin Lum. He said that if the company became listed, the Lum family would lose the freedom to manage the company as they wished, including supporting their own long-held values and beliefs. These values, he said, were managing for the long term and adopting a paternalistic management style. Other directors said that the new listing rules that would apply to the board, including compliance with the stock market's corporate governance codes of practice, would be expensive and difficult to introduce.

The flotation went ahead in 2011. In order to comply with the new listing rules, Lum Co took on a number of non-executive directors (NEDs) and formed a unitary board. A number of problems arose around this time with NEDs feeling frustrated at the culture and management style in Lum Co, whilst the Lum family members found it difficult to make the transition to managing a public company with a unitary board. Gustav Lum said that it was very different from managing the company when it was privately owned by the Lum family. The human resources manager said that an effective induction programme for NEDs and some relevant continuing professional development (CPD) for existing executives might help to address the problems.

Required

(a) Compare the typical governance arrangements between a family business and a listed company, and assess Crispin's view that the Lum family will 'lose the freedom to manage the company as they wish' after the flotation. **(10 marks)**

(b) Assess the benefits of introducing an induction programme for the new NEDs, and requiring continual professional development (CPD) for the existing executives at Lum Co after its flotation. **(8 marks)**

(c) Distinguish between unitary and two-tier boards, and discuss the difficulties that the Lum family might encounter when introducing a unitary board. **(7 marks)**

(Total = 25 marks)

12 Oland (12/12)   49 mins

After a recent financial crisis in the country of Oland, there had been a number of high profile company failures and a general loss of confidence in business. As a result, an updated corporate governance code was proposed, with changes to address these concerns.

Before the new code was published, there was a debate in Oland society about whether corporate governance provisions should be made rules-based, or remain principles-based as had been the case in the past. One elected legislator, Martin Mung, whose constituency contained a number of the companies that had failed with resulting rises in unemployment, argued strongly that many of the corporate governance failures would not have happened if directors were legally accountable for compliance with corporate governance provisions. He said that 'you can't trust the markets to punish bad practice', saying that this was what had caused the problems in the first place. He said that Oland should become a rules-based jurisdiction because the current 'comply or explain' was ineffective as a means of controlling corporate governance.

Mr Mung was angered by the company failures in his constituency and believed that a lack of sound corporate governance contributed to the failure of important companies and the jobs they supported. He said that he wanted the new code to make it more difficult for companies to fail.

The new code was then issued, under a principles-based approach. One added provision in the new Oland code was to recommend a reduction in the re-election period of all directors from three years to one year. The code also required that when seeking re-election, there should be 'sufficient biographical details on each director to enable shareholders to take an informed decision'. The code explained that these measures were 'in the interests of greater accountability'.

Required

(a)   Examine how sound corporate governance can make it more difficult for companies to fail, clearly explaining what 'corporate governance' means in your answer.   **(10 marks)**

Martin Mung believes that Oland should become a rules-based jurisdiction because the current 'comply or explain' approach is ineffective as a means of controlling corporate governance.

Required

(b)   Explain the difference between rules-based and principles-based approaches to corporate governance regulation, and argue against Martin Mung's belief that 'comply or explain' is ineffective.   **(8 marks)**

(c)   Explain what 'accountability' means, and discuss how the proposed new provisions for shorter re-election periods and biographical details might result in 'greater accountability' as the code suggests.   **(7 marks)**

(Total = 25 marks)

13 Sarbanes-Oxley (12/13)   49 mins

The Sarbanes-Oxley legislation in the United States was introduced in 2002, partly in response to the earlier failure of the American energy company, Enron. It was decided by United States legislators that compliance should be enforceable under law rather than under listing rules. At the time it was being debated, some said that the legal enforceability of Sarbanes-Oxley would be unfair to smaller companies without the infrastructure needed to generate internal control data and to report on it. One example of this was the debate over s.404 of Sarbanes-Oxley, which mandated external reporting on the adequacy of internal controls. Before a size criterion was later introduced, this applied equally to all companies but now smaller companies are partly exempted from this requirement.

In its advice on this requirement, the United States Securities and Exchange Commission (SEC) published the following comments.

> 'The rules we adopted in June 2003 to implement s.404 of the Sarbanes-Oxley Act of 2002 ('Sarbanes-Oxley') require management to annually evaluate whether internal control over financial reporting (ICFR) is effective at providing reasonable assurance and to disclose its assessment to investors. Management is responsible for maintaining evidential matter, including documentation, to provide reasonable support for its assessment. This evidence will also allow a third party, such as the company's external auditor, to consider the work performed by management.'

Required

(a)   Distinguish between rules and principles-based approaches to the regulation of corporate governance, and explain the disadvantages of a rules-based system such as Sarbanes-Oxley in the United States.   **(7 marks)**

(b)   Define 'agency' in the context of corporate governance and discuss the benefits to shareholders of 'maintaining a system of internal control over financial reporting' in a rules-based jurisdiction.   **(10 marks)**

(c)   Construct the case to exempt smaller companies from the full reporting requirements of s.404 of the Sarbanes-Oxley Act 2002.   **(8 marks)**

(Total = 25 marks)

14 Help-with-life (12/13)   49 mins

'Help-with-life' (HWL) is a charitable organisation established ten years ago. Its stated purpose is, 'to help individuals and families with social problems and related issues.' Its work, in a large city with people from many countries and backgrounds, involves advising, counselling, giving practical support to service users (the people who come for help). Over the years it has been operating, HWL has realised that the best outcomes are achieved when the staff member understands and sympathises with the service users' social norms, ethical and cultural beliefs.

40% of HWL's funding comes from local government. This means that HWL has to account for its use of that portion of its funding and comply with several rules imposed by local government. One of these rules concerns demonstrating appropriate diversity amongst the managers of services such as those delivered by HWL. It requires the charity management team to involve the widest feasible range of people and to reflect the demographic make-up of the community.

HWL has recently had to replace a number of executive and non-executive members of its board. The external auditor suggested that setting up a nominations committee would help in these board appointments. The CEO, Marian Ngogo, has always stressed that all directors should share the ethical values of HWL and agree to take reduced rewards because, 'every dollar we pay a director is a dollar less we are spending on service delivery.' She stressed that the culture in a charity was very different from a commercial ('for profit') business and that staff and directors must share the ethical stance of HWL and had to accept a different approach to social responsibility if they joined.

Required

(a) Explain the roles of a nominations committee and describe how the Help-with-life (HWL) nominations committee might approach the task of nominating and appointing new directors. **(8 marks)**

(b) Explain the advantages of diversity on the board of HWL. **(8 marks)**

(c) Explain 'corporate social responsibility' (CSR) and discuss the ways in which CSR and the ethical stance might differ between HWL and a commercial 'for profit' business. **(9 marks)**

(Total = 25 marks)

15 Chambon (12/14)   49 mins

The independent board of governors (an independent oversight body comprised of local residents, parents and other concerned citizens) of the state-funded Chambon school for 11- to 16-year old children met to consider its most recent set of public examination results. A key responsibility placed upon the school's governors is the delivery, to its local government authority, of a report on exam performance in a full and timely manner. A report on both the exam results and the reasons for any improvement or deterioration over previous years are required from the governors each year. Accordingly, this annual meeting on exam performance was always considered to be very important. Although the school taught the national curriculum (a standard syllabus taught in all schools in the country) as required of it, the exam results at Chambon had deteriorated in recent years and on this particular occasion, they were very poor indeed.

In order to address the weaknesses in the school, Chambon's budget had increased in recent years and a number of new teachers had been employed to help improve results. Despite this, exam performance continued to fall. A recent overspend against budget was funded through the closure of part of the school library and the sale of a sports field.

One member of the board of governors was Sally Murol. She believed that the local government authority might attempt to close Chambon school if these exam results were reported with no convincing explanation. One solution to avoid this threat, she said, was to either send the report in late or to select only the best results and submit a partial report so the school's performance looked better than it actually was. There is no central computerised exam results service in the country in which Chambon is located by which the local authority could establish the exam performance at Chambon school.

A general feeling of the governors' meeting was that perhaps the school needed some new leadership and it was time to remove the existing headteacher. Mr Besse had been in the role for many years and his management style was thought to be ineffective. He was widely liked by staff in the school because he believed that each teacher knew best how to manage their teaching, and so he tried not to intervene wherever possible. Mr Besse had sometimes disagreed with the governors when they suggested changes which could be made to improve exam performance, preferring to rely on what he believed were tried and tested ways of managing his teaching staff. He was thought to be very loyal to longstanding colleagues and had a dislike of confrontation.

Required

(a) Explain, using evidence from the case, the characteristics which identify Chambon school as a public sector organisation and assess how its objectives as a public sector organisation have not been met. **(10 marks)**

(b) Explain the roles of a board of governors in the governance of Chambon school and discuss, in the context of Sally Murol's suggestion, the importance of transparency in the board of governors dealings with the local government authority. **(9 marks)**

(c) Discuss the potential advantages to Chambon school of replacing the headteacher in seeking to address its problems. **(6 marks)**

(Total = 25 marks)

16 New Ideas Company (12/14)

49 mins

New Ideas Company (NIC) was launched early this year as a result of a scientific breakthrough at a university. The company was located in a relatively small regional city, some distance from the main centres of population. Because the initial capital needed was large, the scientists behind the company decided to float the company on the stock exchange and the take up of shares was very good. This meant that the initial capital needs were fully funded. The business itself was highly technical, with many shareholders only weakly understanding the science behind the company. Upon reading the share prospectus, some analysts believed that NIC was a relatively risky business and that it could fail within two years unless a very good management team, including suitable non-executive directors (ideally locally based), was in place.

None of the scientists involved in NIC had any experience of business before and had to learn about the roles of a board and how to effectively run a company. Dr Ranjana Foo, the lead scientist who made the scientific discovery, was thought to be the logical person to become chief executive but she herself questioned her suitability for the role. She said she was happiest working alone and in the quiet environment of her laboratory, and was not inclined to invest valuable time learning about running a business as she was not good at relating to a wide range of people.

Colleagues said of Ranjana that, being a good scientist, she was excellent at detail but sometimes struggled to see the bigger picture on a project. Always popular, however, Ranjana liked to think that all of her colleagues liked her and she tended to avoid confrontation and conflict wherever possible. One potential director of NIC was an experienced local businessman, Dr Idris. Upon being approached about the position, he said that he may have a conflict of interest because he was a major shareholder in one of the potential suppliers of the capital equipment which NIC would be purchasing.

Required

(a) Assess Ranjana Foo's suitability to become chief executive officer (CEO) of New Ideas Company (NIC). Your answer should include an explanation of the roles and personal qualities of a CEO. **(10 marks)**

(b) Explain the benefits, specifically to NIC, of the appointment of 'suitable non-executive directors' and discuss the difficulties which the company may encounter in non-executive recruitment. **(9 marks)**

(c) Explain 'conflict of interest' and briefly discuss how a major shareholding in a potential supplier could be a conflict of interest to Dr Idris were he to become a director of NIC. **(6 marks)**

(Total = 25 marks)

17 Hafnium Company (6/15)

49 mins

A major corporate governance code contains the following entry on audit committees.

> 'The board should establish formal and transparent arrangements for considering how they should apply the corporate reporting and risk management and internal control principles and for maintaining an appropriate relationship with the company's external auditors.

> The board should establish an audit committee of at least three, or in the case of smaller companies, two, independent non-executive directors. In smaller companies the company chairman may be a member of, but not chair, the committee in addition to the independent non-executive directors, provided he or she was considered independent on appointment as chairman. All audit committee members should be considered independent upon appointment to the committee. The board should satisfy itself that at least one member of the audit committee has recent and relevant financial experience.'

When Hafnium Company floated on the stock exchange, it attempted to establish the audit committee required by the listing rules. It was unable to recruit a non-executive director with the requisite financial experience so it appointed experienced non-executive director, Sophie Xu, as the committee chairman. Sophie Xu was a technical engineer. She was appointed to the board of Hafnium because of her expertise in the technology used by Hafnium and she understood the company's business model and its systems. But she did not understand financial matters.

Sophie Xu told colleagues that she did not understand much about the concept of independence. She said that in her own field of engineering, colleagues inside and outside a certain company often supported each other and that this was often encouraged. As a community of specialists, they often found that helping each other was an important part of professional life over the years. Accordingly, she said she did not really understand why independence was important for audit committee members. She also said that she did not understand much about the company's relationship with the external auditors.

Required

(a)   Define 'independence' in the context of audit committees, and explain why audit committee members should be 'considered independent' at the time of their appointment.   **(8 marks)**

(b)   Discuss how the inability of Hafnium Company to recruit a person with 'recent and relevant financial experience' might threaten the effectiveness of the audit committee's contribution to shareholder value.
                                                                                                                  (8 marks)

(c)   Explain the nature of an 'appropriate relationship with the company's external auditors' and discuss how Hafnium Company's audit committee should respond if it believes the relationship to be too close.
                                                                                                                  (9 marks)

                                                                                                          (Total = 25 marks)

18 Scapa Holdings (Mar/Jun 16)   **49 mins**

Arthur Jellicoe has been the chief executive officer (CEO) of Scapa Holdings, a listed company, for over 15 years, during which time the company has been very successful in capturing market share and achieving levels of profitability well in excess of it direct competition. Much of this success has been credited specifically to the way Arthur has managed the company. So when he advised the board at its last meeting that he plans to retire at the end of the year, there was real concern about appointing his successor. Scapa Holdings is particularly aware that any uncertainty which may arise during the CEO transitional period could result in a fall in share price, which they clearly wish to avoid.

The remuneration policy at Scapa Holdings includes a provision for awarding significant share options to executive directors when the company attains high levels of performance. For many years the targets set by the remuneration committee have been exceeded, so Arthur has accumulated a large number of share options which he can exercise any time over the next year. As part of his retirement planning, Arthur has consulted with an independent financial adviser who has recommended that he exercises his share options before he retires because they will deliver a tax efficient capital gain which he can then invest for his future. Clearly it will be in Arthur's best interest to choose an exercise date when the share price is trading at its highest. So when a new contract opportunity was tabled by the sales director, which would clearly increase the company's share price this year, Arthur was an enthusiastic supporter. Unfortunately, the finance director advised the board that its bank loan contained a restrictive covenant requiring the company to maintain interest cover of four times its pre-tax profit. Although Scapa Holdings has always been able meet this loan condition, the finance director is concerned that the further investment in the working capital needed for the proposed new contract presented a significant risk of breaching the loan covenant.

To address this issue the CEO suggested that inventory could be valued differently in order to report a higher profit figure, and thereby increase the level of interest cover. He further suggested that 'this minor policy change would not be opposed by shareholders' as it would undoubtedly increase the value of the share price. He also advised the board that he was sure that he could use his longstanding friendship with the engagement partner of Scapa Holdings' auditors, who he had trained with as an accountant many years ago, to convince the audit team to agree with the higher inventory valuation during the forthcoming audit.

Required

(a)   An inherent risk in any listed company is that its directors have the power to pursue their own personal interests, which may not be aligned with their fiduciary duties towards shareholders.

      Explain the term conflict of interest in this context, and using information from the scenario, discuss how Arthur Jellicoe's behaviour presents a clear conflict of interest, stating what course of action he should take.
                                                                                                                  (8 marks)

(b)   Describe the agency relationships at Scapa Holdings, and explain how clear accountability could increase trust between principal and agent thereby reducing agency costs.   **(9 marks)**

(c)   Explain the meaning of 'probity' when maintaining professional business relationships as described in the scenario, and criticise the ethical behaviour of Arthur Jellicoe with respect to probity.   **(8 marks)**

                                                                                                          (Total = 25 marks)

INTERNAL CONTROL AND RISK

Questions 19 to 31 cover internal control and risk, the subject of Part B of the BPP Study Text for Paper P1.

19 H&Z (6/09)

49 mins

John Pentanol was appointed as risk manager at H&Z Company a year ago and he decided that his first task was to examine the risks that faced the company. He concluded that the company faced three major risks, which he assessed by examining the impact that would occur if the risk were to materialise. He assessed Risk 1 as being of low potential impact as even if it materialised it would have little effect on the company's strategy. Risk 2 was assessed as being of medium potential impact whilst a third risk, Risk 3, was assessed as being of very high potential impact.

When John realised the potential impact of Risk 3 materialising, he issued urgent advice to the board to withdraw from the activity that gave rise to Risk 3 being incurred. In the advice he said that the impact of Risk 3 was potentially enormous and it would be irresponsible for H&Z to continue to bear that risk.

The company commercial director, Jane Xylene, said that John Pentanol and his job at H&Z were unnecessary and that risk management was 'very expensive for the benefits achieved'. She said that all risk managers do is to tell people what can't be done and that they are pessimists by nature. She said she wanted to see entrepreneurial risk takers in H&Z and not risk managers who, she believed, tended to discourage enterprise.

John replied that it was his job to eliminate all of the highest risks at H&Z Company. He said that all risk was bad and needed to be eliminated if possible. If it couldn't be eliminated, he said that it should be minimised.

The risk manager has an important role to play in an organisation's risk management.

Required

(a)   (i)   Describe the roles of a risk manager.   **(4 marks)**

       (ii)   Assess John Pentanol's understanding of his role.   **(4 marks)**

(b)   With reference to a risk assessment framework as appropriate, criticise John's advice that H&Z should withdraw from the activity that incurs Risk 3.   **(6 marks)**

Jane Xylene expressed a particular view about the value of risk management in H&Z Company. She also said that she wanted to see 'entrepreneurial risk takers'.

Required

(c)   (i)   Define 'entrepreneurial risk' and explain why it is important to accept entrepreneurial risk in business organisations.   **(4 marks)**

       (ii)   Critically evaluate Jane Xylene's view of risk management.   **(7 marks)**

                                                (Total = 25 marks)

20 YGT (6/11)

49 mins

The board of YGT discussed its need for timely risk information. The consensus of the meeting was that risk consultants should be engaged to review the risks facing the company. One director, Raz Dutta, said that she felt that this would be a waste of money as the company needed to concentrate its resources on improving organisational efficiency rather than on gathering risk information. She said that many risks 'didn't change much' and 'hardly ever materialised' and so can mostly be ignored. The rest of the board, however, believed that a number of risks had recently emerged whilst others had become less important and so the board wanted a current assessment as it believed previous assessments might now be outdated.

The team of risk consultants completed the risk audit. They identified and assessed six potential risks (A, B, C, D, E and F) and the following information was discussed when the findings were presented to the YGT board:

Risk A was assessed as unlikely and low impact whilst Risk B was assessed as highly likely to occur and with a high impact. The activities giving rise to both A and B, however, are seen as marginal in that whilst the activities do have value and are capable of making good returns, neither is strategically vital.

Risk C was assessed as low probability but with a high potential impact and also arises from an activity that must not be discontinued although alternative arrangements for bearing the risks are possible. The activity giving rise to Risk C was recently introduced by YGT as a result of a new product launch.

Risk D was assessed as highly likely but with a low potential impact, and arose as a result of a recent change in legislation. It cannot be insured against nor can it be outsourced. It is strategically important that the company continues to engage in the activity that gives rise to Risk D although not necessarily at the same level as is currently the case.

In addition, Risks E and F were identified. Risk E was an environmental risk and Risk F was classed as a reputation risk. The risk consultants said that risks E and F could be related risks. In the formal feedback to the board of YGT, the consultants said that the company had to develop a culture of risk awareness and that this should permeate all levels of the company.

Required

(a)   Criticise Raz Dutta's beliefs about the need for risk assessment. Explain why risks are dynamic and therefore need to be assessed regularly.   **(8 marks)**

(b)   Using the TARA framework, select and explain the appropriate strategy for managing each risk (A, B, C and D). Justify your selection in each case.   **(6 marks)**

(c)   Explain what 'related risks' are and describe how Risks E and F might be positively correlated.   **(5 marks)**

The risk consultants reported that YGT needed to cultivate a culture of risk awareness and that this should permeate all levels of the company.

Required

(d)   Explain and assess this advice.   **(6 marks)**

(Total = 25 marks)

21 Zogs (6/12)   49 mins

John Louse, the recently retired chief executive of Zogs Company, a major listed company, was giving a speech reflecting on his career and some of the aspects of governance he supported and others of which he was critical. In particular, he believed that board committees were mainly ineffective. A lot of the ineffectiveness, he said, was due to the lack of independence of many non-executive directors (NEDs). He believed that it was not enough just to have the required number of non-executive directors; they must also be 'truly independent' of the executive board. It was his opinion that it was not enough to have no material financial connection with a company for independence: he believed that in order to be truly independent, NEDs should come from outside the industry and have no previous contact with any of the current executive directors.

In relation to risk committees, he said that in his experience, the company's risk committee had never stopped any risk affecting the company and because of this, he questioned its value. He said that the risk committee was 'always asking for more information, which was inconvenient' and had such a 'gloomy and pessimistic' approach to its task. He asked, 'why can't risk committees just get on with stopping risk, and also stop making inconvenient demands on company management? Do they think middle managers have nothing else to do?' He viewed all material risks as external risks and so the risk committee should be looking outwards and not inwards.

Since retiring from Zogs, Mr Louse had taken up a non-executive directorship of SmallCo, a smaller private company in his town. In a meeting with Alan Ng, the new chief executive of Zogs, Mr Ng said that whilst risk management systems were vital in large companies like Zogs, fewer risk controls were needed in smaller companies like SmallCo.

Required

(a) Define 'independence' in the context of corporate governance and critically evaluate Mr Louse's comment that greater independence of non-executive directors is important in increasing the effectiveness of board committees. **(8 marks)**

(b) Describe the roles of a risk committee and criticise Mr Louse's understanding of the risk committee in Zogs Company. **(9 marks)**

(c) Assess whether risk committees and risk mitigation systems are more important in larger companies, like Zogs, than in smaller companies like SmallCo. **(8 marks)**

(Total = 25 marks)

22 Dubland (6/13)   49 mins

Because of a general lack of business confidence in Dubland, its major banks had severely restricted new lending. This lack of lending extended to small and large businesses, and also to individuals in society. Press statements from the banks often referred to the need to mitigate financial risks and the need to maintain capital adequacy. Over time, the lower lending produced some negative consequences in the wider Dubland economy.

Responding to these problems, the Dubland finance minister remarked that, 'financial risks may not only cause companies to fail but they can also cause problems in wider society. Banks, in particular, need to be more aware of their financial risks than most other sectors of the economy. They have to manage a unique set of risks and I strongly urge the directors of banks to institute robust risk management systems as part of their corporate governance.'

'As finance minister, however, I also believe that banks have a vital role in supporting the economic strength of this country. They hold cash deposits and make short and long-term loans, which are vital to other businesses. Taking risks is a normal part of all business operations and our banks need to accept this risk when it comes to lending.'

Ron Ng, the chief executive of BigBank, Dubland's largest bank, said that continuous and ongoing risk assessment was necessary. He said that despite the finance minister's call for higher lending, his only duty was to BigBank's shareholders and it was this duty that guided BigBank's reduced lending.

Required

(a) Explain the meaning of 'risk assessment' as used by Ron Ng and discuss, in the context of the case, the need for risk assessment to be 'continuous and ongoing'. **(8 marks)**

Ron Ng believed that his 'only duty' as BigBank's CEO was to the BigBank shareholders.

Required

(b) Describe 'fiduciary duty' in the context of the case and critically evaluate the issues raised by Ron Ng's belief. **(7 marks)**

(c) Explain the term 'financial risk' and discuss how management of these risks can be embedded in a large organisation such as BigBank. **(10 marks)**

(Total = 25 marks)

23 Franks & Fisher (Examiner question)   49 mins

The board of Franks & Fisher, a large manufacturing company, decided to set up an internal control and audit function. The proposal was to appoint an internal auditor at mid-management level and also to establish a board level internal audit committee made up mainly of non-executive directors.

The initiative to do so was driven by a recent period of rapid growth. The company had taken on many more activities as a result of growth in its product range. The board decided that the increased size and complexity of its operations created the need for greater control over internal activities and that an internal audit function was a good way forward. The need was highlighted by a recent event where internal quality standards were not enforced, resulting in the stoppage of a production line for several hours. The production director angrily described the stoppage as 'entirely avoidable' and the finance director, Jason Kumas, said that the stoppage had been very costly.

Mr Kumas said that there were problems with internal control in a number of areas of the company's operations and that there was a great need for internal audit. He said that as the head of the company's accounting and finance function, the new internal auditor should report to him. The reasons for this, he said, were because as an accountant, he was already familiar with auditing procedure and the fact that he already had information on budgets and other 'control' information that the internal auditor would need.

It was decided that the new internal auditor needed to be a person of some experience and with enough personality not to be intimidated nor diverted by other department heads who might find the internal audits an inconvenience. One debate the board had was whether it would be better to recruit to the position from inside or outside the company. A second argument was over the limits of authority that the internal auditor might be given. It was pointed out that while the board considered the role of internal audit to be very important, it didn't want it to interfere with the activities of other departments to the point where their operational effectiveness was reduced.

Required

(a) Explain, with reference to the case, the factors that are typically considered when deciding to establish internal audit in an organisation. **(10 marks)**

(b) Construct the argument in favour of appointing the new internal auditor from outside the company rather than promoting internally. **(6 marks)**

(c) Critically evaluate Mr Kumas's belief that the internal auditor should report to him as finance director. **(4 marks)**

(d) Define 'objectivity' and describe characteristics that might demonstrate an internal auditor's professional objectivity. **(5 marks)**

(Total = 25 marks)

24 Gluck and Goodman (12/08) 49 mins

Susan Paullaos was recently appointed as a non-executive member of the internal audit committee of Gluck and Goodman, a public listed company producing complex engineering products. Barney Chester, the executive finance director who chairs the committee, has always viewed the purpose of internal audit as primarily financial in nature and as long as financial controls are seen to be fully in place, he is less concerned with other aspects of internal control. When Susan asked about operational controls in the production facility Barney said that these were not the concern of the internal audit committee. This, he said, was because as long as the accounting systems and financial controls were fully functional, all other systems may be assumed to be working correctly.

Susan, however, was concerned with the operational and quality controls in the production facility. She spoke to production director Aaron Hardanger, and asked if he would be prepared to produce regular reports for the internal audit committee on levels of specification compliance and other control issues. Mr Hardanger said that the internal audit committee had always trusted him because his reputation as a manager was very good. He said that he had never been asked to provide compliance evidence to the internal audit committee and saw no reason as to why he should start doing so now.

At board level, the non-executive chairman, George Allejandra, said that he only instituted the internal audit committee in the first place in order to be seen to be in compliance with the stock market's requirement that Gluck and Goodman should have one. He believed that internal audit committees didn't add materially to the company. They were, he believed, one of those 'outrageous demands' that regulatory authorities made without considering the consequences in smaller companies nor the individual needs of different companies. He also complained about the need to have an internal auditor. He said that Gluck and Goodman used to have a full time internal auditor but when he left a year ago, he wasn't replaced. The audit committee didn't feel it needed an internal auditor because Barney Chester believed that only financial control information was important and he could get that information from his management accountant.

Susan asked Mr Allejandra if he recognised that the company was exposing itself to increased market risks by failing to have an effective audit committee. Mr Allejandra said he didn't know what a market risk was.

Internal control and audit are considered to be important parts of sound corporate governance.

(a) (i) Describe **five** general objectives of internal control. (5 marks)

    (ii) Explain the organisational factors that determine the need for internal audit in public listed companies. (5 marks)

(b) Criticise the internal control and internal audit arrangements at Gluck and Goodman as described in the case scenario. (10 marks)

(c) Define 'market risk' for Mr Allejandra and explain why Gluck and Goodman's market risk exposure is increased by failing to have an effective audit committee. (5 marks)

(Total = 25 marks)

25 Saltoc (12/09)   49 mins

After a major fire had destroyed an office block belonging to Saltoc Company, the fire assessment reported that the most likely cause was an electrical problem. It emerged that the electrical system had suffered from a lack of maintenance in recent years due to cost pressures. Meanwhile in the same week, it was reported that a laptop computer containing confidential details of all of Saltoc's customers was stolen from the front seat of a car belonging to one of the company's information technology (IT) mid-managers. This caused outrage and distress to many of the affected customers as the information on the laptop included their bank details and credit card numbers. Some customers wrote to the company to say that they would be withdrawing their business from Saltoc as a result.

When the board met to review and consider the two incidents, it was agreed that the company had been lax in its risk management in the past and that systems should be tightened. However, the financial director, Peter Osbida, said that he knew perfectly well where systems should be tightened. He said that the fire was due to the incompetence of Harry Ho the operations manager and that the stolen laptop was because of a lack of security in the IT department led by Laura Hertz. Peter said that both colleagues were 'useless' and should be sacked. Neither Harry nor Laura liked or trusted Peter and they felt that in disputes, chief executive Ken Tonno usually took Peter's side.

Both Harry and Laura said that their departments had come under severe pressure because of the tight cost budgets imposed by Peter. Ken Tonno said that the last few years had been 'terrible' for Saltoc Company and that it was difficult enough keeping cash flows high enough to pay the wage bill without having to worry about 'even more' administration on risks and controls. Peter said that Harry and Laura both suffered in their roles by not having the respect of their subordinates and pointed to the high staff turnover in both of their departments as evidence of this.

Mr Tonno asked whether having a complete risk audit (or risk review) might be a good idea. He shared some of Peter's concerns about the management skills of both Harry and Laura, and so proposed that perhaps an external person should perform the risk audit and that would be preferable to one conducted by a colleague from within the company.

Required

(a) Describe what 'embedding' risk means with reference to Saltoc Company. (6 marks)

(b) Assess the ability of Saltoc's management culture to implement embedded risk systems. (8 marks)

(c) Explain what external risk auditing contains and construct the case for an external risk audit at Saltoc Company. (11 marks)

(Total = 25 marks)

26 COSO (6/10)   49 mins

The Committee of Sponsoring Organisations (COSO) of the Treadway Commission is an American voluntary, private sector organisation and is unconnected to government or any other regulatory authority. It was established in 1985 to help companies identify the causes of fraudulent reporting and to create internal control environments able to support full and accurate reporting. It is named after its first chairman, James Treadway, and has issued several guidance reports over the years including important reports in 1987, 1992 and 2006.

In 2009, COSO issued new 'Guidance on monitoring internal control systems' to help companies tighten internal controls and thereby enjoy greater internal productivity and produce higher quality reporting. The report, written principally by a leading global professional services firm but adopted by all of the COSO members, noted that 'unmonitored controls tend to deteriorate over time' and encouraged organisations to adopt wide ranging internal controls. It went on to say that, the 'assessment of internal controls [can] ... involve a significant amount of ... internal audit testing.'

After its publication, the business journalist, Mark Rogalski, said that the latest report contained 'yet more guidance from COSO on how to make your company less productive by burdening it even more with non-productive things to do' referring to the internal control guidance the 2009 report contains. He said that there was no industry sector-specific advice and that a 'one-size-fits-all' approach to internal control was 'ridiculous'. He further argued that there was no link between internal controls and external reporting, and that internal controls are unnecessary for effective external reporting.

Another commentator, Claire Mahmood, wrote a reply to Rogalski's column pointing to the views expressed in the 2009 COSO report that, 'over time effective monitoring can lead to organisational efficiencies and reduced costs associated with public reporting on internal control because problems are identified and addressed in a proactive, rather than reactive, manner.' She said that these benefits were not industry sector specific and that Rogalski was incorrect in his dismissal of the report's value. She also said that although primarily concerned with governance in the USA, the best practice guidance from COSO could be applied by companies anywhere in the world. She said that although the USA, where COSO is based, is concerned with the 'rigid rules' of compliance, the advice ought to be followed by companies in countries with principles-based approaches to corporate governance because it was best practice.

Required

(a)   Distinguish between rules-based and principles-based approaches to internal control system compliance as described by Claire Mahmood and discuss the benefits to an organisation of a principles-based approach.

(7 marks)

Mr Rogalski is sceptical over the value of internal control and believes that controls must be industry-specific to be effective.

Required

(b)   Describe the advantages of internal control that apply regardless of industry sector and briefly explain the statement, 'unmonitored controls tend to deteriorate over time'. Your answer should refer to the case scenario as appropriate.   **(10 marks)**

The COSO report explains that 'assessment of internal controls [can] ... involve a significant amount of ... internal audit testing.'

Required

(c)   Define 'internal audit testing' and explain the roles of internal audit in helping ensure the effectiveness of internal control systems.   **(8 marks)**

(Total = 25 marks)

27 Yaya (12/12)   49 mins

In Yaya Company, operations director Ben Janoon recently realised there had been an increase in products failing the final quality checks. These checks were carried out in the QC (quality control) laboratory, which tested finished goods products before being released for sale. The product failure rate had risen from 1% of items two years ago to 4% now, and this meant an increase of hundreds of items of output a month which were not sold on to Yaya's customers. The failed products had no value to the company once they had failed QC as the rework costs were not economic. Because the increase was gradual, it took a while for Mr Janoon to realise that the failure rate had risen.

A thorough review of the main production operation revealed nothing that might explain the increased failure and so attention was focused instead on the QC laboratory. For some years, the QC laboratory at Yaya, managed by Jane Goo, had been marginalised in the company, with its two staff working in a remote laboratory well away from other employees. Operations director Ben Janoon, who designed the internal control systems in Yaya, rarely visited the QC lab because of its remote location. He never asked for information on product failure rates to be reported to him and did not understand the science involved in the QC process. He relied on the two QC staff, Jane Goo and her assistant John Zong, both of whom did have relevant scientific qualifications.

The two QC staff considered themselves low paid. Whilst in theory they reported to Mr Janoon, in practice, they conducted their work with little contact with colleagues. The work was routine and involved testing products against a set of compliance standards. A single signature on a product compliance report was required to pass or fail in QC and these reports were then filed away with no-one else seeing them.

It was eventually established that Jane Goo had found a local buyer to pay her directly for any of Yaya's products which had failed the QC tests. The increased failure rate had resulted from her signing products as having 'failed QC' when, in fact, they had passed. She kept the proceeds from the sales for herself, and also paid her assistant, John Zong, a proportion of the proceeds from the sale of the failed products.

Required

(a)   Explain typical reasons why an internal control system might be ineffective.   **(5 marks)**

(b)   Explain the internal control deficiencies that led to the increased product failures at Yaya.   **(10 marks)**

(c)   Discuss the general qualities of useful information, stating clearly how they would be of benefit to Mr Janoon, and recommend specific measures which would improve information flow from the QC lab to Mr Janoon.   **(10 marks)**

(Total = 25 marks)

28 Blup (6/13)   **49 mins**

When Blup Co (a listed company involved in water supply) decided to establish an internal audit function, in line with new listing rules, the board approached Karen Huyer, an external consultant. She explained that internal audit is especially important in highly regulated industries but that it could also offer benefits to companies regardless of the industry context.

Karen was particularly keen to talk to John Xu, the head of the audit committee. John explained that because Blup Co was a water supply company and was thus highly regulated, he considered it important that all of the members of the audit committee were professional water engineers so that they fully understood the industry and its technical challenges. All three members of the audit committee were non-executive directors and all were recently retired members of the Blup executive board. When Karen asked about the relationship with external auditors, John said that they had an 'excellent' relationship, saying that this was because the external audit practice was run by the chairman's son-in-law.

Karen said that one of the essential functions of internal audit is to provide assurance that the internal controls which underpinned financial reporting are effective. She said that effective internal controls are necessary for maintaining the integrity of financial reporting and that the new internal audit function could help with that.

Required

(a)   Discuss the importance of internal audit in a highly regulated industry such as the water industry that Blup Co operates in.   **(7 marks)**

(b)   (i)   Criticise the ways in which Blup Co's audit committee has failed to meet best practice.

        (ii)   Explain why the audit committee is responsible for overseeing the internal audit function.

The total marks will be split equally between each part.   **(12 marks)**

(c)   Discuss how effective internal controls can provide assurance on the integrity of financial reporting.   **(6 marks)**

(Total = 25 marks)

29 Bob Wong (6/14)

49 mins

Bob Wong was fortunate to inherit some money and decided he wanted to invest for the long term in one or more investments so he would have a higher income in retirement. He was not a specialist in accounting and had little understanding of how investments worked.

Bob studied an investment website which suggested that he needed to be aware of the level of risk in an investment and also that he needed to know what his basic attitude to risk would be. This meant he needed to decide what his risk appetite was and then select investments based on that.

When Bob studied share listings in newspapers, he noticed that they were subdivided into sectors (eg banks, pharmaceuticals, mining, retail). He noticed that some sectors seemed to make higher returns than others and he wanted to know why this was. One website suggested that risks also varied by sector and this was partly explained by the different business and financial risks which different sectors are exposed to.

One website said that if a potential investor wanted to know about any given company as a potential investment, the company's most recent annual report was a good place to start. This was because, it said, the annual report contained a lot of voluntary information, in addition to the financial statements. Bob could use this information to gain an understanding of the company's strategy and governance. The website suggested that the contents of the corporate governance section of the annual report would be particularly helpful in helping him decide whether or not to buy shares in a company.

Required

(a) Explain 'risk appetite' and 'risk awareness', and discuss how Bob's risk appetite might affect his choice of investments. **(8 marks)**

(b) Explain 'business risk' and 'financial risk' and discuss why risks might vary by sector as the website indicated. **(8 marks)**

(c) Distinguish, with examples, between mandatory and voluntary disclosure in annual reports, and assess the usefulness of corporate governance disclosure to Bob in selecting his investments. **(9 marks)**

(Total = 25 marks)

30 Loho Company (12/14)

49 mins

After a period of expansion into several overseas markets and some structural decentralisation, Loho Company was considering its internal audit and internal control needs. Although privately owned and therefore not subject to listing rules, Loho's auditors had often suggested that a formal internal audit function would be beneficial.

The launch of several new products and a rapid increase in exports had raised a number of problems at Loho. These included problems in meeting order deadlines, whilst a number of operational constraints had meant that some orders had been delivered to customers late. The increase in overseas business had also, according to Sonja Tan, the financial director, increased the overall risk profile of the business. Credit risk had risen substantially as had a range of risks associated with exporting and overseas investment. In addition to a growth from 150 to 600 employees in its home country, Loho also had recruited a further 200 people overseas in order to facilitate business in those countries.

As part of her continuing professional development (CPD), Sonja Tan, the finance director who was also a professional accountant, had been to a seminar on improving internal controls (IC). She believed that at this point in its growth, Loho could benefit from tighter internal controls. Speaking about this to the board on her return from the seminar, she reminded her colleagues that sound internal controls could only provide 'reasonable assurance' and that any IC system had inherent limitations and could never be totally effective whatever changes were made to improve them. This came as a surprise to some board members who assumed, because internal controls were often very expensive, that they should be guaranteed to be fully effective.

Required

(a) Construct the case for establishing an internal audit function at Loho Company. **(10 marks)**

(b) Explain the reasons why many internal controls can never be guaranteed to be fully effective and discuss why ICs being 'very expensive' are no guarantee of their effectiveness. **(9 marks)**

(c) The finance director Sonja Tan learned about improved internal controls as part of her continuing professional development (CPD).

Required

Explain the advantages of continuing professional development (CPD) for professional accountants such as finance director Sonja Tan. **(6 marks)**

(Total = 25 marks)

31 Branscombe Co (Sep/Dec 15)   49 mins

Branscombe Co has been supplying and fitting premium bathrooms and kitchens in hotel chains throughout Effland for the past 20 years. The company started as a small family concern, but because of the rapid growth it experienced and an associated need for additional capital, it was recently listed on the national stock exchange by an initial public offering.

To remain fully compliant with the Effland corporate governance code, the board established audit, remuneration and nomination committees which were solely populated by independent non-executive directors. However, it did not consider it necessary to create a separate risk committee because the board believed that the remit of the audit committee included all aspects of risk management policy. This explanation was formally submitted to the shareholders at its first general meeting, who agreed with the board's proposal.

As part of its expansion strategy, the board of Branscombe Co decided it needed to enter overseas markets, and in particular the developing country of Geeland. The reason that Geeland was selected as a suitable market was because it had experienced rapid economic growth and domestic prosperity following the discovery of rich, offshore mineral deposits. Unfortunately, this small island nation has never enjoyed stable democratic government and is notorious for corrupt business practices, with customs officials regularly demanding bribes from both importers and exporters. As a result, Geeland has a poor international credit rating. In order to attract both domestic and foreign inward investment, the government of Geeland operates with very low levels of indirect tax, which has stimulated the island's tourist industry and led in turn to a significant increase in hotel building.

Following a successful tendering exercise, Branscombe Co was awarded the contract to supply all of the bathroom equipment for a 200-room hotel, currently under construction in a remote area of the island. The total value of the supply contract amounted to Geeland $1,800,000, and it was to be paid in three equal instalments as the bathrooms were delivered to the hotel. The contract assigns responsibility for shipping the goods the 3,000 km from Effland to the island solely with Branscombe Co, and no payment will be made until an agreed volume of goods clears Geeland customs. A further problem is that the Geeland dollar is quite volatile, but recently it has been strengthening against the Effland dollar. As all contract payments are to be made in Geeland currency, Branscombe Co is exposed to foreign exchange risks.

The many contract-related issues amount to significant risks to Branscombe Co requiring effective management if the supply contract is to be a success and contribute to the company's ambitious growth targets.

Required

(a) Explain the function and roles of a risk committee within an effective corporate governance framework, and discuss the advantages which a risk committee could add to the governance of Branscombe Co. **(10 marks)**

(b) Explain the term risk appetite, and assess how the risk appetite of Branscombe Co has influenced both its corporate strategy and the risks it has chosen to bear. **(7 marks)**

(c) Explain how Branscombe Co could effectively control the strategic and operational risks which arise from the Geeland supply contract. **(8 marks)**

(Total = 25 marks)

PROFESSIONAL VALUES AND ETHICS

Questions 32 to 50 cover professional values and ethics, the subject of Part C of the BPP Study Text for Paper P1.

32 Anne Hayes (6/08)

49 mins

It was the final day of a two-week-long audit of Van Buren Company, a longstanding client of Fillmore Pierce Auditors. In the afternoon, Anne Hayes, a recently qualified accountant and member of the audit team, was following an audit trail on some cash payments when she discovered what she described to the audit partner, Zachary Lincoln, as an 'irregularity'. A large and material cash payment had been recorded with no recipient named. The corresponding invoice was handwritten on a scrap of paper and the signature was illegible.

Zachary, the audit partner, was under pressure to finish the audit that afternoon. He advised Anne to seek an explanation from Frank Monroe, the client's finance director. Zachary told her that Van Buren was a longstanding client of Fillmore Pierce and he would be surprised if there was anything unethical or illegal about the payment. He said that he had personally been involved in the Van Buren audit for the last eight years and that it had always been without incident. He also said that Frank Monroe was an old friend of his from university days and that he was certain that he wouldn't approve anything unethical or illegal. Zachary said that Fillmore Pierce had also done some consultancy for Van Buren so it was a very important client that he didn't want Anne to upset with unwelcome and uncomfortable questioning.

When Anne sought an explanation from Mr Monroe, she was told that nobody could remember what the payment was for but that she had to recognise that 'real' audits were sometimes a bit messy and that not all audit trails would end as she might like them to. He also reminded her that it was the final day and both he and the audit firm were under time pressure to conclude business and get the audit signed off.

When Anne told Zachary what Frank had said, Zachary agreed not to get the audit signed off without Anne's support, but warned her that she should be very certain that the irregularity was worth delaying the signoff for. It was therefore now Anne's decision whether to extend the audit or have it signed off by the end of Friday afternoon.

Required

(a)   Explain why 'auditor independence' is necessary in auditor-client relationships and describe **three** threats to auditor independence in the case.   **(9 marks)**

Anne is experiencing some tension due to the conflict between her duties and responsibilities as an employee of Fillmore Pierce and as a qualified professional accountant.

Required

(b)   (i)   Compare and contrast her duties and responsibilities in the two roles of employee and professional accountant.   **(6 marks)**

        (ii)   Explain the ethical tensions between these roles that Anne is now experiencing.   **(4 marks)**

(c)   Explain how absolutist (dogmatic) and relativist (pragmatic) ethical assumptions would affect the outcome of Anne's decision.   **(6 marks)**

(Total = 25 marks)

33 Hogg Products (12/08)

49 mins

Hogg Products Company (HPC), based in a developing country, was recently wholly acquired by American Overseas Investments (AOI), a North American holding company. The new owners took the opportunity to completely review HPC's management, culture and systems. One of the first things that AOI questioned was HPC's longstanding corporate code of ethics.

The board of AOI said that it had a general code of ethics that HPC, as an AOI subsidiary, should adopt. Simon Hogg, the chief executive of HPC, disagreed however, and explained why HPC should retain its existing code. He said that HPC had adopted its code of ethics in its home country which was often criticised for its unethical business behaviour. Some other companies in the country were criticised for their 'sweat shop' conditions. HPC's adoption of its code of ethics, however, meant that it could always obtain orders from European customers on the

BPP
LEARNING MEDIA

guarantee that products were made ethically and in compliance with its own highly regarded code of ethics. Mr Hogg explained that HPC had an outstanding ethical reputation both locally and internationally and that reputation could be threatened if it was forced to replace its existing code of ethics with AOI's more general code.

When Ed Tanner, a senior director from AOI's head office, visited Mr Hogg after the acquisition, he was shown HPC's operation in action. Mr Hogg pointed out that unlike some other employers in the industry, HPC didn't employ child labour. Mr Hogg explained that although it was allowed by law in the country, it was forbidden by HPC's code of ethics. Mr Hogg also explained that in his view, employing child labour was always ethically wrong. Mr Tanner asked whether the money that children earned by working in the relatively safe conditions at HPC was an important source of income for their families. Mr Hogg said that the money was important to them but even so, it was still wrong to employ children, as it was exploitative and interfered with their education. He also said that it would alienate the European customers who bought from HPC partly on the basis of the terms of its code of ethics.

Required

(a)   Describe the purposes and typical contents of a corporate code of ethics.   **(9 marks)**

'Strategic positioning' is about the way that a company as a whole is placed in its environment and concerns its 'fit' with the factors in its environment.

(b)   With reference to the case as appropriate, explain how a code of ethics can be used as part of a company's overall strategic positioning.   **(7 marks)**

(c)   Assess Mr Hogg's belief that employing child labour is 'always ethically wrong' from deontological and teleological (consequentialist) ethical perspectives.   **(9 marks)**

(Total = 25 marks)

34 Policy speech (6/09)   **49 mins**

In a major policy speech, Government finance minister Mrs Wei Yttria said that the audit and assurance industry's work should always be judged by the effect it has on public confidence in business. She said that it was crucial that professional services such as audit and assurance should always be performed in the public interest and that there should be no material threats to the assurer's independence. Enron and other corporate failures happened, she said, because some accountants didn't understand what it was to act in the public interest. She stressed that it was important that firms should not provide more than one service to individual clients. If a firm audited a client then, she said, it shouldn't provide any other services to that client.

Mr Oggon Mordue, a financial journalist who had worked in audit and assurance for many years, was in the audience. He suggested that the normal advice on threats to independence was wrong. On the contrary in fact, the more services that a professional services firm can provide to a client the better, as it enables the firm to better understand the client and its commercial and accounting needs. Mrs Yttria disagreed, saying that his views were a good example of professional services firms not acting in the public interest.

Mr Mordue said that when he was a partner at a major professional services firm, he got to know his clients very well through the multiple links that his firm had with them. He said that he knew all about their finances from providing audit and assurance services, all about their tax affairs through tax consulting and was always in a good position to provide any other advice as he had acted as a consultant on other matters for many years including advising on mergers, acquisitions, compliance and legal issues. He became very good friends with the directors of client companies, he said. The clients, he explained, also found the relationship very helpful and the accounting firms did well financially out of it.

Another reporter in the audience argued with Mr Mordue. Ivor Nahum said that Mr Mordue represented the 'very worst' of the accounting profession. He said that accounting was a 'biased and value laden' profession that served minority interests, was complicit in environmental degradation and could not serve the public interest as long as it primarily served the interests of unfettered capitalism. He said that the public interest was badly served by accounting, as it did not address poverty, animal rights or other social injustices.

Required

(a)   Explain, using accounting as an example, what 'the public interest' means as used by Mrs Yttria in her speech.   **(5 marks)**

This requirement concerns ethical threats. It is very important for professional accountants to be aware of ethical threats and to avoid these where possible.

Required

(b) (i) With reference to the case as appropriate, describe five types of ethical threat. **(5 marks)**

(ii) Assess the ethical threats implied by Mr Mordue's beliefs. **(8 marks)**

(c) Assess Ivor Nahum's remarks about the accounting profession in the light of Gray, Owen & Adams' deep green (or deep ecologist) position on social responsibility. **(7 marks)**

(Total = 25 marks)

35 John Wang (12/09)   49 mins

John Wang is a junior partner and training manager at Miller Dundas, a medium sized firm of auditors. He oversees the progress of the firm's student accountants. One of those under John's supervision, Lisa Xu, recently wrote in her progress and achievement log about a situation in an audit that had disturbed her.

On the recent audit of Mbabo Company, a medium sized, family-run business and longstanding client of Miller Dundas, Lisa was checking non-current asset purchases when she noticed what she thought might be an irregularity. There was an entry of $100,000 for a security system for an address in a well-known holiday resort with no obvious link to the company. On questioning this with Ellen Tan, the financial controller, Lisa was told that the system was for Mr Martin Mbabo's holiday cottage (Martin Mbabo is managing director and a minority shareholder in the Mbabo Company). She was told that Martin Mbabo often took confidential company documents with him to his holiday home and so needed the security system on the property to protect them. It was because of this, Ellen said, that it was reasonable to charge the security system to the company.

Ellen Tan expressed surprise at Lisa's concerns and said that auditors had not previously been concerned about the company being charged for non-current assets and operational expenses for Mr Mbabo's personal properties.

Lisa told the engagement partner, Potto Sinter, what she had found and Potto simply said that the charge could probably be ignored. He did agree, however, to ask for a formal explanation from Martin Mbabo before he signed off the audit. Lisa wasn't at the final clearance meeting but later read the following in the notes from the clearance meeting: 'discussed other matter with client, happy with explanation'. When Lisa discussed the matter with Potto afterwards she was told that the matter was now closed and that she should concentrate on her next audit and her important accounting studies.

When John Wang read about Lisa's concerns and spoke to her directly, he realised he was in an ethical dilemma. Not only should there be a disclosure requirement of Mr Mbabo's transaction, but the situation was made more complicated by the fact that Potto Sinter was senior to John Wang in Miller Dundas and also by the fact that the two men were good friends.

Required

(a) Explain the meaning of 'integrity' and its importance in professional relationships such as those described in the case. **(5 marks)**

(b) Criticise Potto Sinter's ethical and professional behaviour in the case. **(10 marks)**

(c) Critically evaluate the alternatives that John Wang has in his ethical dilemma. **(10 marks)**

(Total = 25 marks)

36 Happy and healthy (6/10)   49 mins

'Happy and healthy' is a traditional independent health food business that has been run as a family company for 40 years by Ken and Steffi Potter. As a couple they have always been passionate campaigners for healthy foods and are more concerned about the quality of the foods they sell than the financial detail of their business. Since the company started in 1970, it has been audited by Watson Shreeves, a local audit firm. Mr Shreeves has overseen the Potters' audit for all of the 40-year history (rotating the engagement partner) and has always taken the opportunity to meet with Ken and Steffi informally at the end of each audit to sign off the financial statements and to offer a briefing and some free financial advice in his role as what he calls, 'auditor and friend'. In these briefings, Mr

Shreeves, who has become a close family friend of the Potters over the years, always points out that the business is profitable (which the Potters already knew without knowing the actual figures) and how they might increase their margins. But the Potters have never been too concerned about financial performance as long as they can provide a good service to their customers, make enough to keep the business going and provide continued employment for themselves and their son, Ivan. Whilst Ken and Steffi still retain a majority shareholding in 'Happy and healthy' they have gradually increased Ivan's proportion over the years. They currently own 60% to Ivan's 40%. Ivan was appointed a director, alongside Ken and Steffi, in 2008.

Ivan grew up in the business and has helped his parents out since he was a young boy. As he grew up, Ken and Steffi gave him more and more responsibility in the hope that he would one day take the business over. By the end of 2009, Ken made sure that Ivan drew more salary than Ken and Steffi combined as they sought to ensure that Ivan was happy to continue in the business after they retired.

During the audit for the year ended 31 March 2010, a member of Watson Shreeves was performing the audit as usual when he noticed a dramatic drop in the profitability of the business as a whole. He noticed that whilst food sales continued to be profitable, a large amount of inventory had been sold below cost to Barong Company with no further explanation and it was this that had caused the reduction in the company's operating margin. Each transaction with Barong Company had, the invoices showed, been authorised by Ivan.

Mr Shreeves was certain Ken and Steffi would not know anything about this and he prepared to tell them about it as a part of his annual end of audit meeting. Before the meeting, however, he carried out some checks on Barong Company and found that it was a separate business owned by Ivan and his wife. Mr Shreeves's conclusion was that Ivan was effectively stealing from 'Happy and healthy' to provide inventory for Barong Company at a highly discounted cost price. Although Mr Shreeves now had to recommend certain disclosures to the financial statements in this meeting, his main fear was that Ken and Steffi would be devastated if they found out that Ivan was stealing and that it would have long-term implications for their family relationships and the future of 'Happy and healthy'.

Required

(a)   Explain how a family (or insider-dominated) business differs from a public listed company and, using evidence from the case, explore the governance issues of a family or insider-dominated business.

(10 marks)

(b)   Mr Shreeves is a professional accountant and auditor. Explain why he is considered a professional by society and describe the fundamental principles (or responsibilities) of professionalism that society expects from him and all other accountants. **(7 marks)**

(c)   Discuss the professional and ethical dilemma facing Mr Shreeves in deciding whether or not to tell Ken and Steffi about Ivan's activity. Advise Mr Shreeves of the most appropriate course of action. **(8 marks)**

(Total = 25 marks)

37 JGP (12/10)   49 mins

At a board meeting of JGP Chemicals Limited, the directors were discussing some recent negative publicity arising from the accidental emission of a chemical pollutant into the local river. As well as it resulting in a large fine from the courts, the leak had created a great deal of controversy in the local community that relied on the polluted river for its normal use (including drinking). A prominent community leader spoke for those affected when she said that a leak of this type must never happen again or JGP would suffer the loss of support from the community. She also reminded JGP that it attracts 65% of its labour from the local community.

As a response to the problems that arose after the leak, the JGP board decided to consult an expert on whether the publication of a full annual environmental report might help to mitigate future environmental risks. The expert, Professor Appo (a prominent academic), said that the company would need to establish an annual environmental audit before they could issue a report. He said that the environmental audit should include, in addition to a review and evaluation of JGP's safety controls, a full audit of the environmental impact of JGP's supply chain. He said that these components would be very important in addressing the concerns of a growing group of investors who are worried about such things. Professor Appo said that all chemical companies had a structural environmental risk and JGP was no exception to this. As major consumers of natural chemical resources and producers of potentially hazardous outputs, Professor Appo said that chemical companies should be aware of the wide range of ways in which they can affect the environment. CEO Keith Miasma agreed with Professor Appo and added that because JGP was in chemicals, any environmental issue had the potential to affect JGP's overall reputation among a wide range of stakeholders.

When the board was discussing the issue of sustainability in connection with the environmental audit, the finance director said that sustainability reporting would not be necessary as the company was already sustainable because it had no 'going concern' issues. He said that JGP had been in business for over 50 years, should be able to continue for many years to come and was therefore sustainable. As far as he was concerned, this was all that was meant by sustainability.

In the discussion that followed, the board noted that in order to signal its seriousness to the local community and to investors, the environmental audit should be as thorough as possible and that as much information should be made available to the public 'in the interests of transparency'. It was agreed that contents of the audit (the agreed metrics) should be robust and with little room left for interpretation – they wanted to be able to demonstrate that they had complied with their agreed metrics for the environmental audit.

Required

(a) Explain 'sustainability' in the context of environmental auditing and criticise the finance director's understanding of sustainability. **(6 marks)**

(b) Explain the three stages in an environmental audit and explore, using information from the case, the issues that JGP will have in developing these stages. **(9 marks)**

(c) Define 'environmental risk'. Distinguish between strategic and operational risks and explain why the environmental risks at JGP are strategic. **(10 marks)**

(Total = 25 marks)

38 Ann Koo (6/11 amended) 49 mins

The IESBA code of professional ethics (2013), adopted as being relevant to ACCA members and students, contains the following advice.

'A professional accountant in business or an immediate or close family member may be offered an inducement. Inducements may take various forms, including gifts, hospitality, preferential treatment, and inappropriate appeals to friendship or loyalty. Offers of inducements may create threats to compliance with the fundamental principles [of professionalism].'

Executive director and qualified accountant Ann Koo was in charge of awarding large outsourcing contracts for a large public listed company. When her family fell into debt, she looked for a way to make some additional income. When her company was seeking to place a contract for a large outsourced service, without inviting other tenders from which to select, she accepted a bid from one supplier who said it would pay her $50,000 as a 'thank you' once the contract was awarded. She justified her behaviour by reminding herself that she obtained her job partly because she was an accountant and that she had worked extremely hard to obtain her accounting qualification. She believed she was entitled to make a 'higher personal return' on her investment of time and effort in her accountancy training and through successful qualification as a professional accountant.

Required

(a) Briefly describe the five types of ethical threats in the IESBA code of professional ethics (2009) and discuss how accepting excessive 'gifts' or 'hospitality' can give rise to some of these threats within this case. **(9 marks)**

(b) Criticise Ann Koo's beliefs and behaviour, and explain why accepting the $50,000 conflicts with her duty to uphold the public interest. **(10 marks)**

The IESBA code also highlights the need for: 'up-to-date education [for directors] on ethical issues and the legal restrictions and other regulations around potential insider trading.'

Required

(c) Explain what 'insider dealing/trading' is and why it is an unethical and often illegal practice. **(6 marks)**

(Total = 25 marks)

39 Biggo (12/11)

When Biggo Manufacturing (a public listed company) needed to build an extension to its factory, it obtained planning permission to build it on an adjacent field. The local government authority was keen to attract the new jobs that would go with the expansion and so granted the permission despite the objections of a number of residents, who were concerned that the new factory extension would mean the loss of a children's play area.

When the board of Biggo met after the building approval had been given, the chief executive read out a letter from Albert Doo, leader of the local government authority, saying that although permission to build had been given, the company should consider making a sizeable contribution towards creating a new children's play area in a nearby location. Mr Doo said that Biggo 'should recognise its social responsibility'. He said that the company should consider itself a citizen of society and should, accordingly, 'recognise its responsibilities as well as its legal rights'.

One of Biggo's directors, Robert Tens, said he thought the request was entirely reasonable given the displacement of the play area. He also said that they could use the donation strategically to help cultivate the company's reputation locally to help in future recruitment. It might also, he said, help to reduce resistance to any future expansion the company might need to make.

Margaret Heggs, in contrast, argued that the company should not make the donation as it was likely that company profits would be low in the current year. She said that the acquisition of the land and the gaining of planning permission were done through the normal legal channels and so the company had no further contractual or ethical duties to the local government, nor to the local community. She said that Biggo provided local employment and produced excellent products and so it was unreasonable for the request for a donation to have been made. 'This board is accountable to the shareholders of Biggo and not to the local community or the local government authority', she said.

Required

(a)   Explain the meaning of 'rights' and 'responsibilities' in the context of Biggo and describe how these terms are interpreted at the two ends of the Gray, Owen & Adams 'continuum'.   **(10 marks)**

(b)   Justify, using evidence from the case, which of Gray, Owen & Adams's positions are best described by the comments made by Robert Tens and also Margaret Heggs.   **(6 marks)**

(c)   Define 'social responsibility' as used by Albert Doo. Contrast how short and long-term shareholder interest perspectives may affect Biggo's attitude to the requested contribution for the children's play area.   **(9 marks)**

(Total = 25 marks)

40 Jojo (6/12)

Jojo Auditors is an audit practice with five partners. The five partners have worked together for several years and, as well as being work colleagues, are personal friends with each other. At Jojo it is customary for the performance of all student accountants to be appraised after their first year of a training contract using a range of criteria including examination success, technical ability and professionalism. Three levels of outcome are possible:

1.   'Good', allowing students to continue with no issues
2.   'Some concerns', meaning students are counselled and then allowed to continue
3.   'Poor', where students are dismissed from the audit practice

The appraisal committee is comprised of three people: managing partner Jack Hu, the training manager (both of whom are professional accountants) and the person responsible for human resources. The committee receives confidential reports on each student and makes decisions based on the views of relevant engagement partners and also exam results. It is normally the training manager who makes the recommendation and in most cases his appraisal is agreed and then acted upon accordingly. Because the appraisals are confidential between the student and the firm, the list of students and their appraisal categories are not publicised within the firm.

When the 2010 intake was being appraised last year, one student was appraised by the training manager as 'poor' but was not dismissed. Polly Shah was unpopular among other students because she was considered lazy and technically weak. She also failed a number of her exams. Other students who were appraised as 'poor' were dismissed, but Polly received a brief counselling session from Jack Hu and then returned to her duties. Polly stayed for another year and then, having failed more exams, left Jojo to pursue other career interests outside accounting.

Polly's departure triggered some discussion amongst Jojo's partners as to why she had been retained when other poor performers had not. It later emerged that Jack Hu was a close friend of Polly's parents and had enjoyed free holidays in the Shah family's villa for several years. Because he was the managing partner, Mr Hu was able to insist on retaining Polly, despite the objections of the training manager and the human resources representative, although the training manager was reported to be furious at the decision to retain Polly.

Required

(a) Define 'conflict of interest' and assess the consequences of Mr Hu's behaviour after Polly Shah's appraisal.

(10 marks)

(b) Describe four ethical safeguards that could be used in Jojo to prevent a recurrence of the events like those described in the case.

(8 marks)

The case raises issues of the importance of senior management performance measurement. In a public company, this refers to directors, and in a privately-owned partnership like Jojo, it refers to partners. The managing partner (Mr Hu's position) is equivalent to the role of chief executive.

Required

(c) Explain the typical criteria used in the performance measurement of individual directors and discuss the reasons why individual performance measurement of partners may be difficult to implement at Jojo.

(7 marks)

(Total = 25 marks)

41 RDC (12/12)
49 mins

Railway Development Company (RDC) was considering two options for a new railway line connecting two towns. Route A involved cutting a channel through an area designated as being of special scientific importance because it was one of a very few suitable feeding grounds for a colony of endangered birds. The birds were considered to be an important part of the local environment with some potential influences on local ecosystems.

The alternative was Route B which would involve the compulsory purchase and destruction of Eddie Krul's farm. Mr Krul was a vocal opponent of the Route B plan. He said that he had a right to stay on the land which had been owned by his family for four generations and which he had developed into a profitable farm. The farm employed a number of local people whose jobs would be lost if Route B went through the house and land. Mr Krul threatened legal action against RDC if Route B was chosen.

An independent legal authority has determined that the compulsory purchase price of Mr Krul's farm would be $1 million if Route B was chosen. RDC considered this a material cost, over and above other land costs, because the projected net present value (NPV) of cash flows over a ten-year period would be $5 million without buying the farm. This would reduce the NPV by $1 million if Route B was chosen.

The local government authority had given both routes provisional planning permission and offered no opinion of which it preferred. It supported infrastructure projects such as the new railway line, believing that either route would attract new income and prosperity to the region. It took the view that as an experienced railway builder, RDC would know best which to choose and how to evaluate the two options. Because it was very keen to attract the investment, it left the decision entirely to RDC. RDC selected Route A as the route to build the new line.

A local environmental pressure group, 'Save the Birds', was outraged at the decision to choose Route A. It criticised RDC and also the local authority for ignoring the sustainability implications of the decision. It accused the company of profiting at the expense of the environment and threatened to use 'direct action' to disrupt the building of the line through the birds' feeding ground if Route A went ahead.

Required

(a) Use Tucker's 'five question' model to assess the decision to choose Route A.

(10 marks)

(b) Discuss the importance to RDC of recognising all of the stakeholders in a decision such as deciding between Route A and Route B.

(8 marks)

(c)   Explain what a stakeholder 'claim' is, and critically assess the stakeholder claims of Eddie Krul, the local government authority and the colony of endangered birds.   **(7 marks)**

(Total = 25 marks)

42 Lobo (12/13)   49 mins

A technological failure occurred at Lobo Company last year. A new computer system which was designed to control Lobo's complicated operational facility broke down shortly after it was installed. This meant that the company was unable to carry out production processes normally for several days.

The cause of the failure was later found to have been a system specification error made by Frank Bub, the operations director and a professional engineer. He had seriously miscalculated the capacity needed for the new system and had ordered a computer system which was unfit for purpose. Not only had this resulted in the loss of several days of production and a loss of loyalty and goodwill from customers and others, it also cost a large amount to repair and upgrade the system to be able to cope with the actual demands placed upon it.

Frank Bub acknowledged that he had over-ridden normal procurement procedures in purchasing the system. But he was thought by his colleagues to be such a competent engineer, it was not felt necessary for anybody else in the company to discuss the purchase with the suppliers. His fellow directors believed that Mr Bub would exercise the judgement needed to purchase and implement the new system. Because the system was needed urgently, there was no time to run it in 'pilot mode' or to test it on site before it was fully installed. When he was asked about the failure, Frank Bub said that he decided to buy the system in question because an old friend had recommended it and that he saw no need to take further advice beyond that.

The non-executive directors met after the incident and collectively decided that Frank Bub, who had nine months remaining on his renewable three-year contract, had lost the confidence of the board and should leave the company at the earliest opportunity. It was decided to move him to a non-critical role until such time as it was possible to remove him as cheaply as possible.

Required

(a)   Directors may leave the service of a board in several ways.

   (i)   Describe the main ways in which the directors of companies can leave the service of a board.
                                                                                                              (3 marks)

   (ii)   Justify an appropriate way for Frank Bub to leave the board of Lobo Company, based on the circumstances of the case.   **(5 marks)**

(b)   Briefly explain 'technological risk' and discuss the problems which led to the technological failure at Lobo, commenting on how these might affect shareholder confidence in the entire board.   **(8 marks)**

You may assume that, as a professional engineer, Frank Bub is bound by the same fundamental principles of professional ethics as a professional accountant and must act in the wider public interest.

Required

(c)   Discuss the fundamental principles of professional ethics which Frank Bub failed to observe and explain how an awareness of his duty to the public interest may have prevented his errors.   **(9 marks)**

(Total = 25 marks)

43 Hum and Hoo (6/14)   49 mins

Hum and Hoo is an established audit practice in Deetown and has a large share of the audit services market among local businesses. Because Deetown is a relatively isolated area, many clients rely on Hum and Hoo for accounting and technical advice over and above the annual audit. This has meant that, over time, Hum and Hoo has also developed expertise in compliance advice, tax, strategy consulting and other professional services.

Because non-audit work is important to Hum and Hoo, staff have 'business growth' criteria strongly linked with bonuses and promotion. This means that many of the professional accountants in the firm actively seek to increase sales of non-audit services to businesses in the Deetown area, including from audit clients. The culture of the firm is such that everybody is expected to help out with any project which needs to be done, and this sometimes means that staff help out on a range of both audit and non-audit tasks. The lines between audit and non-audit services are sometimes blurred and staff may work on either, as workload needs demand. Managing partner Cherry Hoo told staff that the non-audit revenue is now so important to the firm that staff should not do anything to threaten that source of income.

Cherry Hoo said that she was thinking of beginning to offer a number of other services including advice on environmental reporting and the provision of environmental auditing services. She said she had spoken to local companies which were looking to demonstrate their environmental sustainability and she believed that environmental reporting and auditing might be ways to help with this. She said she was confused by the nature of environmental reporting and so was not sure about what should be audited.

Required

(a)   Explain 'ethical threat' and 'ethical safeguard' in the context of external auditing, and discuss the benefits of effective ethical safeguards for Hum and Hoo.   **(8 marks)**

(b)   Explain 'environmental audit' and assess how environmental reporting and auditing might enable companies to 'demonstrate their environmental sustainability' as Cherry Hoo suggested.   **(8 marks)**

(c)   Some corporate governance codes prohibit audit firms such as Hum and Hoo from providing some non-audit services to audit clients without the prior approval of the client's audit committee. This is because it is sometimes believed to be against the public interest.

Required

Explain 'public interest' in the context of accounting services and why a client's audit committee is a suitable body to advise on the purchase of non-audit services from Hum and Hoo.   **(9 marks)**

(Total = 25 marks)

44 Mahmood (6/14)   49 mins

Mahmood is a junior employee of Tzo Company (a large, listed company). Tzo is a processor of food labelled as containing only high quality meat. The company enjoys the trust and confidence of its customers because of its reputation for high quality products. One day, when passing through one area of the plant, Mahmood noticed some inferior meat being mixed with the normal product. He felt this must be unauthorised so he informed his supervisor, the factory manager, who told Mahmood that this was in fact a necessary cost reduction measure because company profits had been declining in recent months. Mahmood later found out that all stages of the production process, from purchasing to final quality control, were adapted in order to make the use of the inferior meat possible.

The factory manager told Mahmood that the inferior meat was safe for humans to eat and its use was not illegal. However, he told Mahmood that if knowledge of the use of this meat was made public, it would mean that customers might stop buying the products. Many jobs could be lost, probably including Mahmood's own. The factory manager ordered Mahmood to say nothing about the inferior meat and to conduct his job as normal. Mahmood later discovered that the main board of Tzo was aware of the use of the inferior meat and supported its use in seeking to reduce costs and maintain profits. In covering up the use of the inferior meat, the factory produced a fraudulent quality control report to show that the product was purely based on high quality meat when the company knew that this was not so.

When Mahmood heard this, he was very angry and considered telling an external source, such as the local newspaper, about what he had seen and about how the company was being dishonest with its customers.

Required

(a)   Explain how Mahmood might act, in each case, if he were to adopt either conventional or post-conventional ethical assumptions according to Kohlberg's definitions of these terms. Your answer should include an explanation of these two terms.   **(8 marks)**

(b)   Construct an ethical case for Mahmood to take this matter directly to an external source such as a newspaper.   **(8 marks)**

(c)   Some jurisdictions have a compulsory regulatory requirement for an auditor-reviewed external report on the operation and effectiveness of internal controls (such as s.404 of Sarbanes Oxley).

Required

Explain how such a requirement may have helped to prevent the undisclosed use of the inferior meat at Tzo Company.   **(9 marks)**

(Total = 25 marks)

45 Rosey and Atkins (6/15)   49 mins

Rosey and Atkins (R&A) is one of the largest institutional investors in the country. Its investment strategy has traditionally been to own a minor shareholding in each of the top 200 companies on the stock exchange. The R&A shareholding is typically between 2% and 10% of each company and it manages funds for over two million clients (people and businesses who buy into share funds managed by R&A).

Established over 200 years ago, R&A has always believed itself to be socially responsible. As part of its CSR strategy, R&A recently purchased 100% of the shares in a national housebuilder, Natcon, which it owned as a direct holding and did not include in its managed funds. Natcon, in turn, owned a large amount of land suitable for future low cost housing development. The R&A website reported that the reason for this purchase was to address the board's concerns over a shortage of affordable housing in the country which R&A felt they could help to address by having outright ownership of Natcon. R&A reported that there was a large social need for affordable homes, and it hoped to create many hundreds of new low cost homes each year.

Natcon wanted to build a large estate of new homes in the town of Housteads and the local government authority granted the required building permission. But the nearby University of Housteads strongly opposed it because it believed the new houses would ruin what was considered to be a panoramic view from the university campus which helped it to recruit staff and students to the university. Both the Housteads local government authority and the University of Housteads had money from reserves invested as clients (ie fund investors) with R&A, but with the university having a substantially smaller investment in the fund than the local government authority. The local government authority also owned shares in R&A, meaning that it was both an investor in funds and a shareholder in R&A.

Required

(a)   Distinguish between private and institutional shareholders, and discuss the agency problems which might arise when an institutional shareholder such as R&A holds money in funds on behalf of clients (ie investors in R&A funds).   **(7 marks)**

(b)   Explain the difference between 'corporate social responsibility (CSR) strategy' and 'strategic CSR', and construct the argument that the purchase of Natcon (the house builder) is an example of strategic CSR.   **(10 marks)**

(c)   Explain how stakeholder claims are sometimes in conflict and, using a suitable stakeholder analysis framework, assess the competing claims of the local government authority and the University of Housteads in the proposed housing development.   **(8 marks)**

(Total = 25 marks)

46 Pulpo (6/15)   49 mins

Pulpo is a local pulp and paper factory. As a subsidiary of a major international company, Pulpo has not produced a social and environmental report for itself, but instead provided data which was fed into the parent company's group report. There was some discussion about Pulpo having an environmental report on its own website but no resources were provided for its development, so nothing ever materialised.

Mary Wong was the manager at Pulpo whose responsibility was to monitor and report on environmental emissions. It was her responsibility to monitor emissions and to feed data into the company's internal control systems on resource consumption (energy and water) and waste. It was a job she enjoyed because it enabled her to express her personal concern for the environment in her work. When she took over her role two years ago, she was told that the company had very ambitious voluntary emission targets and that they would eventually be reduced to make the company even more environmentally responsible over time. Mary found this exciting and it was on this basis that she agreed to accept the appointment. Because of the sensitive nature of some of the data she managed, her employment terms and conditions included a confidentiality clause in which she agreed never to publicly disclose the environmental targets or the company's performance against them.

When investment in new manufacturing capital was delayed because of a deteriorating profit performance, Mary was informed that the emissions target would be temporarily increased because the ageing equipment would not be able to maintain the low level of emissions. Dismayed by this change, she complained to the company chief executive but was told that she had to accept the higher emissions until the company could afford its factory investment, which could be several years in the future.

She decided that the most effective way to deal with this change was to publicise it to the local newspaper and to the nearby residents' association, both of whom had been longstanding critics of the factory's impacts on the environment. The public reacted angrily to the disclosure as it was already considered a 'dirty' factory which often emitted fumes and effluent, which polluted the local river. When the board of the company discovered her actions, she was dismissed for breach of her terms and conditions in publically disclosing the confidential information.

Required

(a)   Distinguish between Kohlberg's conventional and postconventional ethical responses and explain, with reasons, which ethical approach Mary Wong took in her decision to publicise the change in emissions target.

(9 marks)

(b)   Construct the case for Pulpo to now publish an environmental report on its own website in addition to that provided by the parent company.

(8 marks)

(c)   Explain the meaning of 'internal control' and discuss why a sound internal control system is necessary in managing Pulpo's environmental footprint.

(8 marks)

(Total = 25 marks)

47 Plantex (Sep/Dec 15)   49 mins

Plantex is a large international pharmaceutical company which has been at the forefront of research into developing cures for many tropical diseases. The nature of its business means that continuous and significant financial investment is required for research and development activities, for which its shareholders expect sizeable returns.

At a recent meeting of the board of Plantex, the finance director, Rachel Tang, submitted a paper on integrated reporting <IR> for discussion and consideration. She advised the board that Plantex had only ever disclosed the minimum information which it was required to by law, but recent developments in the International Integrated Reporting Framework has made a very strong case for broadening the amount of published corporate information.

The primary objective of <IR> is to demonstrate the clear link between a firm's competitive strategy, governance system and financial performance, alongside the social, environmental and economic context within which the firm operates. Rachel Tang claimed that by integrating these different areas, the board of Plantex would be in a far better position to allocate its valuable resources more effectively and thereby make more environmental and socially sustainable decisions.

The chairman was highly supportive of the proposal as he had been trying to encourage a corporate citizenship agenda at recent board meetings. He suggested that <IR> would demonstrate that Plantex took corporate social responsibility seriously by being more transparent, accountable and responsive to its stakeholders' demands.

Rachel Tang further asserted that <IR> would have the effect of simplifying published financial information, with excessive detail being removed and critical information being highlighted. If Plantex voluntarily adopted <IR>, its shareholders, and other stakeholders, would better understand how the firm was really performing and so be able to make a meaningful assessment of the firm's long-term strategy. This openness could encourage further investment and strengthen the firm's competitive position.

The chief executive, Stanley Broadway, suggested that this all sounded very good in theory, but he found it hard to justify the extra expense without any recognisable return to shareholders. He said it was 'just another costly management fad that distracted the company from its real purpose – making money for its shareholders!'

Required

(a) Explain the concept of corporate citizenship and assess the rights and responsibilities of Plantex as a corporate citizen of society. **(7 marks)**

(b) Describe the differing opinions about integrated reporting <IR> of Rachel Tang and Stanley Broadway and assess them using the relevant Gray, Owen & Adams positions on social responsibility. **(6 marks)**

(c) (i) Describe the advantages to Plantex and its stakeholders of adopting <IR>. **(6 marks)**

    (ii) Explain how using an <IR> approach will provide information about the six capitals including the resources and relationships on which Plantex depends. **(6 marks)**

(Total = 25 marks)

48 MRA (Sep/Dec 15)   49 mins

When MRA was shortlisted for a valuable contract for the development of a coastal defence system for another country, it was contingent on the payment of a facilitation fee to an official in the defence ministry. Clearly this was an unusual request but it was also made very clear that MRA would not be awarded the contract, worth $2 billion over 10 years, unless the relatively modest sum of $1 million was paid immediately.

Recently, business activity in the defence sector had been very slow, and MRA was about to announce around 500 staff redundancies. Therefore news that this contract was about to be awarded came as a great relief to the board of MRA, as the jobs would now be secured. However, only the chief executive officer (CEO) and operations director knew about the facilitation fee, so an emergency meeting of the board was convened with only one item on the agenda.

Due to the very sensitive nature of the matter at hand, it was decided not to make a formal record of the discussions at the board meeting. This was more likely to result in a frank exchange of views and encourage all directors to express their opinions openly.

The CEO, Charlie Desborough, explained the dilemma to the board, making it very clear that without this contract there would be no way to protect jobs. The finance director, Jake Neilson, said that he was personally very uncomfortable with the idea of paying a facilitation fee, which was in effect a 'bribe'. As a professional accountant he was bound by a code of ethics which strictly prohibited making such payments, therefore he could not sanction the payment under any circumstances.

The HR director, Sarah Shue, took a far more pragmatic stance. She acknowledged that any form of corruption was utterly deplorable; however, it was a fact of life in many countries. She asserted that if the board of MRA decided not to make the payment and forego the contract, then it could be assured that a competitor would not adopt such a high-minded position. The net effect was that by avoiding a relatively small payment, the firm would be doing a disservice to both its employees and its shareholders, who would undoubtedly suffer a reduction in their shareholder value. She maintained that sometimes it is necessary to take difficult decisions in business that are for the greater good, and so suggested that the payment to the official should be made.

Required

(a) (i) Compare relativism and absolutism and explain the significance of individual or personal differences in guiding ethical behaviour under each approach in a given scenario such as the situation at MRA. **(5 marks)**

    (ii) Explain the ethical theories of deontology and teleology or consequentialism, and analyse which of the approaches have been adopted by Sarah Shue and Jake Neilson. **(6 marks)**

The involvement of directors in bribery and corruption can seriously undermine the relationships of trust upon which corporate governance is based.

Required

(b) (i) Assess how bribery and corruption could undermine confidence and trust in MRA, with reference to the principles of corporate governance. **(8 marks)**

    (ii) Describe best practice measures which could be employed by MRA to combat bribery and corruption. **(6 marks)**

(Total = 25 marks)

49 Angus Fortune (Mar/Jun 16)

Angus Fortune, an ACCA qualified accountant, is a director of a medium-sized consultancy company and he heads up the business advisory division. Angus qualified 15 years ago and has worked for his current employer for nearly eight years, where he is viewed by his colleagues as a knowledgeable and experienced professional. His reputation for always offering good quality advice to clients, together with his work ethic and loyalty, earned him promotion to the board last year.

In recent discussions with Peter Wise, the managing director, it was agreed that as part of his continuous professional development (CPD) as a director, Angus should attend an overseas conference on tackling internet fraud, a line of business activity the company was keen to develop.

After the opening session, which gave delegates details of the content of the three-day conference, Angus realised that he already knew everything which was going to be covered from his private studies. So he decided instead to spend his time more productively at a local library reading up on issues which would directly help him with a forthcoming major assignment. He phoned Peter before leaving the conference explaining what he planned to do, but Peter said that he would still like him to attend the conference as he was bound to pick up new areas of useful and relevant knowledge. However, Angus still decided to leave after the morning coffee break.

He was observed leaving by one of the conference organisers, despite remaining signed in for the whole all day. At the start of Day 2, Angus returned to sign the attendance register again, but then immediately proceeded to leave the conference building. He was approached by the conference organiser who advised Angus that he really ought to report his absence. Angus explained to the conference organiser that he already knew much of the content of the conference, and so felt that it would be waste of his time if he stayed. Instead, he explained, he planned to spend the time more productively researching subject matter which better suited both his personal development and his company's needs.

On reflection, the conference organiser decided to report Angus's absence.

Required

(a) Evaluate the benefits of CPD to Angus Fortune, and describe the features of effective CPD. **(10 marks)**

(b) With reference to Kohlberg's theory of human moral development, describe conventional level reasoning and discuss how Kohlberg's conventional level arguments could be used to justify the conference organiser's decision to report his absence. **(8 marks)**

(c) Evaluate Angus's actions at the conference against the fundamental ethical principles which should have guided his behaviour as a professional accountant. **(7 marks)**

(Total = 25 marks)

50 WSK (Mar/Jun 16)

WSK produces chemicals for use in the agricultural sector, some which are highly toxic in both liquid and gaseous states. They need to be safely stored on site after processing until they are shipped out to customers either by road or rail.

Analysis of recently published data, detailing the frequency and impact of earthquakes around the world, suggest that the likelihood of a strong earthquake occurring in the area where WSK has its only manufacturing and chemical storage facility is high. This very serious claim was made by the operations director at a recent board meeting following consultation with the senior scientific team. It has always been recognised that the WSK factory was situated in an area where earthquakes could occur, but the area had not experienced any major tremors for several years.

The possibility of an earthquake which could destroy the WSK factory and then cause a major environmental incident was of grave concern to the board, who decided that it needed to be fully evaluated and then effectively managed. The board asked the scientific team to calculate the probability of a toxic chemical emission being caused by an earthquake together with the consequential effects on the local environment and population, many of whom depended on WSK for employment and commercial activity. However, the scientific team were unable to provide any objective analysis to support their initial claim, they merely offered their best guess of what they perceived the risk to be.

The board concluded that this was inadequate, so they tasked the internal audit team to conduct an environmental audit, and to determine WSK's environmental footprint.

Required

(a) Evaluate the difficulties of risk perception, and describe the problems with the perception of risk shown by the scientific team at WSK. **(8 marks)**

(b) Explain the stages and benefits to WSK of conducting an environmental audit, and assess the importance of then reporting good quality information to the board. **(10 marks)**

(c) Explain the term environmental footprint, and assess how the activities of WSK contribute to its footprint. **(7 marks)**

(Total = 25 marks)

51 Rowlands and Medeleev (6/08)

97 mins

Rowlands & Medeleev (R&M), a major listed European civil engineering company, was successful in its bid to become principal (lead) contractor to build the Giant Dam Project in an East Asian country. The board of R&M prided itself in observing the highest standards of corporate governance. R&M's client, the government of the East Asian country, had taken into account several factors in appointing the principal contractor including each bidder's track record in large civil engineering projects, the value of the bid and a statement, required from each bidder, on how it would deal with the 'sensitive issues' and publicity that might arise as a result of the project.

The Giant Dam Project was seen as vital to the East Asian country's economic development as it would provide a large amount of hydroelectric power. This was seen as a 'clean energy' driver of future economic growth. The government was keen to point out that because hydroelectric power did not involve the burning of fossil fuels, the power would be environmentally clean and would contribute to the East Asian country's ability to meet its internationally agreed carbon emission targets. This, in turn, would contribute to the reduction of greenhouse gases in the environment. Critics, such as the environmental pressure group 'Stop-the-dam', however, argued that the project was far too large and the cost to the local environment would be unacceptable. Stop-the-dam was highly organised and, according to press reports in Europe, was capable of disrupting progress on the dam by measures such as creating 'human barriers' to the site and hiding people in tunnels who would have to be physically removed before proceeding. A spokesman for Stop-the-dam said it would definitely be attempting to resist the Giant Dam Project when construction started.

The project was intended to dam one of the region's largest rivers, thus creating a massive lake behind it. The lake would, the critics claimed, not only displace an estimated 100,000 people from their homes, but would also flood productive farmland and destroy several rare plant and animal habitats. A number of important archaeological sites would also be lost. The largest community to be relocated was the indigenous First Nation people who had lived on and farmed the land for an estimated thousand years. A spokesman for the First Nation community said that the 'true price' of hydroelectric power was 'misery and cruelty'. A press report said that whilst the First Nation would be unlikely to disrupt the building of the dam, it was highly likely that they would protest and also attempt to mobilise opinion in other parts of the world against the Giant Dam Project.

The board of R&M was fully aware of the controversy when it submitted its tender to build the dam. The finance director, Sally Grignard, had insisted on putting an amount into the tender for the management of 'local risks'. Sally was also responsible for the financing of the project for R&M. Although the client was expected to release money in several 'interim payments' as the various parts of the project were completed to strict time deadlines, she anticipated a number of working capital challenges for R&M, especially near the beginning where a number of early stage costs would need to be incurred. There would, she explained, also be financing issues in managing the cash flows to R&M's many subcontractors. Although the major banks financed the client through a lending syndicate, R&M's usual bank said it was wary of lending directly to R&M for the Giant Dam Project because of the potential negative publicity that might result. Another bank said it would provide R&M with its early stage working capital needs on the understanding that its involvement in financing R&M to undertake the Giant Dam Project was not disclosed. A press statement from Stop-the-dam said that it would do all it could to discover R&M's financial lenders and publicly expose them. Sally told the R&M board that some debt financing would be essential until the first interim payments from the client became available.

When it was announced that R&M had won the contract to build the Giant Dam Project, some of its institutional shareholders contacted Richard Markovnikoff, the chairman. They wanted reassurance that the company had fully taken the environmental issues and other risks into account. One fund manager asked if Mr Markovnikoff could explain the sustainability implications of the project to assess whether R&M shares were still suitable for his environmentally sensitive clients. Mr Markovnikoff said, through the company's investor relations department, that he intended to give a statement at the next annual general meeting (AGM) that he hoped would address these environmental concerns. He would also, he said, make a statement on the importance of confidentiality in the financing of the early stage working capital needs.

Any large project such as the Giant Dam Project has a number of stakeholders.

Required

(a) (i) Define the terms 'stakeholder' and 'stakeholder claim', and identify from the case FOUR of R&M's external stakeholders as it carries out the Giant Dam Project. **(6 marks)**

(ii) Describe the claim of each of the four identified stakeholders. **(4 marks)**

(b) Describe a framework to assess the risks to the progress of the Giant Dam Project. Your answer should include a diagram to represent the framework. **(6 marks)**

(c) Using information from the case, assess **three** risks to the Giant Dam Project. **(9 marks)**

(d) Prepare the statement for Mr Markovnikoff to read out at the AGM. The statement you construct should contain the following.

(i) A definition and brief explanation of 'sustainable development'. **(3 marks)**

(ii) An evaluation of the environmental and sustainability implications of the Giant Dam Project. **(8 marks)**

(iii) A statement on the importance of confidentiality in the financing of the early stage working capital needs and an explanation of how this conflicts with the duty of transparency in matters of corporate governance. **(6 marks)**

Professional marks for layout, logical flow and persuasiveness of the statement. **(4 marks)**

Internal controls are very important in a complex civil engineering project such as the Giant Dam Project.

Required

(e) Describe the difficulties of maintaining sound internal controls in the Giant Dam Project created by working through sub-contractors. **(4 marks)**

(Total = 50 marks)

52 Swan Hill (12/08)   97 mins

The scientists in the research laboratories of Swan Hill Company (SHC, a public listed company) recently made a very important discovery about the process that manufactured its major product. The scientific director, Dr Sonja Rainbow, informed the board that the breakthrough was called the 'sink method'. She explained that the sink method would enable SHC to produce its major product at a lower unit cost and in much higher volumes than the current process. It would also produce lower unit environmental emissions and would substantially improve product quality compared to its current process and indeed compared to all of the other competitors in the industry.

SHC currently has 30% of the global market with its nearest competitor having 25% and the other 12 producers sharing the remainder. The company, based in the town of Swan Hill, has a paternalistic management approach and has always valued its relationship with the local community. Its website says that SHC has always sought to maximise the benefit to the workforce and community in all of its business decisions and feels a great sense of loyalty to the Swan Hill locality which is where it started in 1900 and has been based ever since.

As the board considered the implications of the discovery of the sink method, chief executive Nelson Cobar asked whether Sonja Rainbow was certain that SHC was the only company in the industry that had made the discovery and she said that she was. She also said that she was certain that the competitors were 'some years' behind SHC in their research.

It quickly became clear that the discovery of the sink method was so important and far reaching that it had the potential to give SHC an unassailable competitive advantage in its industry. Chief executive Nelson Cobar told board colleagues that they should clearly understand that the discovery had the potential to put all of SHC's competitors out of business and make SHC the single global supplier. He said that as the board considered the options, members should bear in mind the seriousness of the implications upon the rest of the industry.

Mr Cobar said there were two strategic options. Option one was to press ahead with the huge investment of new plant necessary to introduce the sink method into the factory whilst, as far as possible, keeping the nature of the sink technology secret from competitors (the 'secrecy option'). A patent disclosing the nature of the technology would not be filed so as to keep the technology secret within SHC. Option two was to file a patent and then offer the use of the discovery to competitors under a licensing arrangement where SHC would receive substantial royalties for the 20-year legal lifetime of the patent (the 'licensing option'). This would also involve new investment but at a slower pace in line with competitors. The licence contract would, Mr Cobar explained, include an 'improvement sharing' requirement where licensees would be required to inform SHC of any improvements discovered that made the sink method more efficient or effective.

The sales director, Edwin Kiama, argued strongly in favour of the secrecy option. He said that the board owed it to SHC's shareholders to take the option that would maximise shareholder value. He argued that business strategy was all about gaining competitive advantage and this was a chance to do exactly that. Accordingly, he argued, the sink method should not be licensed to competitors and should be pursued as fast as possible. The operations director said that to gain the full benefits of the sink method with either option would require a complete refitting of the factory and the largest capital investment that SHC had ever undertaken.

The financial director, Sean Nyngan, advised the board that pressing ahead with investment under the secrecy option was not without risks. First, he said, he would have to finance the investment, probably initially through debt, and second, there were risks associated with any large investment. He also informed the board that the licensing option would, over many years, involve the inflow of 'massive' funds in royalty payments from competitors using the SHC's patented sink method. By pursuing the licensing option, Sean Nyngan said that they could retain their market leadership in the short term without incurring risk, whilst increasing their industry dominance in the future through careful investment of the royalty payments.

The non-executive chairman, Alison Manilla, said that she was looking at the issue from an ethical perspective. She asked whether SHC had the right, even if it had the ability, to put competitors out of business.

Required

(a)   Assess the secrecy option using Tucker's model for decision-making.   **(10 marks)**

(b)   Distinguish between strategic and operational risks, and explain why the secrecy option would be a source of strategic risk.   **(10 marks)**

Mr Cobar, the chief executive of SHC, has decided to draft two alternative statements to explain both possible outcomes of the secrecy/licensing decision to shareholders. Once the board has decided which one to pursue, the relevant draft will be included in a voluntary section of the next corporate annual report.

Required

(c)   (i)   Draft a statement in the event that the board chooses the secrecy option. It should make a convincing business case and put forward ethical arguments for the secrecy option. The ethical arguments should be made from the stockholder (or pristine capitalist) perspective.   **(8 marks)**

        (ii)   Draft a statement in the event that the board chooses the licensing option. It should make a convincing business case and put forward ethical arguments for the licensing option. The ethical arguments should be made from the wider stakeholder perspective.   **(8 marks)**

        Note. Professional marks for the persuasiveness and logical flow of arguments: two marks per statement.
                                                                                                             (4 marks)

Corporate annual reports contain both mandatory and voluntary disclosures.

Required

(d)   (i)   Distinguish, using examples, between mandatory and voluntary disclosures in the annual reports of public listed companies.   **(6 marks)**

        (ii)   Explain why the disclosure of voluntary information in annual reports can enhance the company's accountability to equity investors.   **(4 marks)**

                                                                                                   (Total = 50 marks)

53 Global-bank (6/09)

Global-bank is a prominent European bank with branches throughout Europe and investment arms in many locations throughout the world. It is regarded as one of the world's major international banks. Through its network of investment offices throughout the world, fund managers trade in local investment markets and equities. Futures and derivative traders also operate. Its primary listing is in London although it is also listed in most of the other global stock markets including New York, Hong Kong, Frankfurt and Singapore. As with similar banks in its position, Global-bank's structure is complicated and the complexity of its operations makes the strategic management of the company a demanding and highly technical process. Up until the autumn of 20X8, investors had a high degree of confidence in the Global-bank board as it had delivered healthy profits for many years.

In the autumn of 20X8, it came to light that Jack Mineta, a Global-bank derivatives trader in the large city office in Philos, had made a very large loss dealing in derivatives over a three-month period. It emerged that the losses arose from Mr Mineta's practice of ignoring the company trading rules which placed limits on, and also restricted, the type of financial instruments and derivatives that could be traded.

The loss, estimated to be approximately US$7 billion, was described by one analyst as 'a huge amount of money and enough to threaten the survival of the whole company'. As soon as the loss was uncovered, Mr Mineta was suspended from his job and the police were called in to check for evidence of fraud. The newspapers quickly reported the story, referring to Mr Mineta as a 'rogue trader' and asking how so much money could be lost without the bank's senior management being aware of it. It turned out that Mr Mineta's line manager at the Philos office had ignored the trading rules in the past in pursuit of higher profits through more risky transactions. Mr Mineta had considerably exceeded his trading limit and this had resulted in the huge loss. It later emerged that Mr Mineta had been dealing in unauthorised products which were one of the riskiest forms of derivatives.

At a press conference after Mr Mineta's arrest, Global-bank's chief executive, Mrs Barbara Keefer, said that her first priority would be to ask the Philos office why the normal internal controls had not been effective in monitoring Mr Mineta's activities. It emerged that Mr Mineta had in the past been one of Global-bank's most profitable derivatives traders. Some journalists suggested to Mrs Keefer that the company was happy to ignore normal trading rules when Mr Mineta was making profits because it suited them to do so.

Another derivatives trader in the Philos office, Emma Hubu, spoke to the media informally. She said that Mr Mineta was brilliant and highly motivated but that he often said that he didn't care about the trading rules. Miss Hubu explained that Mr Mineta didn't believe in right and wrong and once told her that 'I'm in this job for what I can get for myself – big risks bring big returns and big bonuses for me.' She also explained that the culture of the Philos office was driven by Mr Mineta's line manager, Juan Evora. She said that Mr Evora knew that Mr Mineta was breaking trading rules but was also very profits driven and kept compliance information from head office so that the nature of Mr Mineta's trading was not uncovered. The compliance information was required by head office but several failures to return the information had not been acted upon by head office. Mr Evora's bonus was directly linked to the size of the Philos office's profits and all of the derivatives traders, including Mr Mineta, were regularly reminded about the importance of taking risks to make big returns. Miss Hubu said that trading rules were not enforced and that head office never got involved in what went on in Philos as long as the annual profits from the Philos derivative traders were at or above expectations.

It emerged that the lack of correct information from Philos and elsewhere meant that Global-bank's annual report statement of internal control effectiveness was not accurate and gave an unduly favourable impression of the company's internal controls. In addition, the company's audit committee had been recently criticised by the external auditors for a lack of thoroughness. Also, the audit committee had recently lost two non-executive members that had not been replaced.

The amount lost by Mr Mineta made it necessary to refinance the Global-bank business and when the board recommended a US$5 billion rights issue, some of the institutional investors demanded an extraordinary general meeting (EGM). Global-bank's largest single shareholder, the Shalala Pension Fund, that held 12% of the shares, was furious about the losses and wanted an explanation from Mrs Keefer on why internal controls were so ineffective. When the Shalala trustees met after the losses had been reported, it was decided to write an urgent letter to Mrs Keefer expressing the trustees' disappointment at her role in the internal control failures at Global-bank. The letter would be signed by Millau Haber, the chairman of the Shalala trustees.

At the EGM, Mrs Keefer made a statement on behalf of the Global-bank board. In it she said that Mineta had been a rogue trader who had wilfully disregarded the company's internal controls and was, in breaking the company's trading rules, criminally responsible for the theft of company assets. She denied that the main Global-bank board had any responsibility for the loss and said that it was a 'genuinely unforeseeable' situation.

Kohlberg's theory of the development of moral reasoning contains three levels, with each level containing two stages or 'planes'. It is a useful framework for understanding the ways in which people think about ethical issues.

Required

(a)   (i)   Explain the three levels of Kohlberg's theory.   **(6 marks)**

      (ii)   Identify the level that Mr Mineta operated at and justify your choice using evidence from the case.
                                                                                                        (4 marks)

      (iii) Identify, with reasons, the stage (or 'plane') of Kohlberg's moral development most appropriate for a
             professional bank employee such as Mr Mineta as he undertakes his trading duties.   **(2 marks)**

(b)   Explain **five** typical causes of internal control failure and assess the internal control performance of Global-
      bank in the case scenario.   **(10 marks)**

(c)   Analyse the agency relationship that exists between the board of Global-bank and the trustees of the Shalala
      Pension Fund.   **(4 marks)**

(d)   Distinguish between narrow and wide stakeholders and identify three narrow stakeholders in Global-bank
      (based on Evan & Freeman's definition) from information in the case. Assess the potential impact of the
      events described on each narrow stakeholder identified.   **(10 marks)**

(e)   You have been asked to draft a letter from Millau Haber, chairman of the Shalala trustees, to Mrs Keefer as a
      result of concerns over the events described in the case. The letter should explain the roles and
      responsibilities of the chief executive in internal control, and criticise Mrs Keefer's performance in that role.
                                                                                                        (10 marks)

      Note. Professional marks are available in part (e) for the structure, content, style and layout of the letter.
                                                                                                        (4 marks)

                                                                                                 (Total = 50 marks)

54 Mary Jane (12/09)   **97 mins**

The Mary Jane was a large passenger and vehicle ferry operating between the two major ports of Eastport and Northport across a busy section of ocean known as the 'Northport route'. Prior to this, the Mary Jane had operated for many years in the much calmer waters of the 'Southsea route' but she had been transferred to the Northport route because her large size meant that more profit could be made by carrying more passengers and vehicles per journey. She was capable of carrying up to 1,000 passengers, 300 cars and 100 lorries per trip. The Mary Jane belonged to Sea Ships Company, a long established international company with a fleet of five ships operating on routes in other parts of the world. The Mary Jane had large doors at both the front and rear. Vehicles would drive in through the rear doors in Eastport and when she arrived in Northport, the Mary Jane would dock the other way round so that the vehicles could drive straight out using the forward doors. There were two doors at each end, upper and lower, and it was important that all four doors were securely closed before setting out to sea.

As with all marine operations, the safety procedures aboard the Mary Jane were subject to regulation, but her design left one weakness which was eventually to prove a disaster. From the main control bridge of the ship, it was not possible to see the front or rear doors, which meant that it wasn't possible to check from the main control bridge that they were closed upon departure from a port. On the night of 7 November, the Mary Jane was leaving Eastport in a storm for a crossing to Northport, a journey which should have taken five hours. It was dark and the weather was very poor. When she was only a few kilometres out from the Eastport harbour, water entered the car decks through the upper rear doors that had been left open after the Mary Jane had left port. The stormy conditions meant that the waves were very high and on this occasion, high enough so that when a large wave hit, the water entered through the open rear doors. Once enough water had entered her car decks, the Mary Jane began to lean to 30 degrees before completely falling over onto her side. The speed of the event, less than two minutes, meant that escape via lifeboats wasn't possible and the Mary Jane sank with the loss of many lives.

Among the survivors was first officer Ned Prop. Mr Prop later told how a recent change to staff reporting procedures had produced a situation in which the responsibility for checking that the rear doors were closed before sailing had changed. He said that, under the new system, two people were responsible for safety on the car deck but each person assumed that the other had checked that the upper rear doors had been closed. A reporting system in which each department head (car deck, navigation, etc) on the ship separately reported readiness for sea to the captain at the beginning of each journey had been abandoned because it was too inconvenient to operate. Mr Prop said that the normal procedure was that if they didn't hear anything to the contrary by the departure time, he and Captain Mullet assumed that all was well throughout the ship and they could put to sea.

Mr Prop told how procedures on board ship often relied on 'human teamwork' rather than 'following paperwork systems'. It also emerged that, on the day of the disaster, a mistake in loading vehicles onto the wrong decks had delayed the ship's departure and created pressure to leave as soon as possible after all the vehicles were loaded. Mr Prop said that this too may have been a contributory factor to the confusion over who should have checked that the rear doors were closed. Mr Prop's superior officer, Captain Mullet, was drowned in the disaster. Sea Ships Company, the Mary Jane's owner, was one of the longest established and most respected companies listed on the stock exchange. Although best known for its ferry operations, it had diversified into other activities in recent years. It was considered by investment analysts to be a 'steady and reliable' investment and the company chief executive, Wim Bock, had often said that Sea Ships Company employed 'the highest standards of corporate ethics'. It also valued its reputation as a well-run company and believed that the company's value was primarily due to its reputation for 'outstanding customer care'. The board often claimed that Sea Ships was a socially responsible company.

When Sea Ships' board met to discuss how to proceed after the disaster, Wim Bock said that the company could expect to receive substantial claims from victims' relatives. He also reported that, because of a regrettable oversight in the company's legal department, only a proportion of that liability would be covered by the company's insurance. There would also be punitive fines from the courts, the size of which would, a legal adviser said, reflect the scale of Sea Ships' negligence in contributing to the disaster. The finance director, Jill Wha, reported that if the company met the expected uninsured liabilities in full, even if reduced on appeal, it would severely threaten future cash flows as it would most likely have to sell non-current assets (most of its ships) to settle the claims. If large punitive fines were also imposed after the legal process, Mr Bock said that the company may not survive.

The government ordered an enquiry and a senior official was appointed to investigate the disaster. In her conclusions, enquiry chairman Caroline Chan said that in addition to the human error in not ensuring that the upper rear doors had been closed, it had also emerged that the Mary Jane had been travelling above the local shipping speed limit out of Eastport harbour. The excess speed had caused increased turbulence in the water and this was made much worse by the storm on the night in question. The combination of these factors meant that water gradually entered the open upper rear doors and this eventually caused the ship to lean and then capsize. Mrs Chan said that contrary to the board's perception of itself as a well-run company, she had encountered a 'culture of carelessness' at Sea Ships and that the internal control systems were inadequate for safely operating a fleet of ships. She reserved particular criticism for the board of Sea Ships saying that it was unbalanced, lacked independent scrutiny and, because none of the existing directors had ever served on board a ship, lacked representation from technically qualified nautical officers.

After the enquiry was concluded, but before the level of claims and punitive damages had been set by the courts, a document emerged within the company confirming that certain independent advice had been received from an external consultant. The advice was received at the time of the Mary Jane's transfer from the Southsea route to the Northport route. Because the Northport route is a much rougher area of sea, the advice concerned structural changes to the Mary Jane that would make her safer in rougher seas. Had the advice been followed, the Mary Jane would have had additional doors inserted inside the car deck to act as a second internal bulkhead to prevent water flooding the whole deck. Water would still have entered through the open rear doors on the night of 7 November, but would have been kept sealed in that rear section of the car deck and the Mary Jane would not have sunk. The company had received the advice but had not acted upon it as it would have required an expensive refit for the Mary Jane. This advice was then 'lost' in the company and only emerged later on.

The independent consultant's advice was that the Mary Jane should have received structural work to make her safe for operating in the rougher seas of the Northport route. Sea Ships Company did not act on the advice.

Required

(a) Using the seven-step American Accounting Association (AAA) model for ethical decision-making, examine the company's dilemma on whether or not to disclose this information publicly. **(14 marks)**

(b)   Using information from the case, identify and analyse the internal control failures at Sea Ships Company and on the Mary Jane.   **(12 marks)**

(c)   Assess the contribution that non-executive directors might have made in improving the corporate governance at Sea Ships Company.   **(8 marks)**

(d)   Draft a memo from chief executive Wim Bock to the senior officers on the other ships in the Sea Ships fleet informing them of vital internal control and risk issues following the loss of the Mary Jane. The memo should include the following, all placed in the context of the case.

   (i)   An assessment, based on information in the case, of the importance for the board of Sea Ships to have all the information relating to key operational internal controls and risks.   **(6 marks)**

   (ii)   An explanation of the qualitative characteristics of information needed by the Sea Ships' board for the assessment of internal controls and risks.   **(6 marks)**

Note. Professional marks will additionally be awarded in part (d) for drafting a memo that is clear, has a logical flow, is persuasive and is appropriately structured.   **(4 marks)**

(Total = 50 marks)

55 Hesket Nuclear (6/10)   97 mins

Hesket Nuclear (HN) is a nuclear power station in Ayland, a large European country. The HN plant is operated by Hesket Power Company (HPC), which in turn is wholly owned by the government of Ayland. Initially opened in the late 1950s, the power station grew in subsequent decades by the addition of several other facilities on the same site. HN now has the ability to generate 5% of Ayland's entire electricity demand and is one of the largest nuclear stations in Europe. At each stage of its development from the 1950s to the present day, development on the site was welcomed by the relevant local government authorities, by the businesses that have supported it, by the trade union that represents the majority of employees (called Forward Together or FT for short) and also by the national Ayland government. A nuclear reprocessing facility was added in the 1980s. This is a valuable source of overseas income as nuclear power producers in many other parts of the world send material by sea to HN to be reprocessed. This includes nuclear producers in several developing countries that rely on the cheaper reprocessed fuel (compared to 'virgin' fuel) that HN produces.

HPC is loss-making and receives a substantial subsidy each year from the government of Ayland. HPC has proven itself uneconomic but is deemed politically and environmentally necessary as far as the government is concerned. The government of Ayland has reluctantly accepted that large subsidies to HPC will be necessary for many years but considers nuclear power to be a vital component of its energy portfolio (along with other energy sources such as oil, gas, coal, renewables and hydroelectric) and also as a key part of its 'clean' energy strategy. Unlike energy from fossil fuels (such as coal, gas and oil), nuclear power generates a negligible amount of polluting greenhouse gas. HN also provides much needed employment in an otherwise deprived part of the country. The HN power station underpins and dominates the economy of its local area and local government authorities say that the HN plant is vital to the regional economy.

Since it opened, however, the HN power station has been controversial. Whilst being welcomed by those who benefit from it in terms of jobs, trade, reprocessing capacity and energy, a coalition has gradually built up against it comprising those sceptical about the safety and environmental impact of nuclear power. Some neighbouring countries believe themselves to be vulnerable to radioactive contamination from the HN plant. In particular, two countries, both of whom say their concerns about HN arise because of their geographical positions, are vocal opponents. They say that their geographical proximity forced them to be concerned as they are affected by the location of the HN plant which was not of their choosing.

The government of Beeland, whose capital city is 70 km across the sea from HN (which is situated on the coast), has consistently opposed HN and has frequently asked the government of Ayland to close HN down. The Beeland government claims that not only does 'low-level' emission from the site already contaminate the waters separating the two countries but it also claims that any future major nuclear 'incident' would have serious implications for the citizens of Beeland. There is some scientific support for this view although opinion is divided over whether Beeland is being irrational in its general opposition to HN.

The government of Ceeland is also a vocal opponent of HN. Ceeland is located to the north of Beeland and approximately 500 km away from Ayland. Some nuclear scientists have said that with such a large stretch of water between the HN plant and Ceeland, even a much-feared incident would be unlikely to seriously impact on Ceeland. Some commentators have gone further and said that Ceeland's concerns are unfounded and 'borne of ignorance'. FT, the trade union for HN employees, issued a statement saying that Ceeland had no reason to fear HN and that its fears were 'entirely groundless'.

HN's other vocal and persistent opponent is No Nuclear Now (NNN), a well-organised and well-funded campaigning group. Describing itself on its website as 'passionate about the environment', it describes HN's social and environmental footprint as 'very negative'. NNN has often pointed to an environmentally important colony of rare seals living near the HN plant. It says that the seals are dependent on a local natural ecosystem around the plant and are unable to move, arguing that the animals are at significant risk from low-level contamination and would have 'no chance' of survival if a more serious radioactive leak ever occurred. NNN points to such a leak that occurred in the 1970s, saying that such a leak proves that HN has a poor safety record and that a leak could easily recur.

Each time an objection to the HN power station is raised, FT, the trade union, robustly defends the HN site in the media, and argues for further investment, based on the need to protect the jobs at the site. Furthermore, the radiation leak in the 1970s led to FT uniting with the HPC board to argue against those stakeholders that wanted to use the leak as a reason to close the HN site. The combination of union and HPC management was able to counter the arguments of those asking for closure.

HN places a great deal of emphasis on its risk management and often publicises the fact that it conducts continual risk assessments and is in full compliance with all relevant regulatory frameworks. Similarly, FT recently pointed out that HN has had an 'impeccable' safety record since the incident in the 1970s and says on its website that it is 'proud' that its members are involved in ensuring that the company is continually in full compliance with all of the regulatory requirements placed upon it.

The board of HPC, led by chairman Paul Gog, is under continual pressure from the government of Ayland to minimise the amount of government subsidy. Each year, the government places challenging targets on the HPC board requiring stringent cost controls at the HN power station. In seeking to reduce maintenance costs on the expiry of a prior maintenance contract last year, the board awarded the new contract to an overseas company that brought its own workers in from abroad rather than employing local people. The previous contract company was outraged to have lost the contract and the move also triggered an angry response from the local workforce and from FT, the representative trade union.

FT said that it was deplorable that HPC had awarded the contract to an overseas company when a domestic company in Ayland could have been awarded the work. The union convenor, Kate Allujah, said that especially in the nuclear industry where safety was so important, domestic workers were 'more reliable' than foreign workers who were brought in purely on the basis of cost and in whose countries safety standards in similar industries might not be so stringent. HPC said that it had done nothing illegal as the foreign workers were allowed to work in Ayland under international legal treaties. Furthermore, it argued that pressure by FT to raise wages over recent years had created, with the government's subsidy targets, the cost pressure to re-tender the maintenance contract.

On HN's 50th anniversary last year, NNN published what it called a 'risk assessment' for the HN power station. It said it had calculated the probabilities (P) and impacts (I) of three prominent risks.

Risk of major radioactive leak over the next 10 years: P = 10%, I = 20
Risk of nuclear explosion over the next 50 years: P = 20%, I = 100
Risk of major terrorist attack over next 10 years: P = 10%, I = 80

Impacts were on an arbitrary scale of 1–100 where 100 was defined by NNN as 'total nuclear annihilation of the area and thousands of deaths'.

The governments of Beeland and Ceeland seized upon the report, saying that it proved that HN is a genuine threat to their security and should be immediately closed and decommissioned. HN's risk manager, Keith Wan, vigorously disagreed with this assessment saying that the probabilities and the impacts were 'ridiculous', massively overstated and intended to unnecessarily alarm people. HN's public relations office was also angry about it and said it would issue a rebuttal statement.

Required

(a)   Distinguish between voluntary and involuntary stakeholders, identifying both types of stakeholders in Hesket Nuclear. Assess the claims of **three** of the involuntary 'affected' stakeholders identified.   **(12 marks)**

The trade union, Forward Together, has had a long relationship with HN and represents not only the main workforce but also the employees of the maintenance company replaced by the foreign workers.

Required

(b)   Explain the roles of employee representatives such as trade unions in corporate governance and critically evaluate, from the perspective of HPC's board, the contribution of Forward Together in the governance of HPC. **(10 marks)**

(c)   Explain what an agency relationship is and examine the board of HPC's current agency relationship and objectives. Briefly explain how these would differ if HPC was a company with private shareholders. **(10 marks)**

As a part of HPC's public relations effort, it has been proposed that a response statement should be prepared for the company's website to help address two major challenges to their reputation.

Required

(d)   Draft this statement to include the following.

(i)   Referring to the NNN report, explain why accurate risk assessment is necessary at Hesket Nuclear. **(8 marks)**

(ii)   Explain what a social and environmental 'footprint' is and construct the argument that HN's overall social and environmental footprint is positive. **(6 marks)**

Note. Professional marks will additionally be awarded in part (d) for drafting a statement that is clear, has a logical flow, is persuasive and is appropriately structured. **(4 marks)**

(Total = 50 marks)

56 ZPT (12/10)   97 mins

In the 2009 results presentation to analysts, the chief executive of ZPT, a global internet communications company, announced an excellent set of results to the waiting audience. Chief executive Clive Xu announced that, compared to 2008, sales had increased by 50%, profits by 100% and total assets by 80%. The dividend was to be doubled from the previous year. He also announced that based on their outstanding performance, the executive directors would be paid large bonuses in line with their contracts. His own bonus as chief executive would be $20 million. When one of the analysts asked if the bonus was excessive, Mr Xu reminded the audience that the share price had risen 45% over the course of the year because of his efforts in skilfully guiding the company. He said that he expected the share price to rise further on the results announcement, which it duly did. Because the results exceeded market expectation, the share price rose another 25% to $52.

Three months later, Clive Xu called a press conference to announce a restatement of the 2009 results. This was necessary, he said, because of some 'regrettable accounting errors'. This followed a meeting between ZPT and the legal authorities who were investigating a possible fraud at ZPT. He disclosed that in fact the figures for 2009 were increases of 10% for sales, 20% for profits and 15% for total assets which were all significantly below market expectations. The proposed dividend would now only be a modest 10% more than last year. He said that he expected a market reaction to the restatement but hoped that it would only be a short-term effect.

The first questioner from the audience asked why the auditors had not spotted and corrected the fundamental accounting errors and the second questioner asked whether such a disparity between initial and restated results was due to fraud rather than 'accounting errors'. When a journalist asked Clive Xu if he intended to pay back the $20 million bonus that had been based on the previous results, Mr Xu said he did not. The share price fell dramatically upon the restatement announcement and, because ZPT was such a large company, it made headlines in the business pages in many countries.

Later that month, the company announced that following an internal investigation, there would be further restatements, all dramatically downwards, for the years 2006 and 2007. This caused another mass selling of ZPT shares resulting in a final share value the following day of $1. This represented a loss of shareholder value of $12 billion from the peak share price. Clive Xu resigned and the government regulator for business ordered an investigation into what had happened at ZPT. The shares were suspended by the stock exchange. A month later, having failed to gain protection from its creditors in the courts, ZPT was declared bankrupt. Nothing was paid out to shareholders whilst suppliers received a fraction of the amounts due to them. Some non-current assets were acquired by competitors but all of ZPT's 54,000 employees lost their jobs, mostly with little or no termination payment. Because the ZPT employees' pension fund was not protected from creditors, the value of that was also severely reduced to pay debts which meant that employees with many years of service would have a greatly reduced pension to rely on in old age.

The government investigation found that ZPT had been maintaining false accounting records for several years. This was done by developing an overly-complicated company structure that contained a network of international branches and a business model that was difficult to understand. Whereas ZPT had begun as a simple telecommunications company, Clive Xu had increased the complexity of the company so that he could 'hide' losses and mis-report profits. In the company's reporting, he also substantially overestimated the value of future customer supply contracts. The investigation also found a number of significant internal control deficiencies including no effective management oversight of the external reporting process and a disregard of the relevant accounting standards.

In addition to Mr Xu, several other directors were complicit in the activities although Shazia Lo, a senior qualified accountant working for the financial director, had been unhappy about the situation for some time. She had approached the finance director with her concerns but having failed to get the answers she felt she needed, had threatened to tell the press that future customer supply contract values had been intentionally and materially overstated (the change in fair value would have had a profit impact). When her threat came to the attention of the board, she was intimidated in the hope that she would keep quiet. She finally accepted a large personal bonus in exchange for her silence in late 2008.

The investigation later found that Shazia Lo had been continually instructed, against her judgement, to report figures she knew to be grossly optimistic. When she was offered the large personal bonus in exchange for her silence, she accepted it because she needed the money to meet several expenses related to her mother who was suffering a long-term illness and for whom no state health care was available. The money was used to pay for a lifesaving operation for her mother and also to rehouse her in a more healthy environment. Shazia Lo made no personal financial gain from the bonus at all (the money was all used to help her mother) but her behaviour was widely reported and criticised in the press after the collapse of the company.

The investigation found that the auditor, JJC partnership (one of the largest in the country), had had its independence compromised by a large audit fee but also through receiving consultancy income from ZPT worth several times the audit fee. Because ZPT was such an important client for JJC, it had many resources and jobs entirely committed to the ZPT account. JJC had, it was found, knowingly signed off inaccurate accounts in order to protect the management of ZPT and their own senior partners engaged with the ZPT account. After the investigation, JJC's other clients gradually changed auditor, not wanting to be seen to have any connection with JJC. Accordingly, JJC's audit business has since closed down. This caused significant disturbance and upheaval in the audit industry.

Because ZPT was regarded for many years as a high performing company in a growing market, many institutional investors had increased the number of ZPT shares in their investment portfolios. When the share price lost its value, it meant that the overall value of their funds was reduced and some individual shareholders demanded to know why the institutional investors had not intervened sooner to either find out what was really going on in ZPT or divest ZPT shares. Some were especially angry that even after the first restatement was announced, the institutional investors did not make any attempt to intervene. One small investor said he wanted to see more 'shareholder activism', especially among the large institutional investors.

Some time later, Mr Xu argued that one of the reasons for the development of the complex ZPT business model was that it was thought to be necessary to manage the many risks that ZPT faced in its complex and turbulent business environment. He said that a multiplicity of overseas offices was necessary to address exchange rate risks, a belief challenged by some observers who said it was just to enable the ZPT board to make their internal controls and risk management less transparent.

Required

Because of their large shareholdings, institutional investors are sometimes able to intervene directly in the companies they hold shares in.

(a) (i) Explain the factors that might lead institutional investors to attempt to intervene directly in the management of a company. **(6 marks)**

(ii) Construct the case for institutional investors attempting to intervene in ZPT after the first results restatement was announced. **(6 marks)**

(b) Distinguish between absolutist and relativist approaches to ethics and critically evaluate the behaviour of Shazia Lo (the accountant who accepted a bonus for her silence) using both of these ethical perspectives. **(10 marks)**

The ZPT case came to the attention of Robert Nie, a senior national legislator in the country where ZPT had its head office. The country did not have any statutory corporate governance legislation and Mr Nie was furious at the ZPT situation because many of his voters had been badly financially affected by it. He believed that legislation was needed to ensure that a similar situation could not happen again. Mr Nie intends to make a brief speech in the national legislative assembly outlining the case for his proposed legislation and some of its proposed provisions.

Required

Draft sections of the speech to cover the following areas.

(c) (i) Explain the importance of sound corporate governance by assessing the consequences of the corporate governance failures at ZPT. **(10 marks)**

(ii) Construct the case for the mandatory external reporting of internal financial controls and risks. **(8 marks)**

(iii) Explain the broad areas that the proposed external report on internal controls should include, drawing on the case content as appropriate. **(6 marks)**

Professional marks will be awarded in part (c) for the structure, flow, persuasiveness and tone of the answer. **(4 marks)**

(Total = 50 marks)

57 Bobo (6/11) 97 mins

The Bobo car company decided to launch a new model of car to compete in the highly competitive 'economy' market. Although Bobo was a long-established and profitable car manufacturer with a wide range of vehicles in other markets (such as family cars, four-wheel drives, etc), it had not entered the economy market because it believed profit margins would be too low. Company research showed that this was the car market segment with the smallest unit profits. The appointment of James Tsakos as chief executive changed that; however, as he believed that Bobo should offer a model in every category of car. It was announced that the new economy car, when launched, would be called the 'Bobo Foo'. The key concepts in the new model were conveyed to the design team led by executive director and head of design, Kathy Yao: cheap to buy, economical to run, cheap to repair, easy to park, fun to drive.

At the outset, James Tsakos met to discuss the new model with Kathy Yao. Because it was to enter the economy market, the minimisation of unit costs would be absolutely paramount. Mr Tsakos had some posters printed to hang in the design offices that read: 'The Bobo Foo – keep it cheap!' They were all signed personally by Mr Tsakos to emphasise the message to the design team as they were designing the car.

As well as repeating the 'Keep it cheap' message as often as possible, Mr Tsakos also instructed Kathy Yao that rather than the usual 43 months it took to develop a new model of car 'from the drawing board to the road', he wanted the Bobo Foo ready in 25 months. This, again, was about saving on costs to increase the eventual unit profits once the Bobo Foo was on sale. The design team was placed under a lot of pressure by Mr Tsakos, and Kathy Yao became stressed with the demand to complete the project in such a short time period. She privately told colleagues that the period was too short to ensure that all design features were safety tested. (This case took place before rigid safety regulations were imposed by governments so legal issues can be ignored.)

Kathy Yao's team worked out that one way of reducing manufacturing costs would be to position the car's fuel tank slightly differently from usual. She calculated that a small amount could be saved on producing each unit of production if the fuel tank was placed behind the rear axle rather that on top of the axle as was the normal practice. Along with other cost saving measures, this was incorporated into the finished prototype. In order to shorten the time to market, the factory started to be prepared for production of the Bobo Foo (called 'tooling up') as soon as the completed design was available but before the prototype was fully tested.

When the prototype Bobo Foo went through a range of crash tests, the positioning of the fuel tank was shown to be a potential fire risk in the event of a rear collision. No action was taken in the light of this observation because, as part of the low-cost strategy for the Bobo Foo, the factory had already been tooled up and was ready to begin production. The board decided that it would have been too expensive to retool the production line to a modified design and so it went into production as it was.

The Bobo Foo quickly became a big seller and sold half a million units of the model a year, making it appear that the Bobo Foo was another successful product for the Bobo Company. Some time later, however, a lorry crashed into the back of a Bobo Foo containing three young women. Upon impact, the fuel tank was ruptured causing a fire in which all three passengers in the car were killed. The company then began to receive other claims from lawyers acting for people killed or injured by fires started by several rear-end collisions and fuel tank damage. Bobo accepted legal advice to pay compensation for each injury or loss of life caused by the fuel tank design fault.

The board then met to discuss the options for the Bobo Foo. Kathy Yao said her team had worked out that the cars could be made safe by adding some reinforcing metalwork around the tank area. Vernon Vim, the finance director, said that there were two options in the light of what Kathy had said. First was the 'universal recall' option. The company could recall, at its own expense, all Bobo Foos to make the modifications suggested by Kathy Yao and retool the production line to ensure safe positioning of the fuel tank on all future cars. The second option, the 'compensation option', was not to recall the existing cars nor to make changes to the production line but to continue to pay full compensation to victims or their families if, or when, a serious or fatal liability arose as a result of fuel tank damage from rear collisions.

Vernon Vim produced some calculations to illustrate the dilemma. They showed that, assuming that the Bobo Foo will be produced for ten years, the universal recall option would amount to $750 million over those ten years whilst the compensation option was likely to amount to approximately $200 million in total.

Vernon Vim said that even allowing for substantial errors in the calculation, there was still at least a three-fold difference in cost between the two options. Because the board's bonuses were partly based on the company's annual profits, he said that the board should simply continue to pay compensation claims and not issue the universal recall. He reminded the board that the difference between the two options was half a billion dollars over ten years.

Kathy Yao said that the company should consider the universal recall option and think about retooling the production line to ensure the safe repositioning of the fuel tank on future production. It was important, she believed, for customers to know they could trust Bobo cars for their safety and that customers associated the brand with social responsibility. She said this was an important part of the company's strategic positioning and that the company should comply with the expectations that society has of a large company like Bobo.

Chief executive James Tsakos was concerned about complying with the expectations of shareholders and with how events might affect the company's share price and longer term prospects. The company's reputation as a strong investment was very important and any long-term damage to the brand would be very unfortunate. He said that issuing a universal recall would send out a terrible signal to the financial markets and would damage confidence.

After a lengthy and heated discussion of the two options, it was decided that the 'compensation option' would be adopted. This was for financial reasons and it was decided that any discussion of the decision in public should be avoided because of the potential risk to reputation that may arise.

An unknown member of the board, outraged by the decision, informed the media about the choice the board had made and about the design process that led to the Bobo Foo (thereby acting as a 'whistleblower'). With a great deal of resulting negative publicity for Bobo on TV, radio and in the press, the institutional shareholders demanded an extraordinary general meeting to discuss the relevant issues with the board. In particular, the shareholders wanted to hear the chief executive explain why the board took the decision it did. In particular, they wanted to hold James Tsakos accountable for the decision: to establish how he understood his role as chief executive and how he arrived at the decision not to issue a universal recall on the Bobo Foo.

Required

(a)   The fuel tank risk with the Bobo Foo was subsequently classified by an insurance company as a product and a safety risk.

Explore the circumstances leading to the fuel tank problem. Identify and explain internal control measures capable of mitigating the risk in future car development projects.

Note. Ignore any possible legal or regulatory issues that may arise. **(12 marks)**

(b) Explain Kohlberg's three levels of moral development and identify, with reasons, the levels of development exhibited by James Tsakos, Kathy Yao and Vernon Vim. **(12 marks)**

(c) Distinguish between annual general meetings (AGMs) and extraordinary general meetings (EGMs). Explain the purpose of each and the advantages of holding an EGM to discuss the issues raised by the whistleblower. **(8 marks)**

(d) Prepare a statement for Mr Tsakos, the chief executive, to read at the EGM to address the following areas.

   (i) An explanation of the roles of the chief executive in managing the issues described in the case at Bobo Company. **(8 marks)**

   (ii) A defence of the company's decisions on the Bobo Foo from a 'pristine capitalist' ethical perspective (using Gray, Owen & Adams's framework). **(6 marks)**

Note. Professional marks will additionally be awarded in part (d) for drafting a statement that is clear, has a logical flow, is persuasive and is appropriately structured. **(4 marks)**

(Total = 50 marks)

58 Coastal Oil (12/11)   97 mins

Coastal Oil is one of the world's largest petrochemical companies. It is based in Deeland and is responsible alone for 10% of Deeland's total stock market value. It employs 120,000 people in many countries and has an especially strong presence in Effland because of Effland's very large consumption of oil and gas products and its large oil reserves. Coastal Oil is organised, like most petrochemical companies, into three vertically integrated business units: the exploration and extraction division; the processing and refining division; and the distribution and retailing division.

Because of the risks and the capital investment demands, Coastal Oil has joint venture (JV) agreements in place for many of its extraction operations (ie its oil and gas rigs), especially those in the deep-water seas. A joint venture is a shared equity arrangement for a particular project where control is shared between the JV partners. In each of its JVs, Coastal Oil is the largest partner, although operations on each rig are divided between the JV member companies and the benefits are distributed according to the share of the JV.

As a highly visible company, Coastal Oil has long prided itself on its safety record and its ethical reputation. It believes both to be essential in supporting shareholder value. Its corporate code of ethics, published some years ago, pledges its commitment to the 'highest standards' of ethical performance in the following areas: full compliance with regulation in all jurisdictions; safety and care of employees; transparency and communication with stakeholders; social contribution; and environmental responsibility. In addition, Coastal Oil has usually provided a lot of voluntary disclosure in its annual report and on its website. It says that it has a wide range of stakeholders and so needs to provide a great deal of information.

One of the consequences of dividing up the different responsibilities and operations on an oil or gas rig is that Coastal Oil does not have direct influence over some important operational controls. The contractual arrangements on any given oil rig can be very complex and there have often been disagreements between JV partners on some individual legal agreements and responsibilities for health and safety controls. Given that Coastal Oil has JV interests in hundreds of deep-water oil and gas rigs all over the world, some observers have said that this could be a problem should an accident ever occur.

This issue was tragically highlighted when one of its deep-water rigs, the Effland Coastal Deep Rig, had an explosion earlier this year. It was caused by the failure of a valve at the 'well-head' on the sea floor. The valve was the responsibility of Well Services, a minor partner in the JV. Eight workers were killed on the rig from the high pressure released after the valve failure, and oil gushed into the sea from the well-head, a situation that should have been prevented had the valve been fully operational. It was soon established that Well Services' staff failed to inspect the valve before placing it at the well-head at the time of installation, as was required by the company's normal control systems. In addition, the valve was attached to a connecting part that did not meet the required technical specification for the water depth at which it was operating. The sea bed was 1,000 metres deep and the connecting part was intended for use to a depth of up to 300 metres. There was a suggestion that the need to keep costs down was a key reason for the use of the connecting part with the inferior specification.

Reports in the media on the following day said that the accident had happened on a rig 'belonging to Coastal Oil' when in fact, Coastal Oil was technically only a major partner in the joint venture. Furthermore, there was no mention that the accident had been caused by a part belonging to Well Services. A journalist did discover, however, that both companies had operated a more lax safety culture on the deep-water rigs than was the case at facilities on land (the 'land-side'). He said there was a culture of 'out of sight, out of mind' on some offshore facilities and that this meant that several other controls were inoperative in addition to the ones that led to the accident. Information systems reporting back to the 'land-side' were in place but it was the responsibility of management on each individual rig to enforce all internal controls and the 'land-side' would only be informed of a problem if it was judged to be 'an exceptional risk' by the rig's manager.

The accident triggered a large internal argument between Coastal Oil and Well Services about liability and this meant that there was no public statement from Coastal Oil for seven days while the arguments continued. Lawyers on both sides pointed out that liability was contractually ambiguous because the documentation on responsibilities was far too complex and unclear. And in any case, nobody expected anything to go wrong. In the absence of any official statement from Coastal Oil for those seven days, the media had no doubts who was to blame: Coastal Oil was strongly criticised in Effland with the criticism growing stronger as oil from the ruptured valve was shown spilling directly into the sea off the Effland coast. With no contingency plan for a deep-water well-head rupture in place, the ruptured valve took several months to repair, meaning that many thousands of tonnes of crude oil polluted the sea off Effland. Images of seabirds covered in crude oil were frequently broadcast on television and thousands of businesses on the coast reported that the polluted water would disrupt their business over the vital tourist season. Public statements from Coastal Oil that it was not responsible for the ruptured valve were seemingly not believed by the Effland public. Senior legislators in Effland said that the accident happened on 'a rig belonging to Coastal Oil' so it must be Coastal Oil's fault.

A review by the Coastal Oil board highlighted several areas where risk management systems might be tightened to reduce the possibility of a similar accident happening again. Finance director, Tanya Tun, suggested that the company should disclose this new information to shareholders as it would be value-relevant to them. In particular, she said that a far more detailed voluntary statement on environmental risk would be material to the shareholders. The annual report would, she believed, be a suitable vehicle for this disclosure.

Because of the high media profile of the event, politicians from Effland involved themselves in the situation. Senator Jones's constituency on the coast nearest the rig was badly affected by the oil spill and many of his constituents suffered economic loss as a result. He angrily retorted in a newspaper interview that Coastal Oil's CEO, Susan Ahmed, 'should have known this was going to happen', such was the poor state of some of the internal controls on the Effland Coastal Deep Rig.

As the oil spill continued and the media interest in the events intensified, CEO Mrs Ahmed was summoned to appear before a special committee of the Effland national legislature 'to explain herself to the citizens of Effland'. The Coastal Oil board agreed that this would be a good opportunity for Mrs Ahmed to address a number of issues in detail and attempt to repair some of the company's damaged reputation. The board agreed that Mrs Ahmed should provide as full a statement as possible on the internal control failures to the special committee.

Required

(a) Describe the general purposes of a corporate code of ethics and evaluate Coastal Oil's performance against its own stated ethical aims as set out in its code of ethics. **(10 marks)**

(b) Explain, using examples, the difference between voluntary and mandatory disclosure, and assess Tanya Tun's proposition that additional voluntary disclosure on environmental risk management would be material to the shareholders. **(10 marks)**

In preparing to appear before the special committee of the Effland national legislature, CEO Mrs Ahmed has been informed that she will be asked to explain the causes of the accident and to establish whether she can give assurances that an accident of this type will not re-occur.

Required

(c) Prepare a statement for Mrs Ahmed to present before the committee that explains the following.

   (i) The internal control failures that gave rise to the accident. **(10 marks)**

   (ii) The difference between subjective and objective risk assessment (using examples). Argue against Senator Jones's view that Mrs Ahmed 'should have known this was going to happen'. **(8 marks)**

(iii) 'Health and safety' risk and the factors that can increase this risk in an organisation **(4 marks)**

(iv) Why Coastal Oil cannot guarantee the prevention of further health and safety failures, using the ALARP (as low as reasonably practicable) principle **(4 marks)**

Note. Professional marks will be awarded in part (c) for logical flow, persuasiveness, format and tone of the answers. **(4 marks)**

(Total = 50 marks)

59 Hayho (6/12)   97 mins

Hayho is a large international company with direct investments in 65 countries. It is a manufacturer of high technology products, with each Hayho factory typically employing over 3,000 people. Hayho factories also support local supply chains employing many more people so each Hayho plant is considered a vital part of the regional economy in which it is located.

Several years ago, Hayho was widely criticised for its operations in Arrland, a developing country with an oppressive and undemocratic government. Investigative journalists produced material showing the poor conditions of workers, and pollution around the Hayho factories in Arrland. They also showed evidence suggesting that Hayho had paid bribes to the Arrland government so that local opposition to the Hayho operation could be forcefully stopped. After this episode, the company became very sensitive to criticism of its operations in developing countries. A press statement at the time said that Hayho, in future, would always uphold the highest standards of integrity, human rights and environmental protection whilst at the same time 'responsibly' supporting developing countries by providing jobs and opportunities to enable greater social and economic development.

The board of Hayho is now deciding between two possible large new investments, both directly employing about 3,000 people. Both options have a number of advantages and disadvantages and Mr Woo, Hayho's finance director, has recently made clear that only one can be chosen at this stage. The two options are of similar investment value and are referred to as the 'Jayland option' and the 'Pealand option'.

The 'Jayland option' is to build a new large factory in Jayland and to recruit a completely new local workforce to work in it. Jayland is a developing country with few environmental and labour regulations. It has a poorly developed education and training system, and is generally considered to be undemocratic. Its president, Mr Popo, has been in office since he seized power in a military coup 30 years ago. Human rights organisations say that he maintains order by abusing the rights of the people and cruelly suppressing any dissent against him. In early exploratory talks between Hayho and the Jayland government, Hayho was given assurances that it could pursue its activities with little regulation from the government as long as the Jayland president, Mr Popo, received a personal annual 'royalty' (effectively a bribe) for allowing Hayho to operate in his country.

Finance director Mr Woo said that some stakeholders would probably criticise Hayho, perhaps in the international media, for investing in Jayland. Hayho may be accused of supporting the dictatorship of Mr Popo in that country, especially if the 'royalty' was ever discovered. Mr Woo calculated that the NPV (net present value) of projected pretax returns of the Jayland option over a ten-year period was $2 billion but that there was also a risk of potential political instability in Jayland during the lifetime of the investment.

The 'Pealand option' is to buy an existing plant in Pealand which would then be refurbished to facilitate the manufacture of Hayho products. This would involve 'inheriting' the workforce of the previous owners. Pealand is a 'new democracy', and a transitional economy, having gained its independence ten years ago. In an attempt to purge the corrupt business practices associated with its past, the Pealand government has become very thorough in ensuring that all inward investments, including Hayho's factory purchase, meet exacting and demanding standards of environmental protection and work conditions. Mr Woo, the finance director, said that the NPV of projected pre-tax returns over a ten-year period was $1 billion for the Pealand option but that the risk of political instability in Pealand was negligible. Both of the returns, the forecast $2 billion for Jayland and the $1 billion for Pealand, were considered to be acceptable in principle.

Mr Woo also said that there were issues with the two options relating to the effectiveness of necessary internal controls. Whichever option was chosen (Jayland or Pealand), it would be necessary to establish internal controls to enable accurate and timely reporting of production and cost data back to head office. So a number of systems would need to be put in place to support the production itself. One staff member, Emily Baa, who had previously worked in Jayland for another company, gave her opinion to the board about some of the issues that Hayho might encounter if it chose the Jayland option. She said that Jayland was very under developed until relatively recently and explained how the national culture was unfamiliar with modern business practice and behaviour. She said that property security may be a problem and that there was a potential risk to assets there. She also said that, in her opinion, there was a lack of some key job skills among the potential workforce in Jayland such as quality control and accounting skills. She explained that quality control skills would be necessary to ensure product specifications were met and that accounting skills would be necessary for the provision of internal and external reporting. As a manufacturer of very technologically advanced products, a number of stringent international product standards applied to Hayho products wherever in the world they were produced.

Meanwhile, news that Hayho was considering a large investment in Jayland leaked out to the press. In response, Hayho's chief executive, Helen Duomo received two letters. The first was from a prominent international human rights lobbying organisation called 'Watching Business' (WB). In the letter, the lobby group said that because of its 'terrible track record' in Arrland and elsewhere, Hayho was being carefully monitored for its 'unethical business practices'. WB said its interest in Hayho's activities had been rekindled since it had received intelligence about the possible investment in Jayland and warned Mrs Duomo not to make the investment because it would provide credibility for the 'brutal dictatorship' of Mr Popo.

Whilst Mrs Duomo, known for her forthright manner, would normally dismiss threats from groups of this type, she knew that WB had a lot of support among senior politicians and legislators in many parts of the world. She believed that WB could achieve some power through mobilising public opinion through effective use of mass media, such as newspapers and television. WB was also respected as a research organisation and its advice was often sought by politicians and trade organisations.

Mrs Duomo said she was frustrated whenever anybody got in the way of her accountability to the Hayho shareholders, but that some interests could not be ignored because of their potential to influence. WB fell into this category.

The second letter she received was from the head of Quark Investments, Hayho's single biggest institutional shareholder. The letter sought to remind Mrs Duomo that the Hayho board was employed by its shareholders and that Mrs Duomo should be determined and resolute in maximising shareholder returns. The letter encouraged the board not to be diverted by 'well meaning but misinformed outsiders concerned with things that were actually none of their business'.

Aware that she had to manage two competing demands placed on her, Mrs Duomo sought advice from Emily Baa, who had experience of life in Jayland. So she asked Emily Baa to prepare some notes for the next board meeting to clarify whom the board of Hayho was actually accountable to and how it might respond to the letter from WB.

Required

(a) Explain 'risk appetite' and demonstrate how different risk appetites might affect the selection of investments between Jayland and Pealand. **(6 marks)**

(b) Use the AAA (American Accounting Association) seven-step model to examine the ethical decision whether to select the Jayland option or the Pealand option. **(14 marks)**

(c) Describe the general purposes of an internal control system and, based on Emily Baa's views, assess the main internal control challenges that Hayho might encounter if it chose the Jayland option. **(12 marks)**

(d) Prepare briefing notes from Emily Baa to prepare chief executive of Hayho, Helen Duomo, for the board meeting as requested in the case. The notes should cover the following.

   (i)   A discussion of the meaning of accountability at Hayho and of how the Mendelow framework can be used to predict the influence of the Watching Business pressure group; **(7 marks)**

   (ii) A brief explanation of the agency relationship between the board of Hayho and Quark Investments, and advice on why the demands from Watching Business should be carefully considered. **(7 marks)**

Note. Professional marks will be awarded in part (d) for the clarity, flow, persuasiveness and structure of the briefing notes. **(4 marks)**

(Total = 50 marks)

60 P&J (12/12)

P&J is a long established listed company based in Emmland, a highly developed and relatively prosperous country. For the past 60 years, P&J has been Emmland's largest importer and processor of a product named X32, a compound used in a wide variety of building materials, protective fabrics and automotive applications. X32 is a material much valued for its heat resistance, strength and adaptability, but perhaps most of all because it is flexible and also totally fireproof. It is this last property that led to the growth of X32 use and made P&J a historically successful company and a major exporter.

X32 is mined in some of the poorest developing countries where large local communities depend heavily on X32 mining for their incomes. The incomes from the mining activities are used to support community development, including education, sanitation and health facilities in those developing countries. The X32 is then processed in dedicated X32 facilities near to the mining communities, supporting many more jobs. It is then exported to Emmland for final manufacture into finished products and distribution.

Each stage of the supply chain for X32 is dedicated only to X32 and cannot be adapted to other materials. In Emmland, P&J is the major employer in several medium-sized towns. In Aytown, for example, P&J employs 45% of the workforce and in Betown, P&J employs 3,000 people and also supports a number of local causes including a children's nursery, an amateur football club and a number of adult education classes. In total, the company employs 15,000 people in Emmland and another 30,000 people in the various parts of the supply chain (mining and processing) in developing countries. Unlike in Emmland, where health and safety regulations are strong, there are no such regulations in most of the developing countries in which P&J operates.

Recently, some independent academic research discovered that X32 was very harmful to human health, particularly in the processing stages, causing a wide range of fatal respiratory diseases, including some that remain inactive in the body for many decades. Doctors had suspected for a while that X32 was the cause of a number of conditions that P&J employees and those working with the material had died from, but it was only when Professor Harry Kroll discovered how X32 actually attacked the body that the link was known for certain. The discovery caused a great deal of distress at P&J, and also in the industries which used X32.

The company was faced with a very difficult situation. Given that 60% of P&J's business was concerned with X32, Professor Kroll's findings could not be ignored. Although demand for X32 remained unaffected by Kroll's findings in the short to medium term, the company had to consider a new legal risk from a stream of potential litigation actions against the company from employees who worked in environments containing high levels of X32 fibre, and workers in industries which used X32 in their own processes.

In order to gain some understanding of the potential value of future compensation losses, P&J took legal advice and produced two sets of figures, both describing the present value of cumulative future compensation payments through litigation against the company. These forecasts were based on financial modelling using another product of which the company was aware, which had also been found to be hazardous to health.

	In 5 years	In 15 years	In 25 years	In 35 years
	$m	$m	$m	$m
Best case	5	30	150	400
Worst case	20	80	350	1,000

The finance director (FD), Hannah Yin, informed the P&J board that the company could not survive if the worst-case scenario was realised. She said that the actual outcome depended upon the proportion of people affected, the period that the illness lay undetected in the body, the control measures which were put in place to reduce the exposure of employees and users to X32, and society's perception of X32 as a material. She estimated that losses at least the size of the best case scenario were very likely to occur and would cause a manageable but highly damaging level of losses.

The worst case scenario was far less likely but would make it impossible for the company to survive. Although profitable, P&J had been highly geared for several years and it was thought unlikely that its banks would lend it any further funds. Hannah Yin explained that this would limit the company's options when dealing with the risk. She also said that the company had little by way of retained earnings.

Chief executive officer, Laszlo Ho, commissioned a study to see whether the health risk to P&J workers could be managed with extra internal controls relating to safety measures to eliminate or reduce exposure to X32 dust. The confidential report said that it would be very difficult to manage X32 dust in the three stages of the supply chain unless the facilities were redesigned and rebuilt completely, and unless independent breathing apparatus was issued to all people coming into contact with X32 at any stage. FD Hannah Yin calculated that a full refit of all of the company's mines, processing and manufacturing plants (which Mr Ho called 'Plan A') was simply not affordable given the current market price of X32 and the current costs of production. Laszlo Ho then proposed the idea of a partial refit of the Aytown and Betown plants because, being in Emmland, they were more visible to investors and most other stakeholders.

Mr Ho reasoned that this partial refit (which he called 'Plan B') would enable the company to claim it was making progress on improving internal controls relating to safety measures whilst managing current costs and 'waiting to see' how the market for X32 fared in the longer term. Under Plan B, no changes would be made to limit exposure to X32 in the company's operations in developing countries.

Hannah Yin, a qualified accountant, was trusted by shareholders because of her performance in the role of FD over several years. Because she would be believed by shareholders, Mr Ho offered to substantially increase her share options if she would report only the 'best case' scenario to shareholders and report 'Plan B' as evidence of the company's social responsibility. She accepted Mr Ho's offer and reported to shareholders as he had suggested. She also said that the company was aware of Professor Kroll's research but argued that the findings were not conclusive and also not considered a serious risk to P&J's future success.

Eventually, through speaking to an anonymous company source, a financial journalist discovered the whole story and felt that the public, and P&J's shareholders in particular, would want to know about the events and the decisions that had been taken in P&J. He decided to write an article for his magazine, *Investors in Companies*, on what he had discovered.

Required

(a)   Define 'social footprint' and describe, from the case, four potential social implications of Professor Kroll's discovery about the health risks of X32.   **(10 marks)**

(b)   Describe what 'risk diversification' means and explain why diversifying the risk related to the potential claims against the use of X32 would be very difficult for P&J.   **(10 marks)**

As an accountant, Hannah Yin is bound by the IESBA fundamental principles of professionalism.

Required

(c)   Criticise the professional and ethical behaviour of Hannah Yin, clearly identifying the fundamental principles of professionalism she has failed to meet.   **(9 marks)**

(d)   Writing as the journalist who discovered the story, draft a short article for the magazine *Investors in Companies*. You may assume the magazine has an educated readership. Your article should achieve the following.

   (i)   Distinguish between strategic and operational risk and explain why Professor Kroll's findings are a strategic risk to P&J.   **(8 marks)**

   (ii)   Discuss the board's responsibilities for internal control in P&J and criticise Mr Ho's decision to choose Plan B.   **(9 marks)**

   Note. Professional marks will be awarded in part (d) for the structure, logical flow, persuasiveness and tone of the article.   **(4 marks)**

                                          (Total = 50 marks)

61 Hoppo (6/13)   **97 mins**

A report was recently published by an international accounting organisation on the future of certain rare chemicals used in industrial processes. The report said that some of these chemicals, crucial to many industrial processes, were now so scarce that there was a threat to supply chains for items such as computer circuitry and the rechargeable batteries used in electronic goods. One of these scarce and rare chemicals, the highly toxic trans-Y13 (TY13), has become increasingly rare and, therefore, very expensive. It requires careful processing and, although used in small quantities in each product, its high cost means that even small inefficiencies in its treatment can disproportionately affect final product costs.

The report's conclusions included this statement: 'Put simply, we are living beyond the planet's means. Businesses that use these materials will experience new risks. It may even become seen as socially unacceptable to use some of these materials. Finally, if supply stops, then manufacturing stops.'

One company which depends on a continuous and reliable supply of TY13 is Hoppo Company. Hoppo is a listed company based in the highly developed country of Essland. It has, for several years, designed and developed its products in Essland and then outsourced manufacturing to another company, Red Co, which is based in the developing country of Teeland. This means that Red Co manufactures Hoppo's products for an agreed price and to Hoppo's designs and technical specifications.

Because Red Co is based in Teeland (a developing country with lower land and labour costs than Essland), working with Red Co has offered Hoppo cost advantages over manufacturing its products in its home country. As a company which outsources many of its functions, Hoppo tries to ensure that in each case of outsourcing, working conditions and environmental responsibility are the same at each outsourcing company as they would be if carried out in its highly-regulated home country of Essland.

Hoppo itself is one of the most valuable companies on the Essland stock exchange and has strategically positioned itself as a company that is seen as a trustworthy and responsible producer, that is also responsible in its social and environmental behaviour. In its press statements and annual reports, it has frequently highlighted the high value it places on integrity and transparency as fundamental values in its corporate governance. It has recently considered producing an annual environmental report, as it believes its shareholders would value the information it contains.

Red Co is an experienced producer of electronic circuits and has a long history of working with TY13. It has relationships with the main TY13 suppliers going back many years, and these relationships ensure that it can normally obtain supplies even during periods when world supply is short. Because the supply quality of TY13 varies widely, Red Co has developed finely-tuned methods of ensuring that the TY13 received is of suitable quality. The performance of the finished product is very sensitive to the quality of the TY13 and so this pre-production testing is considered vital. In addition, TY13's toxicity and high cost mean that other systems are put in place at Red Co to ensure that it is safely stored until needed for manufacture.

Earlier this year, however, two issues arose at Red Co which caused Hoppo to reconsider its outsourcing relationship. The first one was the publication of an international media report showing evidence that, despite Hoppo's claims about having the same working conditions at all of its outsourcing clients, labour conditions were unacceptably poor at Red Co. Because labour regulations were less stringent in Teeland, Red Co had been forcing employees to work excessively long hours without breaks, and other measures that would not have been permitted in Essland. It was reported that workers were being bullied, and threatened with dismissal if they complained about their working conditions.

The second problem was a leakage of unprocessed TY13 from the Red Co factory. Not only was this seen as wasteful and careless, it also poisoned a local river, killing many fish and contaminating local farmland. The community living nearby said that it would be unable to use the contaminated land for many years and that this would affect local food supply.

When a journalist, Bob Hob, discovered information about these two issues, the media interpreted the story as a problem for Hoppo, partly because of its reputation as a responsible company. Hoppo's own research had shown that many of its customers valued its environmental reputation and that some of its key employees were attracted to Hoppo for the same reason.

Some important customers began to associate Hoppo directly with the problems at Red Co, even though it was Red Co which had actually been responsible for the employee issues and also the TY13 leak. Hoppo's share price fell when some investors considered the problems to be important enough to undermine future confidence in Hoppo's management and brand value.

In an effort to protect its reputation in future, Hoppo began to review its outsource arrangement with Red Co. The board considered the options for taking manufacturing under its own direct control by building a new factory in another low-cost country, which would be owned and operated by Hoppo. It quickly realised that stopping the outsourcing relationship with Red Co would mean the loss of about 1,000 jobs there and could also raise the likelihood of legal action by Red Co against Hoppo for loss of contract. As Hoppo's manufacturing contract is so valuable to Red Co, some people thought it likely that Red Co would sue Hoppo for loss of future earnings, despite the terms of the contract being legally ambiguous. This lack of clarity in the contract arose because of differences in Essland and Teeland law and as a consequence of poor legal advice that Hoppo received when drawing up the contract. It was believed that any legal action would be widely reported because of Hoppo's international profile and that this may result in some unfavourable publicity.

When considering its options for a directly-owned factory, Hoppo's plan was to build a modern and efficient plant with 'state of the art' environmental controls. Yuland was chosen as a suitable country and Hoppo narrowed the choice down to two possible sites in Yuland for its new factory: Ootown and Aatown. The mayors of both towns wrote to Hoppo's chief executive saying that they would welcome any potential investment from Hoppo. In addition, the mayor of Ootown asked for a 'personal gift' (relatively immaterial although not a trivial amount to Hoppo but a large amount of money locally) to facilitate a trouble-free passage of the necessary planning permission for a new Hoppo factory in the town.

When deciding between Ootown and Aatown In Yuland, the general view was that, all other things being equal, Ootown was a better location. But there was some discussion about whether the 'personal gift' requested by the mayor of Ootown was ethical. The board thought that the decision was an important one and so took some time to reflect before reaching a decision on whether to continue with Red Co or to build a new factory in either Ootown or Aatown.

Having become aware that investing in Ootown and paying the money to its mayor was being considered by Hoppo, a member of the chief executive's office staff informed the journalist, Bob Hob, and a story appeared in an Essland national newspaper saying, 'Hoppo considers paying a bribe to get preferred site in Yuland.' Bob Hob made remarks challenging Hoppo's claims about integrity and transparency, and suggested that recent events had shown that it had demonstrated neither. Public discussion then took place on the internet saying that Hoppo, previously considered a highly ethical company, had been corrupt and incompetent, both in allowing Red Co to breach employment and environmental best practice, and then to consider paying a bribe to the mayor of Ootown.

It was decided that, in seeking to restore its reputation, the company needed to publish a detailed press statement responding to the issues raised in the media. Because Hoppo's reputation for integrity and transparency were considered to be strategically important and had been questioned, it was decided that the statement should also contain reassurances about these important themes.

Required

(a) Briefly explain 'related' and 'correlated' risks. Explore the correlation between legal risk and reputation risk for Hoppo if it were to cancel its contract with Red Co. **(10 marks)**

(b) Describe an environmental report, including its purpose and contents, and discuss the potential advantages of an environmental report for Hoppo and its shareholders. **(10 marks)**

(c) Briefly explain how internal controls can be strategic in nature. Explain, using detailed examples from the case, why developing sound internal controls over the supply and processing of TY13 would be important if Hoppo opted to build its own factory in Yuland. **(10 marks)**

(d) Draft the press release as discussed in the case. It should:

 (i) Define and explain the importance of 'integrity' and 'transparency' in the context of the case.
 (6 marks)

 (ii) Construct an argument against paying the bribe to the mayor of Ootown from both business and ethical perspectives. Your ethical arguments should include both deontological and consequentialist perspectives. **(10 marks)**

 Note. Professional marks will be awarded in part (d) for the format, tone, logical flow and persuasiveness of the press release. **(4 marks)**

 (Total = 50 marks)

62 Wyland (12/13)
97 mins

When the 1,000 km Hiaka pipeline in Wyland was built ten years ago, the route took it, overground, the full length of Hiakaisland, one of Wyland's largest offshore islands. Owned and operated by Hiaka Energy Company (HEC), its construction was significantly over budget and suffered lengthy delays, but the pipeline has since become a vital source of economic growth on Hiakaisland and beyond. Its purpose is to connect the oil platforms off the north coast of the island with the deepwater port of Hiakatown in the south. A land pipeline to the south is needed because sea ice in the north prevents shipping access during the winter months. The oil carried by the pipeline is loaded onto several ships each day at Hiakatown port. Most of the oil from Hiakaisland is sent to the neighbouring country of Exland, with oil from Hiakaisland representing 90% of Exland's total oil consumption. Because the contract with HEC is so important to the government of Exland, the terms of supply are subject to legal enforcement with regard to prices charged, delivery terms and the quality of the oil delivered. Because most of its output goes to export, HEC is a major source of foreign currency for Wyland.

Hiakaisland is a globally important natural habitat with a dramatic and rugged terrain. It is monitored by several international scientific agencies, some of which were very critical of the decision to build the pipeline in the first place. It is one of very few locations in which some wildlife species threatened elsewhere are still in abundance. There are healthy populations, for example, of bears, elk and otters. One well-respected international wildlife organisation (called Save Our Wilderness or 'SOW') produced a report saying that the Hiaka pipeline was not environmentally sustainable and that, over time, it would deteriorate and create an unacceptable environmental risk to Hiakaisland. It said that both the company (HEC) and the government of Wyland needed to adopt longer-term time perspectives and consider the potential environmental consequences of the pipeline. The government of Exland, elected every four years, disputed this, saying that SOW's definition of sustainability was too narrow and that it should also consider the economic sustainability of Exland. The position of the board of HEC is that its operations should be 'as sustainable as is economically possible'.

Wyland is a developing country with few labour regulations and very little legislation on employee pay and conditions. This has enabled HEC to use a large proportion of poorly-paid immigrant labour to build and maintain the pipeline, thereby reducing its construction and operating costs. Because of the multinational nature of much of the semi-skilled workforce, there are often language difficulties, especially when conveying messages to staff working on the pipeline and on the oil platforms. HEC has a requirement that all staff should speak the language of Wyland, but this has proven to be impossible to enforce.

As the main employer on Hiakaisland, HEC employs 5,000 people including some on offshore oil platforms, others in the main southern town of Hiakatown, and others still at a number of remote locations the length of the island at strategic points situated along the pipeline. Because of the remoteness of much of the work on Hiakaisland, conditions are harsh for many of these workers. HEC employees often work in freezing temperatures and live in encampments with intermittent logistical support. Motivation and morale are often low among these maintenance employees.

There have been poor industrial relations because of this lack of support. Workers resent the company's management in Hiakatown for the harsh conditions. These poor relationships have also made it difficult for management to try to enforce the Wyland language requirement upon the immigrant labour. The remote locations and poor conditions also meant that the company has found it difficult to recruit the skilled technical people it needs to inspect and maintain the pipeline. There is a shortage of qualified engineers and technical staff in Wyland, with many preferring to work in the cities rather than in the more difficult conditions on Hiakaisland.

HEC is one of Wyland's biggest businesses and is listed on the Wyland Stock Exchange. Because of the nature of the energy market, shareholders have come to expect a good annual return on investment in terms of dividends. One market analyst recently commented that a focus on short-term returns has not been good for the company's long-term strategy and that shareholders should be prepared to expect lower dividend yields as a result.

In order to address the many challenges which the company faced, HEC appointed a new chief executive and risk manager last year. Gavin Hoo was appointed chief executive and Gerry Jupp joined as risk manager. Born and educated in a highly developed country, Mr Hoo had a strong track record in the energy industry and took over at HEC on what was considered a good reward package for his home country. On Hiakaisland, however, the level of reward was very large by local standards, making him the highest paid person not just in the company, but in the entire regional economy of Hiakaisland. When the reward figure was later published in the annual report, the local press and some trade unions were angry, believing that his reward was 'outrageous' and that he lived in luxury whilst unskilled immigrant workers 'froze' in the maintenance parties working along the length of the pipeline. Some critics pointed to the fact that it was significantly cheaper to live on Hiakaisland than in the major cities on the Wyland mainland and that this was not reflected in Mr Hoo's rewards at all.

Meanwhile, risk manager Gerry Jupp set about examining the company's many risks. One of his first tasks was to assess some of the risks which may affect the operation of the pipeline, and he took technical advice on these to arrive at probabilities of the risks arising over the next ten years. It was recognised that there was some subjectivity involved in these measurements.

- Risk 1: Risk of terrorist attack on any part of the pipeline causing severe spillage and complete supply disruption: 10%.

- Risk 2: Risk of geological movement and/or earthquake capable of severing the pipeline in more than one place causing severe long-term supply disruption: 5%.

- Risk 3: Risk of technical failure of a joint in the pipeline causing a temporary supply disruption of a few hours but no leakage of oil: 10%.

- Risk 4: Risk of animal or natural damage to pipeline (eg by bears, elk or adverse weather) causing superficial damage to pipeline but no disruption to supply: 60%.

Unfortunately, Risk 4 was realised shortly after Gerry Jupp produced his calculations. At the point where it crossed the Gojo river in northern Hiakaisland, the pipeline had a long and unsupported section. During a winter storm, a connection was slightly displaced resulting in a minor oil leak. Although not serious in itself and quickly repaired, the 'Gojo incident' did raise concerns and showed that the pipeline was vulnerable. Seeking to protect both the pipeline and the environment on Hiakaisland, the Wyland government's industry minister wrote to CEO Gavin Hoo asking him to respond to rumours about poor internal controls in HEC and to introduce measures to reduce the chances of a repetition of the 'Gojo incident'.

In response to the industry minister's letter, the HEC board reviewed internal controls and two resolutions were agreed. The first was that the company should establish a formal internal audit function and second, that a full review of any barriers to sound internal controls in the company should be carried out. Although a formal internal audit function was not required by statute law or any stock exchange listing rule in Wyland, the board agreed that it would be good practice, especially if the security and maintenance of the long Hiaka pipeline could be included in the scope (terms of reference) of the internal audit function to be established. It was decided that in responding to the minister, Mr Hoo should convey both the board's resolve on internal audit and also an honest review of the problems for achieving sound internal controls in the unique situation the company was in on Hiakaisland.

Required

(a)   The term 'sustainability' can be understood in different ways.

   (i)   Explain the concept of 'sustainable' as used by 'Save our Wilderness' (SOW) and contrast this with the concept of economic sustainability as discussed by the government of Exland.   **(4 marks)**

   (ii)   Using information from the case, discuss the tensions which exist between these two concepts.

   (8 marks)

(b)   Assess the four risks described by Gerry Jupp and propose a suitable risk management strategy for each. Briefly explain why subjective judgement may limit the accuracy of his risk assessments.   **(10 marks)**

(c)   Briefly explain the meaning of 'labour market conditions' in the context of executive pay and critically evaluate the decision to award Mr Hoo such a high level of reward in comparison with local rates of pay on Hiakaisland.   **(10 marks)**

(d)   Prepare the letter from Gavin Hoo, the chief executive of Hiaka Energy Company (HEC), to the Wyland industry minister. The letter should:

   (i)   Explain the reasons why the implementation of sound internal controls has been difficult at HEC.

   (8 marks)

   (ii)   Basing your answer on the main roles of internal audit, discuss the ways in which an internal audit function might provide assurances in order to make an effective contribution to HEC.   **(6 marks)**

   Note. Professional marks will be awarded in part (d) for the format, tone, logical flow and persuasiveness of the letter.   **(4 marks)**

   (Total = 50 marks)

63 World Justice (6/14)

Several years ago, World Justice, a well-known charity, published a report on the activities of three major food companies in their marketing of manufactured baby foods in some of the poorer developing countries. The report, provocatively called 'Killer Companies', said it had evidence that the three companies were 'aggressively mis-selling' manufactured baby food products in these poorer countries. It was argued in the report that several problems arose with the use of these products in poorer countries which negatively affected the health of the babies, with many babies reportedly dying as a result. These problems included the use of contaminated water in the preparation of the baby food, an inability of parents to read the instructions, making up product at insufficient concentrations (thereby malnourishing the child) and aggressive selling to health facilities in those countries. Doctors often advised against the use of these products for babies because natural feeding solutions were considered safer and more beneficial in most cases.

When the 'Killer Companies' report was published, it was widely reported upon and received a lot of social and political attention. Two of the three companies named in 'Killer Companies' immediately decided to withdraw from the business but the third company, Xaxa Company (Xaxa hereafter), recognised what it believed to be an opportunity to take the market share left by the other two. It set about increasing its production capacity accordingly. When asked by journalists why Xaxa had not also withdrawn from the criticised business activity, the chief executive issued a press statement saying that it was a profitable business opportunity and, as the steward of shareholder value, he owed it to the shareholders to maximise their returns.

When it became widely known that Xaxa had decided to expand and develop its baby food business in poorer developing countries, Mothers Who Care (MWC), a national charity concerned with infant nutrition, organised a campaign against Xaxa. Strongly believing in the natural feeding of infants, MWC initially organised protests outside the Xaxa head office and also encouraged the public to boycott a wide range of Xaxa products in addition to the baby food products. MWC members started to use the phrase, 'Xaxa kills babies' in the hope that it would become widely adopted.

As one of the country's largest companies and operating in many countries, Xaxa has a large issued share volume with the majority being held by institutional investors. Whilst the overall group profits remained strong, some shareholders began to feel concerned about the baby food issue. One prominent fund manager, Hugh Oublie, organised a meeting for institutional shareholders holding large volumes of Xaxa shares and 50 such institutional shareholders attended the meeting. The group became known as the 'Oublie Group'. Although all members of the Oublie Group wanted to retain their holdings in Xaxa because of the otherwise good returns, a number of questions were framed which they decided to put to the Xaxa management:

(i)   Could the company explain the strategic logic of pursuing the baby food business in poorer developing countries?

(ii)   Was the board concerned about potential reputational damage with phrases such as 'Xaxa kills babies' being used widely and in the media?

(iii)   Would the Xaxa board consider withdrawing from the baby food business in poorer developing countries because of the alleged health impacts on children in those countries?

The company issued a statement through its investor relations department, replying that the strategic logic was based on what activities provided the most profit to shareholders regardless of the effects on other claims against the company strategy. Second, the board was not concerned with reputation risks because it believed that these were 'temporary concerns' which would soon be forgotten. Third, no, the board would not withdraw from the baby food market in those countries because, with the loss of two competitors, profit margins were likely to be higher and competition less. The Oublie Group expressed its dissatisfaction with this reply and said it might seek to influence the appointment of non-executive directors (NEDs) to the Xaxa board to increase the scrutiny of the executive members and their discussions on the subject.

Hugh Oublie appeared on television to say that he felt the board of Xaxa lacked balance. He said that, although profitable and a good employer in its home country, the non-executive scrutiny of company strategy had been poor for some time and the board had no meaningful sense of ethics at all. He believed that all of the executive board was dedicated to the mission to produce what he called 'profit at any social cost'. He further believed that none of the non-executive board members was strong enough to question the strategy and raise the problem of baby food as an ethical issue. It was this lack of non-executive scrutiny which Hugh Oublie believed was a major cause of

Xaxa's unwillingness to reconsider its baby food activity. He said that he had been a long-serving observer and shareholder of Xaxa and he had noticed the company becoming more inward-looking and self-reliant in recent years. He believed this trend was very unhelpful. In addition, he expressed concerns, on behalf of the Oublie Group, about the strategic management of Xaxa and his belief that the board lacked concern for medium-term business risks brought about by the baby food marketing.

As World Justice and MWC continued their campaigns against Xaxa, some other groups became aware of the baby food situation in poorer developing countries. A television programme reported how Xaxa products were actually being used in some of the poorer countries. It claimed to confirm the problems highlighted in 'Killer Companies' and it highlighted a number of other Xaxa products which consumers might stop buying if they wanted to put pressure on Xaxa's management to change their policy on baby food.

Partly in response to these pressures, the Xaxa board decided to consider two new initiatives. The first of these was to consider introducing a corporate code of ethics. By carefully drafting this and placing it prominently on its website, the board believed that it could achieve a number of favourable outcomes including improving its reputation.

The second initiative was to consider instituting a full risk audit system in response to the negative publicity it had experienced, especially from MWC, whose members were considered to be natural customers of Xaxa's other products. Private research commissioned by Xaxa showed that the baby food business was damaging Xaxa's reputation and possibly the willingness of some talented people to apply for jobs with the company. Political support for other company plans had also suffered, such that a recent planning application to set up a new factory by Xaxa, in a business area with no connection with baby food, had received opposition. Protestors, mainly local activists and MWC members, opposed the application with placards saying 'Xaxa kills babies'. Because the idea of risk auditing was a new initiative for Xaxa, the board has asked a local consultancy to produce guidance on the benefits of risk audit and the benefits of an external, rather than an internal, risk audit.

Required

(a) The underlying principles of corporate governance include transparency, judgement and reputation.

Explain these three terms and assess the Xaxa board's performance against each one. **(9 marks)**

(b) Explain the purposes of a corporate code of ethics and examine how the adoption of such a code might make Xaxa reconsider its marketing of baby food in poorer developing countries. **(11 marks)**

(c) Institutional investors are potentially influential stakeholders in a company such as Xaxa.

Required

(i) Explain why institutional investors might attempt to intervene in the governance of a company.

(ii) Discuss the reasons why the Oublie Group should attempt to intervene in the governance of Xaxa following the events described in the case.

Note. The total marks will be split equally between each part. **(10 marks)**

(d) Produce notes from the consulting company for the Xaxa board in response to its need for guidance on risk audit. The notes should address the following:

(i) Discuss, in the context of Xaxa, the stages in a risk audit. **(8 marks)**

(ii) Distinguish between internal and external risk audit, and discuss the advantages for Xaxa of an external risk audit. **(8 marks)**

Note. Professional marks will be awarded in part (d) for the clarity, logical flow, style and persuasiveness of the notes. **(4 marks)**

(Total = 50 marks)

64 Cheapkit (12/14)

Cheapkit is a large clothes retailer in a major developed country. Its business strategy is based around vigorous cost leadership and it prides itself on selling fashionable garments for men, women and children at very low prices compared to its main rivals. For many years, it has achieved this cost leadership through carefully sourcing its garments from developing countries where labour is cheaper and where workplace regulation is less than in its home country.

As a company with a complex international supply chain, the board of Cheapkit regularly reviews its risks. It has long understood that three risks are of particular concern to the Cheapkit shareholders: exchange rate risk, supply risk and international political risk. Each one is carefully monitored and the board receives regular briefings on each, with the board believing that any of them could be a potential source of substantial loss to the shareholders.

For the past decade or so, Cheapkit has bought in a substantial proportion of its supplies from Athland, a relatively poor developing country known for its low labour costs and weak regulatory controls. Last year, 65% of Cheapkit's supplies came from this one country alone. Athland has a reputation for corruption, including government officials, although its workforce is known to be hard-working and reliable. Most employees in Athland's garment industry are employed on 'zero hours' contracts, meaning that they are employed by the hour as they are needed and released with no pay when demand from customers like Cheapkit is lower.

Half of Cheapkit's purchases from Athland are from Cornflower Company, a longstanding supplier to Cheapkit. Owned by the Fusilli brothers, Cornflower outgrew its previous factory and wished to build a new manufacturing facility in Athland for which permission from the local government authority was required. In order to gain the best location for the new factory and to hasten the planning process, the Fusilli brothers paid a substantial bribe to local government officials.

The Fusilli brothers at Cornflower felt under great pressure from Cheapkit to keep their prices low and so they sought to reduce overall expenditure including capital investments. Because the enforcement of building regulations was weak in Athland, the officials responsible for building quality enforcement were bribed to provide a weak level of inspection when construction began, thereby allowing the brothers to avoid the normal Athland building regulations.

In order to save costs, inferior building materials were used which would result in a lower total capital outlay as well as a faster completion time. In order to maximise usable floor space, the brothers were also able to have the new building completed without the necessary number of escape doors or staff facilities. In each case, bribes were paid to officials to achieve the outcomes the Fusilli brothers wanted.

Once manufacturing began in the new building, high demand from Cheapkit meant that Cornflower was able to increase employment in the facility. Although, according to Athland building regulations, the floor area could legally accommodate a maximum of 500 employees, over 1,500 were often working in the building in order to fulfil orders from overseas customers including Cheapkit.

After only two years of normal operation, the new Cornflower building collapsed with the loss of over 1,000 lives. Collapsing slowly at first, the number of people killed or injured was made much worse by the shortage of escape exits and the large number of people in the building. As news of the tragedy was broadcast around the world, commentators reported that the weakness in the building was due to the West's 'obsession with cheap clothes'. Cheapkit was criticised as being part of the cause, with many saying that if retailers in the developed world pushed too hard for low prices, this (the collapse of the building) was one consequence of that. In response, Cheapkit's public relations department said that it entered into legal contracts with Cornflower in order to provide its customers with exceptional value for money. Cheapkit said that it was appalled and disgusted that Cornflower had acted corruptly and that the Cheapkit board was completely unaware of the weaknesses and safety breaches in the collapsed building.

One of those able to escape the building was Jess Lui, who was also the leader of a national pressure group 'Protect workers' rights' (PWR) lobbying the Athland government for better working conditions and health and safety practices for workers in the country. Having seen hundreds of people killed and injured in the collapsed building, she believed that although the government could do more, much of the blame lay with Cheapkit and the pressure it continually placed on Cornflower to keep its prices low. Jess questioned whether multinational companies such as Cheapkit should be allowed to exert so much economic pressure on companies based in developing countries. As concern over the state of other workplaces in the developing world became an increasing concern in the media, Miss Lui wrote a letter to the board of Cheapkit, which she also sent to newspapers and other media. Many of the newspapers and television channels reproduced the letter and it became a talking point in many countries because of the issues it raised.

In the letter, she said that Cheapkit was an unethical company because it supplied a market in its home country which was obsessed with cheap clothes. As long as its customers bought clothes for a cheap price, she believed that no-one at Cheapkit cared about how they were produced. She said that the constant pressure on prices had created a culture of 'exploitative wages', including at Cornflower.

Miss Lui received a lot of support after her comments on Cheapkit's accountability. She said that large international companies such as Cheapkit needed to recognise they had accountabilities to many beyond their shareholders and they also had a wider fiduciary duty in the public interest. The defective Cornflower factory in Athland, she argued, would not have existed without demand from Cheapkit, and so Cheapkit had to recognise that it should account for its actions and recognise its fiduciary duties to its supply chain as well as its shareholders.

At the same time as events in Athland unfolded, the business journalists reporting on the events and Cheapkit's alleged complicity in the tragedy also became aware of a new innovation in business reporting called integrated reporting, an initiative of the International Integrated Reporting Council (IIRC). Jess Lui read one article which said that integrated reporting might increase an organisation's accountability and require it to account for a wider set of concerns than was traditionally the case. This new understanding led to her including the following comment in her letter to Cheapkit.

> '... as the leader of the PWR, it is always in my interests to gain as much information as possible from Cornflower and the other businesses with which it transacts, including, in this case, Cheapkit. Perhaps the integrated reporting initiative offers the advantage of a wider reporting model for businesses, to include accountability for a much more diverse set of concerns than has been the case in the past. The integrated reporting model appears to substantially enhance the existing business model and it would be in the interests of broader accountability if Cheapkit, and other businesses in the garment supply chain, were to adopt this new reporting approach. Anything that requires businesses to report on their wider impacts on society and the environment is a good thing as far as social pressure groups like PWR are concerned.'

The board of Cheapkit discussed the issues raised by the well-publicised discussion of Miss Lui's open letter and the comments from business journalists about integrated reporting. The board was, in principle, a supporter of the Integrated reporting initiative and thought it would be useful to explain its position on a range of issues in a press release.

Required

(a) Discuss the stakeholder claims of Cornflower's employees and customers, and how these claims may be in conflict. **(7 marks)**

(b) Explain 'corruption' in the context of the case and discuss how corruption at Cornflower contributed to the collapse of the building and the loss of life. **(10 marks)**

(c) Cheapkit's board believed that its major risks were exchange rate risk, supply risk and international political risk.

Required

Explain each of these risks and how each may be of importance to Cheapkit's shareholders. **(9 marks)**

(d) The board of Cheapkit felt that the reputation of the company had been damaged following publication of Jess Lui's letter. It was decided that it should make a public response to her comments and also respond to points about integrated reporting raised by the business journalists, both of which had received a lot of supportive comment in the media.

Required

Draft a press statement from the board of Cheapkit to include the following content:

(i) An explanation of Cheapkit's role as a 'corporate citizen' given its international supply chain. **(6 marks)**

(ii) An explanation of 'accountability' and 'fiduciary duty' as used in the case, and a discussion of how these are relevant to Cheapkit using a shareholder or 'pristine capitalist' perspective. **(6 marks)**

(iii)   A description of the basic framework of integrated reporting, and the potential benefits to Cheapkit's different stakeholders, of reporting on different capital types. **(8 marks)**

Professional marks will be awarded in part (d) for clarity, tone, logical flow and persuasiveness of your statement. **(4 marks)**

(Total = 50 marks)

65 Lysus (6/15)   97 mins

Lysus surgical supplies was founded 20 years ago by entrepreneur Simon Mara who has been the company's chief executive since the outset. Incorporated as a private company, Lysus began by importing small surgical devices such as syringes and bandages, and selling them to hospitals, clinics and medical facilities. But the company began to grow rapidly when Mr Mara realised the potential of a growing market in knee and hip joint replacements as the population in many countries was rapidly ageing due to the wider availability of more effective, low cost medicines. Fifteen years ago, he began to manufacture the surgical hip and knee joints used for most joint replacement surgery. As a company operating in the surgical supplies industry, Lysus has always been subject to regulation and must complete compliance reports every year to declare that it is using surgical grade materials for its manufacturing and also that it maintains the requisite level of hygiene in its processes. These reports are a legal compliance matter and must be signed by two directors.

Lysus surgical supplies has been a private family (or 'insider') company throughout its history. Owned jointly by Simon Mara, his wife and brother, Mr Mara owns 51% of the shares, his wife, 20% and his brother 29%. All three are directors of Lysus surgical supplies. As the company grew, they sought to employ members of the extended family as much as possible, partly to provide them with jobs and partly to 'give a feeling of family' in the company. It was often described as a 'tight-knit' culture with family members occupying the senior positions and with few appointments made from outside the company to important roles. When the company grew to a certain size, Mr Mara decided that he needed a qualified accountant on the board of directors to help with investment appraisals, costings, cash flow management, compliance issues and financial reporting. He eventually appointed Amy Tsang, a relatively inexperienced but ambitious person to the board. This was her first role as finance director.

Simon Mara was known to be a strong and domineering person. Some former employees described him as a bully who was unable to discuss matters in a calm manner. He was described as quick to anger and capable of intimidating even his senior colleagues such that they would feel unable to challenge him at all. This was also the case with Amy Tsang, the new finance director. She found him overbearing and impossible to challenge. She always did as he asked, even when she felt uncomfortable with what she was being asked to do.

When the joint replacement industry became more competitive, Mr Mara had the idea that he could reduce the company's unit costs by switching some of the surgical-grade materials used in manufacture for a cheaper industrial grade instead. Such a switch would be undetectable to the surgeons using the artificial joints but did increase the risk of fracture and deterioration once the replacement joints were used in a patient. Mr Mara asked Amy Tsang, as an accountant and finance director, to produce detailed costing calculations for the switch and to forecast how this change would affect profits. She also calculated the costs of retooling the factory to allow the industrial grade material to be used. Later, on Mr Mara's instruction, she approved the investment and oversaw the changes in manufacturing and the purchasing processes, in the full knowledge that such changes were both illegal and unethical. Mr Mara assumed that because many of the senior employees were family members, and that he could control Amy Tsang, that the switch to industrial grade material would go undetected.

The problem came to the public attention some time later when joints made from the inferior material began to deteriorate and immobilise previously mobile patients. The industrial grade material used in the joints often caused infection in patients and some vulnerable patients died of the effects of the product failure.

John Qua was the investigative journalist who brought the problems at Lysus to national attention. He thought that the problems arose as a result of a probity risk and that the probity or integrity failure was on the part of Mr Mara and Amy Tsang. Mr Qua's mother had received a Lysus hip joint and subsequently experienced a great deal of pain and distress when the joint deteriorated, producing some unfortunate side effects including blood poisoning. Although his mother was able to have the joint safely removed and replaced by a better quality artificial joint, John Qua researched further and found other patients who had not been so fortunate. It was John Qua's investigations into Lysus which alerted the regulatory authorities to the use of the inferior materials in the joints. It soon emerged that the cause of the increased failure of the implants was the use of the inferior industrial-grade material.

When the regulator responsible for the safety of surgical supplies discovered, thanks to John Qua's research, why the joints degraded, they investigated the use of the inferior materials. The legal officers investigating the case noted that two directors had signed the most recent compliance reports, certifying that the company was fully compliant with material usage and quality standards. These were Simon Mara and Amy Tsang.

John Qua was angry with Lysus surgical supplies, because of how his mother and others had suffered. He was particularly angry with Simon Mara and Amy Tsang. As a business journalist, he often wrote articles on the behaviour and performance of listed companies. He became convinced that it was in the public interest for producers of surgical supplies, such as Lysus, to be subject to the regulatory requirements of listed companies. In a published article, he wrote:

> '…whenever I look at company failures such as that at Lysus, I become increasingly convinced that robust ways of embedding risk awareness and risk management are essential in all companies and not just in listed companies. It was the fact that Mr Mara could get away with his offences that is most worrying. He bullied a young accountant, Miss Tsang, into highly unprofessional behaviour, and without the systems in place to enable the offence to be challenged internally, he initially got away with it. Had a whistleblowing system been in place, or a separation of roles at the head of the company, Mr Mara could not have done this terrible thing. Someone would have challenged him and told him not to be so unethical and arrogant.

> The result is that, with such a high impact business risk having been realised, innocent people working for Lysus may lose their jobs whilst patients may have to suffer the effects of this for many years.'

Once the case came to the public attention, Mr Mara was arrested and prosecuted for the illegal sale of non-compliant surgical materials. Amy Tsang was also prosecuted and then investigated by her professional accounting body. After an appeal, she was 'struck off ', thereby preventing her from working as an accountant in the future. The company itself was wound up after sales declined, and all 130 employees lost their jobs. Patients continue to suffer the effects of the defective joint replacements and will do for several years into the future.

Required

(a) Distinguish between the governance of a family-owned company like Lysus and a publicly listed company, and explain how Mr Mara may not have committed the offences he did if Lysus had been a publicly listed company **(10 marks)**

(b) Criticise Amy Tsang's behaviour as the finance director and a qualified accountant, and explain how she acted against the public interest. **(10 marks)**

(c) Briefly explain why some risks vary by industry sector and discuss why legal risk might be more relevant to surgical suppliers like Lysus than in some other industry sectors. **(8 marks)**

(d) Write an article for the specialist magazine *Investors in Companies* which covers the following points. You may assume that the magazine has an educated readership.

    (i) Discuss the potential benefits which an effective non-executive chairman could have brought to Lysus. **(8 marks)**

    (ii) Explain, in the context of the case, how risk awareness, including probity risk, might be embedded in a company like Lysus. **(10 marks)**

Professional marks will be awarded in part (d) for tone, format, flow and persuasiveness of the article.
(4 marks)

(Total = 50 marks)

66 Care Services Company (Sep/Dec 15)

Care Services Company (CSC) is a private company, owned by Dr Sam Tan and his wife, Sonja. Sam, a qualified medical doctor, has been involved with the care of elderly and vulnerable adults for over 30 years and set up CSC five years ago to try to improve the quality of care in his locality and to also build a business which he could then sell when he retired. The company employs 180 people in total with 165 of those being the carers who visit service users (usually the elderly, disabled or those with learning difficulties) in their own homes to help with personal needs.

The services provided by CSC are outsourced to them by the local government authority and the government health service. CSC receives funding from these bodies in line with national government policy which determines that care is best delivered by specialist companies such as CSC, rather than directly by the government. Contracts to care providers such as CSC are awarded on a three-year basis. The criteria for provider selection are partly on the basis of cost and partly on the basis of the perception of the quality of the care provided.

Because they deliver important social services and health care, CSC and other companies providing personal care are subject to a rigorous regulatory regime. These regulations apply to all care services, whether provided directly by the government or by companies such as CSC who provide the outsourced care services. All carers, for example, must undergo compulsory training on a wide range of issues. Each potential employee must be checked for past criminal convictions, whilst high standards of hygiene and professional behaviour are expected at all times.

As time passed, rival care service companies entered the market. As a result, CSC experienced increased competition for contracts and it lost some of its care contracts with some government agencies to competitor care providers. Because the award of contracts was partly based on the perception of the company itself, and not just its care quality, Dr Tan came to believe that the governance of the company might be something which should be reconsidered. He believed that the perception of sound governance was necessary to ensure confidence in its services from both its service users and those government bodies outsourcing the service.

Accordingly, he decided to adopt best practice in corporate governance with the creation of a small executive board augmented by the appointment of a number of non-executive directors, along with a committee structure. Natasha Mbana, the current co-ordinator of the company's care services, was made chief executive and Dr Tan proposed that he himself might become the new non-executive chairman. Over time, a total of five non-executive directors were appointed to the board of CSC and they were each paid a small annual fee for their services. All of the non-executives were retired members of large public listed company boards with little experience of public sector service delivery. They all lived in the locality in which CSC was based and Dr Tan believed their presence on the board would look impressive when it came to CSC renewing its service contracts.

As a company fulfilling public sector contracts for care service delivery, pay rates for carers are often relatively low. This also applies to the financial rewards of the senior management in CSC who receive much less in salary and benefits than those with equivalent responsibilities in the private sector. CEO Natasha Mbana says that she accepts a lower level of reward because she believes in the 'public sector ethos' and believes that CSC provides a vital public service. When the new non-executive directors saw what she earned, they noted that she was on much less than the market rate for a chief executive and that she should receive a substantial increase in her rewards to recognise her contribution to the company. Dr Tan said that this might not be possible and that the new non-executive directors should recognise that rewards in the public sector are often much less than those in large listed companies.

Last year, a problem arose for care providers when a small number of companies were exposed by the media for very poor practice. CSC was not implicated in the allegations, but some other companies in the industry were accused of making inadequate or very brief visits to service users, or missing out visiting some service users altogether, under time pressure to see other service users. Most service delivery contracts specified a minimum visit period of 30 minutes per patient and that carers needed to provide a minimum standard of care on each visit, including attending to the service user's personal needs, food, drinks and medication. But because of the pressure to complete their other duties, carers sometimes ignored these minimum periods and thereby failed to fulfil service users' personal needs.

This meant that affected service users were left in discomfort, without food, water and medicines, and sometimes in considerable pain. This caused a lot of anger among the public, and led the country's health minister to ask about the internal controls in care provider companies. The health minister expressed the view that the most vulnerable in society had been let down badly, and the reputation of the care industry was badly damaged. Many companies, including CSC, became aware of public resentment and, in some cases, public hostility.

The manager of 'We care', another care supplier, went on television to explain that there were a number of structural problems with providing care under the government contracts. He said it was difficult to recruit carers and the low pay often meant that it was difficult to retain them. Furthermore, the pressure to deliver the outsourced care services was intense with carers having to hurry from one service user to another to complete their work. It was no surprise, he said, that service users often received less care than they needed because the demands on each carer were so high.

Aware that this scandal threatened the reputation of the whole care services industry, Dr Tan decided that it might be beneficial for CSC to develop and publish a code of ethics which would apply to the company and all of its carers. He was aware that the reputation of all care providers might be affected by the bad practice of a few companies and he wanted to ensure that CSC was well-thought of so it could compete successfully for future contracts and continue to enjoy the support of its service users.

In response to the negative publicity, a number of care providers held a conference and it was decided that Dr Tan, as a doctor and a senior figure in the industry, should write to the health minister on behalf of them all. In particular, they asked Dr Tan to address the issues of the internal controls in care provisions and the measures which providers would be undertaking to ensure there would be no repetition of any bad practices. They thought this a worthwhile measure to attempt to convince the health minister that providers had addressed his concerns.

Required

(a) Explain the meaning of corporate governance and agency relationships, and contrast how the objectives of corporate governance differs between a large listed company and a smaller company delivering public sector services such as Care Services Company (CSC). **(8 marks)**

(b) The non-executive directors believed that Natasha Mbana was underpaid in her position as chief executive officer (CEO) of Care Services.

Required

Explain what 'market rate' means and explain why Natasha Mbana's rewards as CEO of a public sector service provider are likely to be lower than for a CEO of a large listed public company. **(10 marks)**

(c) Explain the importance of reputation to CSC, and discuss the potential benefits of the proposed corporate code of ethics for CSC. **(12 marks)**

(d) Draft a letter from Dr Sam Tan to the government health minister, which includes the following:

   (i) An explanation of the importance of internal controls in CSC and other care service providers.
   (8 marks)

   (ii) A proposal recommending suitable internal control changes which would help to address the service delivery failures described in the case. **(8 marks)**

   Professional marks will be awarded in part (d) for the layout, flow, tone and structure of the letter.
   (4 marks)

   (Total = 50 marks)

67 Philo (Mar/Jun 16) 97 mins

In the city of Philo, the closure of a large factory released a large amount of land very close to the city centre which was bought by the Philo local government authority. As an area of high unemployment due to closures of heavy industry including shipbuilding and coal mining, Philo had an unemployment rate higher than the national average. As such, the local government authority was always keen to see new investments which would create high quality jobs. Although the former factory land had a potentially high commercial value if sold to housing developers, the local government authority offered the local university the chance to buy it for a favourable rate due to what it could offer the town as a whole. It was hope that the university would buy the land, creating a new development called 'Science First' on the old factory site which would in turn create 500 jobs.

As a city, Philo was well known for its science and engineering history, with many innovations, inventions and science developments having been made in the city going back over 200 years. Philo University saw investment in science as strategic to its future and as a key part of its competitive advantage. The Philo local government authority discussed the possibility of developing the former factory site with the university. After a series of meetings between the university and the local government authority, the university bought the land, as co-owners with the local government authority, with the full support of the local authority for building laboratories and related buildings on the site. They agreed the name Science First for the development and jointly formed a company of the same name for the investment.

It was planned to build four large science laboratories on the site for medical, pharmacological and technology research. Science First Company also wanted to develop a cluster of science-based businesses on the site and offered discounted rents as well as negotiating lower local taxes, to attract these business to the site. One of these new businesses, Topscience Company, had received international attention because of a key breakthrough it had made in medical research. Topscience was very concerned about how its building would appear on promotional photographs and it noticed that just beyond the science park, and within a few metres of its new building, were a number of blocks of poor quality social housing, owned by the Philo local government authority and accommodating rental tenants. Topscience asked if the local government authority would require Science First Company to re-landscape the area around the flats and knock them down in favour of green spaces more in keeping, in Topscience's opinion, with the image of a science park. They suggested they would not be able to locate to the Science First development in Philo unless this was done.

Anxious not to be seen to be doing anything to hinder the park's development, the Philo local government authority agreed to Topscience's demands and issued a notice to quit for all of the local residents affected by the potential demolition of the flats. Upon hearing of the plan to demolish the flats, the head of the local residents' association, Ann Tang, was outraged. She criticised the Philo local government authority for a lack of fairness and transparency in their dealings with the residents. She said that the local authority was so concerned about the science park's development that it did not care about social housing residents and that this was a betrayal of the authority's ethical responsibilities. Ann Tang also said that if the flats were demolished, there would be a loss of a 'close-knit, effective and cohesive' community of people who did not deserve to lose their homes in this way, all for the sake of a science development in which they, the local residents, had no say and did not vote for.

Ann Tang also acquired some figures which showed that, in order to invest in the Science First Company, the local government authority had to take budgeted funding from other services including the cancellation of a proposed new public library in the area where Ann Tang lives. Local residents, who were excited about the new library development, planned to use the new library as a lending library, as a place to study, as a café where people could meet and enjoy time with friends, and as a place for other services to be provided including 'mums and toddlers', 'unemployment clubs' and art classes. The cancellation of this library development would also mean that the ten jobs in the library would not now be created.

In seeking to address the challenges from the residents' association and others, the local government authority asked the finance director of Science First Company, accountant Kathy Wong, to produce a balanced assessment of the contribution of the Science First development to the city and the region. The local government authority, co-owners of Science First Company, insisted that she produce a balanced assessment which could also be published for the benefit of local residents. As a director of the development, however, she felt she ought to produce a report which clearly showed the benefits of the park to the city of Philo. Accordingly, she produced a report which concentrated on the benefits to Philo of the Science First development, in terms of the creation of jobs, marginal revenues and improved reputation for both the university and the city. Kathy Wong's report concluded that the park was of substantial benefit and should be supported by the local government authority, by the university and by local residents, who, she argued, should understand the strategic benefits of the development to the city.

Ann Tang criticised Kathy Wong for not taking into account the costs to residents and other local services of the Science First development. She said that the true social cost of the development was negative because it threatened to destroy homes and it would entail the cancellation of the proposed library. It would also have a negative effect on local infrastructure, including the diversion of roads, footpaths and bus routes.

The Philo local government authority, as a democratic body, is controlled by elected representatives from a range of different political parties, each of whom represents a portion of the total city population. Despite their political differences, the majority of elected representatives strongly supported the Science First development.

Some of the elected representatives on the Philo local government authority decided that it was right to consider the various stakeholders in the Science First development. Some elected representatives, especially those representing residents around the development, wanted to minimise the damage to local communities. They decided that the three main stakeholders to be considered were the Science First Company, the residents' association and the potential library users.

The head of the Philo local government authority, Simon Forfeit, sought to address the concerns of the elected representatives in a meeting of the elected members in which he set out the case for why the Philo local government authority had so strongly supported the Science First development. He said he recognised that in allowing and encouraging the Science First development, it was clear there would be local problems to address, but that the strategic interests of the city of Philo required this development. The city's reputation as a science city would, in his view, be enhanced by the Science First development. He argued that public sector organisations had complicated objective-setting processes which have to prioritise some interests over others. He said that he 'can't please everybody all the time and in any planning decision there are winners and losers.'

Mr Forfeit said that a local government authority had many obligations and had to serve the interests of local taxpayers who fund its work, and also the people who use its services. At the same time, it had to act in the long-term strategic interests of the city, which was why it so strongly supported the Science First development. The quality of jobs attracted by the science site, being highly skilled and highly paid, meant that the local government authority had no choice but to support and invest in the development even though some of the effects on local residents might be perceived as negative. In addition to the 500 new jobs, which will be advertised locally, Mr Forfeit said that the site would also provide space for expansion of the businesses which locate to the site. Mr Forfeit said that in addition to Topscience, other companies attracted to the site included companies producing electric vehicles, advanced medical solutions and other companies in growth sectors.

Required

(a) (i)   Analyse the stakeholder claims of Science First Company, the residents' association and the potential library users, using the Mendelow matrix to plot these three stakeholders in the Science First development.   **(9 marks)**

     (ii) Explain how the potential library users and residents' association might attempt to increase their influence as stakeholders in the Science First development.   **(4 marks)**

(b) Critically evaluate the contribution to the public interest of the new Science First development to the city of Philo.   **(10 marks)**

(c) Explain the role of accountants in society and criticise Science First Company's finance director, Kathy Wong, in her assessment of the Science First development.   **(8 marks)**

(d) The head of the local authority was criticised by the residents' association for lacking transparency and fairness in its dealings with the residents.

     Required

     Draft a statement on behalf of the head of the Philo local government authority, for their website, which covers the following issues:

     (i)   Explanations of transparency and fairness and their importance in public sector governance.
                                                                                                                                                                   (6 marks)

     (ii) An analysis of the complexities of performance measurement for public sector organisations and an explanation of how the 3Es model can be a used for this purpose.   **(9 marks)**

     Professional marks will be awarded in part (d) for flow, tone, persuasiveness and structure of the statement.
                                                                                                                                                                   (4 marks)

                                                                                                                                                       (Total = 50 marks)

Answers

Note. These answers have been written by BPP and are based on Study Text content that the examination team has reviewed.

1 Sentosa House

Text references. Chapters 1, 2 and 5.

Top tips. This question is likely to be a good example of the question design that the examiner will use. The company circumstances are very closely integrated into the question requirements. This is also a good illustration of how a scenario might have to be analysed from the viewpoint of a specific stakeholder.

Note the marking scheme in (a): you will get 2 marks for a clear definition in (a) but just knowing the definition won't be enough to pass that part. The key elements that incur agency costs are means of obtaining information and controls established over the agent. Most of the marks are available for relating agency costs to the scenario and discussing why they might be increased.

In (b) you need to think about threats to value and the various problems associated with a cavalier attitude towards control – including risks to your own reputation for being associated with it.

(c) sees the risk committee as having a similar monitoring remit to the audit committee, and hence needing to be composed of non-executive directors. This is not necessarily the case under many corporate governance regimes, and companies may have more flexibility in the role they give to risk committees and staffing risk committees with executive directors. However to pass this part you have to focus here on the circumstances described in the question.

(d) represents a core point in relation to principles-based regimes. It illustrates the significance of listing rules and investor reaction. Remember also that a principles based-regime implies companies comply or explain why not. Stating that the company hasn't complied because compliance isn't compulsory is **never** an adequate explanation.

Easy marks. All question parts appear to be of roughly equal difficulty. (b) though has a lower level question verb than the other parts – describe (see Gareth Owen's article in the front pages) so is less demanding in terms of application skills required.

Marking scheme

			Marks
(a)	2 marks for definition of agency costs	2	
	1 mark for each problem identified and briefly discussed	5	
			7
(b)	1 mark for each relevant point identified and briefly described on conditions for intervention	7	
	1 mark for each relevant point made on Eastern Products	3	
			10
(c)	1 mark for each relevant point made		4
(d)	1 mark for each relevant point made		4
			25

(a) **Definition of agency costs**

Agency costs arise from the need of **principals** (here shareholders) to monitor the activities of agents (here the board, particularly the chairman). This means that principals need to **find out what the agent is doing**, which may be difficult because they may not have as much information about what is going on as the agent does. Principals also need to **introduce mechanisms to control the agent** over and above normal analysis. Both finding out and introducing mechanisms will incur costs that can be viewed in terms of money spent, resources consumed or time taken.

BPP
LEARNING MEDIA

Problems with agency costs in Eastern Products

Attitudes to risk

The first reason for increased agency costs is that the company's attitude to risk is a major area of concern on which Sentosa requires **more information**, since the **risk appetite** appears significantly greater than what would normally be expected in this sector.

Unwillingness of chairman to be monitored

Agency costs will certainly increase because Thomas Hoo is **unwilling to supply any information about the reasons for his policies**, certainly indicating arrogance and also a **lack of willingness to accept accountability**. This means that Sentosa will have to **find out from other sources**, for example any non-executive directors who are on the board. Alternatively they may contact other investors and take steps to put more pressure on Thomas Hoo, for example by threatening to requisition an extraordinary general meeting.

Inadequacy of existing mechanisms

Agency costs will also increase because existing mechanisms for communicating concerns appear to be **inadequate**. There are **insufficient non-executive directors** on the board to exert pressure on Thomas Hoo. There is **no risk management committee** to monitor risks. The investor relations department is **insufficiently informed and unhelpful**. Thomas Hoo has abruptly dismissed the one-off phone call. Because of the seriousness of the concerns, ideally there should be **regular meetings** between Thomas Hoo and the major shareholders, **requiring preparation** from both parties and increasing agency costs.

Combining shareholder concerns

Thomas Hoo may be able to ignore shareholder concerns, because of the **shareholding patterns**. Although institutional shareholders are concerned, those who want to take action may not together hold a sufficiently large shareholding to enforce their views. Building a shareholder alliance will also increase agency costs.

(b) ### Active intervention

Active intervention by an institutional shareholder by making an attempt, for example, to change the board is regarded as a serious step, and may result in a **significant increase in agency costs**. However there are a number of reasons why it might happen.

Threats to value of shareholding

Institutional shareholders may intervene if they perceive that management's policies could lead to a fall in the value of the company and hence the **value of their shares**. There could be concerns over strategic decisions over products, markets or investments or over **operational performance**. Although they can in theory sell their shares, in practice it may be difficult to offload a significant shareholding without its value falling. Here although Eastern Products is currently making high returns, Sentosa may judge that the **risk of a major strategy** going wrong is **too high**.

Lack of confidence in management integrity

Institutional investors may intervene because they feel management cannot be trusted. At worst they may fear **management fraud**; this could be a worry in this scenario given that Thomas Hoo has done away with a key component of the control system (the risk committee) without good reason.

Failure to control management

Institutional investors may take steps if they feel that there is **insufficient influence** being **exercised by non-executive directors** over executive management. The disappearance of the risk committee is also a symptom of this problem.

Lack of control systems

Intervention would be justified if there were **serious concerns about control systems**. Thomas Hoo's actions may indicate a fundamental flaw in control arrangements with management able to bypass whatever systems are in place.

Failure to address shareholder concerns

Even if there is no question of dishonesty, there may be intervention if institutional investors feel that management is **failing to address their legitimate viewpoints**. Institutional investors' own investors may exert pressure on them **not to invest in high-risk companies**, or **companies with a poor ethical reputation**. Thomas Hoo is solely focused on returns whilst **failing to address the issue of risk**.

Failure to comply with stock market requirements

Eastern Products' failure to comply with corporate governance concerns appear to be quite blatant. The institutional investors may be concerned that they will **suffer criticism** if they are perceived as conniving in these breaches because they have not taken action. It may also **threaten the value of their shareholding** if the stock market turns against Eastern Products.

(c) **Importance of risk committees**

Risk committees are considered to be **good practice in most worldwide governance regimes**, particularly in situations like this where there are doubts about the attitudes of executive management. A risk committee staffed by non-executive directors can provide an **independent viewpoint** on Eastern Products' overall response to risk; a significant presence of non-executive directors, as required by governance guidelines, would be able to **challenge Thomas's attitudes**.

Determining overall exposure to risk

The first contribution the committee can make is to pressure the board to determine what constitutes **acceptable levels of risk**, bearing in mind the likelihood of the risks materialising and Eastern Products' ability to **reduce the incidence and impact** on the business.

Monitoring overall exposure to risk

Once the board has **defined acceptable risk levels**, the committee should **monitor whether Eastern Products is remaining within those levels**, and whether **earnings are sufficient** given the levels of risks that are being borne.

Reviewing reports on key risks

There should be a regular system of reports to the risk management committee covering areas known to be of **high risk**, also **one-off reports** covering conditions and events likely to arise in the near future. This should facilitate the monitoring of risk.

Monitoring the effectiveness of the risk management systems

The committee should **monitor the effectiveness of the risk management systems**, focusing particularly on **executive management attitudes towards risk** and the **overall control environment and culture**. A risk management committee can judge whether there is an emphasis on effective management or whether **insufficient attention** is being **given to risk management** due to the pursuit of high returns.

(d) **Significance of principles**

In a principles-based jurisdiction, corporate governance is underpinned by certain basic ethical concepts such as **integrity and accountability**. These should be applied willingly and clearly are not designed as an excuse for non-compliance.

Principles and requirements

In most principles-based jurisdictions, the general guidance is often combined with specific stock market requirements as here with the **number of non-executive directors**. Companies have to comply with requirements if they are to continue to enjoy a stock market listing.

Comply or explain

Other, less specific, requirements are based on what would normally be regarded as **best practice** and thus investors would expect companies to comply with them. If companies don't, they should supply good and clear reasons for non-compliance. This Eastern Products has failed to do.

Investor reaction

Even if reasons are supplied, investors can challenge them. Ultimately, if not satisfied, they **can put pressure on Eastern Products' share price** by selling their shares.

2 Frank Finn

Text reference. Chapter 3.

Top tips. Directors' remuneration is the type of subject that you are very likely to see in this exam as it is (always) topical and there's lots of corporate governance guidance covering it. In (a) 8 marks is quite a generous allocation for the role of the remuneration committee; the answer brings out what it does, the issues and complexities with which it has to engage, and the key corporate governance responsibilities of accountability (here the reporting requirements) and compliance. Your answer on cross-directorships needs to bring out the key principle (independence) and show how independence is breached. This scenario is a good illustration of why governance reports require remuneration committees to be chaired by independent non-executive directors.

In (b) the description of remuneration brings out the most important issue of links with performance, but also another important issue, that of directors getting benefits on better terms than employees. Note the stress on trying to balance short and long-term priorities; the weighting of each is not easy to determine, particularly for a sales director whose short-term performance will be significant.

In (c) evaluate means you have to cover the arguments for and against. The arguments for the proposal take an absolutist view of the rules, reinforced by arguments stressing the beneficial consequences (simple solution, better for reputation).

The arguments against the proposal stress that there is doubt about malpractice and also other consequences (loss of experience unbalancing the board). Remember under most governance codes not all non-executive directors have to meet the independence criteria, but there need to be sufficient independent non-executive directors on the board to constitute a strong presence and to staff the key corporate governance committees.

Overall (c) is a good example of weighing up a strong ethical solution against a maybe weaker, but more practical, one.

Easy marks. The descriptive sections on remuneration committee and directors' remuneration certainly offer most of the marks you need to pass this question. Remember however that in your exam, the marks may be more tilted towards application. The mark allocation for explaining (a level 1 verb) appears to be generous.

Marking scheme

			Marks
(a)	(i)	1 mark for each valid point made for demonstrating an understanding of cross directorships	2
	(ii)	Award up to 2 marks for each valid point made on roles of remuneration committees	8
	(iii)	Award up to 2 marks for each valid point on undermining the roles	4
			Max 12
(b)		1 mark for each component of a director's remuneration correctly identified	4
		1 mark for each relevant point describing how Finn's remuneration might be more aligned to shareholders' interests	5
			Max 8
(c)		Award 1 mark for each point evaluating the proposal from Hanoi House	1
		Arguments in favour – up to 3 marks	3
		Arguments against – up to 3 marks	3
			Max 5
			25

(a) **Complying with laws and best practice**

To ensure that executive directors do not set their own remuneration, governance codes such as the UK Corporate Governance Code suggest that the committee should be **staffed by independent non-executive directors**, who have no personal interests other than as shareholders. The committee should also ensure **compliance with any relevant legislation**, for example prohibition of loans to directors.

Establishing general remuneration policy

The remuneration committee is responsible for establishing remuneration policy, acting on behalf of shareholders, but for the **benefit of both the board and shareholders**. They should consider the **pay scales for directors**, including how much the remuneration offered by comparable companies should influence remuneration levels in its own company. It also includes considering **what relation remuneration should have to measurable performance** or enhanced shareholder value and **when** directors should receive performance-related benefits.

Determining remuneration packages for each director

The committee needs to establish packages that will **retain, attract and motivate directors** whilst taking into account the interests of shareholders as well. The committee should consider how **different aspects of the package are balanced**, also what **measures** are used to assess the performance of individual directors.

Determining disclosures

The committee should also consider what **disclosures** should be made in the remuneration committee report in the accounts, generally in the corporate governance section. The report normally includes **details of overall policies** and the **remuneration of individual directors**.

Cross-directorship

Cross-directorships are when two or more directors **sit on the boards of the same companies**; there may also be **cross-shareholdings** in both companies. The cross-directorship undermines the role of the remuneration committee because Mr Ng, its chairman, is linked with Frank Finn as fellow directors of another company. He does not have the necessary **independence** since Frank Finn, in his role as director of DEF, may be responsible for determining Mr Ng's salary. Both may therefore be tempted to act in their own interests by voting the other a high salary.

(b) **Basic salary**

Basic salary is the **salary laid down** in the director's contract of employment. The terms are determined by the contract and the original salary is not generally related to performance (although increases in it may be). Shareholder interests can be promoted by ensuring that contracts of employment are **not of excessive length**; however if remuneration packages are heavily weighted towards basic salary, as here, they may be criticised for not providing enough incentives for directors to perform well.

Performance related bonus

Directors may be paid a cash bonus for **good performance**. Performance measures need be determined carefully so that they are in **shareholders' interests**, are not **subject to manipulation of profits**, do not focus **excessively on short-term results** and **reward the individual contribution of Mr Finn**. However given that Mr Finn is a sales director, **rewards based on revenues or profits** would play an important part in rewarding performance, on an annual or more frequent basis.

Shares and share options

Share options give directors the **right to purchase shares at a specified exercise price over a specified time period in the future**. If the price of shares rises due to good company performance so that it exceeds the exercise price, the directors will be able to purchase shares at lower than their market value. Share options can be used to align Mr Finn's interests with shareholder wishes to maximise company value. They can also be used to **reward long-term performance** whereas bonuses can be used to reward short-term performance, by specifying that the options may not be exercised for some years (the UK Corporate Governance Code recommends not less than three years).

Benefits in kind

Benefits in kind could include a **car, health provisions** and **life assurance**. It may be difficult to relate these elements to directors' performance and indeed one symptom of the breakdown of the agency relationship is the directors being rewarded with excessive 'perks'. There is also the issue that these measures may be **unpopular with employees** who are not enjoying the same terms. Thus the remuneration committee should ensure that the value of these benefits is not excessive compared with other elements of the package.

Pensions

Some companies pay pension contributions for directors. As pension contributions tend to be linked to **basic salary**, they are not usually connected with performance, and again there may be a concern about directors receiving **preferential treatment,** with Mr Finn and others' pension contributions being paid at a higher rate than those of staff. The UK Corporate Governance Code stresses that the remuneration committee should consider the pension consequences and associated costs to the company of basic salary increases and changes in pensionable remuneration.

(c) **Nature of issues**

The issues are how best to deal with a **conflict of interest** and also whether it is fair for the two directors to suffer detriment.

Arguments in favour of Hanoi House's position

Integrity

Resignation of both directors would arguably demonstrate that they are acting with **integrity** and are **putting their companies' interests before their own**. It would also demonstrate **ABC's strict adherence** to the **principles of good corporate governance**.

Removal of threat to independence

Given that corporate governance reports suggest that cross-directorships are a threat to independence, resignation is the **simplest way to remove that threat**.

Reputation risk

ABC and DEF may be vulnerable to criticisms that **'fat cat' directors** are operating on a 'you scratch my back, I'll scratch yours' basis. Resignation would **restore confidence in the remuneration committee**.

Arguments against Hanoi House's position

Evidence of malpractice

Although cross-directorships are against corporate governance best practice, it looks excessive to suggest that there is **evidence of malpractice. Frank Finn's package** may have been **poorly designed**, but this may not have been deliberate.

Loss of Mr Ng

Swanland Investments makes the legitimate point that the two directors' contribution will be lost. It emphasises the complexities of corporate governance, the need to choose between the **better functioning of the board** against the **threat to independence**.

Role of other directors

Swanland's proposals emphasise that the remuneration committee does not just consist of Mr Ng; there should be **other independent non-executive directors** on it who are capable of coming to a fair decision even without Mr Ng.

3 Seamus O'Brien

Text references. Chapters 2 and 3.

Top tips. (a) is textbook material; knowledge of the UK Corporate Governance Code is particularly helpful. Your answer needs to demonstrate that the main role of the chairman is to run the board effectively. If you had just listed the chairman's ideas in a single-line bullet point list without any detailed description, you would have scored a maximum of 2 marks for this part.

In (b) you should bring out the problem of unfettered power that can result from the chairman and chief executive being the same person; this has been a significant issue in a number of corporate governance scandals. The points about the time available, separation providing two viewpoints and two sets of experience, and chairman's role as a link with the non-executive directors and shareholders are also important. The chairman will need to show detachment from executive management to provide accountability and give investors confidence, and can never do this if he is chief executive as well. The discussion on accountability needs to bring out the methods of enforcement.

As in Questions 1 and 2, the requirement to evaluate in (c) means reviewing the arguments for and against. The main arguments in favour of local codes are that governance guidance should reflect local conditions. The arguments against local variation come mainly from a globalist perspective, although also you have corporate governance practice reflecting activity elsewhere, here the international convergence in accounting guidance.

Easy marks. (a) should be five of the easiest marks on this paper.

Examiner's comments. The question highlighted which students had a basic knowledge of corporate governance, but struggled when answering questions with higher level verbs. In (a) students needed to explain (ie provide evidence of understanding of the role over and above an identification).

Good answers to (b) focused on the benefits arising from a separation of roles reducing the unfettered power of a single individual. Students appeared to be surprised by the second requirement on increased accountability to shareholders. Students need to be aware that questions 'will often ask them to think about something in the exam that they may not have read directly in the study guides or been taught in class.' (b) is a good illustration of the sort of question structure that students should expect in future exams.

Marking scheme

			Marks
(a)	1 mark for each relevant role clearly identified		Max 5
(b)	'Cross mark' points made in these answers.		
	Benefits of separation of roles: Up to 2 marks for each point identified and assessed as an argument	Max 10	
	Accountability and separation of roles: 1 mark for each point made explaining the comment	Max 4	
			Max 12
(c)	'Cross mark' points made/issues raised in the two parts of the answer		
	1 mark for each relevant point made on why corporate governance provisions should not vary by country	Max 5	
	1 mark for each relevant point made on why corporate governance provisions might vary by country	Max 5	
			Max 8
			25

(a)   **Running the board and setting its agenda**

The chairman is responsible for ensuring that the board **meets regularly** and **runs effectively** when it meets. The chairman should **encourage active participation** by all members of the board and **promote good relations between executive and non-executive directors**.

Ensuring the board receives accurate and timely information

Good information will enable the board to **take sound decisions** and **monitor the company effectively**.

Communicating with shareholders

Financial statements in many jurisdictions include a **chairman's statement** that must be compatible with other information in the financial statements. The chairman may also be **responsible for signing off the financial statements**.

Ensuring that sufficient time is allowed for discussion of controversial issues

The chairman should ensure that board meetings **focus on strategic matters**, and that the board takes account of the key issues and the concerns of all board members. The board should have enough time to **consider critical issues** and not be faced with unrealistic deadlines for decision-making.

Taking the lead in board development

The chairman is responsible for **addressing the development needs** of the board as a whole and enhancing the effectiveness of the whole team, also **meeting the development needs of individual directors**. The chairman should ensure that the induction programme for new directors is **comprehensive, formal and tailored**. The chairman should also ensure the performance of the whole board, board committees and individuals is **appraised at least once a year**.

(b)   **Benefits of splitting the roles**

Authority

There is an important difference between the authority of the chairman and the authority of the chief executive, which having the roles taken by different people will clarify. The chairman **carries the authority of the board** whereas the chief executive has the authority that is **delegated by the board**. Having the roles separate emphasises that the chairman is acting on behalf of the board, whereas the chief executive has the authority given in his **terms of appointment**. Having the same person in both roles means that **unfettered power** is concentrated into one pair of hands; the board may be ineffective in controlling the chief executive if it is led by the chief executive. The chairman provides a second **effective viewpoint** and also contributes his or her own **experience**, augmenting the board.

Time considerations

An important argument in favour of splitting the roles of chairman and chief executive is that both are very demanding functions. In large, complex organisations no one individual will have the time to do both jobs effectively. Splitting the roles means that the chairman is responsible for the functions of **leading and running the board** described in (a), the chief executive for **running the organisation and developing its strategy**.

Leadership of non-executive directors

Governance reports emphasise the importance of a strong, influential presence of **independent non-executive directors**. A **non-executive chairman** can provide effective leadership for the non-executive directors.

Information for non-executive directors

The chairman is responsible for obtaining the information that other directors require to **exercise proper oversight**. If the chairman is also chief executive, then directors may not be sure that the information they are getting is sufficient and objective enough to support their supervision. The chairman should ensure that the board is receiving sufficient information to make **informed decisions**, and should put pressure on the chief executive if the chairman believes that the chief executive is not providing adequate information.

Information for markets

Having a separate chairman means that there is a division of roles between the person **responsible for communicating business performance to markets** (the chairman), and the person **responsible for that performance** (the chief executive).

Protection of minority shareholders

A separate chairman can also ensure that executive management pays **sufficient attention to the interests of minority shareholders** and protects their interests. Seamus O'Brien's comment about family reasons highlights a situation where a separate chairman is particularly important; in companies where a founding family dominates executive management, shareholders who are not family members often feel that their interests are neglected.

Accountability

Definition

Accountability means ensuring that the chief executive is **answerable for the consequences** of his actions.

Role in appraising chief executive

A separate chairman can take responsibility for regularly appraising the chief executive's performance. The chairman may also be responsible for advising the remuneration committee on the chief executive's remuneration, having taken **account of shareholder views**.

Focal point for non-executive directors

If the non-executive directors or shareholders have **concerns about the way executive management** is running the company, a chairman not involved in executive management can offer an effective point for reporting these concerns. If however the chief executive is also the chairman, the non-executive directors may doubt his objectivity, as he is ultimately responsible for managing the company.

Ensuring accountability to shareholders

The UK Corporate Governance Code and other reports stress the role of the chairman in seeking the **views of shareholders** and ensuring **effective communication with them**. This provides a means for shareholders to raise concerns about the chief executive, and the chairman, as board representative, can **ultimately be held to account for this**.

Ensuring legal accountability

As representative of the board, the chairman can be **held responsible in law** for its activities including the supervision exercised over the chief executive.

(c) **In favour of variation**

Varied board structures

Vincent Viola rightly highlights one key international difference, that what are felt to be appropriate corporate governance structures vary by country. In the UK for example a **single board is** responsible for all aspects of corporate governance. In other jurisdictions a **supervisory board** is **responsible for review and safeguarding stakeholder interests**, a **management board** for **executive decisions**. It is difficult for a single international code to encompass these different arrangements.

Impact of local culture

Vincent Viola also raises another issue, that to be more effective corporate governance needs to reflect **local cultural issues**. For example the King report in South Africa was designed to reflect issues that are seen as important in South Africa's development such as collectiveness, consensus and fairness. This also extends to different concepts of accountability.

Legal systems

The effectiveness of governance codes should be reinforced by legal sanctions being available against miscreant directors. Governance codes therefore need to be **compatible with differing legal regulations and systems** in different countries.

Costs

The costs of following a very structured international regime (such as one based on **Sarbanes-Oxley**) may be **very burdensome** for **companies based in less developed countries**, who are not operating worldwide.

Against variation

Concerns of global companies and investors

Companies trade across several different jurisdictions and many investors invest in different countries. Having to comply with the provisions of a number of different local codes will **increase compliance costs for companies** who are **operating in many jurisdictions**. Many European companies, for example, have expressed concern about the costs of complying with Sarbanes-Oxley, if they have interests in America, as well as their own local European codes. In addition local codes may not be able to deal with **cross-jurisdiction issues** of concern to investors, such as impediments to cross-border shareholdings.

Compatibility of financial reporting rules

A key part of debates about corporate governance has been the need to **develop robust financial reporting rules,** since investors' concerns with unreliable accounting information has meant that they have questioned corporate governance arrangements. Developments in international accounting standards are aiming to **promote greater international harmony in accounting practice**, and international convergence on governance would be consistent with this.

Investor protection

Consistent corporate governance practice worldwide can also **encourage investment**, since it should ensure investors are **treated equally in different jurisdictions**. A major concern of many international investors has been the **different levels of protection** given to domestic and foreign investors under local governance regimes.

Investor confidence

More fundamentally investors may **not have the confidence to invest in regimes** that allow local, very flexible, interpretations. They may migrate to countries where good governance is emphasised and backed by effective codes, rather than countries that 'do not care as much' and which therefore **allow bad practice**.

4 West vs Leroi

Text references. Chapters 2 and 8.

Top tips. Perhaps the most important point in (a)(i) is the lack of flexibility as this leads into (a)(ii). It's no use setting out rules that companies can't comply with because of lack of local infrastructure. Our answer also brings out the point that a principles-based approach encourages governance to develop as the companies expand, and addresses the issue raised of international investor confidence by pointing out that there are globally recognised international codes that are principles-based. Many students found the wording to (a)(ii) unclear, but the examiner was generous in rewarding students who misinterpreted the question, but produced valid arguments to support their interpretation.

In spite of the mention of Sarbanes-Oxley in the requirements to (b), your answer doesn't need to be based on what's in the Act. Basing the answer on Turnbull or other governance guidance covering external reporting would have earned you the marks you need. Note that (b) is not talking about the external auditors' letter of weakness/management letter to management.

(c) is largely framed in terms of costs-benefits, considering whether the costs will be beyond small companies, and even if small companies can afford them, whether the benefits will warrant the costs.

Note that both (a)(ii) and (c) require construction of arguments ie you only cover the points that support the view (if you had been asked to discuss, you would have had to cover fairly the points for and against). The examiner has indicated that questions asking students to construct a case will feature regularly in this exam. You should think of these types of questions as essentially asking 'Tell me why'.

Easy marks. (a)(i) and (b) should have been some of the easiest marks in this exam as they just represent textbook knowledge.

Marking scheme

				Marks
(a)	(i)	1 mark for each essential feature briefly described		3
	(ii)	1 mark for each relevant point made on the advantages of principles-based	Max 4	
		2 marks for each relevant point on developing countries	Max 6	
				10
(b)		2 marks for each relevant area of content identified and briefly described		8
(c)		1 mark for each relevant valid argument put forward		4
				25

(a) (i) **Rules-based approaches**

Lack of flexibility

Rules-based approaches allow **no leeway**; the key issue is whether you have complied with the rules.

Visibility

It should be easy to **assess** whether or not a company has complied with the rules.

Aspects of governance emphasised

Rules-based approaches emphasise aspects of governance that can be verified easily, such as whether there is an **audit committee**. They place less emphasis on areas such as organisational culture that cannot be governed by clear rules.

(ii) **Overall compliance**

A principles-based approach emphasises to businesses the need to comply with the **overall spirit of governance codes**. It thus is more likely to encourage the **continuous improvement** that is particularly important in developing countries, especially in areas which are not easily covered by rules. Adopting a rules-based approach means that the focus is on conformance with a possibly limited set of rules.

Lack of local resources

A rules-based approach will only be effective if companies can draw on **sufficient local resources** to fulfil those rules. This may not be the case in developing countries. For example requiring all companies to set up an audit committee including non-executive directors with financial knowledge will be ineffective if there is an insufficient pool of individuals within the country who are willing to serve on audit committees.

Varying circumstances

Companies in developing countries are likely to develop their governance structures at different speeds as their businesses develop. Requiring all companies to meet the standards that are necessary for the **largest, most developed companies**, will not be **cost-effective**.

Local legislation

Professor Leroi highlighted the discussions going on at government level. A **rules-based approach to corporate governance** may only be effective if it is backed by government legislation; governments may not be willing to introduce this legislation because of the cost to the taxpayer and corporate sector.

International appeal

If companies in developing countries follow a recognised international principles-based code, for example the **OECD code**, this may inspire more confidence in investors than if they follow a local, rules-based, code. Investors will be judging against an internationally recognised benchmark. Also the emphasis in international codes on comply or explain encourages **transparency** by companies. This should also increase confidence because the accounts should explain clearly the company's current state of corporate governance.

(b) According to UK corporate governance guidance, the report should include the following disclosures.

Acknowledgement of board responsibility

The directors should acknowledge that they are responsible for the **company's system of internal control** and **reviewing its effectiveness**.

Management of risks

The board should disclose the **existence of a process for managing risks, how the board has reviewed the effectiveness of the process** and that the **process accords** with **guidance**.

Aims of control systems

The report should explain that the control system is **designed to manage** rather than **eliminate the risk of failure** to achieve business objectives, and can only provide **reasonable and not absolute assurance** against material misstatement or loss.

Review of control systems

The report should give a **summary of the process** that the directors (or a board committee) have used to **review the effectiveness of the system of internal control** and consider the **need for an internal audit function** if the company does not have one. The reports should also disclose the process the board has used to deal with **material internal control aspects of any significant problems** disclosed in the annual accounts.

Weaknesses in control systems

The report should give information about those **weaknesses in internal control** that have resulted in **material losses, contingencies or uncertainties**, which require disclosure in the financial statements or the auditors' report.

(c) **Elaborate control systems**

The requirements of Sarbanes-Oxley and other worldwide governance guidance imply that businesses are reporting on **elaborate control systems** involving for example various board committees and varied means of assessing compliance. These systems are more complex than a small business with a few, **relatively straightforward activities**, would need.

External reporting

To be worthwhile, external reporting must be supported by a reliable assessment of how controls are operating. For smaller companies, this assessment will require **excessive time and resources** and will not be justified by the benefits it will deliver. Small companies would not have the resources to employ an internal audit department.

Audit costs

Some governance requirements, for example the Sarbanes-Oxley legislation, require auditors to attest the internal control report to give accounts users **greater assurance**. Paying for this exercise will be a significant extra cost, in addition to the audit fee, for small companies.

Shareholder assurance

A significant proportion of the shares of many small companies will be held by shareholders who are **directors or actively involved in management** and who do not need a report to inform them about the control systems.

5 TQ

Text reference. Chapter 3.

Top tips. (a)(i) illustrates the links between F4 and P1 – remember F4 material is assumed knowledge. Death, dissolution of the company and prolonged absence are other ways you could have mentioned. Knowledge of the law can help in (ii), as well as a questioning approach – how do you prove incompetence? The examiner is likely to test the assessment of poor performance by directors again in the future.

The key points in (b) are that the chairman's statement should demonstrate the accountability and the independence of the chairman.

In (c) and (d) the examiner's comments about how he uses the verb 'criticise' are very important. What he is looking for is not just, for example, a comment that the remuneration package is bad, but that it is deficient in comparison with what is regarded as best practice. The key yardstick in (c) is alignment of remuneration package against shareholders' interests, which demonstrates the package is totally unsatisfactory.

In (d) the four criteria for non-executive directors under the Higgs report – strategy, scrutiny, risk and people – are a useful framework for generating ideas. Higgs also provides a description of an effective chairman, which you can bring into your answer.

Easy marks. (a)(i) if you still remembered F4. Note though the examiner's comments about bullet points. Just providing three or four word bullets when the examiner wanted a sentence of explanation of each way would have cost you a couple of marks.

Examiner's comments. (a)(i) on the ways in which a director can leave a company was well done in most cases although as elsewhere, bullet lists were not well-rewarded. In (a) (ii), poorer answers said that it was easy to remove a serving chief executive from service. Better answers were able to draw out some of the issues surrounding the costs of removal, difficulties in proving incompetence and so on.

A common problem for (b) was failing to see that the question was asking candidates to assess the importance of the chairman's statement in the context of the case. The point was that the chairman had a particular duty to report truthfully to shareholders, and not to conceal information on executive performance that was material to shareholders. The question was not asking about the general purposes of a chairman's statement in an annual report.

(c) and (d) were both pitched at level 3 outcomes in which candidates had to show how the situations in question fell short of expectations or best practice. Overall, (c) was done better than (d). Good performance in 'criticise' questions relies on two things: a sound knowledge of the expectation or best practice against which to measure, and careful study of the case scenario.

Marking scheme

			Marks
(a)	(i)	1 mark for each way identified and explained. Half for identification only	Max 4
	(ii)	1 mark for each relevant discussion point made	4
(b)		1 mark for each relevant comment made	5
(c)		1 mark for each relevant point of criticism clearly made	4
(d)		1 mark for each relevant point of criticism clearly made	8
			25

(a)   (i)   **Ways in which company directors leave a board**

Resignation

Directors can leave the board if they **resign by notice in writing**.

Disqualification

Directors may be disqualified from acting as a director if they are **disqualified by legislation or courts**, they become **bankrupt** or enter into an arrangement with creditors, or they become of **unsound mind**.

Failing to seek re-election

Directors leave a board when they are required by the **retirement by rotation** provisions in company constitutions to **seek re-election**, but they decide not to offer themselves for re-election.

Voted out

Directors also leave a board if they are nominated for re-election at an annual general meeting, but members **vote against their re-election**. Directors may be also removed from office by **ordinary resolution at a general meeting** of which **special notice** has been given to the company.

  (ii)   **Service contract**

As an employee, a chief executive will have a service contract. If Mr Smith had been removed from office before the end of his contract, TQ could have faced **legal action and possible compensation for loss of office**. TQ may find it difficult to satisfy the courts that the chief executive was **incompetent**. This particularly applies to strategic decision-making where the success of decisions can only often be assessed in the longer-term, and where company failure does not provide a reliable indicator of incompetence.

Retirement by rotation

The chief executive may be required to **submit himself for re-election regularly** at annual general meetings, at which time members will have the opportunity to remove him from office. However provisions in the company's constitution may exempt the chief executive from retirement by rotation.

Special meeting of company

Some members may wish to force the chief executive's departure from office by voting him out at an extraordinary general meeting. However although some members were disgruntled, they may **not have been sufficient in number or voting powers** to be able to call a general meeting. In addition a director who is also a member may have **weighted voting rights** given to him under the constitution for such an eventuality, so that he can automatically defeat any motion to remove him as a director.

Resignation

It therefore follows that perhaps the quickest way to ensure the chief executive leaves office is to **persuade him to resign**. This could be done by the rest of the board stating that they have **lost confidence** in him. Here it seems the other directors were too cowed by Mr Smith to force the issue.

(b)   **Accountability and independence**

The chairman's statement is a separate document in the accounts that enables the chairman to demonstrate that she is acting in the **interests of shareholders**. Her commentary can also demonstrate an **independent view** of the company's affairs, drawing attention to issues that the chief executive would prefer not to be raised.

Performance of chairman

The statement can provide information about how the **chairman is exercising her role**. This information, along with analysis of the **quality and reliability of the other information in the statement**, provides the shareholders with material to enable them to judge the performance of the chairman.

Corporate governance

The chairman's statement could have provided information to shareholders about how corporate governance was operating in the company. In particular it could have explained how Mr Smith was **exercising his role**. It could also have commented on the **implications and consequences of the departure of the non-executive directors and the failure to replace them**.

Wider information provision

The chairman's statement could have included disclosures covering wider areas than those required by law or regulations. These could have given stakeholders a **better idea of the environment** within which TQ was operating and how it was responding. This should have enabled Investors to carry out a more informed analysis of the **strategies** the company was pursuing, **reducing information asymmetry** between directors and shareholders. The chairman's statement could also have been focused on **future strategies and objectives**, giving readers a **different perspective to compulsory information** that tends to be **focused on historical accounting data**.

Assurance about executive management

The chairman's statement could have provided investors with further yardsticks to **judge the performance of executive management, in particular the chief executive**.

(c) **Basic salary**

Most of Mr Smith's package is basic salary, and as such it is **unrelated to company performance and hence value to shareholders**. It therefore shields him from suffering the consequences of the poor strategic decisions he has allegedly made.

Car

The excessive amount spent on the car does **not appear to have resulted in any benefit** for TQ or its shareholders. Having such an expensive car does not appear to have been necessary for Mr Smith to perform his duties. If the car is viewed as a reward, again it is a reward that is unrelated to company performance.

Share options – long-term performance

The share options appear to have rewarded Mr Smith for TQ's performance over **too short a period of time**. They would have become worthless had he had to wait longer, and TQ had then gone into administration.

Share options – immediate exercise

In addition the benefits of share options, tying a **part of Mr Smith's remuneration package to TQ's performance**, disappeared as soon as Mr Smith exercised the options and could immediately sell the shares. Some benefit could have been retained if Mr Smith had been required to keep the shares for a period after the options were exercised, thus still maintaining his interest in ensuring TQ performed well and maintained a high share price.

(d) **Strategy**

If the shareholders' allegations are correct, then Miss Hoiku has **failed to criticise the strategies** proposed by the chief executive, perhaps because she is frightened of him. The Higgs report suggests that the chairman and other non-executive directors should **scrutinise and challenge the strategies proposed by executives.** The chairman has responsibility for ensuring that the board spends **sufficient time discussing risk management issues**.

Scrutiny of chief executive's activities

As chairman Miss Hoiku should have **scrutinised Mr Smith's performance effectively**. She should have assessed his achievements against targets such as profit or revenues. She should also have **formally appraised his performance at least annually** and raised concerns about excessive time spent away from headquarters. **No effective appraisal** appears to have been carried out.

Agency problems

Miss Hoiku was also responsible for representing shareholder interests and ensuring that there was **goal congruence** between the **objectives of the shareholders** and the **activities of the chief executive**. Instead she has allowed a significant agency problem to develop, with the chief executive effectively voting himself a generous package that **bears little relation to what shareholders require**.

Risk management systems

The chairman should oversee the board's assessment of TQ's risk management systems. It is clear here that an **effective assessment did not take place,** since the problems with implementing strategy and **coordination of operational procedures** that derived from the absence of the chief executive were not resolved.

Failure to replace non-executive directors

The failure to replace the non-executive directors probably breaches local requirements about the proportion of non-executive directors on the board. Miss Hoiku should have ensured that the process for **recruiting new non-executive directors began** as soon as the existing directors announced they were leaving.

Committee system

The departure of the non-executive directors has resulted in a further **breach of governance best practice**. A key board committee (the remuneration committee) has not operated due to the lack of non-executive directors on the board and thus **Mr Smith's package has not been effectively scrutinised**.

Executive directors' remuneration

A remuneration committee should have been in place to **scrutinise the remuneration of the chief executive and other executive directors**. In the committee's absence Miss Hoiku was responsible for challenging executive packages rather than meekly accepting Mr Smith's proposals for his own package.

Shareholder communications

Miss Hoiku should have taken the lead in communicating with shareholders and making a considered response to shareholder concerns. Instead there appears to have been **no attempt to address shareholder concerns**, and **no explanation for this failure**. The chairman's statement appears inadequate.

6 Tomato Bank

Text references. Chapters 1, 3 and 9.

Top tips. The problems in (a) are fairly well signposted in the scenario, emphasising the examiner's comments about the need for careful analysis of the scenario. To score high marks you need to demonstrate an understanding of the qualities and duties of non-executive directors.

The latter part of (b) brings out the agency problem which underlies the whole question. It also considers the best ways of ensuring that the remuneration package can be an effective mechanism for passing judgement on the directors' performance. Judging over a longer period provides stronger evidence, and removing entitlement on a vote of no confidence by the shareholders ensures shareholder opinions are taken into account.

You could have used other frameworks as a basis for answering (c). Again concepts of agency and responsibility are important, and enhanced by the director's poor conduct.

Easy marks. Certainly the remuneration package elements in (b), although note that you had to give some description to get a mark for each. Merely listing each item would have given you half a mark at best.

Examiner's comments. (a) and (b) were done quite well overall but (c) was done poorly by most candidates.

In (a), I was pleased to see that many candidates were able to do well on this question with case analysis skills being well demonstrated by successful candidates. On questions containing verbs such as 'criticise', careful analysis of the case is usually essential in preparing good answers.

In (b), the first task, largely bookwork, was done better than the second. There were ample points in the case to pick up on and careful study of the case was rewarded with higher marks than those who merely relied on 'lists' of points.

(c) was badly done by most candidates. Although Mr Woof was legally entitled to receive the pension value, the question specifically asked candidates about the ethical case. Mr Woof could have accepted a reduction in the value of his pension in recognition of his failure as CEO. This was done poorly by a majority of candidates, thus somewhat underscoring the importance of developing ethical reasoning skills in preparation for P1 exams.

Marking scheme

		Marks
(a)	2 marks for each criticism identified and discussed	Max 10
(b)	1 mark for each component identified and described (0.5 marks for identification only)	Max 5
	1 mark for each relevant point of explanation of the benefits of a balanced package for Mr Woof	Max 5
		10
(c)	1 mark for each relevant point made	Max 5
		25

(a)   **Failure to consider risks**

The remuneration committee was too heavily influenced by the favourable publicity surrounding Woof. It failed to consider the **consequences** of Woof failing to deliver. Although Woof had previously been successful, this may have been by taking very risky strategies. The committee failed to consider whether Woof's package was **compatible** with the desirable risk **appetite** of the bank.

Agreeing to non-performance related element

A significant part of Woof's package was the pension element. It was not related to the bank's performance and shareholders' interests. Woof was still entitled to it despite the bank's problems, and there was **no downside risk** for him. The committee could have made the granting of the pension dependent on Woof leaving office in a satisfactory way, and not being forced out for failure.

Lack of scrutiny of elements

The committee failed to scrutinise the individual elements of the package. In particular they failed to take into account the fact that a significant part of the package was **payable after only two years**, but Woof's performance could only be judged fairly over a longer time period. The directors also should have considered whether the **balance of the different elements of the package** was appropriate.

Influenced by Woof and finance director

The committee failed to take an **objective view** of the package, but allowed itself to be **influenced by Woof's lobbying and pressure from the finance director**. Governance reports recommend that the committee is made up of non-executive directors so that they can take a **view of directors' remuneration** that is **independent** of executive directors. Instead committee members **failed to scrutinise and challenge** the proposals put forward by the finance director.

Lack of independence

Two of the non-executive directors were former colleagues of Woof's. They lacked the **independence** required by governance best practice to judge what his package should be. They should therefore have taken no part in the decisions on his remuneration.

(b)   **Elements of reward package**

Basic salary

Basic salary will be in **accordance with the director's contract of employment** and is not related to the performance of the company and the director. It is determined by the **experience of the director** and the **market rate** that other companies are prepared to pay.

Short and long-term performance related bonuses

Directors may be paid a cash bonus for meeting **performance targets**. It may well be linked to the level of **accounting profits**. The bonus level may be limited to a **fixed percentage of salary or pay**.

Shares and share options

Directors may be **awarded shares** in the company with time limits on when they can be sold. They may alternatively be awarded **share options**, the right to purchase shares at a specified exercise price over a specified time period in the future. If the price of the shares exceeds the exercise price when the options can be exercised, the directors will be able to buy shares at lower than market value.

Benefits-in-kind

Benefits-in-kind can include a car, health provisions, life assurance, holidays, expenses and loans.

Pension contributions

Companies may pay directors' pension contributions. Directors may be in a **separate scheme** from employees, and have their contributions paid at a higher rate. A pre-arranged pension benefit might also be paid after a certain number of years' service.

Why more balanced package would have been appropriate

Agency costs

A package more dependent on company performance would have reduced **agency costs**. Agency costs arise out of the need for shareholders to monitor the performance of their agent (CEO) and are enhanced if the agent's interests are not aligned with theirs. A package based on results would bring the CEO's **interests more into line with shareholders**, and reduce the need for **scrutiny**.

Investors' expectations about risk

The package appears to have encouraged Woof to **pursue a high risk high growth strategy**. This will have been contrary to the **interests and expectations** of shareholders who held Tomato's shares as a **low-risk element** in a balanced portfolio. To counter this excessive risk-taking, the package could have depended on an assessment by internal audit of the **riskiness** of the sources of funding, and judgements by the remuneration committee of whether these risks were too high.

Long-term elements

It seems Woof's performance could only be judged fairly **over a number of years**, since the **demand for mortgages** is over the long-term (often 25 years). However much of the package was payable before a judgement could be made.

Past performance

In a sense the pension entitlement was awarded based on Woof's good performance at other banks. However his historic performance did **not guarantee future profit increases** for Tomato's shareholders, and his package should have been based more on what he achieved at Woof.

Manner of departure

A further way of adding balance to the package would be to have made some or all of it **conditional** on the way in which **Woof left office**. The agreement could have provided for a loss of entitlement if Woof left office as the result of a shareholders' vote.

(c) **Accountability to shareholders**

As the agent of shareholders, Woof is accountable to them for the performance of the bank. A decision to accept a reduction indicates his **responsibility for strategic decisions**, and acknowledges that he is answerable for the consequences of his poor management.

Expectations

The case for a reduction is enhanced by Woof **knowing** that he was taken on because his reputation led the directors to believe the bank would generate much better results under his leadership. He **encouraged these expectations** by his promises of sustained growth for many years. Though the pension element was not explicitly linked to performance, Woof was given it because other directors believed that it was needed for him to agree to become CEO and deliver the growth.

Responsibility for results

The case for Woof giving up some of his pension is enhanced the **level of direct responsibility** he has for the bank's problems. Although poor economic conditions beyond Woof's control could have led to the failure of the sources of funds, Woof's excessive risk-taking has made a bad situation worse for the bank.

Flaws in granting process

A further argument for Woof returning his pension was that the procedure for granting it was **unsatisfactory**. The directors making the decision were too concerned to attract him and failed to give his package the **independent and thorough scrutiny** required.

Level of morality

Judged by Kohlberg's scale of morality, Woof appears to be operating at pre-conventional level 1, seeing the situation in terms of the rewards to which he has an **entitlement**. If he was viewing the decision at a desirable post-conventional level 3 he would take into account the views of society that he was morally not entitled to the pension or even decide independently that he should not be rewarded for failure.

7 KK

Text references. Chapter 3.

Top tips. The requirements for this question require careful reading as it's particularly easy to produce a general answer for (b) and (c) that contains much irrelevant material. In (a) the requirement to discuss suggests 2 marks will be available for each conflict of interest that you cover. Note the problem with the cross-directorship would apply even if KK did not purchase from SS.

The temptation in (b) is to base the answer around all of the Higgs report categories (strategy, scrutiny, risk and people). The answer however needs to focus on NEDs' contribution to discussions about strategy and also risk. The last point about reassurance is important in the context of the agency relationship between shareholders and executive directors. Effective NEDs can lower other agency costs.

It would be easy for an answer to (c) to be a unorganised list of disclosures. The focus needs to be on the performance and functioning of the board, as this is the main concern of Fin. Some of the headings used in the answer are similar to those in the UK Corporate Governance Code, although we also discuss communication with shareholders.

Easy marks. Identifying the conflicts of interest in (a) should have been straightforward as they are very clearly highlighted in the scenario.

Examiner's comments. (a) asked candidates to explain what a conflict of interest was and then to discuss the conflicts of interest that would arise if John Soria, the nominee for the position, became the NED of KK Company. This was done well overall, with many candidates scoring well on both tasks.

There was a difference in (b) between candidates who attempted to analyse the case and carefully consider what the question was actually asking, and those who seemed to think that questions asking about the non-executives should be answered in terms of the four general roles (people, risk, strategy, scrutiny). The question asked specifically about how NEDs would benefit the KK board during a period of growth and this required candidates to carefully consider the particular circumstances in question. Those candidates that carefully considered the case and the particular advantages that NEDs could bring during a period of rapid growth achieved the highest marks.

(c) was actually asking something quite straightforward: what would a good corporate governance section of an annual report contain. In many countries, a substantive CG section is either mandatory or prescribed under listing rules. Reports often have several pages of content called 'corporate governance' or similar. This underlines the importance of candidates being aware of a range of reporting issues. Inspecting the annual reports of most large companies would be a way of becoming familiar with corporate governance reports. One common error was to answer as if the question was asking about the contents of an annual report (chairman's statement, income statement, etc). It was asking about the corporate governance section in an annual report and not about the annual report in its entirety.

Marking scheme

			Marks
(a)	Explanation of conflict of interest 2 marks for each potential conflict of interest identified and explained	2 Max 6	
			8
(b)	2 marks for each advantage assessed		Max 7
(c)	2 marks for each section explained Explanation of information needs of Fin Brun	Max 8 2	
			10
			25

(a) **Conflicts of interest**

Non-executive directors (NEDs)' conduct and decision-making should be determined by the best interests of the company that they manage and its shareholders. A conflict of interest is an external pressure or commitment that **undermines the independence** of NEDs and could lead them to make decisions that are not in the best interests of the company or shareholders.

Conflicts of interest in KK

Personal relationships

John has very strong links with KK's board, being brother-in-law of the chief executive and friends with the rest of the board. John may not therefore wish to come into conflict with the board if it **threatens family harmony or friendships**. John may also be more inclined to take what KK board members tell him on trust because he relies on his close personal knowledge of them. Thus he may fail to query doubtful conduct or decisions when he should do so.

Relationship with supplier

John's non-executive directorship can be expected to strengthen the links between KK and Soria Supplies. (SS). A close supply chain relationship may in practice benefit both companies. However the underlying conflict of interest is that as directors of both companies, John and also Susan are expected to **promote the best interests of both**, and these may come into conflict. In particular it could ultimately be in KK's best interests to stop using SS because, for example, other suppliers offer better terms. John and Susan could not be involved in this decision because of their commitment to SS.

Cross-directorships

The cross-directorships of John and Susan (executive director of KK is NED of SS and vice-versa) are by themselves a threat to independence, even if there were no other links between KK and SS. The problem is that non-executive directors will **sit in judgement on executives** when, for example, they consider their remuneration. Having one director judge another when the other director is also judging the first director is a conflict of interest, since directors' decisions could clearly be determined by their own interests rather than their companies.

(b) **Advice on strategy**

NEDs with wide knowledge of the industry such as John has, could help advise on the **appropriateness** of **expansion strategies**. Here the right NEDs could supply what other directors are lacking, **knowledge of particular overseas markets and experience of developing a presence in these markets**.

Advice on risk

Experienced NEDs should also be able to offer an **informed opinion** about the **riskiness of rapid expansion** into new markets. Because KK is growing quickly, it is likely to face new or much increased exposure to many different risks. The NEDs may have greater knowledge of some of these risks than the less experienced executives. The NEDs should also advise on whether the increase in risk exposure has been too high, given the **returns** available and the **appetite of shareholders for new risks**.

Advice on risk management

Because the NEDs have had experience of other companies, they should also be able to **benchmark KK's risk and control management systems** against systems elsewhere, and try to ensure that they are developing along with the expansion in business. The expansion in director numbers may help, but will not be enough by itself. A **risk committee**, staffed by NEDs, could be valuable for KK.

Reassurance to investors

Experienced and effective NEDs should also offer shareholders comfort that Ken Kava does not have unrestrained powers of decision-making. Shareholders will want to believe that NEDs are **scrutinising future plans**, and **challenging strategies** that they believe to be inappropriate. For KK, experienced NEDs are particularly important for shareholders because of the **lack of experience** of many of the executive directors, which appears to mean that executives lack the confidence to challenge Ken.

(c) **Board details**

Shareholders will be interested in how the board is functioning as a **forum for decision-making** and **monitoring**. The report should contain details about the workings of the board including the frequency of, and attendance at, board meetings, and how the board's performance has been evaluated. The report should also detail changes in the composition of the board, including particularly explanations of why directors have **left the board suddenly and unexpectedly**.

Non-executive directors and board committees

Shareholders will be looking for evidence that NEDs are a strong, objective presence on the board. The report should explain whether NEDs are considered to be **independent**. NEDs will also be particularly involved in **key board committees**, the **nomination, audit, remuneration and risk committees**. The report therefore should contain details about the terms of reference and composition of these committees, as well as the frequency of meetings. Each of the main committees should provide a **report on their activities during the year**.

Accounts and audit

The report should contain certain specific disclosures for shareholders' reassurance. These include a statement of the **board's responsibility for the preparation of accounts and that the company is a going concern.** The report should contain details about any **accounting issues** that have arisen, for example the impact of changes in accounting standards or a restatement of the accounts. There should be information about **relations with auditors**, including reasons for change and steps taken to ensure auditor objectivity and independence if auditors have provided non-audit services. If the company does not have an **internal audit** function, the report should say why. The report should also include a statement about the **board's review of internal controls**.

Communication with shareholders

The report should include information about **relations with shareholders** and how communication channels have been maintained. The report can be a means of providing shareholders with the information that they have said they need. This particularly applies to the **business review,** which should give shareholders information about how the directors view **historic performance and their plans for future strategy**. This is particularly important where, as with KK, the company is developing rapidly.

Fin Brun's information needs

Fin Brun is correct in asserting that it is likely to be difficult to determine individual directors' performance from the accounts. The accounts can however provide some information to reassure Fin. The accounts should disclose why directors have been **nominated for election or re-election**. The accounts should disclose the **bonuses paid to directors,** which should have been objectively determined by a remuneration committee staffed by NEDs. These will provide an indication of how the remuneration committee has viewed performance. The report could also include **biographical details** about the directors and also details of their **main responsibilities and objectives**. This information together should help Fin determine whether directors appear to be qualified for board membership and their board roles. The accounts could also give more details about the **process for appraising individual directors**, including the frequency of assessment, the criteria used and how the results of the appraisal are actioned. These should help reassure Fin that a rigorous system is in place.

8 HHO

Text references. Chapters 1 and 3.

Top tips. Most of the differences discussed in (a) relate to issues mentioned in the scenario.

The main omission from the scenario is the role of trustees. It is important to bring out in (b) the links between transparency and accountability to different classes of stakeholder, particularly donors. It might have been helpful to think, when answering (b), about why you give money to particular charities, and what you expect to see those charities doing. Transparency here, as in other questions in this exam, is also seen as a means of reducing or halting damaging publicity about the organisation.

In (c) the answer discusses most of the major roles of the audit committee. As always, your answer needs to bring in material from the case as a justification for discussing each role. The compliance role of the audit committee is perhaps wider than it would be for a limited company, with more focus on compliance with the expectations of stakeholders and not just laws and regulations.

Easy marks. Definitions such as the definition of transparency in (b) should always be worth a couple of straightforward marks.

Examiner's comments. (a) should have been straightforward to candidates that were familiar with the relevant part of the study guide and who had studied the relevant technical article. This part was done quite well by many of those who attempted Question 3.

(b) offered more of a challenge because after a relatively straightforward opening (to define transparency), a higher level verb ('construct') invited candidates to examine the case in detail, to pick out those things that were wrong at HHO and to use those issues to argue in favour of greater transparency.

Marking scheme

		Marks
(a)	0.5 marks for identification. 2 marks for each area of difference identified and explained	Max 6
	Differences in governance structures	Max 3
		9
(b)	2 marks for definition of transparency	
	2 marks for each point made for greater transparency	Max 8
(c)	2 marks for each relevant area of internal audit explained	Max 8
		25

(a) **Purpose**

The main purpose of companies is to earn a return for shareholders. Directors and staff aim to **maximise long-term cash flows**. Success is measured by **earnings per share, cash flows and share price movements**.

Charities exist to fulfil the charitable purpose for which the charity is set up. To be able to operate as a charity, this purpose will have to be a **socially beneficial or benevolent purpose as defined by the law**. Funds are donated to the charity to support its charitable purpose. The charity's governance should thus not only be concerned with maximising the income received, but also the expectations of donors about how their donations will be used.

Regulations

Companies will be subject to **companies' legislation** that applies locally, including regulations about how the company should be administered and the contents of the company's financial reports. Larger companies listed on a local stock exchange will be subject to listing rules and required to comply with the local governance codes, which include additional requirements such as the need for board committees.

Charities will be subject to a different statutory regime. They will need to fulfil the requirements of the local charitable authority to be able to operate as a charity. **Charitable status** confers certain privileges, for example exemption from taxation, that companies do not have. The **accounting information required from charities** is also likely to differ from that required for companies. In this country the information that charities have to disclose is significantly less than companies, but the same is not true in other regimes.

Stakeholders' expectations

Society expects a business to be **run profitably and efficiently** and to supply goods or services that society requires. A business is expected to **create value** for shareholders, and treat other key stakeholders, particularly employees, suppliers and customers, fairly. A business will be successful if people want to work for it, suppliers supply resources and customers buy what it offers.

A charity's main stakeholders include donors, beneficiaries and employees. All of these will be concerned about the extent to which, and the ways in which, the charity **fulfils its benevolent purposes**.

Governance arrangements

Companies are **governed by a board of directors**. Listed companies are expected to include non-executive directors as well as executive directors on their board. The shareholders can hold the board accountable through **votes at general meetings,** including votes on whether to re-elect directors and whether to approve directors' remuneration arrangements. In many countries a single board oversees the company.

Charities may have a board of executive directors to run its **operations**. However the fulfilment of the charity's purposes is **overseen** by a **board of trustees**. The trustees interpret how the charity's purposes and fiduciary duties should be applied. The trustees may include **representatives of beneficiaries**. However in many instances, as with HHO, trustees will have to look after the interests of beneficiaries who cannot represent themselves. The trustees themselves hold the executive board **accountable** for running the charity in **accordance with the charity's purposes**. This includes being sensitive to whether the executive board is acting in its own interests and not the charity's, by, for example, earning excessive salaries.

(b) **Transparency**

Transparency means **open and clear disclosure** of relevant information to stakeholders, and also not concealing information when it may affect decisions. It implies a **default position of information provision rather than concealment**.

Reassurance of donors

Donors provide the charity with the bulk of its income. They will wish to see that the charity is spending **its money in accordance with its aims and purposes**, and their monies have funded the projects promoted by Horace Hoi. In many countries multiple charities exist to promote animal welfare. The proportion of money being spent on improving animal welfare by each charity will be a major influence on donors' decisions on which charity to support. In addition donors may also be influenced by the level of detail provided by different charities, gaining greater reassurance from charities that give much more detail than HHO has provided. The lack of detail given by HHO may be counter-productive and suggest the charity has something to hide.

Reduction of criticism

As well as being influenced by the data the charity itself provides, donor decisions will also be influenced by other information. Press criticism poses a **substantial threat to the reputation of the charity** and **could lead to a significant fall in donations and other support**. Better information would demonstrate to the media that HHO took donors' concerns seriously. It would also decrease the risk of inaccurate speculation by journalists damaging the charity.

Position of Horace Hoi

Horace Hoi's role has come under particular scrutiny and concerns have been raised about his **stewardship of the organisations' resources.** Donors and others are concerned that he is receiving excessive rewards and is spending money unnecessarily, for example on the private jet. The failure to join other charities in disclosing more information can be seen as demonstrating a poor attitude to governance. The accounts should be used to explain the business case for **potentially controversial expenditure**, for example the need for Horace Hoi to be transported rapidly around the world.

(c) ### Role of audit committee

The audit committee can help create a **culture** that emphasises discipline and control in governance. The audit committee can also contribute to improving significantly the culture of **transparency**. The committee's role will be strengthened if it consists of independent trustees or non-executive directors, at least some of whom have financial knowledge. Directors with these qualities should be able to **resist pressure** from Horace Hoi and make **informed judgements on key areas**.

Review of financial statements

The audit committee can play a particularly important role in HHO by reviewing the quality of financial information. The committee can put pressure on the other directors to **increase the level of detail of financial reporting** towards the full disclosure made by other charities. It can also review the accounting systems that provide information for the public and authorities, and press for improvements in these.

Review of internal controls

The audit committee can also look at other aspects of internal control. It should focus on the **control of the expenses** that do not relate directly to specific charitable projects, as these are a sensitive issue. It should press for **proper budgeting** of this expenditure and follow-up by executive management if actual expenditure exceeds budgets. It should also obtain evidence about the system of expenditure authorisation, focusing on **authorisation of large amounts** and **expenditure which may not be necessary** for the charity's main purpose. The audit committee also needs to assess whether adequate controls are in place to **limit the risk of fraud and non-compliance with regulations**.

Fraud

The audit committee should also consider the risk of **fraud**. Because of the sensitivities surrounding expenditure levels at HHO, the audit committee should establish a **whistleblowing channel**, enabling staff to report suspicions of fraud directly to the audit committee. The audit committee should also be able to **instigate an investigation** into fraud itself, without the approval of executive directors being required. Here there seems to be a need for the audit committee to **investigate remuneration arrangements for directors** and the **activities of Horace Hoi,** assessing whether he has misused the charity's income to fund his personal lifestyle.

Compliance and ethics

The audit committee should obtain evidence that HHO is **complying with the regulations and codes** that apply in this country to an organisation with charitable status. It should also check for compliance with voluntary codes, for example that the charity's appeals are line with the sector's best practice and do not mislead donors. More widely it could itself review **large transactions for reasonableness,** measured against the expectations of the charity's donors.

9 Geeland

Marking scheme

		Marks
(a)	Distinguishing between rules and principles-based approaches	4
	2 marks for each argument in favour of or against remark	Max <u>10</u>
		Max 12
(b)	2 marks for point of explanation (½ mark for identification only)	
		Max 8
(c)	1.5 marks for each relevant point of assessment (½ mark for identification only)	<u>5</u>
		<u>25</u>

(a) **Rules-based approach**

A rules-based approach, known as **box-ticking**, requires companies to comply with regulations. There are **no exceptions** apart from those allowed for in the regulations. A rules-based approach is generally underpinned by law. Companies which do not comply will face **legal sanctions**.

Principles-based approach

A principles-based approach is likely to be underpinned by some company law, but the principles will also cover areas not included in legislation. Principles-based approaches emphasise the **objectives of governance**, rather than good governance being achieved by taking a number of prescribed actions.

Companies operating under a principles-based code cannot however just ignore it. The code will often be incorporated into listing rules. They have to state that they have complied in their accounts or identify and explain the areas where they have not complied. Investors will then decide whether they accept the company's justification for non-compliance and may take action that impacts upon share price.

Geeland's approach

The guidance in the Geeland code clearly identifies that the code is **principles-based**, as it states that there is more to governance than complying with rules. Good governance requires broad principles which should be applied flexibly to individual companies.

Arguments in favour

Areas of application

A principles-based approach can **extend more widely** than a rules-based approach and can focus on areas where it would be unrealistic to apply rules. For example a principles-based approach can require directors to undertake professional development to extend their knowledge and skills without laying down how many courses they should go on each year. A principles-based approach can require boards to maintain good relations with major (institutional) shareholders without laying down how much contact there should be each year.

Cost to companies

A principles-based approach is also less costly in terms of time and expenditure. Companies in a rules-based jurisdiction may have to invest considerable time and monies in developing information and reporting systems that evidence compliance. There is evidence that companies have turned away from US stock markets, where they would be under the rules-based, Sarbanes-Oxley, regime on the grounds of cost of compliance. To be effective also, a rules-based regime has to have bodies to **monitor and enforce compliance**. The costs of maintaining these bodies are often passed on to companies in the form of listing costs.

Flexibility of approach

A principles-based approach can require companies to maintain adequate structures, for example effective risk management systems, but allow what is adequate to vary by company or industry. For example in some industries companies will avoid hazardous activities and will not therefore require **elaborate health and safety control systems**. Other industries, for example extractive industries, inevitably involve hazardous activities and so require complex risk management systems, to ensure that risks are reduced to levels that are as low as reasonably practicable.

Flexibility in application

Principles-based codes can allow for flexibility in application of provisions in circumstances where non-compliance can be justified. Companies may have to deal with a period of transition, for example where a Chairman leaves the board suddenly and it takes time to recruit a permanent successor. In these circumstances having the same person act as Chairman and Chief Executive on a temporary basis may be felt to be the most **practical solution**. Provided the non-compliance is explained clearly, investors may accept the justification.

Arguments against

Consistency of approach

A rules-based approach means all companies are **complying with the same standards**. It should be easy for investors to see that **compliance** has been **achieved**. Comparison between companies should be **straightforward**. Some investors may have **more confidence in a rules-based approach** as a result. It is also therefore easier to enforce a rules-based approach on companies.

Broad principles

The principles in a principles-based code may be so broad as to mean that companies have excessive leeway in following the code. Some companies may therefore try to do as little as possible to comply with the code, and therefore gain **cost and competitive advantage** over other companies that have been more conscientious.

Compulsory requirements

Where principles-based codes include specific recommendations, for example that the role of **chairman and chief executive be split**, there may be confusion over whether these recommendations are compulsory or not. Recommendations that are underpinned by company law requirements will be compulsory, but the status of recommendations that are not underpinned may be unclear. In some countries, the adoption of governance codes by stock exchanges means that specific recommendations in codes have been seen as **listing rules requiring compliance**. Companies that lack compliance expertise may find it difficult to judge whether and how they should comply.

Explanations

Explanations for non-compliance may not be adequate for shareholders. Shareholders **may not understand** the **reasons for, and consequences of, non-compliance**. Accounts may provide unclear explanations, with directors knowing that, even if some shareholders are unhappy, their positions are guaranteed by having the support of sufficient large shareholders.

(b)   **Power**

Having the same person in both roles means that **power** is **concentrated** in one person. A common feature of governance scandals that have prompted the development of guidance has been an individual exercising excessive power. The board may be **ineffective in controlling the chief executive** if it is led by the chief executive. For example the chairman is responsible for providing information that the other directors require to manage the company. If the chairman is also chief executive, the directors cannot be sure that the information they are getting is **sufficient and accurate**. Separation of the role also means that the board can **express its concerns more effectively** by providing a point of reporting for the non-executive directors.

Accountability

The board cannot make the chief executive **truly accountable** for management if it is chaired and led by the chief executive. The chairman carries the **authority of the board** and the chief executive carries **authority delegated by the board**. Separating the roles emphasises the chief executive's accountability to the board's leader, the Chairman, and also the shareholders whose interests the Chairman represents. Separation should **reduce the risk of conflicts of interest** where the Chairman/Chief Executive focuses on his own self-interest.

Demands of roles

Splitting the posts between different people reflects the reality that both jobs are **demanding roles** and no-one person will have the **skills and the time** to do both jobs well. The chief executive can concentrate on running the company's operations, developing business and risk management strategy, reviewing investment policy and managing the executive team. The chairman can concentrate on running the board effectively and ensuring that directors develop an understanding of the views of major investors.

Under governance best practice, the chairman should be an independent non-executive director, and hence well-placed to adopt a **supervisory and monitoring role**.

Governance requirements

Splitting the roles **ensures compliance with governance requirements and reassures shareholders**. Investor confidence is important in maintaining company value and sometimes compliance with governance best practice is needed to maintain confidence. Although Marks and Spencer in the UK sought to justify Sir Stuart Rose acting as Chairman and Chief Executive for a few years, a number of institutional investors objected to this arrangement, saying that such a leading UK company should set an example by complying with this important governance requirement, rather than explaining why it had not complied.

(c)   **Comply or explain**

Compliance with governance requirements

Anson has fulfilled the requirements of the listing rules to identify areas of non-compliance. The statement **clearly highlights the issue** where Anson has not complied. It unambiguously states that it is not in accordance with governance best practice. It specifies as well that Mr Klunker is the individual concerned.

This may be significant for shareholders who may be less concerned about the breach because they have confidence in Mr Klunker.

Why it has happened

However the statement does not state clearly **why** Anson has not complied. It does not explain the reasons for the company benefiting from having Mr Klunker in control. The statement that the company has maintained robust corporate governance is also vague. Stating the company understands the concerns of shareholders is not the same as saying that the company has responded to them.

Time limit to non-compliance

However shareholders will be reassured by the fact that Anson is planning to **comply with governance requirements in future**. Anson has made a clear commitment to separate the roles and has set a time limit on this.

10 Dale Gas

Text references. Chapters 3 and 6.

Top tips. This question was designed to highlight the governance issues that can occur with organisational changes such as privatisation. The scenario contains a lot of information that you can use when answering (a) including Mrs Evans's strategic skills, the views of shareholders, Mrs Evans's abilities, market rate (the case mentioned other companies of similar size), government regulations that had previously constrained her pay, and the opinions of some that believed the doubling of her reward to be unreasonable. Remember in (a) that the purposes of offering someone the right remuneration package are the three issues stated – to attract them to the company, to keep them loyal and keep them motivated. The rest of the answer brings in factors that would apply to any chief executive and also the factors highlighted in the scenario – stakeholder reaction and constraints on government.

(b) may seem at first to be a fairly difficult requirement. The market risk here relates to the share value of Dale Gas – it is the risk of loss due to an adverse movement in the market price of the share. The loss of a key executive can increase market risk because it can unsettle investors or threaten the value of those assets upon which future cash flows, and hence market values, depend. Market risk is dependent on the reaction of shareholders and there is a lot in the scenario about why shareholders regard Mrs Evans favourably that you can bring in here.

Perhaps the most important point in (c) is the practical point that proxies save institutional and other shareholders the time and agency cost involved in attending uncontroversial AGMs. It would be impossible for a fund manager like Tom Nwede to attend the annual general meetings of every company in the managed funds. If institutional investors have confidence in the board of a company, they may be prepared to allow the chairman to vote on their behalf in order to avoid the need to study each motion and attend in person.

Easy marks. The definitions in (b) and (c) should offer a few straightforward marks,

Examiner's comments. It seems when some candidates see questions such as part (a), they enter into a description of the components of a reward package, even if it is clearly not required. This requirement had two clear tasks, to explain the purposes of a CEO's reward package (not its components) and then to review the factors that might influence the level of the rewards for Mrs Evans. Most candidates were able to explain the ideas of attract, retain and motivate as the main purposes of a reward package, although those that only listed the terms without reference to the case did not receive good marks. More difficult for some candidates was the second part of the requirement. There was a lot in the case to use in answering this requirement. The secret to getting the marks was to carefully examine the case and to use that as the basis for the answer. Some merely listed the main points without explaining from the case and those answers were not so well rewarded.

Part (b) was less well done. The first task should have been straightforward as it was a simple definition, but it seemed to confuse many candidates.

A common problem with part (c) on proxy voting was to recognise that it involved voting without attending the general meeting but then to fail to explain the advantages.

			Marks
(a)	1 mark for each purpose	Max 3	
	2 marks for each influencing factor reviewed in context (½ mark for identification only)	Max 8	
			Max 10
(b)	Definition of market risk	2	
	2 marks for each relevant point of justification	Max 8	
			10
(c)	Definition	2	
	1 mark for each advantage	Max 3	
			5
			25

(a) **Purposes**

Attract

Remuneration packages are designed to persuade an individual with **appropriate skills, knowledge and experience** to join the company. If the package is too low, the company will not be able to recruit a chief executive with the qualities it desires. If it is pitched too high, it may attract applicants who lack the required qualities.

Retain

Packages are designed to **retain the chief executive's services** and to avoid the **discontinuity** arising from a chief executive leaving unexpectedly to take a role with another company that offers more generous remuneration.

Motivate

Reward packages should motivate chief executives to remain loyal and to lead the company to achieve objectives that are **consistent with shareholders' interests**. This may be done by **linking part of remuneration to achievements,** for example bonus to profit levels.

Influences on Mrs Evans' remuneration

Previous performance

Past performance in the role will influence the salary levels of a chief executive. Here Mrs Evans is felt to have **performed very well**. This has influenced the value that the remuneration committee has placed on her services. In particular she has demonstrated strategic and communication skills and gained the trust of employees and investors, which will all be very important in the new circumstances of Dale Gas.

The market rate

Remuneration will be influenced by the remuneration paid to chief executives in comparable positions, in other words what Mrs Evans would be paid if she moved to an **equivalent position in another company**. The remuneration committee believes that doubling Mrs Evans's salary would bring her package into line with what other public companies of similar size are paying.

Government constraints

The scenario highlights that **government constraints** were an influence on the chief executive's salary when the company was a nationalised monopoly. These constraints may be imposed by **legislation**, or governments may **impose a pay policy** on salaries to limit expenditure levels or avoid political unpopularity from having a government servant paid what is viewed as an excessive amount.

Stakeholder views

Some organisations may take into account the **views of stakeholders such as the small shareholders** in this case. This is most likely in a case of a public interest organisation, such as a charity, where the use of funds raised for non-charitable purposes is very sensitive. However it may be an issue here if a large salary increase occurs at the same time as significant price increases to consumers and the new company is vulnerable to the charge of continuing to exploit a monopoly position.

(b)   **Market risk**

Market risk is the risk of loss on capital markets due to an adverse movement in the market value of an asset, here the shares in Dale Gas. Market value will be sensitive to a number of factors, including views on the leadership of the company. If Mrs Evans were to be replaced, the share price and return on investment could fall.

Advantages of retaining Mrs Evans

Tom Nwede's belief

Tom believes that it is important for the future of Dale Gas and the market value of its shares that Mrs Evans be retained and motivated by an appropriately increased salary.

Knowledge of sector

Investors need assurance that the company is being directed and its strategies being developed by a board that includes directors with expertise in the gas industry, particularly during a time of change. Retaining Mrs Evans would mean that the leading executive director in Dale had the **necessary expertise** in the sector.

Knowledge of company

Mrs Evans also provides **continuity in the leadership of the company** because of her previous experience of the nationalised supplier. She can **guide the new directors** who are unfamiliar with the company. Mrs Evans is also well-known to the company's key internal and external stakeholders.

Strategy

The board's role of developing strategy would be especially important as Dale enters the private sector and seeks to **reposition itself strategically**. Mrs Evans clearly has the **strategic skills** necessary to lead this development and the **communication skills** to keep institutional investors informed of what is being planned.

Internal communication

Mrs Evans' skills will also be important in **maintaining internal morale**. The uncertainty and culture changes resulting from privatisation are likely to unsettle staff. Key individuals may leave. Staff who are left behind may become demotivated and resist change. Mrs Evans' communication skills, and the trust staff have in her, appear to mean that she is the most likely person to **persuade staff to adapt to the new circumstances**. The belief that Mrs Evans is able to implement a necessary change in attitudes is likely to enhance the confidence of investors.

(c)   **Proxy voting**

A **proxy** is a person appointed by a shareholder, who is **unable or unwilling to attend company general meetings**, to exercise the votes of that shareholder at the meetings. The shareholder completes a proxy form that transfers the right to vote to a board member or another person. The proxy may or may not have **specific instructions** on how to vote on each motion.

Advantages

Attendance

Institutional shareholders often hold shares in hundreds of companies. It is impractical to expect their representatives to attend every annual general meeting. Even if they could, the **associated agency costs** would be considerable and the usefulness of being present would be limited if all the votes were routine. Using a proxy means that **their votes can be exercised**, in accordance with best practice.

Representative of shareholders' views

If only those who attend the annual general meeting are allowed to vote and only a small number of shareholders attend, the votes taken may **not be representative** of the views of the shareholder body as a whole. Proxies mean that the views of those not attending the annual general meeting are reflected in the general meeting votes and the votes should thus be more representative of shareholder opinion.

11 Lum

Text references. Chapters 2 and 3.

Top tips. The scenario provides a number of clues of issues to discuss in (a), particularly the lack of formal requirements, such as the appointment of non-executive directors and the focus on the long-term. Note that as a listed company, the views of other stakeholders and society as a whole may become more important, as well as the requirements of external stakeholders.

To score well in (b), you need to bring in where possible the problems that Lum has found in operating as a limited company, in order to show why induction and CPD are required.

In (c), there are different ways in which multi-tier boards can work, but the scenario makes clear that the supervisory board was in overall control of strategy.

Easy marks. The first part of (b) is drawn from the guidance in the Higgs report.

Examiner's comments. The first task of part (a) was done quite well overall but candidates sometimes failed to recognise the importance of listing rules in the second task.

For part (b) a common error was to discuss the contents of an induction programme when the question specifically asked for an assessment of the benefits. Another common error was to treat the two under the same heading when in fact the two (induction and CPD) are quite different and serve different needs within a company. I was surprised to see that many candidates struggled to achieve high marks in part (c) on unitary and two-tier boards, despite this topic having been on previous P1 papers. There was evidence that some candidates did not understand the roles of NEDs on the two types of boards nor how the two approaches might affect the control that the Lum family might have over the company after flotation.

			Marks
(a)	4 marks for contrasting family and listed	4	
	2 marks for each relevant point of assessment	Max 6	
			10
(b)	1 mark for each contribution of induction	Max 4	
	1 mark for each contribution of CPD	4	
			8
(c)	4 marks for distinguishing between (2 marks for each)	Max 4	
	1 mark for each difficulty discussed	Max 7	
			Max 7
			25

(a) **Comparison between family business and listed company**

Legal formalities

In most jurisdictions, family companies are only subject to limited legal requirements affecting their governance. Listed companies face **greater statutory requirements and also are subject to listing rules**. These are designed to give investors assurance about the way listed companies are governed and hence increase their confidence in their investment.

Formality

Family company boards are likely to run informally because they are **not accountable** to **external shareholders outside the small family group**. Governance arrangements for listed companies have to be much more formal, in order to ensure their **accountability to external shareholders** who are not involved in the company. Hence for example listed companies are subject to regulations that require them to report information about the board of directors, such as the number of meetings each year and the work of board committees.

Composition and structure

Many family companies will have **no non-executive directors**. Many governance codes require listed company boards to be **balanced between executive directors and non-executive directors**. For example the UK Corporate Governance Code requires at least 50% of the board to be independent non-executive directors. Family companies may not need to operate any board committees as they have enough time to discuss all important issues. Listed companies are required to have a **number of committees**, partly to monitor the activities of executive directors and ensure their remuneration is fair.

Objectives

The boards of family companies will need to take account of the wishes of the few major shareholders. Often this group will want the company to **invest for the long-term**. The board of a listed company will have to address **varying requirements of different shareholder groups and other stakeholders**. Some may want **longer-term capital gains** but others will require **strong short-term profits and dividends**.

Impact of flotation

Long-term values and beliefs

Whether the board will still be able to manage in accordance with its beliefs will depend on how shareholders view these beliefs. Shareholders, for example, may believe that the board is **excessively focused on the long-term** and instead needs to focus more each year on **achieving a target profit**. This may mean that the board is forced to take action on a business segment that investors perceive has **under-performed one year**, rather than accepting that the segment be allowed to build up resources for longer-term success.

Impact of institutional investors

A significant proportion of Lum's shares may well be held by financial institutions. They will require **regular information from Lum, including briefings on financial results**, and explanations from Lum if its financial performance or behaviour does not meet their expectations.

Meeting expectations

Lum will have to demonstrate it meets the expectations of the stock market. Because a listed company's activities are **more visible in society**, it also becomes increasingly **subject to society's expectations**. This may mean that it has to change the way it acts and is organised in a number of areas, to fulfil the requirements of society and key stakeholder groups.

Paternalistic management style

Crispin Lum emphasised the paternalistic management style of Lum prior to the flotation. The directors may **not be able to manage in this way** if the company becomes listed. Investors may require a **stricter approach** to dealing with employees and Lum to focus more on **controlling labour costs**. Employees may expect better-defined management procedures, with **more formal human resource structures and policies** being introduced.

(b)   **Benefits of induction**

Better-informed NEDs

Non-executive directors (NEDs) need to be given information about Lum to enable them to develop an understanding of its **business and its markets**, and hence to be able to make informed contributions at board meetings. This includes information about Lum's business strategy and model, its products and markets, major competitors, major risks and performance indicators.

Management and culture of the business

Particularly as there have been problems with NEDs becoming frustrated, induction also needs to include guidance on how the company is managed, including how the board is **structured and exercises its responsibilities**. NEDs also need to develop an understanding of the company's **management style and culture**. This does not mean that they necessarily will accept all aspects of it, but it should give them a better understanding of what the executive directors are trying to achieve.

Establishing communication with personnel

Again because of the clashes with established members of the board, induction should enable the NEDs to establish strong links with the **company's personnel**. This includes meetings with board members outside the boardroom, meetings with other senior managers and visits to company sites other than headquarters.

Stakeholder relationships

Induction also should enable NEDs to build up **understanding of Lum's stakeholders**, including customers and suppliers. Most importantly, induction should enable NEDs to **build relationships** with stakeholders with whom they will be dealing, such as the external auditors, or whose interests they are representing, for example institutional investors.

Benefits of CPD

Purpose of CPD

The main purpose of CPD is for directors to **extend their knowledge and skills on an ongoing basis**. This means that it should aim to **enhance areas of performance** where directors appear to be struggling or to brief directors on **developments in the business environment** and changes in the requirements that the company faces.

Compliance

As discussed, as a listed company, Lum became subject to a **significantly greater number of regulations**. Lum's directors should have been given training about the **differences in legal requirements** facing a listed company as opposed to a private company. They should also have been briefed on the **requirements of listing rules and corporate governance codes**.

Personal skills and leadership

The problems in establishing relationships with the NEDs suggest that board members should have training in personal skills, including dealing with people whose **perspectives and requirements do not coincide with theirs**. Also as it seems that existing directors are struggling to manage the company, they need **training in different leadership styles** so that they can guide Lum more effectively, rather than relying on a paternalistic style that is no longer appropriate.

Investor requirements

Lum's board should also have had training in **managing relationships with the investors** who now have shares in Lum. This would include the **requirements of institutional investors** and how to enhance relationships with them. It also includes **methods of communication** with shareholders, particularly the management of general meetings, which may be more difficult occasions now that the number of shareholders is much larger.

(c)   **Unitary board**

Legal responsibility

All participants in a unitary board have **equal legal responsibility for management of the company and strategic performance**. This requires active involvement not just by executive directors, but also non-executive directors who are supervising and monitoring executives.

Involvement in decision-making

All directors will be **members of a single board and attend the same board meetings**. They should all **participate in decision-making and have equal access to information**.

Two-tier board

Separation of duties

A two-tier board provides a clear **separation of duties** between the executive or operational board, which runs the operations of the company, and the supervisory board, which monitors the executive board. The supervisory board is also responsible for legal and regulatory compliance issues.

Responsibility for strategy

The supervisory board will be **responsible for developing business strategy**. The executive board will be **responsible for executing this strategy**.

Difficulties for the Lum family

Different ways of operating

A unitary board means that **all directors will be entitled to participate in decision-making** on all areas. Beforehand the supervisory board, which only consisted of Lum family members, exercised control of the company, but now the Lum family is having to get used to others participating in controlling the company. Governance requirements aim to prevent boards being controlled by a small group of directors and the Lum family may find this frustrating.

Slower decision-making

With a unitary board, **notice of board meetings is required and the board often meets on fixed dates**. This may mean that **decision-making is slower**, and it means that the directors can **respond less quickly to changing circumstances**, which again may annoy the Lum family.

Change in board culture

The Lum family has to get used to **working in a different way on a unitary board**. The Lums must consult with, and achieve the agreement of, non-family members and also justify their decisions and actions to the rest of the board.

12 Oland

Text references. Chapters 1 to 3.

Top tips. The definition included in the answer to (a) is a combination of the Cadbury and IESBA definitions of governance. The rest of (a) picks up on the key themes of maintaining effective control, dealing with risks and maintaining relationships with shareholders and other key stakeholders.

Note in (b) that the requirement is to argue against – so you only need to include one side of the case. The key distinction is enforcement by law authorities versus enforcement by investors. 'Comply or explain' should give investors the information they need to make a balanced judgement on non-compliance.

Some of the arguments in (c) are also in favour of retirement by rotation, but you should remember that retirement by rotation is designed to change the board by slower evolution than having all directors up for election every year.

Easy marks. The definitions and explanations at the start of each part should guarantee 6 or 7 marks in this question.

Examiner's comments. All the themes raised in this question had been on previous P1 papers and so well-prepared candidates who had worked through the past papers would have seen similar requirements before.

Weaker answers to (a) listed the key underpinning concepts in the study guide. It wasn't clear how this approach was attempting to answer the requirement about making it more difficult for companies to fail and so these answers were not well-rewarded. Good answers reflected upon the essential features of good governance and then, importantly, considered how each of these made a company more robust and less likely to get into financial difficulty.

In (b) the distinction between rules and principles-based approaches was well understood by most candidates but the second task was less well-done by some.

In (c) most candidates could explain accountability successfully. The other tasks were less well done. It was important to understand the link between accountability as a concept and the mechanisms of calling it to account. Again the ability to apply a piece of knowledge was key to gaining good marks.

Marking scheme

		Marks	
(a)	Explanation of corporate governance somewhere in answer	2	
	2 marks for each point examined on corporate governance and failure	10	
			Max 10
(b)	Distinguishing between rules and principles	2	
	2 marks for each argument supporting comply or explain	6	
			8
(c)	Explanation of accountability	2	
	2 marks for each relevant discussion point on greater accountability	7	
			Max 7
			25

(a) **Definition of corporate governance**

Corporate governance is the system by which companies are **directed and controlled.** It focuses on the relationships between a company's directors, shareholders and other stakeholders. It provides the structure through which the **objectives of the company** are **set**, and the **means of achieving those objectives and monitoring performance** are **determined**.

Promotion of relationships with shareholders

Good governance should ensure alignment of the **interests of shareholders and directors**. It should minimise the chances of agency problems arising through directors pursuing their own interests and **threatening the company's future** by **reckless behaviour**, or failing to pursue the best long-term strategies for the company.

Risk management

If a company is to achieve its objectives, it must have systems in place for the **identification, evaluation and mitigation** of risk. These systems should particularly highlight risks that may have serious impacts upon the future of the company, so that effective action can be taken to deal with them.

Control systems

As part of risk management good governance should ensure that **effective controls** that protect the business are being operated. These include controls that ensure that business assets are being **safeguarded** and resources are **not being wasted on unprofitable activities,** but are being used efficiently and effectively.

Promotes reporting

A well-governed company will demonstrate transparency by providing financial information that is **accurate and fair** and also additional, voluntary, disclosures. These will help investors and other key stakeholders make informed decisions about the company. Full disclosure will also encourage **accountability**, as directors and senior managers will know that stakeholders have the **information available to scrutinise their stewardship effectively**.

Promotes stakeholder confidence

If a company is believed to be well-governed, then those who deal with it can have **trust** in their relationships with it. It is particularly important for shareholders to have confidence, as a loss of belief will lead to the company's market price falling, maybe threatening its future. There are also other important stakeholders, such as taxation authorities or industry regulators, who can be a serious threat to companies that they do not believe to be sound and therefore take action against them.

Attracts funding

Good governance can be a means of **attracting additional funding** into a company. More sources of funds may be available and the **costs** of different sources of funds should be **low**. This should enhance solvency as more cash will be available over the longer-term, and liquidity, as fixed finance costs should be low.

(b)   **Difference between rules-based and principles-based approaches**

A rules-based approach emphasises **definite, measurable actions**. It does not judge a company by underlying issues which cannot be the subject of regulation. Compliance with the rules is **compulsory and enforceable in law**. Penalties will be imposed on companies that break the rules. A principles-based approach is also not optional, but **compliance is enforced by stock market or investor pressure**, not legal sanctions. A principles-based approach emphasises the **achievement of objectives** and accepts the possibility that different actions may be equally effective in achieving the desired objectives.

Arguments against Martin Mung's belief

Circumstances of non-compliance

Martin Mung's belief appears to be based on the view that companies can ignore the requirements of principles-based codes. This is not true. As explained above markets and investors generally **expect compliance**. Non-compliance should mostly occur in unusual circumstances or transitional situations, for example an unforeseen, sudden, change in a board of directors.

Appropriateness of response

Principles-based codes also allow companies to develop approaches that are the most **appropriate and cost-effective** for their own circumstances. There may be specific reasons why a particular company may not comply with what would often be regarded as governance best practice.

Enforcement of transparency

'Comply or explain' requires companies to provide reasons for, and full details of, areas of non-compliance with the code. This **enhances transparency**. Full disclosure enables investors and others to make an **informed judgement** on whether they accept the reasons for non-compliance.

Market reaction

Real-life experience suggests that markets will not simply allow bad behaviour. Significant institutional investors in particular can put considerable pressure on companies by selling shares, raising issues at general meetings or direct intervention. They have the strong motivation of **protecting the value** of their investment. They will also wish to gain assurance that **non-compliance** has been **resolved**, rather than just enforcing punishments on companies that have broken the rules.

Legislation may be ineffective

By emphasising principles, a 'comply or explain' approach may **ensure wider compliance** than a rules-based approach. There have been several instances of companies failing who fulfilled the accounting regulations in force at the time, but nevertheless failed to report accurately and fairly as would be required by a principles-based approach.

(c)   **Accountability**

Accountability refers to whether a **company and its directors** can be held to be **answerable** for their actions, particularly to shareholders as directors are shareholders' **agents**. The measures proposed aim to give shareholders greater power to make directors answerable and to **impose their will upon boards**.

Impact of new proposals

Removal of underperforming directors

Making re-election compulsory every year gives investors the chance to **remove under-performing directors quickly**. Directors will be aware that their achievements will be judged every year by investors and that they do not have the right to remain on the board. However, there is a risk that directors' performance will be

considered solely on the basis of the results of the last year, and that investors will be less focused on judging how directors have ensured longer-term success.

Directors' rewards

There will also be **compatibility** between the period for which directors' remuneration is assessed and the period over which investors judge directors' performance. Making annual re-election compulsory should also remove the need to compensate directors for loss of office. Directors will simply not be re-elected, rather than having their contracts terminated prematurely and being able to seek compensation.

Evolution of board

Annual re-election allows for more **rapid changes in the composition of the board**. If shareholders feel that the board collectively has become complacent and less in-touch with shareholder requirements, they can alter its composition quickly. It also gives shareholders greater opportunity to promote changes in the underlying characteristics that the board as a whole has, for example making the board more diverse.

Biographical details

Publication of details of potential directors should enable shareholders to make an informed judgement about whether they have the **knowledge and experience** necessary to make an **effective contribution** to the board. Once directors have been elected, shareholders may be able to judge whether the contribution that they appear to have made seems to be in line with what they could have been expected to do.

13 Sarbanes-Oxley

Text references. Chapters 1, 2, 7 and 8.

Top tips. The key points to bring out in (a) are flexibility and cost. Note though that a comply or explain approach is not completely flexible – companies are expected to comply and generally non-compliance will be for a good reason and only temporary. The point about enforcement is also significant, although it will depend on how nuanced the rules-based approach is, whether all transgressions are pursued vigorously and the varying penalties that may be employed for different breaches.

(b) stresses the importance of underlying information flows (remember the ACCURATE mnemonic in the information flows). These support the three areas where shareholders require assurance – assurance on management of resources, reliability of accounting figures and compliance with governance regulations.

(c) is about the high fixed costs v the limited benefits of requiring full compliance, based on the limited impact that failure by a small company will have.

Easy marks. All of part (a) and the definition of agency in part (b) should have been straightforward.

			Marks
(a)	Distinguishing between rules and principles	4	
	1.5 marks for each disadvantage explained (0.5 marks for identification only)	3	
			7
(b)	Definition of agency	2	
	2 marks for each relevant discussion point	8	
			10
(c)	2 marks for each relevant point convincingly made		8
			25

(a) **Approaches to corporate governance**

There are two main approaches to corporate governance, a rules-based approach and a principles-based approach, with the United States' Sarbanes-Oxley Act being the main example of a rules-based approach.

Rules-based approach

Under a rules-based approach **compliance is compulsory** with all aspects of governance regulations. There are no exceptions allowed. The emphasis is on fulfilling the rules and providing **evidence of compliance**. If companies fail to comply with legislation, they face **criminal sanctions**.

Principles-based approach

A principles-based approach is applied by stock exchanges. It focuses on **achieving certain objectives** associated with good corporate governance. The standards expected are generally set out in a **corporate governance code**. It can allow companies to **comply or explain**, providing information of reasons for not fulfilling certain aspects of the governance code and giving details of when they expect to achieve compliance. A principles-based approach can be applied to aspects of governance such as organisational culture where it would be difficult to formulate rules. Shareholders will judge any lack of compliance and may take action, for example selling their shares or putting pressure on management.

Disadvantages of rules-based approach

Lack of value

A rules-based approach applies equally to all types of company. It takes no account of **differences in size**. A rules-based approach does **not allow for transitional situations or unusual circumstances**. It may prescribe mechanisms or requirements that are inappropriate or very expensive for certain companies. Costs of compliance may **outweigh considerably the benefits to shareholders**. Resources may be disproportionately used in demonstrating compliance with rules that are of little significance for the company.

Limitation of scope

The emphasis of rules-based approaches is on **achieving compliance rather than continually improving practice** in areas such as reporting to stakeholders. Companies may not be concerned with important aspects of governance that are not covered by the rules. Rules-based approaches may not deal well with doubtful situations. Directors may argue that they are allowed to take actions if they are not forbidden to do so by the rulebook, even if the actions appear to be dubious practice.

Imposition of sanctions

Legal authorities will impose penalties on companies for not complying. Shareholders will not be involved in enforcement, although governance guidance is designed to protect their interest. Criminal proceedings against non-compliant companies may **fail to consider whether shareholders would regard non-compliance as acceptable**. It is also arguably more **economically efficient** for those who have the greatest economic interests in the company, the shareholders, to enforce governance best practice.

(b) **Agency**

Agency refers to the relationship between principal and agent where the principal employs the agent to carry out a **service on the principal's behalf**. In the case of corporate governance, this refers to the **separation of ownership and control** of the company. The shareholders (the principals) employ the directors (the agents) to manage the affairs of the company in which the shareholders have invested. Directors are responsible for **maximising the long-term value** of the company and **regularly providing accurate and complete information** to shareholders of how they have fulfilled their responsibilities.

Benefits of maintaining a system of internal control

Information provision

A key aspect of the system will be **timely availability of sufficient information**. This serves a number of purposes that are important to shareholders. It means that directors are more likely to make **better-informed decisions** if they are based on reliable data. It also allows for the **monitoring** of directors. Strong information can provide a **reliable audit trail** for auditors to use to assess the company's affairs.

Benchmarking

Fulfilment of the requirement provides a **standard to shareholders that gives them confidence that the company is being well-run**. It enables directors to demonstrate that they have been effective stewards of the company's resources. It provides assurance that the company has the internal systems in place that are necessary to support a long-term strategy of value maximisation.

Compliance with accounting rules

An effective internal control system also **underpins the external reports** that shareholders and other stakeholders will use to judge the company. This gives shareholders confidence that the information given in the report is true and fair and that reports **fulfil accounting standards and other regulations**. Systems should not only provide evidence that compliance has been considered but also provide **reliable information** that can be used to ensure compliance, allowing auditors to give an unqualified audit report and shareholders to be able to rely on the information.

Compliance with governance regulations

An effective financial reporting control system also allows companies to **demonstrate compliance with governance regulations or best practice**. As well as compliance with regulations relating to control systems, a compliant control system also ensures that the company can provide **strong evidence of compliance** with other aspects of regulations. Particularly in a rules-based regime, this will give shareholders **confidence** that there is a low risk that the company will suffer legal penalties and reputational damage for non-compliance.

(c) **Relevance of provisions**

The provisions of Sarbanes-Oxley are designed to compel the largest listed companies to provide the information required to reassure shareholders and regulators about their accounting systems. However smaller companies, with **simpler systems and less complicated circumstances**, do not need to provide the same volume of detail to reassure stakeholders that systems are in place. In addition smaller listed companies often do not have a wide range of shareholders, with managers, who are aware of the company's circumstances, holding a significant proportion of the shares.

Consequences of smaller company failures

The failure of a smaller company will have **less of an impact on the wider economy** than the listed economy. The number of shareholders will be fewer. The losses to external shareholders are likely to be less, since it is less likely that shares in a smaller company will form a large part of individual shareholders' portfolio. Job losses and damage to other stakeholders such as suppliers and customers is likely to be less for a smaller company. Failure by a smaller company will not have the impact upon economic confidence that failure by a large company such as Enron will have.

Excessive costs

Given that the impact of a smaller listed company failing will be less than a large company, the **costs involved in ensuring full compliance** will be **less proportionate** than for a larger company. The **set-up and fixed maintenance of the necessary systems will have to be absorbed by fewer units** produced and sold than for larger companies, meaning that the overheads appear excessive. The costs of report preparation and management time in ensuring compliance will also be largely fixed.

Deterrent

The high costs of compliance and the responsibilities placed on directors may mean that directors of smaller companies are unwilling to seek a listing. This means that the companies **will not obtain funds** from offering their shares to the public, **limiting the financial resources available** for them to invest and grow. If many companies are deterred for this reason this will limit economic activity and employment in the economy. Alternatively firms that have interests abroad may seek a listing on a foreign stock market with a more sympathetic governance regime.

14 Help-with-life

Marking scheme

			Marks
(a)	1 mark for each role	5	
	1 mark for each approach to nomination	3	
			8
(b)	2 marks for each advantage explained		8
(c)	3 marks for explanation of CSR	3	
	2 marks for each relevant difference discussed. 0.5 marks for identification only	6	
			9
			25

(a) **Roles of the nominations committee**

Balance between executives and non-executives

The committee is responsible for ensuring that there is an **appropriate balance** between the different types of director. This includes ensuring that the company fulfils requirements such as the UK requirement for at least half of the members of listed company boards to be independent non-executive directors. More generally, the committee will consider whether non-executives have a **significant enough presence** on the board for their views to carry weight.

Skills, knowledge and experience required by board

The committee will consider whether the board members between them have **all the attributes necessary** to run the organisation effectively. This includes knowledge of the main business functions and also here knowledge and experience of dealing with social problems.

Need for continuity and succession planning

One aspect of the nominations committee's work is to ensure that the board is **renewed by changes of membership**, but that these occur smoothly over time. The situation described here, of replacing a number of directors quickly, is one that a committee should try to avoid. The committee should also consider planning for changes in specific board roles, for example grooming another non-executive director to take over if the Chair is to retire soon.

Desirable size of board

The committee should also consider what the **desirable size of the board is for it to be able to function effectively**. This should be weighed against the need for the board collectively to have sufficient breadth of experience to be able to run the company effectively and represent a range of different views.

Diversity of backgrounds

The committee should have regard to any **legal or political requirements affecting the composition of the board**, for example here the demands of local government. The committee should also consider recruiting members with the knowledge and experience of the cultures from which the beneficiaries of the charity's activities come.

Recruitment methods

The new directors need to have the skills and attributes to contribute effectively to the board, share the charity's ethical values and also be prepared to take reduced rewards. A number of methods can be used.

Recommendations of current board members

The nominations committee could ask current board members if they have **any contacts** who would be willing to serve on the board. Current board members should have a good idea of whether their contacts share HWL's ethical values and would be easy to work with on the board.

Use of human resources

HWL's **human resources function could work with nominations committee members** to draw up a specification for the qualities that a new director would need to have and what their role would be. They would also decide on the best means of recruitment, for example where advertising would be placed and what form the recruitment process would take.

Use of external consultants

HWL might not be keen to use external consultants because of the costs involved. However consultants may have knowledge of, and access to, a **wider pool of candidates** than the current board. They may be particularly useful if HWL is trying to fill a specific board role, for example Finance Director. Consultants' databases may also be able to identify suitable directors serving on other charity boards or people who are looking for opportunities to serve in this area.

(b) **Diversity policy**

Diversity policy aims to ensure that the board **fairly represents the demographic balance** of the stakeholder interests that it serves.

Advantages of diversity policy

Legitimacy of HWL

HWL relies on the **financial and other support of the society** in which it operates to be able to function effectively. It can be said to have a **social contract** with society. To **achieve legitimacy** in society's eyes, the board needs to be **representative** of the range of viewpoints within society. If the board is dominated by a particular demographic group, it could lose the backing of groups who are not represented on it and be vulnerable to accusations of unduly favouring certain groups in society.

Local government requirements

A diverse board will fulfil the requirements of local government. This will mean that HWL **does not come under political pressure to make changes** on its board and ensures that it continues to receive the funding that it requires.

Aims of HWL

HWL is committed to give support to the range of beneficiaries it serves. To do this effectively, staff members have to be able to **empathise** with the beneficiaries' differing norms and beliefs. A diverse board with members with differing cultural backgrounds is more likely to **appreciate the issues that staff are dealing with** and hence be able to supervise the charity's activities.

Talent

A commitment to diversity improves HWL's chances of finding and using the best available talent on its board rather than limiting itself. It should make it easier to find board members who possess the **necessary knowledge and skills** to be able to oversee the charity effectively.

Range of opinions

A diverse board is more likely to **have a range of opinions and avoid a consensus** that means awkward issues are not raised. The board collectively is likely to have an **independence of mind** that challenges plans from different viewpoints and ensures that long-term strategies are effectively developed.

(c) ### Corporate social responsibility

Corporate social responsibility means the extent to which the organisation **goes beyond its responsibilities imposed by law**, and considers its ethical duties towards society and its members and its obligations to behave in ways that benefit society and do not harm it.

The range of measures that an organisation can take to fulfil its perceived duties is wide. It includes **equitable treatment of a range of stakeholders** whose interests the organisation's activities significantly affect, even though those stakeholders may not have significant power over the organisation. This includes provision of good salaries and working conditions for employees and fair treatment of suppliers. It also includes **avoiding adverse impacts** such as externalities and **making positive contributions** that enhance society, for example charitable donations. It also involves **demonstrating accountability to society** by publishing more information than is required by law.

Corporate social responsibility can be seen as a **key part of strategy**. The company may gain through attracting customers and other stakeholders to deal with it if it is perceived to be strongly ethical. Social responsibilities can be built into the company's **mission statement**, meaning that the company views acting responsibly as integral to the way it does business. The mission statement can be supported by guidance such as a code of ethics which enforces these values on employees.

Differences between HWL and a with profit business

Central purpose

Acting with socially responsible ends in mind is the **prime objective of HWL**. It was founded to fulfil a **benevolent purpose**. It does not charge for what it provides and therefore does not balance services given with payments made. A company's prime objective is to maximise long-term returns for its shareholders. For a company its social responsibility commitment influences how it achieves that objective.

Measurement of success

HWL will measure its success by the **level and quality of help** it has managed to give. It will also consider whether it has **fairly allocated its resources** across the different groups it serves. A company is likely to measure its success in financial and market terms. Customer satisfaction may be a measure that a company uses, but that is measuring the satisfaction by customers who have an economic, rather than a charitable, relationship with the business.

Values and beliefs

HWL requires its directors and staff to **share its ethical stance** and **accept a culture that is very different from a commercial business**. The prime quality required of employees is **understanding of, and empathy with, beneficiaries**. Directors must accept that they are **making economic sacrifices** by accepting low remuneration if they belong to HWL's board. A commercial organisation would expect employees to have values that are **consistent with the commercial success of the organisation**. Directors' remuneration is likely to be **influenced by what the market rate is for their role** and directors are likely to wish to increase their income over time, rather than sacrifice income so that the company can do more to help the stakeholders with whom it deals.

15 Chambon

Text references. Chapters 1 and 2.

Top tips. Public sector governance is a recent addition to the P1 syllabus and it is therefore important that you read the examiner articles that have been published on this area.

Easy marks. The first part, identifying the characteristics of a public sector organisation, should be straightforward.

Examiner's comments.

The case scenario in Question 2 was about a public school and the requirements focused on public sector governance issues. The scenario concerned a school having to submit a performance report to the local government authority but one member of the board of governors, Sally Murol, suggested submitting a partial report to prevent the feared closure of the school. There were also issues with the effectiveness of the head teacher, Mr Besse.

Part (a) should have been straightforward for any candidates familiar with the characteristics of a public sector organisation. To answer this well, candidates needed to study the case to pick out the characteristics which identified Chambon school as a public sector organisation. Poorer answers listed the points as bullets but the verb at the beginning of the question was 'explain'. This meant that to gain high marks, each relevant point had to be explained and not just stated.

In part (b), it was evident that had the governors followed Sally Murol's suggestion about submitting a partial report, the governors would have failed in its duty of transparency. In fact it would have submitted what is essentially a fraudulent report. In public sector organisations, governors are put in place to deal with integrity and transparency with the funders of the work (in this case the local government authority) and to facilitate the effective running of the organisation. There were two requirements in this part. The first was to explain the roles of a board of governors, which should not have been difficult for well-prepared candidates. The second requirement was to discuss the importance of transparency for the governors in its relations with the local government authority. This second requirement was less well answered, although it was relatively straightforward to candidates who had studied the importance of transparency in agency relationships.

Part (c) concerned the possible replacement of the head teacher at Chambon school. The case highlighted several problems with Mr Besse and the requirement was to discuss the potential advantages of replacing him. The case contained several issues that were relevant to the discussion, and many candidates failed to adequately study the case and therefore missed some factors relevant to the discussion.

Marking scheme

		Marks
(a)	1 mark for each explanation of Chambon as a public sector organisation to a maximum of 4 marks; half mark for identification only 2 marks for assessment against objectives to a maximum of 6 marks	
		10
(b)	1 mark for each role of governors to a maximum of 4 marks 2 marks for each point on transparency to a maximum of 4 marks 1 mark for evidence of understanding of transparency (anywhere in the answer)	
		9
(c)	2 marks for each advantage to a maximum of 6 marks	
		6
		25

(a)   **Characteristics of a public sector organisation**

The following information from the case identifies Chambon as a public sector organisation.

- Funding – the school is state-funded, which means that the money needed to run the school comes from taxation.

- Purposes and objectives – to provide education for 11- to 16-year old children; there is no profit motive.

- Performance – the school is required to provide an annual report on exam performance to the local education authority (not to shareholders as in the private sector).

- Ownership – the school is subject to a national curriculum set by central government, and may be threatened with closure by the local authority if it fails to meet its exam performance targets.

- Stakeholders – the independent board of governors is comprised of local residents, parents and other concerned citizens.

How Chambon is meeting its objectives as a public sector organisation

Chambon's success in meeting its objectives can be assessed by using the public sector value for money, or 'three Es' model , to determine whether it is achieving economy, efficiency and effectiveness.

Economy is defined as obtaining inputs of the appropriate quality at the lowest price available. Chambon has had its budget increased in recent years so that it can improve the exam results. A number of new teachers were employed but despite this performance continued to deteriorate, so much so that a budget overspend led to the closure of part of the school library and the sale of a sports field. Chambon has not therefore been successful in achieving economy.

Efficiency means delivering the service to the appropriate standard at minimum cost, time and effort. Despite the fact that Chambon's budget was increased and more teachers were employed, exam performance continued to fall. In other words, inputs in the form of income and teaching staff have not been converted to an increase in outputs in the form of exam performance.

The third element of the three 'Es' model is effectiveness, which means achieving the desired objectives as stated in an entity's performance plan. Chambon school is state-funded, it teaches the national curriculum and is subject to national government and local authority scrutiny. Its primary responsibility is to provide education for 11- to 16-year old children. Whether the achievement of this objective can be measured solely in exam results is debatable. We can, however, conclude that pupils have lost part of the library and a sports field, thereby reducing the effectiveness of the learning environment.

(b)   **Roles of board of governors**

The main role of the board of governors is to provide independent oversight of the running of the school. There are several aspects to this role:

- Ensuring that the school complies with the local authority's requirement to report on exam performance. In order to do this the board must ensure that systems are in place to collect and collate this information in an appropriate format for both internal and external reporting.

- Reporting promptly, truthfully and without bias within the timeframe set by the local authority.

- Being answerable to all interested parties on the topic of school performance and to provide explanations for the continued deterioration in exam results.

- Responsibility for how the school is run, including leadership and staffing, and the quality of education provided for its pupils.

- Appointing senior staff, including the headteacher, and monitoring their performance. The board should look into the criticisms of Mr Besse and decide on what action to take.

- Budget setting and monitoring, to ensure that the school has adequate resources and that expenditure is controlled.

The importance of transparency

Transparency means open and clear disclosure of relevant information to stakeholders, not concealing information, open discussion and adopting a default position of information provision rather than concealment.

The board of governors is obliged to report on exam performance in a full and timely manner, and should therefore reject Sally Murol's suggestion that the report be delayed or modified.

The school is state funded and must therefore inform its funding body how it has spent the money allocated to it and how it has performed. If successful it should be able to show that public funding has obtained value for money in the provision of education by the school.

As there is no central information gathering system for exam results, the accuracy of the information provided to the local authority is crucial. It is likely that this information is used for future planning and funding decisions and could therefore have an impact on the country as a whole.

(c) **Replacement of headteacher**

The current headteacher, Mr Besse, has been in post for many years. He is said to be loyal and popular with staff as he does not believe in interfering with what teachers do, and he also dislikes confrontation. These qualities may be positive ones but could also point to an unwillingness to address poor performance amongst the teaching staff. Such a culture could lead to poor practices becoming embedded and difficult to challenge. A new leader would be forced to confront this culture and change it if it was having a negative effect on the performance of the school.

The appointment of a new head would signal a willingness on behalf of the school and the board to make a fresh start and bring in new ways of working in order to improve exam performance. Any members of staff underperforming would have targets put in place and monitored over time against key performance indicators.

A new headteacher, appointed by the board of governors, would be in a position to work together with all the stakeholders represented on the board in order to put the necessary changes in place. Mr Besse may have been acting in the school's best interest but may also have been unwilling to confront failure and to change long-standing behaviour.

16 New Ideas Company

Text references. Chapter 3.

Top tips. The information in the case is fairly detailed and understanding the characteristics described is crucial in making the assessment needed in the question.

Easy marks. Each part of this question has some potentially easy marks: part (a) for the role of CEO; part (b) for the benefits of NEDs, and part (c) for an explanation of conflict of interest.

Examiner's comments.

The case in Question 3 was about New Ideas Company (NIC), a university 'spin-off' company arising from an important discovery at the university. The case described the situation of Dr Ranjana Foo, an excellent scientist but with clear limitations as a business leader. Part (a) asked about Ranjana Foo's suitability to be the chief executive of NIC. In order to achieve a high mark on this part, candidates needed to know about the roles and personal qualities necessary to be an effective CEO, and also to study the case to gather the information on her suitability for the role. The case made clear on several occasions that she did not have the necessary qualities to lead the company, whilst nevertheless being a very good scientist. Less-prepared candidates listed the roles of a CEO as a bullet list and this approach did not attract high marks. This type of question demonstrates the importance of sound knowledge of the study guide, and also the necessity of studying the case. It was not possible to achieve a high mark in this part without studying the case in detail.

Part (b) was about non-executive directors (NEDs). For a small and risky company such as NIC, the role of NEDs could be decisive in its success or failure. Some candidates, perhaps on seeing the words, "non-executive directors" framed their answer in terms of the four general roles of NEDs (strategy, scrutiny, risk, people) but this was not what the question was asking. There were two tasks in this requirement. The first was to explain the benefits to NIC of suitable NEDs and the second was to discuss the difficulties, given the information in the case, that NIC might have in making NED appointments. In each task, it was necessary to situate the answer in the specific context of NIC. General lists of the advantages of NEDs were not what was required. Likewise, the second task required candidates to consider the issues that NIC might encounter – again, a general response was not a well-rewarded answer. The case contained information about NIC's location, its risk problems, etc. that would make it difficult to appoint suitable NEDs.

Part (c) was about a potential conflict of interest that one proposed NED might encounter. This requirement, worth 6 marks, was less well done than the first two requirements in Question 3. Most candidates were able to explain 'conflict of interest' to some extent but many were less confident on the second task which was to discuss the specific conflict of interest that Dr Idris is likely to encounter. Again, a short time studying the case would have enabled candidates to gather the information from the case necessary to answer this task. It shouldn't be difficult to discuss a conflict of interest when one of the directors also owns a large shareholding in a potential supplier to NIC, but many were seemingly unable to spot this.

Marking scheme

		Marks
(a)	Up to 2 marks for each role and quality to a maximum of 8 marks. Half mark for identification only	
	1 mark for each point of unsuitability explained to a maximum of 4 marks Half mark for identification only	
		Max 10
(b)	1 mark for each benefit of NEDs at NIC to a maximum of 3 marks Up to 2 marks for each difficulty in recruitment	
		9
(c)	Up to 2 marks for explanation of conflict of interest Up to 2 marks for each relevant point made on Dr Idris's conflict of interest To a maximum of 4 marks	
		6
		25

(a) **CEO roles**

The main roles of a CEO are as follows.

- Business strategy and management

    The CEO will take the lead in developing objectives and strategy having regard to the organisation's stakeholders, and will be responsible to the board for ensuring that the organisation achieves its objectives, optimising the use of resources.

- Investment and financing

    The CEO will examine major investments, capital expenditure, acquisitions and disposals and be responsible for identifying new initiatives.

- Risk management

    The CEO will be responsible for managing the risk profile in line with the risk appetite accepted by the board. He will also be responsible for ensuring that appropriate planning, operational, and control systems and internal controls are in place and operate effectively. The CEO has ultimate ownership of the control systems and should take the lead in establishing the control environment and culture.

- Establishing the company's management

    The CEO will provide the nomination committee with his view on the future roles and capabilities required of directors, and make recommendations about the recruitment of individual directors. He will also be responsible for recruiting and overseeing the management team below board level.

- Board committees

  The CEO will make recommendations to be discussed by the board committees on remuneration policy, executive remuneration and terms of employment.

- Liaison with stakeholders

  Like the chairman, part of the CEO's role will be to deal with those interested in the company. The chairman's focus though will often be on dealing with shareholder concerns, whereas the CEO will also be concerned with other major stakeholders who impact upon the company's operations, for example its most important customers.

Suitability of Ranjana Foo

Ranjana is probably not the most suitable person for the CEO role, because of some of the characteristics that she herself has made clear.

Her strengths lie in the scientific field and she is technically competent, but this does not necessarily mean that she would be capable of other technical challenges such as investment and financing decisions.

She prefers to work alone in a quiet environment and would therefore not relish the prospect of board meetings and the need to debate and negotiate with other board members.

She is good at detailed work but can sometimes miss the bigger picture, so she would not be comfortable developing a strategy for NIC as a whole and for taking the company forward.

She dislikes confrontation and would therefore hold back from making unpopular although necessary decisions and in putting her point across to other board members and stakeholders.

(b) **Benefits of NEDs**

Non-executive directors can bring a number of advantages to a board of directors.

Experience and knowledge

They may have external experience and knowledge which executive directors do not possess. The experience they bring can be in many different fields. They may be executive directors of other companies, and have experience of different ways of approaching corporate governance, internal controls or performance assessment. They can also bring knowledge of markets within which the company operates.

Perspective

Non-executive directors can provide a wider perspective than executive directors who may be more involved in detailed operations.

Reassurance

Good non-executive directors are often a comfort factor for third parties such as investors or creditors.

Compliance

Appointing non-executive directors ensures compliance with corporate governance regulations or codes.

Dual roles

The most important advantage perhaps lies in the dual nature of the non-executive director's role. Non-executive directors are full board members who are expected to have the level of knowledge that full board membership implies. At the same time they are meant to provide the so-called strong, independent element on the board.

Difficulties in recruiting NEDs

Non-executive directors do not have the same financial incentives as executive directors in general, and there are specific difficulties identified in the scenario.

Firstly, NIC is located in an isolated area, where the small population alone could be a barrier to finding suitable qualified and independent people for the role.

Secondly, what NIC does is highly technical so it will be difficult to recruit people with the necessary technical knowledge. Without this knowledge it will be difficult for NEDs to explain to shareholders how the company is protecting and increasing their investment.

Finally, the business itself is risky and could fail within two years unless good management practices, including NEDs, are put in place. This puts added pressure on NEDs in this company as the founders are scientists, not business people.

(c) **Conflict of interest**

A conflict of interest in the context of directors' duties most often means a situation where directors face influences that tempt them not to act in the best interests of the company.

As agents, directors have a general duty to try to avoid a conflict of interest. In particular:

- The directors must retain their freedom of action and not fetter their discretion by agreeing to vote as some other person may direct.
- The directors owe a fiduciary duty to avoid a conflict of duty and personal interest.
- The directors must not obtain any personal advantage from their position as directors without the consent of the company for whatever gain or profit they have obtained.

As far as Dr Idris is concerned, he is a shareholder in the company that will potentially supply NIC's equipment; he can not therefore be impartial with regard to any dealings with this company. Obtaining a good price for goods for NIC would have a negative effect on the overall profits of the supplying company and would therefore affect his shareholding.

Were he to be involved in awarding the contract in the first place he would look favourably on the company in which he has invested and would not be able to come to an unbiased and independent decision.

17 Hafnium Company

Text references. Chapters 2, 8

Top tips. Corporate governance is a key part of the syllabus and is frequently examined.

Easy marks. You should be very familiar with the concept of independence and the role of audit committees so part (a) should be reasonably straightforward.

Examiner's comments.

The case scenario in this question was about a code's provisions on audit committees. A key part of the provision was about the independence of audit committee members and part (a) asked about this. The requirement was for candidates to define independence in the context of audit committees and then (for the second task), to explain why audit committee members should be considered independent at the time of their appointment. Weaker answers defined independence in general terms (not necessarily in the context of audit committees) but to get full marks on this, it was necessary to define independence in that context.

The second task in part (a) was about the importance of being considered independent upon appointment to an audit committee. This is important because the audit committee's value is because it is independent of the main board and able to receive internal control and internal audit reports. The audit committee must also monitor the company's relationship with the external auditor (which part (c) touches on).

Part (b) was about the provision in the code to appoint someone with 'recent and relevant financial experience' to the audit committee. In this case, the requirement meant that candidates had to study the case to determine why, in the case of Hafnium Company, the difficulties in recruiting someone with this quality might threaten the effectiveness of the audit committee's contribution to shareholder value. Audit committees add to shareholder value by being independent, by receiving and processing reports on internal audit and internal controls, and by continually reviewing the nature of the relationship between the company and its external auditors. The committee also has a role in ensuring the integrity of the processes underpinning financial reporting and hence, a person with recent and relevant financial

experience is necessary to understand these various roles. Without this capability, the effectiveness of the committee, and hence its ability to add value to shareholders, would be compromised.

Part (c) asked about the nature of the relationship between the company and its external auditors, which was a straightforward task for many candidates. It should be independent, detached, professional and regularly reviewed. The second task in the requirement was about what the audit committee might respond if it believes the external auditor relationship to be too close. In this case, the audit committee can recommend that the audit contract be put out to tender so that others auditors can bid for the work, thereby removing the problem of having an overfamiliar relationship between auditor and client. The second task was not done as well as the first, although a moment spent thinking and planning the answer might have been beneficial for many candidates in planning their approach to this requirement.

Marking scheme

		Marks
(a)	Up to 2 marks for definition of independence 2 marks for each relevant point on independence of AC members.	8
(b)	Up to 2 marks for each relevant point made.	8
(c)	1 mark for each relevant point on appropriate relationship to a maximum of 3 marks. 2 marks for each relevant point on AC response to a maximum of 6 marks.	9
		25

(a) **Define independence**

Independence is a quality possessed by individuals and refers to the avoidance of being unduly influenced by a vested interest. This freedom enables a more objective position to be taken on issues compared to those who consider vested interests or other loyalties. In the case of the independence of the members of an audit committee, it is important that members are not influenced by the company's finance function or other members of the executive board.

The independence of audit committee members can be threatened by over-familiarity with, for example, executive directors, which is why many corporate governance codes have measures in place to prevent over-familiarity. These include restrictions on share option schemes for non-executives directors (NEDs), time-limited appointments and bans on cross-directorships. Other restrictions, depending on jurisdiction and code, include salaries being set at an appropriate level for NEDs, a compulsory number of years after retirement from a company before being eligible for a NED role (if ever), and no close personal relationships between executives and non-executives.

Independence of audit committee (AC) members

Independence brings with it a helpful ignorance of any factions or points of friction in the company's management of internal control or risk. By bringing a 'fresh pair of eyes' to the important areas of audit committee oversight, the committee can act without bias or prejudice. With an important input into financial reporting, for example, the audit committee needs to ensure the accuracy of reporting and the robustness of the systems supporting that reporting. Without the 'baggage' of knowing the history of a certain system, AC members can assess its fitness for purpose as if assessing the system for the first time.

Members need to be free of vested interest to act solely in the interests of shareholders and not of any faction in the company. Members are not representing any particular part of the company (eg the board, trade unions or certain interests with which a certain member might have sympathy) but the strategic interests of the shareholders. The audit committee must be able to scrutinise, review and act upon reports on internal controls and internal audit without the fear of upsetting friends or colleagues inside the company who he or she may know informally or through other networks.

The independence of the audit committee members serves to *reassure investors* and other non-executive directors in that it makes the governance of the company appear to be more robust and trustworthy. A key purpose of an audit committee is to provide an independent oversight of important governance systems in a listed company, and shareholders and regulators usually place a high value in having an effective audit committee in place. It is important, then, that it is independent, and seen to be independent, to provide maximum reassurance to shareholders in constraining the potential excesses and vested interests of executive directors.

(b) **Inability to recruit a person with 'recent and relevant financial experience'**

First, it shows that *the company may be having trouble with compliance* and this is not a good start to the company's life as a listed company. A shareholder might ask why Hafnium Company was unable to recruit NEDs to ensure compliance with the listing rules. This will negatively affect the shareholders' perceptions of the competence of the management of Hafnium Company and hence their willingness to invest in the company and trust the board with strategic decisions.

Some of the functions of an audit committee require some financial experience and the committee would not be operating as it should be if this expertise is not available. It needs to *review the annual accounts of the company*, for example, and this requires knowledge of how accounts are constructed and the regulatory framework around this. If this expertise is not present on the audit committee, they will not be able to provide the scrutiny necessary and this opens the company up to potential fraud or error in this important task.

The audit committee also has an important role in the *oversight of the relationship between the company and its external auditors*. Although Sophie Xu has a good understanding of Hafnium Company's business model (which is very helpful), she does not necessarily understand the nature or importance of this relationship with the external auditor. As a key part of underpinning the shareholders' trust in the accuracy of the company's accounting systems and audited accounts, an effective and independent auditor is essential. If Sophie Xu is unable to contribute to this role because of a lack of financial and accounting knowledge, the shareholders' confidence in the committee will be reduced.

The audit committee also has a role in *receiving reports on internal controls and risk management systems*. It is likely that, as an engineer who understands the Hafnium Company business model, Sophie Xu will be well equipped to understand some of these reports. Her lack of financial experience, however, might mean she is not equipped to understand the internal controls linked to the accounting systems or financial measurements. Likewise, risks arising from financial exposures such as exchange rates, debt to equity, credit and cash flow may be outside her understanding. These risks can substantially threaten shareholder value and the audit committee's inability to meaningfully process the information could reduce its value to shareholders.

(c) **Nature of the relationship**

It is important that the relationship between the audit committee and the external auditor is appropriate in that it should *not be close and it should be free from any ethical threats to independence*. This means the auditor must have no familiarity threats, self-interest threats or other interests which might compromise its independence.

The audit committee, acting on behalf of the shareholders, needs to ensure the *independence and effectiveness of the external auditor* in its important role as the party providing assurance of financial statements and the systems which support them. The audit committee has the power, in its role as the body overseeing the relationship between the company and the external auditor, to recommend replacement of the auditor if it believes audits are in any way lacking independence or rigour. This means that the audit committee must adopt a *default position of being sceptical* of the external auditor so as to always assure the shareholders of the independence of the relationship at all times.

Audit committee response to too close a relationship

There are several possible responses for an audit committee which believes that there may be an inappropriate relationship between the company and the external auditor. It is not uncommon for human relationships between company employees and external auditors to be friendly and cordial, perhaps with accountants in the two organisations having longstanding friendships and professional associations.

Depending upon the extent of the perceived threat to independence, the audit committee has several options it can pursue.

Many audit firms, sometimes underpinned by regulation, have a policy in place to rotate the audit staff conducting the audit for a given company. This is to ensure that the engagement partner (the senior auditor overseeing the audit at a certain company) does not become too familiar with the client such that it might threaten the independence of the auditor–client relationship. The simplest way to refresh the relationship and remove the independence threat is for the audit committee to advise the board to liaise with the auditor to ensure its engagement partner rotation policy is fully effective or request the rotation of a particular engagement partner if it perceives that the current occupier of that position is too close to a senior person in the company.

Second, the audit committee can recommend to the board that a policy be instituted *where the audit contract goes out to tender every so many years*. Some corporate governance codes provide for this, and the intention in each case is to ensure that the auditor is continuously aware that there is nothing to be gained by investing in the relationship with the client because the contract will be independently awarded every so many years. This not only provides better financial value for the shareholders (audit firms compete, including on price, for the audit contract) but also helps to maintain a certain distance between auditor and client.

In an extreme case, where the audit committee believes that the independence of the auditor is seriously threatened, the audit committee can recommend the immediate replacement of the auditor. This is usually considered to be a last resort and it would only be enacted if serious independence threats were observed and the board was thought to be unresponsive to a resolution on the issue, but it provides shareholders with the assurance that the audit committee can act, on their behalf, to ensure an effective financial audit in each case.

18 Scapa Holdings

Marking scheme

		Marks
(a)	Up to 4 marks for a detailed explanation of conflict of interest in corporate governance [1 mark only for definition]. Up to 2 marks for each conflict of interest point discussed in the scenario; maximum of 6 marks.	8
(b)	1 mark for explaining the agency concept. Up to 4 marks for describing the agency relationship at Scapa Holdings. Up to 2 marks for explaining agency costs. Up to 2 marks for each point which explains how accountability reduces agency costs at Scapa Holdings; maximum of 4 marks.	9
(c)	2 marks for explanation of probity in business relationships. Up to 2 marks for each criticism of Arthur Jellicoe's behaviour with respect to probity; maximum of 6 marks.	8
		25

(a) Company directors have a fiduciary duty to act in the best interests of the shareholders who have appointed them to their position. They act as agents of the shareholders [the principals], and as such are delegated the power and authority to make decisions which will ultimately increase shareholder value over the longer term. A director owes a duty to all shareholders not to place him/herself in a situation where personal self-interest conflicts with the interests of the company, and vicariously its shareholders. Conflict of interest is when one's personal interest is at variance with one's professional duty of care.

In the context of corporate governance, directors must avoid the temptation to be influenced by factors which might not be in the best interests of the company. This could include:

- Obtaining some personal advantage by virtue of their position as director, possibly to the detriment of the company;

- Avoiding the influence of external parties, such as from a cross-directorship, when this comes into direct conflict with the best interest of the company; and

- Directors contracting with their own company, except where permitted by the articles of association and where the directors' interest is fully disclosed.

In the scenario it can be clearly observed that the motivation and actions of Arthur Jellicoe are underpinned by his impending retirement. He is using his position of power on the board of Scapa Holdings to influence the decision to revalue the inventory and thereby inflate the reported earnings. This in turn should have the effect of increasing the company's share price and the value of the share options which Arthur holds, which he has been advised to exercise before his retirement.

Although the rise in share price would be advantageous to all shareholders, it is the motivation behind Arthur's actions which creates the conflict of interest. He appears to be willing to use his longstanding friendship with the auditor's engagement partner to put pressure on the audit team to accept the revaluation of inventory, even if its accounting basis maybe dubious. When Arthur has exercised his options, made the tax efficient capital gain by selling the shares, and then retired as CEO, he will have no further interest in any consequential damage his actions may have caused to Scapa Holdings. In particular, if a further readjustment is subsequently required which could reduce profits to a level which breaches the loan interest cover covenant, placing the company in financial distress.

Consequently, Arthur should declare his interest and leave any decision about revaluing inventory to the remainder of the board. He will avoid the associated conflict of interest, and be seen to be acting in the best interests of the company's shareholders.

(b) The directors of Scapa Holdings, collectively referred to as the board, are charged with managing the affairs of the company by its shareholders. Directors, individually and collectively, have a duty under corporate governance to provide entrepreneurial leadership and run the company to the betterment of the shareholders.

The veil of incorporation ensures that Scapa Holdings is a separate legal entity from both its directors and shareholders, thus protecting the personal assets of owners and investors from lawsuits. This separation also restricts how much direct influence the shareholders have over directors in discharging their responsibilities. This is particularly important for a listed company where the shareholders simply view the company as an investment vehicle, so they may sell their shares at any time to rebalance their portfolio if required.

Agency theory describes the relationship between the shareholders, known as the principal, and the directors, their agents, and it is derived from the concept of separation between ownership and control. At Scapa Holdings the shareholders employ the directors using a contract of service to act as their agents and to manage the company on their behalf. The agents are granted both expressed and implied authority to deal with third parties on behalf of their principal, and they are held accountable under corporate governance for their actions and outcomes.

Should a situation arise, as described in the scenario, where the interests of the principal and agents are not necessarily aligned, an agency problem arises. The CEO of Scapa Holdings appears to be willing to take risks on behalf of the shareholders, who may have a very different attitude to risk taking. He has adopted a very short-term view of business performance to serve his own needs rather than focusing on maximising shareholder value over the longer term. This situation compromises the agency relationship and it may require an intervention by the principal to take steps to exercise some control over their investments, resulting in agency costs.

Agency costs can include:

- The time and expense of reviewing published information, and then attending meetings to monitor and scrutinise the board's performance;

- Paying for the services of independent experts and advisers;

- External auditor's fees; and

- Transaction costs associated with managing their shareholding in Scapa Holdings.

These agency costs could be reduced when direct action is taken to resolve the alignment of interest problem, which would improve board accountability. The employment of sufficient independent non-executive directors to monitor and scrutinise the executive members of the board should have a positive influence on their behaviour and inspire confidence from shareholders. In particular, a remuneration committee could devise and propose reward packages for executive directors which motivate them to act in the best interest of the shareholders they represent.

The direct link between rewards and performance confers an obligation on directors to account for their actions and activities to shareholders. This should prove that they are discharging their duties in line with shareholders' expectations of risk and reward. Any clear breach of agent accountability could result in the ultimate sanction of removing the offending directors from office and replacing them.

(c) Probity means honesty and making decisions based on integrity. Probity is a fundamental corporate governance principle and is concerned with telling the truth and thereby not misleading shareholders or any other stakeholders. For an individual, it suggests that they should act ethically with integrity, by always conducting their business dealings in an honest and straight forward manner.

Arthur Jellicoe has not behaved ethically with respect to probity. His attempt to persuade other board members to increase the value of inventory was purely for personal benefit; yet he did not explain his reasoning to them. In pursuance of his personal agenda he has acted dishonestly, certainly not displaying the ethical characteristics expected from a CEO (or any director). His suggestion that this was only a 'minor policy change' was designed to give an unfair impression of the effect of the revaluation to shareholders and other users of financial information, so misleading them away from his prime motives.

The gravity of the situation was compounded by the CEO offering to place undue influence on a longstanding friendship with the engagement partner of Scapa Holdings' auditors thereby ensuring that the policy change was accepted as presenting a true and fair view of the company's financial performance. Of course, this would mean that if the partner convinced his audit team to agree to the higher inventory valuation at the next audit, his friend would become culpable in this breach of probity.

Finally it is disclosed that Arthur Jellicoe trained as an accountant many years ago. Therefore he is bound by a code of ethics which requires him not to act with self-interest or pressurise others to act to his advantage. His actions both display unprofessional behaviour and a profound lack of integrity which could result, if proven, in disciplinary action and sanctions against him.

19 H&Z

Text references. Chapters 5 and 7.

Top tips. (a)(i) is basic book knowledge, but note the examiner required a description of the roles, which meant more than a single line bullet point list. On this occasion most students provided sufficient detail.

Some of the points in (ii) may appear slightly odd, but they do indicate that the risk manager's role goes beyond assessment of risks and simple recommendations. It does though bring into question H&Z's recruitment policies, recruiting someone to an important role whose understanding was so fundamentally flawed. Note also that a key theme of the June 2009 exam in which this question appeared was the shortcomings of important individuals, here the risk manager and in other questions the chairman and chief executive.

In (b) the very strong hint in the question is for you to explain the likelihood-consequences matrix (the risk management framework) and then apply it. Risk appetite is an important issue to mention.

In (c) the requirement to evaluate requires (almost) the same number of points for and against. The answer includes the concept of STOP errors, a topic highlighted by the examiner as very important.

Easy marks. The role of the risk manager in (a)(i) and the likelihood-consequences matrix are what the examiner would describe as 'bookwork'.

Examiner's comments. Again, the parts based on bookwork were better responded to than those requiring higher levels of intellectual engagement.

Most candidates did well on describing the roles of a risk manager in (a)(i) but many then failed to see anything wrong with John Pentanol's understanding of his own job.

In (b), the most helpful risk assessment framework is the impact/likelihood (or hazard/probability) framework and this was the one that candidates should have employed in this answer. The point was that John had only measured the impact of the risks (paragraph 2) and had completely ignored their probabilities. Many candidates correctly described the risk assessment framework but then failed to note the flaw in John's analysis, thereby failing to gain high marks for this part.

(c)(i) was about the necessity of accepting risk as a part of a successful strategy. Most candidates who attempted this question were able to define entrepreneurial risk but fewer were able to develop the theme of why it was important to accept it in business organisations.

(c)(ii) was a 'critically evaluate' question in which the answer should have contained arguments for and against Jane Xylene's view on risk management. Markers allowed for a range of responses to this question but in each case were looking for evidence of evaluation of Jane's view (not mere repetition of her remarks, for example).

Marking scheme

				Marks
(a)	(i)	1 mark for evidence of understanding in each type of role (0.5 marks for identification and 0.5 for description)		Max 4
	(ii)	1 mark for each relevant assessment comment on John's understanding of the role		4
(b)		Evidence of understanding of risk assessment (impact/hazard and probability)	2	
		Recognition of uncertainties over impact and probability information and description	2	
		Importance of return and recognition of lack of return/benefit information and description	2	
				6
(c)	(i)	Definition	2	
		Explanation of its importance	2	
				4
	(ii)	1 mark for each relevant point made in the case for Jane Xylene's view	Max 4	
		1 mark for each relevant point made in the case against Jane Xylene's view	Max 4	
				Max 7
				25

(a) (i) **Establishing a RM framework**

The framework should **cover all aspects of risk** across the organisation, integrating enterprise risk management with other business planning and management activities and framing authority and accountability for enterprise risk management in business units. Development of policies includes the **quantification of management's risk appetite through specific risk limits**, **defining roles and responsibilities** and **participating in setting goals for implementation**.

Promoting enterprise risk management competence

This includes **training managers and staff** to help them develop risk management expertise and, **helping managers align risk responses with the entity's risk tolerances**.

Dealing with insurance companies

The risk manager needs to deal carefully with insurers because of **increased premium costs, restrictions in the cover available** (will the risks be excluded from cover) and the **need for**

negotiations if claims arise. If insurers require it, the risk manager needs to demonstrate that the organisation is actively taking steps to manage its risks.

Risk reporting

The risk manager is responsible for **implementing risk indicators and reports,** including losses and incidents, key risk exposures, and early warning indicators. He should **facilitate reporting by operational managers**, including **quantitative and qualitative thresholds**, and **monitor** this reporting process.

(ii) **Flaws in risk assessment**

It is understandable that John wanted to carry one of the most important tasks quickly. However by doing it as soon as he started at H&Z, it seems he didn't give himself sufficient time to understand the company's **background and strategic aims**. The fact also that he had not had time to establish a risk management framework will have meant that his assessment of risk is based on inadequate information.

Form of advice

John's advice to the board is expressed too strongly. The board has responsibility for **taking key strategic decisions** and John is exceeding his remit by telling them so bluntly to stop the activity associated with Risk 3.

Support for advice

John's advice does not appear to be **backed by the supporting information** necessary for the board to take an informed decision on the risk.

Risk management

John is not responsible for **eliminating or minimising all the highest risks** facing the company. Some risks, for example the risks of operations being disrupted by natural disasters are risks John cannot influence much, if at all. John will also need to consider whether some high impact risks **cannot be effectively lessened**, but could be **transferred**, for example to **H and Z's insurers**.

(b) **Probability-impact/Likelihood-consequences matrix**

This matrix is used to group risks and assess their relative importance. As such, it is a useful tool when you are considering, as John is, the **impact of major risks**.

Consequences (Impacts or hazard)

This diagram maps two continuums on which risks are plotted. The **nearer the risk is** towards the **bottom right-hand corner** (the high-high corner), the **more important** the risk will be. This profile can then be used to set priorities for risk mitigation.

Failure to consider probability

The most significant failure in John's approach to assessing risk is his failure to consider the **likelihood** that the risk will materialise. As Jane points out, in order for H&Z to continue in business, it will have to bear some **significant entrepreneurial risks**. However the investments can be justified if the risks are **low**.

Risk and return

John has also failed to take into account what the directors have established as the company's **risk appetite**. The directors may believe that taking significant risks is justified by the possibility of achieving **high returns** from the associated activities. Risk elimination or minimisation may not always achieve high returns. Instead better returns may be achieved by **risk reduction or transfer**.

Uncertainties of assessment

John has also not taken into account inevitable **uncertainties in the data used** to make the likelihood-consequences assessment. His strongly-expressed view fails to take into account the importance of the assumptions made, the likelihood of different scenarios and other issues surrounding the assessment.

(c) (i) **Entrepreneurial risks**

Entrepreneurial risks are the risks that arise from **carrying out business activities,** for example the risks of a major investment failing to deliver required returns or profits being lessened by competitor's activities.

Acceptance of entrepreneurial risks

Few if, any, business activities are risk free. For example in all business situations other than a monopoly, the business will face **risks arising from competition**. Also **shareholders** will have invested in a business on the grounds that they wish to **achieve higher returns** than those offered by risk-free investments. A business can only earn these returns if it takes risks.

(ii) **Benefits vs costs**

Jane correctly identifies the needs to balance the benefits of risk management against costs. **Expenditure on over-elaborate risk management systems** may not be warranted by the **losses they prevent** or the **disruption to operating activities** that they cause.

Opportunity costs

Jane also correctly identifies the problems with taking a completely pessimistic view of risk, treating all risks as pure risks with only negative consequences. **Speculative risks**, the risks relating to doing business are risks from which **good or harm** may result. The upside of these risks needs to be taken into account when managers decide how to deal with them.

STOP errors

Jane's views also reflect the existence of **STOP errors**, of the adverse consequences of failing to take an opportunity that should have been pursued.

Lack of understanding

However Jane does not appear to understand the benefits of risk management and why corporate governance guidance insists that listed companies have appropriate risk management structures in place. Directors need to gain assurance that the decisions they take about **what risks** should be **borne** and how the **risks borne** should be **managed** are enforced. The risk management function helps to **give them this assurance**. The risk management function also **provides information** to the board to help decide on the risk implications of strategy, and also to operational managers so that they can recognise and deal with risks when they arise.

Risk-return relationship

Jane seems to be operating at the other extreme to John, and as such has an equally flawed view of the risk-return relationship. **Shareholders** may require risks to be taken so that they can achieve an adequate return, but they will also judge some risks to be too high for the **potential returns from taking them**. Jane does not appear to recognise any limits to H&Z's **risk appetite**. John is right in saying that there are some risks that are too great for the company to bear, that will threaten its existence, and cannot be justified whatever the return.

Risk management strategies

Jane incorrectly views risk avoidance and the forbidding of activities as the only strategies recommended by risk managers. Risk managers can **recommend risk reduction strategies** that will increase the chances of commercial success, for example piloting a new product to a small audience before it is launched.

20 YGT

Text references. Chapters 5 to 7.

Top tips. The examiner used the question to examine some of the new study guide content on risk, in particular the dynamic nature of risk and the idea of related risk.

(a) mentions dynamic risks, so you should be looking for signs in the scenario of risks that have changed recently. It is clearly stated that Risks C and D have been affected by recent events. As you're asked to criticise Raz's beliefs, you should also be looking for evidence that the risk assessment provided useful information, and the scenario again clearly emphasises that it did.

In (b) the descriptions of the risks are worded carefully to make clear where each fit on the impact/likelihood risk assessment map. None are marginal. Once the risks are correctly plotted on the map, the risk strategies should have been clear and the scenario again helps by indicating which activities are vital and which peripheral.

In (c) the point was that in some cases, increased environmental losses can result in deterioration of a company's reputation (ie a rise in reputation risk). Because both risks rise and fall together, they can be said to be positively correlated. However that does not mean their relationship is exact because of the different consequences that they have.

The key themes to bring out in (d) are that risk awareness is a way of thinking and that everyone in the organisation must have it. Being aware of risks that apply to day-to-day operations can be as important as awareness of strategic risks, and perhaps awareness of operational risks can easily be taken too much for granted.

Easy marks. The examiner highlighted coming up with criticisms in (a) and plotting the risks on the continuum in (b) as areas where easy marks should have been obtained.

Examiner's comments. (a) and (c) were done quite well on the whole and (b) and (d) were very variable.

For (a), many candidates were able to discuss the notion of risks arising as an organisation's environment changes but fewer were able to gain the 'criticise' marks.

Marking scheme

			Marks
(a)	2 marks for each evaluation point made	Max 4	
	2 marks for each point identified and explained on dynamic	Max 4	
			8
(b)	0.5 marks for correct strategy selection for each risk. 1 mark for each risk strategy correctly explained and justified method of risk embeddedness		Max 6
(c)	2 marks for explanation of related and correlated risks	2	
	2 marks for each description of why correlated	Max 4	
			Max 5
(d)	1 mark for explanation	1	
	2 marks for each relevant point for assessment	Max 6	
			Max 6
			25

(a) **Raz Dutta's beliefs**

Both Raz Dutta's assertions are incorrect.

Risks don't change much

It is untrue to say that the risks YGT faces do not change much. The new product, for example, has given rise to Risk C and the change in legislation has given rise to Risk D. Risk assessment is needed to translate these events in the environment into an analysis of the **consequences for YGT and the likelihood** that these consequences will occur.

Risks hardly ever materialise

The risk assessment that the consultants carried out revealed that this assertion is **incorrect,** which justified the assessment being made. Risk B is assessed as **highly likely to occur and with a high impact**. The risk assessment should **prompt action to be taken quickly**, perhaps abandoning the activity.

The assessment has also revealed that Risk C will have a high potential impact if it materialises. The risk assessment should therefore **prompt the board to weigh up this assessment** against **the low probability** of the risk materialising and see whether it is worth taking the alternative actions mentioned.

Why risk assessment is dynamic

Risk continuum

Most businesses **operate on a continuum** somewhere between highly static and highly dynamic. Few businesses operate very near the static end of the continuum, because of the **changing forces** in the outside world and the need for them to respond. These may include any or all of the PESTEL factors (political, economic, social, technological, environmental, legal). Risks may become more or less likely to materialise or have increased or decreased impact. Stricter legislation, for example, may increase the impact of the risk of non-compliance because it introduces tougher penalties for breaking the law.

Strategic decisions

The product launch, and the risks associated with that launch, will have arisen because YGT is seeking to gain a **competitive advantage**. Competitors are likely to take action in response to the product launch, resulting in further changes in risk levels.

Operational changes

The risks from the external environment will also prompt changes in the **organisation's activities and operations,** such as the introduction of procedures to comply with new legislation. Changes will carry their own risks, for example modifications in production processes when a new product is introduced may make machine breakdowns more likely.

(b) **Risk A**

Risk A should be **accepted**. Although the activity is marginal and could be abandoned, the **high returns** generated outweigh the low likelihood and impact and justify continuing with the activity.

Risk B

Risk B should **probably be avoided**. Although it generates high returns, it is not vital to YGT's continued existence. It is unlikely that the risk appetite determined by the directors should permit YGT to continue to be involved in an activity that is peripheral and which will probably generate large losses.

Risk C

Risk C should be **transferred**. Although it might have a high impact, it cannot be avoided. The scenario mentions alternative actions being taken. These could include insurance or outsourcing production, if the risk is associated with manufacture.

Risk D

Risk D should be **reduced**. Some action has to be taken to **avoid the business suffering frequent, small losses**. This action clearly cannot include transferring the risk. As the risk is associated with a change in legislation, the action could be whatever is necessary to comply with the new rules. The action could also include reducing the activity or carrying it out in a different way. The directors would need to weigh up the benefits of continuing to carry out the activity at the present level against the increased costs of doing so, and repeat this assessment at other levels or for other methods of performance.

(c) **Related risks**

A related risk is a risk that is **not independent of other risks**. Its level is linked to the level of the other risk, and its level will change as the level of the other risk changes. **Correlation** is an example of a relationship between risks.

Environmental risk links with reputation risk

Environmental risks are exposures to losses through the **impacts** the organisation makes on the environment or the **resources it consumes**. The organisation may suffer bad publicity, and hence a risk to its reputation, as a result of environmental risk arising. **Reputation risk** is thus likely to be **positively correlated** to environmental risk because they have a **common cause**, an impact or event that adversely affects the environment. Actions taken to reduce the likelihood of adverse environmental impacts or events occurring will also decrease the likelihood of reputation risk materialising.

Environmental risk distinction from reputation risk

The losses incurred from environmental risks materialising are separate from the losses resulting from damage to reputation. Environmental risk losses may include **clean-up costs or legal penalties**, reputation risk losses may include **lost sales** as customers boycott the business. The impact of reputation risk materialising is also not only dependent on the environmental impact or event that has occurred, but also how people have **reacted to it**. If there is no reaction, then reputation risk has not materialised.

(d) **Risk awareness explanation**

Risk awareness is the ability of an organisation and its personnel to recognise the risks facing the business. To be effective, there needs to be **risk awareness throughout the organisation**. Staff need to be thinking without prompting about the risks involved in what they are doing. Risk awareness needs to influence the ways they carry out their activities on a **day-to-day basis**.

Risk awareness assessment

Presence throughout the organisation

Risks are present in different ways within the organisation. They do not just arise from the strategic decisions directors make. There will be **risks present at every level of operations**. A culture of risk awareness will help employees understand the risks that affect them and identify these risks when they arise.

Dynamic risks

Directors and employees need to be aware that risks can change over time as a **result of changes in operations or changes in the business environment**. The most recent risk assessment may quickly become outdated. If employees have an awareness that risks can change, it will help them identify when risks have changed and this will aid risk assessment in the future.

Lack of board awareness

The fact that Raz Dutta feels that risk assessment is unnecessary indicates a **lack of awareness at board level** that will hinder the effective implementation of risk awareness lower down. This could mean that staff do not spot relevant risks and thus the company's exposure is higher than it should be. Alternatively they could wrongly assess risks and take unnecessarily costly actions to combat them.

21 Zogs

Text references. Chapters 1, 3, 4 and 5.

Top tips. In (a) the key point in the definition of independence is freedom from personal or vested interests. Such interests may arise through long connections with others (remember that familiarity is one of the threats to fundamental principles in accountancy ethical codes). The key issue to discuss in the rest of (a) is not the need for directors to be independent but how useful it is for non-executive directors to come from outside an industry. The outsider director may lack prejudice but he may also lack knowledge and experience. Note there is overlap in (a) with arguments in favour of board diversity, such as challenging entrenched views from a different perspective.

Careful analysis of the scenario is clearly beneficial in (b). If you look closely, you can see there are four distinct points being made in the second paragraph and these are the issues you need to discuss. The views include some basic misconceptions, such as risk = risk avoidance and risk management is concerned solely with losses.

(c) focuses on the relative impact of risks materialising on large companies, their shareholders and society. A very important purpose of risk management systems is risk reduction by prevention of problems. The separation of shareholders from management, and board from operations are also important issues in large companies that small companies don't face. You should certainly have scored 2 marks for raising costs v benefits issues that are fundamental to any discussions on control systems.

Easy marks. The roles of the risk committee in the first part of (b) should have been easy marks but note the examiner's comments. If you are asked to describe, a single line bullet point (the headers in our answer) is insufficient. You need to develop each point by providing a couple of sentences of further description.

Examiner's comments. For part (a) it was disappointing to see that some candidates answered a question that was not set. Some wrongly produced a list of the roles of NEDs (strategic, risk, people and scrutiny) and some discussed regulation. Because independence is such an important concept in corporate governance, I was pleased to see that most candidates were able to define it. The second part of part (a) was less well done with a wide range of approaches being taken.

The most common error with the first task in part (b) was to disobey the verb (which was 'describe'). It was clear that many candidates knew these roles but a short bullet list is not a description. The best way to answer a question such as this is to start with the single short sentence and then to expand that with a description to show that the thing being described is fully understood. Other common errors in this task included discussing the factors that determine whether the company should establish a risk committee, and also regulatory and listing rule issues with risk committees. Neither of these was asked for in the requirement.

For the second task in part (b), some candidates were able to extract the quotations from the case but were then unable to enter into a meaningful criticism of the views expressed. These answers received fewer marks than those able to include the criticisms.

The answer to part (c) should have included points including strategic and regulatory issues but this part was the weakest for many candidates. Some sought to explain, often without using a meaningful argument, that large and small companies were the same with regard to risk systems and such answers were not well rewarded.

Marking scheme

			Marks
(a)	2 marks for definition of independence	2	
	1 mark for each argument for and against (allow cross marking)	Max 6	
			8
(b)	1 mark for each role described	Max 5	
	1 mark for each point of criticism	Max 4	
			9
(c)	2 marks for each explanation of Mr Ng's belief		Max 8
			25

(a)   **Definition of independence**

Independence means **not being influenced by a personal interest** in a situation. It links with objectivity and should mean not allowing bias, conflict of interest or undue influence of others to override professional judgement. Non-executive directors (NEDs) can lack independence because they become too close to the executive directors and most governance codes include guidelines to try to prevent this.

Mr Louse's views on independence are **stricter** than those found in most governance codes. In many companies NEDs come from the same industry sector and are able to provide industry experience and knowledge, whilst still being considered independent.

Arguments in favour of independence

Lack of prior interests

Outside NEDs should not have had prior interests in terms of **friendships or material business relationships** with other directors. Outside NEDs can thus challenge board proposals and behaviour by directors without fearing that their interests will be jeopardised by offending other directors. This means that they can **monitor without favouritism the performance of executive management**.

Challenging groupthink

NEDs from outside the industry will have had different career experiences and have been subject to different influences than directors who have all remained in the same industry. NEDs from outside may be in a position to **challenge groupthink**, the assumptions that directors from within industry would automatically make. Outside NEDs may also provide **sensitivities to a wider range of viewpoints and issues**, such as threats to reputation.

Lack of prejudices

Outside NEDs will not have built up **assumptions and prejudices** about policies or individuals. This means they should be able to scrutinise proposals without **bias and favouritism**. They are more likely to require explanations and justifications rather than trusting executives whom they have known for a long time.

Arguments against independence

Lack of familiarity with industry

NEDs from outside the industry may take time to learn enough about the industry to be able to **contribute effectively** to strategy and may lack **credibility** with the rest of the board. NEDs from inside the industry will have from the start the **knowledge of issues** necessary to provide well-grounded advice on strategy. In some industries NEDs will also need **technical expertise** to be able to contribute effectively in certain roles, for example as members of a risk or audit committee. Again this may take time to acquire.

Contacts

NEDs recruited from within the same industry may have **networks of contacts** that it might be useful for a company to acquire. Their knowledge of personalities within the industry and the demands of the industry may be particularly useful if they are members of the nomination committee, involved in board recruitment.

(b)   **Roles of risk committee**

Approving the organisation's risk management strategy

The risk committee will agree an **overall approach to tackling the portfolio of risks** across the company. The committee will be particularly concerned with the strategic risks arising from the organisation's business strategy. The risk committee will generally therefore work with the main board in deciding on risk management strategy.

Reviewing reports on key risks prepared by business operating units, management and the board

The reporting system operated should allow for **regular reports to the risk committee** on major risks. There should also be scope for **urgent reporting** if certain risks are judged to have reached a serious level and directors need to take immediate action to manage them. Reports should come in from operational functions and also finance and technical functions such as research and development.

Monitoring overall exposure to risk and ensuring it remains within limits set by the board

Overall exposure means **total possible losses**. Acceptable exposure will vary according to the risk appetite the organisation has, which in turn will be determined by factors such as the **industry** within which the organisation operates. For important risks, the committee will be concerned both with the **exposure** the company faces and the **residual risk**, the remaining exposure after risk management action has been taken.

Assessing the effectiveness of the organisation's **risk management systems**

The risk committee will examine **operational data** to determine how effectively systems have managed risks and also review the **assessment of new systems** which have not yet coped with risks materialising. Their assessment will also be based on data from **internal audit work**. The committee may direct internal audit towards reviewing areas of particular concern within systems.

Approving statements on risk and internal control

The risk committee will be particularly concerned with statements that are required by legislation and governance codes, but should **review any statement on risk that is issued externally**. The risk committee is likely to work with the audit committee in reviewing these statements.

Criticisms of Mr Louse's views

Avoidance of risks

There are many risks facing companies which a risk committee cannot prevent, including risks inherent to operating within the business or risks arising from location. However it can ensure that an **effective strategy** is in place to **limit the risks that do affect the business**.

Information requirements

The risk committee is a board committee. Its members, as directors, are responsible to shareholders for ensuring risks are being managed effectively. To gain assurance that this is happening, the risk committee needs to have **sufficient information** from operational managers, so that the committee can hold operational managers accountable if they are responsible for failings.

Gloomy and pessimistic view

The risk committee must take into account the likelihood of risks materialising and the magnitude of consequences if they do. They may take into account **possible losses**, but will do so in order to ensure that the correct risk management policies are chosen and priorities are established effectively. The committee will also take into account **upsides**, events turning out better than expected, that are relevant for some risks.

All serious risks are external risks

There are a number of internal risks which could **seriously threaten a company's existence**. Negligent treatment of the company's assets could result in damage or destruction. Failings in health and safety could lead to **restrictions being placed on operations** or the company being shut down. Lax IT procedures could result in **major disruption to business or hackers stealing key information**. The risk committee needs to obtain assurance that these risks are being managed effectively.

(c) **Compliance issues**

Large listed companies such as Zogs are subject to **greater compliance requirements** than small companies with regard to risk management systems. Companies operating under the Sarbanes-Oxley legislation have to be able to demonstrate that they have effective controls over financial reporting. The compliance requirements are based on the impact of a significant risk damaging or wiping out a large company, with its shareholders incurring large losses and the stock market itself being damaged. The **aggregate loss** to shareholders in a smaller company if a major risk materialises will be **much less**. In addition, most shareholders in large companies have no day-to-day involvement in the company. They will still however **require assurance** that their investment is not being **recklessly put at risk**. Complex risk management systems, properly disclosed in accounts, help provide that assurance.

Reflection of complexity of company structure

Boards in both large and small companies have ultimate responsibility for obtaining assurance that their companies are being properly managed. However they do so in different ways. In large companies risk management systems are part of the complex systems that result from delegation down the management structure. The risk management systems ensure that subordinates are carrying out their **responsibilities effectively** and provide evidence to the board that it cannot obtain through visiting every site daily. In smaller businesses, the directors will be **much more involved in operational management** and will gain assurance about how risks are being managed from that involvement.

Reflection of size and complexity of risks

The complexity of risk management systems in larger companies often reflects the **complexity of the risks being managed**, as well as the magnitude of the consequences if risks materialise. In, for example, a treasury function, an elaborate system of authorisation and trading limits will often be required to give assurance that risks are being limited to an acceptable level. These elaborate systems would not be appropriate in smaller companies where magnitude of potential losses is smaller and the risks are easier to understand.

Cost-benefit analysis

The costs of elaborate systems may be justified in larger companies because of the **magnitude of the losses** they prevent or reduce the risks of occurrence. The costs of elaborate systems would not be justified in smaller companies because they might considerably outweigh any losses from risks materialising. Costs will include **fixed costs of set-up and variable costs connected with the resources required** to implement systems. However some controls and monitoring will be needed in smaller companies, to guard against surprises and ensure that business opportunities are taken when they arise.

Conclusion

Elaborate risk management systems are more important in larger companies, but all companies require some form of risk monitoring and basic risk management to safeguard their position and remain competitive.

22 Dubland

Text references. Chapters 1, 5, 6, 7 and 11.

Top tips. (a) reflects the examiner's interest on contemporary issues in risk, with banks having to adjust their lending policies as the recession develops being a current concern.

Critically evaluate in (b) means giving both sides of the argument, making sure that you give enough weight to the arguments against. You can score well if you realise that fiduciary duty has both legal and ethical strands. These two strands may lead to lack of certainty and conflicting views. Note the element of self-interest for banks in boosting the economy.

Embedding risk is another favourite topic of the examiner. The measures discussed in (c) can apply to most large companies. The aim is to get managers and staff always to think risk, rather than regarding risk assessment as a detached activity.

Easy marks. There are some relatively easy marks in each part, the definitions of risk assessment, fiduciary duty and financial risks balancing the other requirements.

Examiner's comments. In (a) weaker answers discussed the whole risk auditing process when the question was only about risk assessment. Weaker answers to the second part of (a) did not attempt the second task but better answers showed how frequent and unpredictable environmental changes create changes to an organisation's risk profile.

Candidates who were able to see what (b) was asking (the stakeholder/shareholder debate) often achieved good marks but weaker answers attempted to define fiduciary duty but offered little discussion beyond that.

Weaker answers to (c) made an attempt to explain financial risk but then failed to develop the second task on embedding risk. Stronger answers were able to place the idea of embedding risk into the context of the case and with regard to BigBank's situation in particular.

ACCA examiner's answer. The ACCA examiner's answer to this question can be found at the back of this Kit.

			Marks
(a)	1 mark for each relevant point on risk assessment	4	
	2 marks for each relevant point, in context, on the need for ongoing	4	
			8
(b)	2 marks for description of fiduciary duty, plus 1 mark for context of case	3	
	1 mark for each relevant argument in favour of Ron Ng's statement	2	
	1 mark for each relevant argument against Ron Ng's statement	2	
			7
(c)	Explanation of financial risks	4	
	2 marks for each point about embedding risks at BigBank discussed	6	
			10
			25

(a)   **Risk assessment**

Risk assessment is the process of analysing the significance of risks, in order to decide **what action should be taken to manage individual risks** and how risk management actions should be prioritised.

Risk assessment has two aspects to it – assessing the **likelihood or probability** of the risk materialising and assessing the **consequences (value of the loss)** for the business if the risk materialises. A bank may consider that its largest customers are unlikely to default on their loans but the consequences for the bank will be severe if they do. Smaller customers may be more likely to default on their loans but the financial loss per customer to the bank will be less.

Risk assessment provides the basis on which risk management actions can be taken. Banks such as BigBank may choose to **avoid risks** by not lending to certain customers if the probability of default and the financial loss that would be incurred is unacceptable. For customers where risks are assessed as lower, banks may take measures to **reduce risk**, such as requiring customers to provide regular financial information and placing conditions upon loans that are made.

Continuous and ongoing

Dynamic

Risk assessment needs to be continuous and ongoing because of the changing nature of the environment in which **BigBank operates**. The current recession in Dubland is resulting in continuous changes in the **level of business confidence and activity**. These changes impact upon the liquidity and financial stability of BigBank's customers and hence the risks BigBank faces when dealing with them. The initial assessment made of customers' financial situation may have to be revised often as their financial circumstances change.

Changing risk management strategies

Up-to-date risk assessments may also be needed to underpin changes in **risk management strategies**. As the environment changes, risks that were previously managed by risk reduction measures may be avoided altogether, for example lending for certain purposes may no longer happen. Changes in risk management strategies may be a consequence of reduced appetite for risk by directors or they may be imposed by pressure from shareholders to reduce bank exposure to liquidity risks.

(b)   **Fiduciary duties**

A fiduciary duty is a duty of **care and trust** which one person or entity owes to another. It can be a legal or ethical obligation. In a business context it would often mean a financial duty of care, for example a duty not to jeopardise a bank's liquidity by lending to high-risk customers.

In law it is a duty imposed upon certain persons because of the position of **trust and confidence** in which they stand in relation to one other. For example doctors have a duty of care towards their patients.

Difficulties can arise if there is no clear **legal fiduciary duty** but there is arguably an ethical duty. What the ethical duty is may depend on an individual's view of ethical responsibilities. There may also be problems if a **legal fiduciary duty to one group of stakeholders conflicts** with what appears to be an **ethical fiduciary duty to another group**, as in this situation.

Evaluation of Mr Ng's position

In favour of his position

Legal duty towards shareholders

Mr Ng is adopting a **pristine capitalist position** by arguing that BigBank's directors have a fiduciary duty in law to act in the best interests of shareholders who own the bank, as the directors are managing the bank's affairs on the shareholders' behalf as their agents. The directors are thus obliged to **give shareholder interests priority** over the interests of other stakeholders. This means pursing profit maximisation and not jeopardising shareholder investment by taking excessive risks.

Ethical duty towards shareholders

Mr Ng also appears to be arguing that BigBank's board has an **ethical fiduciary duty** to protect shareholders' property, since they are incurring risks in investing in banks and are entitled to rewards. Taking action in accordance with the interests of other stakeholders and thus reducing the profits available to shareholders constitutes theft from shareholders.

Against his position

Context

One argument against Mr Ng's position is that banks do not operate, and shareholders do not receive returns, in a vacuum but in the **context of a wider economy**. Banks' directors thus have an ethical duty to take into account promotion of the strength of the economy, since the economy provides the opportunities for banks to make profits, including, as the minister says by making loans and hence earning interest. There is also argument, put forward by the minister, that banks are going beyond their duty to shareholders if they limit risks too much, since shareholders can only expect a return if they are prepared to take risks.

Strategic interests

Apart from the ethical issues, failing to take into account the interests of stakeholders with which the bank deals may not be in the longer-term interests of shareholders. Reducing lending may contribute to **reduced activity in the economy and lower demand for the bank's services**, limiting returns for shareholders.

(c)   **Financial risks**

Financial risks include the risks that an organisation will incur **excessive costs or suffer losses** as a result of the financing activities it undertakes, or that its cost of capital will rise. Financial risks also include risks relating to the **capital structure** of the organisation, risks that the organisation will be unable to raise the finance it requires, it will have insufficient cash to meet its obligations and ultimately it will not be able to **function as a going concern**.

Examples of financial risks include **currency risk**, the risk of loss due to changes in exchange rates and **interest rate risk**, the risk of incurring higher finance costs. Risks connected with financial stability include **credit risk,** the risk of debtors failing to meet their obligations and **liquidity risk,** the risks of cash inflows not matching cash outflows in the short-term. Risks connected with financial structure include **gearing risk**, the risk of being unable to meet commitments connected with debt.

Embedding financial risk management

Embedding financial risk management means that it should be **taken for granted** at all levels of the organisation. This means it should not be a separate activity but be seen as a normal part of everyone's activities.

Training and communication

Risk awareness needs to be built into training courses. Staff who join should be **briefed** on the key risks that are relevant to their jobs, covering their possible impacts and how they should be managed. Training on risks also needs to be **organised systematically** for current staff to ensure that they are kept up to date on the risks affecting the bank. Management also needs to discuss risks and risk responses in regular communications with employees.

Job descriptions and appraisal

Staff's **job descriptions** should make clear the extent of their responsibilities for risk management. If this is to be fully effective, their **annual performance objectives** should also include objectives relating to risk, and risk management needs to be considered as part of the appraisal and reward systems.

Performance indicators

Identification of risk needs to be built into the key performance indicators used in the business. Indicators should be designed so that significant risks are **monitored regularly** and **flagged as requiring immediate action**, if required.

Discussions

Risk issues need to be **built into management discussions on strategy or operations**. Employee guidance should include requirements for employees to consult with others across the organisation when new events or risk conditions are identified.

23 Franks & Fisher

Text references. Chapters 4 and 8.

Top tips. There are a number of clear hints in the scenario (the internal control problems the lack of appreciation by the board of internal audit's role) directing you towards using the Turnbull list in (a). The marking scheme is quite generous in terms of rewarding basic knowledge as opposed to application to Franks & Fisher.

(b) is a good illustration of what we say in the front pages about the need to read questions carefully. You are only being asked to make the case for appointing externally, not for appointing internally. However part of the case for appointing externally is a negative one; it's not a good idea to appoint internally because of failure to be objective/independent, also possible lack of expertise.

(c) illustrates that you need to look out for words such as critically in question requirements. They will generally mean that the bulk of your answer to that part will discuss problems with the views. The issue of internal audit reporting relationships is likely to feature in many exams, so you must have the arguments clear in your mind. You would gain credit for making the alternative suggestion that internal audit reports to an independent NED heading the audit committee.

(d) illustrates the importance of being able to define certain terms succinctly, having regard to the question context. If you couldn't think of any factors, think what could lead to **internal** auditors not judging situations fairly.

Easy marks. If you had good knowledge of the Turnbull report, you should have been able to generate ideas for (a) quite easily.

			Marks
(a)	1 mark for each factor identified and briefly discussed	7	
	1 mark for each factor applicable to Franks & Fisher	3	
			10
(b)	1 mark for each relevant point identified and briefly described		6
(c)	1 marks for each relevant point made		4
(d)	2 marks for definition of objectivity	2	
	1 mark per relevant characteristic identified and briefly described	3	
			5
			25

(a) **Turnbull report**

The UK Turnbull report lists a number of considerations which will be taken into account when deciding whether to establish an internal audit department; most are relevant here.

Scale and complexity of operations

This has clearly increased recently with **rapid growth** meaning more products and activities being taken on, and possibly more that can go wrong. Internal audit review can act as a check on the decision-making processes, that all the **implications of the change in business** have been **fully considered**.

Number of employees

Increases in employee numbers are an indication of changes in size and the need for **development of human resource systems**, which internal audit would wish to evaluate.

Changes in organisational systems

Overall control systems will have to develop, and **internal audit** will be an important part of this change. Internal audit may be particularly needed as a check on the development of other parts of the system; with rapid growth, there is a danger that information systems for example may not develop in a way that is best for the company.

Changes in key risks

Changes in products and activities will bring changes in risks. There will be **risks associated with the production and sales of the new products**, such as production stoppages, health and safety considerations and distribution difficulties. There may also be **changes in the general risks** that Franks and Fisher faces, with possibly the **increased risk of inefficiencies and diseconomies of scale**. Internal audit can **review the adequacy** of the **overall risk management systems for** coping with these changes and carry out work on specific areas of high areas.

Problems with internal systems

The breakdown has highlighted possible problems with **quality standards**. The recent changes may mean that they would be **inadequate anyway even if rigorously enforced**. However they have not been employed conscientiously, and this calls into question whether other parts of the control systems are working as effectively as they should be. Internal audit should definitely investigate this.

Unacceptable events

Clearly the production breakdown was an unacceptable event because of its **consequences and its avoidability**. Franks & Fisher is trying to establish itself in various product markets and therefore disruption in supply could have particularly serious consequences. If internal audit recommendations can reduce the chances of this happening in future, clearly this will be a major benefit.

Cost-benefit considerations

The fact that the board are talking about limiting internal audit's work may indicate that cost-benefit considerations are significant. Fears that internal audit will interfere with operational departments may well be exaggerated, and well-directed internal audit work should **bring benefits**. However if internal audit's work is going to be seriously limited, it may not be worthwhile employing an internal auditor.

(b)   **Arguments in favour of external recruitment**

Other experience

An external recruit can bring **fresh perspectives** gained from working elsewhere. He can use his experience of other organisations' problems to **identify likely risk areas** and **recommend practical solutions** and **best practice from elsewhere**.

Independence of operational departments

An internal recruit is likely to have built up **relationships and loyalties** with people whom he has already worked, perhaps owing people favours. Equally he could have **grievances or have come into conflict with other staff**. These could compromise his independence when he comes to audit their departments.

Prejudices and biases

An internal recruit is likely to have **absorbed the perspectives and biases** of the organisation. He thus may be more inclined to treat certain individuals or departments strictly, whilst giving others the benefit of the doubt when maybe that is not warranted.

Auditing own work

Recruiting internally could mean that the internal auditor has to **audit the department** for which he worked, or **even his own work**. These would mean that he **lacked the detachment** necessary **to be objective**. This would not be a danger with an external recruit not previously involved with operations.

(c)   **Inappropriateness of reporting to Mr Kumas**

There are a number of reasons why internal audit should not report to Mr Kumas.

Independence of internal audit

Internal audit's **independence** as a check on internal controls will be compromised by having to report to Mr Kumas, because he has **responsibility for operations** as an **executive director**. Instead internal audit should report to the chair of the audit committee, on the grounds he is, or should be, an **independent non-executive director** with no operational responsibilities. The corporate governance codes emphasise the importance of this.

Employment of internal audit

If internal auditors report to Mr Kumas, he will have **responsibility for establishing their pay and conditions**. Thus they will have a significant personal interest in not producing adverse findings and hence antagonising him.

Work of internal audit

Part of internal audit's work will be on the **finance function** for which Mr Kumas is responsible. If Mr Kumas is in charge of internal audit as well, he may be able to ensure that internal audit coverage of the finance function and his own work is **not as rigorous** as it should be, and may be able to **water down or suppress adverse audit findings**.

Using Mr Kumas' help

Even if internal audit did not report to Mr Kumas, he would **still have to supply them with the budgets and other control information** he has and generally provide assistance. However internal auditors should not rely on him for audit knowledge as they should themselves possess **sufficient knowledge and experience** to carry out their responsibilities effectively.

(d) **Definition of objectivity**

Objectivity means **not letting bias, conflict or undue influence of others** to override professional or business judgements. It implies detachment and not letting personal feelings intrude into professional judgements.

Demonstrating objectivity

Lack of favouritism

Internal auditors should **not accept gifts nor undue favours** from the departments that they are auditing.

Fairness

Internal auditors should avoid the perception that they are out to **'hit' certain individuals or departments**. They should **not take sides**, not being influenced by office politics in determining the work carried out and the reports given.

Not responding to intimidation

Internal auditors should choose which areas to audit based on their objectives and risk analysis, **and not be kept away** from certain areas by aggressive managers. Internal audit should also **cover the whole management process** and **not just audit the operational areas**.

Valid opinion

Internal auditors should aim to deliver a report that satisfies the needs of their principal (the audit committee). This means **producing a report based on all relevant factors** rather than one **designed to please operational departments**.

24 Gluck and Goodman

Text references. Chapters 4, 7, 8.

Top tips. (a) is very straightforward. You may have grouped the objectives of internal control under different headings, but your answer should have said much the same as ours. Other organisational factors relating to internal audit that the Turnbull report identifies include number of employees and problems with internal control systems.

In (b) the verb is criticise, a higher level verb, indicating you not only have to identify the problems but show why they are issues. Hence the mark scheme allocates 2 marks per point with the second mark being available for developing the point. In many scenarios, as here, the examiner drops some very clear hints about the problems; you need to highlight. They include blatant breaches of governance provisions (finance director chairing audit committee) failure to fulfil risk management responsibilities and also a lack of understanding of the importance of scrutiny by the internal audit function and audit committee.

The definition of market risk in (c) is taken from the BPP Study Text and is similar to the definition in IFRS 7, that market risk is the risk that the fair values or cash flows of a financial instrument will fluctuate due to changes in market prices. A wider definition of market risk would be risks from any of the markets in which the company operates, including resources, product and capital markets. Under this definition lack of an audit committee would have a strong impact upon the capital market risks affecting the company, since it would erode confidence that the company was a sound investment and hence affect its share price.

Easy marks. (a) is very much derived from the Turnbull report.

Examiner's comments. The first ten marks, (a) (i) and (a) (ii), were both level 2 verbs asking about what should have been core knowledge. I draw attention to the level of the verb because it was on misjudging this that some otherwise well-prepared candidates failed to gain marks. It was insufficient to merely identify the content requested in Q3 (a).

It was frustrating for markers, who always seek to award marks and give the benefit of the doubt where possible, to see an answer from a candidate who clearly knew the answers to these parts but then failed to develop their answers according to the verb. Some candidates demonstrated their knowledge using a bullet list or a single paragraph for all five objectives.

(b) was the core of this question and employed the verb 'criticise'. In order to produce a criticism of something, the critic must know what good and bad practice is. Importantly, to criticise does not involve simply regurgitating the points in the case that were evidence of poor practice. That is only part of the answer. To produce a critique, candidates should discuss each point, perhaps in the context of other things (in the case of the exam scenario, regulations and code provisions) and why each point is important. One valid point of criticism in the case scenario, for example, was that the audit committee chairman considered only financial controls to be important. So the criticism begins with recognising that fact. In order to gain other marks, however, it is important to add why the criticism is valid. In this case, the audit committee chairman has failed to recognise the importance of other control mechanisms such as technical and operational controls.

In (c) I was surprised to see a lot of candidates unable to define market risk when it is clearly listed in the study guide as an examinable area. It was obviously difficult for candidates to explain its importance if they were unable to produce a correct definition. I would remind candidates and tutors that any part of the study guide may be examined and that all of it should be taught, learned and revised prior to the exam.

Marking scheme

			Marks
(a)	(i)	0.5 marks for the identification of each objective 0.5 marks for brief description (Maximum of 1 mark per objective)	5
	(ii)	0.5 marks for the identification of each factor 0.5 marks for brief description (Maximum of 1 mark per factor)	5

			Marks
(b)	1 mark for identification of each criticism 1 mark for reason as to why identified behaviour is inappropriate (Maximum of 2 marks per criticism)		10
(c)	Definition of market risk – 1 mark for each relevant point made	Max 2	
	No audit committee and risk – 1 mark for each relevant point made	Max 3	
			5
			25

(a) (i) **Objectives of internal control**

Facilitate operations

Internal controls should ensure the organisation's operations are conducted **effectively and efficiently**. In particular they should enable the organisation to respond appropriately to **business, operational, financial, compliance** and other **risks** to achieving its objectives.

Safeguard assets

Controls should ensure that assets are optimally utilised and stop assets being **used inappropriately**. They should prevent the organisation **losing assets** through **theft or poor maintenance**.

Prevent and detect fraud

Controls should include measures designed to prevent fraud such as **segregation of duties** and **checking references** when staff are recruited. The information that systems provide should **highlight unusual transactions or trends** that may be signs of fraud.

Ensure quality of internal and external reporting

Controls should ensure that records and processes are kept that generate a **flow of timely, relevant and reliable information that aids management decision-making**. They should ensure that published accounts **give a true and fair view**, and other published information is **reliable** and **meets the requirements** of those stakeholders to whom it is addressed.

Ensure compliance

Controls should ensure that the organisation and its staff comply with **applicable laws and regulations**, and that staff **comply with internal policies** with respect to the conduct of the business.

(ii) **Need for internal audit**

Scale, complexity and diversity of operations

Internal audit is more likely to be found in bigger, more diverse organisations, since the more complex the operations, the more that can go wrong. If operations are complicated, a key task of internal audit will be to assess the system as a whole to see if **risk management and internal controls** are **properly focused**.

Changes in key risks

If the business is developing in new areas, an internal audit assessment of how effectively it is **handling changes in risk** can be very valuable.

Increased number of unexplained or unacceptable events

Internal audit may have to investigate events that **cause problems with accounting records**, and problems that **delay production or result in inferior quality goods or services**.

Compliance with external requirements

An internal audit presence may be required to **comply with stock market or regulatory requirements**.

Cost-benefit considerations

The **costs** of employing internal auditors (salary, management time lost dealing with internal audit) should **not outweigh the benefits** internal audit work can bring.

(b) **Problems with internal control and audit arrangements**

Work of audit committee

The work of the internal audit committee is too heavily focused on financial controls. There appears to be **no review of other important aspects of the risk management systems,** such as the operational and quality controls in the production facility. The assumption that if the accounting systems are fully functional, then all other systems can be assumed to be working correctly, is extremely dubious.

Finance director chairing audit committee

The finance director should **not chair the audit committee**. One of the key aspects of the audit committee's work should be to review the financial statements and systems, for which the finance director is ultimately responsible. If the financial director chairs the audit committee, he is thus responsible for reviewing his own work, which means that the financial systems are not **independently scrutinised**.

Lack of information for audit committee

The audit committee appears not to be trying to obtain the information it needs to review internal systems effectively. In particular it trusts Mr Hardanger to **manage the production facility effectively**, rather than demanding the compliance information suggested by Susan Paullaos. As the production facility is a key element in the business, the committee **cannot rely on Mr Hardanger's reputation** as a good manager.

Lack of internal audit function

Gluck and Goodman's board has not given the question of whether to have an internal audit function the **serious consideration demanded by governance reports.** The board's belief that internal audit work duplicates the work of management accounting shows a flawed understanding of the different purposes of the two functions, in particular that internal audit should be **examining the quality of the management accounting function's work**.

Lack of support from chairman

The audit committee clearly does not have the support of Mr Allejandra. Ultimately the audit committee should report to him. As Mr Allejandra is a non-executive director, he should be aware of the need for non-executive directors generally, particularly board committee members, to **scrutinise** the performance of executive management.

(c)   **Definition**

Market risk is the risk of loss due to an **adverse movement in the market value** of an asset – a stock, bond, loan, foreign exchange or commodity – or a derivative contract linked to that asset.

Audit committee and market risk

Review of risk

The audit committee is failing to review risks other than those connected with the accounting systems. If it fails to identify market risk that exists, it means that the risk exposure will **not be effectively managed**.

Lack of expertise

Even if the committee's remit is extended to review other risks, it still may not highlight market risk if its members **lack experience of the areas affected by the risk,** or if, as here, they do not even know what market risk is. One reason for having an increased presence of non-executive directors is that they bring wider experience of other business environments, including finance environments, which may help the audit committee conduct a more effective review of risk.

Inability to have recommendations implemented

Even if the audit committee correctly identifies risks and makes appropriate recommendations for dealing with them, it will be ineffective if it **cannot enforce the recommendations**. In this situation, Mr Allejandra's lack of support undermines the audit committee in the eyes of the rest of the board and company, and means that the audit committee may well find it difficult to ensure its recommendations are implemented by managers and staff such as Mr Hardanger.

25 Saltoc

Text references. Chapters 5 and 8.

Top tips. Although this question is primarily about risk awareness, management and audit, the scenario also illustrates the interactions between different elements of a company's systems that the examiner is keen to stress – here how board squabbling has undermined corporate governance and effective risk management.

In (a) the talk about embedding risk should have led you to discuss culture, and there are also obvious cultural problems as demonstrated by the loss of the computer data and the chief executive's attitude to risk management. The use of performance management as part of the control systems is not stressed particularly in the P1 syllabus, but is worth bearing in mind in promoting risk management, as the participation of all staff is required.

(b) explores the cultural factors that can undermine risk management, with most of the problems flowing from the lack of unity and the pressurising of board members.

In (c) as well as obtaining recommendations for better risk management, you also need to consider the need to reassure customers (who are mentioned in the scenario) and shareholders (who will naturally be concerned with their shares' value). Having an independent review is particularly important here as internal politics have compromised everyone working for the company.

Easy marks. The explanation of an external risk audit should have provided easy marks in (c), and you should go back over this area if you struggled.

Examiner's comments. (a) was not just asking for a description of embeddedness, but specifically mentioned 'with reference to Saltoc Company'. Many candidates failed to gain the application marks showing again the importance of carefully reading the question.

Time spent studying and scrutinising the case usually resulted in better answers to (b). It was not possible to gain a high mark without a careful study of the Saltoc culture based on the evidence of the case. Some candidates attempted a general discussion either about culture in general or about the importance of risk embeddedness but neither of these were well rewarded.

In (c) many candidates were able to get the 'contains' marks but then did less well on making the case for risk auditing at Saltoc. Given that the examiner had written an article on this, he was surprised and disappointed that some candidates were unable to recall the four stages in risk auditing. Candidates also had to study the case in order to place themselves in a position to make a convincing argument for external risk auditing. Again, a detailed analysis of the case was necessary to gain the highest marks.

Marking scheme

			Marks
(a)	1 mark for each relevant point describing embeddedness	Max 3	
	1 mark for each relevant point of application	Max 3	
			6
(b)	2 marks for each issue identified and discussed in context (1 mark for recognition only)		Max 8
(c)	1 mark for each point of explanation of external risk auditing	Max 3	
	2 marks for each relevant point in the construction of the argument (1 for recognition, 1 for development and application to the case)	Max 8	
			11
			25

(a) Interaction with control systems

To have risk embedded in a system implies that appropriate steps need to be taken to assess and manage risks. This means that **risk management** should be seen as an **essential part** of an organisation's control systems. The operation of other control systems should reflect the requirement to manage risks effectively. With Saltoc the budgeting process needs to take account not only of the **costs of risk management** but of the **consequences of risks materialising** if management is inadequate.

Promoting risk culture

A further part of embedding risk culture is to make sure that all staff think about potential risks and consequences of risk materialising while they are carrying out their day-to-day work. The aim is that staff take **simple steps** that are not costly or bureaucratic, but can avoid serious risks materialising. The obvious example with Saltoc is **not leaving a computer containing sensitive data** in a **location** where it can **easily be stolen. Clear communication**, particularly a **clear risk policy**, and **targeted staff training** can all help promote awareness of risk.

Performance management

To reinforce managers and staff's awareness of risks, **metrics** should be built into the performance assessment system so that risk management is regarded as a normal part of employees' **job descriptions**. The **appraisal process** should include **accountability** for how risks have been managed, for example Laura being assessed on the effective operation of IT security arrangements.

(b) Conflict between directors

A significant barrier to effective implementation of risk management is the clear division in the board. For risk management to work a **coherent, unified approach** is required from the whole board. Here it seems Peter is most concerned with point-scoring over other directors. He also seems to be using his power over finances to reduce costs and make his own performance look good, while starving other directors of the **financial resources they need to manage risks effectively**.

Blame culture

There seems to be a widespread **blame culture** in place. When the disasters have occurred, the board has **not taken effective steps** to address the problems, but instead has concentrated on trying to blame each other.

CEO's view of risk management

Ken's view that risk management and control means **even more administration is misguided**. It explains why risk management has not been given a high enough priority, as other directors may well wish to comply with the chief executive's views, and it is difficult to see Ken leading attempts to embed more effective risk management. Ken seems to be unaware that effective risk management involves taking steps to manage **risks to company value**. The last few years may have been terrible for Saltoc, but the failure to manage these risks effectively could have even more devastating consequences.

Ability of managers to enforce risk management

If Peter is right, and Harry and Laura do not have the respect of their staff, then this will be a further barrier to **embedding risk systems**. A key aspect of Saltoc's control environment should be that the **tone** is set from the top, with management demonstrating through their words and actions **commitment to effective risk management**. However staff will only follow the example that managers should be setting if they respect them and that may not be the case here.

Staff problems

The frequent staff turnover will also not help the implementation of a risk culture. New staff will require **induction and training** and will also take time to gain the **necessary experience** to think about how to avoid effectively the risks that relate to their work.

(c) **External risk auditing**

External audit

External audit means that the work will be carried out by **independent auditors** who are **not directors or employees** of Saltoc. The audit may be carried out by the firm that audits Saltoc's accounts, by another firm of accountants or by other risk specialists.

Identification and assessment of risks

Risk audit involves **identifying the main risks** affecting Saltoc. The risk audit should assess the **probability** of these **risks crystallizing** and their **likely impacts**.

Review of management and controls

The auditors will assess the operation and effectiveness of the risk management processes and the internal **controls** in operation to **limit risks**. A comprehensive risk audit will extend to the **risk management and control culture**.

The case for external risk auditing

Clear assessment of weaknesses

The recent problems have highlighted clear weaknesses in Saltoc's risk management systems such as **inadequate maintenance** and **deficiencies in the risk awareness** of staff with the result that Saltoc has been **exposed to the risks arising from the loss of data**. An external risk audit would assess the extent of the weaknesses. Internal personnel may have become **too familiar** with Saltoc's systems, and therefore be unable to see how they might change.

External expertise

External auditors would be able to bring **knowledge and experience** of other companies' methods of managing risks, something which internal auditors might well lack. External auditors would therefore be better able to **benchmark Saltoc's systems** against best practice elsewhere and base recommendations for improvements upon this.

Objectivity

External auditors would be able to take an **unbiased view** of Saltoc's problems. Their recommendations would not be affected by the **internal politics** at Saltoc, and they would not feel the need to protect their own positions and blame others for any problems.

Assurance to stakeholders

The **shareholders** of Saltoc are likely to be extremely worried by the threats to the value of the shares caused by the recent incidents. **Customers** are considering withdrawing their business from Saltoc. An investment by Saltoc in a risk audit should provide these stakeholders with the assurance that Saltoc will take **effective action** to remedy the risk management deficiencies, and may **reduce the damage** to Saltoc's **reputation**.

26 COSO

Text references. Chapters 2, 4, 7 and 8.

Top tips. Principles v rules is often discussed in this exam in the context of corporate governance, but it shouldn't have been difficult to apply it to internal controls. Comply or explain is a key difference, as is the emphasis on applying objectives v utilising specific controls. Key benefits to stress in the second part are flexibility and the cost-effectiveness of only having to operate necessary controls.

In (b) your answer needs to demonstrate why certain key features of operations apply whatever the industry. The second part brings out the importance of performance measurement of individuals in control systems.

Hopefully you should have remembered the first part of (c) from your F8 studies. The second part of (b) needs to bring out how internal audit testing contributes to an assessment of control systems design and operation generally, and also focuses on certain key features of systems, some of which you discussed in (b).

Easy marks. Hopefully the definitions of the principles and rules based approaches.

Examiner's comments. (a) was quite well answered overall although some became confused in their answers with rules and principles-based approaches to corporate governance in general. The second task was more challenging. This 'to an organisation' was important as it placed a particular perspective on where the benefits were obtained.

In (b) some less well-prepared candidates introduced a bullet list of 'purposes of internal control' from their study texts. This wasn't quite what the question was asking. In the context of the case, candidates were required to comment on the non-industry specific advantages. Most candidates who attempted the second part of (b) were able to provide something here but others seemed unprepared to explain a phrase that they had perhaps not encountered before, despite it being an important theme in internal control.

In (c) the COSO advice was simply used to introduce a notion that should have been familiar to a well-prepared P1 candidate. The first task on defining internal audit testing was done well by many candidates but the second task less so.

Marking scheme

			Marks
(a)	2 marks for distinguishing between rules and principles and 1 for application to the case	3	
	1 mark for each relevant advantage/benefit of principles-based	Max 4	
			7
(b)	1 mark for recognition of each advantage and 1 for development of that point	Max 8	
	2 marks per point for explanation of the statement	Max 4	
			10
(c)	2 marks for definition of internal audit testing	Max 2	
	2 marks for each internal role identified and explained	Max 8	
			Max 8
			25

(a)   **Rules-based approach**

A rules-based approach means what an organisation does is prescribed by legislation and compliance is **enforceable in law**. A rules-based approach will mean that organisations are **required to operate specific internal controls**, whatever their individual circumstances. It requires the **one size fits all approach**.

Principles-based approach

A principles-based approach is often based on stock market regulations, but non-compliance is allowed if it is fully disclosed. It means that the organisation's control systems should fulfil **general objectives**. To achieve these objectives however, organisations can adopt whatever controls are best and cost-effective for them.

Benefits of principles-based approach

Appropriate controls

The approach allows organisations to adopt the controls that are appropriate for them, based on their **size and risk profile**.

Avoidance of unnecessary controls

Organisations will **not have to spend money and time** complying with irrelevant legislation and operating controls that will not provide any benefits for them.

Development of principles

A principles-based approach allows **business sectors** to develop their own guidelines to meet the internal control challenges that are relevant to their sector.

Comply or explain

A principles-based approach allows companies some **flexibility and temporary periods of non-compliance** provided they disclose what they're doing. This puts the **emphasis on investors** making up their own minds about what businesses are doing.

(b)   **Facilitate effective and efficient operations**

Whatever the business sector, well-designed internal controls should ensure that operations **run well**. They should do this by addressing the **risks to achieving objectives** that the organisation faces. These include waste and production of poor quality goods or services.

Ensure quality of internal and external reporting

Controls over accounting can help ensure the **correct and accurate processing of transactions** that is necessary to support reliable accounting records and ultimately true and fair reporting under local legislation. They should also help guarantee the quality of other external reports. They should also ensure that information is **captured and distributed in appropriate form and in good time.**

Ensure compliance with laws and regulations

All businesses have to comply with some laws and regulations. Internal controls should help them **address and demonstrate compliance**.

Aid shareholder confidence

Knowledge that internal controls are operating effectively should give investors and other stakeholders comfort that managers are **discharging their stewardship responsibilities effectively**. This should help reduce shareholder monitoring and agency costs. It should also provide comfort to other finance providers about the risk to their finance, resulting in a **lower business risk premium** and **lower cost of capital** as a result.

Deterioration of controls over time

Performance metrics

Continued operation of controls is most likely when they are monitored and the results used as part of the **performance measurement** of those who are supposed to be operating them. If they are not monitored, compliance becomes less likely over time as individuals' situations change.

Changing circumstances

Unmonitored controls will deteriorate, become less useful, over time, because **business circumstances change**. The controls in place will no longer be a **proactive** response to the problems the business faces. Even if they remain relevant, their **tolerance levels** may need to change.

(c) **Internal audit testing**

Internal audit testing means **obtaining evidence** about the operation of the accounting and internal control systems. It involves the use of audit techniques based on set measures and outcomes. It is part of the monitoring process over internal controls.

Roles of internal audit

Risk and control systems analysis

Internal audit work will involve **identification of significant business and financial risks**. It also includes **assessing the design of control systems** to ascertain whether they are appropriate for managing the risks faced and **testing internal control systems** to ensure that they are operating effectively.

Examination of financial and operating information

Internal auditors will test the **reliability and timeliness** of information. This includes review of the means used to identify, measure, classify and report information. It may also involve testing specific items (transactions and balances) for accuracy.

Review of compliance

Internal auditors will test **compliance with laws and regulations** and with internal policies and directives. Internal auditors may have to test the evidence provided of compliance to external regulators. It will also review compliance with specific internal requirements (authorisation levels), and measure actual performance against internal standards (safety measures or environmental issues).

Review of the implementation of corporate objectives

Internal auditors can analyse business planning, assess whether standards and objectives are relevant and review the implementation of corporate objectives. They can also **evaluate how well specific policies are operating,** such as communication of information.

27 Yaya

Text references. Chapters 7 and 8.

Top tips. In (a) the point about controls deteriorating over time due to changed circumstances (or perhaps less conscientious application) is a significant justification for monitoring.

(b) focuses on the issues of a lack of segregation of duties (partly due to collusion) and ineffective monitoring due to poor information flow and, it has to be said, management negligence.

(c) illustrates how you should make use of a mnemonic, here the ACCURATE mnemonic about qualities of information. You don't need to bring in all the categories for full marks, though most are relevant. You also need to apply each category you choose to the situation in the question.

Easy marks. The answer to (a) is very largely bookwork, but remember a point stressed by the examiner a number of times that you have to explain each point (a couple of sentences) to achieve a full mark. A single line bullet point will achieve half a mark at best.

Note the examiner commented that on a P1 paper containing so much detail, where you need to analyse the case and engage with higher level cognitive verbs, it is very important that bookwork marks are obtained where available. This underlines the importance of revising the main lists, themes and concepts in the study guide.

Examiner's comments. (a) was done well overall because it was mainly bookwork. (b) was a typical P1 question and had been asked in various forms several times before. Well-prepared candidates were able to gain good marks on this requirement with the best approach being to carefully pick out the IC failures, one at a time, with a separate paragraph dedicated to each.

(c) was done less well. Weaker answers used a mnemonic to list the qualities of useful information, but did not score highly as they failed to engage with the value to Mr Janoon. Weaker answers to the second part were general or vague, whereas a good answer considered the specific needs of Mr Janoon and was framed in this way.

Marking scheme

		Marks
(a)	1 mark for explanation of each relevant point. 0.5 marks for identification only	5
(b)	Up to 2 marks for each internal deficiency explained	10
(c)	Up to 1.5 marks for each quality of information discussed in the context of the case — Max 6 2 marks for each relevant measure proposed — Max 4	10
		25

(a) Reasons why an internal control system can be ineffective

Mistakes or poor judgement

The successful operation of many controls depends on the **people operating them**. Staff may fail to operate controls because, for example, they are tired or **do not understand** what they have to do. They may **make errors** operating controls, for example incorrectly failing an item they have tested.

Collusion between staff

Segregation of different tasks is a key aspect of control systems, as is the **involvement of more than one staff member in activities** so that staff know that someone else will see what they are doing. Fraudulent collusion between staff, as here, undermines segregation and oversight. John Zong did not report Jane Goo's fraud because she involved him in it.

Management over-ride

Senior management may be able to insist that certain activities or transactions are not subject to controls that would normally operate. Staff operating the controls may **lack the authority or be unwilling to challenge** senior managers.

Coping with unusual situations

Control systems may be designed to cope with an organisation's **routine transactions**. If transactions occur that are out of the ordinary, it may be difficult to apply controls. Similarly if unforeseen circumstances arise, normal controls may become irrelevant.

Deterioration over time

Controls may be designed to cope with a set of circumstances and business environment that **changes over time**, making the controls less relevant. Staff also may become less conscientious about applying controls over time, particularly if they are dissatisfied with the organisation.

(b)   **Internal control weaknesses**

No check on Jane's activities

No-one **reviewed the compliance work** that Jane had done to see if it was correct. There was **no need for a second signature**. **No-one saw the quality control reports** after they had been filed. Jane was thus able to file fraudulent reports.

Failure to deal with products that had failed

Yaya relied on Jane Goo to **dispose of the products** that had failed. It did not insist that the goods were returned and disposed of independently. It thus gave Jane the **opportunity** to sell the products that she incorrectly claimed had failed.

Opportunity for collusion between Jane and John

There was collusion between Jane and John. Both considered themselves to be **poorly paid** and both **derived financial benefit** from the fraud. The **isolation of the QC facility** meant that for the fraud to be successful, only two people needed to be involved.

Identification of increased failure rate

There was **no automatic reporting** of the increase in the failure rate. An **acceptable failure rate** had **not been established**. Hence there was no trigger that the rate was excessive. Since the failure rate increased gradually, it did not become noticeable for quite some time.

Failure of supervision

Ben Janoon failed to carry out a **number of supervisory checks**. He did **not visit the site very often**, did **not insist on automatic reporting** and **failed for a long time to spot an increase in failure rates**. Possibly as he designed the systems, he had misplaced confidence that they would work properly.

(c)   **Qualities of information**

Accurate

Information needs to be **accurate, complete, unbiased and reliable**. Ben Janoon needed to be able to trust the information that he was receiving. If Ben Janoon had had accurate information, he would have been able to assess whether there was a problem with products failing quality checks.

Cost-beneficial

The value of the information needs to **outweigh the costs of collecting it**. Clearly there would be costs involved in scrapping faulty products. Therefore feedback from the QC lab could enable Ben Janoon to see why products were failing and isolate where in the production process problems might be occurring.

User-targeted

Readers of the information need to be able to **understand it** and clearly **grasp the salient points**. This is particularly important when the user does not have the same level of knowledge as the preparer of the information. Although Ben Janoon did not have a science degree, the QC lab ought to be able to supply a summary of the results of its testing that he could **understand** and based on which he could **make decisions**.

Relevant

Information needs to be relevant to the user's requirements, with anything that is not useful excluded. This means that the QC lab should report anything that **impacts upon Ben Janoon's responsibility for operations**. This includes overall impressions of quality, as well as changes in failure rates.

Timely

Information needs to be **available when it is needed**. The user needs to have time to **process the information and use it for decision-making**. If, for example, there had been a sudden large increase in the failure rate of products, Ben Janoon would need to be informed immediately due to the costs involved.

Specific measures

More frequent reports

Ben Janoon could require the QC lab to provide **regular reports**, weekly or monthly, of failure rates and other metrics. These would help identify upward trends requiring investigation at an earlier stage.

Greater detail

The information supplied could have been **much more detailed**, with a breakdown of why products had failed, ideally **measured against precise metrics**. This would have provided useful operational information for Ben Janoon and made it more difficult for Jane Goo to fake results, as she would have to have supplied reasons for each failure. The information also ought to be in a format specified by Ben Janoon to ensure that he, and not Jane Goo, controlled the information flow.

Physical contact

Ben Janoon could make **more frequent visits** to the QC lab to see what was going on there. One reason for the QC lab staff feeling that they could get away with the deception was that they were rarely visited and their work was not monitored in other ways. The QC lab needs to be seen as a more important function at Yaya. Moving it to a more central site may assist this.

28 Blup

Text references. Chapters 7 and 8.

Top tips. In (a) you may well have identified the compliance burden as an important area for internal audit to consider, but note also the importance of internal audit providing independent assurance that the company's reporting is reliable.

The three issues in (b) were fairly well-flagged in the scenario. Lack of financial knowledge will always be a core weakness in any audit committee, but here also it wouldn't be sufficient for the committee just to consist of financial experts – it is necessary, as Blup has done, to include technical expertise as well. Recruiting as non-executives previous executive directors can result in a self-review threat as well as a familiarity threat. In (ii) the audit committee acts as a link between internal audit and the board's strategy-setting, as well as giving internal audit the backing it needs to operate effectively.

In (c) the question requirements ask for a discussion of assurance provided. This isn't just about establishing information systems, it's also making sure that the people who operate them have the knowledge and capability to do so. Assurance is further enhanced by audit work, so the system needs to generate a clear audit trail.

Easy marks. A couple of easy marks for the definition of internal audit.

Examiner's comments. Overall it was disappointing to see some candidates resorting to memorised lists rather than answering the question set.

In (a) for example the question was not asking about the importance of internal audit but to consider the importance of internal audit in responding to regulation in highly-regulated industries. This task required candidates to consider the roles of internal audit in a specific industry situation. Higher scores were awarded to candidates able to do this more successfully and this, again, underlines the importance of answering the question actually set rather than the one they wish had been set.

In (b) weaker answers wrote in general terms rather than analysing the content of the case. On seeing the words 'internal audit function' weaker candidates produced a list of the purposes or function of internal audit. Better answers considered the relationship in terms of internal audit helping to achieve the strategic aims of the company, remaining independent of those being audited, operating with the necessary board-level authority and meeting the compliance needs of the company as determined by the audit committee.

It was disappointing to see (c) being poorly answered, especially when the subject matter was so important in corporate governance. The most common answer to this was a brief discussion of the general importance of internal controls and this was clearly not what the question was asking.

ACCA examiner's answer. The ACCA examiner's answer to this question can be found at the back of this kit.

			Marks
(a)	Up to 2 marks for explanation of internal audit anywhere in the answer	2	
	2 marks for each point on regulated industry	6	
			Max 7
(b)	(i) 2 marks for each relevant criticism	6	
	(ii) 2 marks for each relevant issue on audit committee and internal audit	6	
			12
(c)	2 marks for each relevant discussion point		6
			25

(a) Internal audit

Internal audit is an **independent appraisal function** within an organisation that examines and evaluates its activities. It acts as a **service**, helping employees carry out their responsibilities. Its remit includes review of accounting systems, internal controls, risk management, compliance and value for money.

Internal audit in regulated industries

Compliance

Internal audit is particularly important for organisations in regulated industries because they need to comply with **stringent external requirements**. Non-compliance may result in very serious consequences, for example loss of a licence to operate or substantial fines. Internal auditors therefore need to focus on whether systems to ensure compliance are **appropriate** and **operate effectively**, and **investigate suspected incidents of non-compliance**. This monitoring and testing role is required to provide management with sufficient assurance that compliance is taking place.

Information provision

As well as compliance with technical regulations, organisations in regulated industries are required to produce information and reports for regulators. Regulators require **assurance** that the organisation's information systems are **capable of producing reliable information** and the **information produced is correct**. Appraisal of systems and examination of information by an internal audit function that is independent of those producing that information provides that assurance.

Reputation

Apart from legal penalties, a regulated organisation's reputation for **compliance and fair dealing** is also a **strategic asset**. Failure to comply may lead to pressure from government that may threaten the organisation's continued existence in its current form. Non-compliance may also result in protests by consumers and pressures to compensate them if failure to meet regulations has damaged their interests.

(b) (i) Lack of financial knowledge and experience

Karen's comments about the importance of controls over financial reporting highlights the **lack of financial expertise** that the three non-executive directors have. All three may be qualified to advise on technical risks relating to the water industry, but the comfort they can give on financial reporting is limited. The Sarbanes-Oxley legislation requires one member of the audit committee to be a **financial expert** and other jurisdictions have similar requirements.

Lack of independence

Most jurisdictions require audit committee members to be independent non-executive directors. However none of the directors on Blup's audit committee would qualify as independent under generally-accepted practice, since they have all **recently been executive directors**. Some jurisdictions impose a time limit before a retired executive director can become a non-executive. In any case there are obvious ethical issues. Early on, the non-executive directors may be considering the consequences of board decisions made when they were executive directors. Relationships built up with other executives may also impair their objectivity.

Independence of audit partner

One key function of the audit committee is to consider **threats to external auditor independence**. Blup's audit committee appears not to have done this. They have not identified a situation where a close personal relationship between the lead partner and chairman poses a problem of familiarity, which is identified as a threat to independence in professional codes.

(ii)   **Objectives of internal audit**

The audit committee is responsible for setting the **objectives and terms of reference of internal audit**. As directors on the full board, audit committee members will also be involved in establishing Blup's strategic objectives. They thus should be able to ensure that internal audit work is **focused on areas that are important to the strategy of the company** and that audit work concentrates on **risks that threaten achievement** of strategic aims.

Compliance requirements

The audit committee should also be able to ensure that sufficient internal audit attention is given to reviewing **compliance with the regulations that the company faces**. Here certainly the industry knowledge that audit committee members have should ensure that internal audit work is directed into **the** right areas.

Independence

Reporting to the audit committee and being able to communicate with the audit committee without executives being present **helps maintain the independence of the internal audit function**. Audit committee members have no executive responsibilities, and so audit committee members will have **no self-interest** in diverting internal audit's attention away from their area of the business. This should mean that internal audit is not compromised by pressure from operational management.

Authority

Reporting to the audit committee means that internal audit has authority **delegated from the audit committee**. This should give internal audit the power it needs to enforce its demands and obtain the access it requires to people and documents.

(c)   **Importance of financial reporting**

Shareholders rely on financial reporting as the **basis for making decisions about their investment** in the company. They therefore need to have confidence in this information. To provide shareholders with this assurance, most corporate governance codes require companies to report on controls over financial reporting.

Information systems

Effective internal controls should ensure that companies produce **timely, relevant and reliable information** that underpins accurate financial accounts and aids management decision-making. Controls ensuring that assets and transactions are recorded completely and appropriately measured, accounting entries are recorded correctly and that cut-off has been applied properly should ensure that systems produce information that can be trusted and that uncertainties surrounding figures are minimised.

Personnel

Effective personnel controls can help give significant assurance about financial reporting. They can ensure that **accountability for key tasks** such as producing information is clearly defined. Controls can ensure that organisational structures have **segregation of duties** built in as an important check on activities. They should also ensure that staff have **sufficient knowledge and competence** for the tasks that they undertake, in particular that everyone is well-briefed on current financial reporting requirements.

Audit trail

Financial reporting controls should also assist in providing a **detailed audit trail** that can be followed by internal or external auditors. This should make it easy for auditors to **analyse the reliability and correctness of the information** provided and means that their work can provide greater assurance. If auditors find errors, a detailed audit trail may make it easier to assess how the errors occurred and make correction of errors easier.

29 Bob Wong

Marking scheme

		Marks
(a)	2 marks for explanation of risk appetite 2 marks for explanation of risk awareness 1 mark for each relevant point on Bob's choice (max 4 marks)	8
(b)	2 marks for explanation of business risk 2 marks for explanation of financial risk 2 marks for each relevant point on risks varying by sectors	8
(c)	2 marks for distinguishing between mandatory and voluntary Half mark for each example given (max 2 marks) 2 marks for each relevant assessment (max 6 marks)	9 25

(a)   **Risk appetite**

This describes a person or an entity's attitude towards risk; from being risk averse (low risk appetite) to being risk seeking (high risk appetite) with all variations in between the extremities. In broad terms high risk investments are considered to bring better returns, whilst low risk investments tend to bring in lower rates of return. Bob will need to consider his attitude towards risk before he can decide what type of investment is most suitable for him.

Risk awareness

People and organisations cannot be expected to avoid risks unless they aware of which risks exist in the first place and how the level of risk varies from one type of investment to another. Bob must consider the merits of higher risk investments versus those with a lower risk profile in order to develop a portfolio that suits his personal risk appetite.

Effect on choice of investment

If Bob decides that he is risk averse he will look for investments that provide a predictable rate of return coupled with low levels of uncertainty. Typically such investments will yield a lower return over time compared with higher risk investments. An example of a low risk investment would be a corporate bond paying a fixed percentage interest over a fixed number of years.

If on the other hand Bob is risk seeking, he will be prepared to take on higher risk investments in order to obtain higher rates of return. These investments will involve more uncertainty and the returns will be less predictable. Examples include stocks and shares, especially in new companies or those expanding into emerging markets. The appeal of higher returns is tempered by the possibility of capital losses as well as gains.

As a newcomer to the world of investments, Bob might at this stage wish to consider a varied portfolio of investments, with a balance between steady returns and more volatile investment products.

(b) Business risk

This is a general risk that affects the survival of a business organisation. It can arise from a number of sources, for example the business model itself, business strategies, the activities of the organisation, the sector in which the organisation operates, or risks to the going concern status.

Financial risk

This arises from the way in which a business is organised financially, that is how it manages working capital, how its debt to equity ratios are organised, and its level of borrowings. The day to day management of cash flows is important in order to ensure that all monies are collected and debts owed are paid in a timely manner. Failure to manage cash flow effectively is all too often a reason why new and rapidly growing enterprises fail.

Variation of risk by sector

The type of sector in which a business operates will have an influence on the types of risks it faces. A company in the publishing industry, for example, will face very different risks compared to a pharmaceutical company which is in a much more heavily regulated environment.

Sectors in different environments – the geographical location can be either stable or uncertain, as can restrictions regarding the movement of capital and exchange rates. Companies in stable environments with strict regulations and a strong customer base will be lower risk that those in more dynamic, hi-tech and turbulent external environments.

Sectors with different business models – the approach to making profits will differ between sectors. Service industries will depend primarily on skilled personnel who are able to deliver an intangible product, whilst a manufacturing industry will be dependent on machinery and an efficient manufacturing process. Risks facing service industries include technological changes and skills shortages, whilst manufacturers could face risks such as product obsolescence.

Sectors with different financial structures, strategies and cost bases – these can be simple or complex, depending on the sector and the activity. Highly-geared companies, for example, are more at risk from interest rate changes than companies that have lower gearing. The nature of the activity may make it necessary to borrow large sums, for example to finance large construction projects.

(c) Mandatory disclosure

These are required either by statute, financial reporting standards or stock market listing rules and include the primary financial statements and the auditor's report. Disclosures relating to directors' remuneration, the composition of the board and a 'comply or explain' statement are requirements in some jurisdictions.

Voluntary disclosure

Companies may choose to disclose more than that which they are required to do by law etc. What is disclosed will depend on what the company wishes to share with shareholders and the wider public, for example future plans and prospects, social and environmental impacts, charitable activities and so on.

Usefulness of corporate governance disclosure

Bob will need to consider a number of aspects of corporate governance disclosure in his investment decisions:

- Composition of the board of directors – ratio of NEDs to executive directors, experience of individuals on the board

- Risk reporting – what are the risks the company is facing, what has been put in place to manage those risks

- Decisions on remuneration and bonus payments – there are agency risks where executive directors' pay and bonuses is closely aligned with the company's performance

- Compliance statement – to what extent is the company compliant with principles-based corporate governance codes

- It will also be important for Bob to look for any breaches of codes, statutes or rules, which might indicate a higher risk relating such companies.

30 Loho Company

Text references. Chapters 3, 4 and 8.

Top tips. The main thrust of this scenario is change resulting from expansion and the need for internal controls.

Easy marks. There is a fairly easy list to learn for some good marks in part (b).

Examiner's comments.

The case in Question 4 was about Loho Company which had recently undergone some internal changes and restructuring. These changes meant that its situation had become more complicated, thereby changing its need for internal controls. The scenario describes a number of risk changes and also a situation in which the finance director (Sonja Tan) has explained the limitations of some internal controls.

Part (a) should have been straightforward for candidates who were aware of the criteria for changed internal controls in an organisation. The case was seeded with a number of these changes that meant it would be favourable for Loho Company to review its internal audit needs. Given the changes (increased risks, more employees, more decentralised, etc) there was clearly a case for strengthening the internal audit function in Loho. The task was to construct the case which means to argue in favour of it based on evidence from the case. Weaker answers listed the criteria for strengthened IA but failed to fully analyse the case from evidence. The task was not to argue for internal audit but to do so in the context of Loho Company and this was missed by some candidates. This should act a reminder to study the case for evidence if this is what the requirement is asking candidates to do.

Part (b) referred back to the case and a point made by Sonja Tan, the finance director. Whilst she believed that Loho needed tighter internal controls, she also emphasised that internal controls could only provide 'reasonable assurance' and each had inherent limitations that can affect their effectiveness. For 9 marks, this requirement asked candidates to explain why this is the case and to discuss why controls being 'very expensive' is no guarantee of effectiveness. So the requirement contained two tasks.

Candidates receiving the most marks were able to link their answer into the case. There are a number of reasons why internal controls can never be fully effective and this was book work to a certain extent with those able to link it back to the case of Loho receiving the most marks. The second task, to discuss why expense is no guarantee to effectiveness, was more difficult for many candidates as it required considering the specification of the control. An internal control has to be specified correctly for the thing it is controlling. It can be over-specified, which means the organisation receives poor value for money for the control, or underspecified, meaning that the control is not sufficiently effective. So the first task was done better than the second in some cases.

The final part of question 4 was about continuing professional development (CPD). Most professionals, including accountants, have a CPD requirement built into their continuing registration with their professional body and so it was surprising that some candidates made only a weak attempt on this question (although many produced excellent answers). CPD is an essential part of continuing professional competence and important in any professional career.

Marking scheme

		Marks
(a)	Up to 2 marks for each relevant argument	
		10
(b)	1 mark for each reason identified and explained to a maximum of 5 marks	
	Half mark for identification only	
	2 marks for each relevant discussion point in relation to cost to a maximum of 6 marks	
		Max 9
(c)	2 marks for each relevant point made to a maximum of 6 marks	
		6
		25

(a) **Case for establishing internal audit function**

The Turnbull report in the UK stated the criteria to consider when deciding on the need for internal audit, and the following are relevant to Loho Company.

- Scale, diversity and complexity of operations

  Loho has grown recently and has developed new products and new markets overseas, both of which are major areas of uncertainty on the Ansoff matrix. The company is experiencing some problems as a result of this growth in activity. An effective internal audit function can provide information on different aspects of operations to help with understanding the complexities in Loho's business model.

- Number of employees

  Loho has increased its home country employees from 150 to 600 and has also recruited a further 200 employees overseas. These and existing employees will need systems in place to ensure that their performance is monitored and that they are adequately rewarded in accordance with their contracts of employment.

- Changes in organisational structure

  Growth has resulted in Loho Company becoming more decentralised, meaning that authority is delegated away from head office. This raises the issue of control in regional offices and internal audit can help to ensure uniformity of approach and compliance with control procedures.

- Changes in key risks

  Trading overseas carries a number of risks, especially in a period of rapid expansion. Loho may be using different currencies, which carries an exchange rate risk and, as Sonja Tan had realised, there is a credit risk related to the increase in exports. Internal audit can help to ensure that appropriate controls are put in place to manage these risks, for example by putting in place criteria for extending credit and enforcing payment terms.

- Increased number of unexplained or unacceptable events

  The launch of several new products and the rapid increase in exports has meant that Loho has had difficulties in meeting its orders. In time this could lead to a loss of orders if customers are dissatisfied. Effective controls could help to ensure that inventory levels are adequate and that orders are dispatched promptly.

(b) **Effectiveness of internal controls**

An internal control framework in any organisation can only provide the directors with reasonable assurance that their objectives are reached, because of inherent limitations, including:

- The costs of control not outweighing their benefits (Sometimes setting up an elaborate system of controls will be too costly when compared with the financial losses those controls may prevent.)
- Poor judgement in decision-making
- The potential for human error or fraud
- Collusion between employees
- The possibility of controls being by-passed or overridden by management or employees
- Controls being designed to cope with routine and not non-routine transactions
- Controls being unable to cope with unforeseen circumstances
- Controls depending on the method of data processing – they should be independent of the method of data processing
- Controls not being updated over time

Cost of internal control

The fact that internal controls are expensive to implement is not a guarantee that they will achieve the desired effect.

The design of a control is a primary driver of its effectiveness. If it is too complicated or difficult to implement, staff will be tempted to take short cuts or to ignore the control completely if it hinders day to day operations. Internal audit can help in the design of controls that meet the needs of the organisation without putting too great a burden on staff.

Controls that are over-specified can be treated as a mere box-ticking exercise, generating a great deal of paperwork or electronic records, without achieving the primary aim of addressing risk.

No matter how expensive a control is to implement, it can be circumvented or ignored by staff, either wilfully or accidentally.

(c) **Continuing professional development**

The Higgs report points out that to remain effective, directors should extend their knowledge and skills continuously. The report suggests that professional development of potential directors ought to concentrate on the role of the board, obligations and entitlements of existing directors and the behaviours needed for effective board performance.

For existing directors, significant issues that professional development should cover on a regular basis include:

- Strategy
- Management of human and financial resources
- Audit and remuneration issues
- Legal and regulatory issues
- Risk management
- The effective behaviours of a board director such as influencing skills, conflict resolution, chairing skills and board dynamics
- The technical background of the company's activities so that directors can properly appreciate the strategic considerations (for example in fast evolving fields such as financial services or technology)

The Higgs report suggests that a variety of approaches to training may be appropriate including lectures, case studies and networking groups.

Sonja Tan is a professional accountant, and as such she will need to comply with her professional institute's requirements regarding CPD. This will include keeping her skills and knowledge up to date and developing new skills as her role demands. By doing so she will comply with the fundamental ethical principle of displaying professional competence and due care.

31 Branscombe Co

Marking scheme

		Marks
(a)	4 marks for a description of the function and roles of a risk committee.	
	2 marks per advantage of a risk committee to Branscombe, up to a maximum of 6 marks.	
		10
(b)	Up to 3 marks for an explanation of risk appetite.	
	Up to 2 marks for each influence assessed, up to a maximum of 6 marks.	
		7
(c)	2 marks per well explained point on relevant risks and how to manage them. Only 1 mark if not applied to the scenario.	8
		25

(a) The primary function of a risk committee is to recommend to the board a sound system of risk oversight, management and internal control.

Its roles include:

1. The recommendation to the board of a risk management strategy which identifies, assesses, manages and monitors all aspects of risk throughout the company.

2. Reviewing reports on key risks prepared by business operating units, management and the board, and then assessing the effectiveness of the company's internal control systems in dealing with them.

3. Advising the board on risk appetite and acceptable risk tolerances when setting the company's future strategic direction.

4. Advising the board on all high-level risk matters and monitoring overall exposure to risk and ensuring it remains within limits set by the board.

5. Informing shareholders, and other key stakeholders, of any significant changes to the company's risk profile.

Although not a prescribed requirement in corporate governance codes and legislation, a risk committee would ensure the robust oversight of the management of risk throughout the company. In its absence, its duties and responsibilities would be discharged by the mandatory audit committee.

The establishment of a risk committee could be advantageous to the governance of Branscombe Co in a number of ways:

1. **Formalise business practices**

Establishing a sub-committee at board level would ensure that risk is high on the company's agenda when devising strategy and making key business decisions. The recent successful Geeland tender

may have been considered differently by the company if all of the inherent risks associated with the contract were identified and assessed from the outset.

A formal risk management process would have required Branscombe Co to evaluate its exposure to risk, including exchange rate risk, when considering any business opportunity so that only those opportunities within the company's risk tolerances would be progressed.

2. **Focus attention**

Risk is the likelihood that business activities may not go according to plan. Sometimes the outcomes may exceed expectations but there is also a downside to risk which exposes the company to potential losses and financial distress. The establishment of a separate risk committee helps the board to ensure that adequate risk management systems are in place to meet every eventuality. A risk committee would take the lead in promoting awareness and driving through the required changes.

By agreeing to set up a risk committee, Branscombe Co will be clearly raising the profile of risk throughout the company, and helping to inculcate a more risk aware culture amongst all staff. In turn, this should to lead to less dysfunctional decision-making and improve overall business performance.

3. **Reduce control breaches**

Through the establishment of a formal reporting system, the risk committee monitors internal control compliance and considers any breach of the company's agreed risk appetite. Any resultant action plans designed to address significant breaches of the company's principal risk policies should reduce the likelihood and frequency of control breaches.

At Branscombe Co, it is unclear if it currently has any structured risk management procedures and internal control systems. However, its ambitious expansion plans necessitate robust procedures and practices to manage the vast array of different risks it faces; this includes a hedging strategy to manage its exposures to volatile foreign exchange rates, as this could reduce its profitability from the Geeland venture and put a strain on its cash flows and working capital.

4. **Improve communication**

An effective risk management framework integrates all business planning and management activities across the company, which in turn correctly aligns power and authority with responsibility and accountability lines. A risk committee, established at the apex of this framework, will set a tone of risk awareness at the top which then permeates down through the whole organisational structure. This flow of communication ensures that everyone is adequately informed of their responsibilities and so they are more likely to discharge their duties correctly.

The risk committee is required to formally report to shareholders annually on the effectiveness of the company's risk management strategy, and report any material control breaches which may have occurred, together with resultant actions taken to avoid a recurrence. Such communication adequately informs shareholders, and other stakeholders, as to how well risk is being managed by the company.

(b) **Risk appetite**

Risk appetite can be explained as the nature and strength of risks which an organisation is prepared to accept or seek. It comprises two key elements:

(i) The level of risk which the company's directors consider desirable; and
(ii) The capacity of the company to actually bear the level of risk.

A company which opts for riskier ventures to attain higher returns is said to be risk seeking, whereas with a more cautious approach is risk averse.

At Branscombe Co, it is apparent that the company has adopted a risk seeking approach to making strategy. The board has decided that the best way for the company to achieve ambitious levels of growth, and satisfy the demands of its shareholders, is to adopt a higher risk appetite. In effect, this means that the risk tolerance boundaries have been set so that most business opportunities would be viewed as acceptable under these criteria.

The selection of Geeland as a suitable country for expansion was driven by the opportunities presented from the boom in its economic fortunes and generous indirect tax incentives offered by the Geeland government, rather than the risks associated with operating in an unstable political system in which corruption is evident. Clearly the board of Branscombe Co, when weighing up the pros and cons of this venture, determined that the potential benefits outweighed the identified risks and so submitted a successful tender for the hotel contract. However, the resultant supply contract has placed a significant burden of risk on Branscombe Co in terms of logistics and the transportation of equipment, payment terms and foreign exchange exposure. Provided that sound internal control systems have been set up to manage all aspects of risk associated with this contract, then the risk seeking policy adopted should deliver the expected return to the company.

(c)   The Geeland supply contract presents a number of strategic and operational risks for Branscombe Co which could be controlled as follows:

Trading risk

International trade presents its own special risks due to the increased distances and times involved. The types of trading risk include:

1.   Physical risk of goods being lost, stolen or damaged in transit, or the legal documents accompanying the goods going missing;

2.   The customer refusing to accept the goods on their delivery; and

3.   Cancellation of an order whilst in transit.

To overcome the trading risks described above, Branscombe Co could employ local agents in Geeland to liaise with the management and project team for the new hotel, and coordinate the shipment of goods to meet the precise requirements of the client. This means that only those items actually required will be despatched and they will be accepted on delivery. Additionally, it might be prudent to take out an insurance policy covering the value of goods which could be lost or damaged on the long journey to Geeland, as well as any liquidated damages which might be claimed by the customer for non-delivery.

Probity risk

There is a general risk of unethical behaviour by one or more persons involved in a business activity, and as Geeland has a bad reputation for corrupt business practices, the risk is high. It might be that corrupt officials require a 'facilitation payment' to be made to them to allow the goods to pass through import controls in Geeland. It would never be acceptable to make such a payment and indeed in many jurisdictions paying a bribe is illegal, so Branscombe Co must make this clear in its code of practice. To overcome this possible probity risk, the contract should be drafted to make it clear that the client should undertake the local administrative measures necessary for the importing of and acceptance of goods on their arrival at the island.

Political risk

The unstable legacy of political administrations in Geeland suggests a possible political risk. Should there be a change of government, the incentives which encouraged Branscombe Co to trade with Geeland could be withdrawn and the contract could become less attractive. It would be inappropriate to lobby, engage or ally the business with any foreign government or political party; by adopting a policy of political neutrality Branscombe Co would be less likely to be negatively affected by any change in the Geeland government.

Foreign currency risk

There is always the risk of a loss arising from exchange rate movements between the time of entering into an international trading transaction and the time of cash settlement. When Branscombe Co remits an invoice to its client in Geeland $, it will be exposed to foreign currency risk. Any further strengthening against the Effland $ will mean that the final amount receivable will be of less value than at the time of entering into the transaction.

If this risk is considered material, Branscombe Co may wish to hedge its exposure. There are a number of hedging methods designed to counter the effect of movements in exchange rate including forward contracts and money market hedges.

32 Anne Hayes

Marking scheme

				Marks
(a)	1 mark for each relevant point on importance of independence made and briefly described. Half mark for mention only		Max 3	
	1 mark for each threat to independence identified		Max 3	
	1 mark for each threat briefly described		Max 3	
				9
(b)	(i)	1 mark for each organisational duty identified and briefly described	3	
		1 mark for each professional duty identified and briefly described	3	
		1 mark for each contrast or comparison drawn up	2	
				Max 6
	(ii)	1 mark for each point made on inclination towards role as employee	Max 2	
		1 mark for each point made on inclination towards professional duty	Max 2	
				4
(c)	4 marks for evidence of understanding the two positions (whether as a definition or in the other parts of the answer)		4	
	2 marks for explanation of how the positions affect outcome		2	
	Cross marks between these two to reflect adequacy of overall answer			
				6
				25

(a) **Necessity for independence**

Reliability of financial information

Corporate governance reports have highlighted **reliability of financial information** as a key aspect of corporate governance. Shareholders and other stakeholders need a trustworthy record of **directors' stewardship** to be able to take decisions about the company. Assurance provided by independent auditors is a key quality control on the reliability of information.

Credibility of financial information

An unqualified report by independent external auditors on the accounts should give them more **credibility**, enhancing the appeal of the company to investors. It should represent the views of independent experts, who are not motivated by personal interests to give a favourable opinion on the annual report.

Value for money of audit work

Audit fees should be set on the basis of charging for the work **necessary to gain sufficient audit assurance**. A lack of independence here seems to mean important audit work may not be done, and thus the shareholders are not receiving value for the audit fees.

Threats to professional standards

A lack of independence may lead to a failure to **fulfil professional requirements** to obtain enough evidence to form the basis of an audit opinion, here to obtain details of a questionable material item. Failure by auditors to do this **undermines the credibility of the accountancy profession** and the standards it enforces.

Threats to independence

Familiarity with client

Zachary Lincoln has been partner in charge of the audit for **longer than the period recommended by most governance reports** (between five and seven years). His familiarity appears to have influenced his judgement, leading him to make the dubious assumption that because there has been no problem on this audit in the past, there cannot be a problem now.

Personal friendship – self interest

Zachary Lincoln appears to be **allowing his personal friendship** with Frank Monroe to **bias his judgement** on whether to investigate the questionable payment. There is a **self interest threat** involved in Zachary's wish to maintain the friendship, and also a **lack of objectivity**.

Non-audit services – self interest

Governance codes identify **provision of non-audit services** as a potentially significant threat to auditor independence. This scenario illustrates why; a **qualified opinion** on Van Buren's accounts may mean that the company stops using Fillmore Pierce to provide consultancy services. Thus it is clearly in Fillmore Pierce's **self interest to give an unqualified audit report**, and therefore it seems doubtful that the firm is truly independent.

(b) (i) **Obedience**

As an employee Anne owes the duty of **obedience** to her **managers**, and should comply with reasonable orders provided they do not breach her professional duties.

As a professional accountant Anne should comply with the **technical and ethical standards established by her professional body**, even if these conflict with what she is being required to do in the workplace.

Interests of employer and profession

As an employee, Anne has a responsibility to **promote the interests of her employer**. These include the **commercial, fee-earning, interests**, making efforts to obtain new work and keep existing clients happy.

As a professional accountant, Anne has a responsibility to maintain the good name of her accountancy body. This includes acting **honestly and objectively**, and not allowing herself to be associated with misleading information or a misleading report.

Obligations of employment and membership

As an employee, Anne owes a general duty to '**fit in**', be part of a team and behave in ways that are in accordance with the **organisational culture** of her employer.

As a member of a professional accounting body, Anne owes the duty to act in accordance with the **norms** of that body, including its stress on **professional behaviour**.

(ii) **Acting non-commercially**

The main tension between the roles that Anne is experiencing is that if she acts in accordance with professional standards, and pursues a full explanation for the payment, she will not be acting in her employer's **commercial interests**. The audit will go on longer than budgeted, meaning that the assignment is **less profitable**. She also risks upsetting the client and **putting future income at risk**.

Anne's own interests

There is also the issue of whether Anne should take into account her own interests and if so how she should do this. She may feel that in order to make her life **easier as an employee** of Fillmore Pierce, she should allow the report to be signed. Against this is the **possibility of suffering disciplinary action** by her professional body if she allows the audit report to be signed, and it later turns out to be misleading.

(c) **Absolutist assumptions**

Definition

Absolutist dogmatic assumptions are based on the idea that there are **rules** which should be followed in all circumstances, **whatever the consequences**. This means that if an individual is facing an ethical dilemma, there should be a **'right' solution** to that dilemma.

Van Buren situation

Absolutist assumptions would indicate that an audit provides **independent assurance** on a business. Because of this, all material audit queries need to be resolved if an **unqualified audit report** is to be given.

Conclusion using absolutist assumptions

Resolving the query is the right course of action to take and thus should be pursued, even if it means a longer audit and problems with the client.

Relativist assumptions

Definition

A relativist position would be that there are a variety of ethical beliefs and practices, and that the ethics that are most appropriate in a given situation will depend on the conditions at that time. A **pragmatic consequentialist** position would consider the **consequences** of the various options available, and choose the option that on balance **produced the greatest benefits** or the **least degree of harm**. This may be benefits or lack of harm in general, or it may be defined more narrowly to mean benefits or lack of harm to Fillmore Pierce or even just to Anne herself (which would be egoism).

Van Buren situation

Using relativist assumptions would mean that Anne needs to assess the **consequences** of pursuing this point. The relativist viewpoint would take into account the argument that **not all audit trails** can **end neatly**. It would also consider the **other circumstances** surrounding the audit, including **previous experience of the client** and **personal knowledge of Frank Monroe**. That said, the relativist view would also consider the possible **adverse consequences to the reputation of Anne Hayes and Fillmore Pierce** if the firm gives an unqualified report when it later turns out it should not have done.

Conclusion using relativist assumptions

The decision using relativist assumptions therefore requires the weighing up of **different possible consequences**. Because of this, the outcome of the decision cannot be predicted easily.

33 Hogg Products

Text references. Chapters 9 and 10.

Top tips. Note in (a) that the purposes of the code of ethics are underlying themes across the whole of this exam. You could also have mentioned communication and other relevant purposes. Your discussion on contents could have included discussion of other key stakeholders such as suppliers of finance, other aspects of relations with the stakeholders identified in our answer (only buying from suppliers who provide quality guarantees or who meet ethical standards).

In (b) the examiner helpfully defines strategic positioning, although it is not so easy to see how many points you are required to make (five at maximum to generate seven marks). Our answer contains a combination of general points (a strong code of ethics means customers can have confidence in HPC's fairness) and specific issues linked to some of the content discussed in (a).

In (c) don't worry if you don't have all the points we identified; (c) will have been marked quite generously. The way to approach both viewpoints is to give a general description and then bring in the material from the scenario. The requirement to use the broad teleological viewpoint means that you can generate marks by looking at variations of the consequentalist viewpoint.

Easy marks. Using the contents of the example code of conduct in Chapter 10 of the Study Text would have generated most of the marks you needed in (a).

Examiner's comments. This question was the least attempted question on the paper and also the poorest done in terms of marks. The poor quality of many answers to this question suggests that candidates may have some difficulty with this section of the syllabus and this should be a challenge for future candidates and their tutors.

The content for (a) is clearly covered in published material so I was surprised that candidates overall did poorly on it. Some candidates confused corporate with professional ethics and introduced the elements of professional ethical behaviour (integrity, etc) in place of the contents of corporate codes of ethics (policies towards suppliers, customers, etc).

Many candidates who attempted (b) showed some misunderstanding of the term in question ('strategic positioning') despite it being briefly explained in the question itself. The question was referring to the ways in which some organisations use ethical behaviour and ethical reputation as a key part of the way they are perceived by their stakeholders.

In (c) the requirement was to 'assess' a particular belief (that employing child labour is 'always wrong') from deontological and teleological (consequentialist) ethical perspectives. It was therefore necessary to know what the two ethical perspectives were and also to be able to apply them. Where candidates did attempt this question, many answers consisted of a page or so of notes containing semi-remembered definitions of the two terms. The fact that some candidates entered into definitions of consequentialism by detailing 'egoism' and 'utilitarianism' demonstrated that the question was either misunderstood or that those candidates were unprepared for this question. Well-prepared candidates should not only be aware of the ethical theories but also use and apply them.

Marking scheme

			Marks
(a)	For purposes of corporate codes of ethics – 1 mark for each relevant point made	Max 3	
	For contents – 1 mark for application of each to case	Max 6	
			9
(b)	1.5 marks for relevant point made and explained		Max 7
(c)	For deontological assessment, 1 mark for each relevant point made	Max 5	
	For teleological assessment, 1 mark for each relevant point made	Max 5	
			Max 9
			25

(a) **Purposes of code of ethics**

Establishment of organisation's values

Ethical codes form part of the organisation's underlying environment. They develop and promote values that are linked to the organisation's mission statement.

Promotion of stakeholder responsibilities

Codes also demonstrate whom the organisation regards as **important stakeholders**. They show what action should be taken to maintain good **stakeholder relationships** (such as keeping them fully informed).

Control of individuals' behaviour

By **promoting or prohibiting certain actions**, ethical codes form part of the human resources mechanisms by which employee behaviour is controlled. Ethical codes can be referred to when employee actions are questioned.

Contents of ethical codes

Broad principles

Codes generally open with a wide statement stressing that it is company policy to conduct all of its business on ethical principles and it expects its employees to do likewise.

Role of employees

Codes normally stress the **core role of employees** in the organisation, often stating that they are the organisation's most important component. Because of this, the **duties of employees** to **follow the organisation's ethical ideals** are stressed in codes. Codes will also set out the concepts such as trust, respect, honesty and equality to which employees are expected to commit.

Relations with other stakeholders

Relations with customers and suppliers are often highlighted, since they are primary stakeholders with whom many employees deal. Codes stress the need for dealing with **customers courteously and politely** and **responding promptly** to their **needs**. They define relations with suppliers as being based on **mutual respect and truthfulness**, and stress various aspects of fair dealing including paying suppliers on time and in accordance with agreed terms of trade.

Legal and regulatory standards

Codes normally stress that it is company policy to **comply with industry legal and regulatory standards** and that employees are expected to do so. This emphasises that compliance should be regarded as **conventional behaviour**.

Fair business practices

Codes often develop wider ethical standards by stressing that the company aims to act as a good **corporate citizen in the markets** in which it operates. This is often defined as meaning being committed to open markets, promoting responsible competitive behaviour and prohibiting actions that undermine fair markets such as seeking or participating in questionable payments or favours.

Corporate social responsibility

Ethical codes often include statements that **define the basis** of the **organisation's corporate social responsibility commitment**. This may include commitments to **promoting sustainable development** and **preventing waste of natural resources**.

(b)   **Ethical company**

Having a strong code of ethics, communicated throughout the business, to which employees are expected to adhere means that external stakeholders should be sure that they are dealing with people who **do business fairly**. Part of HPC's appeal to European customers seems to be that its strong code means that it has an outstanding ethical reputation and that it is a trustworthy business partner.

Social responsibility

Taking a **strong stance on responsibility and ethics** can enhance appeal to consumers in the same way as producing the right products of good quality can. Here HPC's chief executive believes that HPC has gained orders from European customers because it does not use child labour, orders which its local competitors cannot obtain as they do employ children.

Response to customers

As codes of ethics emphasise the importance of responding to customer requirements, drafting parts of the code to comply with customer wishes demonstrates that businesses are **responsive to customers**. Again HPC is obtaining orders from European customers on the basis of being able to give them guarantees that HPC is complying with their wishes.

Avoidance of sweatshop labour

Central to many codes is the guarantee that labour will be treated fairly, and prohibiting sweatshop conditions shows that labour is valued. HPC can link this with its positioning on **product quality**, emphasising that employees are treated well and as a result produce high quality products.

Position of market leadership

As well as making specific commitments in its code, the strength of a code of ethics may be determined by where the business **wishes to position itself** overall in its market. Here HPC seems to wish to be the **market leader** locally, and as such has a stronger code of ethics than any of its competitors.

(c)   **Deontological viewpoint**

The deontological (Kant) viewpoint would stress that a decision such as whether to employ child labour was **absolutely right or absolutely wrong**, depending upon the ethical principle(s) that was relevant. This would mean that if it is **wrong in some circumstances**, then it is **always wrong**, even if in some situations there may be some arguably favourable consequences.

Child labour

Mr Hogg's viewpoint is that employment of child labour is ethically wrong by itself. This is partly based on the grounds that it exploits children as they **lack the ability to give informed consent to the terms** under which they are employed. They also do not have the physical and mental resources to cope with employment, and are traditionally paid much less than adult workers doing the same jobs.

Interruption of education

Mr Hogg has identified a further ethical principle, that a child's best hope in life is to receive a **proper education**. Child labour employment is therefore wrong since it denies children the chance to receive that education.

Contrary to code of ethics

In addition HPC has been able to **establish trading relations with European customers** on the basis of an ethical code prohibiting child labour. Deciding subsequently to use child labour could be seen as wrong, since HPC would not be honouring a commitment that underpins the trading relationship.

Capitalist viewpoint

However if the pure capitalist view is taken as to what is absolutely right, then HPC has a duty to its shareholders to **maximise profits**. Taking actions for reasons other than profit maximisation is morally wrong. Here as employment of child labour is legal, then if it ensures profits are maximised by minimising labour costs, then it is the right decision to take.

Teleological viewpoint

The teleological viewpoint stresses that the **consequences** of actions should be considered when an ethical decision is made. The correct ethical decision may vary according to the **situation**. The complication is to decide which consequences are most important, and the significance of the various parties affected by the ethical decision.

Capitalist viewpoint

A consequentalist version of the capitalist viewpoint would be that pursuit of profit maximisation by all companies **generates the maximum amount of economic wealth**. The economic wealth can be distributed so that everyone benefits.

Wages

Mr Tanner raised the issue of HPC providing opportunities for children to **earn income** to support their families. The important consequences are thus that HPC is providing the opportunity for families to **increase their standard of living**.

Better working conditions

Mr Tanner also has highlighted the issue that HPC provides **better working conditions** than any of its competitors. If therefore children will work for HPC's competitors if HPC will not employ them, then the argument is that it is better for HPC to employ them as they will be treated better there than anywhere else.

Interference with education

Use of the teleological view may mean acknowledging that employment of child labour could have adverse consequences for the children's education. However it could be argued that these are **outweighed by the economic benefits** to children and their families, or that HPC can take steps to ensure **damage to education is minimised** by providing teaching and training itself.

34 Policy speech

Text references. Chapters 10 and 11.

Top tips. The definition in (a) is adapted from the IESBA definition.

(b)(i) is mostly a test of knowledge. However the question does invite you to use material from the scenario and it's best to avoid here making any reference to Mr Mordue's speech, since you'll be covering that part of the scenario in (ii). In (ii) we have also based our answer round the structure of the five threats. However the examiner's comments confirm that it would have been equally acceptable to structure your answer round the content of Mr Mordue's speech and then bring into your discussion the threats.

You may have found the requirement in (c) difficult to understand. What the examiner seems to want is an assessment of the remarks from the perspective of a deep ecologist.

Easy marks. You should have scored 5 out of 5 for the straightforward descriptions required in (b)(i).

Examiner's comments. The five general ethical threats asked for in (b)(i) were, where attempted, usually correct. Bullet lists of the threats were not well rewarded because they didn't respond to the verb 'describe'.

There was a wide range of responses to (b)(ii) in which candidates had to 'assess' the ethical threats implied by Mr Mordue's beliefs. Some candidates answered it by relisting the general threats and considering how Mr Mordue's beliefs might represent each threat. Others worked through Mr Mordue's beliefs and showed how each one was an ethical threat. Both approaches were rewarded by markers as long as they showed evidence of understanding of how some of Mr Mordue's beliefs were ethically wrong.

(c) on the deep green perspective was done poorly overall. Many candidates were able to say something about the deep green perspective but very few could show how Mr Nahum's remarks were deep green in nature. I would encourage candidates and their tutors to practise applying theories to cases as this tends to be how theory is tested.

Marking scheme

				Marks
(a)		Definition/evidence of understanding of public interest	2	
		Explanation/application to accounting	3	
				5
(b)	(i)	1 mark for each type of ethical threat described (½ for identification only)		Max 5
	(ii)	2 marks for assessment of each ethical threat in the case highlighted by Mr Mordue		8
(c)		Up to 2 marks for each area of agreement identified and assessed		Max 7
				25

(a) **Definition**

The **public interest** is the **collective wellbeing** of the community of people and institutions that the professional accountant serves, including the business and financial community and others who rely on the work of professional accountants.

Trust

Trust is a key issue in terms of the public interest as it relates to accountants. The working of capital markets depends upon **reliable financial information,** as does business decision-making affecting jobs and supply. The public has to be able to believe that accountants' opinions are given on a basis of sufficient work and that they are **unaffected by external pressures**.

Audit and assurance

Mrs Yttria is arguing that accountants who provide audit or assurance services must be able to demonstrate clearly their **detachment from the client**. They cannot do this if they are providing other services to the client.

(b) (i) **Self-interest**

Self-interest means the accountants' own interests being affected by the **success of the client,** or the **continuation of the accountant-client relationship**. An example would be a financial interest in a client.

Self-review

Self-review means the accountants auditing or reviewing work that they **themselves have prepared**. This could include auditing work that has been prepared as part of a non-audit service, something that prompts the suggestion that firms should not provide more than one service to a client.

Advocacy

Advocacy means **strongly promoting the interests of the accountants' clients** and undermining the accountants' objectivity. Accountants can be seen as acting in the client's, rather than the public, interest.

Familiarity

Familiarity means dealing with a client's affairs for a long time and developing a close relationship. This can lead to **reliance on previous knowledge** rather than a questioning approach to information supplied.

Intimidation

Intimidation means conduct of the assignment or conduct towards the client being **influenced by pressure exerted by the client**.

(ii) **Self-interest**

Mr Mordue's comment about a firm providing multiple services highlights one threat to self-interest. If a firm providing audit and other services disagrees with the client over the accounts that it is auditing, it faces the risk of **not just losing the income from the audit**, but perhaps also the **much greater income from providing other services**. Mr Mordue's comments highlight how well financially firms can do out of providing multiple services.

Self-review

If the accountants provide other services that materially affect the content of the accounts, then they will have to **audit figures that they themselves have prepared**, for example valuations.

Advocacy

Mr Mordue mentioned providing **legal advice**. There are two problems. Firstly providing that advice could be seen as promoting the client's interests rather than the public interest. Secondly the accounts may need to contain **provision for, or disclosure about, legal actions**. This will depend on the likelihood of the success of legal action, which could in turn depend on the advice Mr Mordue had

given. Therefore there is a clear possibility of the accountant not wishing to undermine the advice he has given by taking a prudent view of the issues' treatment in the accounts.

Familiarity

Mr Mordue **highlights his friendships** with his clients. Although he would claim that this made it more likely that clients would listen to his advice, critics could suggest the friendships meant that he placed **excessive trust** in what he was told, and would be **unwilling to raise awkward issues** that could jeopardise the friendships. The **provision of other services** may mean that accountants are less rigorous in auditing information with which their firm has been involved.

Intimidation

Mr Mordue comments that he got to know his clients very well and presumably they got to know him very well. This could mean that if they wished to **intimidate him** into giving advice that they wanted to hear, they would have a good idea of how to do so, by for example threatening to replace his firm as auditors.

(c)   **Economic priorities**

Mr Nahum is arguing that if accountants serve the **economic interests of clients**, then their priorities are fundamentally flawed. The deep ecologist perspective argues that giving the economic objectives of capitalists any priority over social and environmental degradation is immoral.

Environmental degradation

Mr Nahum's highlighting of environmental degradation links to the deep ecologist view that business must **not threaten the habitats of other species** or worsen the living conditions of humans affected by their activities.

Animal rights

The emphasis on the need for accountants to **address animal rights** is an important distinction between the deep ecologist and other positions, as it places animal rights on an equal plane with humans.

Poverty

The stress on making the relief of poverty and other social injustices a priority links in with the deep ecologist view that all humans, **living and yet-to-be-born,** are stakeholders in business. Businesses need to **recognise the needs of all stakeholders** rather than subjugating their requirements to the current economic interests of shareholders.

35 John Wang

Text references. Chapters 1 and 10 provide some help.

Top tips. This scenario is similar to Anne Hayes (Q44), but the focus is on internal relationships and the perspective in (c) is unexpected. (a) is the sort of question the examiner likes, requiring a definition of a key concept and then exploring what it means. Here the question examines why it is much easier to conduct professional relationships if trust is present. Giving the definition would only have scored 2 out of 5 marks.

Thinking about the stakeholders involved in corporate governance and the auditors' duty to them is helpful in (b), although you can get quite a number of marks for discussing potential breaches of law and accounting rules in which Potto is colluding. It would have been possible to obtain full marks without mentioning IAS 24 (or FRS 8) but the examiner directed that up to 2 marks could be awarded for referring to these standards.

In (c) critically evaluate means you have to put some arguments in favour of both alternatives, even though the arguments are heavily weighted towards John taking further action. Failure to act with integrity can ultimately result in the partner, the firm (and their institute) suffering a serious loss of reputation, which is one of the strong arguments in favour of pursuing the issue.

Easy marks. You ought to be able to define integrity and the other ethical concepts discussed in Chapters 1 and 10.

Examiner's comments. (a) should have been relatively straightforward. Most candidates that attempted this question were able to define integrity but fewer were able to apply that knowledge to the case. Accordingly, some did not gain the marks for applying integrity to professional relationships.

(b) and (c) were less well done overall. Both employed level three verbs and required a careful analysis of the case. In (b) there were five clear ethical and professional 'issues' in the case attributed to Mr Sinter and it should have been straightforward for candidates to pick these out. However this question was not done well overall, perhaps because candidates felt too time-pressured to spend time reading the case in detail and yet this was necessary to answer the question correctly. Where case analysis is essential for gaining marks, it is better to invest time studying the case to the required level rather than writing a long but unfocussed answer that fails to address the question.

In (c) it was necessary to know what John Wang's alternatives were before they can be evaluated. A dilemma, by definition, is a choice between two options (in the same way that a trilemma would have three choices) so there were two main options to be considered. In recognising that some other options were theoretically possible (such as consulting a third party for advice), markers allowed some latitude. Confronting Potto Sinter was the correct option in context and it was disappointing to note that some candidates failed to recognise this.

Marking scheme

			Marks
(a)	Explanation and meaning	2	
	1 mark for each explanation of importance	Max 3	
			5
(b)	1 mark for each criticism identified in the context of the case.		
	1 mark for the development of the criticism with reference to practice or application		Max 10
(c)	1 mark for recognition of each option	Max 2	
	2 marks for each relevant argument for or against either alternative	Max 8	
			Max 10
			25

(a) **Integrity**

The Cadbury report defines integrity as meaning **straightforward dealing** and **completeness**. IESBA's fundamental principles define integrity as being **straightforward and honest** in all business and professional relationships. Integrity means resisting any pressure to act unethically.

Importance in professional relationships

Reliability

Integrity should mean that colleagues should be able to **rely on a professional's word** and be sure that his **intentions are ethical**.

Promotion of control environment

As a partner, and hence being someone who is in charge of management, at Miller Dundas, Potto should be particularly concerned to promote integrity. Not only is his own integrity more important because of his position of power, but also he should set an example to other staff in order to **promote an ethical environment** at the firm on which clients and others can rely.

Efficiency and effectiveness

Integrity means that time does not have to spend checking the statements of a professional colleague against other evidence. Instead it should mean that other partners or staff who are unsure of an issue should feel they can obtain unbiased advice from Potto.

(b) **Agreeing to corruption**

It appears that Potto could be implicated in a **misappropriation of company funds** for Martin Mbabo's personal use. He has either agreed to this or accepted a weak explanation, raising issues about his **integrity or professional competence**.

Duty to shareholders

Potto seems to have allowed his relationship with Martin to override his duty to the rest of the shareholders. Potto is reporting to the shareholders to give them assurance of Martin's **stewardship** of the company and that he has acted reliably as their agent. He should therefore have taken an **objective** view of Martin's conduct and he has failed to do this.

Duty to tax authorities

As well as a duty to shareholders, Potto has a **duty to stakeholders** who have a legal or other right to rely on the reliability and completeness of information in the accounts. This particularly applies to the tax authorities in any regime, and in many regimes Potto could be charged with **colluding in tax evasion**.

Duty to professional colleagues

Potto has let down his partners and staff in a number of ways. Lisa's query was justified and Potto's initial response would have given the impression that he was **not taking the query seriously**. Potto then accepted what appeared to be an inadequate explanation, and **did not provide any reason** for his decision. Not only was this **poor conduct of professional relationships**, it was also a partner setting a **poor example** to a student.

Failure to fulfil accounting and auditing standards

Potto has breached auditing standards by allowing an **unqualified report** to be issued on accounts with a breach of accounting standards. IAS 24 requires all related party transactions to be disclosed regardless of value.

(c) **The alternatives are:**

(i) **Take no further action**

John could decide not to raise the issue with Potto. Possible arguments in favour of this are as follows.

Respect for Potto's judgement

Although Potto has failed to explain himself well, that may not mean that his decision was wrong. As a senior partner, Potto has **experience and knowledge of the client** that Lisa and John lack.

Destruction of working relationships

A confrontation with Potto without sufficient evidence is likely to destroy not only Potto and John's friendship, but also mean they **cannot work together in future**. It undermines the basis of trust that underpins the partnership in which they and others participate. Because of Potto's seniority, a dispute would also damage John's position in the firm. However, if John allows these considerations to be the main influence in his decision, he clearly would appear to **lack objectivity** and have yielded to the threat of **intimidation**.

(ii) **Confront Potto**

John's other alternative is to confront Potto and **demand an adequate explanation**. If Potto does not provide one, John would have to raise the matter with the other partners. Arguments in favour of this include:

Complicity in Potto's actions

The strength of the evidence suggests that at least John should seek an explanation from Potto, even if he accepts it in the end. At present it seems that if John takes no further action, then he, like Potto, is **complicit** in possible fraud, tax evasion and breaches of accounting, auditing and ethical standards.

Duty to other partners

If the transaction is found to be wrong, then sanctions may be taken not only against Martin and Mbabo Co, but also against Potto and Miller Dundas for failing to report the transaction and incorrectly giving a clean audit report. The firm may suffer **financial penalties** and a **loss of reputation** that would affect all partners. John therefore has a **duty to other partners** to deal with a potentially serious problem as soon as possible.

Duty to Lisa

As a training partner, John has a duty to Lisa to take her concerns seriously and make sure that they are **adequately addressed**. This is particularly important here as Potto has already set such a poor example. If John takes no action, Lisa may take the issue further herself, reporting her concerns to other partners or external authorities. John's position in the partnership and reputation may be damaged if he is found to have failed to investigate Lisa's concerns adequately.

Conclusion

John has a clear duty to seek an **adequate explanation** from Potto and take the matter further if Potto does not provide one.

36 Happy and healthy

Text references. Chapters 2 and 10.

Top tips. It's not easy to tell the split of marks between the two requirements in (a) (2:8) and you may well have spent too long differentiating a family business and public company. The points in the rest of (a) are fairly well sign-posted in the scenario (non profit maximisation, Ivan taking over, likely conflict).

In (b) 2 marks seems a miserly allocation for quite a challenging definition. Note the stress on what the accountant is expected to possess and the belief that the accountant will act in the public interest. A brief mention of relevant scenario detail will improve your answer to (b), though not all of the basic principles are relevant to the situation.

The recommendation in (c) confirms what Mr Shreeves appears to have already decided (he seems to know he has to recommend disclosures in the financial statements). This is perhaps the clearest issue you need to discuss. The other issues discussed are complications – split loyalties and an (arguably) ethical desire not to cause hurt. The discussion required in (b) should also have suggested that professionalism and the public interest needed to be brought into the discussion.

Note that speaking to Ivan before speaking to his parents could be construed as tipping off under money laundering legislation.

Easy marks. If you didn't know the fundamental principles of professionalism in (b) you need to learn them.

Examiner's comments. (a) was, in particular, about governance. It drew on content that should have been familiar to candidates that had carefully studied the study texts and many candidates were able to gain some marks for this distinction.

The first task in (b) was seemingly more challenging than the second. Most well-prepared candidates were able to do the second task. Fewer were able to explain the position of professionals in society and the importance of the public interest to a professional like Mr Shreeves.

(c) was done poorly overall. It required candidates to bring their ethical reasoning skills to bear on a problem. There were a number of professional and ethical issues that were relevant to the decision and it was a discussion of these that was required. More detailed preparation for ethical reasoning tasks would have benefited candidates and this should represent a challenge to tutors and future P1 candidates.

			Marks
(a)	1 mark for each relevant point distinguishing between a family and listed business	Max 2	
	2 marks for each relevant point of explanation identified and discussed	Max 8	
			10
(b)	1 mark per relevant point explained on accountants as professionals	Max 2	
	1 mark for each relevant fundamental principle of professionalism	Max 5	
			7
(c)	2 marks for each relevant issue identified and discussed	Max 6	
	1 mark for each relevant point made of the 'advise' point	Max 2	
			8
			25

(a) **Differences from public company**

Shareholder base

The majority of shares in a family company are held by a **small number of members of the family**. The shares in a public company are available to buy and sell on the stock market. As a result the shareholder base is likely to be much more widely dispersed, although in practice institutional shareholders could hold a significant proportion of shares.

Management

The family shareholders are likely to be **actively involved** in running the **company**. In a public listed company, there is a **split between management and ownership**. Most or all of the shares will be held by shareholders who take no part in the management of the company and instead they employ executive directors on service contracts to run the company on their behalf.

Governance issues

Agency

Because the shareholders are also managers, **agency costs** should be **reduced** as outsider shareholders do not need to check on managers whose interests may be different. However agency issues are not entirely absent if a manager-director operates **without adequate supervision** from the others, as here. The greater informality may allow a director to pursue his own interests without this being identified by the other directors, as has happened with Ivan.

Emphasis on financial performance

Manager/shareholders may be more flexible about when profits are earned. As with the Potters, they may seek to **satisfice** (ensure the company makes a certain level of profits) rather than **maximise profits**, which outsider shareholders would demand. Manager/shareholders may choose to **pursue other objectives instead**. Here the Potter family prefer to run the company to provide employment for themselves and a good service for their customers.

Succession planning

There are **unlikely to be formal mechanisms** for recruiting directors from outside to carry on the business. If the business is to continue, new family members have to take over from those who are retiring. This can **simplify long-term succession planning**, if new members are willing to assume responsibility. Ken and Steffi clearly hope that this is happening, with Ivan gradually being given greater responsibilities until he takes the business over. However Ivan appears to have other plans, throwing the company's future into doubt.

Mechanisms for resolving conflict

Family unity may be required for the company to continue to operate. There may be **no formal mechanisms for resolving conflicts** on the board. If the directors clash, the company may be deadlocked. Here it seems that a dispute over Ivan's conduct is probable, and it is difficult to see how a split with his parents would be resolved. Although his parents may be able to vote Ivan off the board as they hold a majority of shares, Ivan's holding of 40% is likely to give him a veto over several important issues affecting the company.

(b) **Why Mr Shreeves is regarded as a professional**

Mr Shreeves is regarded as a professional because he is making judgements, the value of which depends upon the **education, practical experience and professional and ethical qualities** that he holds himself out to have by virtue of calling himself an accountant and belonging to an accountancy institute. Society also expects these judgements to be exercised in the **public interest,** and the interests of his clients.

Fundamental principles

Professional competence and due care

Professionals have a duty to maintain **professional knowledge and skill** at a level required to ensure that they provide competent professional service **based on current developments in practice, legislation and techniques.** Professionals should **act diligently** and in **accordance with applicable technical and professional standards**, including **relevant ethical standards**.

Integrity

The public expects professionals to be **straightforward** and **honest** in all business and professional relationships. This means when they identify dishonest conduct such as Ivan's, they would not be expected to keep quiet and allow it to continue, but to deal with the problem.

Professional behaviour

Society expects professionals to **comply with relevant laws and regulations** and avoid any action that discredits their profession.

Confidentiality

Society expects professionals to **respect the confidentiality of information** acquired as a result of professional and business relationships and **not disclose any such information** to third parties without proper or specific authority or unless there is a **legal or professional right or duty to disclose**.

Objectivity

Professionals are expected not to allow **bias, conflicts of interest** or **undue influence** of others to override professional or business judgements. They are expected not to let **personal friendship** lead them away from the best course of action, which may be a problem with the Potter family.

(c) **Nature of problem**

Mr Shreeves appears to have **sufficient evidence** to establish that Ivan has been defrauding Happy and healthy. To seek explanations from Ivan may make Mr Shreeves liable under local money laundering regulations for **tipping off**. Mr Shreeves has therefore to decide whether to tell Ken and Steffi.

Public interest and interests of shareholders

One potential problem that can be identified is that Mr Shreeves **cannot act in the interests of the shareholders as a whole**. Ivan's interests clearly differ from his parents. Bringing the issue to light could also threaten the company's future. However considerations of **professionalism** and the **public interest** make Mr Shreeves' duty clearer. He is expected to act with **integrity,** and therefore act in accordance with the interests of the injured shareholders. Here the nature of the injury and conduct are clear. Ivan seems clearly to have committed a **fraud** and there is a clear **breach of trust** between him and his parents.

Professional competence

As well as being potentially fraudulent, the transactions with Barong are related party transactions which are **disclosable under accounting standards and possibly law**. Mr Shreeves does appear to understand that these rules mean he has to recommend disclosures.

Personal conflicts

The nature of Mr Shreeves' friendship complicates his decision. Even if Mr Shreeves wishes to do what is right professionally, he wants to **avoid causing hurt** to Ken and Steffi. They may decide not to pursue Ivan for the losses to Happy and healthy, but their relationship with their son may be destroyed.

Recommendation

Mr Shreeves must disclose what has happened to Ken and Steffi. He will be acting with **integrity** by disclosing the fraud. He will also demonstrate he is acting with **objectivity** by making the disclosure, since if the directors were not related and he was not a close friend, he would wish to disclose to the directors not involved in the fraud what had happened.

37 JGP

Text references. Chapters 6 and 11.

Top tips. In (a) the definition of sustainability is largely based on the definition given in the Brundtland report. (a) targets the view that businesses' effects on the environment aren't significant and they should not be constrained in their pursuit of profits by environmental requirements.

The three stages in (b) are three key stages in any audit: (1) planning (deciding what you will do) (2) testing/measuring (3) reporting. The examiner wrote a technical article in 2009 on this area.

In (c) the definition of environmental risk extends to the impact of the environment upon the organisation as well as the organisation upon the environment. The scenario gives plenty of clues on why environmental risks are strategic – impact on key stakeholders and factors seriously affecting the entire industry. Strategic and operational risks were covered in a 2008 article in *Student Accountant*, once again demonstrating the importance of studying articles carefully.

Easy marks. The definitions of, and distinctions between, strategic and operational risks, have been examined before. They are essential knowledge for this paper.

Examiner's comments. This question was mainly concerned with sustainability and environmental themes although part (c) introduced some content on risk. Many candidates did well on part (a) which was pleasing to see. Explaining what 'sustainability' meant was straightforward for well-prepared P1 candidates although some could not see the way in which the finance director had misunderstood the term. He thought it meant going concern and so equated sustainability with the business being financially sustained rather than the environmental sustainability of the company.

(b) was about environmental auditing. I addressed this topic in detail in a technical article for *Student Accountant* in March 2009 so was surprised that this question was not answered well by the majority of candidates. Environmental auditing is an important element of environmental management and in reassuring investors and other stakeholders concerned with an organisation's environmental risk. It is important that candidates and tutors carefully study technical articles – they may contain content relevant to exams!

(c) was done better overall. The 'strategic/operational' risk distinction has appeared before and there was a technical article on this by Nick Weller in September 2008. The final task, to explain why the environmental risks at JGP are strategic, was less well done although a careful analysis of the facts of the case should have enabled an answer to be arrived at if the candidate knew what strategic risks are.

		Marks
(a)	Explanation of sustainability	4
	Criticism of the FD's understanding	2
		6
(b)	3 marks for each of the 3 stages of the audit (1 mark for explanation of the stage, 2 marks for exploration)	9
(c)	Definition of environmental risk	2
	Distinction between strategic and operational risks	4
	2 marks for explanation of each reason why environmental risks are strategic at JGP	4
		10
		25

(a)   **Sustainability**

Sustainability is ensuring that economic activities and development **meet the needs of the present without compromising the ability of future generations to meet their own needs**.

For businesses, sustainability means that the businesses' inputs and outputs should have **no irredeemable effects** on the environment. It involves developing strategies so that the organisation only uses resources (inputs) at a rate that allows them to be **replenished**, in order to ensure that they will continue to be available. Emissions of waste should be confined to **levels that do not exceed the capacity of the environment** to absorb them. It also involves recycling to **reduce the impact of product manufacturing** on natural resources. Sustainability can be assessed by measures such as triple bottom line reporting, **measuring financial, social and environmental performance**.

Finance Director's views

The Finance Director limits the definition of sustainability to **financial sustainability**, that based on past performance and current financial position, JGP should continue to go on making profits and operate as a going concern. The first problem with this view that it assumes that JGP will continue to be able to, or be allowed to, **pursue its strategies and operate in the way that it has done in the past**. Difficulties with resources (certain chemicals no longer being allowed or shortage of local labour) may mean that JGP has to make fundamental changes to its strategies or operations. In addition, in the context of environmental auditing, sustainability refers to whether JGP's environmental footprint is acceptable and sustainable, and that is the main issue here.

(b)   **Audit planning**

Audit planning involves deciding on the **areas (metrics) that the audit will cover and the measures that will be used**. The decision is more difficult because there are **no mandatory audit standards and no compulsory auditable activities** in an environmental audit. The scope of the audit will be influenced by the need to **produce sufficient evidence to satisfy key stakeholders**. This will determine the **targets** auditors consider when assessing performance and what and how much evidence is obtained, which in turn impacts upon the **length and cost of the audit**. A decision that has to be made at the planning stage is whether to extend the audit to **JGP's supply chain**. Not only will there be logistical audit issues in obtaining supplier co-operation and arranging the timetable with suppliers, the audit process may have serious impacts upon relations with suppliers that JGP's board may wish to consider.

Testing and measuring

The second stage of the audit is **measuring performance against the metrics established** at the planning stage of the audit. In order to increase the credibility of the audit, auditors are likely to focus on measuring **quantitatively** against targets where possible, for example in areas such as resource usage, waste disposal or emissions. However other areas of concern, for example how the business is perceived by key stakeholders, will **not be easy to measure quantitatively**.

Reporting

The last issue is deciding how the results of the audit should be reported. This means considering not only the **contents**, but also **to whom** the report should be circulated. Given the board wishes to make as much information as possible available to the public, it seems likely that the audit report will be included in the company's annual report, its primary document for communicating with stakeholders. The board will need to consider how the audit report will be included within the full environmental report that JGP makes. This report is likely to include a **high level of detail** to satisfy all significant stakeholders, but the board may need to take into account the **differences in information requirements of investors and other local community stakeholders**.

(c)   **Environmental risk**

Environmental risk is the risk of loss to the business arising out of the **impacts of the natural environment upon it, or the impact of its operations upon the natural environment**. It includes the **effects of natural phenomena** such adverse weather or resource shortage. It also includes the risk of **fines** for polluting the environment, and also the risk of **incurring costs and using resources** to clean up the effects of operations or to dispose of waste. Environmental risk can also refer to the **consequences of bad publicity**, including loss of support from the community, boycotts of its products and employees leaving the company.

Strategic and operational risks

Strategic risks

Strategic risks derive from the **decisions the directors take** about the **organisation's objectives** and are the risks of **failing to achieve those objectives**. They link in with how the organisation is **positioned in relation to the sector in which it operates**. Many strategic risks are long-term and cannot be avoided if the business is to trade. They have **high hazards and high returns**.

Strategic risks include **longer-term risks** deriving from decisions the board takes about what **products or services** to supply, including the risks connected with developing and marketing those products. They also include risks connected with key sources of finance. **Reputation risk** can also be an important strategic risk, as here.

Operational risks

Operational risks are risks connected with the **internal resources, systems, processes and employees** of the organisation. They relate to the problems that can occur in the organisation's day-to-day business activities, such as human error or information technology failure.

Operational managers and employees will have responsibility for **managing operational risks**, whereas **management of strategic risks** will be the responsibility of the **board and senior management**, since they are taking the strategic decisions on which strategic risks depend.

Why environmental risks are strategic

Impact on primary stakeholders

Environmental risk is strategic because it affects the ways JGP is **viewed by its primary stakeholders**, those without whose support JGP will have difficulty continuing. These include here **the local community** because it supplies the key resource of labour. Withdrawal of community support could mean the loss of key staff and problems filling vacancies. The other significant primary stakeholders are **investors**. Loss of their support may result in them selling their shares and affecting JGP's market price. They may also seek to engineer changes in objectives by, if necessary, forcing changes in JGP's board.

Industry characteristics

Professor Appo's comments highlight environmental risks as structural risks that **underlie** the **entire chemical industry**. The methods of chemical processing used mean that the consequences of risks materialising are much higher than for other industries, leading in turn to **serious financial and reputational consequences**. Professor Appo emphasises also that JGP's and its suppliers' **usage of resources** may have serious environmental implications. JGP's strategies may be affected by the need to change the resources it uses, a shortage of resources or significantly greater resource costs.

38 Ann Koo

Marking scheme

			Marks
(a)	0.5 marks for identification, 1 mark for each threat identified and briefly described	5	
	2 marks for each relevant threat discussed	Max 4	
			9
(b)	2 marks for each criticism identified and developed	Max 8	
	2 marks for understanding of public interest	2	
			10
(c)	3 marks for evidence of understanding of insider dealing/trading	3	
	3 marks for explanation of why it is unethical	3	
			6
			25

(a) **Conflicts of interest**

Self interest

Self-interest occurs when accountants' decisions are **influenced by their own interests**, or those of close family members.

Self review

Self-review is when decisions and judgements are **reviewed by the same accountant** who made them or who prepared the data supporting them.

Advocacy

Advocacy is when accountants promote a position or opinion **to so great an extent** that their **objectivity appears to be compromised**.

Familiarity

Familiarity is when a **close or long-standing friendship undermines the objectivity** of an accountant's judgements.

Intimidation

Intimidation is an accountant being **deterred from acting objectively** by actual or perceived threats.

Application to case

Self-interest

Ann has clearly acted in her own self-interest, by letting her decision to choose the supplier be **influenced by her family's financial needs**. It has meant that she has **failed to show objectivity** when taking the decision and not acted with **integrity.**

Advocacy

Ann's objectivity may also be impaired by **having to justify her decision** and defend the behaviour of the supplier if the supplier does not perform adequately. She may continue to defend the supplier's interests even though it is best for her company to take action against the supplier.

Intimidation

Ann may also face a threat of **intimidation**. The supplier, or someone else who gains knowledge of the bribe, may attempt to blackmail Ann by threatening to reveal that she took a bribe. This could mean that further decisions she makes are influenced by the threat of her conduct being revealed. She may be pressurised into awarding further contracts to the supplier, even though this is not in the best interests of her company.

(b)   **Criticisms of Ann's beliefs and behaviour**

Illegality

The first criticism is that Ann has **deliberately acted illegally** in taking a bribe. Accountants have a duty to obey the law, even if it conflicts with their own interests. What makes Ann's behaviour more serious is that many governments have recently tried to promote the interests of society by strengthening anti-bribery laws, sending a clear signal that bribery should not be tolerated by society.

Fairness

Ann has not acted fairly in deciding between the competing contractors on the basis of her **personal interest** rather than the **objective criteria** of the value that they offer. Tucker's model, for example, highlights fairness as a key consideration when making an ethical decision.

Best interests of shareholders

Ann has not acted in the interests of her employers and the shareholders whose interests she is expected to promote. Their interests require that Ann should have ensured that all bidding suppliers had an **equal chance to win the contract**. Fair competition between suppliers would have offered Ann's employers the best chance of achieving value for money.

Low level of morality

By putting her desire to achieve a higher personal return first, Ann has acted on a **lower level of morality** than is expected by society. Kohlberg's framework puts making ethical decisions on the basis of personal benefit on a lower level than making them in accordance with the expectations of her professional peers (as expressed in her professional body's ethical code) or the expectations of society (as expressed in its laws). The rules laid down by government and professional bodies distinguish between legitimate pursuit of the career opportunities available and the earning of undeserved rewards through corrupt practice. The use made of the illicit rewards is not relevant.

Public interest

Ann has taken on **responsibilities as a company director and an accountant** which mean that others **rely** on the work that she does. In accepting these roles, Ann thus has a **duty to promote the common well-**

being, and not put her own interests first if they conflict with the interests of society. This applies whatever the pressures are to pursue her personal interests.

(c)   **Insider trading**

Insider dealing is **using inside information** as a basis for deciding to buy or sell shares in the stock market. Inside information is information that is specific and precise, has not yet been made public, and, if made public, is likely to have a significant effect on the share price. It is **price-sensitive information**. Directors will often know whether a company's current share price is over or under valued through knowing information that has not been released to investors. They will be guilty of insider trading if they deal in shares before they release the information publicly.

Why insider trading is unethical and illegal

Distortion of trading

Insider trading means that the market for trading shares may be seen as **unfair** and distorted in favour of those who have inside information. If investors are aware that insider dealing is happening, they may be less inclined to participate. Their lack of access to inside information means that the increased risks they face are not worth the returns they believe they can earn.

Agency

Insider dealing represents an **abuse of the directors' position as agents**. Directors are misusing knowledge, which they have gained as a result of accepting responsibilities as directors, to enrich themselves.

Conflict of interest

If directors believe that they can use information for their own benefit, this may mean that they make decisions in accordance with their own interests rather than the **interests of the shareholders which they should be promoting**. This may mean, for example, that they choose options that will guarantee them short-term gains rather than options that are likely to provide the best long-term value for shareholders. For example, directors may recommend that shareholders accept a takeover bid because they have previously bought shares in the company in the knowledge that the takeover bid would be made, and would make significant gains if the bid went ahead and the share price rose.

39 Biggo

Text references. Chapters 2 and 11.

Top tips. This is a fairly typical question for this paper as it involves a project that has positive and negative impacts.

(a) is a reminder about rights as well as responsibilities. An important point here is how far the business is entitled to the support of society and what it needs to do to earn that support. The Gray, Owen and Adams discussion is very much in terms of rights and responsibilities, ranging from absolute economic rights to perhaps no meaningful economic rights at all. You needed to discuss the issue of the play area in the context of the extreme positions to gain high marks. The examiner highlighted that merely explaining the seven positions did not result in good marks.

It is quite easy for your answer to (b) and (c) to cover much the same ground, given the similarities between the pristine capitalist and the short-term shareholder interest, and the expedient and the long-term shareholder interest perspectives. Hopefully in (b) you did recognise and discuss the clear indications of the position of each director. The emphasis on responsibilities to shareholders and no other responsibilities apart from meeting legal requirements is a clear sign of the pristine capitalist viewpoint. The argument that showing social responsibility can be justified as being for the company's strategic benefit is characteristic of the expedient position. Note that both positions do not see social responsibility as inherently justified, but the expedient position acknowledges that in the real world, stakeholders other than shareholders may have considerable power over the company.

In (c) the short-term position does not really look beyond the next profit statement. Note that the examiner included detail in the scenario that reinforced this position. Biggo was facing low profitability and therefore could not afford the expenditure. It was listed and its market price might be vulnerable. The longer-term perspective can be justified as being in the best interests of shareholders by maximising longer-term value. Here strategic considerations, principally here good stakeholder relations, come into play and the plan for future expansion means that these are particularly important.

Easy marks. Quite difficult to see in this question.

Examiner's comments. This was the least attempted question in Section B of the paper. Part (a) began with what should have been a fairly straightforward requirement, which was to explain the meaning of rights and responsibilities. This is a key part of the citizenship of a business and is actually also a theme in earlier F-level ACCA papers. The more difficult task was to describe the ways in which rights and responsibilities are interpreted by pristine capitalists and deep greens. A common mistake In this question was to list and describe the seven positions on the continuum. Again, a careful reading of the question should have avoided that error. Part (a) is a good example of how theory (the Gray, Owen and Adams continuum) needs to be applied in a P1 question. It is not sufficient just to know what the theories are. To gain high marks, candidates also need to be able to use what they know to describe the two positions from a particular perspective, in this case, in terms of what the two positions say about rights and responsibilities.

Part (b) was done better than part (a) overall which was pleasing. Where candidates sometimes went wrong was to get Margaret Heggs right but Robert Tens wrong, sometimes identifying him as a social contractarian. Again, a close and detailed reading of the case should have prevented such an error.

Part (c) was sometimes treated as a bit of an afterthought with some answers being very short, despite it being worth 9 marks. Most who attempted it were able to gain some of the marks for defining social responsibility. The tasks about short and long term shareholder interests were often not done well. To achieve high marks, candidates had to engage with the case and to show how the decision would have different issues in the short term and, with the management of certain key stakeholders, in the longer term.

Marking scheme

			Marks
(a)	1 mark each for an explanation of rights and responsibilities and up to 3 marks each for explaining these in the context of Biggo	Max 6	
	½ mark each for identification of the two ends of the continuum	1	
	½ mark each for explanation of terms (pristine capitalist and deep green)	1	
	2 marks each for descriptions of the pristine capitalist and deep green ends of the continuum	Max 4	
			Max 10
(b)	1 mark for correct identification of position of each person	Max 2	
	2 marks for justification for selecting position of each person from the case information	Max 4	
			6
(c)	1 mark per relevant point on social responsibility	Max 3	
	Recognition of short and long-term perspectives	Max 2	
	Discussion of short-term effects	2	
	Discussion of long-term effects	2	9
			25

(a) **Citizenship**

Albert Doo's concept of citizenship is that it extends to companies as well as to individuals.

Rights

The rights that a corporate citizen has include **being able to take actions that are lawful and to enjoy the protection of the law**. As a company, Biggo's rights include the right to exist as a separate legal entity and carry on a lawful business. Society will grant it protection under the law and will also permit it to develop and expand.

Responsibilities

Responsibilities are the **duties owed to society** by the citizen as a consequence of the citizen belonging to the society and enjoying rights within it. In order to enjoy the protection, Biggo has to **comply with the laws** that affect it. It also has to recognise that it is **developing its business within society** and must therefore act in accordance with society's norms.

Gray, Owen and Adams's viewpoints

Gray, Owen and Adams identified seven viewpoints on social responsibility and relationships with stakeholders, the viewpoints differing on who were regarded as **important stakeholders** and a business's **rights and responsibilities**. There is greater emphasis on rights at the pristine capitalist end of the continuum and on responsibilities at the deep ecologist end.

Pristine capitalist position

This position emphasises the business's rights to pursue economic ends with the support of society and the law. It **limits business's responsibilities** to achieving maximum value for shareholders by producing goods and services profitably. It does not acknowledge wider responsibilities to society beyond compliance with its laws. It would see a business incurring costs to pursue social responsibility ends, as conflicting with its responsibilities to its shareholders.

Deep ecologist position

By contrast the deep ecologist position is that a business has no **greater rights to existence or consumption of resources** than the rest of humanity and other species. It does not have the right to exploit social and environmental systems for the ends of wealth creation. It has a fundamental responsibility to act in accordance with the **interests of human and non-human stakeholders** and cannot pursue economic objectives that threaten the interests other stakeholders. It would therefore be morally wrong for Biggo to build on the play area, as it would be exploiting the resource of land in conflict with the rest of the community's right to enjoy the use of that land.

(b)   **Robert Tens**

Robert Tens is arguing from an **expedient viewpoint**. This position is that the **business's strategic and economic interests are of prime importance** and the business does not have an implicit duty to be socially responsible. However the business has to recognise that its activities have some **adverse consequences**, for example displacement of the play area. These may be unpopular with the stakeholders with whom the business deals. The expedient position is that it may therefore be necessary to show a limited degree of social responsibility, for example to make the donation, **in order to maintain or enhance the business's wider strategic interests**, for example here to reduce the risk of future local opposition.

Margaret Heggs

Margaret Heggs is arguing from a **pristine capitalist position**. This viewpoint only recognises **accountability to shareholders** and does not recognise accountability to the local community (the social ecologist position) or the local authority (the social contract position). The focus is on **maximising profits for shareholders** and, as a by-product, providing other economic benefits such as employment and products. Provided the business operates correctly through legal channels, it does not have wider responsibilities and should not get involved in costly social responsibility activities, such as the donation for the play area.

(c)   **Social responsibility**

This phrase means that companies should act in the **general public interest** as well as the specific interests of shareholders. Social responsibility can be interpreted narrowly (as by Margaret Heggs) or widely (as by Albert Doo). It can refer to how the company is **governed** or the impact the company has on the **natural environment** through consumption of resources or through its externalities. In this instance the focus is on Biggo's **social footprint**, the impact it is making on the local community.

Johnson and Scholes

Johnson and Scholes drew distinctions between different social responsibility stances based on whether they acknowledged responsibility to shareholders or other stakeholders, and whether they were exercised over the short or the long-term.

Short-term shareholder interest

A short-term shareholder perspective would see the company's principal concerns as being profits or dividends in the near future, perhaps up until the **end of the next financial year**. Its actions would be judged on the basis of the impact they had on **profitability**. Hence the requested donation would not be viewed favourably as it would reduce profits without having any obvious financial benefits. Biggo is currently facing a period of low profits and probably low dividends as well. It has to keep costs under control and **cannot afford to make unnecessary expenditure**, such as the donation. As a public listed company, it has to be especially sensitive to the impact on share price of low profits and dividends.

Long-term shareholder interest

A longer-term perspective would emphasise the importance of pursuing strategies that maximise shareholder value over a number of years. It would not see socially responsible actions such as the donation as **inherently beneficial**, but accept that they could be justified on the grounds of the **strategic opportunities** they provided, particularly here the opportunities arising from good relationships with key stakeholders such as the council and local community. These might include:

- **Benefits from a good public image**, persuading consumers to look favourably on the company and attracting high-quality new employees. The donation might therefore be seen as promotional expenditure

- **Reducing the possibility of future opposition** to Biggo's activities from the local community or local government. It appears that Biggo may need planning permission for future expansion, which it cannot take for granted that it will receive, and in any case it has to co-exist with the local community.

40 Jojo

Text references. Chapters 3 and 10.

Top tips. The examiner has set a number of questions on ethical issues affecting relationships within an accountancy practice. (a) brings out the wider responsibilities partners (particularly managing partners) have towards their firms. These include, but are not confined to, giving a professional service to clients. Note also the point that has come up in other questions that a partner/director acting unethically compromises relationships within the firm and can cause particular difficulties for subordinates such as the training manager or HR representative (or, on other occasions, a junior partner).

(b) takes an area where you may have learnt a list and asks you to select relevant items from that list. CPE, rules about conflicts of interest and involvement of other partners/directors are all generally important safeguards. Transparency can also act as a deterrent.

The key points the first part of (c) brings in are that performance must be measured both in terms of conduct in the individual role and contribution to the management committee. Underlying the answer to the second part is the idea that a group of partners (also directors) that has been together for a long time may not have the ability or desire to be brutally honest about each others' failings.

Easy marks. The criteria for measuring directors' performance in (c) are widely used, and so you should know them.

Examiner's comments. In part (a) most candidates were able to make an attempt at a definition, but the second task was less well done. Rather than considering the consequences, some candidates continued writing about how conflicts of interest can occur and this was clearly not what the question was asking. It is important to realise that corruption and malpractice in business have serious consequences for a range of people. Some of the consequences affected Jack Hu himself, showing that bad practices are often self-defeating as well as being a very bad example to others.

Part (b) was not well answered overall. Candidates who reflected on how the events arose in the first place and how these might be addressed, received the best marks for this part. Again, short bullet points with little detail (ie no description), were not well rewarded.

Part (c) was done poorly overall. Perhaps candidates had considered the performance of boards but not of individual directors of those boards.

Marking scheme

			Marks
(a)	2 marks for definition of conflict of interest	2	
	2 marks for each consequence discussed. ½ mark for identification only	Max 8	
			10
(b)	2 marks for each relevant safeguard identified and described		Max 8
(c)	1 mark for each relevant point on typical criteria	Max 4	
	1 mark for each relevant point made on implementation difficulty	Max 4	
			Max 7
			25

(a) **Conflict of interest**

A **conflict of interest** is when a person's freedom to act is **limited by the need to protect a contrary interest**. This contrary interest undermines what should be objective decision-making. Here Mr Hu faced a conflict between carrying out an agreed policy of his firm by dismissing an unsatisfactory student, Polly Shah, and his interest in continuing to enjoy free holidays.

Consequences for the firm

Failings of Mr Hu

Mr Hu failed to exercise his **responsibilities as managing partner** properly. His conflict of interest meant that he failed to enforce the firm's policies properly. He thus **failed to act in the best interests** of the firm.

Undermining training manager and HR representative

Mr Hu forced the training manager and human resources representative **to go against their objective professional judgement** by insisting on retaining Polly. He thus **undermined their positions** by forcing them to be associated with decisions that they believed to be wrong. He also upset the training manager and this could have led to the training manager leaving the firm.

Poor service to clients

The clients which Polly Shah dealt with may have received a **poor service** because of her failings. If so, this would have meant that the firm **breached professional ethical requirements** to act with competence and care. If Polly worked on audits, it is possible that her poor attitude and technical weaknesses led to the audit failing to fulfil auditing standards and Jojo thus failing to meet its duty of care to shareholders. It also may have resulted in the loss of some clients because of the unsatisfactory service that they were given.

Fairness to students

The students of Polly's intake did **not receive fair treatment** because of the clear favouritism shown to her. Polly's performance was **not judged by the same standards** as other students. This may have **demotivated the other students** and made them **question the fairness of the assessment process**. Jojo's reputation as a good employer of students could have suffered as a result.

(b) **Ethical safeguards**

Continuing professional education

It is possible that Mr Hu did not realise that he had a conflict of interest. Undertaking CPD training on **ethics, specifically avoidance of conflicts of interest**, should mean he is better informed in future.

Partners' interests

To comply with professional regulations, Jojo will have procedures in place for partners to declare potential conflicts of interests that relate to dealings with clients. The firm should **extend these rules** and require partners to **declare any interest** that relates to the decisions they take on internal matters to the rest of the partners, who could then decide on whether it was appropriate for partners with the interest to be involved in the decision-making.

Involvement of second partner in training committee

Mr Hu was able to enforce his views on the training manager and HR representative because he was a partner and they were not. If a second partner was on the committee, Mr Hu would be **less likely to pull rank**. Alternatively partnership rules could state that a decision to retain a student graded as poor by the training manager would need to be signed off by a second partner.

Brief partners and managers

Without going into full details about the appraisals, the appraisal committee could brief other partners and managers **broadly on their results**. This would make the decision-making process **more transparent** and would put pressure on the committee to **justify apparent inconsistencies** such as retaining Polly. It would also enable staff managers to provide targeted guidance to students who had been retained but whose performance was unsatisfactory in some areas.

(c)   ### Criteria for directors' performance

The criteria used will vary between types of companies, and the same criterion may not, for example, be as important for small companies as large, listed companies.

Independence

The case highlights the importance of freedom from conflicts of interest. Independence is particularly **important for non-executive directors** who have to fulfil **independence criteria** laid down by governance codes. However if executive directors have interests that constrain their decision-making, for example that their future in the company is linked to the retention of a particular customer, this calls into question their contribution. There is also the issue of **internal independence**, whether directors push too aggressively the interests of the function that they lead and fail to take a wider view across the whole company.

Participation in board meetings

An important measure in all companies will be the degree to which the director **participates actively in board meetings**. This includes asking questions and insisting on being given full information on areas which appear unclear. It also covers **participation in committees**, for example non-executive directors with financial knowledge belonging to the audit committee.

Development

As all directors should undertake **relevant continuing professional education,** they should be assessed on the training they have had. For example any director with financial responsibilities or members of the audit committee should be appraised on whether they have updated their knowledge of accounting and auditing standards. The appraisal process should also take into account how they have enhanced their knowledge of the business through developing relationships with key staff.

Performance in their roles

The **individual performance** of directors will also be judged. The criteria used will vary by role, although all executive directors should be judged in terms of their **commitment** to their role and their **competence** in it. Executive directors should also be judged in terms of the wider contribution they have made to implementing organisational strategy.

Difficulties in performance measurement at Jojo

Informality

A small partnership has an **informal structure**, with all the partners actively involved in management. There are no non–executive directors who are not involved in day-to-day management and who could therefore look objectively and independently at how the partners are performing. There is also no HR partner who could perform this role. The HR staff do not have **partner status** and so **lack the authority** to carry out appraisals.

Mr Hu's performance

Mr Hu's performance has clearly been deficient. However as managing partner he **exercises authority** over the other partners. It would be difficult for one of them to hold him accountable for failings and to

recommend performance improvements if Mr Hu disagrees with the assessment. The bonds of **friendship and co-operation** that have built up between the partners over many years also make it less likely that they will hold Mr Hu to account.

Lack of outside pressures

As a privately-run partnership there are no pressures from external investors to introduce an **effective appraisal system**. Shareholders in a listed company will expect a formal system of measuring directors' performance to be in place as part of ensuring their accountability, but here the partners are primarily **accountable to each other**.

41 RDC

Text references. Chapters 1 and 9.

Top tips. The discussion on the profitable and legal aspects in (a) is fairly straightforward. Fairness can relate both to the decision actually taken and the criteria used to make the decision. Generally in problems using Tucker, there may be no one solution that is 'right' and you have to consider different viewpoints, so bringing in Gray, Owen and Adams' extreme viewpoints is useful for the 'right' question here. The discussion on sustainability brings out the conflict between environmentally sustainable and socially sustainable. Note that 2 marks were awarded for a conclusion.

(b) is about analysing stakeholders in order to identify which stakeholders have (or should have) influence over RDC's actions. Each of the first three points relates to an important category of stakeholder, power to approve (primary), desire to take action (active) and most affected by the organisation's strategy (narrow). Dealing with conflict in this part is seen in terms of identifying and minimising disagreements, possibly therefore trying as hard as possible to avoid having to decide between conflicting claims.

In (c) stakeholder claims are used to enforce outcomes that stakeholders desire or avoid undesirable outcomes. In order to assess the claims you need to consider on what basis the claims are legitimate and also whether the stakeholders may not be able to enforce their claims because they do not understand them or cannot voice their concerns.

Easy marks. You would have got limited credit for getting the five Tucker questions right in (a), even if you provided very limited discussion.

Examiner's comments. In (a) some candidates merely listed the five questions with little attempt to engage with the case. A similar version of (b) was on a previous paper, so it was disappointing to see that many candidates performed poorly. A common, but incorrect, response was to frame the answer around the Mendelow matrix. Perhaps the word stakeholder triggered the assumption that the answer must involve the Mendelow matrix – but this was not so, except to highlight that some stakeholders are more influential than others. The question specifically asked about the importance of recognising all the stakeholders in a decision and therefore concerned stakeholders as sources of risk, disruption and reputation loss. A careful reading of the wording of the question was necessary to get the actual meaning of what was required.

For (c) the examiner wrote a technical answer about stakeholder claims in early 2008 and it was pleasing to see that most candidates could explain the notion of a claim. The second task was done less well, with weaker answers just repeating information from the case.

Marking scheme

			Marks
(a)	1-2 marks for a discussion of each point. ½ mark for identification only	10	
	2 marks for balanced summary	2	
			Max 10
(b)	2 marks for each relevant point discussed. ½ mark for identification only		8

(c)   2 marks for explanation of stakeholder claim   2
       2 marks for assessment of each claim   6
                                                                                        Max 7
                                                                                          25

(a)   **Is the decision**

       Profitable

       Route A is a profitable choice. Projections demonstrate that its Net Present Value is positive $5 million,
       $1 million more than if Route B was chosen. However both routes have **additional, uncertain costs** which
       complicate the analysis. With Route A RDC may be faced with costs arising from direct action by the protest
       group. With Route B, RDC could have been faced with the costs of defending a legal action.

       Legal

       The local government authority has given planning permission for Route A, so RDC seems to have fulfilled
       its requirements. RDC does **not appear to face the threat of legal action** with Route A that it could have
       faced if it had chosen Route B.

       Fair

       RDC has had to **decide between the conflicting claims of different stakeholders**, the birds versus Eddie
       Krul and his workers. Choosing Route A ignores the birds' rights to access their feeding grounds and may
       threaten their existence. Choosing Route B means depriving Eddie Krul of a farm that he wants to keep and
       causing his workers to lose their jobs. Arguably it has taken the decision not out of an **objective assessment**
       of the strength of each claim, but because Route A is more profitable and it has been influenced by Eddie
       Krul's threat of legal action.

       Right

       If a **pristine capitalist view** is taken that RDC's duty is to choose options that **maximise shareholder value**,
       then the choice of Route A appears to be correct. However, from the viewpoint of a **deep ecologist,** the
       decision is **wrong** because RDC should **not disrupt the existence of other species in any circumstances**.
       From a **social and economic viewpoint** however, the decision appears to be right as the line will improve
       transport and boost economic activity and the construction work will provide employment opportunities.
       Route A does not have the adverse consequences of closing the farm that Route B would have had,
       including loss of employment and loss of a source of local food.

       Sustainable

       The decision to choose Route A appears to be the **less environmentally-sustainable decision**. It could
       threaten the existence of an endangered species and **disrupt the local ecosystems**, with possible
       unforeseen consequences. Choice of Route B would though have had implications for social sustainability,
       with loss of jobs at the farm and adverse impacts on the local community. Arguably the investment in rail is
       an investment in a relatively sustainable form of transport that should reduce the number of cars on the
       roads.

       Summary

       Whichever decision RDC chose would have had **negative implications** for some stakeholders. It chose to
       prioritise profitability and minimising the impact on the local community over the effect on the birds and the
       associated ecosystems.

(b)   **Conflict between different stakeholders**

       In a situation where there are a number of possible stakeholder claims, it is important to recognise and
       analyse the importance of all stakeholder groups for the following reasons.

       Stakeholder approval

       RDC needs to recognise first which stakeholders have the **power** to **approve the decision** before it can start
       work on the project and how much **interest** in the project those stakeholders will show. Here the stakeholder

with the **power** is the local government authority, which has the responsibility of granting planning permission. RDC would have had to **fulfil any requirements laid down by the local government authority** before it could go ahead.

Stakeholder action

RDC needs to identify which stakeholders are likely to **take action** that will have a **major impact upon the success** of the investment. This means here in particular the risk of the pressure group being **able to disrupt the project** and how great **the adverse consequences of disruption would be**. RDC also has to weigh up how much disruption the pressure group could cause against the delays possibly imposed by legal action by Eddie Krul.

Reputation issues

From an ethical and reputation viewpoint, RDC not only needs to consider the amount of influence each stakeholder has but also the **impact upon each group**. There may be disapproval from society if the **adverse impact on vulnerable stakeholders appears particularly great** and RDC may face protests or political pressure. It is therefore also important to identify stakeholders such as the Save the Birds pressure group who hope to use this threat to reputation to pressurise RDC.

Conflicting stakeholder claims

It is important to be aware of all stakeholders when, as here, the claims of influential stakeholders are likely to come into **conflict**. In order to have a clear rationale for deciding between stakeholder claims, RDC needs to assess the **relative influence** of each stakeholder upon the project and where disagreements are likely to occur. It can then try to minimise the threat of disruption from stakeholders by trying to **resolve the disagreements** between them.

(c) **Stakeholder claim**

A stakeholder is any person who **affects** or is **affected** by the activities of an organisation. A claim is the **outcome** that the **stakeholder seeks** or the outcome which would **benefit the stakeholder most or harm it least**. This therefore brings in claims by stakeholders who do not understand or cannot voice the claims that they have, for example here the rare birds.

Eddie Krul

Eddie Krul's claim is that RDC should avoid his farm. The **legitimacy** of his claim is based on the **fairness** argument that his farm has been **owned by his family** for four generations and the **economic argument** that he provides local employment opportunities. Since he **understands his claim** and is able to **voice his concerns**, he is clearly able to enforce his claim.

Local government authority

The **legitimacy** of the local government authority's claim is based on its being given the power by law to **grant or deny planning permission**. Its decision on whether to use its claim appears to have been determined by the **economic benefits** that would accrue to the region. Since the local government authority has the power to influence how the investment is undertaken, arguably it has **not made good use of its claim** in that it has not expressed an opinion and not required RDC to implement effective safeguards to protect the bird colony.

Bird colony

The legitimacy of the bird colony's claim is based on the **threat to its existence**. However there may be concerns that RDC will **fail to recognise this claim** because the birds **lack the ability to understand their claim and cannot vocalise it themselves**, although the pressure group can advocate it for them.

42 Lobo

Marking scheme

			Marks
(a)	½ mark for each way briefly described	3	
	1 mark for each relevant point made	5	
			Max 8
(b)	2 marks for explanation of technological risk	2	
	2 marks for each problem at Lobo discussed. ½ mark for identification only	4	
	2 marks for comment on shareholder confidence	2	
			8
(c)	2 marks for each fundamental principle identified and discussed. ½ mark for identification only.	6	
	1 mark for each relevant point on awareness of public interest	3	
			9
			25

(a)   (i)   **Resignation**

A director may voluntarily resign, giving written notice of his or her resignation.

Not offering himself/herself for re-election

When the director is due to stand for re-election under provisions in the company's constitution for retirement by rotation, the director may decline to put his or her name forward for election again.

Not being re-elected

A director may stand for re-election but not be re-elected.

Disqualification

A director may be disqualified from holding office, either through provisions in the company's constitution, or by the courts or authorities.

Dismissal from office

A director may be dismissed from office for misconduct or incompetence, or for prolonged absence.

Insolvency of company

A director may leave office if the company becomes insolvent or is not able to pay for the services of a director.

(ii) **Not being re-elected**

The best way would be for Frank to **continue in office until his contract expires** and the other directors then not to recommend that his contract be renewed. This is the best solution for the following reasons.

Natural termination

It brings his term of office to a natural end. Forcing him out before the contract expires could be **complicated and involve the board in a time-consuming legal dispute**. It may be difficult to show objectively how Frank failed as a director.

Cost

Assuming Frank is not entitled to compensation if his contract is not renewed (rather than being terminated prematurely), then allowing Frank to remain in office for nine months may be the **least costly option**. Lobo will still have to pay his salary, but will not face a large compensation claim or the possibility of significant legal costs if a dispute goes to court.

Damage limitation

Lobo is able to ensure that Frank's actions **do not have any more adverse impacts on it**. He can be placed in a non–critical role as has been suggested. Alternatively he could be sent on **gardening leave**, agreed absence until his term of office expires.

Responsibility of other directors

Allowing a natural ending also **avoids disputes about the extent of Frank's responsibility** compared with how much responsibility the rest of the board has for what has happened. The situation is certainly unclear. In law, directors are entitled to place some reliance on the expertise of other directors or expert third parties that they employ. However the board has a **collective responsibility** to supervise the activities of individual directors and ultimately a joint responsibility for major decisions taken. The decisions Frank took were too important to be made by a single director.

(b) **Technological risk**

Technological risk is the **risk of damage to an organisation's interests through problems or limitations with the technology it uses**. Strategically it can mean that the business does not achieve its objectives due to the inability of its technology to **support what it is trying to achieve**. Technological risk can also mean **disruption to the company's operations** such as data loss caused by failure of the technology or the choice of technology that is impractical for operational purposes. Technology may mean information technology or it can extend to engineering and designs.

Problems leading to technological failure

Technical errors

Frank made a **serious technical error** which resulted in a **systems misspecification** and choice of a system that was **not fit for purpose**. It could not handle loads that would normally be placed on it and thus it failed. The shareholders might be less inclined to blame the rest of the board for the technical errors, as the other directors reasonably relied on Frank's expertise. However they might question how someone who was capable of serious technical errors came to be appointed in the first place to such a significant role.

Purchasing

Frank was allowed to make the purchasing decision alone rather than **involve others in the company**. Shareholders may blame the other directors for their failings here. The decision to purchase should have been made collectively rather than being left to Frank. The rest of the board should have considered the advice of Frank carefully, but asked him to **demonstrate that he had considered alternative systems** and the **reasons for his recommendations**. The other directors could also have obtained other views and perhaps insisted that the recommendations be made by a project team rather than a single person.

Lack of testing

The problems over the purchase were enhanced by a **failure to test the system properly** when it went live. A pilot run would have picked up problems and avoided the disruption. Again the shareholders may query the lack of direction from the rest of the board. Shareholders may believe that the pressures to implement the system quickly demonstrated **generally poor planning**. The board should have been discussing the situation regularly and this should have highlighted the need for enough time to be taken to ensure the system would work. Shareholders may also again query the lack of supervision over Frank, that the other directors **allowed the system to go live without obtaining evidence** from Frank that it would work properly.

(c) **Professional competence and due care**

Frank made a major technical error that resulted in an incorrect specification being made and hence the wrong system being chosen. This was **not the sort of error** that someone of his experience occupying a senior position **should have made**. In addition he did **not have his calculations checked** by someone with sufficient expertise. Proper checking would have meant that the error was identified before it could cause damage.

Objectivity

Frank showed a lack of objectivity by **totally relying on the advice of an old friend whose judgement** may have been biased or may not have had the knowledge necessary to make the best recommendation. Frank **did not show any scepticism about his friend's recommendations**, obtain independent evidence about the system or discuss its purchase with anyone else. Frank **did not consider alternatives**. He should have considered at least three solutions to ensure the system chosen was a good choice for Lobo.

Professional behaviour

Frank demonstrated a lack of professional behaviour in that he overrode normal purchasing procedures. He **failed to consider alternatives**. He also was **reckless** in forcing through the implementation of the system without adequate testing procedures to ensure that it worked properly. Procedures in these areas are an important part of control systems, ensuring that the organisation obtains value for money and makes purchases that are fit for purpose.

Acting in the public interest

Expectations of society

Those that call themselves professionals, whether professional accountants or engineers, are given a place of privilege in society. They can differentiate themselves because of the expertise they claim to possess, obtaining work and being able to charge fees at a particular level because of the value that they are meant to provide. In return for this privileged position, society has expectations that it expects professionals to fulfil, including the **ultimate expectation to act in the public interest** at all times.

Professional expertise

In order to deserve the title, society has the expectation that individuals who call themselves professionals should have the **expertise** to support that claim and demonstrate that expertise in the actions they take and the decisions they make. Frank should have taken steps to ensure that those who relied on his expertise were not mistaken in doing so.

Stakeholders

Society also expects that professionals will act in a way that serves the interest of legitimate stakeholders and **does not jeopardise those interests by bias or negligence**. Here the legitimate stakeholders would have included customers and employees who were adversely affected by problems with the system.

43 Hum and Hoo

Marking scheme

		Marks
(a)	2 marks for explanation of ethical threat	
	2 marks for explanation of ethical safeguard	
	2 marks for each importance factor identified and discussed (max 6)	
		8
(b)	2 marks for explanation of environmental audit	
	2 marks for each point of assessment of environmental reporting (max 4)	
	2 marks for each point of assessment of environmental audit (max 4)	
		8
(c)	3 marks for explanation of public interest in the context of prof. services	
	2 marks for each relevant point on audit committee (max 6)	
		9
		25

(a)   **Ethical threat**

Any factor which may reduce the effectiveness of a professional person's ability to act in the public interest without threatening independence can be counted as an ethical threat.

Both the ACCA and IESBA Codes of Ethics identify five ethical threats: self-interest, self-review, advocacy, familiarity and intimidation. Since external auditors conduct their work on behalf of shareholders and provide them with an independent auditor's report, it is particularly important that auditors are free from ethical threats.

Ethical safeguard

Any measure put in place to to prevent the occurrence of an ethical threat is an ethical safeguard. Safeguards can be either wide-ranging, imposed on the profession as a whole by legislation or regulation, or they can be devised by individual firms.

Benefits of ethical safeguards

Hum and Hoo are facing a number of ethical threats with regard to the provision of non-audit services, not least of which is the threat to independence. They need to put in place effective safeguards to protect the firm and its staff and these safeguards need to be transparent.

Having safeguards in place will enhance the trust placed by the shareholders in the audit firm and will demonstrate that independence remains undiminished. Without their good reputation, the role of accountants and auditors can be called into question.

Finally, having safeguards in place will enable the firm to deliver both audit and non-audit services without facing the difficulties imposed by ethical threats.

(b) **Environmental audit**

The purpose of an environmental audit is to give assurance that the information provided in the company's environmental report gives a true and fair view of the environmental policies and performance during the reporting period. Items in the environmental report can include the use of resources such as energy and water, commitment to using renewable sources of energy, carbon emissions, waste and recycling policies and achievements.

Demonstrating environmental sustainability

As Cheery Hoo correctly states, environmental reporting tends to be voluntary and does not come under a specific accounting standard. It is therefore up to the company to decide how much it wishes to disclose in an environmental report. The more disclosure, with measurable inputs, outputs, recycling targets and outcomes, etc, the easier it will be to audit the results as the success of environmental policies will be tangible.

The company may have aspirational targets in its report, for example a commitment to researching the feasibility of renewable energy, which will be harder to audit. The problem with aspirational targets is that the company could face criticism of pandering to the green movement without making any real steps towards sustainability in real terms.

The environmental report should enable a company to demonstrate its green credential as long as what is reported is measurable, is supported by reliable data and can therefore be audited.

(c) **Public interest**

To act in the public interest means to act for the collective wellbeing of society as a whole. Accountants should serve the interest of their own clients, shareholders, governments and other stakeholders. Accountants need to be aware that, when conducting an audit, they need to be impartial and unbiased because they are employed by shareholders to act on their behalf. It is important for the public at large that accounts are true and fair and that auditors express an independent view that is professional and unbiased.

Approval by audit committee

Some codes of corporate governance, such as Sarbanes-Oxley, specify that some non-audit services can be provided by the external audit firm but only with the express consent of the client's audit committee. There is similar provision in other codes regarding the acceptability of external auditors taking on non-audit work for their audit clients.

Suitability of audit committee

- The audit committee is responsible for the independence of the external audit and is in a position to make a judgement as to whether non-audit work could jeopardise that independence.

- The presence of non-executive directors (NEDs) on the audit committee will improve impartiality as they have no vested financial interest in the company.

- It is the responsibility of the audit committee to represent the interest of the shareholders in the face of any vested interest executive directors might have in the short-term performance of the company.

The audit firm itself is responsible for determining whether providing non-audit services would constitute a threat to independence. If the client is a public interest entity, such work is expressly forbidden by the ACCA Code.

44 Mahmood

Text references. Chapters 4 and 9.

Top tips. Pay particular attention to the verbs used in the requirement; this gives an indication of the intellectual level and therefore the depth expected in the answer.

Easy marks. Explanation of Kohlberg's levels.

Examiner's comments. This question dealt with an employee's ethical dilemma over concerns about product quality, and the potential implications of whistleblowing.

Part (a) asked how Mahmood might act if he was acting with Kohlberg's conventional and post-conventional assumptions. Most candidates that attempted this were able to explain these two terms, but fewer were able to link the two motivations to behaviours that Mahmood might adopt. The central point here was that if Mahmood was conventional in his morality, he would see the moral position as being to comply with his orders as an employee and he would certainly therefore not inform the press. But if he were post-conventional, he might see a higher or universal good in not deceiving the public, in which case he might go to the newspaper. Post-conventional behaviour normally incurs a high personal cost for the person adopting that behaviour and in this case, the high cost would be borne by Mahmood himself and his colleagues, all of whom might lose their jobs.

Part (b) was not done very well overall. The requirement was to construct a case for Mahmood to take the matter of the use of the inferior meat to the newspaper. This involved carefully considering the ethical issues that the use of the meat raised but some candidates used the Tucker or the AAA framework to attempt to make sense of it. Such attempts were not well-rewarded because they failed to construct the case as the requirement asked for. Both Tucker and the AAA framework are ethical decision-making tools and so were not suitable for this task. To 'construct' is a level three verb in terms of intellectual outcome and is one that P1 candidates should prepare for. Practising these requirements from past papers is, of course, an excellent way of preparing for requirements such as this one.

The final requirement, part (c), was based on the notion of externally reporting on internal controls. The point here is that a reporting requirement, especially if underpinned by statute, can affect and drive internal behaviour. When a company has to externally report on internal controls, it is necessary to convey the robustness of internal controls to shareholders and to include compliance reports as a part of that reporting. The inclusion of inferior meat in Tzo's products is in part because of weak internal controls and so the need to convey their robustness to shareholders would help to prevent such failures. This requirement was not done well by many candidates. Some seemed to think it was about Sarbanes-Oxley and some answered by listing the benefits or characteristics of internal controls, both of which were incorrect approaches.

ACCA examiner's answer. The ACCA examiner's answer to this question can be found at the back of this kit.

Marking scheme

		Marks
(a)	2 marks for each explanation of Kohlberg's levels 2 marks for each explanation of how Mahmood would act	
		8
(b)	2 marks for each relevant argument	8
(c)	2 marks for each relevant argument	9
		25

(a) **Conventional ethical behaviour**

The three stages of ethical development according to Kohlberg are: pre-conventional, conventional and post-conventional.

In a conventional ethical response the person facing an ethical dilemma will comply in full with the rules that apply or with the instructions that have been given. For Mahmood this will involve doing exactly as he has been ordered to do by his manager. There is no need for him to think beyond this; in his place in the hierarchy it is sufficient for him to comply with the instructions from higher up the organisation.

A post-conventional response involves looking beyond laws and regulations and to consider universal principles of ethics such as justice, fairness, compassion and decency. In adopting this approach Mahmood might think he has a moral duty to inform customers that inferior meat is passed off as a premium product by Tzo Company and that this is based on a conscious decision by the board of the company (ie it is not accidental).

Mahmood has voiced his concerns within the company but has had no satisfaction; in order to act on his higher values his only option is to inform an external source such as a newspaper. He should be aware, however, that such action often comes at a high cost, in this case the potential loss of employment for himself and for his co-workers.

(b) **Ethical case**

It is clear from the scenario that the company is deliberately misleading its customers, and as an employee Mahmood is part of this deception. Although the inferior meat is not necessarily a health risk, it is not acceptable that customers are paying for one thing and are getting another.

The board of Tzo know what they are doing as this is a decision made by them, so Mahmood is unlikely to find a sympathetic ear in the higher echelons of the company. Raising the issue internally could be risky as Mahmood could lose his job.

There is also the issue of reporting to external agencies; reports are being falsified and again the board of directors is aware of this practice. External agencies such as those responsible for ensuring the quality of meat products are acting in the public interest so deceiving them is a very serious matter.

The company is not acting truthfully with regard to its shareholders, employees, customers, external agencies and the public as a whole. The damage to reputation when, perhaps inevitably, the extent of the deception is revealed, will be considerable.

(c) **IC report and preventing the fraud**

External reports on the effectiveness of internal controls are intended to convey the robustness of a company's internal controls to an external audience, usually the shareholders. In order to prepare the report the company must have in place the necessary systems and information sources; the mere existence of these can help in controlling behaviour of employees and management.

The board must take control of the process and be responsible for the system of internal controls; they are then less likely to abuse or over-ride those controls that are in place. Reports on internal control create accountability for ensuring that the controls are operating properly and that quality is maintained throughout the production process.

With adequate and properly monitored controls in place, the use of inferior meat would not be possible without disclosing that fact; failure to disclose or making a false claim would be in breach of regulations.

A report on the effectiveness of internal controls requires the directors to explain the processes used to assess the effectiveness and to comment on any deficiencies found. As the report is subject to auditor review the auditors will need to be provided with a full audit trail and evidence to support the assessment of the directors.

From the point of view of Tzo their reputation and the trust of shareholders and customers is at stake if they fail to address this potentially high risk situation.

45 Rosey and Atkins

Text references. Chapters 1, 11

Top tips. CSR is a relatively new part of the P1 syllabus, and the examining team has written an article on this topic. Make sure you keep up to date with such articles as they provide an excellent resource for your studies.

Easy marks. Discussing competing stakeholder claims should be within the capability of a well-prepared candidate.

Examiner's comments.

The case in question 2 was about Rosey and Atkins (R&A), which was based on a real life investment company based in Europe. Its strategy was to invest in many of the country's largest companies and it had over two million clients who invested in the funds managed by Rosey and Atkins. The case explains how the company invested in Natcon, a national house builder, in order to build affordable homes in certain locations. The case goes on to explain how Natcon bought land near the University of Housteads and that this had given rise to some debate about the use of the land.

Part (a) asked candidates to do two tasks. The first was to distinguish between private and institutional shareholders and many candidates made a good attempt at this. The second, slightly more ambitious task was to discuss the agency problems brought about by R&A holding investments on behalf of clients. A typical weak approach was to define agency but this was not what was required. Because R&A holds funds and clients buy parts of those funds, a number of agency issues arise because the clients do not themselves own the shares directly.

Part (b) examines a relatively new section of the study guide (E2d) on CSR strategy and strategic CSR. There was a technical article on this and so it was disappointing to read many answers that did not seem to know what these two terms meant. The first task in this requirement was to explain the difference between these two terms. The second was to construct the argument that the purchase of Natcon was an example of strategic CSR. This task was less well-done by many candidates, perhaps because they were unsure of the difference between the two terms. Obviously it was important to know the difference between these terms before this question can be meaningfully answered. This underlines the importance of studying the technical articles as they relate to P1.

Part (c) asked about stakeholders. The requirement contained two tasks. The first was to explain how stakeholder claims are sometimes in conflict (meaning that different stakeholders want mutually-exclusive outcomes for an organisation and therefore one must 'win' and the other therefore loses. The task was then to 'assess the competing claims' (as discussed in the case scenario) of the local government authority and the University of Housteads. Many candidates were able to address the first task but others only weakly addressed the assessment of the competing claims of the two stakeholders. A common approach was to explain the claims of the two stakeholders without meaningfully discussing the competing claims.

Marking scheme

		Marks
(a)	Up to 3 marks for distinguishing between private and institutional 2 marks for each relevant point on agency issues	
		7
(b)	Up to 2 marks each for explanation of CSR strategy and strategic CSR to a maximum of 4 marks Up to 2 marks for each relevant argument	
		10
(c)	2 marks for explanation of stakeholder claims in conflict 2 marks for evidence of understanding of the Mendelow (power/interest) matrix 2 marks for assessment of each of the two stakeholders	
		8
		25

(a) **Private and institutional shareholders**

Shares in public listed companies are held by a range of individuals and institutions. In most stock exchanges, it is convenient and relatively cheap to buy or sell shares (usually on an internet-based application) and many individual people often buy and sell shares in companies in this way. A second type of shareholder is the institutional shareholder. This is an organisation, rather than an individual, and accordingly, the number of shares held is usually much higher than individual 'private' shareholders hold. Some investors buy shares directly in companies through the stock exchange whilst others purchase a small part of a larger fund, such as that at R&A.

Institutional shareholders tend to be large financial institutions with large capital sums and include pension funds, insurance companies, banks, and specialised investment companies. They have many clients buying into a certain fund, such as the one at R&A, and this fund is then managed in some way with the agreement of the clients who have placed money into that fund. The fund attracts a management cost (to pay for the transactions and the fund management costs) which is deducted from the gains (or losses) made.

Agency issues and institutional shareholders

The agency problem exists whenever there is a separation between the ownership and management of a company. It is called a 'problem' because it is partly the role of management to ascertain the wishes of the shareholders in order to most effectively manage the strategy to maximise shareholder satisfaction.

The agency problems are potentially more complex with institutional shareholders than when private shareholders buy shares directly in companies.

Because R&A owns shares on behalf of clients, the final shareholders are one stage removed from the shareholdings. In other words, the R&A clients might find it more difficult to convey their preferences to the companies they hold shares in and must effectively delegate this responsibility to the fund manager employed by R&A. This means that individuals or organisations who buy into R&A funds do not receive company information for each of the shares held by the fund and not everything which the individual companies do may meet with the expectations of each client of the fund. In addition, it is difficult for the boards of those companies to determine the wishes of the clients because they are 'concealed' behind the fund manager and the confidentiality systems of R&A.

There are many shareholders who are members of each fund. Although it is likely that they all share the general objective of capital growth, there may be disagreements on corporate social responsibility (CSR) matters such as the extent to which R&A should be investing in house building companies in order to deliver a certain social good. A shareholder seeking, for example, to maximise long-term returns might not see the purchase of the house builder as a priority or necessarily one which can add most value to their portfolio. In this regard, because the R&A client is a member of the R&A fund, no client would have a direct voice in supporting or challenging company policy (on CSR or on other strategic matters such as the purchase of Natcon).

The shares held in a certain fund might change over time as some shares are purchased and others are divested by the fund manager. This means that the client (the investor in the fund) might not know the identity of the companies the fund is currently holding. Unless the investor is very active, by say, checking the composition of the fund on a weekly basis (usually on the internet), it is likely that they would not know which shares they indirectly own and this would restrict their ability to hold principals to account, even if this was their intention and desire.

(b) **Distinguish between CSR strategy and strategic CSR**

To have a strategy for CSR is to have a set of policies which guide and underpin CSR activities. This means that some causes or areas of activity are favoured over others, in line with the strategy adopted. So, for example, a company might have a policy to invest in some communities or charitable causes and not others. The policy or strategy may be agreed based on a number of issues: perhaps the preferences of the employees, the preferences of senior people in a business, or the preferred outcomes may be chosen based on strategic concerns.

When CSR is undertaken to maximise its effects on the long-term economic benefit of the business, it can be described as strategic CSR. When CSR activities are strategic, they generally support the main business areas of the business. So a financial company such as a bank might favour financial education causes whilst a medical supplies company might prefer medical or nursing research causes or overseas medical efforts. It would be seen as strategically wasteful to use CSR to support activities which are not aligned to the core activities. An assumption underpinning strategic CSR is that all assets in a company belong to the shareholders and so all activities, including CSR, should be configured in such a way as to support shareholder value.

Argument that the purchase of the house builder is strategic CSR

The purchase of the house builder is described in the case as a departure from R&A's longstanding strategy of investing in listed companies as part of its holding of passive funds. In arguing that it is nevertheless strategic and therefore in the long-term economic interests of the R&A shareholders, several points can be made.

The case scenario describes a 'shortage' of low cost housing and whenever demand exceeds supply, prices rise. This has the capacity to make the prices chargeable for the new properties higher than might be expected and the large reserves of land (land bank) are also likely to increase in value over time if demand continues to exceed supply. So although it may be described as a CSR measure by R&A, it is likely that substantial returns may be made on the investment at the same time

As with other CSR initiatives, the development of affordable homes may make some *reputational capital for R&A*, especially as it frames its purchase in terms of meeting a social need. If the housing developments are conveyed to the public as R&A exercising its social responsibility, it may increase the company's profile generally, and also enhance the favourable perception by which R&A is viewed. These joint effects may make it more likely that people will invest in R&A either as shareholders or clients, thereby ensuring the company makes an economic return on its CSR.

Because R&A is an investment company which purchases shares but does not control the companies it invests in, the outright purchase of a company represents a diversification of its business activities. It could be argued that such a diversification represents a strengthening of the robustness of R&A's business as it means that risk and return become more widely spread.

(c)   Stakeholder claims are the outcomes sought in a given situation by a specific stakeholder. If a stakeholder has a voice (such as a university, a local government authority, a trade union, etc), then the claim can be articulated clearly in terms of which outcome is being sought. If it does not have a voice (such as future generations), then its claim is less certain and the best outcome is not always clear. Stakeholder claims are often in conflict. This means that two stakeholders want different outcomes in a certain situation. The university in the case does not want new housing to be built whilst R&A and the local government authority are both in favour of the development. This is an example of stakeholder claims in conflict because both preferences cannot be accommodated; one must 'win' over the other.

In any stakeholder situation, including those which are in conflict, the influence can be ascertained by the Mendelow matrix. This is one way of mapping the influence of stakeholders. Identified stakeholders are assessed according to their relative power and interest. Those stakeholders with the highest combination of these variables are those with the most influence over outcomes.

The local government authority has a higher structural power than the university because of its ability to grant or withhold planning consent. This is a statutory power devolved to local government authorities from central government, although it is usually required that local consultation be entered into before final approval is granted. It also has limited power as a shareholder of R&A and possibly some influence as an investor in R&A's funds. As an external stakeholder being an authority interested in the construction of low cost housing and both a client and a shareholder of R&A, there are considerable conflict issues. It has a social obligation to see the development approved as this will allow lower cost housing to be built where most needed. The local government authority's interest in the activities of R&A therefore derives from two sources: its interest in providing low cost housing and its concern for the profitability of the R&A company in which is holds shares.

The university has less power over the planning decision because it has no statutory power, is not a shareholder in R&A directly and has a lesser investment in R&A's funds than the local authority as an R&A client. It is likely that the views of such an important local institution would be taken into account, however, because a successful university is important in the development of Housteads as a town. The local government authority must balance the claims of a number of stakeholders when taking decisions of this type, including the economic interests of R&A. The interest of the university is *over the spoiled view from one of its buildings* (sometimes referred to as a visual amenity). The university is of the opinion that the new houses will reduce the view over countryside currently enjoyed. The weight given to the value of the view over and against the social value of the new housing development to the local government authority and the local community is an ethical matter and one which, in this case, seems to have been decided in favour of the development.

46 Pulpo

Text references. Chapters 4, 9, 11

Top tips. The application of ethical theories features often in the P1 exam and you should not only be familiar with them but should also be able to apply them to the scenarios in exam questions.

Easy marks. Part (c) on internal control should not cause any problems as this is a core part of the syllabus.

Examiner's comments.

The final question on this paper included themes on environmental reporting, Kohlberg's levels of moral development and internal control. The case scenario was about Pulpo, a local pulp and paper factory which has been criticised for its own local environmental performance. Mary Wong, who cared about the company's environmental impact, acted as a whistle blower because of the company's suspension of an emissions target.

Part (a) was based on Kohlberg's analysis and it contained two tasks. The first was to distinguish between conventional and post-conventional ethical responses. There were some excellent answers to this whilst some others just produced a general description of Kohlberg's framework which was not what was required. The second task was to explain, with reasons, which ethical approach Mary Wong took in her decision to publicise the change in emissions targets. Because this required Mary Wong to question the value of the current management and because she acted alone in publicising the changes, she acted in a post-conventional manner. It is often the case that post-conventional behaviour attracts a personal cost to the person so acting, and in this case, Mary Wong was sacked for her behaviour. Many candidates were able to identify her post-conventional behaviour but fewer were able to discuss the reasons for this which was also required by the question. It may be the case that some candidates, upon seeing 'Kohlberg' in a requirement, assume that all they have to do is reproduce the framework to get the marks but this is not so. Again, candidates needed to carefully study the question to see what is being asked for in the requirement and then crafting their answer in line with what is being asked for.

Part (b) was a 'construct the case' requirement. This requirement is very similar to the verb 'justify' or to argue for something with supportive evidence. Candidates were required to construct the case for Pulpo to publish its own environmental report for local consumption, mainly because of the local stakeholders who had concerns over the factory's environmental performance. A common, if weaker, performance was to discuss environmental reporting in general terms but not to construct the case for Pulpo to produce its own report for local consumption because of its own local challenges. There were some excellent answers to this requirement, however and it was a pleasure to see those.

Part (c) asked about the importance of internal control in managing Pulpo's environmental performance. The relevant point here is that a number of important internal control measures need to be managed, and information obtained, to enable the environmental footprint to be managed and reported upon. Again, there were two tasks in the requirement. The first was to explain the meaning of internal control. Some candidates repeated a list of the benefits of internal control (safeguarding assets, etc.) but this was not the correct approach: the requirement was to explain the meaning of internal control which was not the same as listing the benefits. The second task was to discuss why a sound internal control system was necessary in managing Pulpo's environmental footprint, and this necessitated a discussion of the role of internal control in underpinning many of Pulpo's internal functions and reporting. This second task was less well done by some candidates.

Marks

(a) 4 marks for distinguishing between Kohlberg's levels
1 mark for correct identification of the level Mary adopted
2 marks for each relevant point of reason

Max 9

(b) 2 marks for each relevant argument made and developed

8

(c) Up to 2 marks for explanation of internal control
Up to 2 marks for each relevant point on IC controlling environmental footprint

8
25

(a) **Kohlberg's levels of ethical development**

Kohlberg's three levels of human moral development are the preconventional, the conventional and the postconventional. Each level is characterised by certain beliefs about what an ethical act is and the extent to which conventional rules and regulations should be observed.

At the conventional level, morality is understood in terms of compliance with either or both of peer pressure/social expectations or regulations, laws and guidelines. A high degree of compliance is assumed to be a highly moral position. A person who is ethically engaged at the conventional level will consider it important to learn the rules and expectations which apply to them and then comply in detail. These can concern legal rules, social norms and accepted standards of behaviour.

At the postconventional level, morality is understood in terms of conformance with 'higher' or 'universal' ethical principles as perceived by the person being considered. Postconventional assumptions often challenge existing regulatory regimes and social norms, and so postconventional behaviour is often costly in personal terms. The nature of the 'higher' ethical principles is subjective and specific to the person.

Mary Wong's behaviour

Mary Wong would have been considered conventional if she had considered it an ethical 'good' to comply with her instruction to maintain the confidentiality of the data. The case, however, describes a situation in which Mary Wong acted according to a postconventional motive. Several aspects of her behaviour can be cited in support of this.

She did not comply with the terms and conditions of her employment, which would have prevented her from making any information public. The company's preference to keep internal information confidential to itself was presumably intended to prevent too much external scrutiny from local communities whilst maintaining a good performance against environmental targets. A conventional ethical response would have been to have maintained this confidentiality in the belief that compliance with existing rules, regulations and constraints was the ethical good.

But Mary Wong believed that some things were more important than obeying rules, however well-intentioned those rules may be. Having taken her concerns to the highest authority in the company and receiving no satisfaction, she judged it a greater good to disregard the constraints of her contractual terms and conditions, and expose what she saw as an injustice to the wider community. Her belief was likely to be concerned with their right to know about how the emissions might affect them, and as someone who had a strong internal motivation for environmental matters, her outrage outweighed her concern for her job.

Mary Wong paid a high personal price for her actions by being dismissed from her job. Those acting from a postconventional motivation often manifest this by disobeying or exceeding existing regulatory constraints (such as by organised disobedience, whistleblowing, etc). It is therefore common for such people to be sanctioned, either by the state, by an employer or by whichever organisation or group is affected by their actions. They assume for themselves an ethical position higher or more important than those of others and, accordingly, often bear the disapproval of the majority.

(b)   **The case for Pulpo to publish an environmental report**

Given the recent problems which Pulpo has been having, there is a strong case for increased environmental disclosure directly relating to Pulpo. The first point to make is that the company already gathers data on environmental matters to supply to the parent company for its own group environmental report. This means that the systems must therefore be in place to produce environmental data and so the *marginal costs will be relatively modest*, and mainly concerned with drafting information pages and having them published on the website.

It will increase the appearance of transparency at Pulpo, and help to repair the damaged relationships with the residents' association and the newspaper. Mary Wong's disclosures clearly angered these groups and so a lack of trust is likely to exist towards Pulpo as a result. Measures capable of restoring trust and legitimacy include increased disclosure and efforts to increase the transparency of the company, especially to those who have been historically critical of it.

An environmental report framed in terms of explaining the inputs, processes and outputs, including waste, would help Pulpo to explain its business model and possibly provide information to address the environmental challenges. These might include helping to offset criticisms about the smell and the water pollution which are perceived to be a problem by local residents. If, for example, the company provides a full explanation of why fumes are generated and what those fumes are, whilst perhaps not fully satisfying residents, they may at last understand why they are necessary.

The publication of environmental information may help to improve the local reputation of Pulpo, which appears to have had some recent reputation problems. If it wishes to continue to enjoy the support of the local community, from which it presumably draws a lot of its labour, its reputation locally will be important. If a company such as Pulpo begins to lose the implicit or explicit support of the local community, it may suffer in terms of being able to recruit employees and in terms of local support when, for example, building planning permission is needed or similar developments which may have an impact on the local environment.

(c)   **Explanation of internal control**

At its simplest, an internal control is any action or system put in place by management which will increase the likelihood that organisational objectives will be met and assets safeguarded. Internal control measures are put in place to control the internal activities in an organisation so that they achieve the purposes intended. By having internal activities co-ordinated and configured appropriately, with means of measuring and reporting on compliance levels, waste (ie non value-adding activity) is minimised and efficiencies are gained which increase the effectiveness of the organisation in meeting its strategic purposes.

Internal controls and environmental footprint

Internal controls are important in controlling all internal activities, including the systems and procedures which underpin Pulpo's environmental footprint.

One of the most obvious ways in which internal controls are necessary for controlling environmental footprints is in the operational controls which measure and determine the input consumption and the production of emissions. It is only by the accumulation of accurate environmental consumption and emissions data that the footprint can be identified and therefore monitored, scrutinised and improved. Internal controls capable of making these measurements (say in terms of energy, water and raw material consumption, and waste emissions) are therefore essential in measuring and therefore controlling the environmental footprint.

Internal controls can also be used in the management of the plant and equipment which is used in the production of pulp and paper. The case says that the ageing equipment in the factory is a source of increased emissions, and this implies that the maintenance and replacement cycles of machinery is a major factor in Pulpo's environmental footprint. Internal controls which measure the efficiency of the factory equipment, how much material it consumes and how much waste it produces can be measured. This data, in turn, can be used to adjust maintenance and replacement times to help control the environmental footprint.

Sound internal controls are a key part of the normal efficient management of operations. They are also necessary for producing accurate information upon which regular reporting is based. These make internal controls able to act as an 'early warning system' for any inefficiency in environmental systems which help to control the environmental footprint. By having an effective continuous monitoring of internal systems, there will be an automatic awareness of targets and early signs of any internal threats to the meeting of those targets.

47 Plantex

Marking scheme

				Marks
(a)	Up to 2 marks for a description of the concept.			
	Up to 3 marks for an explanation of rights.			
	Up to 3 marks for an explanation of responsibilities.			
			Max	7
(b)	Up to 3 marks for description and evaluation of each person using Gray, Owen & Adams positions on CSR.			6
	Only 1 mark if the position is only described.			
(c)	(i)	1 mark for each <IR> advantage to Plantex described up to a maximum of 4 marks.		
		1 mark for each <IR> advantage to stakeholders to a maximum of 4 marks.		
				6
	(ii)	Up to 6 marks for explaining the importance of the capitals used in <IR>.		6
		½ mark for identifying the capitals only.		
				25

(a) Corporate citizenship is an approach which can be adopted by any business with the aim of shaping its core values so that they more closely align the decisions made each day by its directors, managers and employees with the needs of the society in which the business operates.

There are three principles which take into account successful corporate citizenship:

(i) Minimising any harm caused to society by the decisions and actions of a business, which could include avoiding harm to the natural environment as well as the social infrastructure. The very nature of Plantex's business operations means that it is promoting health and well-being among wider society through the development of life enhancing pharmaceuticals.

(ii) Maximising any benefit created for society as a consequence of normal business activity. Any successful business will stimulate local economic activity and increase employment, but a good corporate citizen will do this with greater sensitivity to its environmental and social impacts.

(iii) Remaining clearly accountable and responsive to a wide range of its stakeholders, thereby combining business self-interest with a greater sense of responsibility towards society at large.

By embracing the corporate citizenship agenda, Plantex is able to recognise its fundamental rights and acknowledge that it has responsibilities towards the wider community.

Rights

Plantex has the right to exist as a separate legal entity and carry out its lawful business within a society. By further extending these fundamental rights to a corporate citizen means that Plantex is able to enjoy the full protection of the law as long as it acts within the law. In effect, society grants Plantex the necessary protection under the law to enable it to develop, expand and succeed as a business.

Responsibilities

Responsibilities are the duties which are owed to society by the corporate citizen as a consequence of it belonging to that society, and thereby enjoying the rights and privileges afforded it. In order to enjoy this level of protection, Plantex must comply with all laws that affect it, and conduct its business in accordance with the society's behavioural norms.

Plantex's shareholders and management would normally determine the extent to which it is socially responsible for meeting their legal, ethical and economic responsibilities. However, corporate citizenship goes further by ensuring a better quality of life in the communities in which the business operates, while still preserving profitability and wealth creation for shareholders.

(b)   Gray, Owen and Adams argue that there is always an ethical dimension to any business decision. Consequently, when different individuals in Plantex expressed different views on the relative merits of integrated reporting <IR>, these can be described and evaluated with reference to their social responsibility positions.

Rachel Tang

The finance director, Rachel Tang, presented a very strong argument in favour of <IR> from an expedient perspective. She suggests that by providing this additional information to shareholders and key stakeholders it will strengthen the firm's competitive position and possibly attract additional investment.

However, Rachel Tang's views could also be described as those of a social ecologist because she equally recognises that a benefit of <IR> is greater efficiency in allocating scarce natural resources. The adoption of <IR>, as proposed by Rachel, would mean that decision-makers in Plantex would become more aware of their corporate social responsibilities.

Stanley Broadway

The chief executive, Stanley Broadway, takes a fundamentally different position. He considers that the extra resources required to generate <IR> information would merely deplete shareholder funds and add no intrinsic value to the business. Consequently he opposes the initiative and considers it to be an ethically irresponsible waste of shareholders' funds.

He adopts a typical pristine capitalist approach focusing on maximising profits and seeking economic efficiency. He is unable to see any merit to Plantex of producing additional <IR> information, emphasising the view that the only purpose of the firm is to maximise shareholder wealth and there has been no request from shareholders for any additional voluntary information.

(c)   (i)   Through an understanding of the connections between a business's operations and the environments in which it operates, Plantex's management is able to take more environmentally and socially sustainable decisions and allocate its scarce non-renewable resources more effectively. Consequently the information contained within <IR> enables investors and other stakeholders to better understand how a firm is holistically performing.

The following are recognised advantages to Plantex of adopting <IR>:

Decision-making. The connections made through <IR> enable investors to better evaluate the combined impact of the diverse factors, or 'capitals', affecting the business. This in turn should result in better investment decisions by the shareholders, and more effective capital allocation by the firm.

Reputation. The greater transparency and disclosure of <IR> should result in a decrease in reputation risk, which in turn should result in a lower cost of, and easier access to, sources of finance.

Harmonisation. <IR> provides a platform for standard-setters and decision-makers to develop and harmonise business reporting. This in turn should reduce the need for costly bureaucracy imposed by central authorities.

<IR> also provides the following advantages to Plantex stakeholders:

Communications. The additional information would help to strengthen communication links between Plantex and its key stakeholders. This would enable the alignment of interests between the firm and its stakeholders to be assessed and improved as necessary.

Relationships. The information will lead to a higher level of trust from, and engagement with, a wide range of stakeholders. This emphasis on stakeholder engagement should lead to greater consultation with stakeholder groups and enable the company to handle their concerns more effectively.

Accountability. Due to the broader perspective required by <IR>, both in terms of the resources and relationships which it takes into account and the longer timeframe over which value creation is considered, it makes Plantex more accountable as stewards of society's common resources, in particular human, natural and social capital.

(ii) **Capitals**

<IR> simplifies accounting information, as it dispenses with unnecessary levels of detail and focuses attention on more critical information. <IR> aims to make visible the 'capitals', resources and relationships, on which Plantex depends. It also illustrates how Plantex utilises and impacts on those 'capitals' and effectively transforms them.

There are six 'capitals' described in the <IR> framework:

1. **Financial capital**. This comprises the pool of funds available to Plantex, which includes both debt and equity finance. This description of financial capital focuses on the source of funds, rather than its application which results in the acquisition of manufactured [revenue] or other forms of finance.

2. **Manufactured capital**. This is the human-created, production-oriented equipment and tools used in production or service provision, such as buildings, equipment and infrastructure. This would include the specialist equipment used by Plantex for the development of new drugs. Manufactured capital draws a distinction is between inventory (as a short-term asset) and plant and equipment (tangible capital).

3. **Intellectual capital**. This is a key element in an organisation's future earning potential, with a close link between investment in R&D, innovation, human resources and external relationships, as these can determine the organisation's competitive advantage. Plantex depends heavily on intellectual capital as it is key to its ongoing success, developed pharmaceuticals become patented products which ultimately derive value to the firm and its shareholders.

4. **Human capital**. Is understood to consist of the knowledge, skills and experience of the company's employees and managers, as they are relevant to improving operational performance. Pharmaceutical companies like Plantex are knowledge intense businesses which rely heavily on the innovation and creativity of the talented scientists who work within it.

5. **Natural capital**. This is any stock of natural resources or environmental assets which provide a flow of useful goods or services, now and in the future. Plantex will require access to refined, pure chemicals in order to create its pharmaceutical solutions.

6. **Social and relationships capital**. Comprises the relationships within an organisation, as well as those between an organisation and its external stakeholders, depending on where social boundaries are drawn. These relationships should enhance both social and collective well-being.

48 MRA

Marking scheme

				Marks
(a)	(i)	Up to 3 marks for explanation of relativism.		
		Up to 3 marks for explanation of absolutism.		
		Maximum of 2 marks in total if no reference to the scenario.	Max	5
	(ii)	Up to 2 marks for description of deontology.		
		Up to 2 marks for description of teleology.		
		Up to 2 marks for analysis of Sarah Shue's position.		
		Up to 2 marks for analysis of Jake Neilson's position.		
			Max	6
(b)	(i)	1 mark for each governance principle assessed at MRA. ½ mark if no reference made to confidence and/or trust at MRA.		8
	(ii)	1 mark per described best practice measure.		6
				25

(a) (i) **Ethical relativism** is the broad acceptance that nothing is objectively right or wrong, but depends on the circumstances of the situation and the individuality of the person facing the situation or dilemma.

It suggests that an ethical position held by one person may be viewed as right for them, but may be wholly unacceptable to another person in the same situation. Relativism therefore insists that what is considered true by an individual replaces the search for an absolute truth by denying the existence of objective moral standards. Rather, according to ethical relativism, individuals must evaluate actions on the basis of what they feel is best for themselves.

Ethical relativism takes account of who is making the ethical decision and what their psychological, cultural and moral background is and accepts that different people will form different moral opinions of the most ethical approach to be taken in any given situation.

At MRA, the HR director appears to have taken an ethically relativist approach, because her pragmatic attitude about the need to secure jobs appears to ignore the fundamental wrong of paying a bribe.

Ethical absolutism is concerned with whether an action or conduct is right or wrong. Therefore, from the standpoint of ethical absolutes, some things are always right and some things are always wrong, no matter how one tries to rationalise them. Ethical absolutism requires that individuals always defer to a set of rules to guide them in the ethical decision-making process. It holds that whether an action is ethical does not depend on the view of the person facing the dilemma; instead it depends on whether the action conforms to the given set of ethical rules and standards.

Absolutism takes no account of who is making the ethical judgement, but defers to universal principles which should guide anyone's behaviour in the situation, regardless of their background. The finance director is a clear proponent of ethical absolutism, as he cannot agree to pay the bribe no matter what the circumstances or consequences are.

(ii)   **Deontological ethics** focuses on actions and rules and lays down criteria by which these actions may be judged in advance. In this respect it is similar to ethical absolutism, but it is primarily concerned with the decision-making process itself rather than the broad principles underpinning it. It is also accepted that the outcome of the decision taken is not relevant to the decision itself.

Deontological ethics is based on the idea that facts themselves are neutral; they are what they are and should not suggest what action should be taken. The criteria by which a situation is judged should always be independent from the facts themselves.

Teleology does not focus on any action taken or how well the action adheres to a system of rules. Teleological ethics, often referred to as consequentialism, is more concerned with the end result. The essence of all forms of teleological ethics is best expressed using utilitarianism as 'the greatest good for the greatest number'. This approach differs from deontology in that there is no set of hard and fast rules in place; actions are viewed as ethical depending on individual circumstances and the consequential effects, so is more consistent with a relativist approach.

The ethical dilemma about whether or not to pay the bribe to secure a large defence contract for MRA has been considered fundamentally differently by Sarah Shue and Jake Neilson.

Sarah is very pragmatic in her approach acknowledging that if the business is to successfully compete, it must be flexible in how it acts in different situations. She considers the $1 million payment as an undesirable necessity in this situation, otherwise the $2 billion contract would be awarded to a competitor. The consequences of this would be that

500 employees would be made redundant, probably at a cost to MRA far in excess of $1 million, and the firm's shareholders would forego the gains arising from this lucrative 10-year deal. Sarah holds a very teleological position as her focus is purely based on the consequences of the decision.

Jake Neilson supports a pure deontological approach because he chooses to defer to the principles within his professional code of ethics. Governed by adherence to strict rules, he is unable to accept that any situation justifies the payment of a bribe. He ignores the consequential effects of not being awarded the contract because he feels that paying a bribe sets an unacceptable precedent which cannot be tolerated.

(b)   (i)   Corporate governance involves establishing trustworthy relationships between various parties in the management and operation of a commercial business. Key to successful governance arrangements is the recognition of fundamental principles upon which both decisions and disclosures should be based. However, bribery and corrupt activities undermine these principles and diminish the value of corporate governance in a number of ways:

1.   **Integrity** requires that a firm conducts straightforward and honest dealings with all of it stakeholders. If MRA were to agree to pay the bribe, it would become complicit in a dishonest action purely designed to serve its own interests at the expense of others.

2.   **Fairness** suggests that a business respects the rights and views of all stakeholders with legitimate interests. It is difficult to reconcile how by paying a bribe MRA would be serving the interests of all stakeholders in an even-handed way.

3.   **Judgement** is concerned with making decisions using objective and reliable information which enhance the firm's prosperity. Although it is not explicitly stated, it could be reasonably be presumed that the directors of MRA would ultimately benefit personally from the award of the $2 billion contract, therefore they need to be very cautious when judging the situation on its merits.

4.   **Independence** further develops the principle of judgement by requiring an action to be based on objective criteria which service the interests of the firm, its shareholders and other legitimate stakeholders. The arguments presented by both the CEO and HR director do appear to be considering the employees and shareholders, but are certainly not giving due regard to the wider public interest.

5.   **Openness** suggests that actions, decisions and information should be conducted and presented in a transparent manner. The secrecy under which the MRA board meeting was

conducted fundamentally contradicts this principle, and suggests a secret agenda is being pursued. Such secrecy does not inspire confidence and trust.

6. **Probity** requires that individuals act truthfully, and without misleading others. Should the board of MRA eventually decide to pay the bribe, it will have to be done covertly, and by default it will mislead other stakeholders.

7. **Responsibility** involves having an explicit and implied duty to deal with an issue. This means that individual directors at MRA cannot allow others to decide about paying the bribe and assume they are not responsible for the decision.

8. **Accountability** holds that decision-makers are answerable for the consequences of actions. This would in effect mean that the directors of MRA will be jointly and severally liable should they decide to pay the bribe, and this could result in criminal proceedings being taken against them.

9. **Reputation** is the perception or expectation that others hold about a firm, and there is little doubt that the reputation of MRA would be damaged if it paid the bribe and this knowledge were made public.

It is clear that the MRA board faces a challenging dilemma and needs clear guidance and support to ensure that they act both legally and correctly.

(ii) The following best practice measures could be employed to both reduce and combat bribery and corruption in MRA:

1. **Top-level commitment**. The board must foster a culture in which bribery is never acceptable and it is understood that the achievement of business objectives should never be at the expense of unethical and corrupt behaviour. Consequently it should not make the $1 million payment to the foreign official.

2. **Proportionate procedures**. Procedures should be implemented which are proportionate to the bribery risks faced by the firm and its activities. These should also be transparent, practical, accessible, effectively implemented and enforced by management.

3. **Risk assessment**. A formal and documented audit of both the internal and external risks of bribery and corruption should be periodically undertaken. This should be incorporated into the firm's generic risk management procedures and reported upon annually to shareholders.

4. **Due diligence procedures**. Bribery risks can be mitigated by exercising due diligence. Any personnel operating in sensitive areas require greater vigilance; this includes all board members and any personnel involved in procurement and contract work.

5. **Communication**. Internal and external communications ensure that bribery prevention policies and associated procedures are embedded into the firm's culture and understood by everyone. Employees at all levels should undertake regularly anti-bribery compliance training so that they remain constantly aware of the risks.

6. **Monitoring and review**. Internal audit, tasked by the audit committee, should monitor and review bribery prevention procedures and recommend improvements where necessary. This control loop can then gauge if actions taken have been effective in reducing bribery and corruption at MRA.

49 Angus Fortune

		Marks
(a)	Up to 2 marks for each benefit of CPD for Angus Fortune, up to a maximum of 6 marks. Up to 2 marks for each descriptive point for effective CPD, up to a maximum of 6 marks.	10
(b)	Up to 4 marks for describing conventional level reasoning [2 marks per sub level]. Up to 4 marks for a description of conventional responses.	8
(c)	Up to 2 marks for each principle evaluated, or ½ mark if not applied to scenario.	7
		25

(a) CPD is the systematic maintenance, improvement and broadening of knowledge and skills, and the development of personal qualities necessary for the execution of professional and technical duties throughout an individual's working life. Angus, being both a company director and a professional accountant, will benefit from undertaking CPD in a number of ways:

1. CPD is concerned with maintaining his knowledge and skills base so that he remains effective in his current role by focusing on necessary competencies. This in turn will ensure that he is able to discharge his duties and responsibilities as a company director and professional, and improve overall performance in his current role.

2. By keeping his professional qualifications up-to-date, he will improve his competence in a wider context benefiting both his personal and professional roles. CPD can improve and broaden knowledge and skills to support future professional development, and so it will increase Angus's capacity to take on new and challenging roles as a director.

3. By updating his knowledge and skills on existing and new areas of business practice, like tackling internet fraud, he will be able to contribute towards the development of the company. In effect, CPD can act as a catalyst for improving and enhancing business performance.

4. By undertaking CPD, Angus demonstrates a commitment to his profession and his company. By using the networking opportunities from attending a conference, he could develop business links which will help the company in the future.

Features of effective CPD

Individual professionals should be responsible for organising and conducting their own CPD so that it meets their particular needs. This can be achieved by determining what form of training or other intervention delivers the necessary output. ACCA operates a professional development matrix to assist its members, like Angus, analyse their roles and responsibilities, and then prioritise learning needs. The matrix comprises four elements:

Planning. The process will commence with Angus analysing his current role and then identifying the competencies which are needed to deliver the required level of performance for that role. A development plan is then devised which involves prioritising elements of the role which need most attention, but also addressing any emerging areas. When Angus decided to undertake private study to help him prepare for a forthcoming assignment, rather than attending the conference, he clearly was planning his CPD around his emergent job needs.

Action (inputs). The actual CPD undertaken should satisfy the following requirements:

- Relevance of the actual learning activity to the role;
- Understanding how the learning outcomes will apply to the workplace;
- Providing evidence that the learning activity was undertaken, and in part independently verified.

If Angus had attended all three days of the conference, he would have received verification that a number of hours of CPD had been completed, whereas by studying on his own Angus can only self-certify his CPD.

Results (outputs). On completion Angus should compare the results of his learning activities against his development plan, and self-assess whether the CPD has met his pre-determined objectives. Clearly this is only possible some time afterwards, and in the case of Angus could be gauged against how successful his future performance proves to be, particularly if he is given an assignment dealing with tackling internet fraud.

Reflection. As part of the iterative CPD process Angus should examine the evolving requirements of his role, as these will become a key feature of future planning. This ensures that all CPD he undertakes in the future remains relevant to his role and the needs of the company and its clients.

(b) Laurence Kohlberg devised a theory which explained the rationale behind human moral reasoning, where he was less concerned about the actual decision taken but rather the cognitive process which arrived at each judgement. Kohlberg described the development of individual moral and ethical reasoning through three discrete levels: pre-conventional, conventional and post-conventional.

At the conventional level, individuals aim to conform to social norms, so when deciding on a course of action they will consider what is expected of them and act accordingly. The level can be further viewed in two ways:

- **Interpersonal accord and conformity.** Sometimes referred to as the 'good boy–good girl' orientation, this stage focuses on living up to social expectations and accepted roles in society. Due consideration is given to the expectations of peers with an emphasis on conformity when arriving at an appropriate decision.

- **Social accord and system maintenance.** As individuals progress towards this more advanced stage of moral development, focus shifts towards a sense of duty and responsibility by observing law and order, adhering to rules and respecting authority.

In the situation described in the scenario where Angus Fortune decides to absent himself from the conference for reasons of his own choosing, and despite this being contrary to the instructions of his employer, it places the conference organiser in a difficult position. However, by applying Kohlberg's conventional level thinking it will make the decision taken by the conference organiser easier to arrive at and justify.

When Angus was booked onto the conference, a legally binding contract was made between his company and the conference organisers to deliver the content of the conference to Angus for the price paid. When Angus signed into the conference but then immediately proceeded to leave, it became apparent that he was trying to mislead his employer that he actually attended the conference. So the dilemma facing the conference organiser was whether or not to report Angus's absence to his company.

If conventional thinking uses interpersonal accord and conformity, the conference organiser may take a precedent from the expectations of his colleagues, who are likely to consider it to be a core part of their role to report known absences. However, assuming social accord and system maintenance is adopted, the conference organiser may decide it to be his/her moral duty to report the irregularity to Angus's employer, not simply because of any contractual obligations but because they believe it to be the right and proper thing to do.

(c) Angus Fortune, being a member of ACCA, is required to observe the highest standards of professional conduct and comply with the ACCA *Code of Ethics and Conduct*. This code contains, among other things, the key fundamental principles which should be used to govern acceptable behaviour. Consequently, when Angus chose to spend his time at private study rather than attending the conference as per Peter's instructions, these underpinning ethical principles could be used as criteria to evaluate the ethics of his decision.

Professional behaviour. As a qualified accountant Angus should avoid any action which may discredit the profession. The ACCA Rulebook requires that all members show due consideration towards everyone they come into contact with in a professional capacity. So it could be argued that by misleading the conference organisers Angus had acted discourteously, and unethically.

Integrity. Integrity implies honesty, truthfulness and fair dealing with all parties. By taking the decision not to attend the conference, Angus is clearly misleading his employer and acting dishonestly as it is contrary to explicit instructions. Therefore this represents a clear ethical breach of trust.

Professional competence. All professional accountants have an ongoing duty to maintain their professional knowledge and skills base at a level required to ensure that clients or employers receive a competent professional service. It could be reasonably argued that when Angus elected to undertake his own CPD through carefully considered private study, he demonstrated a commitment to update his knowledge in a way which would be most useful in his current role. His motives appeared honourable and in the best interests of his employer rather than purely serving his own interests.

Objectivity. Objectivity requires that an individual should not allow bias, conflicts of interest or the undue influence of others to compromise their professional or business judgement, and infers independence of action. Angus certainly did not act because of the influence of others as his decision was made from his own reasoning, and with the best of intentions.

50 WSK

		Marks
(a)	Up to 3 marks for evaluating difficulties of risk perception. 1 mark for a definition only. Up to 2 marks for each problem with the subjective risk perception described, up to a maximum of 6 marks.	8
(b)	Up to 2 marks for each stage explained, up to a maximum of 4 marks. 1 mark for each benefit to WSK explained, up to a maximum of 4 marks. 1 mark for each use of information by the WSK board, up to a maximum of 4 marks.	10
(c)	Up to 3 marks for explaining environmental footprint. Up to 2 marks for each activity contributing to WSK's footprint to a maximum of 6 marks.	7
		25

(a) Risk perception is the belief held by an individual or collectively by a group like the WSK scientific team, whether rational or irrational, about the chance of a risk occurring and/or about the extent, magnitude, and timing of its effects.

Risk perception is subjective by its very nature, which means it is difficult to accurately quantify either the likelihood or scale of impact of any identified risk. Therefore the 'best guess' made by the team of scientist about the likelihood of a major earthquake in the vicinity of the factory was highly subjective and unverifiable. This presented the board of WSK with the difficult decision of whether or not to accept the expert findings of the scientific team, and then act to limit the potential damage and harm which would be caused by such an event.

The board would need to commit a high level of expenditure to mitigate any damaging consequences of an earthquake. However, the limited data available offers no empirical or verifiable evidence that an earthquake near the factory will occur in the foreseeable future. However, if an earthquake struck, the consequences could be devastating to WSK and the local population if there were a leak of toxic chemicals into the atmosphere or water system.

There are many uncontrollable natural variables which influence the likelihood and impact of an earthquake. Therefore the range of outcomes varies from a minor quake which would not even be noticed to a great earthquake for which no precautionary measures could avoid its damage to the factory, including the release of toxic chemicals into the environment.

The board has to decide if they are happy to live with the unknown risk of a major earthquake or to commit significant resources to minimise the impact on the company and its natural environment. The risk perception of the scientific team does not help to clarify their dilemma.

(b)   Environmental audits are structured investigations which can quantify an organisation's environmental performance and position by a systematic and objective evaluation of how well the company, its management and equipment are performing with respect to the primary aim of aiding the natural environment. An environmental audit comprises three key stages:

1.   Agreeing suitable metrics for the organisation, which detail what specifically should be monitored and the best way this is to be achieved. In the scenario of WSK, this is likely to be concerned with the measurement of any chemical leakages from its manufacturing processes and storage facilities.

2.   The audit team then measures actual performance against the agreed metrics using a representative sample related to the level of risk and the confidence required in the results. A mixture of compliance and substantive testing will provide the necessary evidence. Clearly the audit will have to be very thorough at WSK and the sample large because of the dire consequences of a toxic leak.

3.   The auditors then compile a report to the board on their findings, detailing the levels of compliance achieved together with any significant breaches they identified. They would use the evidence gathered to determine and recommend improvements to the internal control systems. At WSK, this could include tightening safety procedures for handling chemicals and strengthening their storage arrangements.

Benefits of an environmental audit

The benefits will vary depending on the objectives and scope of the environmental audit, but include:

Improved decision making. WSK will have a better appreciation on how to meet its legal obligations. The audit will enable the board to understand their specific environmental risks and ensure that appropriate measures are taken to manage these risks. For WSK, this is particularly important because of the nature of their business, as they produce and store toxic chemicals. The board can use the findings of the environmental audit to determine the likelihood of a chemical leak, particularly in the event of an earthquake the scale of which cannot be accurately determined.

Resource consumption. Understanding how the company interacts with its natural environment allows it to more efficiently use its resource, particularly non-renewables. This clearly demonstrates that the company is environmentally responsible, and for WSK this could offer a distinct competitive advantage over similar firms by demonstrating that they aware of their impact upon the environment and taking action to mitigate any harm by having a robust environmental policy.

Compliance. An environmental audit will provide independent evidence that the organisation is meeting its specific statutory requirements. This focuses management attention on the inherent risk of non-compliance and ensures that internal control systems are fit for purpose and improved if recommended by the audit report. At WSK, a systematic investigation of the environmental risks associated with all of its chemical processes could help to avoid future breaches and potentially save the company significant money.

Importance of good quality information

The information obtained and used should be *relevant* for specific decision-making rather than producing too much information simply because their information systems can 'do it'. A good way for the board of WSK to ensure that they are not overloaded with erroneous information to clearly specify to the internal auditors the clear objectives of the environmental audit, this way they will only receive reports on matters they are concerned with [like the probably earthquake].

Information needs to be *timely* if it is to be useful. Although the board of WSK has no evidence that an earthquake is imminent, the perceived risk from the expert scientific team suggests that they may need to take action sooner rather than later. Therefore the environmental audit and its findings should be reported without delay.

As far as possible, information should be free from errors, however, accurate information is usually a function of accurate data collection. In the situation described in the scenario it is unlikely that the data collected will be totally accurate, so the board of WSK need to guard against expecting 'perfect' information as it is more important for the environmental audit information to be up-to-date and based on known assumptions.

Information should come from *authoritative* sources to ensure its reliability. It is good practice to quote the source used – whether it be internal or external sources. If estimates or assumptions have been applied, these should be clearly stated and explained.

The board does not have time to trawl through masses of information, so it should be clearly presented, not too long and communicated using an appropriate medium. The environmental audit report should provide a summary of the main findings and resultant recommendations so that its key features can be understood by all board members; however, it might also need to be presented by the auditors so that any questions arising from the report can be answered.

(c) A company's environmental footprint assesses its impact on the natural environment in a variety of ways, including:

- Its resource and energy consumption, with particular concern for unsustainable resources;
- The amount of waste produced and disposed of; and
- The harm or damage caused by emissions to the environment.

Ideally every organisation, commercial or otherwise, should work towards attaining a zero environmental footprint by conserving, restoring and replacing those natural resources used in its operations whilst at the same time taking necessary measures to eliminate pollution and emissions.

To assess the environmental footprint at WSK, it is necessary to consider the core activities of its factory's operations, which can be broadly categorised in the following four ways:

- Delivery of raw materials to the factory from its suppliers will involve their transportation, which by definition will cause fuel consumption and pollution. Care should be taken to order quantities so that the number of shipments required is minimised.

- Chemical production processes which will involve consumption of energy and possible chemical spillages, which can be minimised by following well-designed procedures.

- Storage of finished goods inventory, which must be undertaken with great care to minimise the risk of toxic chemical leakages.

- Shipment of finished goods to customers by rail and road will have an environmental cost associated with the transportation. Rail is generally considered to have a lower environmental footprint than road haulage because of the quantities which can be shipped out by one vehicle.

Once the elements of the environmental footprint have been assessed and evaluated, WSK can take action to reduce the overall impact on the environment, and introduce robust measures which would mitigate the environmental risks arising from the effects of an earthquake.

51 Rowlands and Medeleev

Text references. Chapters 1, 6 and 11

Top tips. Note that (a) required you to identify external stakeholders; employees are internal, not external, stakeholders, so you would not have gained marks for discussing them. However you would also have gained marks in (a) for discussing the claims of shareholders. Remember that there is a **two-way** relationship between the organisation and its stakeholders.

The examiner described (a)(ii) as more ambitious and the question does offer scope for misinterpretation. The term stakeholder claims means what the stakeholder wants R&M to do, not how much power the stakeholder has, for example First Nation not wanting the dam to go ahead.

In (b) the examiner has used the word assessment quite narrowly, to mean considering the likelihood and consequences of each risks (a stage described as risk profiling in the BPP Study Text). This use of assess is problematic, as in Chemco in the pilot paper the examiner takes risk assessment to mean the whole process, from initial identification of risk through to risk consolidation. The clues in this question are that only 6 marks are available, which would not give you time to describe all stages adequately, and the mention of the diagram means that you should concentrate on the profiling stage.

The requirements in (c) clearly oblige you to make good use of the information in the case. Although clearly many risks affect R&M, you shouldn't have discussed them if they weren't mentioned in the scenario.

The requirement in (d) to prepare a statement to be read out at a general meeting will have surprised a lot of students, although the examiner has emphasised that students may be asked to prepare different types of business communication in the exam. The examiner explained what he wanted to see in this statement:

'It would begin with a formal introduction and provide an overview of what he was going to cover. As he spoke, the sections would be connected with narrative designed to make the speech sound convincing, logical and persuasive. It would obviously not contain bullet points (how would they be delivered in a speech).'

(d)(ii) in a sense is really the heart of the question; the examiner chose a big civil engineering project to test environmental implications, asking students to explore the pros and cons of the development. Make sure that you can define sustainability. Bear in mind that flooding habitats and farmland is an environmental impact, whereas forcing First Nation out of their homes is a social impact and therefore you would not have gained marks for discussing it.

The main point to bring out in (iii) is the conflict between the two important ethical principles. Confidentiality is needed for protecting commercial interests.

If you struggled with (e), think about the prevent-detect-correct categorisation of controls; that may help you generate ideas. In our answer culture is a prevent control, budget reports and quality inspections are detect controls and the discussion on dealing with problems is effectively saying that it will be difficult for R&M to remedy delays if they occur.

Easy marks. There are a few easy marks for definitions and descriptions of the risk analysis framework in (b), but overall the question is quite a rigorous test of your application skills.

Examiner's comments. Most candidates did well on (a), although some confused internal and external stakeholders. In (b) some students confused the likelihood-consequences matrix with Mendelow's mapping of stakeholders.

In (c) some students failed to address the specific risks described in the case; the scenario gave details of three risks with enough information to make an assessment, and those risks were what was rewarded: 'It was thus crucial to analyse the case. If a requirement asks candidates specifically to use information from the case as this one did, then they will not be awarded the best marks unless they do what the question requires.'

The professional marks in (d) could make the difference between passing and failing. Students should spend some of the time allocated to professional marks planning how they are going to fulfil the question requirements. Most students were able to define what sustainable development was, although a few thought sustainability referred to R&M being able to continue as a going concern. In (d)(ii) the requirement to discuss environmental and social sustainability implications meant that the question was not concerned with the fate of 'First Nation' nor the archaeological sites.

(e) was about how the lack of internal controls in subcontractors could delay the project's progress. Many students gained marks for discussing issues such as the subcontractors having different corporate cultures, structures and control regimes to R&M.

Marks

(a) (i) 1 mark for each relevant point made on definition of stakeholder — Max 2
1 mark for each relevant point made on definition of stakeholder claim — Max 2
0.5 marks for each stakeholder correctly identified — Max 2

6

(ii) 1 mark for a brief description of each claim — Max 4

(b) 1 mark each for recognition of impact and probability as the two variables — Max 2
1 mark each for explanation of each variable in context — 2
2 marks for a correct diagram (axis labelling may vary) — 2

6

(c) 1 mark for identification of each risk — Max 3
2 marks for assessment of each risk (1 for impact, 1 for probability) — Max 6

9

(d) (i) 1 mark for each relevant point made — 3
(ii) 1 mark for each environmental impact identified (2 positive, 2 negative factors) — 4
1 mark for description of each up to a maximum of 4 — 4

8

(iii) 1 mark for each relevant point on the 'normal duty of transparency' — 3
1 mark for each relevant point on the importance of confidentiality in the case — 4

Max 6

Professional marks for layout, logical flow and persuasiveness of the answer (ie the professionalism of the statement) — 4

(e) 1 mark for each difficulty briefly identified and explained (half mark for mention only)

4
50

(a) (i) **Stakeholder**

Stakeholders are any entity (person, group or possibly non-human entity) that can **affect or be affected by** the achievements of an organisation's objectives, here to build the dam. The relationship is thus **bi-directional**.

Stakeholder claim

Stakeholder claims mean the **demands** that stakeholder interests make upon organisations, based on the view that the impact of companies is so great that they have responsibilities to different sections of society, not just to shareholders. Management has to decide on the **legitimacy and relative strength** of different stakeholder claims.

Four stakeholders

Four stakeholders are:

- Government of the East Asian country
- Stop-the-dam
- First Nation people
- Banks

(ii) **Stakeholder claims**

Government of the East Asian country

The government is the most important **primary stakeholder** in the development, since without its desire to invest in the dam, the project would not go ahead. The government wants the project completed **on time and to budget**. The government evidently believes that the project will service the

greater good of the whole community and also the wider world, and this outweighs the detriment suffered by some other stakeholders.

Stop-the-dam

Members of the Stop-the-dam group are **active stakeholders**, seeking to prevent the dam being built on the grounds that its **negative environmental and social footprint** will be greater than the benefits derived from changing to hydroelectric power. The group would argue that its interest in environmental matters means it can make an **informed assessment** of the consequences of the project. The imperatives to protect the environment mean that it has the right to protest if the project is wrongly given the go-ahead.

First Nation people

The First Nation people are **narrow, involuntary stakeholders**. They too do not want the dam to proceed and wish their current lives to continue. They are protesting that they have had **no say in a decision** that has a fundamental impact on their lives.

Banks

Banks are also **primary stakeholders** since they will be providing the funding that R&M needs to invest in the dam. They wish to provide the funding at a level of **risk** to themselves that is **consistent with the return on lending**. It is clear here that banks are not only concerned about the risk of default; they are also worried about the **threats to their reputation**.

(b) **Risk assessment**

Risk assessment involves considering how significant risks are. This means considering the **likelihood** of risks materialising and the **consequences** of risks materialising, the hazard involved.

The organisation has to **profile risks**, compare them on the basis of their likelihood and consequences. This should indicate to the business the action that should be taken to tackle risks and also **prioritisation** – which risks are the high likelihood, high consequences risks that must be tackled first.

Likelihood-consequences matrix

Consequences (hazard)

(c) **Disruption to the project**

The Stop-the-dam pressure group could take the action described of blocking access to the site, and hiding in tunnels and then having to be evicted before work could continue. This clearly represents a risk to the **progress of operations**, involving delays to the actual work, and staff having to spend time dealing with the protestors.

The **risks of disruption materialising** appear to be **high**, as the Stop-the-dam pressure group is being organised to disrupt the project. The **consequences** may be **low to medium**, depending on the tightness of timetables to complete the dam (is any allowance at all being made for delays from external sources). The consequences will also be influenced by the measures that the country's government is prepared to take to support R&M.

Treatment of First Nation people

The First Nation people are likely to try to undermine the project by highlighting the adverse impact on themselves and the environment that the dam will have. This poses a **reputation risk** to R&M. It may be more difficult for R&M to find business partners, since some may wish to demonstrate their commitment to corporate social responsibility by declining involvement in a questionable project.

The **likelihood** of this risk materialising seems high, as clearly the First Nation people have **strong reasons for protesting**. The **consequences** are **less likely to be high**, since sub-contractors, for example, would have strong business reasons for involvement in such a large project.

Financial risks

The financial risks that R&M faces are that the banks may be reluctant to lend sufficient money to invest in the project, not only because of fears about **bad publicity**, but also **concerns about the viability of the project**. This risk will be more significant if **additional finance** is required during the project or existing finance needs to be renewed; banks will have additional evidence to make their decision and as a result finance may not be available at that point.

The **likelihood** of these risks materialising can be assessed as **low to medium**. It may depend on the **risk attitudes of banks**, how easy it is to discover which banks are financing the project, and also whether the project keeps within budget limits. The **consequences** of finance not being available are **high**; the project will not be able to begin if no finance is available and R&M may expend substantial resources without full reward if funding is withdrawn midway through the project.

(d)   (i)   **Chairman's statement at the annual general meeting**

Good morning. Thank you for attending this Annual General Meeting.

I am speaking to you today to explain our **potential involvement in the Giant Dam project**. I understand that as shareholders, many of you are naturally interested in our involvement; not only is this project one of the largest R&M has ever undertaken, but I know that many of you are concerned with the **impacts upon the environment** that this project will have. I therefore feel that I should demonstrate why this project reflects R&M's commitment to sustainable development.

Because of the **sensitivity of the project**, obtaining the finance necessary has not been straightforward. Therefore I shall also explain issues surrounding the project's funding and our relationship with lenders.

Sustainable development

I shall begin by clarifying what is meant by sustainable development. Sustainable development means investing in developments that will **safeguard the needs of those living in the future as well as those living in the present**. Society has to try to ensure that those living the future have the opportunity to experience the same quality of life as those in the present. Key issues in sustainable development are energy, usage of land and natural resources and waste emissions.

(ii)   **Implications of the Giant Dam project**

Resource depletion

One of the most important benefits of the project is that it means that the country can **rely on hydroelectric power and not fossil fuels**. This has important sustainability implications. Future generations will have **equal opportunities** to our own to use hydroelectric power. On the other hand the supply of fossil fuels is **finite**; if we continue to use them, they will eventually be exhausted and hence unavailable to future generations to use to maintain their lifestyle.

Global warming

The burning of fossil fuels also has a significant impact upon the environment, **inevitably releasing greenhouse gases** and hence **contributing to global warming**. The government places a high priority on **meeting its obligations to reduce carbon emissions**. Effective worldwide action is needed if carbon emissions are to decrease. We believe governments will need to support major projects like the building of the dam to make a sufficient impact on the amount of carbon produced.

Impact on natural environment

At the same time your board is aware that the dam will **destroy several rare plant and animal habitats** and may therefore result in a **wider loss of balanced environmental conditions**. We do regret this. We are also sensitive to the view that building the dam maintains the economic sustainability of the human race by providing a supporting power source, but does so at the expense of the sustainability of other species. However we believe that this needs to be weighed against the **impact on the natural environment of global warming**, with threats to many plants and species being well-documented.

Loss of productive farmland

I also acknowledge that building the dam will **destroy farming land** that has been occupied by the First Nation people for hundreds of years. We acknowledge that the loss of productive farmland will impact upon the country's ability to sustain itself by producing its own food. Again however the long-term **consequences of global warming** could well be much more significant, resulting in the loss of a lot of productive land due to flooding or erosion.

Conclusion

As you can see there are arguments for and against development. Our client, the government, has weighed the arguments up and believes that the country's future prospects and also wider global interests are best served by going ahead with the dam. **Choosing to change the source of power**, the government believes, will make a greater **contribution to sustainability** than preserving the original environment at all costs, which is the belief of the Stop-the-dam pressure group. I emphasise that in accepting the contract, the board is happy that the decision has been made on the basis of full and fair consideration by the government.

(iii) **Confidentiality**

In order to undertake this significant project, we shall require **significant funding**. We shall have to incur early project costs before receiving our first payment from the government. We shall also from the start of the project need to pay our sub-contractors.

It seems likely that we shall only be able to obtain this funding if we keep the **identity of the finance supplier confidential**. Even if this condition is not built into the terms of lending, your board feels honour bound to comply with it. Without the guarantee of early funding we cannot begin this project.

Conflict with transparency

Your board is however aware that keeping the **identity of the finance supplier secret** conflicts with our normal duty of **transparency**. We are committed to disclosing all relevant information to you, not concealing any information that may affect your decision-making, in order to **retain your confidence**.

As suppliers of equity finance, we understand that you will wish to be aware of what the **other main sources of business finance** are and what conditions are placed on its availability; it impacts upon the **risk of your investment**. However although our accounts give details of the length and conditions attached to loan funding, they do not normally disclose the identity of individual lenders.

Resolution of conflict

We believe that obtaining funding from banks on conditions of confidentiality will **minimise the risk to the project** due to lack of continuing funding. Project failure would certainly have a major adverse impact on the **market value** of the company and the **value of your investment**. We shall be taking all the steps necessary to ensure that the Stop-the-dam pressure group does not obtain knowledge of our lender.

Conclusion

I hope I have addressed all the concerns that you have about the Giant Dam project. However I shall willingly answer any questions now or separately after the meeting. Thank you for your time today; are there any questions?

Culture

The subcontractors may not have the same attitudes to risk and control as R&M. The control environment and culture may be **laxer**, with subcontractor staff being encouraged to finish jobs as quickly as possible and failure to operate controls being ignored.

Agency costs

In order to ensure that the subcontractors are working to an acceptable standard, R&M will have to review their work. Given the sensitivity of the project, it is unlikely that self-certification by the subcontractors will be strong enough evidence. R&M will therefore have to incur costs and use staff time sending staff out to check on the subcontractors' work.

Tracking progress

A number of different subcontractors may be used on the project. This will make it difficult to see if the project is within **time and budget limits**, even if the information supplied by subcontractors is reliable, and that cannot be assumed.

Dealing with problems

If problems do arise, for example time going over-budget, R&M may find it difficult to take action to remedy the situation. Subcontractor staff are not under R&M's direct control so it may not be easy to ensure that they **start working more efficiently**.

52 Swan Hill

Text references. Chapters 1, 6, 8 and 9.

Top tips. The mark guide in (a) indicates that it is possible to get 5 marks out of 10 for demonstrating understanding of Tucker's criteria. However the obvious way to demonstrate understanding is to apply the criteria to the scenario. Note that the discussion on fairness links in with the effect on stakeholders.

The key difference in (b) is between the risks that are affected by where the directors position SHC, and those that arise out of normal business activities.

In (c) we have tried to save time by using the same introduction to both sections. You would be rewarded for the introduction as part of the four professional marks. The main thing to emphasise in (i) is the responsibility to maximise profits, whilst in (ii) you need to consider who legitimate stakeholders are. Note the differing perspectives on the need for competition in the two parts.

You may have thought of various alternative disclosures in (d)(i), using your knowledge of financial accounts and corporate governance. The main advantage of voluntary disclosure is increased information provision, and it can also enhance participation by shareholders.

Easy marks. The definitions of strategic and operational risks, and the disclosures in (d), should offer good mark scoring opportunities.

Examiner's comments. (a) was the question that candidates did the best on with many achieving all ten marks. Some candidates failed to gain high marks because of a failure to relate the answer to the case or by misunderstanding one or more of the criteria. Some, for example, wrongly construed 'sustainable' as referring to the continuance of the SHC business rather than the environmental implications of the option.

In (b) there was a recent article in *Student Accountant* on strategic and operational risks by Nick Weller so it was good to see many candidates achieving good marks on the theory. It was disappointing to see that many candidates were less able to use their theoretical knowledge of strategic risk by relating it back to the case. In order to attract maximum marks, candidates had to show how the secrecy option would be a **strategic** risk and not just a general risk.

(c) was the most ambitious component of this question. Candidates therefore had to be aware of what each ethical perspective was 'about' and also to apply it to the case. This application of ethical theory to the case proved difficult for many candidates. A common approach was to attempt to make the business case for the two options and then to include a paragraph briefly providing the candidate's understanding of the two ethical stances but failing to develop those by referring to the case. Again, it is the application of ethical theories to the case that was the reason why many candidates did not perform well in (c). Candidates will usually be required to apply them in some way to get the majority of marks in P1 ethics questions.

(c) also contained 4 professional marks. Candidates should ensure they are familiar with formats. Here some candidates wrote a letter from chief executive Nelson Cobar while in other cases the answer was more like a memo. Neither of these incorrect approaches was rewarded with professional marks.

(d)(i) asked candidates to distinguish between mandatory and voluntary disclosures with examples and it wasn't surprising that most candidates were able to do that to some extent. In (d)(ii) many candidates were unsure as to the link between voluntary disclosure and accountability. Once an item is disclosed it means that stakeholders gain information on which to hold the business to account.

Marking scheme

				Marks
(a)		1 mark for evidence of understanding of each of Tucker's criteria	5	
		1 mark for application of each to case	5	
				10
(b)		1 mark for each relevant point demonstrating understanding of operational risk	Max 3	
		1 mark for each relevant point demonstrating understanding of strategic risk	Max 3	
		1 mark for each reason explaining why the secrecy option is a strategic risk	Max 4	
				10
(c)	(i)	1 mark for each relevant point making the business case	Max 4	
		1 mark for each relevant point making the stockholder (shareholder) case	Max 5	
				Max 8
	(ii)	1 mark for each relevant point making the business case	Max 4	
		1 mark for each relevant point making the stockholder (shareholder) case	Max 5	
				Max 8
	(iii)	Professional marks: up to 2 marks per part		4
(d)	(i)	1 mark for definition of each (mandatory and voluntary)	2	
		0.5 marks for each example up to a max of 2 marks per category (allow latitude for jurisdictional differences)	4	
				6
	(ii)	1 mark for each relevant point made and briefly explained (0.5 marks for mention only)		Max 4
				50

(a)   **Tucker's five criteria**

The stages of Tucker's five question model are to ask is the decision:

Profitable

Edwin Kiama is arguing that the secrecy option is the option offering the chance of the highest profits and so should be pursued for that reason. However SHC's board also needs to take into account the relationship between **profits and risks**, and consider whether the option that offers highest possible profits also involves taking unacceptable risks. Sean Nyngan's viewpoint is that the licensing option is preferable, as it offers **acceptable profit levels** in return for **zero risks**.

Legal

Clearly developing new environmentally-friendly technology in secret is legal. Apart from the risks of not filing a patent, the other legal concern may be the consequences of SHC creating a **global monopoly**. Competition authorities may well be concerned, and may have the power to force SHC to share the technology.

Fair

SHC has valued its relationship with its stakeholders in the **workforce** and the **local community**. However the secrecy decision means that **some stakeholders are likely to benefit at the expense of others**. Certainly SHC's workforce may well benefit from higher profits through their remuneration packages. However the local community may, as an **involuntary stakeholder,** suffer various consequences of SHC's attaining a monopoly such as a significant increase in traffic congestion. There is also the issue of SHC's **position versus its competitors**. Is it fair for SHC to keep all the rewards for its investment in research and development, or should competitors be given the chance to develop the sink method further and benefit their employees and shareholders.

Right

It seems very difficult to treat the secrecy decision as a morally absolute one without having regard for the **consequences**. The issue is whether the board should pursue the secrecy option if it believes certain consequences will result. Alison Manilla for example believes that SHC may not have the right to put its competitors out of business. On the other hand the **pristine capitalist** view would be that secrecy was the right option if it was the **profit-maximising option**.

Sustainable

One of the main justifications for developing the new process is that it will enable SHC to produce lower unit emissions, so in that respect the development is **environmentally sustainable**. However if the secrecy option is pursued and SHC does become the single global supplier, the **carbon footprint** from transporting the products round the world may be higher than if customers continued to be supplied by local manufacturers. SHC's decommissioning its old plant may also have adverse environmental impacts.

(b) **Strategic risks**

Strategic risks derive from the **decisions the directors take** about an **organisation's objectives** and are the risks of **failing to achieve those objectives**. They link in with how the organisation is **positioned in relation to its environment**. Many strategic risks are long-term and cannot be avoided if the company is to trade; they have **high hazards and high returns**.

Strategic risks include **longer-term risks** deriving from decisions the board takes about what **products or services** to supply, including the risks connected with developing and marketing those products. They also include risks connected with key sources of finance.

Operational risks

Operational risks are risks connected with the **internal resources, systems, processes and employees** of the organisation. They relate to the problems that can occur in the organisation's day-to-day business activities such as human error or information technology failure.

Operational managers and employees will have responsibility for **managing operational risks**, whereas **managing strategic risks** will be the responsibility of the **board and senior management**, since they are taking the strategic decisions on which strategic risks depend.

Why secrecy option is a strategic risk

Changes in processes

The secrecy option represents a **fundamental change in the method of operations**, leading to major alteration in SHC's **cost base**, the **technology** it uses and hence its **pricing policy**.

Changes in sales

The much higher volumes of production that the new process will enable may mean that SHC has to change its **distribution networks significantly**. SHC may have to move a much greater number of products to a significantly expanded number of outlets.

Place in market

The secrecy option will also **change the product market** in which SHC operates. SHC may move from being one of a **number of competitors** to a **monopoly supplier**, with a fundamental change in its **risk profile**. However its competitors could take **retaliatory action** with uncertain consequences.

Requirement for funds

The level of capital investment that the secrecy option needs means that SHC is likely to require a **major injection of long-term funds, probably debt**. This appears to mean a significant alteration in SHC's capital structure, with the company becoming more dependent on debt and possibly facing a **significant increase in its finance costs**.

(c)   (i)   **New production method**

Background

Our research and development function has recently made an important discovery connected with the manufacture of our most important product that will revolutionise production of the product. This discovery meant that your board had to take a decision that will have a fundamental impact on the future of the company:

(1)   To **develop the technology ourselves** and keep the technology secret from competitors
(2)   To **share the technology with competitors** under a licensing arrangement

Having given this decision very serious consideration, your board decided to develop the technology ourselves for the following reasons.

Business issues

Enhanced position in marketplace

We believe that implementing the new technology will lead to **significant falls in the company's cost base** and mean that SHC can **meet greatly expanded demand**. This means that SHC can move from being the market leader to taking a **dominant position** in the market, enabling us to gain **pricing power** and **guaranteeing large profit levels** for the foreseeable future. Your board believes that this is the logical outcome of acting competitively, and that our competitors would take the same decision were they to discover a revolutionary new method.

Higher customer satisfaction

We also believe that our customers will benefit through **lower prices and higher quality goods**. These higher levels of customer satisfaction should also generate **increased sales**.

Benefits to shareholders

This fundamental shift in SHC's position will, we believe, result in **significant increases in dividends** and also a major increase in SHC's market valuation and hence in the value of its shares.

Ethical issues

Responsibility to shareholders

Your board is committed to **pursuing shareholders' economic interests**, and hence seeking to maximise profits, since the shareholders are SHC's legal owners who have risked their own money by investing in the company.

Dilution of responsibility to shareholders

Your board also acknowledges its responsibility as **agents** of the company's shareholders. We believe that our loyalty is therefore to our shareholders. If we take into account responsibilities to

other external stakeholders, and as a result take actions that result in lower than optimal profits, we should be **abusing our position as agents**.

Responsibility to employees

We also believe the development offers **major opportunities to our employees**. They can benefit materially and develop their skills. This in turn will aid recruitment in future years. This commitment to our employees will also benefit the locality in which we are situated.

Commitment to competition

Your board believes that society's interests are best served by the pursuit of **economic efficiency**. We believe that economic efficiency is most likely to be attained by companies making every effort to **maximise their own performance** by pursing maximum profits.

(ii) **New production method**

Our research and development function has recently made a most important discovery connected with the manufacture of our most important product that will revolutionise production of the product. This discovery meant that your board had to take a decision that will have a fundamental impact on the future of the company:

(1)   To **develop the technology ourselves** and keep the technology secret from our competitors
(2)   To **share the technology with competitors** under a licensing arrangement

Having given this decision very serious consideration, your board decided to share the technology with competitors for the following reasons:

Business issues

Legal protection

We believe that the option to develop the method ourselves would involve overall risk levels that would be greater than your board regards as acceptable. One risk would be being unable to protect the technology. The need to keep the development secret means that we would be unable to file a patent, and hence possibly **lack legal redress** against competitors who obtained and used the technology.

Financing the development

Developing the technology ourselves would also have required capital investment that would have been larger than anything SHC has previously undertaken. This investment would initially have required a **large injection of debt finance**, raising debt to levels greater than your board deems desirable. We believe that the need to pay interest to service this debt would impact upon the funds available for distribution as dividends.

Low risk of licensing option

By contrast we believe that the licensing option can generate very significant royalties in return for minimal risk. We believe that it can generate a **smoother flow of funds** in the medium to long-term; these funds can be invested in further research and development to enhance our position as market leader.

Consequences of improvement sharing

Finally we believe that enabling our competitors to share our technology means that the process can develop quicker, since several manufacturers will be implementing the processes and **pursuing improvements**.

Ethical issues

In addition we are conscious that there are significant ethical issues connected with the decision. Your board is sensitive to these and in particular to the need to consider the interests of stakeholders whom SHC's activities significantly affect.

Responsibility to local community

SHC has always been committed to working in partnership with the local community. We felt that this partnership might be broken if SHC developed the technology by itself. To do so could have put our competitors out of business, and we are sensitive to the **increased unemployment** that might result. In addition the huge increase in sales that we believe could result from developing the new technology would lead to greatly increased activity around SHC's premises, impacting adversely on the community by for example **causing increased traffic**.

Commitment to fair competition

Your board has always been committed to **fair competition** within the industry. We believe that high customer service levels and commitment to research and development are best stimulated by a number of competitors operating within the industry. We believe that if any company, ourselves or any competitor, held a monopoly, then this would inhibit developments in the industry that benefit customers and other stakeholders.

Wider social responsibility

In addition we believe that the technology could have a major impact on the **environmental footprint of production**, significantly reducing unit emissions. This is perhaps the most important consequence of developing the new method, and therefore your board needed to consider how best to develop the technology to enhance further the positive environmental impact. We have decided that allowing competitors to share our technology is the best way to benefit society, since it will give competitors the opportunity to make further improvements, which could then be shared.

(d) (i) **Mandatory disclosures**

Mandatory disclosures are disclosures that listed companies are required to make by legislation, regulation, accounting standards or stock market requirements. In most jurisdictions the annual report should include the identity of directors and information about the directors including interests in shares. The directors should make a statement of whether the company has **complied with the corporate governance requirements** that apply to it, together with details of, and justification for, any examples of non-compliance. The report should also include **accounting information**, such as a statement of comprehensive income and a statement of financial position, and the audit report on the accounts.

Voluntary disclosures

Voluntary disclosures are disclosures that are not required by regulation but are made to **enhance the usefulness of the accounts** and **provide information of interest to key stakeholders**. Examples include:

- A **chief executive's report** providing a commentary on what has happened and the company's future strategy that is wider and more detailed than required by law or regulation

- A **social and environmental report**, setting out the company's social responsibility objectives and the progress made in fulfilling the targets it has established for itself

- Information about the policies adopted towards the company's employees including **anti-discrimination policies** and ways in which employees are **involved in decision-making**

- Details of the company's **code of business ethics**, and how it affects relations with key stakeholders such as customers and suppliers

(ii) **Wider information provision**

Disclosures covering wider areas than those required by law or regulations should give stakeholders a **better idea of the environment** within which the company is operating and how it is responding to that environment. This should enable investors to carry out a more informed analysis of the company's **strategies**, **reducing information asymmetry** between directors and shareholders.

Different focus of information

Voluntary information can be focused on **future strategies and objectives**, giving readers a **different perspective to compulsory information** that tends to be **focused on historical accounting data**.

Assurance about management

Voluntary information provides investors with further yardsticks to **judge the performance of management**, and its disclosure demonstrates to shareholders that managers are **actively concerned with all aspects of the company's performance**.

Consultation with equity investors

The voluntary disclosures a company makes can be determined by consultations with major investors such as **institutional shareholders** about what disclosures they should like in the accounts.

53 Global-bank

Text references. Chapters 1, 3, 4 and 9.

Top tips. In (a) the switch of the question requirements from levels in (i) and (ii) to stages/planes in (iii) appears to have caught a lot of students out. You need to revise it if it gave you difficulty, and watch out carefully in questions on Kohlberg for the terminology used.

There is a risk that your answer to (b) may overlap with later parts of the question, so you need to plan your answer carefully.

You may have struggled in (c) to understand what was required by the verb 'analyse', which normally means gives reasons for. Here the examiner appears to want commentary on the relationship.

(d) emphasises the importance the examiner attaches to the interests of stakeholders. The different ways in which stakeholders can be grouped is important knowledge. In questions about stakeholders, it seems that the examiner will only give marks for identifying stakeholders who are mentioned in the scenario. Thus here for example no credit would be given for discussing Global-bank's customers, even though they are an important narrow stakeholder.

In (e) it was important to respect the terms of the requirement, and only discuss the chairman's role in relation to internal control. The examiner's comments on professional marks are disappointing, as students should certainly have expected a letter as a possible format.

Easy marks. The levels of Kohlberg at the start of (a) should have been straightforward (and should be revised if they weren't). You should also have picked up without difficulty the marks in (b) for the reasons for control failures, and been able to define wide and narrow stakeholders in (d).

Examiner's comments. (a)(i) should have been 6 relatively straightforward marks for the well-prepared candidate who had not tried to question-spot. Most candidates that got (i) right also got some marks on (ii). In (iii) many candidates failed to recognise the difference between a level and a stage or plane. The Kohlberg framework has three levels, each of which is divided into two stages/planes (stages and planes mean the same thing). Some candidates assumed that the highest level (post-conventional) was the best one to say in an exam answer. This missed the point of the question which was to highlight the importance of compliance in organisations (plane 4 or level 2.2).

In (b) many candidates were able to get some marks on pointing out the internal control problems at Global-bank, even if they couldn't remember the five main causes of internal control failure from the study texts.

(c) on agency theory was probably the part of the question that was the most competently answered overall. Although only worth 4 marks, most answers correctly identified the principals and agents in the case and analysed the agency relationship.

(d) was worth 10 marks and examined stakeholder issues in the case. I wrote an article for Student Accountant on the different ways of categorising stakeholders and was disappointed that many candidates failed to either know the difference between narrow and wide stakeholders or to identify the narrow stakeholders and explain how they are affected by the information in the case. The stakeholder debate is an important part of the P1 study guide and so I would encourage candidates to ensure that stakeholders are well understood.

In (e) a common mistake in the letter itself was to misread the question. The first task in the question was not to explain the roles and responsibilities of the CEO, but rather to explain the roles and responsibilities of the CEO **in internal control**. Lists of general roles of the CEO were not well rewarded. The second part of the task was to criticise Mrs Keefer's performance, to show how her performance fell below that which would be expected or that which conforms with best practice. Of course candidates need to know what good or best practice is before they can criticise it, which is why sound theoretical knowledge underpins case analysis.

The professional marks were awarded for the structure, content, style and layout of the letter. I was disappointed to see that many candidates struggled to lay out a business letter correctly whilst others could lay out the letter but failed to use the type of language typical of a business letter. I would encourage candidates to read the article in a recent edition of Student Accountant on P1 professional marks.

Marking scheme

				Marks
(a)	(i)	2 marks for each Kohlberg level identified and explained. ½ mark for identification only		Max 6
	(ii)	0.5 marks for correct identification of Mineta's level. 1 mark for each relevant justifying point		Max 4
	(iii)	Correct identification of stage 4 in conventional level with brief explanation. 0.5 marks for identification of conventional only	1	
		Explanation of why it is most appropriate level	<u>1</u>	
				2
(b)		1 mark for each cause of failure identified and briefly explained (0.5 marks for identification only)	Max 5	
		1 mark for each internal control failure at Global-bank identified and briefly explained (0.5 marks for identification only)	Max 5	
				10
(c)		Evidence of understanding the principal-agency relationship	1	
		Explanation of principal side	Max 2	
		Explanation of agency side	Max 2	
				Max 4
(d)		Distinguishing between narrow and wide stakeholders	3	
		0.5 marks for each narrow stakeholder identified	Max 1.5	
		2 marks for assessment of the loss and refinancing on each identified narrow stakeholder	<u>6</u>	
				Max 10
(e)		1 mark for each CEO role identified and briefly explained max	4	
		1 mark for each relevant criticism of Mrs Keefer's performance linked to case	Max 6	
				10
Professional marks				
Physical layout of the letter, address and signoff			1	
Flow, persuasiveness and tone			3	
				<u>4</u>
				<u>50</u>

(a) (i) **Pre-conventional**

The decisions individuals make on ethical matters will have nothing to do with the ethical issues involved, but will instead depend on the **personal advantage or disadvantage to the individual**, including rewards, punishments and deals.

Conventional

When taking ethical decisions individuals live up to what they think is **expected of them**, by their **immediate circle**, or by society as expressed in **laws or social customs**.

Post-conventional

Individuals make ethical decisions in terms of what they **believe to be right in line with higher or absolute ethical principles**, not just acquiescing in what others believe to be right.

(ii) **Pre-conventional**

Mr Mineta appears to have operated at Kohlberg's pre-conventional level for the following reasons.

Lack of ethics

Miss Hubu's evidence that Mr Mineta **didn't believe in right and wrong** indicates that his decision-making was not influenced by whether a course of action was ethical.

Reward

Miss Hubu's evidence indicates instead that the decisions made were determined by how much **personal reward** they would bring him.

No pressures to act at conventional level

Mr Mineta **ignored internal control systems** and did not face any pressures to act at a **conventional level,** as trading rules were not enforced in his office. Instead he was encouraged to take risks in return for a trade-off of high rewards.

(iii) **Desired level**

Mr Mineta should have operated at the **Conventional level Stage 4** making decisions in accordance with the ethical norms expressed in **trading rules and internal guidance**. Stage 3 here would not be sufficient due to the possibility of office pressures to ignore the rulebook.

(b) **Poor judgement in decision-making**

Poor control decisions can sometimes be made because the **information** supporting those decisions has been inadequate.

Human error or fraud

Adequate controls may be in place, but staff may **not operate them properly** either through **making mistakes** or in **order to commit a fraud**.

Collusion between employees

A system that depends on one employee checking or monitoring another's work will be ineffective if the employees **connive together** so that the checks are not carried out.

Management over-ride

Managers may **ignore the controls in place** and instruct the staff working for them **not to operate the controls**.

Routine transactions

Control systems may be **designed to deal with routine transactions**. They may **not recognise or highlight problems with non-routine transactions or unforeseeable circumstances**.

Performance of Global-bank

Judgement

Mr Mineta demonstrated **poor judgement** by breaching trading rules.

Failure to apply controls

The controls that should have applied to all traders, **trading limits and authorised products,** were **not applied to Mr Mineta** because his trading made such large profits.

Culture

The culture in the Philos office promoted by the manager, Mr Evora, focused on **maximising profits** at all costs, even if it meant controls were **not enforced or bypassed**.

Information provision

The Philos office did not provide the information to head office that head office needed to **monitor its activities effectively**. Head office did not insist that this information be provided.

Role of head office

Head office **accepted without question the high level of profits** made in Philos, and did not investigate warning signs of potential problems, such as the persistent failure to provide information. It seems also that there were **no whistleblowing channels** that worried employees in the Philos office could use to voice their concerns.

(c) **Agency relationship**

The two parties in the agency relationship are the **agent** and the **principal,** with the agent being **accountable** to the principal.

Principals

In this situation the trustees are the human representatives of the principal, the Shalala pension fund. Their aim is to **maximise the value of the fund**, so that its members' fund values are also maximised. This means maximising the value of Shalala's investments, including its investment in Global-bank. However the trustees cannot do this by managing Global-bank itself. Instead Shalala's agents, Global-bank's directors, run the bank on its behalf and are **accountable to the pension fund**.

Agents

As agents, the directors of Global-bank are responsible for running the bank with the aim of achieving the objectives of their principals, the Shalala pension fund and other shareholders, the **maximisation of long-term value**. The directors have a **fiduciary duty** to act solely in their principals' interests and are accountable to the principals for failure to achieve objectives. Here the bank has failed to achieve the objectives of maximum capital growth because of the failure of internal controls.

(d) **Distinction between narrow and wide stakeholders**

Narrow stakeholders are the stakeholders who are **most affected** by the organisation's strategy and policies, including shareholders, managers, suppliers and important customers. **Wide stakeholders** are those who are **less affected** by the organisation's strategy, including government and the wider community.

Narrow stakeholders

Investors

The impact on investors' interests is that the **market price of their shares has presumably already fallen**. They now face a choice between paying out for additional shares to fund the losses made by Mr Mineta, or refusing to support the rights issue and increasing the risk that the company will become insolvent and wipe out their existing investment. They will presumably wish to gain more assurance before subscribing to the rights issue. The rights issue itself does not guarantee Global-bank's continued existence. If Shalala or other investors refused to subscribe to an issue that goes ahead, then their holding will be **diluted**, reducing their influence over the bank.

Employees

If Global-bank is in financial trouble, many of its employees could **lose their jobs**. Those that remain could find themselves operating under **more restrictive controls**, with **more stringent limits** being placed on their **performance-related bonuses**. Employees based in the Philos office who are found to have known what was going on could **lose their licence to trade**.

Directors

Directors who are up for re-election at the next annual general meeting may find themselves being **voted out of office**. The whole board may face a **vote of no confidence** at a **general meeting**. Even if they avoid this, they may experience **increased scrutiny and intervention by investors**. This may adversely affect their **remuneration or bonuses**. Some or all of the directors may face **local legal sanctions for** making an inaccurate statement about internal control effectiveness.

(e)

Shalala Pension Fund
1 Any Street
Alltown
12 October 20X8

Global-bank
1 Every Road
Capital city

Dear Mrs Keefer

Internal controls at Global-bank

I am writing to express the concerns of the trustees of the Shalala Pension Fund over the losses made in the Philos office and the fall in the value of the shares held by the fund that resulted from this. We do not accept your argument that what happened was a genuinely unforeseeable situation. We are sorry to say that we hold the board responsible for the shortcomings in control, and feel that prime responsibility for these failings must rest with yourself as chief executive.

We would like to define the roles and responsibilities that you should assume in relation to internal control and set out our assessment of how you have discharged those responsibilities.

Risk assessment

As chief executive you should have ensured that the board **assessed and monitored areas of greatest risk** to the company as part of its review of the company's activities. We are sorry to see that the board appeared to have **no idea of the risks** that were being borne in the Philos office, particularly since the area of derivatives trading would normally be an **area of high risk** that the board should monitor.

Risk appetite

The chief executive is **responsible for ensuring** that the activities of the company **reflect the risk appetite** that the board has established. However the situation in Philos appears to illustrate that the board's wishes were **not communicated effectively**. Mr Mineta's activities were not **regarded as those of a rogue trader in Philos,** but as being in accordance with an ethos of taking undesirably high risks to achieve large profits.

Lack of enforcement

The board does not appear to have enforced the control systems that were in place **effectively**. Mr Mineta felt that he could break trading rules unpunished and in addition Mr Evora appears to have totally **ignored normal trading rules** instead of enforcing them.

Monitoring of internal controls

As chief executive you need to ensure that you receive **sufficient information** to be able to **monitor the bank's controls** effectively and **report on its controls fairly in its accounts**. We are very disappointed that you have **failed to obtain the assurance** that controls were operating properly in Philos because of the office's failure to submit the information it should have sent to head office. We are particularly disturbed that this has resulted in an **inaccurate report** on the strength of internal controls.

Audit committee

In addition there are flaws in the bank's corporate governance arrangements that have helped prevent effective scrutiny of the activities of the Philos office. We are disturbed that **no attempt has been made to replace the two directors** who have left the audit committee, especially because this has resulted in criticisms of the effectiveness of the audit committee by the external auditors. We would emphasise that we regard the **proper functioning of the audit committee** as a key control.

Internal audit

We also are disappointed that the **internal audit function** at Global-bank has been ineffective. We regard internal audit as a particularly important part of corporate governance.

I would stress again that we are deeply concerned with the apparent failures of control that the events in Philos have illustrated. We look forward to receiving your response to the comments we have made.

Yours sincerely

Millau Haber
Chairman of the Shalala trustees

54 Mary Jane

Text references. Chapter 9 on the AAA model, Chapters 4 and 5 on internal control issues and Chapter 8 on information.

Top tips. The mark schemes for this exam are worth studying in detail. In most question parts, the examiner draws a clear distinction between demonstrating knowledge and understanding (worth perhaps up to 50%), and demonstrating the higher level skills of analysis and application.

If you couldn't remember the AAA model in (a), be warned that it was examined in the compulsory section of the paper. (Note also that the other decision-making model highlighted in the syllabus, Tucker's five questions, has also been examined in the compulsory section). In the exam, if your mind does go blank, the best method is to analyse the problem logically and hope you will gain some marks for application. If you did remember all the questions, you needed to give at least a comment to demonstrate your understanding. The norms, principles and values in Question 3 relate to care to customers, compliance with law, good governance and acting in accordance with the values the company proclaims it has.

The examiner expected you to consider the case for non-disclosure and so your answer should have considered the threat to shareholders and the company. However a note from the examiner indicated that although some credit would have been given for coherently arguing in favour of non-disclosure as the final decision, you would not have got full marks as 'alignment with the stated values of the company' required disclosure.

In (b) you will need to read through carefully to sort out all the detail in the scenario. It certainly will have helped to have read through the requirements before reading the scenario in detail, as the requirements would have told you that you need to look out for internal control failures, and that is important here as the failures you need to discuss are scattered throughout the scenario. If you did go through the process and identify the weaknesses, you would have scored well. However knowledge dumping the content of the Turnbull report would not have scored marks, as all the points you discussed needed to be derived from the scenario.

In (c) your answer needs to discuss what NEDs bring to Sea Ships and what they can do. Here technical expertise and the lack of independent scrutiny are highlighted in the scenario to help you. As with (b), just dumping your knowledge of the relevant governance report, in this case the Higgs report, and making bland general statements would not have scored marks as the justification needed to be related to the scenario.

In (d) the format of the memo should not have caused you any problems. The introduction should emphasise the regret felt at the tragedy. (i) relates to the strategy and objective setting, and monitoring roles of the board, as well as the need for external reporting to be supported by reliable information flows. There are various ways to describe the qualities of good information in (ii) and the examiner allowed leeway for different descriptions. The mnemonic ACCURATE is one checklist you can use. However (d) was not about implementing risk management and better controls, however desirable that is. If you discussed issues that were not related to information provision, you would not have scored any marks for them.

Easy marks. Hopefully your knowledge of what non-executive directors can provide and do will have helped you in (c). If you struggled to think of points, you must revise this important area.

Examiner's comments. In (a) all of the information needed to conduct the analysis was in the case scenario. Candidates that could only recall some of the seven steps did receive some recognition but it was disappointing to see some candidates reproduce the seven steps but then either ignore or misinterpret the ethical dilemma. A careful reading of the question should have indicated exactly what the requirement was to consider 'whether or not to disclose this information [about the independent consultant's report on structural changes] publicly' but some failed to recognise that this was the dilemma to be considered and thereby did not achieve high marks for this part.

(b) required a careful reading of the case but the internal control failures were relatively clear to many candidates. Some candidates missed out on some of the internal control failures at the Sea Ships Company itself (such as the failure to ensure adequate insurance cover).

In (c) candidates that based their answers on the unique governance situation at Sea Ships were rewarded whilst those that reproduced an auto-response ('strategy, scrutiny, risk and people') tended to achieve few or no marks on this question. Again, it was important to analyse the case and read the question carefully. The question was not asking about the roles of NEDs but rather the contribution they (rather than executive directors) could make given the governance failures at Sea Ships Company.

In (d) the two requirements were poorly done overall with some candidates refusing to attempt them at all. Both areas asked about were well covered in the study texts so I was surprised and disappointed that some candidates did so poorly. The range of answers on (d)(i) suggested that some candidates misinterpreted its meaning. The key words in the question were 'importance of information'. (d)(ii) was also done poorly overall but was relatively straightforward in what it was asking. However many candidates failed to see what the question was asking them to write about. Again a careful reading of each question is crucial.

One of the most disappointing things to report was the poor attempts to gain the professional marks. The question required the answers to be in the form of a memo. The various forms of narrative communication should be taught to, and learned by, P1 candidates. It was evident that many candidates were unsure of how to frame and draft a memo to management and this was reflected in the professional marks awarded. A common error was to write the answer in the form of a letter

Marking scheme

			Marks
(a)	1 mark for recognition and evidence of understanding of each question.		
	1 mark for correct application to case		Max 14
(b)	1 mark for identification of each control failing.		
	1 mark for analysis of each failing		Max 12
(c)	1 mark for recognition of each area where NEDs could improve matters.		
	1 mark per area for application to case		Max 8
(d)	(i)	1 mark for each point on importance.	
		1 mark for application of each point to case	Max 6
	(ii)	For each quality of information, ½ marks for recognition,	
		1 mark for development of quality based on content of case, 1½	
		marks per quality recognised and developed	Max 6

	12
Additional professional marks for the layout, logical flow, persuasiveness and tone of the memo	4
	50

(a)   **Step 1 – What are the facts of the case?**

The Mary Jane ship has sunk with much loss of life. This disaster could have been **prevented** if **structural changes** had been made to the ship to make it safer for the ship to operate in the rough seas of the Northport route.

Step 2 – What are the ethical issues in the case?

The main ethical issue is a conflict in responsibilities to stakeholders. Particularly as Sea Ships has stressed its ethical credentials, there is a **duty to the passengers who survived and the relatives of the victims** to make full disclosure of the circumstances to allow them to arrive at a better understanding of what has happened. On the other hand this exposes the company to a greater risk of huge damages, which will **destroy the value of shareholders' investment**.

Step 3 – What are the norms, principles and values related to the case?

The norms are that the directors have a **duty of care to passengers**, and if that duty has been breached, then passengers and their relatives have a right to know the full circumstances. Sea Ships also should have ensured **compliance with safety legislation** because of the potential risk to life of breaches. It would also be **socially responsible** for Sea Ships to disclose the circumstances so that other shipping lines could take steps to prevent a similar disaster happening with another boat. Sea Ships has claimed to be maintaining the highest standards of corporate ethics, including **integrity and honesty**.

However the directors' primary duty is to **protect shareholder value**, and **keeping the report confidential** may mean that there is less chance of a successful action for negligence and the company's future being threatened by huge fines or damages.

Step 4 – What are the alternative courses of action?

The first alternative is to **publish the consultant's report**.

The second alternative is to **keep the report confidential** and hope that there will be no leak.

Step 5 – What is the best course of action consistent with the norms, principles and values?

If the directors place any value in Sea Ships' **commitment to social responsibility**, then they should **publish the report,** whatever the consequences to Sea Ships and its directors may be. It will be consistent with the **duty of care** to customers, and it will provide other external stakeholders (other shipping lines, insurance companies, regulators) with important information that may help to prevent a similar disaster in future.

Step 6 – What are the consequences of each possible course of action?

If the report is disclosed, the consequences for Sea Ships and its directors will probably be severe. The **fines and damages** may be higher because the report provides additional evidence of **negligence**. These financial penalties may well force the company out of business and at minimum there will a severe loss of shareholder value. The **loss of reputation** may threaten Sea Ships' ability to operate the route in future and threaten the jobs of Sea Ships' workforce. The directors may be liable to prosecution on the grounds of **negligence**.

Non-disclosure may give the company a better chance of continuing, although if the **evidence of other control failures** is made public, the company and directors may be **liable anyway**. Non-disclosure by the board also carries the risk that **someone else**, possibly the consultant who wrote it, will **disclose the report**. This may result in the company and directors incurring **further liability** for non-disclosure of material evidence.

Step 7 – What is the decision?

The board should disclose the report and the circumstances surrounding their failure to act on it. This will act to **protect passengers** who travel on Sea Ships or other lines in the future, and be consistent with the company's ethical values.

The alternative of non-disclosure is very **risky**, as it is likely that the report will be leaked by someone acting according to their conscience or with a grudge against the company. Non-disclosure would also be **against proclaimed ethical and governance values** and will not protect long-term shareholder value.

(b) **Design fault**

The first control failing was that the **design fault** was **highlighted** in the consultant's report, but the **consultant's report** was **not acted upon** because it was 'lost' in the company. This suggests a **serious failure in information provision** within the company.

Problems with loading

Control systems prior to departure also were inadequate as they allowed vehicles to be **loaded wrongly** onto ships. Well-trained staff or physical controls such as better signing would have prevented this happening. These problems contributed to the time pressure that led to the disaster.

Failure to secure doors

The accident was caused by the failure to secure the doors, and the **checks** over door **security** were inadequate. A design flaw meant that no review could take place from the deck of the ship. There was no formal requirement for acknowledgement that the **doors** had been **checked**, instead reliance was placed on someone else carrying out the **check** and the **confusion over responsibilities** meant the control was not carried out.

Reporting system

The ship's reporting system relied on **reporting by exception** – assuming all was well to sail unless the bridge heard otherwise. However if communications were faulty, problems may not have been reported to the bridge. The **previous system of positive reporting** by each department head being required should **not have been abandoned** just because it was **inconvenient to operate**.

Emphasis on speed

The systems were ineffective in allowing captains to give speed of departure and sailing priority over compliance with the law. There were **no control systems** on board to prevent the ships **breaking local speed limits**.

Failure to insure

Controls also failed to operate over Sea Ships' legal department with the result that the liability was not properly insured. The legal department should have **annually reviewed the insurance arrangements** to check that they covered all liabilities and recommended **major changes in cover or terms**.

(c) **Technical expertise**

Caroline Chan's comments highlight one failing of the board, the **lack of technical expertise**. Having a technically qualified nautical officer as a non-executive director would mean that the board was better able to assess the **technical and operating implications** of **major strategic decisions** such as **operating on different routes**.

Independent input

It appears that the current board were very complacent and placed unwarranted trust in the company's control systems. A non-executive director, recruited from outside, would have the **objectivity and independence** required to **challenge the board's strategy and question the company's approach to risk management**.

Improvement in control systems

It is debatable whether the current board could be relied on to review current systems to see how they could be improved, and as Caroline Chan implies, it is poor practice to rely totally on executive directors. Strong non-executive directors can work on board committees (audit and risk) to **monitor exposure to risk** and **review regularly overall control systems**, assessing whether they were as good as the executive directors thought they were. Their outside experience could enable them to **benchmark Sea Ships systems** against better practice elsewhere and therefore recommend improvements. It would also help Sea Ships comply with **local governance requirements** for listed companies.

Legal compliance

Because of the importance of compliance with health and safety legislation, non-executive directors should focus on the company's procedures for complying with **key legislation affecting operations**. They should also review the accounts to check not only compliance with accounting rules, but also that the **narrative in the accounts** gives a **fair picture**, in particular here whether statements about corporate responsibility are warranted by actual performance.

(d) **Memo**

From: Wim Bock, CEO

To: All Sea Ships senior officers

Date: 22 December 20X9

Subject: Information on internal control and risks

(i)   **Colleagues**

I know we are all grieving at the sinking of Mary Jane and of the terrible loss of life. I realise that we all would want to send our sympathies to the families and friends of those involved.

As a result of the tragic events the board has reviewed the internal control systems. One result is that I am writing to you now to remind you of the importance of proper **information provision**.

Board requirements

The board of Sea Ships requires information of good quality in order to be able to discharge its duties effectively. The directors need to place particular reliance on information provision to support the following areas.

Strategy setting

In order to establish **effective strategies**, the directors require **reliable information** about the business environment in which Sea Ships operates. This includes information about the major issues affecting the operation of ships. This allows the board to establish **what changes in working practices or design of the ships** will be necessary if the company is to operate new routes, and to **weigh the costs of these changes against the revenues** that new business may bring.

Monitoring of activities

Governance best practice requires the directors to regularly monitor the company's **activities and performance**, the **risks** it faces and how **efficiently and effectively** the control systems respond to risk. We therefore need information on a regular basis on how control systems are operating, and whether there are any problems or inefficiencies with systems on board ships or elsewhere. If the directors are made aware of issues, then we can take action to address them with your assistance.

Reporting on risks, internal controls and corporate responsibility

The board remains committed to fulfilling the highest standards of corporate governance and ethics. One important aspect of this is transparency, including full reporting of relevant information in the company's annual report. This incorporates a **full report on risks and controls**, including information about weaknesses in control and improvements that are being made. Users of the accounts must be able to place reliance on this report if the company is to repair its reputation. They can only do this if we can provide assurance that report is based on information with a number of qualities, which I shall now go on to discuss.

(ii)   **Qualitative characteristics of information**

In order for the board to be able to make best use of the information you provide, that information must possess a number of features. The content of the information should be **clear** to the board, and the board should quickly be able to establish its **significance**. In particular the information you supply should have the following qualities.

Accuracy and reliability

Firstly to be reliable information must be **correct factually**. It must be **unbiased,** meaning that you should not try to play down news of weaknesses or problems with controls.

Timely

Information should be available when it is needed. This means **submitting routine reports on control and safety on time**. Completion of these reports should not be regarded as a bureaucratic chore but as an essential duty. Also if there are problems of which the directors should be aware, you should **report them immediately** while the directors can take action, for example problems over loading arrangements at ports.

User-directed

Information should be **clearly presented** and not **excessively long**. It should also contain **sufficient explanation of necessary technical and nautical detail** to enable board members without operating experience on ferries to be able to understand it. As already indicated, information needs to be **relevant** for board decision-making.

Complete

You must supply on a **timely basis all the information** you think the board needs to know. I would ask you to supply all necessary details of **risks, systems weaknesses and accidents**, even if you believe that you may cause difficulties for other personnel. It is essential that you do not suppress important information, however bad the news it appears to convey.

The future

The tragic loss of the Mary Jane has emphasised the importance of full provision of information on controls and risks in ensuring the safety of our ships and the commercial future of this company. I know I can rely on your full co-operation in supplying information when required and responding to information when it is provided. If any of you have any questions, please do not hesitate to contact me.

Wim Bock

55 Hesket Nuclear

Text references. Chapters 1, 7 and 11.

Top tips. A general definition of stakeholders would not have been awarded any marks in (a). The scenario makes clear in (a) who are the involuntary stakeholders. The key determinants of strength of claim are proven impact and ability to avoid that impact.

In (b) note that the requirement specified employee representatives/trade union's role in corporate governance so each point you made needed to be relevant to governance. As the answer demonstrates governance includes control systems and representatives can act within these in various ways, highlighting bad board behaviour and helping to manage human resources. The scenario makes it clear that FT's support has greatly benefited HN, but that in exchange perhaps it has used its position to force up wages and cause HPC's board to consider alternative solutions.

Your answer to (c) needs to bring out the competing objectives HN faces. Since the government is the only shareholder, these reflect the government's problems, particularly unemployment reduction versus expenditure (subsidy) reduction.

In (d) both parts of your answer needed to clearly counter NNN's arguments. There is plenty of information in the first couple of paragraphs of the scenario to support arguments by HP. (d)(i) shows how risk management builds on accurate risk assessment, (ii) corrects the impression that NNN's statements give that the footprint is wholly negative. It's difficult to do given limited time but you need to be careful that you don't give NNN opportunity to hit back – any statement about accepting risks could be twisted.

Easy marks. Any definitions in this paper, such as voluntary and involuntary stakeholders and agency should generate 2 or 3 straightforward marks.

Examiner's comments. The issues raised in the case were similar to those present in many such situations in a number of European countries and elsewhere where nuclear facilities are present. As in previous diets, the 50-mark question covered a number of sections of the P1 Study Guide.

In (a) the first task (distinguish) was done quite well in the majority of cases but after that, candidates often became confused over which stakeholders were in which 'camp'. A common mistake was to nominate the anti-nuclear group NNN as an involuntary stakeholder when it is obviously voluntary: it chose to engage with HN of its own free will.

(b) was one of the better questions in terms of candidate answers but the highest marks went to those able to show how FT had helped and challenged HPC using the evidence from the case. It was important to recognise that the union had been helpful to HPC in some respects but unhelpful in others.

In (c) most successful candidates achieved a pass mark on this part although others failed to see the difference between a government being the principal rather than shareholders.

Common errors in (d)(i) were to explain what risk assessment is rather than its importance or to fail to link the answer strongly enough with the case. Those achieving the highest marks were able to show the links with the NNN assessment and the effects that this flawed assessment might have.

For (d)(ii) many candidates were able to explain 'social and environmental footprint' but fewer were able to do well on the second task which was a level 3 intellectual outcome: to construct a case.

Despite my highlighting a poor 'professional marks' performance in previous examiner's reports, many candidates failed to approach the answer as required in order to gain all of these marks. In this case, the required format for the answer was a response statement for a website. This means it was **not** a letter or a report.

Marking scheme

			Marks
(a)	2 marks for distinguishing between the two types of stakeholder	2	
	½ mark for each voluntary stakeholder identified	Max 2	
	½ mark for each involuntary stakeholder identified	Max 2	
	2 marks for each assessment of the three involuntary stakeholders		
	(1 mark for explanation of why it is involuntary and 1 mark for assessment of claim)	6	
			12
(b)	2 marks for each relevant role identified and explained	Max 6	
	Critical evaluation		
	2 marks for each helpful/positive role identified and discussed	Max 2	
	2 marks for each unhelpful/negative role identified and discussed	Max 2	
	2 marks for conclusion/summary	Max 2	
			Max 10
(c)	1 mark for each relevant point on explaining agency relationship	Max 2	
	1 mark for each relevant point in the exploration of HPC's agency with the government of Ayland	Max 6	
	1 mark for each relevant point on HPC as a conventional company	Max 2	
			10
(d)	(i) 1 mark for each relevant point identified and 1 mark for explanation in the context of the case		Max 8
	(ii) 2 marks for evidence of understanding of footprint in context	Max 2	
	1 mark for each relevant positive social and environmental impact convincingly argued for	Max 4	
			6
	Professional marks		4
			50

(a) **Voluntary stakeholders**

Voluntary stakeholders are those who **engage with the organisation of their own free will and choice**, and who can detach themselves from the relationship.

Voluntary stakeholders in HN

They are Forward Together, HN employees, Ayland government, local authorities, HPC board and No Nuclear Now.

Involuntary stakeholders

Involuntary stakeholders are those **whose involvement with the organisation is imposed** and who cannot themselves choose to withdraw from the relationship.

Involuntary stakeholders in HN

They are the Beeland and Ceeland governments, the seal colony and the local community.

Assessment of claims

Beeland's government

Beeland's government is representing its people, and it cannot move all of them and its capital city far away from the plant. The short distance 70 km suggests that it is very possible that **low level emissions** could affect Beeland. Scientific opinion suggests that a major incident could have **serious consequences for Beeland**. The government's claim that it can be affected by the plant is therefore **strong**.

Ceeland's government

Ceeland's government also have to represent its people and some of them would be worried about the plant and their inability to move from where they are. However Ceeland's government's claim is clearly **much weaker than Beeland's**, Ceeland is **much further way from the plant** (500 km) and reliable scientific evidence suggests that even a major incident will not impact significantly upon Ceeland.

Seal colony

Any emissions from the plant could affect the seal colony and more significant incidents may destroy it. Their **dependence on the local ecosystem** means that the seals cannot move away. These factors influence the strength of the claim of the colony. However the most important determinant of the strength of the claim is how much human interests should take priority over non-human interests, which is a matter of individual opinion.

Local community

Some local citizens will have had to put up with the plant being developed nearby, but others will have moved there since and **can move away again**. The plant also provides the local community with **jobs**. The most important factor strengthening the local community's claim is that it will be the most affected by a major incident.

(b) **Role of employee representatives in corporate governance**

Support for management

When board and employee representatives interests are **aligned**, the trade unions' support for the board can **strengthen the business's case against external threats**. For example a board's case against a hostile takeover can be strengthened by trade union opposition to the potential owners.

Critic of poor governance

Employee representatives are part of the safeguards for shareholders or owners over governance, since they are in a **strong position to protest** about aspects of poor governance. For example they will be concerned about a **lax control and risk environment**, which may jeopardise health and safety. They can raise the issues of **poor communication** by directors or **failure to protect whistleblowers who report wrongdoing**.

Control over human resources

Employee representatives can be part of the control systems over the key resource of staff. Most importantly they can advocate staff's interests, and seek to ensure staff are **content and therefore productive**. They can also be involved in **communication of information to staff**, and can be used by the board to ascertain the **views of workers**.

Evaluation of Forward Together's (FT) role

Positive contribution

FT has **consistently supported HPC's board over time** on safety issues. FT has **stressed its members' role in ensuring compliance** and has supported the views put forward that Ceeland's fears are **unfounded**. This may help reassure Ceeland's government, as FT would clearly be concerned if the **risks were substantial**, since its members would be first affected by an incident.

Negative contribution

FT's **attitude** towards staffing issues has been **inflexible**. FT's demands have **driven wages up**, but FT has been **unconcerned with the impact on costs** and the need to stay within its subsidy. The views that foreign workers are not as reliable appear to **lack foundation** and are not based on a valid legal argument.

Conclusion

FT's support for the way HN is operated has strengthened the board's position over time. However FT appears to have **taken advantage of this** by driving up pay so much that the board has been forced to **recruit from overseas**. Whether overseas employees are as experienced as workers from Ayland is questionable.

(c) **Definition of agency relationship**

Agency is a relationship under which a principal engages another person (the agent) to **fulfil the principal's objectives**, and which involves **delegating decision-making authority** to the agent. The agent has a **fiduciary relationship** to its principal.

Board's agency relationship

Agent and principal

HPC's board are acting as the **agents** of its principal, the government of Ayland, the sole owner of HPC.

Accountability to electorate

In turn Ayland's government, and therefore its board, are **accountable to the electorate in Ayland**. Their principal concerns will be the taxes paid to **subsidise HN and their energy supply**.

Objectives

Determined by government

As Ayland's government solely owns HPC, it has the **right to determine its objectives**. These need not be, and are not, solely commercial.

Operational objectives

The most important objective that HPC's board has is that HN needs to be **kept operational** as it is a **key part of Ayland's energy strategy**. This increases the pressure on the board to ensure HN **operates safely**.

Political and environmental objectives

The board is working within the **objectives or constraints determined** by the government. These may change as the government approaches an election and probably will change if there is a change of government.

Social and economic objectives

One reason why HN has stayed open appears to have been that it **provides a great deal of local employment and boosts the local economy**. Ayland's government would have to provide unemployment benefits to many workers if it shut and also cope with other impacts on the area's economy. However the board also faces the economic objective of trying to find ways of **minimising the subsidy** it receives. This has meant that it has had to seek the lower cost solution of using foreign workers, reducing local employment opportunities.

Difference if private shareholders

If HN was owned by private shareholders, it would be assumed that its prime objective was to **maximise profits**. The board would therefore be concerned with **ensuring HP was profitable**. Since HP is currently loss-making, it would mean that the business would need to undergo **substantial restructuring** if it were ever privatised.

(d)   **Statement**

   (i)   **HPC's response to NNN's report**

   We are aware that concerns have recently been raised about the operations of the HN power station following the recent report by NNN. We appreciate the reasons for those concerns. However we believe that NNN's risk assessment was inaccurate and we also strongly disagree with the conclusions of the report, that HN has a wholly negative impact and should be shut down.

   Importance of accurate risk assessment

   Our own risk assessments do not support the figures published by NNN. We feel that we need to emphasise to **stakeholders** the importance we place on accurate risk assessment at HPC and therefore our belief that our assessments are trustworthy.

   Impact of problems

   The most important reason why we seek to assess risks accurately is because we are aware of the **impacts** HPC's activities could have. We appreciate that a major incident could have a devastating effect on the areas affected. We are also concerned about the impact of low-level emissions, since we understand the impact these can have on communities near the power station and on local eco-systems.

   Use of money and resources

   We are also aware that HPC **receives a large subsidy and employs significant resources** in its operations. It is vital therefore that we demonstrate that we are carrying out our activities efficiently and economically as well as effectively. Accurate risk assessment helps us do this by forming the **basis for resource allocation**. Accurate assessment ensures that most resources are allocated to managing effectively the areas of highest risk.

   Methods of managing

   We also need to carry out accurate risk assessments in order to determine **the best ways to manage risks**. It helps us decide which risks should be avoided (because their potential impact is large) and which risks should be reduced by appropriate controls (because the risk is smaller).

   Avoiding over-reaction

   Lastly our risk assessments need to be accurate because we **do not wish to cause concern** by substantially over-rating risks. We believe that the assessment carried out by NNN greatly exaggerates the risks HPC faces and has resulted in unnecessary alarm.

   (ii)   **Social and environmental footprint**

   Our social and environmental footprint relates to the **net impact** we have on local communities and the wider natural environment in which we operate. The net impact is made up of a number of positive and negative interactions. Although NNN has sought to portray our footprint as wholly negative, we believe that we have several positive impacts externally that have to be considered when assessing our net footprint.

   Employment providers

   We remain a **very large employer** in an area where employment opportunities are relatively few. Our contribution to the regional economy is thus very important, and this is recognised by many regional and national stakeholders.

   Clean energy strategy

   Nuclear energy is a **renewable source of energy** and generates a **negligible amount of greenhouse gases**. It is an essential part of the government of Ayland's **clean energy strategy**. We have to fulfil stringent legal regulations that require us to ensure that emissions from HN do not harm the local environment. The alternative to provision of nuclear energy would be the burning of fossil fuels which would generate more pollution and would eventually be exhausted.

Reprocessing fuel

We provide reprocessing facilities for nuclear fuel that enable us to provide developing countries with a much **cheaper source of fuel**. By making it available, we are therefore **promoting economic development** in these countries.

Our safety record

We would remind our stakeholders that we have **fulfilled the high safety standards** to which we are subject. The FT trade union has recently highlighted our clear safety record since the 1970s. We intend to continue to live up to these high standards.

56 ZPT

Text references. Chapters 1 to 3, 8 and 9.

Top tips. The question is based on actual details from corporate governance scandals in America about ten years ago, that led to the development of the Sarbanes-Oxley legislation, including the requirement to report on internal controls over financial reporting.

In (a) a threat to the value of shareholdings is the main reason for intervention, with most of the other reasons ultimately resulting in a loss of value. Note also the thread about institutional shareholders having the opportunity (and maybe the responsibility) to enforce their views.

(b) required you to bring out the differences between absolution and relativism clearly. In (b) an important point with the relativist viewpoint is that although Shazia weighed up her options from an ethical perspective, you should disagree with her decision. Although she was facing conflicting ethical pressures, accountants should never take bribes.

(c)(i) did **not** require a list of the corporate governance failures in ZPT. A key word in the requirement is **by**. It meant that the way you had to make your case was to give examples of the consequences of ZPT going out of business due to its governance failures. The main theme behind (c)(i), which the scenario emphasises, is the loss to innocent internal and connected stakeholders. The other theme reflects what happened in America, the potential disruption to the whole economy of a large company's bankruptcy. This links to market confidence, a key theme in (ii) along with greater accountability and mandatory reporting making it more difficult to tolerate control failures. Our answer to (iii) is mainly based on the Turnbull report. If you used a different framework, it was important nevertheless to stress the responsibility of directors, the processes of internal control and the explanation of weaknesses.

The speech needs to read like a speech, so professional marks will be awarded for tone, flow and persuasiveness. Note the weaknesses highlighted by the examiner.

Easy marks. The examiner has published a question like (a)(i) before. Definitions, such as the different approaches to ethics, should always provide easy marks in this exam.

Examiner's comments. A similar situation happened in 'real life' some years ago and so some candidates may have been familiar with some of the issues already. This does show the value of studying current cases from the business news in preparing for P1 exams as 'real life' themes are sometimes borrowed in framing exam case studies.

(a)(i) was not a requirement to define 'institutional shareholders' as some candidates did (scoring nothing for their efforts in doing so). The content should have been well-known to any well-prepared candidate. For (a)(ii), candidates had to study the case to see which factors applied to ZPT and use these to 'construct the case', which means to produce arguments in favour of investor intervention because of the identified weaknesses.

In (b) from an absolutist perspective, it is obvious that no accountant should ever be complicit in bribery, fraud or mis-statement. From a relativist perspective and this is where the case raises an interesting ethical conundrum, it maybe right in some circumstances to show compassion and to carefully consider the consequences of actions, not merely their legality. Shazia used the money not to enrich herself but to pay for medical treatment for her mother. This in no way excuses her actions but it does raise the issue of trading one ethical good (upholding her professional and legal duties) against another (assisting in the medical care of her mother).

All parts of (c) were done poorly overall. What surprised me about this is that all parts are clearly 'core' areas in the P1 study guide and whilst some candidates addressed the questions correctly and scored highly, many did not.

In (c)(i), it seems that many candidates saw the first part of the requirement but ignored the second part. So they described the nature of 'sound corporate governance' whilst neglecting the second part which was to do this 'by assessing the consequences of the corporate governance failures at ZPT'. This question is essentially probing the main purpose of corporate governance: without sound corporate governance, companies go bust, employees lose their jobs, investors lose their investments and can be financially ruined, and a number of other terrible outcomes. So the 'consequences of CG failure' was often overlooked by candidates, which meant that they failed to gain those marks.

(c)(ii) highlighted that poor internal controls were in part responsible for the situation at ZPT and that mandatory reporting to an agreed reporting framework would have made it much more difficult for the IC failures to have occurred. The accountability created by having to report on internal controls could have made it much more difficult for the ZPT management to have got away with the bad practice that they did.

In (c)(iii) the essential components should have included, in all cases, an acknowledgement statement (whose job is it?), a description of the processes (how is IC done?), it should be accurate and reliable, and, specifically, it should explain any particular IC weaknesses.

The professional marks were awarded for framing the answer to (c) in the form of a speech by a legislator. There was some evidence of improvement in candidates taking this seriously and setting out their answer accordingly, but others made errors like setting it out as a memo or letter, or else by using bullet points (in a speech?) or unlinked statements.

Marking scheme

				Marks
(a)	(i)	1 mark for each reason identified and explained (½ mark for identification only	Max 6	
	(ii)	2 marks for each point identified and argued in context (½ mark for identification only)	Max 6	
				12
(b)		Distinguishing between absolutism and relativism (2 marks for each)	4	
		Evaluation of Shazia Lo's behaviour from an absolutist perspective	3	
		Evaluation of Shazia Lo's behaviour from a relativist perspective	3	
				10
(c)	(i)	2 marks for assessment of each consequence of ZPT's governance failures (1 mark for brief explanation only)	Max 10	
	(ii)	2 marks for each argument identified and made	Max 8	
	(iii)	2 marks for each broad theme identified and explained	Max 6	
				24

Additional professional marks for the structure, flow, persuasiveness and tone of the answer to (c)

4

50

(a) (i) **Active intervention**

Active intervention by an institutional shareholder by making an attempt, for example, to change the board is regarded as a serious step, and may result in a **significant increase in agency costs**. However there are a number of reasons why it might happen.

Concerns about strategy

Institutional shareholders may intervene if they perceive that management's policies could lead to a fall in the long-term value of the company and hence the **value of their shares**. There could be concerns over **strategic decisions** over products, markets or investments or over **operational performance**. They could be concerned that management was taking **excessive risks** or was **unduly risk-averse**. Although institutional shareholders can sell their shares if they are unhappy, in practice it may be difficult to offload a significant shareholding without its value falling.

Poor ethical performance

Institutional investors may intervene because they feel the board cannot be trusted. At worst they may fear **management fraud**. They may also be concerned about the company showing **poor corporate social responsibility**. This may make it vulnerable to social and environmental risks and **harm its reputation** in the long-term.

Poor non-executive performance

Institutional investors may take steps if they feel that non-executive directors are exercising **insufficient influence** over executive management. This is particularly significant when there are concerns over the executive directors, for example a very strong chief executive.

Remuneration concerns

Another sign of limited non-executive influence may be **excessive executive pay**, with non-executive directors on the remuneration committee failing to enforce limits. Shareholders will also be concerned about executive greed and **failure to align remuneration with shareholder interests**.

Internal control failures

Intervention would be justified if institutional investors had **serious concerns about control systems**. They may be worried that control systems do not appear to have changed as the circumstances of the company have changed. They may also be worried about obvious failures, for example high-level fraud or failure to control expenditure on, and development of, major investments.

Compliance failures

The institutional investors may be concerned that they will **suffer criticism** if they are perceived as conniving in breaches of stock market requirements or governance codes because they have not taken action.

(ii) **Threat to share price and investment value**

The downgrading of the results represents a **clear threat to share price** and to the **value of the investment of institutional shareholders** and indeed all other investors. Not only were the results poorer than first announced, they also were below market expectations rather than above. A restatement of this magnitude was not guaranteed to have just a short-term effect on share price, whatever Clive Xu's views. Institutional investors should have intervened to find out why the restatement had happened.

Flaws in accounting and control systems

The restatement calls into question the **accuracy of the accounting and financial control systems.** Institutional investors should have intervened to find out why the systems supported figures used in the initial announcement that were clearly inaccurate. Institutional investors should also have aimed to find out why the auditors failed to identify the misstatement, as it appears that the **audit report may be worthless** and the accounts not therefore verified by an effective independent firm.

Senior management concerns

Again the restatement is of such a magnitude that it calls into very serious question the **competence and integrity of management**. The fact that the authorities were known to be investigating ZPT for **fraud** could have warranted intervention by itself. Even if there was no investigation underway, a misstatement of such seriousness would appear to require the **connivance of at least some of the executive directors**. Some directors, particularly non-executive directors, may have no knowledge of any fraud, but failed to identify problems and intervene. The investors should have been most concerned with the role of Clive Xu, on the grounds that his bonus was based on **artificially inflated figures,** and his failure to repay it raises doubts over his integrity.

(b) **Absolutism**

Absolutism is the view that there is an **unchanging set of ethical principles** that will apply in all situations, at all times and in all societies. The principles should be applied whatever the pressures on the decision-maker.

Relativism

Relativism is the view that a **wide variety of acceptable ethical practices** exist. The ethics that are most appropriate in a given situation will depend on the **conditions** at the time.

Absolutist evaluation of Shazia's actions

Shazia Lo's conduct was ethically correct from an absolutist viewpoint in these ways.

Concern about over-valuation of contracts

She was right to ask herself whether the valuation of contracts was warranted. As a qualified accountant, she is subject to **high ethical and technical standards**, and also **public expectations** that she will act professionally and not be associated with misleading information. Questioning figures that she thought might be wrong fulfils these responsibilities.

Reporting to the finance director

Having become concerned about the problems, Shazia was right to raise the issue with the finance director. She was acting correctly from an absolutist viewpoint in **not being influenced by the impact on her position at ZPT** if her actions were unpopular with management.

Disclosure to press

Threatening to disclose the information outside the company was also correct from an absolutist viewpoint. Again professional ethical guidance makes clear the circumstances in which the **duty to disclose takes precedence over a duty of confidentiality**. These include **false accounting,** since remaining silent would mean that the owners of the company, the shareholders, are being **defrauded**.

Relativist evaluation of Shazia's actions

Shazia's eventual action can be seen from a relativist viewpoint as follows.

Weighing up conflicting ethical outcomes

Relativist viewpoints acknowledge that because a wide variety of ethical practices exist, it is possible that the decision-maker may find that there is a **conflict between two different ethical outcomes**. Here Shazia had to **weigh up** the conflict between the requirement to disclose the fraud, and the morally good ways in which the bonus could be used.

Taking an ethical decision

Shazia's conduct appears to indicate that, having weighed up the two outcomes, she took what appeared to her to be the **best ethical outcome**. She did not keep any of the bonus for herself, but used the money to alleviate her mother's suffering. She gave precedence to reducing her mother's pain over the professional considerations she faced.

Taking the right ethical decision

However it is also possible to question from a relativist viewpoint whether Shazia **weighed up the outcomes correctly**. Her eventual decision meant that she not only **failed to fulfil her professional responsibilities**, she also **accepted a bribe**. The view here is that Shazia should not have had the opportunity to help her mother, since the money she needed to do so was obtained **illegitimately**, through **dishonesty**, and this over-rides the ethically good use of the money.

(c) **Speech on consequences of poor corporate governance**

Introduction

Honourable members, the case I am making today for enhanced corporate governance is a response to the major problems in our country's business environment. These have resulted from the collapse of one or our

largest companies, ZPT, and one of our major audit firms, JJC. Apart from the significant impact on all those involved with ZPT or JJC, we should not underestimate the **general impact on business confidence** in this country.

(i) **Consequences of corporate governance failure in ZPT**

I believe that what happened in ZPT demonstrates the **importance of better corporate governance to prevent the damage caused by management recklessness and incompetence**, The case for stricter regulation can be made by examining in detail the consequences of governance failure at ZPT.

Shareholders

Firstly, ZPT demonstrates that a lack of control over arrogant and negligent directors results in a **loss of shareholder investment**. The shareholders in ZPT received no payments when the company was liquidated. I would remind you that many who lost out were not rich people and big corporations. Instead they were small investors who placed their money in good faith with pension funds and insurance companies, institutional investors, who invested significantly in ZPT. These small investors have seen their potential future income significantly reduced as a result of the collapse. Better governance legislation is needed to protect them.

Employees

Secondly, it will be obvious how much ZPT's and also JJC's employees have lost as a result of the company's collapse. Not only have they lost their jobs without termination payments. ZPT's employees have also **seen the value of their income in old age depleted** because they invested in a pension fund that has proved to be vulnerable to the directors' poor decision-making. We will need to consider stronger protection for employees' pension funds. However for now not only are many of these employees suffering the problems of unemployment, the **burden on our taxpayers is higher**, in terms of unemployment benefit and perhaps future old age support.

Suppliers and customers

Thirdly, those have done business with ZPT have also suffered significant losses. **Suppliers** who provided goods and services have gone unpaid. In the current economic climate this may have threatened their future existence. The lack of money left to repay legitimate business debts indicates that **excessive risks** were taken, and that stricter governance requirements are necessary to force directors to focus on effective risk management. Customers too are **no longer receiving the services and support** for which they have paid, causing personal inconvenience and difficulties to businesses. Again, it is unacceptable that excessive risk-taking has meant that customers have **not received value** in return for their payment.

Impact on wider economy

I would also like to remind you of several broader impacts on our economy. **Confidence in other telecommunications providers as sound investments** has been **damaged**. JJC's failure to report the problems with ZPT may also have caused a **loss of confidence in the audit profession**. This undermines one of the supports to investors being able to deal in shares confidently. Investors need to be sure that the **financial information** they are using as a basis for their decisions is **reliable**. A key source of reassurance is that the information has been effectively and independently verified by strong audit firms. Is an audit firm that also provides lucrative consulting services to its client truly independent? The collapse of JJC has also caused **short to medium-term disruption in the audit profession**. JJC's former clients have needed to find other accountants, and other major firms have struggled to cope. With one fewer major firm, the audit industry has also become less competitive.

Dishonest culture

Supporting better corporate governance will also send out a message that we support a **business culture based on honesty and trust**. The lax governance arrangements in ZPT placed employees in impossible positions. Although we may deplore Ms Lo's conduct in accepting a bribe, we should condemn all the more a system where it was considered best for directors to offer her an inducement. We should also ask ourselves why there were **no internal mechanisms** for Ms Lo to report concerns with impunity, rather than being forced to talk to the media to express her worries.

Better corporate mechanisms, such an audit committee, will ensure channels exist for honest employees to report their concerns in the knowledge that they will receive a fair hearing and not be victimised.

(ii) **Case for mandatory control reporting**

I shall now concentrate on the need for compulsory reporting on internal controls and risks. ZPT's problems arose not only from accounts that gave **inaccurate data**, but accounts that **did not provide sufficient information** about the risks it faced and how these risks were being controlled. There are a number of reasons for requiring major companies to report on risks and controls.

Enhanced confidence

The first reason should be obvious from my previous remarks, that **better reporting improves the confidence of investors**. Investors need to know that boards are **managing risks responsibly**, and that the **information companies provide is reliable**. ZPT's bankruptcy illustrates how rapidly things can go wrong if confidence in directors and controls collapses.

Good practice

Secondly if companies have to report on controls, they know that many investors will scrutinise the report carefully and pursue any weaknesses or problems that the report appears to indicate. This will act as a clear incentive for companies to **eliminate problems by developing effective control systems** and therefore keeping investors happy. The requirement to report annually will mean that review of internal controls has to be a permanent element of companies' systems.

Holding directors to account

Linked in with this, a compulsory report provides ammunition to those that have most power to hold **directors accountable**. These include **stock market regulators**, who can investigate poor practice. They also include **institutional investors** such as pension funds, whose role in ZPT has been criticised significantly. Better reporting would assist greater shareholder activism by institutional investors. It would enable earlier intervention than was possible with ZPT, where the complexities of the group structure and the lack of requirement to report on controls, may have made it difficult for investors to find reasons to intervene.

Need for legislation

Some members might argue that if best practice was publicised rather than enforced by law, that investors would note which companies gave most information and invest in those companies. Companies that were less transparent would see their share prices fall. However there would still be the risk of a similar situation to ZPT developing again. In time there may be another company whose apparently excellent results drive up its share price, with insufficient attention being paid to **possible control weaknesses and lack of transparency** that enable directors to **publish inflated figures**.

(iii) **Content of report on controls**

I do not have time during this speech to do more than outline the broad areas that I believe that a report on internal control should contain. Further details will be included in the bill that I intend to introduce. The areas I recommend have also featured in other guidance on governance around the world, and have resulted in improved reporting in many countries.

Statement by directors

Firstly the report should include an **acknowledgement by the directors** that they are responsible for the company's system of internal control and reviewing its effectiveness. If ZPT's directors had been obliged to make this statement, it would have emphasised to them their **responsibility** for making sure that the systems were working well. Directors making this statement would not easily be able to play down a major restatement of the financial accounts as due to 'regrettable accounting errors'. The statement also emphasises that the board supports the development of effective control systems, and board support is a very important impetus towards developing effective systems.

Process for managing risk

Secondly the statement needs to confirm that there have been **processes in place for managing risks** and highlight and explain any unusual features. Mr Xu alleged some time after ZPT went bankrupt that its complex group structure was a method of managing exchange rate risks. Had ZPT been required to explain this in full, stakeholders would have had a better understanding of how the company was being run, and been able to form their own judgements on whether the structures used were appropriate.

Monitoring by directors

In order to make sure that risk and control systems have been continuing to operate effectively over time, directors **need to review how they have worked**. A major problem identified at ZPT was a **lack of effective oversight** of the controls over the external reporting process. To provide users of accounts with confidence that monitoring has happened therefore, the report on controls needs to include a **summary of the process** that the directors have used to review the effectiveness of control systems. This may include use of a board committee, often the **audit committee**, and also drawing on the work of **internal audit** to support the review.

Problems and weaknesses

If the board review has identified **significant weaknesses in internal control**, then the report needs to give details of these. Significant weaknesses include problems that have resulted in major losses or uncertainties that are, or should be, disclosed in the accounts. One of the major reasons for ZPT's misleading accounts was a failure to follow accounting standards. A board review should have highlighted problems with compliance and explained the implications if these problems had previously affected the accounts.

Conclusion

I would like to thank all of you for your time today. I hope the case I have put for enhanced corporate governance legislation has persuaded you of its necessity. Our economy cannot afford the damage that results from further big corporate scandals. I believe therefore that we have a urgent duty to take steps that will help to prevent another ZPT.

57 Bobo

Text references. Chapters 3, 6, 7, 9 and 11.

Top tips. (a) illustrates the value of systematically reading the scenario as the risks are clearly flagged and some strong hints given about the controls. Any reference in this type of question to cost cutting or rushing work should ring alarm bells and you need to keep an eye out for the consequences of these. Be alert also for signs of intimidation as this illustrates a poor culture and often results in serious consequences. The examiner uses the verb explore to give you some flexibility in how you discuss the issues.

In (b) many students clearly thought that there had to be one person at each Kohlberg level, but this wasn't the case. Vernon's positioning is very clear given his overriding concerns with personal rewards. The key determinant of James's position is that 'he is complying with the expectations of shareholders' ie stakeholders close to the company. Although Kathy's stance appears more ethical than James, she is arguing her position on the basis of the expectations of customers, which places her in the conventional category as well.

In (c) the term extraordinary general meeting is not used in all jurisdictions, but it is clear from the context what is happening. The key justification is that the issues discussed at the EGM must be discussed now and not some months later at the AGM. These will generally be matters that pose a serious immediate risk to shareholder value, such as very poor management decision-making.

With (d)(i) it is important to understand the limitations placed by the question requirements on discussing the chief executive roles. Although the answer covers many of the general roles, it is important to link each of them to James's involvement in the Bobo Foo development. (ii) is an excellent example of the examiner asking students to argue from a viewpoint with which many will have disagreed. With both parts, it is important to try to make as strong a case as possible, emphasising the interests of shareholders and the commercial success of the new car, even though you can see some obvious flaws. Our answer does not mention the failure to act on the test result, which is probably the weakest part of the company's position.

Easy marks. The requirement to explain the different levels of Kohlberg has been examined in a number of questions, and you must revise this area if you struggled with it.

Examiner's comments. As usual, I used the scenario to examine a number of outcomes which not only sampled the study guide and also required candidates to answer at more than one level intellectual level. Also as previously, the requirements were based heavily upon the case, meaning that candidates had to study the case in some detail to gain marks.

In (a) the verb 'explore' was used here to enable candidates to have latitude in responding to this task. Many candidates were able to correctly pick out and explore the causes of the problem. The second task in (a) was less well done than the first task. A careful consideration of the specific problems at Bobo was the secret to gaining marks. Candidates that attempted to answer this using a memorised list of points from a study text or other notes were less well rewarded.

Marking scheme

			Marks
(a)	2 marks for each cause identified and described max	8	
	2 marks for each internal control measure identified and described	Max <u>6</u>	
			Max 12
(b)	2 marks for each Kohlberg level identified and described	6	
	2 marks for each level correctly assigned to a person with evidence,		
	1 mark for correct recognition only	Max <u>6</u>	
			12
(c)	2 marks for distinction between AGMs and EGMs	2	
	1 mark for purpose of AGMs	1	
	1 mark for purpose of EGMs	1	
	1 mark for each advantage	Max <u>4</u>	
			8
			Marks
(d)	(i) 1 mark for each role identified and 1 for placing in context or		
	1 mark for each role identified and briefly explained	Max 8	
	(ii) 2 marks for each point of defence identified and developed	Max 6	
	Up to 4 professional marks for clarity, logical flow, persuasiveness and appropriate structure	<u>4</u>	
			<u>18</u>
			<u><u>50</u></u>

(a) **Cost reduction**

James **emphasised that cost reduction** not safety, was the top priority. This was done to be able to market the car as cheap to buy. James sought to **embed cost savings** as the most important consideration in the thinking of the production team by his poster campaign. **Key decisions** were **determined** by the need to limit costs, particularly the reduction of the testing period, the positioning of the fuel tank and the decision to proceed after the test results.

Reduction in development time

The **significant reduction in the development period** from 43 to 25 months resulted in not enough time being provided to test all the design features satisfactorily. The lack of a sufficient testing period was more significant in relation to the positioning of the fuel tank, since it was proposed in order to save costs and not because it was safe.

Crash test results

The crash tests provided clear evidence that the **positioning of the fuel tank** was **unsafe**. If Bobo had acted in accordance with what the tests indicated, production would have been delayed. However the board decided that **the cost involved in retooling the production line** was the most important consideration in determining whether production went ahead, on the grounds that the directors wished to make a return on the investment as soon as possible

Intimidation

Kathy's actions were determined by the pressures placed on her by James's poster campaign. She was **intimidated** into going ahead with the testing process despite having inadequate time and not protesting about, and making public, the results of the fire safety test. Other directors also failed to raise concerns about the impact of the reduced testing period and the results of the fire safety test. If the board had included strong-minded, independent non-executive directors, they would have felt able to challenge James's decisions.

Internal control measures

Embedding safety

The board needs to ensure product safety is **embedded in the thinking of all staff**. Public statements, such as adverts, should highlight product safety as a key feature of all Bobo's cars. The board should emphasise to staff the need to ensure that products are safe, so that it influences all actions taken by staff. All designs for new cars must include an appropriate safety metric.

Development time

Adequate time needs to be budgeted for testing of vehicles. The minimum period to market should be determined by the time **required to complete thoroughly** all safety tests. The designers should be encouraged to protest if they feel that the testing period allocated is too short.

Testing sign-off

Safety testing, such as the crash test, should be built into the development process at various key stages. As part of the sign-off process before production is allowed to go ahead, management should **obtain evidence that all necessary tests** have been **completed** and **review the results for any problems**. Management must not allow production to go ahead if weaknesses identified by the safety testing have not been rectified.

(b) **Kohlberg's moral development**

Kohlberg provides a framework for classifying responses to ethical issues, based on the moral development of the individual. Kohlberg argued that there are three levels.

Pre-conventional

Pre-conventional development means judging ethical problems in terms of the **drawbacks and benefits** that may affect the individual taking the decision. The individual sees the decision in self-serving terms of whether he or she will be **punished** for ethically wrong behaviour, or **rewarded** for behaving in an ethically acceptable way.

Conventional

Conventional development means taking ethical decisions on the basis of what is **accepted as ethical behaviour** by those who have a relationship with the person taking the decision. It means following the **ethical norms** in the **workplace or the local community**, or **obeying the laws of society** on the grounds that they **codify ethical behaviour** that the community accepts to be right.

Post-conventional

Post conventional development means taking autonomous **ethical decisions** in accordance with **relevant ethical principles**. These ethical principles may be **ethical principles that are applied in the individual's society**, or they may be **universal ethical principles**.

Levels of Bobo management

James

James is exhibiting a **conventional level** of moral development. He believes that the decision should comply with the expectations of those with whom the board has a close business relationship, that is the **shareholders as key stakeholders**. He has argued against the recall option because investors and stock markets would form an adverse view of Bobo as a result.

Kathy

Kathy is exhibiting a **conventional level** of moral development. Her decision again depends on the views of **key stakeholders**. However she is most concerned about **customers**, not shareholders. Her argument is not based on compliance with society's ethical principles as an end in itself. Instead she takes the **pragmatic** line that the decision should be determined by the need to **convince customers** that the cars are safe, and also society that Bobo is acting in line with **society's expectations** about its corporate social responsibility.

Vernon

Vernon is exhibiting a **pre-conventional level** of moral development. He believes that the decision should be determined by the impact on the rewards, the bonuses, that he and the other board members receive. Ethical principles or the expectations of shareholders appear to play no part in his thinking.

(c) **AGM and EGM**

The annual general meeting (AGM) is a **statutorily guaranteed** opportunity for the shareholders of a company to be informed of its affairs and hold its management **accountable**. It is part of the financial calendar of a company.

Extraordinary general meetings (EGM) are one-off meetings, held if there is a **matter of great significance or grave concern affecting the company's present position or its future**. In most jurisdictions, directors can summon an EGM. However if members wish to compel the directors to hold an EGM, they need to hold a certain percentage of share capital holding voting rights.

Purpose of AGM

The AGM is the **most important formal means of communication** with shareholders. AGMs give directors the opportunity to discuss with members the results of the company, present its audited accounts and explain its future outlook. Shareholders vote in proportion to their holdings on the appointment and remuneration of directors, the appointment of auditors and the level of dividends.

Purpose of EGM

EGM are often convened to **discuss issues that cannot wait until the next annual general meeting**. They may be called to allow the shareholders to vote on whether the company should pursue a major business opportunity, such as an acquisition. They may also be called if the company is facing significant risks to its future or the shareholders have major concerns about the decisions directors have taken, to inform shareholders of what is happening and hopefully reassure them.

Advantages of holding EGM

Matters of concern to shareholders

The EGM gives shareholders the chance to be informed about, and discuss, the **safety problems**. The negative publicity surrounding these problems may seriously affect the **value of the shareholders' investment**. Shareholders may also have serious ethical concerns about what has happened.

Accountability

The EGM offers shareholders an opportunity to **hold James to immediate account** for **serious errors of judgement**. These include the decision to proceed with the production of the Bobo Foo despite the safety concerns and the decision not to discuss the choice of the compensation option in public.

Publicity

Although the board tried to keep the decision to pursue the compensation option secret, this has proved counter-productive and has led to much bad publicity. The EGM offers the chief executive and the board a **public opportunity to respond to the bad publicity**. It also offers the board the chance to speak directly to shareholders and answer their questions. It therefore may be a better way to reassure shareholders than written communication.

Resolving the position

The EGM gives shareholders the chance to pass a **vote of no confidence**. If shareholders are not satisfied with the explanations given by James, they can vote him and also other directors out of office. This will quickly **resolve the issues of shareholder dissatisfaction with the board and allow Bobo to move forward,** rather than have uncertainty over the company and board's situation drag on until the next AGM.

(d)   (i)   **Statement at EGM of chief executive's roles**

Thank you for taking the time to come to this extraordinary general meeting. I appreciate that you have a number of serious concerns arising from the recent media coverage about the Bobo Foo. I intend to address these concerns in my statement today.

The first area I shall cover is my own role as chief executive leading the company over the recent period. One of my most important responsibilities is to lead the **development of the company's business objectives and strategy**. I was recruited on the basis that I would oversee Bobo's entry into the economy car market. It was believed that developing a new model for this sector would enhance Bobo's profitability and brand, as a supplier providing cars in all the main market segments.

The second aspect of my role is to **lead the management team** who, amongst other tasks, are responsible for developing new models. Although I was closely involved in the development of the Bobo Foo, the model could not have been developed successfully without the expertise of those involved with all aspects of the project. I believe in particular that Bobo is lucky to have Kathy Yao on the board and in charge of an excellent team of car designers.

As chief executive I am also responsible for overseeing the operational performance of Bobo. This includes **effective management of the company's financial and human resources** and ensuring that appropriate risk management and control systems are in place, weighing the benefits of control systems against their costs. I therefore took a close interest in the development of the Bobo Foo. I emphasised to the management team the factors that were necessary to achieve good performance in the economy car market. The sale of half a million units a year in a very competitive market represents a strong commercial performance.

The last aspect of the role that I want to discuss is my responsibility for dealing with a **range of stakeholders**. This of course very importantly includes addresses the concerns of you, our shareholders. It also means dealing with legal authorities, suppliers and of course customers. It was therefore my responsibility to deal with the legal issues and compensation claims that have been made against Bobo as a result of issues with the Foo's design.

(ii)   **Justification of decision**

I shall now therefore explain the reasons behind our decision not to issue a universal recall of the Foo but to continue dealing with compensation claims.

Firstly, as I have indicated, I have a number of accountabilities to different stakeholders, but my **primary accountability** is to you, our shareholders, as owners of this company. When I am faced with a **range of conflicting views** from different stakeholders, I must remember that my most important responsibility is to **protect shareholder value**. The decisions I take must be taken with this duty always in mind.

The decision not to recall the Foo was therefore taken on the basis of fulfilling my responsibility to take the course of action that would provide the **best value for shareholders.** The detailed calculations that our Finance Director, Vernon Vim, has produced, showed that the expected value of the costs of a universal recall would be approximately $750 million over ten years. This would represent a very significant loss of shareholder value. The costs of continuing to deal with compensation claims are less certain. However on the basis of the incidents with the Foo so far, it is most likely that the costs of the compensation claims would be around $200 million, over half a billion dollars less than the recall option.

I therefore would justify the decision to continue to deal with compensation claims on the basis of the **huge difference between the costs of the two options**. As a result of my fiduciary duty to preserve shareholder value, I had to choose the option that is virtually certain to result in a much smaller loss of shareholder value. I appreciate some of you may have wanted us to take the decision on other criteria. However I hope you will understand that I took a very difficult decision in good faith, on the basis of my responsibilities as chief executive to opt for the most commercially and financially realistic decision.

If any of you have any questions you would like me to answer, I will now gladly do so.

58 Coastal Oil

Text references. Chapters 3, 6, 7 and 10.

Top tips. As with other Section A questions, this case is based on a real-life example.

In (a) as well as being part of the control environment, the corporate code of ethics is also part of strategic positioning (a point emphasised previously by the examiner) as well as influencing relations with stakeholders, which is important in the rest of the question. When you have a question like the second part of (a), it's likely that the company has fallen short in the majority of points emphasised, but you shouldn't necessarily expect that it has fallen short in all aspects.

Compulsory and voluntary disclosures have been examined before in other contexts. Here the voluntary disclosures required specifically relate to issues that affect shareholders' opinion of their investment, including risks, costs and competence of management. Note that the need to take into account shareholders' views is also an important issue in Question 3 of this exam.

If you were worried when answering (c) about making statements that admit liability, that is a valid point. However the examiner appears not to want you to be too concerned about this. The CEO is obligated to explain the causes of the accident and has been instructed to make as full a statement as possible by her board. The situation in (c)(i) can be mitigated by making clear commitments to improve. Otherwise the main task in (c)(i) is scenario analysis as all the control weaknesses are described in there.

If you are still unsure about subjective and objective risk assessment, objective risk assessment means being able to assess likelihood and impact at least reasonably accurately. Otherwise subjective judgement is required. The probabilities of risk events happening are often difficult to estimate and are based on less than scientific assessments that may be difficult for stakeholders to understand. The second part of (ii) deals with the factors that make subjective judgement difficult, although they do not necessarily show Coastal Oil in a good light.

(iii) discusses important issues connected with the control environment and the limitations of what controls can achieve, something that is an issue in (iv) as well. (iv) again is quite difficult to write in circumstances where there has been loss of life. Although cost is an issue when considering ALARP, you cannot make very much of it here.

Easy marks. The purposes of a code of ethics should have been a gentle introduction into this question.

Examiner's comments. As before, a careful and detailed analysis of the case itself was essential to achieve good marks.

The first section of Part (a) should have been relatively straightforward for most well-prepared candidates and indeed, most candidates were able to collect some marks here. Many achieved all five marks. In the second part marks were awarded where candidates were able to show, from the case, how the company had failed to meet its own ethical standards. A common mistake was to list the five areas (full compliance with regulation, etc) but then to describe what the terms meant rather than searching the case for evidence to evaluate the company's performance.

Most candidates were able to gain some marks in the first section of part (b), although quite a lot were not able to say any more than that mandatory was required by law and that voluntary was not. This missed the point about how listing rules also place disclosure requirements on companies, including, in many jurisdictions, details of the company's corporate governance, executive remuneration, etc.

For part (c)(i) the case itself, as in previous questions of this type, was seeded with the information required to provide a comprehensive answer. Because the board agreed that she should provide a full and uncensored statement to the legislative committee, there was no reason for Mrs Ahmed to conceal or play down particular failures. Accordingly, the best answers were those that carefully and systematically explained (ie did more than just identify) each of the five major IC failures in the case. Those that explained internal controls in general terms, perhaps explaining the importance of ICs, received low or no marks because they failed to adequately analyse the case.

Part (c) requirements (ii) and (iv) were done with variable degrees of success. In part (ii), most candidates were able to distinguish between subjective and objective risk assessment but fewer were able to gain the marks for arguing against Senator Jones's view. Part (iv) seemed to be difficult for many candidates. I covered the ALARP principle in a technical article in 2010 and whilst many candidates were able to show some evidence of knowing what it was (sometimes with the help of a simple graph), fewer were able to weave it into the speech as required. Part (iii) on health and safety risk should have been straightforward because it was mainly bookwork. Some candidates defined the term and then did not do so well on explaining the factors.

As usual there were four professional marks available. Some made no attempt to frame their answers in the form of a speech. Others (wrongly) began their answer with 'Dear committee' and ended with 'Yours faithfully'. Another error was to frame it as a memo with 'To: Committee, From: Mrs Ahmed' or similar. It is important to be able to judge the tone of an answer based on what the question asks in terms of format.

Marking scheme

				Marks
(a)		1 mark for each purpose of code of ethics	Max 5	
		1 mark for evaluation of each point max	5	
				Max 10
(b)		Distinguishing between voluntary and mandatory disclosure	2	
		½ mark for each example of mandatory disclosure	Max 2	
		½ mark for each example of voluntary disclosure	Max 2	
		2 marks for each benefit to shareholders identified and assessed (½ mark for identification only)	Max 8	
				Max 10
(c)	(i)	2 marks for each internal control failure identified and explained (½ mark for identification only)	10	
	(ii)	Distinguishing between objective and subjective risk	2	
		1 mark for explanation of each and/or evidence of understanding	Max 2	
		2 marks for each argument developed against the senator's statement	4	
	(iii)	Explanation of health and safety risk	1	
		1 mark for explanation of each factor (½ mark for identification only)	Max 3	
	(iv)	Evidence of understanding of ALARP	2	
		Explanation of why health and safety risks cannot be completely eliminated under ALARP	2	
				26
		Professional marks for logical flow, persuasiveness, format and tone of answer		4
				50

(a) **Purposes of corporate code of ethics**

Establishment of organisation's values

Ethical codes are part of an organisation's **internal environment**. They should be in a form that makes their content easy to remember. They promote **values** that link to the organisation's mission statement and strategic purposes.

Promotion of stakeholder responsibilities

Codes explain who are regarded as legitimate stakeholders and define stakeholder rights and responsibilities. They emphasise the importance of maintaining good relations with stakeholders.

Conveying values to stakeholders

Codes can act as communication devices, increasing the **transparency** of an organisation's dealings with its stakeholders. They help stakeholders understand how the company will react in particular situations.

Control of individuals' behaviour

Codes can promote or prohibit certain actions and therefore help to **control management and employee behaviour**. They are meant to guide internal stakeholders towards acting ethically on a day-to-day basis and achieving ethical outcomes if problems arise.

Promotion of business objectives

Codes can be part of **strategic positioning**. Taking a strong stance on responsibility and ethics and earning a good reputation can enhance appeal to consumers.

Coastal Oil's performance

Compliance with regulations

Coastal Oil aimed to achieve full compliance with regulations in all jurisdictions. The complexity of the arrangements with Well Services meant that **health and safety and environmental regulations** may have been **breached** even though the company was not criminally negligent.

Safety and care of employees

The **lax safety culture and the health and safety failures** on the rigs contributed to the eight deaths and the bereavements for the employees' families. Controls were not operated properly. Coastal Oil's management appears to have been unaware of what was happening on the rigs and did not enforce standards of care on its partner and its managers and employees.

Transparency and communication with stakeholders

Coastal Oil **failed to communicate well** in the days after the explosion. Its priority appears to have been trying to avoid liability rather than providing full information to stakeholders. Many stakeholders would have been anxious to see a statement, including the families of those killed and injured and those living in the surrounding area.

Social contribution and environmental responsibility

Coastal Oil **failed to demonstrate environmental responsibility**. It showed **insufficient commitment to enforcing internal controls** that could have prevented the breach from happening. It had no contingency plan in place for dealing with the effects of a deep-water rupture. The problem took a long time to repair. It caused severe environmental damage, and also had adverse social impacts on the local area's community and economy. Businesses were damaged during the tourist season and the local community therefore had less income to support it.

(b) **Mandatory disclosures**

Company annual reports contain a mixture of mandatory and voluntary disclosures. Mandatory disclosures are those required by legislation, listing rules or accounting standards. They include:

- **Financial statements**
- **Directors' and auditors' reports**

- **Policies** that the company has adopted in particular areas, including the policies it has adopted when preparing its accounts

- **Significant transactions or situations in the context of the accounts,** for example material transactions with related parties or events occurring after the date of the accounts

Voluntary disclosures

Voluntary disclosure can be defined as any disclosure above the **minimum required by legislation and standards**. It can mean giving more information than is required by regulations on particular areas or making disclosures that are not required by regulations. Voluntary disclosures are often narrative in form rather than numerical, as some information that is material to stakeholders cannot be adequately summarised numerically. Examples include:

- **Chairman's statement**

- **Chief Executive's report** going into detail about important aspects of performance

- **Risk reporting** – highlighting the main risks that the company faces

- **Social and environmental reporting** – where guidance is not compulsory but companies may be reporting in line with established good practice

Reasons for voluntary disclosure

Material risks

Even if there had no explosion, shareholders will still welcome detailed disclosure about environmental risk. Interaction with the environment is **inherent** to operating in the oil industry. As sadly demonstrated by the accident, the consequences of risks materialising can be severe and the impact on shareholder value very large. Shareholders therefore require information on the risks that affect Coastal Oil. A detailed statement can also reassure shareholders that Coastal Oil's **risk assessment** policies are effective.

Risk appetite of shareholders

A more detailed environmental report can give shareholders a better idea of the **likelihood and consequences of the risks** the company faces. They can therefore make more informed judgements about whether the overall risk profile of Coastal Oil matches their own appetite for risks, and whether the returns from Coastal Oil are sufficient for the risks of investing in it.

Costs of better systems

Shareholders will wish to see more information about the measures that Coastal Oil will be taking to improve the systems after the disaster, in order to be able to judge what their **costs** will be. Increased costs may have a very material impact on profits, dividends and the value of shareholder investment. Better systems will include better external reporting and this may have a **cost or benefit** too. Greater knowledge about Coastal Oil's activities may have a material impact on market opinion and hence share price.

(c) **Statement to special committee**

Introduction

I would like to start by expressing the deep regret of the board of Coastal Oil for the accident at the Effland Coastal Deep Rig, and the associated loss of life, injuries and environmental damage.

The board accepts the need for **full disclosure** about the circumstances surrounding the accident, in accordance with Coastal Oil's commitment to transparency in its ethical code.

First I want to discuss issues with the internal controls that were operating on the rig.

(i) **Complexity of control arrangements**

Although Coastal Oil accepts its share of responsibility for problems with controls, I would highlight to the committee that we were acting as a **major partner in a joint venture** and did not have complete control over what happened on the rig. Other partners had responsibilities for maintaining controls over operations and safety. However discussions after the accident have highlighted a **lack of clarity in the responsibilities** of ourselves and our joint venture partner. Because we must place

some reliance on the controls maintained by our partner, we acknowledge the need for clearer agreements in future.

Inspection of valve

The second failure of control was a **failure to inspect the valve** that failed before it was installed. The inspection was part of the control systems that our partner, Well Services, operated, but we understand that staff failed to carry out this inspection.

Wrong connecting part

A further issue was the use of a connecting part for the valve that was **not suitable for the depth at which it was operating**. It appears also that the connecting part was not chosen by accident, but was selected on grounds of **cost** despite not having the right specification for that depth.

Information systems

Fourthly, Coastal Oil has had a reporting system in place for rig managers to report problem to management on land (that is land-side management). However rig managers have been allowed to **use their discretion** in reporting problems. It seems that some rig managers have only reported problems to land-side management in exceptional circumstances. Regrettably this can also be seen as part of a picture where rig managers failed to enforce certain necessary controls. The board is considering changing the reporting system and requiring regular reports from rig management, with issues that need to be reported clearly specified. We are also examining how we can obtain greater assurance that the **controls in place are being operated properly**.

Contingency plan

Lastly we acknowledge that there was **no contingency plan** in place to deal with the effects of the explosion and above all to prevent the oil spillage that resulted from the rupture. We failed to take urgent steps to seal the well-head or stop the flow of oil and we very much regret the environmental damage that resulted. Although we believe that the control improvements that we are making will reduce the risks of an accident occurring, we also acknowledge that we need a plan for taking immediate action if the worst occurs.

(ii) **Distinction between subjective and objective risk assessment**

The next area I would like to cover is how we assess risks and respond to Senator Jones's comment that we must have known that an accident would happen. Risk assessment is a complex process, involving the assessment of both the **likelihood** of a risk materialising and the **impact** if it does materialise.

One important distinction in risk assessment is between **objective and subjective risk assessment**. **Objective risk assessment** involves measuring the **likelihood and impact** of risks precisely or at least to a high degree of accuracy. Subjective risk assessment means using judgement to assess risk levels that cannot be determined using objective criteria.

Objective risk assessment

To expand on this definition, objective risk assessment may involve mutually exclusive outcomes, where the probability of each outcome can be assessed with certainty. To take a very simple example, tossing a coin has two outcomes with a 50% chance that each will occur. Impacts of risk occurring can also be measured objectively, for example if a company was to go into liquidation, each shareholder could lose at maximum the amount he paid for his shares.

Subjective risk assessment

By contrast subjective risk assessment involves assessing risks that **cannot be measured with quantitative precision**. The accuracy of the judgement will depend on the **knowledge and skills of the risk assessor**, also the **information available** and the **factors influencing the risk levels**. An example of a subjective likelihood assessment is the risk of a train being late on a particular day. An example of a subjective impact assessment would be how much the stock market might fall during the next month.

Argument against Senator Jones's view

I must respond to Senator Jones's comment that I, as the company's chief executive, 'should have known that the accident was going to happen.' I accept that the Senator is very angry because of the impact of the disaster upon the area he represents. However I must disagree with his comment because it fails to take into account the complexities of risk management.

Subjective assessment of accident

The probability of a workplace accident occurring is not something that can be assessed with precision. It has to be assessed subjectively and I could therefore never therefore be certain that an accident would happen. **Subjective assessment** of the probability and impact of a risk occurring is also very difficult. Coastal Oil operates hundreds of rigs worldwide and does so in conjunction with a number of joint venture partners. The nature of the processes are such that it is very difficult to predict the probability that an accident will happen on any rig, and even more so that an accident will occur on a specific rig such as the Effland Coastal Deep Rig. Similarly it is virtually impossible to predict the scale of the impact if an accident occurs.

Lack of information

Assessment of the risk of accidents was also made more difficult by the information systems we have had in place. As I have already explained, the rig's management informed us of problems **by exception**. They failed to report internal control failures on their rigs to land-side management and hence the board was unaware of these failings. In future we intend that the information that the board receive from the rigs will be enhanced. They will include reports by management on the operation of controls, even if there have been no incidents caused by lapses in control.

(iii) **Health and safety risk**

As a responsible company, we are particularly concerned about the health and safety risks that are connected with our operations. Health and safety risks are the threats of injury or death to employees or others that could arise from our operations.

- Factors increasing health and safety risk
- Health and safety risks can be increased by a number of factors:

  Lack of health and safety policy

  The lack of a policy for dealing with health and safety risks is one factor. However **legislation** in most countries requires companies participating in the oil industry to have effective health and safety policies in place. In addition it is in companies' best interests to enforce policies, because of the loss of working time caused by injuries to employees or the possibility of legal action. We believe that there were robust policies on the rigs.

  Unexpected situation

  The second factor is the failure of policies to deal with an **emergency or unexpected situation**. This can come about, for example, through a lack of emergency procedures or failures of the procedures in place to deal with new threats or impacts that arise because of **changes in technology**.

  Lack of health and safety culture

  The third factor relates to the fact that even if policies and control procedures are appropriate for the demands placed on them, their effective implementation also depends on the **knowledge and the care of the individuals** involved in operations. A lax culture can lead to a lack of care and a failure to operate controls properly. As a board we take very seriously the press reports of a poor health and safety culture on the rigs. We shall be assessing the steps that need to be taken in conjunction with our joint venture partners to improve culture, for example by an enhanced training programme and disciplinary measures.

(iv) **Impossibility of eliminating risk**

I share the committee's desire for an accident like this not to happen again. However, I cannot guarantee that the risk can be reduced to zero. It is impossible for us to avoid undertaking hazardous activities. The controls that we have in place cannot eliminate the risks associated with these activities, since for example the company may face extreme circumstances or errors may be made by staff operating controls. Governance best practice acknowledges that sound control systems can reduce, but not eliminate, risks and that the **costs of operating elaborate controls may outweigh their benefits**.

ALARP

Our risk management procedures are instead based on the **ALARP** (as low as reasonably practicable) principle. This is based on the idea that the **higher the level of the risk**, the **less acceptable** it is. If risks are judged as high, then **effective control measures** are required to reduce their likelihood and impact. We can for example reduce the likelihood of a risk to health and safety materialising by training staff so that they are aware of threats and less likely to make mistakes that will jeopardise safety. We can reduce the impact of a health and safety risk materialising by taking measures to protect staff, for example by insisting that they wear safety clothing.

Judgement

However, as I have already explained, the assessment of the risks that we face is a subjective process. It therefore follows that judgements about the controls necessary to reduce risks are also a matter of **judgement**. This means that I cannot guarantee that the probability of health and safety risks materialising is zero, but it would emphasise that we intend to maintain vigilance in order to keep risk levels low.

Conclusion

Thank you for listening to me today. I will now take any questions.

59 Hayho

Text references. Chapters 1,4,5, 7 and 9.

Top tips. The key distinction in (a) is between risk-averse and risk-seeking companies. The second part of (a) demonstrates the difficulties of weighing risks against returns. Although the Jayland investment may appeal to risk-seekers because of its higher returns, are the risks and the demands Hayho would face too high and would the investment be a reckless use of shareholder funds.

Hopefully in (b) you remembered all the stages of the AAA model. (Go back and learn them if you didn't!) Note the answer covers not just the ethical decision of whether to invest in a country with a corrupt regime, but also duty to shareholders and implications of being under a strict regime in Pealand. As such, there are some arguments for investing in Jayland but the balance is towards Pealand.

To score marks in the second part of (c), you needed to focus on challenges in terms of costs, delays, mistakes and threats to assets.

The requirement for briefing notes in (d) was possibly more straightforward than other Question 1 document requirements. The notes require clear explanations of the key issues. You needed to demonstrate the link between the Mendelow mapping of the pressure group and influence, and show how that influence might in fact threaten the returns that shareholders were concerned about.

Easy marks. The first part of (c) is based on the Turnbull report. However note the examiner's comments about what 'describe' means.

Examiner's comments. Part (a) was done well by most candidates although some failed to explain risk appetite as a continuum, saying instead that risk appetite meant risk seeking. In fact, companies and individuals can have either a high, low or medium risk appetite.

In part (b) a minority chose the wrong framework (employing, for example, the Tucker framework or the Gray, Owen and Adams continuum) but most were able to correctly identify the seven AAA questions. Not all of these were presented in the correct and logical order. Some candidates failed to achieve higher marks here by producing only a shallow analysis of each stage or by confusing the things to consider under each question.

The first task in part (c) was bookwork and should have been straightforward to any well-prepared P1 candidate. It was frustrating that many candidates failed to take into account the verb, 'describe'. It was not enough to 'list' or produce a short bullet list. To get full marks for this first task, markers were looking for a brief description of each general purpose as asked for in the question.

In the second task in part (c) it was not enough just to pick the main challenges out and list them. To get the higher marks, candidates had to assess each in terms of how it would represent a challenge to Hayho.

In part (d)(i) most candidates were able to show evidence of understanding of the Mendelow matrix but fewer were able to use this to show how the variables applied to WB. The point here was to use the evidence in the case to discuss the sources of power and interest specifically for WB and this was done with varying degrees of success.

For part (d)(ii) it was pleasing to see that most P1 candidates had a good idea of what an agency relationship is. The second task was done poorly overall, perhaps because it involved a detailed analysis of the case to establish the sources of WB's influence.

Marking scheme

				Marks
(a)		3 marks for explanation of risk appetite (1 mark for definition, 1 mark for understanding of each preference)	3	
		2 marks for demonstrating risk and return of each option with correct risk appetite preference	4	
				Max 6
(b)		1 mark for each relevant point, wherever made in the answer.		
		½ mark for identification only		14
(c)		1 mark for each purpose of internal control max	4	
		2 marks for each challenge identified and assessed	Max 8	
				12
(d)	(i)	1 mark for each relevant point made on accountability	Max 3	
		2 marks for evidence of understanding of Mendelow's framework	2	
		2 marks for discussion of WB's power, interest and influence	2	
				7
	(ii)	1 mark for each relevant point on agency	Max 2	
		2 marks for each argument on WB's demands	Max 6	
				Max 7
		Professional marks for clarity, flow and structure		4
				50

(a)   **Risk appetite**

Risk appetite is the nature and strength of the risk of loss that a company is prepared to bear. Risk appetite is often defined in terms of a business being **risk-averse or risk-seeking**. A risk-averse business will generally try to reduce risks and is prepared to accept lower returns in exchange for lower risks. A risk-seeking business will seek out high return opportunities, understanding that it will face higher risks as a result.

Risk and return

Jayland option

The Jayland option offers double the return of the Pealand option, but also offers higher risks as well. The **significant risks** associated with the Jayland option are being **forced to pay a bribe or else risking interference from Jayland's government**. If Hayho does pay a bribe, it could be liable to legal action under its home country's **anti-bribery legislation**. There could be a risk of **political instability** affecting operations if there is a revolt against Mr Popo's presidency. There is also a significant threat to the **security of property**. There may be **disruption to operations** in Jayland as a result of staff lacking the required skills and making mistakes. Problems with staff could also **adversely affect the quality of production**.

Pealand option

The Pealand option offers the lower return, but lower risks in important risks such as **political stability, reputation and bribery**. It is possible however Hayho's operations will be affected by the regulations in Pealand requiring **stringent controls**, whereas it could operate with minimal regulation in Jayland.

Choice

The choice between the two options will provide a good indication of whether Hayho is risk-averse or risk-seeking. A risk-averse business could legitimately accept the Pealand option in return for lower returns. A risk-seeking business would be more likely to choose the Jayland option.

(b) **Step 1 – What are the facts of the case?**

Hayho is facing a **choice between two mutually-exclusive investments, both offering an acceptable return**. If it accepts the Jayland investment, with higher returns, there is a risk that it could act unethically. If it accepts the Pealand investment with lower returns, this risk is absent. Instead Hayho will be subject to regulations that require high standards of corporate responsibility in certain areas.

Step 2 – What are the ethical issues in the case?

Hayho has stated that it will demonstrate corporate social responsibility by investing in developing or transitional economies.

If Hayho chooses the Jayland option, it will probably be forced to pay a **bribe to the President and effectively support his corrupt and oppressive regime**. It could also take advantage of the lack of regulations and **treat its labour force harshly**.

In Pealand, although the ethical problems with supporting an oppressive regime are absent, Hayho may face ethical issues when it takes over the existing workforce and needs to **decide how to manage them**.

Step 3 – What are the norms, principles and values related to the case?

Hayho faces a commercial decision and has been reminded that, under its own economy's norms, it has a duty to **maximise shareholder returns**. However it should also **act responsibly when managing risks**.

Significant groups within society are however keen that Hayho acts ethically. Hayho has placed itself under an obligation to behave ethically by stating that it will uphold the **highest standards of integrity, human rights and environmental protection**, while at the same time investing in less advanced countries. These principles would certainly appear to mean **not agreeing to pay bribes**, and could also be taken to mean not **investing in a corrupt country**, although an investment might help that country's economic development.

Step 4 – What are the alternative courses of action?

The first alternative is to **invest in Jayland**, which would mean being able to build its own factory and impose its own culture and working practices. It would also mean, though, operating in an unstable country and having to deal with a workforce that lacked key skills.

The second alternative is to **invest in Pealand**, which would mean taking over the current workforce and subjecting itself to stringent corporate responsibility regulations.

Step 5 – What is the best course of action consistent with the norms, principles and values?

Investing in Jayland would be consistent with some of the norms, the requirement to **maximise returns for shareholders and investing in a developing country**.

However investing in Pealand would appear to be more consistent overall with Hayho's values. It would also involve investment in a **less advanced** country. It would achieve **acceptable returns** for shareholders and could be **justified on commercial grounds** because of its **lower risk profile**. Hayho would avoid the temptation of paying a bribe and being seen to support a corrupt regime, and would instead be **committing to higher standards of corporate social responsibility**.

Step 6 – What are the consequences of each possible course of action?

If Hayho invests in Jayland, it could achieve higher returns. However it faces a significant business threat from **political instability**, a **lax approach to property rights** and an **unskilled workforce**. It could be subject to **criminal penalties for bribery** in its own country and could face calls for a **consumer boycott** because hypocritically supported a corrupt regime.

If Hayho invests in Pealand, it would be choosing an option with lower returns, which might upset some shareholders. Hayho might also find it **difficult to implement the necessary internal controls**. However it could **publicise its investment as being made in accordance with its values** and therefore reduce the pressure from groups such as Watching Business.

Step 7 – What is the decision?

If the board wishes to **follow Hayho's principles and values most closely**, it should invest in Pealand. It would also be taking into account the need to **limit risks to shareholders** and also the lower costs of dealing with an untrained workforce.

(c) **General purposes of an internal control system**

Facilitate its effective and efficient operation

Controls must not be a drag on the business but should aid its success. They should enable a business to **achieve its strategic objectives and respond appropriately to business, operational, financial, compliance and other risks**.

Safeguarding assets

Businesses need to protect the assets they use to generate value. They should have procedures in place to **protect assets** from inappropriate use or from loss, fraud or neglect. They should also have procedures to **ensure that liabilities and sources of loss are identified and controlled**.

Ensure the quality of reporting

In order to produce information upon which reliance can be placed, businesses must **maintain proper records and processes** that **generate a flow of timely, relevant and reliable information**. Internal information such as budgets will assist control of the business. Externally published information should provide assurance to shareholders and markets.

Help ensure compliance with applicable laws and regulations and with internal policies

Businesses must have procedures in place to **comply with company legislation and listing rules, if applicable**. They should also identify and ensure **compliance with other relevant legislation**, whether it is relevant to most businesses (employment laws) or sector-specific. Controls should also ensure compliance with policy statements, such as ethics codes, to ensure a strong culture is maintained and the business is not exposed, for example, to reputation risks from ethical breaches.

Challenges

Local culture

Emily Baa stated that Jayland's national culture is unfamiliar with modern business practice and behaviour. This may mean that there are **basic threats to productivity,** such as poor timekeeping and absenteeism. It may be very difficult to change accepted practices even by training, discipline and reward. **Management**

style may also be a significant issue. Hayho may try to **require local managers to manage in ways that are unfamiliar in the local culture**. Local managers may have difficulty in fulfilling Hayho's requirements and staff may be **dissatisfied** if they feel they are being treated poorly. Again this may hinder business efficiency and productivity.

Property security

The investment in Jayland is a major **commitment of shareholder value**. Hayho must ensure that the components of the investment are being protected. It may be possible to provide security for valuable assets to guard against theft. However, Hayho may find **asset value threatened by inexperienced staff** who do not pay sufficient attention to the maintenance of assets or who use them inefficiently. It may be even more difficult to protect against threats from a **breakdown in the political situation**.

Lack of technical skills

Difficulty in recruiting staff who lack appropriate quality control skills may be a major obstacle to Hayho achieving value from its investment. It will need to ensure that there are sufficient staff with the skills required to guarantee that the products made in Jayland **meet the stringent international standards**. This may involve paying a **premium** to recruit local staff with the necessary skills. Alternatively it could provide **training** to ensure enough staff had the required skills, although it might take some time to achieve this. At least in the short-term, it could try to **persuade staff in other countries** to relocate to Jayland while local staff were trained, but overseas staff may be reluctant to go to an area that is politically unstable.

Lack of accounting skills

Hayho's main board needs to be able to rely on the **information** that it receives from Jayland in order to ensure effective control of its investment and ensure that the investment is accounted for truly and fairly in the group's accounts. If staff lack accountancy skills, they **may not produce reliable management accounting information**, for example variance analysis. They may also **fail to maintain the proper accounting records** that Hayho requires to fulfil its legal responsibilities.

(d)   **Briefing notes for board meeting**

For: Helen Duomo, Chief Executive

Prepared by: Emily Baa, Company Accountant

Date: 4 October 20X2

(i)   **Introduction**

The letters from Quark Investments and Watching Business raise the key issue of the extent to which Hayho is **accountable** to its shareholders and also is more widely accountable to society as a whole.

Definition of accountability

Accountability means whether Hayho and its directors are answerable for its actions to others. Accountability means that Hayho could be asked to **explain its actions** and this may influence the decisions that the directors make.

Power over Hayho

Although some would argue that Hayho is accountable to many current stakeholders, the key issue here is the **enforcement of accountability**, which stakeholders have the **power** to require explanations from Hayho. Clearly the **shareholders** have this power. They own the company and their rights as shareholders are enforceable under company law. However Watching Business may also have sufficient power **because of its influence in society**.

Mendelow's matrix

Mendelow's matrix maps not only the power of stakeholders in Hayho but their level of interest as well. Stakeholders with **high power and high interest** are seen as having maximum influence and Hayho must therefore address their needs.

Watching Business's **power** over Hayho derives from its **influence over legislators and also the wider public**. Its influence over politicians in individual countries may vary depending on which

government is in power. However its high support overall worldwide by politicians cannot be ignored. It is also a well-known organisation that is capable of effectively utilising mass media to promote, for example, a boycott of individual companies by consumers and trade contacts.

However Mendelow's framework also focuses on the **level of interest** that stakeholders have. Power is less significant if the stakeholders have minimal interest in the company. It is though clear that Watching Business has a high level of interest in Hayho as a result of its previous investments. The rumours about the investment in Jayland have increased Watching Business's interest and thus its influence. This high interest is likely to be maintained for the foreseeable future.

This method of analysis clearly therefore implies that Watching Business has a **significant interest in Hayho which it is able to enforce,** and thus its influence cannot be ignored.

(ii) **Agency relationship between Hayho's board and Quark Investments**

The directors of Hayho are employed as agents by the company's shareholders, who own the company. As owners the shareholders have the right to **decide the company's objectives**. The directors are responsible for managing the company in accordance with the shareholders' objectives. The main objective is normally assumed to be **maximisation of returns to shareholders** subject to any constraints imposed by laws and society's values. Quark Investments has thus correctly reminded the board of its responsibilities towards shareholders.

Demands of lobby group

Watching Business does not wish Hayho to take a decision to invest in Jayland, a strategy that may yield high returns for shareholders. It claims that investment in Jayland supports a regime that violates human rights. It is very unlikely to compromise over its claims. Because of Watching Business's high influence over its activities, Hayho has to **consider its claims seriously** when deciding whether to invest in Jayland, whether or not the claims are believed to be valid. The following issues are particularly significant.

Response to society

After the development in Arrland was criticised, Hayho demonstrated its **sensitivity to public opinion** by pledging publicly to uphold high standards. Public opinion could be turned against Hayho by Watching Business's claims that not only was Hayho investing in an oppressive regime, it was also **breaking its previous promises**.

Strategic interests

Hayho's longer-terms **strategic interests** may be harmed by Watching Business's lobbying. Hayho may face **greater regulations and pressures from policymakers** not to ignore human rights concerns. Over the last few years, Hayho has also tried to gain a **strategic advantage** through being associated with high ethical standards and it will lose this advantage if Watching Business is successful.

Reputation risk

Continued adverse coverage in the media may result in consumers **boycotting Hayho's products**, because they do not wish to be associated with a company that is seen as having poor business ethics.

Conclusion

The concerns of Watching Business must be taken seriously when the investment decision is made. If Hayho does decide to invest in Jayland, it must carefully manage threats to its reputation by emphasising the positive ethical reasons for investing there. Although this may not satisfy Watching Business, other interested parties such as politicians may take a more positive view.

60 P&J

Text references. Chapters 4, 6, 7, 10 and 11.

Top tips. Note that in (a) you need to consider the effect on whole communities as well as individuals within them. You are meant to understand from the scenario that a significant change of activities (or liquidation at worst) will be forced upon P&J as a result of Professor Kroll's findings and you need to discuss the consequences of this happening. Some are very clearly highlighted in the scenario – removal of the health threat versus severe loss of employment and community support. The consequences of loss of value to shareholders have been discussed in previous questions and you need to consider the serious impact of loss of wealth, either on people who have made a large investment in P&J or those indirectly affected as a result of their connections with institutional investors in the company. Other issues you could have discussed include loss of tax income from P&J to fund state services, increases in state funding to support affected workers, and impacts on industries that use X32.

The key issue in (b) is how difficult P&J will find it to move away from X32. This is partly a function of the over-commitment (60%), also inflexible facilities and lack of funds for alternative investments.

The requirement in (c) makes it clear that you need to bring in fundamental ethical principles, but remember that you only should bring in principles that are relevant. Here integrity, objectivity and professional behaviour are relevant – confidentiality clearly is not (lack of transparency is part of the problem!). The main issues to bring out in connection with the concepts are accepting inducements, misleading shareholders and betraying their trust – note the emphasis on the shareholders having a high regard for Hannah and this clearly aggravates the situation.

Don't worry too much about adopting snappy journalistic phrases if you have to write an article. The main issues are to ensure that the points made are clear, the language used is not obscure (even if it's an educated audience) and you try to adopt a succinct writing style (lots of short sentences help).

The first part of (d) is concerned with strategic risks as whole company risks. Perhaps the least obvious point is strategic risks affecting strategic positioning, but this has been an issue in other questions. The ethical point behind the second part of the article is the unacceptability of having controls only in countries where they have to be operated – most starkly here because lack of controls poses a clear and proven threat to human life.

Easy marks. Probably the 5 marks available in (d) for quick explanations of the categories in COSO's internal control guidance.

Examiner's comments. In (a) most candidates were able to define what social footprint means. (b) was done poorly. Only a minority was able to describe well what risk diversification means. It was necessary to study the case in some detail as all the reasons for the difficulties were there. Weaker answers attempted to fit the TARA framework into the answer although this was an inappropriate and incorrect response.

In (c) weak answers listed all of the IESBA principles with some attempting to show either their importance (which was not required) or to show how Hannah had somehow breached all of them.

Neither the second part of (d)(i) or (d)(ii) was done well. The second part of (d)(ii) involved being able to apply the idea of strategic risk and to analyse the case to show why these risks are strategic (as opposed to operational).

The examiner was surprised that (d)(ii) was not done so well because five of the nine marks available were effectively testing theoretical knowledge of the board's responsibilities for internal control. Thorough revision should have provided candidates with full knowledge of the board's responsibilities in respect of internal controls and the COSO guidelines were a helpful framework around which to base a correct answer. The second task in (d)(ii) was done poorly even though there were clear criticisms to be made of the plan from an ethical perspective.

There were some excellent attempts from some candidates to gain the professional marks whilst others seem to have made no attempt at all to frame their answers according to the requirement. Making an attempt to gain professional marks can be the difference between a pass and fail.

			Marks
(a)	Definition of social footprint	2	
	2 marks for each implication identified and discussed	<u>10</u>	
			Max 10
(b)	Description of risk diversification	2	
	2 marks for each problem with diversification	<u>10</u>	
			10
(c)	1 mark for each of the fundamental principles breached by Hannah	3	
	Up to 2 further marks for explanation of how each principle is breached	<u>6</u>	
			9
(d)	(i) Distinguishing between strategic and operational risk	2	
	2 marks for each reason why risk is strategic	<u>6</u>	
			8
	(ii) 1 mark for each control responsibility	5	
	2 marks for each relevant criticism	<u>4</u>	
			9
	Professional marks for structure, logical flow, persuasiveness and tone of article		<u>4</u>
			<u>50</u>

(a)   **Definition**

Social footprint is the **impact** that an organisation has on **society, social communities and individuals within communities**. Impacts can be positive (for example, provision of jobs) or negative (for example, loss of amenities or threats to health).

Social implications of Professor Kroll's findings

Threats to health

An effective response to Professor Kroll's findings should lead to internal controls being **introduced to protect the health of workers handling X32 or to curtail the activities of P&J**. These controls over time should **reduce the number of health conditions that have affected employees** and **result in lower mortality**. This will not just impact on those who are exposed to X32, but also the families and carers who have to look after them. Health care facilities will benefit through having resources freed up for other uses if they don't have to deal with patients suffering from X32-related conditions.

Employment and community cohesion

However, if P&J is forced to curtail its activities or go out of business, there could be a serious **loss of employment** in a number of places. In particular the **economic consequences** for the local economy in Aytown could be very serious, as 45% of its workforce are in **danger of losing their jobs**. This could result in other businesses being forced to shut down, significant migration from Aytown to find employment opportunities elsewhere and a loss of community cohesion.

Support for local communities

Community activities could also be affected if P&J is forced to close or contract. In developing countries there could be a **threat to education, sanitation and health facilities** caused by the loss of income from X32 mining. In Beetown the children's nursery, football club and adult education classes could all be forced to close as a result of the loss of support from P&J, resulting in a **serious loss of community facilities**, damaging the community as a whole.

Loss of value of P&J

If P&J's activities are affected, the value of its shares could be **significantly reduced** or even fall to nothing. This would directly affect the **income or wealth of shareholders**. It could also impact on small investors in pension funds or insurance companies that invested in P&J. The small investors could receive **reduced pensions or endowment values** as a result of this loss of value.

(b) **Risk diversification**

Diversification means **spreading risks and return over a number of areas and activities** so that the business will not be affected too seriously by risks materialising in a single area. Risk diversification also involves avoiding having all the business's activities **positively correlated**, which means that everything will turn out **extremely well or badly**.

Reasons why diversification will be difficult for P&J

Balance of business

Currently **60% of P&J's business is connected with X32**. This means that a majority of the assets and the human capital will be geared to dealing with X32 business. At present P&J is very exposed to the risks arising from the health threat that X32 poses. However, a significant move away from X32 would result in a fundamental re-alignment of P&J's product portfolio, which may not be feasible.

Inflexibility of facilities

P&J will not be able to **diversify activities in its mines** as they have been established to mine X32 and nothing else. Processing facilities are also dedicated to X32 production and in some instances it may be impossible for them to be **adapted to alternative uses**. In any case the full refit of processing and manufacturing plants that is necessary to carry on existing activities is not affordable.

Disposal of assets

P&J is unlikely to be able to re-balance its portfolio by selling profitably assets that it cannot adopt for other uses. Now that the health risks of X32 are known, other businesses are **unlikely to want to buy assets** that would require expensive modification, could threaten employees' health and result in significant future liabilities.

Lack of funds

Diversification would have to require **development** of new products, and this would mean investment expenditure would be needed. However it appears that funds will not be available for investment. P&J appears to have **reached the limits of its gearing** and funds are unlikely to be made available by banks. The company has limited retained earnings and investors are unlikely to support a further issue of shares given the risks that P&J currently faces.

(c) Hannah Yin appears to have breached the principles of **integrity**, **objectivity and professional behaviour**.

Integrity

Integrity means being **straightforward and honest** in all business and professional relationships. Hannah has failed to show integrity. She has suppressed information about the worst case scenario. She has also reported Plan B as demonstrating effective social responsibility when it has been designed as a gesture to appease investors, rather than effectively dealing with the problem over the whole company. Her behaviour is aggravated by the fact that the shareholders have placed **trust** in her as a professional. She has abused that trust by taking advantage of the fact that shareholders will believe what she tells them.

Objectivity

Objectivity means **not allowing bias, conflicts of interest or undue influence** of others to **override professional or business judgements or duties**. Hannah Yin has breached objectivity by clearly allowing her decisions to be **influenced by the increased share options**. This gave her an incentive to avoid actions that reduced P&J's short-term share price and hence the value of her share options. She therefore **did not report completely the results of the financial modelling or the costs of the refit**, data that would have been of much interest to shareholders and the markets. She also downplayed without good reason the significance of Professor Kroll's research.

Professional behaviour

Professional behaviour means **complying with laws and regulations and avoiding any action** that discredits the profession. Hannah Yin has **failed to demonstrate professional behaviour**. She has not **reported the situation completely and fairly** to the shareholders. She has **prioritised her personal interests** over her duties as an accountant and company director to the shareholders, to the market that would be concerned about price-sensitive information such as the risks to P&J's existence and the wider public interest that is concerned about X32.

(d)   **P&J – the future?**

No-one would envy the current position of P&J. The situation its directors currently face in relation to X32 is the most serious in the company's history. There are no easy answers, perhaps no answers at all. However sympathy begins to disappear when its board is more concerned with keeping up appearances rather than doing all they can to deal with the issues.

(i)   **Strategic and operational risks**

The difficulties P&J is facing will influence its whole direction in the future. The risks that are troubling the company the most are not **operational risks**, risks arising from within the company affecting parts of the company, affecting internal business processes day-to-day. The most worrying risks are strategic risks, **risks to future profits** arising from the nature of P&J's business, risks that affect the company as a whole. If strategic risks materialise, they can cause not just individual companies, but whole industries, to disappear.

Kroll's findings

The findings of Professor Kroll's report pose a strategic risk to P&J for a number of reasons. Firstly his findings clearly affect all the company. P&J has previously taken the decision to adopt **vertical integration**, which means that it undertakes all stages of the production process, mining, processing and manufacturing. Professor Kroll's findings impact upon each stage.

Secondly it is very difficult now for P&J to **position itself** so that it appeals to its key stakeholders. Banks will not be advancing further funds. Shareholders will be more likely to offload their shares than make a further investment. Customers will be looking in the longer-term for safe alternatives to X32. Current employees will leave for more secure opportunities. It is difficult to see how new employees can be attracted.

All this implies that the most serious strategic issue facing P&J is whether it can **survive at all**. Over time it faces a dwindling in demand and a fall in revenues from X32. It does not have the cash surpluses to make fundamental changes to its production processes or significantly reposition its product base. Most worryingly of all, it faces unknown legal costs and unquantifiable legal liabilities, which may turn out to be enough to wipe almost any company out.

(ii)   **Board responsibilities**

Amidst all these worries, P&J's directors still have to fulfil their responsibilities and maintain effective control over the company. There are a number of things they should be doing, set out in the widely-accepted COSO guidance on internal controls.

COSO guidance

Maintaining an **effective control environment** that supports the operation of controls. This includes providing effective leadership and setting the right tone, emphasising the importance of a responsible attitude towards risk and control and, not least, the need to act ethically.

Having strong **risk assessment procedures** in place to grade risks by likelihood and impact, and to thus identify the most serious risks, such as major threats to health, which require strong and prompt action.

Ensuring that control procedures are **operating effectively over the whole company** and are reducing the risks P&J must bear to levels that are as low as reasonably practicable.

Making sure they have **sufficient information** to be able to oversee P&J, and ensuring that there is **full communication** with staff, so that P&J's staff have the knowledge they need to carry out their responsibilities effectively and operate controls.

Continuously **monitoring controls** and making sure that controls are being implemented properly and modified if they are **ineffective**. With P&J controls that are not operating as they should be could be a matter of life and death.

Form over substance

These responsibilities are serious for the board. Worryingly at present P&J's directors seem concerned with appearance rather than action. So-called Plan B for dealing with the situation is a **partial refit**, aimed at appeasing concerns in Emmland. Emmland has health and safety legislation so P&J introduces controls over X32, but does not introduce the same controls in countries without these laws, taking advantage of weak governments and vulnerable staff. It makes a great play of its social responsibility in Emmland, because that's where its investors are.

And let's remember these controls are not a matter of form-filling and bureaucracy. By not adopting them in developing countries, Mr Ho and his fellow directors are **ignoring the health of its employees**. They will continue to be exposed to X32 as part of their normal employment and their health will continue to be at great risk. The most basic duty that P&J has towards its employees is to provide safe working conditions. Its directors are blatantly ignoring this responsibility in some countries. They are condemning employees to illness and death with full knowledge of what X32 can do.

P&J – what next?

With unknown future liabilities and a board with some worrying ethical questions hanging over it, it seems increasingly difficult to provide any positive answers to questions about P&J's future. Investors and other stakeholders may be more concerned with finding the best ways to disengage rather than suggesting solutions.

61 Hoppo

Text references. Chapters 1, 6, 7, 9, 10 and 11.

Top tips. In (a), remember that for correlation to exist, there must be a relationship so that the risks vary together. Reputation risk will always be correlated to another risk, as it cannot arise unless another risk materialises. The details in the scenario suggest that the correlation is quite strong. However there are complications here. Whilst reputation risk is normally thought of as an adverse risk, there may be an upside if some stakeholders welcome strong action being taken against Red for its poor practices. Note also that reputation may relate to competent business practices as well as ethics. The verb explore is normally used to give you some scope to cover the issues, so you may have made equally valid points to those in our answer.

Key points to bring out in (b) are the report dealing with inputs (possible scarce resources such as TY13) and outputs (emission, pollution, waste etc). Advantages don't just relate to satisfying stakeholders with environmental concerns, reporting also aids decision-making by investors and better systems may result in better decisions being made internally.

In (c) strategic internal controls are controls over factors that affect long-term decisions about the direction of the company's business. The question requires use of detailed examples from the case, and although if you've done P3, it probably makes this part a bit easier, the issues (supply, branding as ethically responsible, pricing and product quality) are fairly well flagged.

In (d) important points that will help get you the 4 professional marks for the press release are a first paragraph that emphasises the key points, the necessary background information to ensure readers fully understand the company's position and a third person narrator. The sections on integrity and transparency include the textbook definition, but they also stress the companys commitment. The business considerations in (ii) focus on the consequences of the destruction of the basis of trust. The deontological case is based round the need for universal rules to underpin business decisions. The consequentalist case is based on the probability of Hoppo having to take further unethical actions.

Easy marks. The contents of an environmental report and its advantages should offer plenty of scope to score quite straightforward marks.

Examiner's comments. In (a) many candidates were able to explain the two terms, although some candidates confused positive and negative correlation of risks. The better answers were able to see and explore the reputational difficulties of legal cases.

The best answers to (b) divided up the two answers and approached them separately. Candidates who had read the technical answer on this would have been well-prepared. There were some very good answers to the first part, but the highest marks were awarded to those able to meaningfully approach the second part, involving examining the specific environmental challenges faced by Hoppo and showing how producing an environmental report could help with these. General answers on the advantages of environmental reporting were less well-rewarded.

(c) required a detailed analysis of the case in order to gather the reasons why such internal controls would be necessary.

Many made a good attempt to gain the professional marks in (d), but it was frustrating to see some candidates setting out their answer as a memo or a letter. It was also important to present the answer as a press release and not just as an exam answer. In a press release for example it would be unusual to see terms like deontological and consequentialist. The model answers present the contents of these two positions but do not use these two terms except as commentary.

A common approach to (d)(i) was to define the two terms but then fail to adequately develop the connection to the case.

The 10 marks for (d)(ii) should have alerted candidates to the need for a fairly detailed consideration of the business and ethical perspectives. A typical answer discussed the essential features of the ethical perspectives, but then did not adequately relate these to the case.

ACCA examiner's answer. The ACCA examiner's answer to this question can be found at the back of this kit.

Marking scheme

				Marks
(a)		1 mark for explaining related risks	1	
		1 mark for explaining correlated risks	1	
		1 mark each for evidence of understanding of legal and reputation risk	2	
		1.5 marks for each issue explored from case exploring link between legal and reputation risk. 0.5 marks for identification only	6	
				10
(b)		Up to 4 marks for description	4	
		2 marks for each advantage	6	
				10
(c)		2 marks for explaining strategic	2	
		2 marks for each internal control explanation in context	8	
				10
(d)	(i)	1 mark for each relevant point explaining integrity in context	3	
		1 mark for each relevant point explaining transparency in context	3	
				6
	(ii)	1 mark for each relevant point on the business case		
		1 mark for each relevant point on deontological arguments		
		(of which 1 mark for evidence of understanding)		
		1 mark for each relevant point on the consequentialist case		
		(of which 1 mark for evidence of understanding)		
				Max 10
		Professional marks for the format, tone, logical flow and persuasiveness of the press release		4
				50

(a) **Related and correlated risks**

Related risks are risks that are connected because the causes of the risk are the same or because one risk links to another.

Correlated risks are two risks that vary together. If positive correlation exists, the risks will increase or decrease together. If negative correlation exists, one risk will increase as the other decreases and vice versa. The correlation coefficient measures the extent of the correlation.

Correlation of legal risk and reputation risk

For Hoppo, legal risk and reputation risk are likely to be correlated. The legal risk is the risk that Red will pursue legal action against Hoppo, with the impacts that Hoppo will have to devote time to contesting the action and may incur costs or damages if it loses the case. The probability of Red pursuing the case is difficult to assess.

Reputation risk is a **change in Hoppo's reputation** that arises as a consequence of another risk crystallizing. Here it is correlated with, and dependent on, the legal risk. It will not arise if Red does not pursue legal action.

There are indications that Hoppo will receive some adverse publicity and suffer a loss of reputation, for the following reasons.

Integrity

Hoppo's reputation for **fair dealing** may be threatened if it is seen to rely on a dubious legal arrangement to release itself from an awkward situation. This threat to reputation is enhanced by being seen in conjunction with Hoppo being known to have considered paying a bribe. Loss of reputation for integrity may result in potential business partners being less willing to work with Hoppo, particularly outsource partners in other legal jurisdictions.

Competence

Hoppo's reputation for competence may also be undermined by publicity about the legal action. Hoppo may be seen as incompetent in **failing to make unambiguous legal arrangements** with a supplier. The legal action also highlights previous failure by Hoppo to manage the supplier relationship properly and identify Red's poor practices. This threat is enhanced by Hoppo's failure to take prompt action when it was offered the bribe. Again a loss of reputation for competence may make potential business partners less willing to work with Hoppo. Hoppo's share price may also fall further if investors lose confidence in its management.

Social responsibility

The legal action will also highlight the adverse social consequences of Hoppo's termination of the contract. The **loss of 1,000 jobs** in a low-cost economy is likely to be highlighted in the press. Ethically-minded consumers may stop buying Hoppo's products as a consequence and the company may become less appealing to potential employees.

On the other hand, legal action might have positive consequences for Hoppo's reputation for the following reasons.

Social and environmental responsibility

Publicity about the legal action will highlight that Hoppo is committed to ensuring that its **manufacturing is conducted responsibly**. It has received bad publicity about the poor working conditions at Red and Red's harmful environmental policies. Terminating the relationship with Red, even if it is by dubious legal means, may enhance Hoppo's reputation with some ethically-minded employees and customers.

(b) **Purpose of environmental report**

The purpose of an environmental report is to disclose a business's **environmental footprint**, the impact its activities have on the environment. By making these disclosures, a business acknowledges its duties as a corporate citizen and demonstrates its stewardship of environmental resources.

Contents of environmental report

An environmental report may be published as part of a business's annual report or as a separate document. It focuses on inputs and outputs, the **consumption of resources** by the business's activities, and the **impact of its production activities and its products** on the environment. It may include **direct and indirect impacts**, covering the impact suppliers such as Red make as well as the impact of the business. The report is likely to include **narrative information** covering objectives of environmental policy, explanations of what the business has done and why targets have or have not been achieved. **Numerical information** may include the amount of emissions or land use.

Advantages of environmental report

Demonstrating responsiveness

Environmental reports can be used to demonstrate a company's **responsiveness** to the concerns of stakeholders and its **accountability**, both to the present world and future generations. Having a reputation as a green company can lead to **marketing opportunities** to customers who value a strong environmental reputation. When a company commits a serious environmental error, it can use its environmental report to provide **reassurance to concerned stakeholders** that it has learned its lessons. For Hoppo an environmental report could include details of how in future it will gain assurance that suppliers are operating in an environmentally-friendly way.

Addressing investor concerns

Publishing an environmental report can be seen as contributing to providing a **balanced and understandable assessment of the company's affairs** for investors. It can **strengthen accountability** to shareholders by providing shareholders with important information about how the company is being managed. In particular Hoppo's report can give investors important data how the company is managing environmental risks and the impacts of these risks on strategy. This can help resolve investors' current doubts about Hoppo.

Impact on internal control systems

The need to specify the impact on the environment means that environmental reports must be integrated with control systems. This means that a company will need to **establish internal measurement systems** that collect and process the data required to support its environmental reports. As well as spurring reductions in environmental impacts, the information generated can be used to develop understanding of how to **reduce cost and waste and improve internal efficiency**. It is particularly important for Hoppo to ensure that its new factory has strong information systems, since this plant is meant to be environmentally state-of-the-art.

(c) **Strategic internal controls**

Internal controls can be strategic in nature if they relate to matters affecting strategic positioning decisions that have a **significant impact on the business's long-term future**. For example controls over sources of supply are important because they affect Hoppo's **ability to produce certain products and pricing decisions**, which will affect its position in its market.

Internal controls in the Yuland factory

Internal controls are necessary in the factory to ensure that inputs of raw materials are **used efficiently**, **waste is minimised** and that **output is of appropriate quality**. There are several reasons why controls are important in the new factory.

Sources of supply

Hoppo depends on a continuous and reliable supply of TY13 and it thus needs to establish strong relationships with suppliers who can be relied on to deliver **material of appropriate quality**. TY13 is a rare commodity and shortages of supply often occur, so if a supplier fails to deliver, Hoppo is likely to struggle to find alternative sources of supply and costs may be even greater. In addition the supply quality of TY13 varies widely and the finished product is very dependent upon the quality of supply. Thus Hoppo needs to identify suppliers who can be relied on to deliver material of appropriate quality.

Costs of waste

Controls are also important because of the **financial impact of inefficiencies**. We are told that even small inefficiencies can **disproportionately affect final product costs**. If TY13 is wasted, either Hoppo will bear the brunt of waste costs or, if the costs of waste are passed on to consumers as price increases, demand will fall. Either way profits may decrease significantly.

Health and safety

TY13 is very toxic. Controls are needed to ensure no leakages occur internally and externally, to guard against **threats to employee health** and the **kind of environmental damage seen in Teeland**. Not only will the local environment be damaged, but Hoppo may suffer **significant financial penalties** and **incur a further loss of reputation and potentially catastrophic damage to its brand values** of being environmentally responsible.

Quality of output

Because of uncertainties over the quality of the material, Hoppo needs to have **equivalent systems of pre-production testing** to those used by Red. Failure to test the material properly may lead to **finished products performing unacceptably**, damaging the reputation of Hoppo's products and causing sales to fall.

(d) **Press release**

Hoppo feels it must respond to allegations made in the media about recent events connected with its review of its manufacturing activities. Hoppo has undertaken this review because of previous concerns raised in the media about poor working conditions at its outsource supplier, Red and also the leakage of toxic material into a local river. Hoppo's directors place high value on maintaining a reputation as a trustworthy and responsible producer and have thus felt compelled to review its relationship with Red and consider taking manufacture under direct control.

This statement provides the opportunity for Hoppo to reassure its stakeholders of its commitment to integrity and transparency. It also allows Hoppo to describe the circumstances surrounding an irregular payment to an individual in Ootown and explain why Hoppo considers making this payment to be wrong.

(i) **Hoppo's commitment to integrity**

Hoppo is committed to being **straightforward and honest** in all its business relationships, dealing fairly with its business partners. This involves a **commitment to strict ethical principles** whatever the pressures to do otherwise and adherence to the highest standards of probity and professionalism. Hoppo believes that integrity is an **essential part of proper corporate governance** and its directors are therefore expected to act with integrity in all their dealings.

Hoppo's commitment to transparency

Hoppo is equally committed to transparency in its business dealings and corporate governance, and welcomes open discussion of its conduct. It is committed to a **default position of information provision rather than concealment**, meaning that it will disclose information unless there are good and legitimate reasons for non-disclosure. Transparency implies **open and clear disclosure of relevant information to shareholders and stakeholders** and not concealing information when it may affect decisions. There are times when Hoppo will be bound by the constraints of commercial confidentiality, but it will not use commercial constraints as an excuse for concealment of dishonest or unethical behaviour.

(ii) **Irregular payment**

Hoppo regrets the perception that its directors were considering paying a bribe. Hoppo wishes to reassure its shareholders and other stakeholders that its **commitment to the highest ethical standards** in its business dealings means that it believes that paying bribes is wrong in all circumstances. Hoppo's board has been considering Ootown as a location for the new factory as it believes there is a strong business case for being based there. However the directors would never allow irregular payments to be made to facilitate a preferred course of action. Because of the seriousness of the allegations, Hoppo's board feels that it needs to set out in detail why it would never agree to paying bribes.

Business considerations

Although there is a business case for investing in Ootown, gaining the chance to invest by paying a bribe is likely to have a number of adverse consequences for Hoppo's business. Hoppo has built its success on a reputation of being **trustworthy and reliable**. It has attracted customers and employees on the basis of this reputation. Becoming known for paying bribes would deter those who wished to deal with, or work for, Hoppo because of its high ethical standards. If Hoppo's directors are believed to be guilty of dishonest behaviour, it would also destroy the **basis of trust between directors and shareholders**. This could adversely affect share price, as investors sold their shares.

More important than business reasons are the ethical reasons for refusing to agree to pay a bribe.

Ethical considerations

(Deontological case)

Hoppo believes that businesses and individuals have moral obligations to act ethically at all times. It sees ethical behaviour as necessary to **underpin relationships in the business world**. If bribery was considered as acceptable and generally no-one could be believed to be acting honestly, then trust in business would be **fatally undermined**. This would make the establishment and maintenance of business relationships, particularly in different environments such as other countries, very difficult. In addition bribery also **undermines business efficiency**, as business decisions are made on the basis of illicit payments rather than what is economically desirable. Some parties may be less inclined to participate in business, if they believe that bribery means that they could not achieve an acceptable return honestly.

Hoppo believes in the strict ethical rule that bribery is **generally wrong for all those involved in business** and that there **are no circumstances** where it would be acceptable to pay bribes.

(Consequentalist case)

Hoppo believes that paying the bribe is also wrong because of what could result if it did make the payment. Firstly it could gain a reputation in Ooland as a company that was prepared to **pay bribes and act dishonestly** to achieve its objectives. This could mean that potential business partners in Yuland who were committed to fair and honest dealing would not wish to deal with Hoppo because of its unethical reputation and because they did not feel that Hoppo could be trusted. Contrawise other parties with poor business ethics might feel **empowered to demand bribes** from Hoppo. Secondly if a bribe is paid and not discovered, the recipient of the bribe has a hold over Hoppo. The recipient could ask for further bribes or make other demands on Hoppo in return for keeping quiet about the original bribe.

Hopefully this statement has addressed all the concerns raised in the media and reassured stakeholders, whose views remain very important to Hoppo.

62 Wyland

Text references. Chapters 3, 6, 7, 8 and 11.

Top tips. (a)(i) brings out the distinction between the concepts as being what should be sustained. You will get some credit for discussing the problem of comparing concepts that are measured in different ways in (a)(ii). However the bulk of (a)(ii) is about incompatibilities – between environmental maintenance and the environmental disruption caused by the steps required for economic development, between human and other species sustainability and between the long and the short-term.

The % given for the risks discussed in (b) are percentages of occurrence but you have also to discuss the potential impacts. The measures of risk reduction are mostly measures to **prevent** problems, not to detect and correct them.

(c) begins with some basic supply and demand analysis but you need then to go on to discuss complications in the demand and supply for labour. The second part of (c) brings out the need to weigh local conditions and sensibilities against the necessity of paying what is considered good global remuneration to attract the right person.

The challenge in the first part of (d) is how to admit problems, some of which have been HEC's fault. It is important to give the impression that these issues will be addressed. The second part should have been easier – hopefully you'll have been able to see how the needs of HEC tie in with the core elements of internal audit's work.

Easy marks. Hopefully most of the professional marks in (d) – you should certainly have been prepared for a letter to come up.

Marking scheme

				Marks
(a)	(i)	2 marks for each explanation of each type of sustainability	4	
	(ii)	2 marks for each relevant discussion point	8	
				Max 12
(b)		1 mark for each risk correctly assessed and 1 mark for each correct strategy proposed with reason (½ mark for identification of strategy only)	8	
		2 marks for each problem with subjectivity	2	
				10
				Marks
(c)		2 marks for an explanation of labour market conditions	2	
		2 marks for each point on a critical evaluation of reward level (arguments either way)	8	
				10
(d)	(i)	2 marks for each IC difficulty discussed and explained. ½ mark for identification only		8
	(ii)	½ mark for each area identified and 1 mark for each discussed in context		6
		Professional marks		4
				50

(a) (i) **Save our Wilderness (SOW)**

SOW's definition focuses on **environmental sustainability**. This means maintaining the ability of the environment to **function as naturally as possible,** to **continue to support all life forms on the planet and maintain its evolutionary potential**. This means not using resources at a faster rate than they can be replenished, and also ensuring that any adverse impacts on the environment can be rectified. For the Hiaka pipeline this means the resources it extracts should be replaced and spills or emissions should be cleaned up.

Government of Exland

The government of Exland's definition focuses on **economic sustainability**, both in terms of the economy as a whole and the sustainability of HEC, a critical player within the economy. This means the ability to sustain and promote economic activity levels. Oil underpins many aspects of an economy's infrastructure, including fuel for transport and heating and thus continuance of oil flows is vital for economic well-being. As 90% of Exland's oil comes from HEC, its economic sustainability is dependent on oil from a single source, since it is unlikely to be able to find alternative sources at a reasonable cost that could make up for the loss of oil from HEC.

(ii) **Fundamental conflict**

The situation here appears to illustrate a basic conflict between economic and environmental sustainability. Whatever measures are taken to limit its impact, the Hiaka pipeline **cannot function without having some adverse impact on the environment**. However if it is shut down it will **limit economic well-being**. The tension is particularly strong here because of the dependence of Exland upon the pipeline for its oil, the large number of jobs on Hiakaisland that the pipeline sustains and the large revenues the Wyland government obtains through selling the oil. Prioritising environmental sustainability will have a massive adverse effect on economic sustainability and also affect social sustainability as well, as people within society react badly to the loss of economic resources.

Human versus other species

A further source of tension is whether the **interests of humans should be prioritised** over the interests of other species. The pipeline can have only adverse consequences for other species, and if their interests were paramount, it would not have been built. The pipeline may have some adverse effects on the humans living in the area, but the judgement has been made that these are outweighed by the positive impacts for society of the availability of oil to sustain economic activity.

Measurement issues

The economic impact of development can be measured and quantified in terms of the impact on the economy. Environmental impact cannot be measured in the same way, so it is difficult to compare the two. In addition, it is much more difficult to **measure environmental impact objectively**. Some environmental impacts will also only be seen in the long-term whereas it is easier to establish short-term economic impacts.

Long-term sustainability

SOW's argument is that oil production is not sustainable, because oil is non-renewable and in the long-term it will no longer be available. Any steps taken by HEC to limit impact will not mitigate this fundamental problem. Arguably then **environmental sustainability is compatible with long-term economic sustainability**, since governments will have to find renewable sources of energy to sustain economic activity. However governments are influenced by the electoral cycle and therefore will continue to prioritise oil production as the best way of maintaining sustainability in the short-term. Companies such as HEC will also be influenced by short-term considerations, such as maintaining strong annual returns to satisfy their shareholders.

(b) **Terrorist attack**

The risk of occurrence has been assessed as **low** at 10% but its impact will be very **high**. Terrorists will wish to cause the maximum disruption possible and complete supply disruption will mean that oil is not delivered for an indefinite period. Possible consequences will include oil and petrol rationing which will have a very serious impact on Exland's economy.

As this is a low likelihood, high impact risk HEC should ensure it has **effective insurance** in place, perhaps in conjunction with the two governments. However, the priority must be to prevent an attack being successful. This will involve a **security presence** at key points in the pipeline and **security cameras** over the rest of the area. HEC should also **liaise with the security services** to obtain indications of heightened threats and take additional steps if the risks are felt to be severe.

Geological movement

The risk of occurrence has been assessed as **low** at 5% but again the impact is potentially **very high**, with an indefinite disruption to supplies.

HEC can do a limited amount to mitigate this risk by using **robust materials and carrying out stress testing**. However the effectiveness of the precautions it can take are limited by current technology and it will not be possible to limit the impacts of the strongest earth movements. HEC, in conjunction with the governments, should therefore seek to **insure the risk**. Exland's government should investigate alternative sources of supply if it materialises.

Technical failure

The risk of technical failure has been assessed as **low** at 10% and the impact is **very low**, with no disruption to supplies.

HEC presumably already carries out some quality reviews of the materials it purchases and carries out maintenance work on the pipeline. These precautions are likely to be **sufficient**. The cost of additional testing or more expensive parts would for this risk outweigh the minimal benefits. HEC should broadly **accept** this risk.

BPP
LEARNING MEDIA

Animal or natural damage

The risk of animal or natural damage occurring has been assessed as **high**, possibly partly reflecting the recent incident, but the impact has been assessed as **low**, with no disruption to supply. The pipeline is situated in exposed countryside that suffers extreme weather regularly. There are plenty of large beasts that could damage the pipeline.

Given this assessment, HEC should take some cost-effective measures to **reduce** the risk. These include **putting up fences or other guards** to deter animals and **reinforcing the pipeline** at points which are most exposed to extreme weather.

Subjective judgement

Risks assessed subjectively often represent a **best guess** compared with risks determined objectively, which can be assessed with accuracy and some certainty. The accuracy of the assessment will depend on the skills and knowledge of the person making the assessment, but uncertainties surrounding the risk mean that the assessment may not be very reliable through no fault of whoever assesses the risk. A subjective judgement may have to be made because of the lack of the kind of evidence that would enable the risk to be assessed with **scientific accuracy**.

For the pipeline the assessment is likely to have based on a combination of problems that the pipeline has had during its **ten years of operation, the experiences of similar operations and assessments of what will happen in the future**. Past evidence may be a reliable guide to some risks, for example the occurrence and impact of extreme weather or damage by animals, but the risk of other disruptions, for example terrorist activities, cannot be predicted from past events.

(c) **Labour market conditions**

Demand and supply conditions

Labour is subject to demand and supply conditions just like any other commodity. At a simple level, the price or salary paid for labour should be at the equilibrium between demand and supply.

Labour is non-homogenous

However the **knowledge and skills possessed by labour are not uniform**. For a senior position such as Chief Executive, a company like HEC will want to employ someone with considerable knowledge and experience of the energy industry and appropriate managerial experience. The number of individuals possessing these qualities, even globally, will be small and this restriction on supply will force the cost of skilled management up.

Labour's preferences

In addition labour is not a passive commodity with no feelings. It has preferences and its decision-making may be influenced by **non-financial factors**. Here the fact that HEC is based in a remote, inhospitable location will deter executives who value comfort and do not want their personal lives disrupted. If they have a choice, they will choose to work in congenial surroundings. Therefore to recruit the right Chief Executive, companies like HEC may have to offer a **premium** as compensation for the non-financial disadvantages associated with taking the role.

Evaluation of decision

For

Inability to recruit

Paying too low a rate of remuneration may mean that HEC **could not recruit the highly skilled and knowledgeable Chief Executive** that it requires. The company is facing considerable challenges at the moment and it is vital to have an experienced Chief Executive. The consequences of poor decision-making by the Chief Executive could be severe, not just for HEC but also the economies that depend on its activities. These costs could be much more than the cost of employing a top-quality Chief Executive who will lead HEC in the right direction.

Global market

The number of executives with the **knowledge and experience** to deal with the challenges that HEC faces is small. Senior executives in the energy industry can **take up appointments in any part of the world**. Therefore it is against **worldwide standards that remuneration should be judged**, even though the global market rate is much higher than is regarded as reasonable in Hiakaisland. The terms offered by HEC have to take into account the fact that the company is competing for executive talent against other companies all over the world.

Against

Level of workers' salaries

Workers at HEC have to work for low salaries in poor conditions. **Morale is low and there are industrial relations problems**. Having a chief executive who is paid not just much more than employees, but also anyone else in the local economy, is likely to depress morale further. It will be difficult for HEC's management to argue in negotiations with the workforce for wage restraint if Gavin Hoo is perceived as being **greedy**. On grounds of **fairness**, arguably Gavin's salary should bear some relation to the salaries being earned by the lowest paid workers. This will demonstrate to employees that management is sensitive to local conditions and also improve media coverage of HEC.

Cost of living

The decision appears to have been influenced by what was considered a **good level of remuneration** in Gavin's home country, a level adequate to maintain a certain standard of living. However **the costs of living are much lower in Hiakaisland** and the standard of living Gavin can enjoy is therefore much higher. This aspect is again likely to **fuel worker discontent** and also lead **shareholders to question** why HEC is paying out considerable sums to finance an over-lavish lifestyle.

(d)

Hiaka Energy
Location
Date

Minister of Industry

Dear Minister

Thank you for your letter about internal controls at HEC. You will be aware that I have recently taken over as Chief Executive. I regard it as one of my most important priorities to ensure that the company has robust internal controls going forward. In this letter I shall set out details of the challenges that the company needs to overcome to establish effective internal controls. I shall also set out details of our plans to establish an internal audit function. We regard setting up an internal audit function as a first priority, as it underpins all the systems we establish.

(i) **Difficulties in internal control**

Nature of terrain

As you will know, the pipeline is 1,000 km in length and thus is a very substantial project to oversee and maintain. Much of the pipeline runs over **inaccessible and rough terrain**, that is often afflicted by poor weather. It can therefore be difficult to monitor the condition of all the pipeline and assess the magnitude of likely threats to it.

Failure to recruit quality staff

I admit that previously staff have **had to endure poor working conditions and have not been paid particularly well**. These have meant that it has been difficult to recruit staff with the technical expertise required to operate certain controls effectively.

Poor morale

I acknowledge also that the morale of HEC's workforce has been low for some time. This has resulted in poor industrial relations and a **lack of trust between staff and management**. I believe that this may have meant that staff have not been motivated to operate controls to the high standards required.

Reliance on foreign labour

HEC has had to recruit foreign labour in order to maintain the levels of staffing required for operations. There have, however, been problems with workers from overseas. HEC has had a requirement in place that all staff employed should speak Wyland's language but this has not been enforced. **Language difficulties** appear to have meant that some staff have not been able to understand the complex technical instructions they have been given and have failed to do as they were told and operate internal controls properly.

(ii)   One change that we are making imminently is the establishment of an internal audit function, that will report to the board of directors. This function will have a number of roles, which I would like to tell you about briefly, and will, I believe, bring a number of benefits to HEC.

Effectiveness of internal controls

An internal audit will carry out a **monitoring** role, assessing the adequacy of HEC's internal control systems and testing the effectiveness of their operations. The nature of HEC's operations means that control systems will necessarily be complex, and it is vital therefore that evidence is obtained through the work of internal audit that the control systems are functioning effectively.

Risk management systems

Similarly internal audit's review of risk management provides evidence that our systems are operating effectively in the challenging environment in which we operate. Internal audit's work will **reinforce the work** that our new risk manager, Gerry Jupp, has been carrying out. Internal audit will **test whether HEC has systematic processes** in place for identification of risk and **effective and thorough strategies** for dealing with the significant risks that have been identified.

Compliance with laws and regulations

HEC operates in a highly-regulated environment. The legal penalties imposed upon the company for breaches could be extremely severe. Internal audit work will review whether the systems HEC has in place are sufficient to **ensure compliance with laws and regulations**, and that staff are fulfilling the requirements imposed upon them. Internal audit will also **review compliance with the contractual terms of the supply agreement** with the government of Exland.

Value for money

Lastly internal audit will review the **economy, efficiency and effectiveness** of operations, to ensure that value for money is being achieved for our **shareholders and customers**. This review will assess the soundness of financial management and also cover areas such as procurement of supplies. Internal audit work will also monitor major work going forward, with a view to ensuring that it is done in time and on budget.

I hope that I have addressed satisfactorily the issues that you have raised about internal controls at HEC. Should you want to discuss further any points I have raised please do not hesitate to contact me. We regard good relations with the Wyland government as vital and I hope this letter establishes a dialogue that will help maintain these.

Yours sincerely
Gavin Hoo

63 World Justice

Text references. Chapters 1, 8 and 10.

Top tips. The case studies in Question 1 are often based on real-life situations. This particular case requires a thorough analysis as the actions of the company are not easily categorised as 'right' or 'wrong'.

Easy marks. The professional marks should be achievable for any well-prepared student.

Examiner's comments. In requirement (a) it was not enough to be able to define the three terms (transparency, judgement and reputation). The requirement was clearly to assess the Xaxa board's performance against each one.

Many candidates seemed to default to assuming that the board's performance against each one was negative, but a careful analysis of the case showed that the company had been relatively transparent about its actions and had been transparent to its shareholders. This underlines the importance of a thorough analysis of the case.

Part (b) was answered poorly by many candidates. The first task was essentially knowledge based and so should have been done well by well-prepared candidates. Most candidates should have been able to explain the purposes of a corporate code of ethics and many did this well. But it was surprising that many answers did not attract these relatively straightforward marks. The second task was poorly done overall. Candidates were asked to examine how the adoption of such a code might make Xaxa reconsider its marketing of baby foods, and this was done well by only a minority of candidates. Some weaker answers attempted to answer this requirement using the Tucker or AAA framework. It was difficult to see what lay behind such attempts but in each such case, they were not well rewarded.

There were two tasks in part (c), both carrying equal marks. Part (c)(i) was essentially a knowledge based question for 5 marks and asked about the reasons for shareholder intervention in the governance of a company. Most candidates were able to gain some marks here but I was disappointed that we were unable to give higher marks for this in many cases. A well-prepared candidate who had worked through the study manual and the past papers should have been able to gain full marks for this part. Part (c)(ii) was more ambitious and required a careful analysis of the case to discuss the reasons why the Oublie Group (a group of influential shareholders) might intervene in the management of Xaxa Company. The case was carefully written to include several reasons why such intervention might be considered necessary. To do this task well required that candidates not only knew what the preconditions for shareholder behaviour were (ie part (a)), but also that they had studied the case to select the reasons from the behaviour of Xaxa Company. This was less well don than part (c)(i).

As in previous P1 papers, part (d) contained the requirement to complete the answer in a certain way to gain some of all of the four professional marks. In this case, answers had to be prepared as notes from the consulting company for the Xaxa board, This means that they had to be written in a way that was easily understandable for the purposes of briefing, and also clear in that the board sought help on the subject of risk auditing. Quite a lot of candidates made no effort to answer the requirements in a suitable manner at all, whilst others, perhaps unexpectedly, set out their answer as a letter or similar.

There were two requirements in part (d). The first (part (d)(i)) asked candidates to discuss the stages in a risk audit. This was essentially a knowledge based requirement but it also asked that the discussion take place 'in the context of Xaxa'. This means that to achieve the highest marks, it was necessary not only to know the main stages in a risk audit but also to analyse the case to place these stages in the context of the case. A common error was to list the main stages in a risk audit as a bullet list without any 'context of the case' and these answers did not attract high marks.

Part (d)(ii) asked candidates to distinguish between internal and external risk audit, and this was done well by many candidates. The second task was to discuss the advantages for Xaxa of an external risk audit. The second task was less well done, with answers often taking a general approach rather than locating the discussion in the context of Xaxa.

ACCA examiner's answers. The ACCA examiner's answers to the June 2014 exam can be found at the back of this Kit.

Marking scheme

			Marks
(a)	1 mark for each explanation		
	2 marks for each assessment of Xaxa's performance		9
(b)	1 mark for each point of explanation (max 5 marks)		
	2 marks for each point on Xaxa reconsidering its position (max 6 marks)		11
(c)	(i)	1 mark for each reason for intervention (max 6 marks)	
	(ii)	2 marks for each relevant point on Xaxa (max 6 marks)	10

(d)   (i)   2 marks for each stage explained and discussed in context   8

        (ii)   1 mark for distinguishing between internal and external audit
              2 marks for each advantage of external risk audit (max 8 marks)   8

        Professional marks   4
                                                                 50

(a) Transparency

Corporations should be open and honest in their dealings with shareholders, taking the default position of disclosing all relevant information unless there is a valid reason for withholding it.

From the information available, Xaxa has been open and transparent in its desire to pursue profit at all cost; the withdrawal of the other two companies in the market has opened up a business opportunity that Xaxa is happy to exploit. Management have made their position clear to shareholders in that their goal is to maximise shareholder returns, and they have replied directly to the Oublie Group's questions on this issue.

Judgement

Management have to apply judgement in the decision-making process, based on their attitude to risk, ethics and likely returns.

In making their decision, the board of Xaxa have adopted a pristine capitalist view of placing profits above any ethical considerations, thereby putting the company's reputation at stake. Their decision goes against the views of MWC and the Oublie Group who question this decision to pursue profits at any cost when the two other companies have withdrawn from this risky market.

Reputation

A company's reputation affects its ability to attract funding, high quality staff and market share. The board must demonstrate to major shareholders that they can place their confidence in management to act in an ethical, fair and reputable manner.

The action of the two other main players in this market suggests that there are significant reputational risks involved in continuing in this market. The board of Xaxa has dismissed the concerns of MWC and the Oublie Group and is determined to ignore the damage that has already been done to the reputation of the company. There have already been calls for a boycott of Xaxa products, and there may be future legal risk if the company were to be sued because of damage done by the product.

(b) Corporate code of ethics

The five main purposes of a corporate code of ethics are:

- To establish the organisation's core values, which underpin its entire structure and help to direct its behaviour as an entity

- To recognise and promote stakeholder responsibilities according to their hierarchy amongst themselves

- To control behaviour and guide decision making, providing employees and management with appropriate ethical guidance when making decisions and helping to prevent unethical behaviour

- To establish the organisation's strategic position, which is based as much on its ethical reputation as on its market and financing strategies

- To convey values and ethical standards to stakeholders, to enable shareholders and employees to compare the corporate ethical stance with their own

Xaxa and the baby food market

Should Xaxa decide to adopt a corporate code of ethics, the company would have to reconsider its position in the light of how this affects its stakeholders. There is clearly dissatisfaction and negative publicity, as demonstrated by the Oublie Group's concerns and the MWC campaign. The company would need to be more outward-looking, and take into account in its decision making the effects of its activities in developing countries and the ethical dilemmas arising.

Taking an ethical stance would make Xaxa reconsider its strategic positioning and consider the damage done to its reputation by continuing to pursue profits in what is now a controversial baby food market. A withdrawal from this market, combined with a clear statement of improved ethical intent, could lessen the threat of damaging protests and boycotts. In future any decisions based on a poor ethical stance could be challenged by stakeholders.

Xaxa must, however, be careful to ensure that adopting a corporate code of ethics is a genuine move towards an improved ethical position rather than being a cynical PR exercise.

(c) (i) **Investor intervention**

The intervention of shareholders is a serious matter because it demonstrates that the agency relationship that puts directors in charge of running the company in the interest of shareholders has broken down. Intervention could take the form of a questions put at the AGM or direct challenge to the chair of the board of directors.

The following are some of the situations where investor intervention may take place.

- Concerns about company strategy; this is a serious situation where the company is acting contrary to shareholders' interest in terms of risks to shareholders' returns or ethical matters

- Poor operational performance given the level of risk the company has been exposed to

- Weak non-executive directors (NEDs) who do not provide sufficient challenge or scrutiny of board decisions

- Serious failure of internal controls that could lead to losses, safety issues or legal challenge. Internal control is the responsibility of management and shareholders may wish to call them to account for any failings

- Compliance failure with regard to laws, accounting standards, or taxation rules and deadlines

- Concerns over governance and ethics in the actions of the board

(ii) **Intervention at Xaxa**

There are three main reasons for intervention at Xaxa:

(1) NEDs are weak when it comes to providing adequate scrutiny of the board's decisions. Their role is to act on behalf of shareholders and to question the board when their strategy puts the company's reputation at risk. The negative publicity regarding the baby food market could also have an impact on Xaxa's market share of other products as a boycott has been threatened. Overall NEDs have been shown to have been ineffective in holding the board to account.

(2) The board has demonstrated that ethical concerns have a low priority when it comes to decision making. They have dismissed the concerns of the Oublie Group and MWC and have put the reputation of the company at risk. If the ethical stance of shareholders, as represented by the Oublie Group, is at odds with that of the board, then there is grounds for intervention.

(3) In pursuing short-term gains by cornering the baby food market, the board may have jeopardised the long-term future of the company. This shows a lack of insight and awareness of how the controversy, seen as a temporary problem by the board, could have the effect of tarnishing the reputation of Xaxa well into the future. The effects may be felt not only in the baby food market but also in other areas of operation, especially if the 'Killer Company' label persists in the public consciousness.

(d)   (i)   **Notes for the Xaxa board**

Prepared for: Board of Directors of Xaxa Company
By: Consulting Company
Date: XX/XX/20XX
Subject: Guidance on risk audit

Introduction

These notes have been prepared in response to your request for guidance on risk auditing and other related issues. Risk audit is a component of sound corporate governance in that it serves to highlight the risks affecting a company and the measures that can be taken to mitigate those risks. Unless specified by local jurisdiction, there are no specific rules as to who should take on this role and both internal and external auditors may be used. Before we distinguish between the two we shall look first of all at the distinct stages of a risk audit.

Risk identification

All risks facing the company must be identified as the first stage in a risk audit. This can be achieved by creating in the first instance a risk register, and then maintaining this up to date as new risks are identified and others become obsolete. In the case of Xaxa specific risks arise from the complexity of the business, operations in different countries, the baby food market, and reputational and product risks.

Risk assessment

For each risk identified, the probability of it occurring and the impact if it does must be plotted. This will enable management to devote resources to high priority risks. The impact of a boycott, for example, could be considerable, whilst the probability of that occurring will depend on the effect of current and future publicity campaigns.

Review of controls

Where appropriate, risks can be controlled or mitigated by introducing controls. The costs and benefits of controls will need to be calculated in relation to the risks they address, as will any shortfalls in resourcing.

Risk audit report

The report will highlight the key risks and will comment on the existing controls in place. Weaknesses in internal controls will be brought to management attention in order to aid future planning and decision making. A key issue for Xaxa will be the effect of its decision to continue operations in the controversial baby food market in developing countries.

(ii)   **Internal and external risk audit**

Internal risk audit is usually carried out by the internal audit function of a company. This function may be staffed by the company's own employees or it may be provided by an external contractor.

In the case of Xaxa, and external risk audit would be more effective for the following reasons.

- Familiarity threat. Internal auditors are part of the company and are therefore influenced by its culture even if they are deemed to be independent. The suggestion that Xaxa is 'inward-looking' makes the case for an outsider's viewpoint to provide the necessary scrutiny.

- Neutrality and independence. External review will provide an impartial mindset.

- Investor confidence. Given the concerns of the Oublie Group, any tension between shareholders and management will be allayed if an organisation from outside the company brings perspective and independence.

- Best practice. External auditors are familiar with a range of companies and can share knowledge and effective practices with the board of Xaxa.

64 Cheapkit

Text references. Chapters 1, 6, 10 and 11 all contain relevant information for this answer.

Top tips. The scenario in this question has some parallels with real world events, and as such it is important to read the details thoroughly so that your answers are specific to the case rather than being generic rote learning, which tends to gain few marks.

Easy marks. There are 4 professional marks available for part (d) but only if the correct format (press statement) is adopted and the argument is presented clearly and logically. As the examiner has pointed out, 4 marks can mean the difference between a pass and a fail.

Examiner's comments.

The case scenario for the compulsory question 1 was about a company (Cheapkit) who sourced its inputs from Cornflower, a producer based in a developing country. In order to control its costs, Cornflower was corrupt in some of its dealings, and this contributed to the building weaknesses that eventually led to the building collapsing, killing many people. This is similar to a real life case that took place a few years ago. The requirements explored a range of issues around these events.

Part (a) asked candidates to discuss the stakeholder claims of Cornflower's employees and customers and how these might be in conflict. The customers include Cheapkit and they rely on very low unit prices from Cornflower in order to be competitive in their own strategies. The case suggests that the need to remain competitive was a factor in Cornflower entering into corrupt practices to keep unit prices low, and these badly affected the health and safety of its employees. The point being explored in the question was that companies have to decide which stakeholders to privilege over others, and in many cases, claims are in conflict meaning that one must be chosen over others. Weaker answers defined stakeholder claim and considered the respective claims of the two stakeholders, but then failed to consider the conflict between the two. Answers that discussed Mendelow and/or the types of stakeholder (active/passive, primary/secondary, etc) missed the point and were not well-rewarded.

Part (b) contained two tasks. The first was to explain corruption. This was done well by most candidates. The second task was to discuss how corruption at Cornflower contributed to the collapse of the building. This involved carefully studying the case and drawing out the corrupt practices that made the collapse of the building more likely. Cornflower's owners, the Fusilli brothers, were corrupt in several was in establishing the new Cornflower building and its fitting out, most of which made it less safe and more likely to fail. This was not difficult for those candidates who took the time to study the case and discuss the various contributory factors. Of course this requirement showed the importance of complying with building regulations and other building requirements in order to ensure the health and safety of employees and the dangers of corrupt practices.

Part (c) asked about three risks that Cheapkit faced. Candidates were required to explain the three risks (exchange rate risk, supply risk and international political risk). In addition, however, candidates were required to explain how each of the three risks might be of importance to Cheapkit's shareholders. A common answer was to explain the three risks and then to offer only a weak explanation of their relevance to shareholders but it should be remembered that the shareholders collectively own the value of a company and so any threat to company value is a threat to the value of a shareholder's investment. According to agency assumptions, a company has no money of its own: all of the value of a company belongs to the shareholders.

Part (d) contained three parts and the requirements asked that the answer be presented as a press statement. As mentioned in the introductory remarks, this was done with varying degrees of success. It has been stressed before in previous examiner's reports that these marks can often make the difference between a pass and a fail, and so it is baffling why so few seem to take this seriously. The default, in many cases, was to (incorrectly) set the answer out as a memo:

From:	Board of Cheapkit
To:	Magazine
Subject:	Press statement

I would encourage tutors to work through these issues with candidates, as these four marks can often be very helpful in accumulating marks on the exam.

In terms of content, 1(d)(i) asked candidates to explain Cheapkit's role as a corporate citizen. This has been examined before on a previous P1 paper and the key was to explain citizenship in terms of the company's rights and responsibilities. Weaker answers described Cheapkit's CSR or ethical postures, which, whilst relevant to a degree, missed the main point of the answer.

Part (d)(ii) asked candidates to explain 'accountability' and 'fiduciary duties' and then, importantly, to relate these concepts to Cheapkit if were to adopt a pristine capitalist perspective. The task here was not to define 'pristine capitalist' but to use this perspective to show how its view of accountability and fiduciary duty would be viewed. Weaker answers defined the three terms and moved on but there were some excellent answers that correctly interpreted accountability and fiduciary duty in terms of a pristine capitalist understanding.

Part (d)(iii) asked candidates to discuss integrated reporting. There was a recent technical article on integrated reporting and it has been on the P1 study guide for some time. It was disappointing to see that many candidates had little idea of this initiative with some, seeing the word 'stakeholders' in the question, assuming it to perhaps be a Mendelow question or similar. Integrated reporting is an international initiative supported by many of the world's most important organisations, including ACCA, seeking to increase the materiality and usefulness of business reporting. It does that in part by specifying the content of business reporting and strongly encouraging reporters to consider the materiality and usefulness of what they report. The six capitals are a part of this, intended to convey to investors and others, the net change from year to year in the quality and stock of those six capitals. This part of question (d) was worth 8 marks and this shows the importance of studying all the study guide including any new additions, included to keep the P1 study guide relevant and up-to-date.

ACCA examiner's comments.

The ACCA's exam answers to the December 2014 exam can be found at the back of this Kit.

Marking scheme

			Marks
(a)		2 marks each for examination of the two claims	
		2 marks for discussion of conflict	
		1 mark for evidence of understanding of stakeholder claim	
		(anywhere in the answer)	
			7
(b)		2 marks for explanation of corruption	
		2 marks each for corruption at Cornflower to a maximum of 8 marks	
		Half mark for identification only	
			10
(c)		3 marks for each risk – one for definition and up to two for importance in context	
			9
(d)	(i)	2 marks for explanation of citizenship in terms of rights and responsibilities	
		2 marks for explaining each in terms of the case to a maximum of 4 marks	
			6
	(ii)	1 mark each for explanation of accountability and fiduciary duty	
		2 marks for each relevant point made on the relevance each to Cheapkit from the pristine capitalist perspective	
			6
			Marks
	(iii)	2 marks for explanation of the basic framework of IR	
		2 marks for each advantage explained to a maximum of 6 marks	
			8
		Professional marks	4
			50

(a)   **Stakeholder claims of Cornflower's employees and customers**

Stakeholders are entities that can affect or be affected by the achievements of an organisation's objectives. It is a two way relationship where each stakeholder group has different expectations and has different claims upon the organisation.

Cornflower's employees will be focused on how the company is performing and on how this will have an impact on their pay and working conditions. Their immediate concern, as voiced by their representative body PWR in the aftermath of the tragedy, is for safer working conditions. They are also subject to a regime of 'exploitative wages' as they are on low pay and zero hours contracts, with poor job security.

Cornflower's customers, including Cheapkit, are concerned with the price and quality of the goods they purchase and with the continuity of supply. Cheapkit's strategy is based around low costs and over 30% of its supplies come from Cornflower. Their focus will therefore be on keeping costs down, including labour costs.

Conflict between employees' and customers' claims

If Cheapkit is to continue with its low cost strategy, this will come into conflict with any attempts in Athland to improve the pay and working conditions of garment workers as this will inevitably result in higher production costs. The dilemma for companies such as Cornflower is that, if costs increase, customers such as Cheapkit will take their business elsewhere and this could result in job losses in the garment industry in Athland.

(b)   **Corruption**

Corruption is defined as deviation from honest behaviour; it undermines the relationships of trust in corporate activities where illegal or unethical means are employed. Bribery is one example of corruption, and the Fusilli brothers have bribed local government officials in order to obtain the best location for their new factory. Other examples include abuse of a system for improper purposes, as has happened in Athland. Corruption leads to, amongst other things, a lack of honesty and good faith, conflicts of interest and damage to reputation.

Although Athland does have building regulations, the regulatory controls are weak and the Fusilli brothers have exploited this situation in a number of ways:

- Building inspectors were bribed when construction began, to overlook the failure of Cornflower to adhere to building regulations. Building regulations exist to keep people safe. These public officials failed in their duty of ensuring that the public interest was protected.

- In constructing the new factory, they used inferior building materials in order to save money on capital expenditure and to complete the project quickly. The use of inferior materials may have contributed to the collapse of the building two years later. Once again public officials are complicit in acting corruptly.

- Bribes were paid again to officials when the Fusilli brothers provided inadequate escape doors and staff facilities. This was driven by the need to maximise the available floor space for production, at the expense of the health and safety of the factory workers. Had there been proper escape routes in place as legally required, the death toll following the collapse of the building might have been less.

- Cornflower ignored the occupancy rules and allowed 1,500 employees to work in a space designed for only 500. This rule does not appear to have been enforced by the relevant health and safety authorities. Pressure on production fuelled by increased demand led to more jobs being created but without proper health and safety measures in place there was little or no protection for these workers in the event of an emergency.

(c)   **Exchange rate risk**

When a company trades with a foreign supplier or customer, it will expose itself to exchange rate or currency risk unless both countries share the same currency (as in the Euro zone for example). Movements in foreign exchange rates create risk in that the final amount payable or receivable will be uncertain.

Cheapkit pays Cornflower and its other Athland suppliers in the currency of Athland; if the exchange rate for this currency increases in relation to Cheapkit's own currency then Cheapkit's costs of buying from Athland will increase. Last year 65% of Cheapkit's supplies came from Athland so an adverse movement in exchange rates could have a significant impact on profit, which will be of concern to shareholders.

Supply risk

This is the risk that Cheapkit will fail to procure the necessary supplies to meet demand from its customers. Cheapkit relies heavily on imports from Athland, and the collapse of the building means that Cornflower will not be able to deliver its orders, at least in the short term. Cornflower produces a third of Cheapkit's products so this loss is significant.

Cheapkit's business strategy is based on providing a range of fashion items at cheap prices. The tragedy in Athland will mean a reduction in the items available in the stores, increased prices or possibly both. This could have an impact of Cheapkit's competitiveness in the market and thus on shareholder value.

International political risk

Political risk is the risk that political action will affect the position and value of an organisation. It is connected with country risk, the risk associated with undertaking transactions with a particular country. Political changes can be favourable or unfavourable.

In Athland the state failed to implement and enforce building and health and safety regulations, and this was a contributory factor in the disaster at the Cornflower factory.

For Cheapkit's shareholders, the weakness of the state means that a significant part of the supply chain is unreliable. A key risk in dealing with suppliers in Athland is the apparent prevalence of bribery and corruption, which could lead to repercussions for Cheapkit personnel if there is UK-style anti-corruption legislation in place. There could also be damage to reputation as a result of dealing with a country where corrupt practices are perceived by consumers to be common.

(d)   **PRESS STATEMENT**

Issued by the board of Cheapkit in response to recent events in Athland

The board of Cheapkit wish to issue the following statement as a response to comments received following the recent tragic events in the Cornflower factory in Athland. The Cornflower factory is one of Cheapkit's major suppliers and we wish to express our condolences and sympathy to all those affected.

We should like to reassure our shareholders and the general public that we are working closely with our contacts in Athland in order to establish why the factory collapsed and to help ensure that such a disaster never happens again.

This statement will address the following issues: Cheapkit's role as a corporate citizen, the relevance of accountability and fiduciary duty, and the benefits of introducing integrated reporting.

(i)   **Cheapkit's role as corporate citizen**

Corporate citizenship is the business strategy that shapes the values underpinning a company's mission and the choices made each day by its executives, managers and employees as they engage with society. Three core principles define the essence of corporate citizenship, and every company should apply them in a manner appropriate to its distinct needs: minimising harm, maximising benefit, and being accountable and responsive to its shareholders. The general concepts of rights and responsibilities are fundamental to the definition of corporate citizenship.

Cheapkit has the right to conduct business with suppliers and customers within the confines of the law in each country in which it operates. We have at all times acted lawfully with respect to our suppliers, customers, employees and shareholders. The tragic events in Athland occurred because of illegal practices in that jurisdiction, and as such were beyond our control.

We recognise our responsibilities as a corporate citizen in our fair dealings with all our stakeholders. Cheapkit has always strived to maximise shareholder wealth by providing value for money for our customers, whilst at the same time acknowledging our duty to secure good working conditions for our employees.

(ii)   **Accountability and fiduciary duty**

Corporate accountability refers to whether an organisation and its directors are answerable in some way for the consequences of their actions. Fiduciary duty is a duty of care and trust which one person or entity owes to another. It can be a legal or ethical obligation. Cheapkit has faced recent criticism in the media with regard to both these issues, and we should like to take this opportunity to address the concerns raised.

As far as accountability is concerned, we owe our primary responsibility to our shareholders; as directors we act on their behalf to protect and maximise their investment in the company. We discharge this duty by pursuing our business strategy of being leading competitors on price in the garments market. Whether our accountability extends beyond this, to include for example the employees of our suppliers, is a matter of opinion. This is clearly the position adopted by Miss Liu, and, whilst we respect her opinion, we do not agree that we should be held responsible for the actions of our suppliers in other countries where we have no authority or influence over business practices.

From a legal point of view our fiduciary duty covers not only our shareholders but our employees and suppliers as well. We must at all times act within the law and comply with the prevailing rules and regulations. Our shareholders can expect us to act on their behalf in their best interest, our employees have the right to fair pay and conditions, and our suppliers can expect fair contract terms and to be paid on time. Again we would question whether our fiduciary duty extends beyond what is required from us by law and regulation. We strongly deny Miss Liu's suggestion that we put pressure on Cornflower to cut corners in order to reduce prices, and thereby contributing to the tragedy at the factory. Our relationship with Cornflower is a contractual one, based on agreed prices and delivery targets, and we can take no responsibility over how the management of Cornflower conduct their affairs in order to fulfil their orders with us.

(iii)   **Integrated reporting**

The aim of integrated reporting is to demonstrate the linkage between strategy, governance and financial performance and the social, environmental and economic context within which the business operates. By making these connections, businesses should be able to take more sustainable decisions, helping to ensure the effective allocation of scarce resources. Integrated reporting is based around the six types of capital that are consumed and created by businesses. These capitals are: financial, manufactured, human, intellectual, natural, and social and relationship.

The board of Cheapkit has expressed enthusiasm for adopting integrated reporting as we believe that this will improve the information that we share with shareholders and other stakeholders. We believe that there are advantages to reporting performance in relation to the types of capital.

The benefits for Cheapkit and it stakeholders include:

- Providing information that is more in line with investor and stakeholder needs, leading to a higher level of trust from, and engagement with, stakeholders.

- Demonstrating our commitment to increasing human capital by investing in our workforce and developing their skills and competencies to enhance their contribution to the continuing success of the company.

- Improving our reputation both at home and in our partner countries through social and relationship capital. This would enable us to face some of the criticism from Miss Liu and other by emphasising our commitment to creating jobs and security of business with our suppliers.

- Creating the internal and external systems, monitoring and reporting requirements to deliver improved accountability to all our stakeholders.

We should like to conclude this statement by thanking all those who have brought matters of concern to our attention, and for the opportunity this has given us to publicly address those concerns.

65 Lysus

Text references. Chapters 1, 3, 6, 10

Top tips. It is very important in this type of question to base your answers on the facts of the scenario rather than setting down chunks of knowledge without context. This is why a thorough read-through, with the requirements in mind, is essential.

Easy marks. As the examiner states (see below) candidates should take full advantage of the generous 4 marks available for a professionally drafted answer to part (d).

Examiner's comments.

The case scenario in question 1 was about a company called Lysus, which made surgical joints. The case describes a situation in which inferior material was used in the manufacture of these joints with some very unfortunate consequences for patients. The requirements were based around some of the regulatory and ethical issues associated with this action. The company's owner, Simon Mara, substituted regulated material for inferior material and the result was that the replacement joints sometimes failed, resulting in some very unfortunate injuries in patients.

Part (a) was worth ten marks and required candidates to distinguish between the governance of a family-owned company and a public listed company. Most candidates were able to do this to some extent but the second task in the question was less well answered by many. It asked candidates to explain how Mr Mara may not have committed the offences he did had Lysus been a public company. This required candidates to discuss the regulation of public companies (under listing rules in a principles-based jurisdiction). This included challenging the 'tight-knit' culture of a family business, the lack of accounting to shareholders, the lack of regulation over family businesses, lack on external scrutiny and expertise, etc. This second task was much less well answered by many candidates, perhaps because it required candidates to apply theory to a real situation, and this seems to have been a challenge to some.

Part (b) asked candidates to criticise Amy Tsang. She was the accountant who was bullied by Mr Mara into helping to facilitate the employment of the inferior materials. In taking part in the bad practice, she also acted against the public interest. In answering this requirement, some candidates based their answers on the fundamental principles of professionalism. By discussing these principles (integrity, objectivity, professional competence and due care, confidentiality and professional behaviour), answers might have covered some of the criticisms of Amy's behaviour but this was not the correct approach. The correct approach was to review the case, and then discuss the criticisms of her behaviour in terms of one issue and then the next. The use of 'lists' are rarely a good approach and candidates would have been better studying the case and discussing her behaviour on a point-by-point basis.

Part (c) contained two tasks: to explain why some risks vary by industry sector (which was largely bookwork) and then, in the context of the case, to discuss why legal risk is a more relevant risk in the surgical supplies industry. The first part was done better than the second part over all. Many candidates were able to explain by risks vary by sector, often in terms of changing business models, different environments, different activities with different risk exposures, etc. It was frustrating that candidates were not able to attract marks on the second task, however, because it wasn't a particularly ambitious requirement. Whenever something as important (to patients) as surgical implants like joint replacements is concerned, anything that goes wrong with the device as a result of poor manufacturing (as was the case at Lysus), then legal risk becomes important because of patients pursuing legal remedies against the company.

Part (d) was to be written in the form of an article for the investors' magazine Investors in companies. This approach has been used before in P1 papers so well-prepared candidates would have studied the correct approach to answering requirements of this type. There were four professional marks for answering the question in the right way. Just for the avoidance of doubt, this meant that a letter, a memo, a report or any other form of format were not correct ways of answering this requirement.

Part (d)(i) required candidates to do two things: to know about the benefits of having an effective non-executive chairman and then to apply this to the situation at Lysus. Weaker answers listed the roles of a chairman (not what was required) whilst the best answers looked at the case of Mr Mara and his deceit, and considered how a strong and effective non-executive chairman would have helped to prevent this happening on the first place. This was one of the reasons why the Cadbury committee in the UK (in 1992) recommended the separation of these two roles after the Maxwell Mirror Group newspapers pension value theft by Mr Maxwell in the United Kingdom. The case of

Lysus, in a different way, represents a similar abuse of executive power. It was frustrating to see some answers introduce the four roles of non-executive directors (people, risk, strategy and scrutiny) as this was clearly not the approach to the requirement. Perhaps some candidates, on seeing the word 'non-executive', assume the roles is the answer to the question. Not so in this case. It is always important to work out what the requirement is asking for and carefully responding to the requirement on a task-by-task basis.

Part (d)(ii) was about embedding risk into Lysus's operations. The question specifically mentioned probity risk, which is the risk of management action that fails to take into account the need for integrity and the highest standards of ethical behaviour. The fact that Mr Mara failed against this standard makes the question all the more relevant. A common failing on this question was to define probity risk but then to only weakly explain how this might be embedded. The correct approach was to stop and think about how this risk might be embedded. I suspect a short time planning the answer would have been a beneficial approach for those who rushed or missed out the second task in this requirement.

Marking scheme

				Marks
(a)	Up to 4 marks for distinguishing			
	2 marks for each relevant point on discussion of family-owned business			
			Max	10
(b)	2 marks for each relevant point of criticism to a maximum of 6 marks			
	2 marks for each relevant point on acting against the public interest to a maximum of 6 marks			
			Max	10
(c)	2 marks for explanation of risks by sector			
	2 marks for each relevant point on legal risk in the sector.			
				8
(d)	(i)	2 marks for each relevant point made.		8
	(ii)	2 marks for each relevant point on 'embedding risk'.		10
	Professional marks			4
				50

(a) Family and listed companies

A family business, when incorporated as a company, is an example of a private limited company. This means that the shares are privately held and are not available for members of the investing public to buy and sell. This is in contrast to a public company, which is listed on a stock exchange and in which members of the public, including private and institutional shareholders, can purchase or sell shares. Being a public listed or public limited company carries a number of requirements, imposed either by statute or the stock exchange, which do not apply to private companies. These requirements include compliance with a number of corporate governance provisions which include the adoption of certain governance structures, adherence with internal control and internal audit standards, and the external reporting of some types of information. A private limited company, in contrast, must comply with company law and tax regulations, but is not subject to listing rules.

Mr Mara's behaviour was highly unethical and also illegal, given the regulatory regime controlling surgical supplies in the country in which he was based. His abuse of his office as CEO of Lysus was made possible by a number of failures, linked in part to the nature and culture of the company.

The first such factor was the 'tight-knit' family culture which enabled the decision to be made and then go unchallenged among the senior management including his wife, brother and Amy Tsang. The unwillingness to appoint from outside meant that senior members of the company became familiar with Mr Mara's management style and may, over time, have come to consider his behaviour as 'normal'. The fact that Mr Mara was such a domineering figure may have become accepted rather than challenged by other directors, partly because of family ties and their prior knowledge of his character and management style. The fact that the company was family-dominated may have made it difficult for others to confront Mr Mara about his style as such an approach may have negatively affected family relationships.

Being a family or 'insider' dominated business meant that the company did not have any external shareholders. This means that there was no need to account to public shareholders for either the performance of the company or its postures on such issues as ethics. External scrutiny of board performance was not present and Mr Mara was therefore not subject to questioning from anybody outside of the company who might have had a different view on his management than the other members of the company.

Because it was not a listed company, there was no regulatory necessity for Lysus to employ governance structures and systems capable of detecting and challenging his irregular behaviour. Had Lysus had, for example, an internal control system which included a control over inbound materials or product design, the replacement of the surgical-grade material with industrial-grade would have been detected and an alert raised as it would have not have been in compliance with the regulations on surgical supplies. Likewise, a formal internal audit system would have been capable of investigating any regulatory non-compliance. This could have then been reported in internal reports and, if deemed necessary, to external authorities.

A criticism common to many family-controlled companies is the lack of external expertise in the form of an effective non-executive presence. Although some companies employ non-executive directors (NEDs) on a voluntary and 'best practice' basis, the private company status of Lysus usually means that there is no regulatory requirement to do so. The purposes of NEDs in a listed company are to represent the strategic interests of shareholders and to populate the main board committees. These committees, in turn, provide a level of assurance to shareholders of probity, transparency and robustness.

(b) **Criticise Amy Tsang's behaviour**

The case describes three ways in which Amy Tsang acted in a manner inconsistent with her status as a qualified accountant. Although described by the case as being in her first senior role as finance director, this was no excuse for acceding to the demands of the overbearing and bullying Mr Mara. Her lack of professionalism was one of the factors which led to the failure of some of the replacement joints and the human suffering which resulted.

In the first instance, and in response to a request from Mr Mara, she performed accounting calculations for the change to industrial-grade materials based on what she knew were illegal materials, unauthorised for the use in surgical joint replacements. This involved calculating the costings and their effects on company profits, and the size and nature of the factory retooling necessary to make the change. As a senior manager in the company, her correct response, when confronted with such a request, should have been to challenge Mr Mara, clearly reminding him that such a change would be both illegal and unethical since it is stated that she was fully aware of this.

Once her calculations had been considered and the effects on profits ascertained, she used her position as finance director to sign off (approve) the investment needed to change the manufacturing process to enable the inferior material to be used. This was a breach of trust conceivably even more serious than the calculations because she approved an investment knowing it would commit the company to the continued use of an illegal material. In retooling the factory so it was capable of using the industrial-grade material, she knowingly approved an action she knew to be illegal. This is a serious breach of the probity expected of a professional accountant.

The third way in which Amy Tsang acted unethically was to sign the compliance reports to the medicines regulator to say that all of the materials and manufacturing were compliant with the licence granted to the company to produce the replacement joints. Mr Mara was equally complicit in this, of course, but as a qualified accountant, professionally bound to the ethical code of such a professional person, this was an act of professional negligence on her part.

Against the public interest

All professionals, including professional accountants, have a primary duty to the public interest. Professionals enjoy a privileged position of high esteem in society, and in return, it is important that they act in such a way as to maintain that position of trust. This includes a commitment to high social values such as human welfare, fairness, justice, integrity and probity, and the wellbeing of society.

In this case, Amy Tsang acted against the public interest in three important ways. First, her actions facilitated the manufacture and use of products which were illegal and unauthorised. These failed to comply with relevant regulations and so the accountant was complicit in illegal actions. Absolute legal compliance is assumed for all professionals and Amy Tsang failed on several counts to live up to this expectation and duty.

Second, because the inferior material was hazardous to the health of some of those who had joint replacements, her actions also meant that many people became ill and some died. The public interest is concerned with the maximisation of benefit to society and a reduction in health is clearly a breach of that trust. In the interest of what Mr Mara considered higher profits (although this ultimately proved to be misplaced), Amy Tsang took actions clearly to the detriment of Lysus's customers and undermined their trust in the company. It may also have increased society's mistrust of surgical suppliers generally, and this may have other, unforeseen, negative consequences.

Her actions partly undermined society's trust in the accounting profession and may have slightly reduced the standing of accountants in society. By taking a full part in the deceit, and approving the changes to the sourcing and manufacture of the products, Amy Tsang was complicit in partially reducing society's trust in professionals and this is against the wider public interest. It is important that professionals of all types, including accountants, act in such a way as to maintain society's trust in the professions.

(c) **Risks vary by sector**

Risks do not apply equally to all companies. This is because risks are associated with particular activities, and companies in different industrial sectors are exposed to different risks because of what they do. So, for example, banks are more exposed to a range of financial risks whilst manufacturing and mining are usually more concerned with health and safety risks. This means that the risk auditing process, usually beginning with risk identification, will be highly context dependent, with different risks being registered depending upon the activities of companies within each sector.

Legal risk in surgical supplies

Companies such as Lysus, which are involved with the manufacture and distribution of surgical supplies, are exposed to certain risks because of their strategic positioning and main activities. Surgical supply companies are engaged with the production of goods which can have profound effects on the patients (for good or bad) and so are positioned quite differently to producers of less health-critical goods such as, for example, stationery supplies. Legal risk is the risk, to a company or individual, of legal action against it. This may result from litigation or regulatory sanction for non-compliance with an impact expressed in terms of fines, asset seizure, social disapproval or other legal penalty including imprisonment of individual directors.

When individuals have a surgical procedure, they expose themselves to a number of vulnerabilities including the quality of the procedures at the health facility, the skills of the medical staff and the quality (ie fitness for purpose) of the replacement devices, if relevant. When the failure of a surgical product, purchased from third parties, causes unnecessary health or mobility problems for a patient, they will often claim that all of the supply chain is accountable for the end result. In the event of any such failure, the patient or his/her family might believe that legal redress is the only way to effectively seek justice for the less-than-successful procedure.

When one or more parts of the process are not fit for purpose, the effects on the patient can be unfortunate, perhaps resulting in ill health, immobility or even death. When a cause of a failure can be clearly identified, such as the fracture or premature deterioration of a replacement device because of defective manufacturing or the employment of an inferior material, then the patient may seek legal redress for the pain and distress caused and also the recovery of costs incurred. It is a fact that an individual can be so personally involved in, and by, a failure which makes the legal risk so prominent in the surgical supplies industry.

(d) (i) **Problems at Lysus**

Every investor knows that the public listed company form is not guaranteed to be a safe and incorruptible form of business, but some governance initiatives seem to have worked to combat the worst excesses. One of the most prominent is the separation of roles at the head of a company and the introduction of a non-executive chairman. The idea for this came in during the early 1990s and has found its way into most of the world's major corporate governance codes.

I can only wonder how events might have been different had such an effective non-executive chairman been in place at Lysus. It seems that chief executive Mr Mara was able to commit the offences he did precisely because there was nobody in the company able to confront him and keep his irresponsible behaviour in check. A non-executive chairman would be able to challenge Mr Mara in a way that no other people in the company were seemingly able to do. The whole purpose of splitting these senior roles is to prevent the investment of unfettered power in a single individual.

In addition, when there is a strong personality like Mr Mara in a private company, it is this person who imprints his or her character on the business culture. An effective non-executive chairman, able to determine the agendas for board meetings and by exercising effective leadership, would be able to influence the culture and 'tone from the top', making

a higher standard of ethical behaviour feel more normal in the company. If staff see their bosses acting unethically and in a dishonest or deceitful way, then it should come as no surprise that this can infect the whole of the company over time.

The presence of a strong figure able to exercise the roles of a chairman would, of course, improve the governance in any company. In the case of Lysus, someone whose job it was to promote openness and debate about strategic ideas and ensure that accurate and clear information was freely circulated in the company could expose misconduct like that demonstrated by Mr Mara. Once ideas are openly discussed, the weaker ones are often criticised and exposed as inadequate. The immunity to criticism which Mr Mara felt, allowed him to believe he could get away with using non-compliant materials, but would soon have been rejected had such an effective chairman been in place.

The sad case of Amy Tsang is a final salutary case in favour of a non-executive chairman. My own view is that she meant well and was a young, ambitious accountant, but she was effectively forced to comply with Mr Mara by his arrogance and bullying. The presence of a non-executive chairman would have given her, and other concerned directors, someone to communicate with about their concerns and give them someone to confide in. With Mr Mara being her only superior manager in the company, she was effectively forced to comply with Mr Mara or leave the company. In hindsight, it would have been better for her if she had left, but that point is irrelevant now.

(ii) Embedding risk awareness

I know it is a bit late to offer advice to Lysus but as someone who has seen several stories like Lysus's in the past, it is worth reminding readers about how situations like this can be avoided. When business risks – those capable of threatening the entire business as a going concern – are realised, the effects are always very unfortunate for those involved. They are often big enough to threaten the business either by a loss of sales or, as in this case, by making the company non-compliant with the regulatory systems which underpin society's trust in the surgical equipment industry.

For those other businesses wrestling with issues such as this, here is the summary of my experience and my advice on improving probity risk awareness. Investments work when we can trust the integrity of directors. When this cannot be assumed, trust in business investments will rapidly deteriorate. As an investment community, these risk-embedding practices should be encouraged in all businesses, whether they are large and listed, or smaller and private.

The whole idea, in my view, is to embed all risk awareness into the normal operations of the company. This means that nothing is 'bolted on' but that all employees are expected to be risk aware at all times. One of the first ways of achieving this is to establish a visible policy on risk awareness, and have this unreservedly supported by management, trade unions and staff. This should encourage everybody to identify risks, including those arising from the behaviour of management, and bring them to the attention of appropriate people without fearing a negative or hostile response. A philosophy and culture of risk awareness would be developed so that everybody recognises the importance of all risks and seeks to address them as far as possible.

Linked to this is the encouragement of open communication and a supportive culture. No-one should think themselves too junior or uninformed to raise a risk issue with management. It is often at the operational levels where risks can have the most unfortunate effects and so many previously unnoticed risks can arise from there. Similarly, management should welcome all discussion of risk as a normal part of their responsibilities and should never dismiss an idea, even if it is something of which management is already aware. It should not be forgotten that it was because of Mr Mara's lack of probity that the employees of the company lost their jobs: their stake in the company was the security of their jobs, and those jobs are now gone.

It is always good practice to establish formal systems such as a risk committee and a risk auditing procedure. The establishment of a risk audit forces the company to identify all risks affecting the business, both internal and external. Once listed on a risk register, each of these can then be assessed according to their perceived probability of being realised and their likely impact. A risk strategy can then be assigned to each risk and any changes to the risk environment can be 'ted' into the system to ensure that it remains current. This also provides a reporting mechanism by which individual managers, including the most senior, can be held accountable for their behaviour in respect of risks. Had Mr Mara known that this probity risk had already been identified and assessed by the risk committee, the outcome may have been very different.

Such risk management systems work when they are embedded into *human resource systems* such as job descriptions and appraisals. If the reporting and management of key risks are treated as a standing item in job descriptions and then considered annually as part of staff appraisals, it will soon become normalised into employees' work roles, and will be considered nothing out of the ordinary. If integrity failures were made something which would attract summary dismissal, for example, the ethical tone in the company may have been improved.

A final way to embed risk awareness in general is to publicise success stories in the company and to reward risk awareness behaviour through whatever mechanisms are appropriate. It would be welcomed if the discovery of a new risk or a change in its assessment was something which employees thought to be an exciting thing and something which might attract an additional day's holiday, a one-off cash payment or a weekend break away somewhere.

I wish the situation at Lysus were different. It is a sorry tale and I only hope that the lessons can be learned by other businesses.

66 Care Services Company

Text references. This is a wide-ranging question with references to topics in Chapters 1, 2, 3, 4, 7, 8, 10 and 11.

Top tips. It is important in this question to apply your answers to the specific context in the scenario. This is a private, family-owned company providing services to the public sector, so an understanding of the public sector 'ethos' will be important. You should also be aware that governance arrangements in private companies will have a different focus from those in large publicly listed organisations, and that agency issues are less prominent.

Easy marks. Part (a) of the question draws largely on knowledge, so you should be able to gain marks here. There are also four professional marks available so make sure that you apply the correct format to aid the professional structure of your argument.

		Marks
(a)	1 mark for explanation of corporate governance and 1 mark for agency.	
	Up to 3 marks for discussion of private sector as contrasted with public sector.	
	Up to 3 marks for discussion of public sector as contrasted with private sector.	
		8
(b)	2 marks for explanation of 'market rate'.	
	2 marks for each explanation of reward difference to a maximum of 8 marks.	
		10

(c)   2 marks for explanation, in context, of reputation.
        1 mark for explanation of each advantage of a corporate code and 1 mark for
        context to a maximum of 10 marks.

                                                                                        12
(d)   (i)   2 marks for each relevant point made, in context, of the importance of   8
                internal controls in the care provision sector.
        (ii)   2 marks for definition of 'ethical safeguard'.
                2 marks for each relevant point on suitable ethical safeguards.

                                                                                         8
        Professional marks.   4
                                                                                        ──
                                                                                        50

(a)   **Definition of corporate governance**

Corporate governance is the system by which organisations are configured, co-ordinated and controlled. This usually involves the characteristics of leadership, the structures, particularly at board level, to help facilitate desirable outcomes, and the behaviours of senior management in the pursuit of those outcomes.

Agency relationships underpin any governance situation, in which there is a separation of ownership and control of an organisation. Agency involves two parties: the principal and the agent. In most situations, the agency is the director responsibility for the performance of the organisation and this party reports to the principal in a fiduciary relationship. The principal is the shareholder in the case of a public company but this is less straightforward in public sector organisations, involving taxpayers and a hierarchy of public sector servants who intermediate on behalf of the state and the taxpayer.

Contrast public and private sector corporate governance

In private sector businesses, corporate governance is partly about delivering acceptable long-term economic returns to investors. In a public listed company, these shareholders are separated from the agents (directors) and so an agency issue may arise. In a private company, agency problems are less likely to exist.

In pursuit of these returns, corporate governance is also concerned with the alignment of agency rewards with shareholder priorities, the enforcement of professional behaviour to maximise investor confidence, and the ethical behaviour with those entrusted with the management of the company's assets. The value of the company is in part contingent upon the competence of its governance, and the market is capable of punishing behaviour or attitudes it finds unacceptable. This might include non-compliance with regulations or the pursuit of strategies considered sub-optimal or unacceptable to shareholders.

In the public sector, corporate governance is similarly concerned with the configuration and co-ordination of activities but it is usually less likely to be concerned with the delivery of long-term shareholder returns. Because public sector organisations usually deliver public services, the strategic focus of management is likely to be about balancing the quality and effectiveness of service delivery with cost constraints.

Because the success of Care Services Company's (CSC) bids for contracts is likely to be based on the commissioning bodies' perceptions of its service delivery quality and the general competence of the organisation, there is likely to be a continuing concern for the experience of service users and the perceived robustness of its governance structures. Accordingly, strategic management is primarily concerned not with maximising returns but rather with effective service delivery within the cost constraints imposed by the commissioning bodies. Gaining and maintaining the full confidence of these bodies and the service users is thus likely to be the focus of corporate governance in CSC. As the long-term goal for the shareholders of CSC is to sell the company to help fund their retirement, being successful in winning contracts will impact the value of the company. Thus, even with this relatively small, privately-owned company, the public sector governance drivers are key.

(b)   **Market rate**

The market rate for a reward is the equilibrium point at which supply and demand curves intersect. This is the price which matches both the supply of suitable candidates for the position and the price which employers are willing to pay for the job. Because the shape and position of supply and demand curves differ between jobs (in other words, the supply of candidates and the willingness to pay varies so much), market rates vary a great deal for different types of jobs. This is why some senior positions attract a very high level of reward and others less so.

The market rate often expresses itself as the 'natural' rate for a given job. It is generally understood, for example, that the market rate for an office cleaner is lower than that for a qualified accountant or a medical doctor. This is because of the supply and demand characteristics, as well as the years of professional training, for those jobs.

Reward differences

It is likely that market rates for chief executives of smaller companies delivering public services will be lower than those for large listed companies for a number of reasons.

Private sector business organisations can generate income with many customers, resulting in large turnovers and variable pricing strategies. Public sector organisations and those, such as CSC, delivering public sector contracts are constrained by government spending budgets. Because public sector spending is often funded by taxation, there is a lot of political and economic pressure to get best value from this revenue and so budgets are often limited. Accordingly, senior salaries in the public sector tend to be substantially below those in large private sector public listed companies. Companies such as CSC, delivering public services on behalf of governments, are similarly constrained by public sector budgets and so there will be less money to pay Natasha Mbana a high salary, even if the board wanted to.

It is often the case that smaller organisations are less able to pay high salaries compared to larger organisations. CSC is relatively small (the case mentions 180 employees, making it a small or medium-sized enterprise) with revenues capped by the values of the government contracts undertaken. Large businesses with many activities arguably require more skilled management than smaller organisations based more around a 'role-based' culture and the market values reflect that. Higher degrees of risk awareness and risk taking require different skills than in a smaller business where the main skill is person management and the scheduling of care visits. Role management is a prominent skill in public sector organisations and, whilst important, requires a different set of skills than entrepreneurial private sector management.

It is likely that, because of the lower rewards on offer, the supply of willing labour is likely to be lower. This means that applicants for each senior position will be likely to accept lower levels of reward than their private sector counterparts. They are also likely to have different motivations in applying for public sector positions in line with what is sometimes referred to as the 'public sector ethos'. With lower salaries on offer and accepted, applicants for the positions will normally have different skills than those who possess the skills and experience of working in the private or corporate sector and whose reward expectations will inevitably be higher.

In some countries, there may be government regulation and legislation which limits public sector incomes with the same applying to those delivering public services such as CSC. With limited budgets and political pressure to get value for money on all public sector contracts, public sector employers are sensitive to what senior management is paid, perhaps fearing that the public may react negatively if they feel the amount to be too high. In some countries, public sector salaries are set by statute and this obviously places a limit on what can be earned by people in those positions.

All these factors combine to justify the salary which Natasha Mbana is paid, and the reasons it is lower than would be paid to the CEO of a large, listed company.

(c) **Reputation**

Reputation concerns the perceptions with which an organisation is viewed by a range of stakeholders. A strong reputation, perhaps for service delivery and robust governance, can be a strategic asset, whilst a weak reputation can be a strong disadvantage. Reputation is one of the important underlying principles in corporate governance. Because there is a separation of ownership and control in many organisations, the reputation which the management of an organisation enjoys with its principals is important in directors or trustees being given the licence to manage the organisation as they see fit, for the long-term strategic benefit of the principals. Reputation is also important for the positioning of an organisation in its environment in terms of society's trust in the organisation as a buyer, supplier, employer, etc.

To CSC, reputation is important in being granted government contracts for care service provision. The company needs to be trusted by those outsourcing the services in that they believe that CSC is competent and has the integrity to provide the services economically, effectively and efficiently. It must also enjoy a strong reputation among service users and their families. Service users often rely heavily upon CSC and so they must be able to trust in CSC staff to deliver the necessary quality of care, on time and with the requisite levels of punctuality and rigour.

Benefits of a code of ethics for CSC

There are several benefits to a corporate (as distinguished from a professional) code of ethics. Although not in itself implicated by the scandal and not cited by the health minister, CSC feels the need to maintain and cultivate its reputation, and Dr Tan believes that the publication of the code might assist with this. CSC's reputation is likely to be a strategic asset in its industry. To the government departments from whom it accepts contracts, CSC's reputation for competence and integrity underpins its credibility as an outsource company. Its reputation is also important for its service users who rely upon the professionalism and competence of its carers. In addition, society, which indirectly pays for the services, needs to have confidence in those delivering care to its most vulnerable members. Accordingly, the reputation of CSC is important in maintaining the confidence of several stakeholders in delivering its services.

A corporate code of ethics is capable of addressing the reputation problems of CSC in several ways.

First, the drafting of a code of ethics helps to establish and promote the organisation's values and provides an opportunity for considering and debating its ethical priorities. If these are contestable, the drafting of the code is a good opportunity for directors to debate their respective opinions and an agreed position to be taken. For care providers such as CSC, there may be a debate, for example, between the need to provide high quality care and the need to be profitable given the values of the contracts it receives from government departments and the regulatory regime it must work within. When there is a conflict between these two pressures, which should take priority?

A code of ethics also promotes the company's responsibilities towards its stakeholders. By recognising the various stakeholders who can affect and be affected by the achievement of CSC's objectives, the relative importance of each can be discussed and, within certain constraints, prioritised. This is likely to be relatively complicated with, for example, the company's responsibilities to its service users sometimes coming into conflict with its responsibilities to its caring staff. The insistence of a minimum duration of visit to each service user may, on occasions, inconvenience caring staff or make other service users wait for attention. Accordingly, a balance may need to be struck between these conflicting claims.

A code of ethics has the ability to control and regulate individual behaviour and guide the actions of employees. Whilst much of the work of a carer is underpinned by regulation, the company might propose voluntary measures to maximise its advantage among government departments outsourcing the care and this might also be of benefit to service users benefitting from the care provision. This might, for example, concern the behaviours and attitudes of carers.

Codes of ethics can sometimes form an important part of the company's strategic positioning with regard to ethical issues. A company's ethical reputation, formed in part by its corporate social responsibility activities, can be a significant part of the way a company such as CSC is strategically positioned in its environment. A company believed by many to be ethical and with a high degree of integrity is likely to have an advantage in some market situations over those with less of a reputation. In the care provision sector in which CSC competes, the cultivation of a strong ethical reputation is likely to be a strategic advantage in gaining and maintaining government care contracts. This, in turn, will enhance company value and provide increased security of employment for CSC's carers.

Codes of ethics can be an effective way to communicate the company's values to stakeholders. Many codes are published on websites or in annual reports and so are publicly visible. This means that those who want to know about the company's postures or policies on certain ethical issues (eg suppliers, employees, service users, etc) can do so and hold the company to account for those stated positions. For CSC, the publication of its codes of ethics would allow it to distinguish itself from competitors without the benefits of such a code. In a situation in which the performance of CSC carers is questioned, the company could point to the relevant section of its code of ethics and remind the public that all of its carers comply with its code. This may have the effect reducing the efficacy of criticisms made against practice.

The proposed corporate code of ethics may serve as a barrier of entry for companies who wish to enter a lucrative and growing market in many developed economies. If barriers of entry are sufficiently high, then a limited number of companies in the sector, such as CSC, might be able to improve their profit margins as they may be able to accrue the well-documented economic advantages of being oligopolies in any industry. With contracts being awarded to responsible companies, the ethical performance of a company and its ability to convey that through a code, may keep some potential competitors out and be a discriminator between companies within the industry.

(d)

Care Services Company
Address line 1
Address line 2
Address line 3
Date

The Ministry of Health
Address line 1
Address line 2
Address line 3

For the attention of the Minister of Health

Dear Minister,

I write on behalf of several companies in the care provision industry in response to your recent well-publicised criticisms of some care provision companies. On behalf of the companies delivering these important services, I have been asked to write to you to outline a number of issues which we hope will not only inform you of the importance we place on effective internal controls, but also to explain how we intend to respond to the recent public concerns over the delivery of these vital care services.

(i)   As the non-executive chairman of Care Services Company (CSC), I can testify to the importance of internal controls within the company I help to lead. At the simplest level, an effective internal control system is necessary to ensure that we can deliver our services on time and within budget. My own company, CSC, has 165 carers providing important care services. There is a complicated scheduling system and effective internal controls are necessary to ensure that all service users are seen as and when necessary, and that the requisite care is provided during each visit.

In addition, the industry is heavily regulated and internal controls are necessary to ensure compliance with regulation. We need to ensure, for example, that all carers are adequately trained, checked for past criminal activity, etc. Compliance is not only necessary for the winning of contracts, but also for the cultivation of public trust in our service provision. You will be aware that care provision companies are subject to the same regulation as other public sector organisations and so internal controls help to ensure compliance with these regulations.

As you will no doubt realise, it is important that the government departments outsourcing these services have confidence in care providers. Our effective internal controls help to provide a reasonable assurance that care provision companies can and do deliver a quality service within the cost framework provided. The companies I represent are aware that they are entrusted by taxpayers to provide a high quality service, and our internal controls help to facilitate this.

We also serve our service users and it is vital that these people have full confidence in our reliability and professionalism. Effective internal controls will enhance the reputation of care services and increase the trust which commissioning bodies, employees and service users have in our business. Belief in the robustness of our internal controls will mean that service users can rely on our services and trust their carers to serve their needs.

(ii)   I have also been asked, on behalf of the companies in the industry, to outline how we intend to deal with some of the criticisms which have been made against a minority of care providers. I should stress, for the record, that my own company, CSC, was not implicated in any of the scandalous service failures. I am, however, able to report on a range of measures which we believe will be effective in ensuring that problems such as those reported upon should not happen again.

Improved internal controls must be instituted wherever there is an ethical threat or a perceived internal control failure. In this case, the fact that serious allegations have been made against a minority of carers delivering public services means that the industry participants must provide measures to prevent the ethical threats from happening again. This is what I mean by an ethical safeguard.

When a serious internal control failure occurs, such as those service failures on which you commented, it is important that the corrective measures are effective. I have been authorised by the companies I represent and by CSC to give a number of assurances which we hope and believe will be effective against future service failures.

In the first instance, carer reporting systems, based on real time recording, will be instituted. These will be capable of capturing the amount of time a carer is actually at a service user's premises and with a compulsory completion of a 'care quality' index. Each carer will be required to sign a record of arrival and departure time, and state the care delivered during the visit. It will be a disciplinary offence to make fraudulent entries on this system and those found to be falsifying entries could be dismissed.

Second, we propose to include formal feedback from service users in the reward and promotion systems for each carer. Wherever possible, service users will be contacted, perhaps at random and perhaps on a regular basis, to provide feedback on their care experiences. A dedicated telephone helpline will be set up to enable dissatisfied users, or their families, to contact their provider at any time. In such a situation, it will be built into a named person's job description to take immediate action to confront the affected carer and ensure that remedial action is taken.

Perhaps the most effective safeguard to ensure the highest levels of care is to create a culture of high care standards such that it is seen as shameful to leave a service user without adequate care. I can also confirm that my own company, CSC, will be instituting a code of ethics which will apply to all areas of our operations. When the highest standards of care are made the norm and inadequate care is made to be unacceptable as part of the culture of an organisation, good practice is embedded. It is my belief that most carers are conscientious people with a strong sense of vocation but this attitude of best practice needs to be observed without exception. This cultural change is something we will attend to as a matter of urgency.

I very much hope that the issues covered in this letter meet with your approval and I look forward to working constructively with the government delivering care provision for many years to come.

Yours sincerely,

Dr Sam Tan

67 Philo

			Marks
(a)	(i)	1 mark for explanation of each stakeholder's claim to a maximum of 3 marks.	
		2 marks for explanation of each stakeholder's position on the Mendelow matrix to a maximum of 6 marks.	9
	(ii)	2 marks for explanation of coalition arrangements.	
		2 marks for application to case.	4
(b)		2 marks for explanation of public interest anywhere in the answer.	
		2 marks for each relevant point of critical evaluation to a maximum of 8 marks.	10

			Marks
(c)		2 marks for each relevant explanation of the role of accountants in society to a maximum of 4 marks.	
		2 marks for each relevant criticism of Kathy Wong to a maximum of 4 marks.	8

(d)	(i)	2 marks for the importance of transparency and fairness in public sector organisations. 2 marks for explanation of transparency. 2 marks for explanation of fairness.	6
	(ii)	Up to 4 marks for understanding of complexity and contestability of public sector objectives. 2 marks for explanation of each of the 3 Es in the context of the case to a maximum of 6 marks.	9
	Professional marks		4
			50

(a) (i) **Mendelow matrix**

The Mendelow matrix is a way of analysing the relative influences of a number of stakeholders in an organisation. In this case, the organisation is the new science park named the Science First development. Influence is conceived of as the result of an estimate of each stakeholder's power and interest. Power is the ability to bring pressure to bear over the objectives and policies of the project and interest is the capital which a stakeholder has invested in the organisation or project (or, an assessment of how much they care or are interested in the development). Higher influence is arrived at by a combination of higher power and higher influence.

Stakeholder claims

Science First Company is seeking to remove any obstacles for the construction of the science park. It believes strongly that the science park is in the strategic interests of the city of Philo and of Philo University. Kathy Wong's report suggested that the board may be unwilling or has become frustrated by local opposition to the development. Science First Company is in a high interest and high power situation and is probably therefore the most influential stakeholder. Its interest is derived from the capital investment in the site, and its power is based on its shareholders including the Philo local government authority, Philo University, both of which are prominent local organisations. The local government authority has control over the planning process and was able to issue a 'notice to quit' notice for residents in the flats affected by Topscience's objection to their presence near the Science First development.

The residents' association represents the interests of local residents affected by the development of the Science First development. The scenario does not say that the residents' association opposes the development of the site, but it feels that the rights of longstanding residents near the site have not been adequately taken into account. Although vocal and with a high degree of interest, it is likely that it has relatively low power. Its interest is based on the fact that the Science First development affects the lives of some residents, especially those whose homes are threatened. The evidence for its low power is based on the observation from the case that it seems unable to resist the proposed demolition of the flats, or any of the other infrastructure changes around the Science First development.

The cancellation of the proposed library was necessitated by the diversion of funds from library services to the Science First development. The loss of the planned library means the loss of a number of community services including a library, a café, and services for parents, art students and others. It will also result in the loss of ten jobs locally which would have been created had the library gone ahead. The potential library users are likely to feel aggrieved at the loss of the planned facility quite intensely and so their interest is likely to be high but, as with the residents' association, their power is relatively low. The low power of the potential library users is suggested by the fact that they were unable to resist the cancellation, and the loss of these important services will be keenly felt locally, especially if residents need to travel away from their local areas to use library services elsewhere in the city of Philo.

(ii)   **Increasing low power stakeholdings**

Low power but high interest stakeholders are, when acting separately, unable to influence objectives because they are unable to move into the influential quadrant of the map because of the structural lack of power.

A common way to increase the aggregated influence of high interest but low power stakeholders is to act together in a type of coalition. This approach has often been tried when stakeholders oppose certain developments, seek to challenge policy changes and similar change initiatives. Stakeholders, often with little in common except their opposition to a certain initiative, act in concert, *co-ordinating* their messages to achieve maximum pressure, to influence local opinion on that which they both oppose. If they were to include other stakeholder also opposed to the science park, their potential influence would be maximised.

In this way, many stakeholders act as one and attempt to mobilise public opinion. In this case, highlighting the local costs of the Science First development on local media and in the streets around the site might serve to challenge the messages conveyed about the site by Philo University, by the Philo local government authority and Science First Company itself. By combining to make their arguments locally, stakeholders with undecided views, such as the local newspapers and some elected representatives, might be influenced to recognise the wider issues surrounding the development and the need for wider consultation. In this way, concessions might have been granted which were favourable to the potential library users and the residents.

(b)   With a development as large and expensive as the Science First development, there are always 'winners and losers' as Mr Forfeit explained. The public interest is a prominent theme in public sector organisations such as the Philo local government authority as well as to professional people including accountants. To act in the public interest is to recognise a fiduciary duty to the benefit of society rather than just a duty to one particular party. For Philo's local government authority, acting in the public interest means recognising that it serves many communities with each having rights and responsibilities. This is not to say that all communities carry equal weight in the local authority's deliberations and it has clearly decided that the Science First development is more important than the rights of local residents. This is likely because the Philo local government authority believes that the public interest is best served with the development of the science site over the concerns of some of the local residents.

The Philo local government authority can see a number of arguments in favour of the development. The attraction of a high profile science development near the city centre would be a way of distinguishing Philo from other cities and repositioning the city as a high-technology city which adds value through scientists, engineers and technologists. The development might also continue the tradition of Philo as a strong industrial and innovation location. This reputation is also likely to create wealth through supply companies to the science development as well as on the science development itself.

For Philo University, the development of the science park will cement its reputation as a prestigious place to study science and it is likely to help recruit some of the world's top scientists and science students to Philo. Having a world-class university will help many sectors of the local economy as well as contributing to the tax revenue of Philo local government authority. Local business, housing developments, shops and restaurants will also benefit, thereby increasing their own employment and paying higher rates of tax.

Perhaps the main public benefit, though, are the jobs which the science park will create. In addition to local jobs in other businesses, the Science First development will create 500 new jobs, all of which were described by Mr Forfeit as 'highly skilled and highly paid'. As a city suffering from high unemployment, any new jobs are welcome and jobs of this quality would be particularly welcome. As well as reducing unemployment, the jobs would help individuals and families participate in society and plan financially for their futures.

There are also arguments which conflict with the above advantages, and these need to be weighed against the benefits. The case describes the outrage of the local residents' association with regard to the loss of the local government authority flats and clearly this was a personal tragedy for the residents of those flats who were required to remove themselves from their homes and community. Described by Ann Tang as a 'close-knit' community, the loss of their homes would have been very painful for the affected residents.

It was also the case that the local government authority budgets allocated to the science development meant that other services had to be reduced. The loss of the proposed local library was clearly an unfortunate example of this, with the loss of several community services as well as the library itself. The fact that local residents did not vote nor give their approval for the science park would have made the loss of the proposed library even more painful and this, in turn, may negatively affect the reputation of the Philo local government authority locally.

(c) **Accountants in society**

As a qualified accountant, Kathy Wong's analysis of the situation would have been seen as trustworthy by many people because of her professional reputation. Her role as a qualified accountant is seen by society as giving her membership of a responsible and respectable profession. This means that her judgement may be accepted without question by many people in the same way it would be for a dentist or a medical practitioner.

This esteem received from society requires, in return, that accountants must be seen to act in the public interest. This means that accountants need to act in accordance with an agreed set of professional values, always maintain the highest levels of integrity, and deal fairly with all parties they engage with. Accountants, along with other professionals in society, are expected to demonstrate unswerving support for these professional values and be beyond reproach, and act independently at all times.

Criticisms

In her report, the local government authority asked her to produce a 'balanced assessment of the contribution of the Science First development to the city and the region'. In producing her report, however, Kathy Wong only meaningfully represented the interests of one constituency in her analysis. If she only considered the Science First development in terms of 'the creation of jobs, marginal revenues and the reputation (of the university and the city)', then she is representing one interest (that of the company) and ignoring or discounting the value of other interests. This is the point which Ann Tang highlighted. Kathy Wong has been criticised for acting in a factional manner and ignoring the effects on those stakeholders not represented by accounting calculations.

The net benefits to the city include an estimation of the advantages and disadvantages calculation including the costs to local residents and the closure of other services in pursuit of the Science First development. Her duty to the public interest includes recognising the diversion of funds to the Science First development from other services including libraries, and the relocation of some residents. A 'balanced assessment' would have included the social costs as well as the economic and reputational benefits and she failed to include these.

(d) (i) Philo local government authority and the Science First development

The local government authority is aware of some discussion in the city over the building of the Science First development. It is of concern that the local government authority has been criticised for a lack of transparency and fairness, when, in reality, these are essential characteristics of an effective local authority. As a public sector organisation, funded by central and local taxation, the Philo local government authority operates in a transparent way in order to ensure that local constituents are consulted and informed on key local decisions. If it failed to be transparent and fair in its decisions, a public sector organisation would fail in its public duty and its legitimacy would be called into question. The social contract which a public sector organisation has with its constituencies relies on these characteristics and it would be open to justifiable criticism were it to fail in these ways.

Transparency is a default position of openness and disclosure rather than concealment. Democratic bodies such as the Philo local government authority are required to debate in public and so the local authority would strongly contest any allegation that it has been lacking in transparency. Because the Philo local government authority exists for the benefit of local citizens, and can only exist with their continuing support, it is necessary to inform citizens of key issues and changes to their service provision and the reasons behind those changes. The scenario explains that the majority of elected representatives are supportive of the Science First development and, accordingly, it means the development enjoys the support of the local government authority. In Philo, an elected representative may be asked to account for her or his views on the development, perhaps by a constituent or the local media and this helps in local transparency.

Fairness is also a central theme in public sector organisations. To be fair is to recognise many interests and to weigh each one against others in an equitable and transparent way. Because a local government authority owes a duty to so many stakeholders, it needs to be fair to all of them. Because they operate using taxpayers' money, public sector organisations need to be fair, and be seen to be fair, in carrying out local policy. It is not always the case that all citizens and causes are treated equally, however, as some interests need to be subordinated for the wider benefit of society, but the local government authority owes a duty to explain any ways in which it balances the interests of different stakeholders over which it has influence.

(ii)   The Philo local government authority recognises that its performance *measurement is more complex* than for a private sector 'for profit' business. With a business, relatively straightforward financial measures are usually good signifiers of success or failure, including, for example, return on equity or return on sales, efficiency measures and productivity measures. For a public sector organisation like the Philo local government authority, financial measures are only one type of many other relevant objectives including the availability and quality of service delivery.

Because public sector objectives are often contested by a range of different stakeholders in society, public sector outcomes are often expressed in terms of value for money or in the delivery of public services such as the provision of public housing, health services, refuse collection, provision of jobs or learning opportunities. In a representative democracy such as in Philo, these outcomes are contested by political parties, with some preferring more or less of some provisions than others. So whilst the residents' association was disturbed by the loss of the proposed library and the block of flats, for example, it was felt by others that these losses were necessary in order to ensure the development of the Science First development.

The 3 Es framework is a way in which public sector objectives can be considered, with the 3 Es referring to the efficiency of the local authority, its effectiveness and its economic performance.

For the Philo local government authority, it must provide an efficient and value-for-money service to local taxpayers. In many cases, its service delivery is prescribed by national government policy whilst other activities, including the support for, and investment in, the science development, are discretionary. We would be very unhappy to run a fiscal deficit (spending more than we receive in tax receipts and block grants) and so we have to observe tight financial limits in delivering the services which our citizens want us to deliver. Efficiency is about delivering outputs for a set level of income, with efficient organisations delivering more on a given level of input than less efficient ones.

The local government authority must also be effective in that it must delivery its required services to a high quality and meet the expectations of service users. The Philo local government authority sees its support for the science development as a key part of its effectiveness as it is unlikely that the development would have been established without its support. In many cases, however, as we have seen with the loss of the adjacent building and the proposed library, the total effectiveness of our service delivery is not evenly spread and sometimes cuts in some services are necessary to provide increases in others. This is always a difficult judgement and public sector bodies are usually very aware of these choices when measuring their performance.

The final E concerns the economic performance or 'economy' of the local government authority. The Philo local government authority receives an income each year based on a settlement from central government and what it raises in local taxation. Within this budget, we must deliver a wide range of local services and employ the skilled people necessary to deliver those services. There is little scope to run a deficit under most public sector organisation terms of reference and in fact most are encouraged to operate at a slight surplus. This often requires painful choices to remain within budget and accordingly, the political choices are often between the 'good' and the 'very good' in terms of how money is spent and this may be little comfort to the residents and library users around the Science First site, but I hope, at least, that this provides some explanation for the local government authority's actions.

As the chief executive of the Philo local government authority, I very much hope I have been able to clarify some issues for local residents. Citizens can, of course, always contact their local elected representative to discuss these matters further.

Mock exams

ACCA Professional Level

Paper P1

Governance, Risk and Ethics

Mock Examination 1

Question Paper
Time allowed: 3 hours 15 minutes
This paper is divided into two sections: Section A   This ONE question is compulsory and must be attempted Section B   TWO questions only to be attempted
Do NOT open this question paper until instructed by the supervisor. Do NOT record any of your answers on the question paper. This question paper must not be removed from the examination hall.

Section A – This question is compulsory and must be attempted

Question 1

SeaShells is a small company operating from an island near continental Europe. SeaShells is a private company with 25 shareholders; its shares are not traded on any stock exchange. The main shareholders of SeaShells include relatives of the company's first CEO, and also private investors from whom the first CEO sought finance and who have since retained their shares. 25% of the share capital is held by members of the current board.

Although SeaShells is a private company, its board is constituted in accordance with good corporate governance practice. Half of the directors are executive directors and half of the directors are non-executive directors who are independent in accordance with the guidance in the UK Corporate Governance Code. The board also operates nomination, remuneration and audit committees. The members of all these committees are all non-executive directors.

The main business of SeaShells is packaging of fresh seafood (fish, oysters, crab etc) and selling these to supermarkets and other retailers. The company employs 750 people, mainly in the packing departments. Packing is labour intensive due to the need to clear and prepare fish etc. by hand prior to packing. Supplies of seafood are obtained from the island's fishing fleet. Previously the fleet supplied a number of companies on the island. However recently a couple of the fleet's other major customers have closed down, and the result is that SeaShells is now the only significant customer of the fleet. SeaShells is also one of the island's major employers. There is some concern that SeaShells' increased demand for seafood is causing over-exploitation of some fish species, and that the population of these fish may 'crash' or decrease dramatically in the near future.

In the last few weeks, the directors of SeaShells have decided to transfer almost all of the packaging of seafood to another country. The seafood will be moved by refrigerated ships to this other country, packaged by workers there and then moved back by ship to SeaShells for resale as before. The rationale behind this move is that labour costs are only 1/10th of the costs on the island. Even taking into account transportation costs, this move will halve the packaging costs of SeaShells. As a result of the move, the workforce will decrease to 200 people. The decision has resulted in significant adverse publicity for SeaShells on the island. The trade union representing the employees has threatened strike action, saying that this is a typical example of exploitative employment practices. However the reaction from customers has been positive as the company can offer reduced prices on many products. A government minister on the island on which Sea Shells is based has recently welcomed developments that limit the price of food to consumers. However the government has recently come under attack from the opposition for allowing jobs to be exported from the island. Both these issues are expected to be campaign issues when an election is held on the island next year.

The directors of SeaShells believe that the decision to transfer the packaging of seafood is correct because, as the CEO explained, the decision is 'best for the company, best for the shareholders and best for the directors'. The CEO has dismissed the objections to the transfer of employment as 'predictable whinging and politician grandstanding.' He has noted that the move has been very popular in the country to which employment will be transferred.

However a couple of the non-executive directors have raised doubts about the move. One has raised the objection that SeaShells depends on sales on its island. However it is removing purchasing power from the island by transferring employment overseas. The other non-executive director has wondered about the impact of moving the packaging operations on SeaShells' environmental footprint and whether it can be regarded as sustainable. He has also wondered about the impact of the move on SeaShells' financial accounts. If the impact on the figures in the accounts is limited, he has raised the issue whether, on grounds of corporate social responsibility, the accounts should include more information about the impact on the environment, or whether this information should be included in a separate report.

The CEO's comment concerning directors is certainly true in terms of directors' remuneration. 75% of the total remuneration package of the directors is based on performance related pay, the main element of this being the net profit of SeaShells. The chairman of the remuneration committee believes that it is important that directors' bonuses can clearly be related to tangible measures. 'Our shareholders want profit, so if the company makes profits, it's only fair that the directors should benefit.' The remaining 25% of remuneration relates to salary and is based on a three year contract with SeaShells. Other (non-salary) remuneration includes company contributions to a pension scheme and a share option scheme, with options being exercisable in five years based on the share price one year ago.

The CEO believes that it is important that the board of SeaShells continues to be staffed by high-calibre executive directors. He believes that the package offered to executive directors must be more than competitive, since SeaShells is a private company. He feels that there is a risk that directors who are seeking to develop their careers may seek to do so in companies listed on an international stock exchange, because of a perception that the opportunities, and therefore the rewards, at these companies are greater. The CEO's arguments have persuaded the remuneration committee and a number of features of directors' remuneration packages are designed to bind them to SeaShells in the longer term.

There have recently been two changes to the board of SeaShells. The Finance Director has retired, and has been replaced by his deputy, who was previously Financial Controller. SeaShells has also recruited a new Marketing Director. The director was previously a senior employee at a large marketing consultancy on the European mainland.

Required

(a)   Explain Mendelow's theory of stakeholder power. Identify the stakeholders involved in the decision to transfer packaging of seafood to another country, and assess the response of each group to this decision.

                                                                                      (14 marks)

(b)   Using Gray, Owens and Adams' viewpoints on social responsibility as a framework for your answer, evaluate the decision to transfer packaging seafood to another country.   **(14 marks)**

(c)   Prepare a memo for the board that:

(i)   Defines the concept of 'sustainability' and assesses the extent to which SeaShells' activities can be considered sustainable   **(7 marks)**

(ii)   Evaluates methods of reporting that can be used by SeaShells to explain the environmental impact of its activities.   **(7 marks)**

                                                (part (c) also includes 4 professional marks)

(d)   Explain corporate governance best practice in terms of directors' remuneration and assess the extent to which remuneration in SeaShells meets these requirements, making any recommendations you consider appropriate.   **(4 marks)**

                                                                                   (Total = 50 marks)

Section B – TWO questions ONLY to be attempted

Question 2

As part of a review of its internal control systems, the board of FF Co, a large textiles company, has sought your advice as a senior accountant in the company.

FF's stated objective has always been to adopt the highest standards of internal control because it believes that by doing so it will not only provide shareholders with confidence in its governance but also enhance its overall reputation with all stakeholders. In recent years, however, FF's reputation for internal control has been damaged somewhat by a qualified audit statement last year (over issues of compliance with financial standards) and an unfortunate internal incident the year prior to that. This incident concerned an employee, Miss Osula, expressing concern about the compliance of one of the company's products with an international standard on fire safety. She raised the issue with her immediate manager but he said, according to Miss Osula, that it wasn't his job to report her concerns to senior management. When she failed to obtain a response herself from senior management, she decided to report the lack of compliance to the press. This significantly embarrassed the company and led to a substantial deterioration in FF's reputation.

The specifics of the above case concerned a fabric produced by FF Co, which, in order to comply with an international fire safety standard, was required to resist fire for ten minutes when in contact with a direct flame. According to Miss Osula, who was a member of the quality control staff, FF was allowing material rated at only five minutes fire resistance to be sold labelled as ten minute rated. In her statement to the press, Miss Osula said that there was a culture of carelessness in FF and that this was only one example of the way the company approached issues such as international fire safety standards.

Required

(a) Describe how the internal control systems at FF Co differ from a 'sound' system of internal control, such as that set out in the Turnbull guidance, for example. **(10 marks)**

(b) Define 'reputation risk' and evaluate the potential effects of FF's poor reputation on its financial situation. **(8 marks)**

(c) Explain, with reference to FF as appropriate, the ethical responsibilities of a professional accountant both as an employee and as a professional. **(7 marks)**

(Total = 25 marks)

Question 3

Chen Products produces four manufactured products: Products 1, 2, 3 and 4. The company's risk committee recently met to discuss how the company might respond to a number of problems that have arisen with Product 2. After a number of incidents in which Product 2 had failed whilst being used by customers, Chen Products had been presented with compensation claims from customers injured and inconvenienced by the product failure. It was decided that the risk committee should meet to discuss the options.

When the discussion of Product 2 began, committee chairman Anne Ricardo reminded her colleagues that, apart from the compensation claims, Product 2 was a highly profitable product.

Chen's risk management committee comprised four non-executive directors who each had different backgrounds and areas of expertise. None of them had direct experience of Chen's industry or products. It was noted that it was common for them to disagree among themselves as to how risks should be managed and that in some situations, each member proposed a quite different strategy to manage a given risk. This was the case when they discussed which risk management strategy to adopt with regard to Product 2.

Required

(a)   Describe the typical roles of a risk management committee.   **(6 marks)**

(b)   Using the TARA framework, construct four possible strategies for managing the risk presented by Product 2.

Your answer should describe each strategy and explain how each might be applied in the case.   **(10 marks)**

Risk committee members can be either executive or non-executive.

Required

(c)   (i)   Distinguish between executive and non-executive directors.   **(2 marks)**

        (ii)   Evaluate the relative advantages and disadvantages of Chen's risk management committee being
                non-executive rather than executive in nature.   **(7 marks)**

                                                                                           (Total = 25 marks)

Question 4

LMN is a charity that provides low-cost housing for people on low incomes. The government has privatised much of the home building, maintenance and management in this sector. The sector is heavily regulated and receives some government money but there are significant funds borrowed from banks to invest in new housing developments, on the security of future rent receipts. Government agencies subsidise much of the rental cost for low-income residents.

The board and senior management have identified the major risks to LMN as: having insufficient housing stock of a suitable type to meet the needs of local people on low incomes; making poor property investment decisions; having dissatisfied tenants due to inadequate property maintenance; failing to comply with the requirements of the regulator; having a poor credit rating with lenders; poor cost control; incurring bad debts for rental; and having vacant properties that are not earning income. LMN has produced a risk register as part of its risk management process. For each of more than 200 individual risks, the risk register identifies a description of the risk and the (high, medium or low) likelihood of the risk eventuating and the (high, medium or low) consequences for the organisation if the risk does eventuate.

The management of LMN is carried out by professionally qualified housing executives with wide experience in property development, housing management and maintenance, and financial management. The board of LMN is composed of volunteers with wide experience and an interest in social welfare. The board is representative of the community, tenants and the local authority, any of whom may be shareholders (shareholdings are nominal and the company pays no dividends). The local authority has overall responsibility for housing and social welfare in the area. The audit committee of the board of LMN, which has responsibility for risk management as well as internal control, wants to move towards a system of internal controls that are more closely related to risks identified in the risk register.

Required

For an organisation like LMN:

(a)   Analyse the purposes and justify the importance of risk management and explain its relationship with the
        internal control system.   **(9 marks)**

(b)   Discuss the importance of a management review of controls for the audit committee.   **(5 marks)**

(c)   Explain the principles of good corporate governance as they apply to the board's role:

        (i)   In conducting a review of internal controls; and
        (ii)   Reporting on compliance.   **(11 marks)**

Illustrate your answer with examples from the scenario.

                                                                                           (Total = 25 marks)

Answers

DO NOT TURN THIS PAGE UNTIL YOU HAVE
COMPLETED THE MOCK EXAM

A plan of attack

We know you've been told to do it at least 100 times and we know if we asked you you'd know that you should do it. So why don't you do it in an exam? 'Do what in an exam?' you're probably thinking. Well, let's tell you for the 101st time. **Take a good look through the paper before diving in to answer questions.**

First things first

What you must do in the first five minutes of reading time in your exam is **look through the paper** in detail, working out **which questions to do** and the **order** in which to attempt them. So turn back to the paper and let's sort out a plan of attack.

We then recommend you spend the remaining time analysing the requirements of **Question 1** and highlighting the key issues in the question. The extra time spent on **Question 1** will be helpful, whenever you intend to do the question. If you decide to do it first, you will be well into the question when the writing time starts. If you intend to do it second or third, probably because you find it daunting, the question will look easier when you come back to it, because your initial analysis should generate further points whilst you're tackling the other questions.

The next step

You're probably either thinking that you don't know where to begin or that you could have a very decent go at all the questions.

Option 1 (if you don't know where to begin)

If you are a bit **worried** about the paper, remember you'll need to do the compulsory question anyway so it's best to get it over and done with.

- You can score well on part (a) of **Question 1** if you use the information in the scenario – there is plenty of information about the stakeholders. There's also enough detail about remuneration to jog your memory in part (d) about corporate governance remuneration requirements.

- There are some marks for general points in **Question 2** and **if** you can remember the key points stressed by the Turnbull report, that will help you here. Don't let the fact that this question ranges quite widely over the syllabus put you off.

- For **Question 3**, (a) and (c)(i), adding to one-third of the marks, are fairly straightforward textbook knowledge. If you don't know what TARA means in (b), then your chances of passing this question will be limited (and you need to revise risk management!). Alternatively you may know what TARA is but struggle to apply it. However don't worry if your suggestions under the TARA headers don't seem very good, as some of the possible TARA strategies are definitely more appropriate than others.

- There's a number of fairly basic points you make in part (a) of **Question 4**, and you can get significant credit in (c) for setting out your knowledge of the corporate governance guidelines. Think when you're planning how you can bring the scenario information in.

What you mustn't forget is that you have to answer **Question 1** and then two questions from Section B.

Option 2 (if you're thinking 'I can do all of these')

It never pays to be over confident but if you're not quaking in your shoes about the exam then **turn straight to the compulsory question** in Section A. You've got to do it so you might as well get it over and done with.

- Make sure you make the most of the information you're supplied with in parts (a) and (d) of **Question 1**; a general answer won't score well. You may well have very good knowledge of the issues covered in parts (b) and (c) but allocate your time carefully; it's important not only to avoid running over time for each question part, but also to ensure you cover a sufficient breadth of points within the time allowed.

Once you've done the compulsory questions choose two of the questions in Section B.

BPP
LEARNING MEDIA

- If you feel that you can answer **Question 2** well, this is encouraging, as it draws on a number of areas across the syllabus. Make sure you make the most of the information given in the scenario, particularly when answering (a).

- **Question 3** contains a number of easy marks in (a) and (c) (i). Make sure again you clearly demonstrate application to the scenario in (b).

- If you've got good knowledge of the corporate governance requirements relating to control reviews, you can score well in **Question 4**. Part (a) is about the fundamentals of risk management, so knowledge of these basics will help you as well. However make sure that you include references to relevant scenario information.

No matter how many times we remind you...

Always, always **allocate your time** according to the marks for the question in total and for the parts of the questions. And always, always **follow the requirements exactly** and indicate which questions you're answering **clearly**.

You've got free time at the end of the exam.....?

If you have allocated your time properly then you **shouldn't have time on your hands** at the end of the exam. If you find yourself with five or ten minutes spare, however, go back to **any parts of questions that you didn't finish** because you ran out of time.

Forget about it!

And don't worry if you found the paper difficult. More than likely other students would too. If this was the real thing you would need to forget the exam the minute you leave the exam hall and **think about the next one**. Or, if it's the last one, **celebrate**!

Question 1

Text references. Chapters 1, 3 and 11.

Top tips. It's a good idea to draw the matrix in (a) as a starter. The way to approach planning the rest of (a) to list all the major stakeholders (and the question makes it clear that the 'usual' stakeholders are all important) and then decide where they fit on the matrix.

If you struggled with (b), learn these viewpoints! The examiner has stressed their importance and may well set similar question parts in the exam. Note that the scenario will have to give you issues that would interest all seven viewpoints. The key questions to ask when considering things from each viewpoint are:

- Do the company's activities have a significant impact?
- Do the impacts they have matter?
- Why do they matter?
- What can the company do to reduce or eliminate the impacts, or provide compensation?

There are various hints to help you answer on sustainability in (c). The issue about unnecessary use of transport is topical, and it's certainly worth keeping an eye on continuing sustainability debates. This question part should represent the maximum amount of detail you need to bring in about sustainability reporting. The main thing to remember is the basics of each framework; what numbers are involved and the narrative element. If you can remember the basics, you should be able to come up with enough examples of the detail in the reports.

(d) is quite a good question part on remuneration as some of the issues involved aren't clear-cut. It's good for example for remuneration to link with performance, but not so good for it to depend largely on short-term financial performance. Asking yourself what the potential problems are and then the key question – why? should enable you to generate sufficient depth of assessment. What you must avoid are simple this is acceptable or unacceptable statements without explanation.

Easy marks. Depends on how well you know the social responsibility material in Chapter 12. There's enough information on remuneration in (d) to give you a number of points to discuss.

Marking scheme

				Marks
(a)		Up to 3 marks for explanation of Mendelow's matrix	3	
		Up to 2 marks for each stakeholder identified and analysed	12	
				Max 14
(b)		Up to 2 marks for each Gray, Owen and Adams position discussed		14
(c)	(i)	Up to 2 marks for definition of sustainability	2	
		Up to 5 marks for assessment of whether company's position is sustainable	5	
	(ii)	Up to 7 marks for evaluation of methods of reporting – to achieve high marks detail must be given of a number of different methods	7	
		Up to 4 professional marks for the form of the answer (memo in which content is laid out in an orderly and informative manner)	4	
				Max 18
(d)		Up to 2 marks for each relevant point. To achieve 2 marks points must include application to company and recommendations		Max 4
				50

(a)   **Mendelow's matrix**

Mendelow classifies stakeholders on a matrix (shown below). The matrix is used to identify the type of relationship the organisation should seek with its stakeholders, and how it should view their concerns. The two axes show the **level of interest** the stakeholder has in the company and the **amount of power** that stakeholder has to influence the decisions of the company

Using these two axes, stakeholders can be divided into four groups as follows.

Section A

Stakeholders in this section have a **low level of interest** in the company and have **minimal power** to influence the decisions of the company.

Government

For SeaShells, Section A stakeholders may include the **government** of the island. As long as SeaShells pays the correct amount of taxes, the government may not be able to interfere with the company.

Section B

Stakeholders in this section have a **high level of interest** in the company, but have **minimal power** to actually influence its activities. This group will normally attempt to influence the company by lobbying groups that have high levels of power.

For SeaShells, stakeholders in this category include the following.

The local community

SeaShells is a major employer on the island. This means the community has an interest in the company **maintaining that level of employment**. It is unlikely therefore that the community will agree with the decision to decrease the number of jobs at SeaShells. However, apart from applying pressure in terms of adverse publicity, the community cannot actually stop SeaShells taking this action.

Suppliers

SeaShells purchases from the fishing fleet on the island. As SeaShells is the **only major customer** of the fleet, then the fleet has little power to affect SeaShells. While in theory the fleet could refuse to sell to SeaShells, the lack of an alternative buyer decreases the effectiveness of this option.

Employees

This group is obviously **interested in the success of the company** as they receive a salary from SeaShells. However, the only method of influencing SeaShells is by **withdrawal of labour**; this is ineffective given that transferring the packing to a different country has this effect anyway for Seashells. The only other option for influencing the company appears to be generating bad publicity, as for the local community above.

Section C

Stakeholders in this section have a **low level of interest** in the company, although they have the **ability to exercise power** over the company if they choose to do so. The group will have to be kept satisfied to ensure that their power is not used.

Shareholders

In SeaShells, this group is likely to include the shareholders. As long as the **return on investment** from SeaShells is **acceptable,** and the directors are running the company effectively, then the shareholders will be happy. Certainly the decision to decrease input costs will be acceptable if this also means increased profits and dividends. Given that knowledge of cost savings is now available, it can be argued that the directors must take this option, or else the shareholders may become dissatisfied and attempt to remove the directors.

Section D

Stakeholders in this section have a **high level of interest in the company** and also a **high level of power.** These stakeholders are therefore able to influence the company. For SeaShells, this group will include customers and directors.

Customers

Customers have high power because they can presumably **obtain supplies of seafood from other companies**. SeaShells must therefore keep this group satisfied or lose important sources of income. The decision to decrease packaging costs will be supported by customers as SeaShells' prices will also fall.

Directors

Directors can influence SeaShells because they **make decisions regarding the running of the company**. In this sense, moving packaging to a different country is in the interests of Seashells, as it provides the company with additional competitive advantage in terms of price and therefore helps ensure its survival.

(b)   **Viewpoints of social responsibility**

Gray, Owen and Adams in their book *Accounting and accountability* identify seven viewpoints of social responsibility. These viewpoints can be applied to many situations, including the actions of companies, as explained below.

Pristine capitalists

Pristine capitalists support the idea that in a liberal economic democracy, the **private property system** is the best system. This means that companies **exist to make profits and seek economic efficiency**. Businesses therefore have **no moral responsibilities** beyond their obligations to shareholders and creditors.

In terms of moving packaging to another country simply on the basis of cost, then SeaShells has acted in terms of this belief; the obligation to maximise shareholder profit has been met and the social issues of making people redundant and the adverse effect on the island community are irrelevant.

Expedients

Expedients believe in a modified liberal economic democracy, noting that economic systems do generate some excesses. This means that businesses have to **accept some, albeit limited, social legislation** and moral requirements, particularly if this is in the businesses' best interests.

SeaShells is potentially caught between two countries here. On the one hand in its home country SeaShells does not appear to be acting morally because the loss of jobs will adversely affect employment and the island's overall economy. However, in the country to which the packaging is being moved, more jobs will be created, potentially in areas of lower employment. In these terms SeaShells is acting morally.

Proponents of the social contract

Proponents of the social contract believe in a **contract between society and organisations**. Both parties must therefore **interact to their joint benefit**.

SeaShells is continuing to provide employment in terms of purchasing fish etc from the fishing fleet – and the island is providing support services to SeaShells (some employment, land etc). SeaShells has possibly breached the contract by removing some employment from the island; some adverse impact in terms of bad publicity is therefore expected.

Social ecologists note that **economic processes** that **result in resource exhaustion, waste and pollution must be modified**. In other words, the transfer of seafood to another country for packaging only to be returned to SeaShells for distribution is not environmentally friendly. To be responsible in this area SeaShells should continue to package the seafood at its current location.

Socialists

Socialists see two classes in society – **capitalists owning businesses exploiting workers**. Within this framework, equality is difficult to achieve. In SeaShells, shareholders and directors appear to be capitalists because they stand to 'win' from the packaging decision. However, the workers on the island stand to 'lose' in that their employment is terminated (although other workers will gain in the overseas country).

Radical feminists

Radical feminists see a trade off between **masculine qualities such as aggression and conflict** and **feminine values of cooperation and reflection**. Moving the packaging work to another country does appear to create conflict. However, whether the feminine view of cooperation is better is unclear – even if say only half the packaging function was moved, there would still be conflict on the island. Similarly, not moving the packaging function could create resentment in the other country as Seashells is not taking advantage of their cost advantage in terms of labour wages.

Deep ecologists

Deep ecologists believe that human beings have **no greater rights to resources or life than other species**. At the extreme therefore the entire business of SeaShells cannot be justified, especially where fish populations are threatened. Similarly, the economic decision to move packaging cannot be justified in environmental terms. The viewpoint that businesses cannot be trusted to maintain something as important as the environment is therefore correct.

(c)
To: Board
From: Accountant
Date: 23 May 20X7
Subject: Sustainability and environmental reporting

Definition of sustainability

Sustainability involves developing strategies so that the company only **uses resources at a rate** that **allows them to be replenished**. This means that those resources will continue to be available into the foreseeable future. Similarly, emissions of waste are confined to levels that do not exceed the capacity of the environment to absorb them.

In other words, sustainability has been defined as ensuring that development meets the needs of the present without compromising the ability of the future to meet its own needs. **Sustainable development** is **development that meets the needs of the present without compromising the ability of future generations to meet their own needs**.

In terms of the activities of SeaShells, they could be termed to be not sustainable on two counts.

Demand on fish stocks

In terms of capitalism, the fishing fleet will continue to try to meet this demand and SeaShells will continue to sell seafood as both parties are making a profit from these activities. However, the warning that some **fish stocks may crash** indicates that fishing and the economic activity of SeaShells as a company are not sustainable. How activities can be amended to be sustainable is unclear, unless there is some way to limit demand for fish or limit the amount of fish actually used by SeaShells.

The transport of seafoods for packaging in another country

The use of fuel simply to take seafood to a different location and back again to be packaged does **not appear to be justifiable economically**, and is not sustainable given that oil is a limited resource.

Disclosures

The extent to which SeaShells may actually want to disclose the environmental impact of its activities is unclear; in other words **entirely voluntary disclosure is unlikely**, particularly in view of the lack of sustainability referred to above. Methods of reporting the environmental impact of SeaShell's activities include the following.

Financial accounts

The basic financial accounts of SeaShells will disclose **the financial impact of its activities**, although these will only show the direct costs in terms of fuel used to transport fish for packaging etc. As many environmental costs are intangible eg pollution or potential over-fishing, these will not be included in the financial accounts, making this method of reporting incomplete.

Full cost accounting

This is a system that allows current accounting to include all **potential/actual costs and benefits** including environmental and possibly social externalities. The aim is to arrive at a 'full cost' of the activities of an organisation.

While the idea is good, it is not necessarily clear what the 'full cost' of an organisation's activities are. Full cost accounting suggests various 'tiers' of costs from the tangible through to the intangible. Using this system SeaShells would disclose not only **actual costs** incurred (transport, wages etc), but also **hidden costs** of maintaining environmental monitoring systems. The accounts would also disclose contingent **liability costs**, such as fines for any environmental damage.

More widely the accounts would show **intangible costs**, including loss of customer goodwill (possible given the packaging policy) and reputation risk (again this risk will be there with the packaging policy). However, it is unclear how these costs will be 'measured'. Lastly the accounts would show **environmentally focused costs** – prevention costs, the costs of ensuring the company's activities have a zero environmental impact. The transport of seafood for packaging is likely to be environmentally negative; there is then the query of how these costs are 'offset' – should SeaShells plant trees to offset CO_2 emissions?

The emphasis on costs and the difficulty of estimating some of those costs again implies that this method of disclosure may not be effective.

CSR/GRI

An alternative to financial reporting is to provide information in a separate, predominantly narrative, report. The Corporate and Social Responsibility (CSR) report in the UK or the recommendations of the Global Reporting Initiative (GRI) are examples of this type of report. The GRI has a vision that reporting on economic, environmental and social importance should become as routine and comparable as financial reporting. The emphasis is therefore on **voluntary disclosure**, but based **on some ethical standards**. The additional information may be expected by society, and therefore perhaps companies should provide it.

SeaShells appears to be under some pressure at present, although this is more in terms of economic pressure on jobs than on environmental reporting. Either additional legislation or social pressure appears to be required to ensure that additional environmental reporting is provided.

(d) **Remuneration**

The overriding requirement is that **adequate remuneration** has to be paid to directors in order to attract individuals of sufficient calibre. Remuneration packages should be structured to ensure that individuals are **motivated to achieve performance levels that are in the company and shareholders' best interests** as well as their own personal interests.

Within SeaShells it is difficult to determine whether total **remuneration is sufficient** to meet this objective. However, the fact that there does not appear to be any problems recruiting directors indicates that remuneration is sufficient, or may even be excessive.

Setting remuneration

Directors' remuneration should be set by a **remuneration committee**, which SeaShells has. The reason for this is to ensure that there is **no bias in setting remuneration levels**.

Performance related remuneration

Corporate governance guidelines indicate that a **significant proportion of the rewards** should be focused on **measurable performance**, which SeaShells does. What is meant by a significant amount is not always stated but 50% is a reasonable figure. A 75% amount may again be considered as excessive.

The other element of guidance regarding the performance element of remuneration is that this should be **balanced and not relate to the short term only**, as short term performance can be manipulated. The current focus simply on net profit is therefore inappropriate.

Share options

Share options give directors the right to **purchase shares at a specified exercise price over a specified time period in the future**. If the price of the shares rises so that it exceeds the exercise price by the time the options can be exercised, the directors will be able to purchase shares at lower than their market value. This provides a good incentive to the directors to increase share prices.

However, corporate governance regulations normally suggest a **three year maximum term** for share options. The five year term in SeaShells may be unrealistic as the **term is too far in the future** to motivate the directors now. Decreasing the term for future option grants should be considered.

Service contract

Length of service contracts can be a particular problem. If service contracts are too long, and then have to be terminated prematurely, directors may receive **excessive payments for breach of contract**. Most corporate governance guidance therefore suggests a 12-month term.

The **current length of service contracts** in SeaShells of three years therefore appears to be **excessive**. Although there is no indication that directors are looking for compensation for loss of office, decreasing the term to one year would be advisable.

Question 2

Text references. Chapters 4, 6 and 10.

Top tips. (a) appears to be in two parts, first description of good control systems and then application to FF. The description paragraphs appear to be quite generously rewarded. Don't assume that this will necessarily be the case in your exam; remember what we said in the front pages about the majority of marks being given in many questions for application of knowledge to the scenario.

The Turnbull report generates a number of ideas for (a). You should note a couple of things which the answer to (a) stresses. Firstly the importance of embedding internal control which has been stressed by the examiner; secondly the need for control systems to respond quickly to changing risks. You may well see scenarios in the exam where the company's business situation is changing, hence its risks are altering, and you will need to explain that the control systems have to respond.

(b) stresses the importance of reputation risk. The level of reputation risk is partly determined by the level of other risks, but, as this answer stresses, it also depends on stakeholder responses. Lost sales is the obvious consequence, but note also the non-financial consequences such as recruitment problems or increased regulator attention.

The key question (c) brings out is when the duty of confidentiality might be overridden. The discussions of professional responsibilities brings out how accountants should have recourse to the basic principles of integrity, probity and public interest in situation where the detail in codes isn't helpful.

Easy marks. The first parts of (a) and (b) are descriptive rather than application based, requiring knowledge of Turnbull and the definition of reputation risk.

Marks

(a) Description of 'sound' control systems – up to 2 marks for each valid
point   6
Explanation of shortcomings at FF – 1 mark for each valid point made   6

            Max 10

(b) Definition of 'reputation risk' – 1 mark for each valid point made   3
Explanation of the financial effects of poor reputation – 1 mark for each
valid point made   4
Recognition of the causes of FF's reputation problems – 1 mark for each
valid point made   2

            Max   8

(c) Responsibilities to employer – 1 mark for each valid point made   4
Responsibilities to professionalism – 1 mark for each valid point made   4

            Max   7
            25

(a) **Control systems**

The Turnbull report sees control framework as being designed to **achieve a number of objectives** and emphasises the need for the control system to be **sound**; an unsound system can undermine corporate governance. **Control systems** are often defined as being made up of two main elements – the **control environment** and **control procedures**.

Compliance with laws and regulations

Control systems should **ensure compliance with applicable laws and regulations**, also with internal policies.

FF's systems clearly have not done this; FF has **failed to follow fire safety standards** and its accounts have **failed to comply with accounting standards**. Also management have **not been able to enforce the objective** of complying with the highest standards of control.

Ensure the quality of internal and external reporting

This requires the **maintenance of proper records and processes** which generate a flow of timely and relevant information.

The qualified audit report that FF has had may be a **failure of controls**, a lack of awareness within the company of the requirements of accounting standards.

Respond to significant and changing risks

The control system should **identify what the most significant risks** are, and be capable of responding quickly to **evolving risks within the business**.

The **lack of compliance with fire reporting standards** suggests a failure within FF's systems to **identify significant risks**, not just the **direct risks of selling unsafe products** but also the **reputation risk** arising from this.

Control environment

The control environment is the **stress** placed by directors and managers, also the management style and **corporate culture and values shared by all employees**.

The Turnbull report comments that internal control systems should be **embedded in the operations of a company** and **form part of its culture**.

The scenario highlights a number of problems with the control environment within FF. Although the board have sought to promote the highest standards of internal control, the **directors failed to respond** when the issue of product safety was raised. In addition Miss Osula asserted that there was an overall **culture of carelessness** within FF.

Control procedures

Control procedures represent the specific **policies and procedures** designed to achieve objectives.

The scenario highlights a number of failings in the control procedures of FF. The **quality control** relating to the **material testing** clearly failed. The qualified audit report suggests a **failure in accounting controls**. Reporting control failings to management is a management control, part of the **system of accountabilities**, and again that failed to work as no action was taken.

(b) **Reputation risk**

Reputation risk is the risk of a **loss of reputation** of an organisation, arising from the **perceptions** others have about the implications of risks materialising. Reputation risk levels depend **not only on the levels of other risks** but **the reaction of stakeholders** to those other risks materialising – how much less of the organisation do stakeholders think, and what actions they take.

Stakeholders and financial consequences

Thus the level of reputation risk depends on the actions that stakeholders can take that can affect the organisation financially. These actions vary by stakeholder.

Shareholders

Shareholders can ultimately sell their shares, more easily if FF is **listed**, if they lack confidence in the way the company is governed. If shareholders holding a significant proportion of shares do this, FF's **share price will fall**.

Customers

If customers are concerned about the safety of FF's products, they are likely to cease buying them, causing **falls in revenues and profits**.

Law enforcement agencies

FF may face **legal action** as a result of failing to comply with standards. This could lead to **fines** and **lawyers' fees** for defending the action. FF may also be ordered to **cease manufacturing** the product that has not complied with standards, again causing **falls in revenues and profits**.

Auditors

Because of the qualified audit report, auditors are likely to scrutinise FF's records more closely in subsequent years, leading to an **increase in audit fees**.

(c) **Ethical responsibilities to employer**

Probity

Accountants should act honestly and not be swayed from fulfilling their duty to the employers by considerations of **personal interests** or **illegitimate pressures** to act other than in their employers' interests.

Professional competence

Accountants should **exercise competence and skill** in the service of the employer and maintain knowledge of best practice, legislation and techniques. Accountants should also **exercise due care** when working in the employer's interests.

Confidentiality

Accountants should respect **confidential information** that they have about their employer and should **not disclose it without proper or specific authority** or **unless there is a legal or professional right or duty to disclose**. This should apply during and after their employment.

Responsibilities towards shareholders and stakeholders

Accountants should seek to fulfil the company's objectives of trying to maximise shareholder value, also **maintaining good relationships** with **other relevant stakeholders**.

Promotion of business interests

Employees have a duty to promote their employer's **legitimate business interests** and not take actions that would be detrimental to their employer.

Responsibilities as an accountant

Public interest

Accountants have a general duty to act in the public interest; at times this may override the **duty of confidentiality**. With FF, Miss Osula's actions could be justified on the grounds that the public needed to know about potential dangers of FF's products.

Professional behaviour

Accountants should **avoid any action that discredits the profession** and **comply with laws and regulations, also ethical codes**. Again Miss Osula's **actions could be justified** on the grounds that to stay silent would have effectively been condoning a breach of regulation.

Question 3

Text references. Chapters 3, 5 and 7.

Top tips. In (a) the marking guide differentiates clearly between a single line bullet point (which would be identifying each role) and a brief (two to three sentences) description which would earn the full mark for each role described. Therefore a six-line bullet point list would earn 3 marks at best.

In (b) it seems clear that the examiner favours the TARA framework. The problem you may have found with using this framework is that certain strategies seem clearly more appropriate than others. However the scenario highlights the disagreements among the risk committee, so it seems reasonable to suppose that the full range would be discussed.

As is actually quite common in exam questions, you are told some details about the products, but not actually told what they are, so don't let that put you off.

It's easy to spend too much time on (c)(i); note it is only worth 2 marks. The main issues in (ii) are weighing up the similarity of the roles of the audit and risk committee and the need for effective scrutiny by executives, against the clear problem of lack of industry knowledge on Chen's committee.

Easy marks. If you had revised risk management committees, the requirements in (a) are straightforward.

Examiner's comments. (a) asked candidates to describe the typical roles of a risk management committee. Some candidates failed to observe the verb ('describe') and produced a list (more like 'identify') thereby failing to achieve full marks. Others, perhaps misinterpreting the task, wrote about the purposes of risk management which is a slightly different thing. For five marks, the time budget of nine minutes should have been enough to write two or three sentences on each role by way of description. Again, I would remind candidates to obey the verb. If a question asks candidates to describe or explain, a bullet list of points is not an appropriate response.

(b) appeared to be straightforward but also required application to the case, and this was where some failed to gain marks.

(c)(ii) was not asking about the pros and cons of NEDs in general. Rather it was asking candidates to consider the pros and cons of the placement of NEDs on a particular committee (the risk management committee) and this raised slightly different issues than the general pros and cons. An approach taken by some candidates was to discuss the general advantages and disadvantages but to then fail to develop these into the more specific case of risk committees. Again, it is important to study what the question is really asking rather than assume that the sense of the task can be conveyed in a cursory glance at the key words in the question.

				Marks
(a)		0.5 marks for each role identified		
		0.5 marks for brief description of each role		6
(b)		0.5 marks for identification of each strategy		
		1 mark for definition of each strategy		
		1 mark for application of each strategy to Chen Products		10
(c)	(i)	2 marks for distinguishing between executive and non-executive directors		2
	(ii)	1 mark for each relevant advantage	Max 4	
		1 mark for each relevant disadvantage	Max 3	
				7
				25

(a) Approving the organisation's risk management strategies and policies

The committee should ensure that risk management strategies and policies are **consistent with overall business strategies** determined by the full board. The committee should also obtain evidence that **risks and risk management strategies** have been **communicated** throughout the organisation, and that appropriate **staff training** has taken place.

Monitoring risk exposure

The committee should take a **portfolio view of risk** across the whole organisation, ensuring that **overall risk levels** do not exceed the levels deemed tolerable by the board, and that **opportunities to diversify and hedge risks** across the company are taken. The committee should also ensure that measures are taken to **limit the most significant risks or risks in particularly vulnerable areas**, for example placing trading limits on treasury function staff.

Reviewing reports on key risks

The committee should receive regular **reports from business operating units** and other key functions such as **information technology and treasury**. The committee should determine from these reports whether **appropriate actions** have been taken to **manage risks**, and the significance of risks crystallising and control failures identified.

Assessing effectiveness of risk management systems

The committee needs to consider whether the **risk management systems** are fulfilling their **objectives**. Reports by internal and external auditors are an important source of evidence for this assessment.

Providing early warning on emerging risk issues

The committee should regularly review the wider business environment, including the activities of key competitors, legal, technological and economic issues. This review should aim to **highlight new risks or alterations in existing risks** that mean that risk management policies or systems need to change.

Reviewing external reports on internal control

The committee needs to satisfy itself that reports on internal control in the financial statements **fairly** reflect the systems in operation and include sufficient detail about **weaknesses in internal control**.

(b) **Transfer**

Transfer means taking action to ensure that **another party** bears some or all of the consequences of risks materialising, in return for that other party receiving some **benefit**.

Chen could **transfer liability for the costs of compensation to an insurance company**, on payment of a **premium** and subject to Chen accepting a **minimum liability**. However the insurance company may insist that Chen also takes action to **reduce risk,** as well as paying the insurance premium, before it accepts the insurance contract. Another method of transfer would be outsourcing manufacture of Product 2, with the outsourcing partner accepting liability for product problems.

Avoidance

Avoidance means **ceasing to undertake the activities** that could result in risks crystallising and the company suffering losses.

Here avoidance of risk would mean ceasing to manufacture Product 2. The cessation could be **temporary**, lasting until the risk committee had obtained sufficient assurance that Product 2 would not fail. Alternatively the committee may consider that the **potential financial consequences** of compensation, plus the damage to Chen Products' **reputation** and **resulting falls in sales** of other products, are so great that Product 2 should be **permanently withdrawn**.

Reduction

Reduction means **reducing the chances of risks materialising**, by for example more stringent control measures or by becoming less dependent on the activity causing the risk.

If Chen was to reduce risks, it would continue to manufacture Product 2. However it would investigate why Product 2 had failed. The results of the investigation might mean that Chen introduced **stricter quality control procedures** or **checks by internal audit** that existing procedures were being applied correctly. Alternatively Chen could manufacture less of Product 2 and more of other products, although the directors would have to weigh up the **potential reduction in compensation claims** against the consequences of switching production to **possibly less profitable products**.

Acceptance

Acceptance means acknowledging that **some risks at a certain level** will be **inevitable** if Chen is to make profits and that the **costs of risk management outweigh the benefits** from reducing or eliminating the compensation claims.

If Chen's risk committee decided to accept risk here, the directors are likely to be acknowledging that some product failure is inevitable and the consequences are not sufficiently serious to warrant Chen taking further action to deal with the risks.

(c) (i) **Executive directors**

Executive directors are **employees** who are responsible for **managing the business** and **developing the company's strategy**, implementing the decisions of the board. Their value to the company lies in their **industry or role knowledge and experience**.

Non-executive directors (NEDs)

NEDs have **no managerial responsibilities** and their role is **part-time**. They are recruited from **wider, external backgrounds**. Their **independent scrutiny of the work of executive directors**, including their work on **board committees**, should provide reassurance to shareholders

(ii) **Advantages of NEDs on risk management committee**

Differing backgrounds and expertise

The variation in experience of NEDs will mean that they have seen **various risk management strategies** in action, and seen how the organisations they have worked for respond to various risks. These insights may be valuable given the changing risks Chen may face, and the need for its risk management to evolve.

Scrutiny of executive directors

A key role of the risk committee is to **scrutinise the operations of the risk management systems**, including the **performance of the executives** responsible for implementing the systems. If NEDs staff the committee, then the scrutiny should be **independent** and form an important part of NEDs' overall responsibilities to scrutinise performance.

Interaction with audit committees

Under governance codes, audit committee members must be NEDs. If the **audit and risk committees** have some common members, this should help ensure both committees take a **consistent approach to risk management issues**.

Discussion of sensitive issues

Having the committee solely staffed by NEDs means that they can discuss sensitive issues **without executives being present**, something identified in governance reports as being important for the audit committee as well.

Disadvantages of NEDs

Lack of experience of Chen's industry

The lack of industry knowledge appears to be the most serious weakness of the committee. As a result the committee's **decision-making** seems **deadlocked**, with no way of determining which of the strategies proposed is most appropriate.

Lack of time

Because of other commitments, NEDs **may not be able to spend enough time considering risk issues**, remembering that they may also have to staff the audit and nomination committees as well as attending full board meetings. Risk committee meetings may not be held frequently enough, and action to counter significant risks may thus be taken too slowly.

Improving risk awareness

Including executive directors on the committee should **improve the understanding of the executives** of the key risk issues that the committee is discussing. It should also provide the NEDs with key information relating to products and systems that helps them **understand the issues** involved in implementing their recommendations in this industry.

Question 4

Text references. Chapters 4, 7 and 8.

Top tips. This question is a very good illustration of our comment in the front pages that questions will cover a variety of organisations. In (a) the link between controls and risk management is highlighted in the question details. The discussion in the first part of (a) should be assisted by examples from the scenario, and in the discussion of risks and controls you need to include some examples of appropriate controls for LMN.

It's necessary to read (b) quite carefully to see what the question wants; a demonstration of how much a review by the professional managers contributes to the work of the audit committee. You have to start off by defining what the work of the audit committee is, then consider how much managers' review contributes compared with other sources of information.

In (c) again you can't be too theoretical; any explanation of principles has to be related to how they impact on the audit committee and board's reviews. Selected examples from the scenario information are also needed here to boost the explanation. If you can remember that the board needs to carry out regular and annual reviews and the main elements of each, you would have scored well in (c) and gone a long way towards passing this question.

Easy marks. No very easy parts, but overall a good example of how to illustrate corporate governance with relevant information from a scenario.

Marking scheme

			Marks
(a)	Up to 3 marks for analysis of purposes of risk management	3	
	Up to 3 marks for justification of importance of risk management	3	
	Up to 3 marks for explanation of interaction of risk management and internal control system	3	
			9
(b)	Up to 3 marks for need for, and significance of, management review	3	
	Up to 2 marks for other sources of assurance	2	
			5
(c) (i)	Up to 8 marks for explanation of different elements of review. To obtain high marks, answer must include details of regular and annual review and relate to information in the scenario	8	
(ii)	Up to 4 marks for explanation of different disclosures. To obtain high marks, answer must include statement of board's responsibilities, what has been done to manage risk and that board has reviewed risk management	4	
			Max 11
			25

(a) Purposes of risk management

Alignment of risk appetite and strategy

LMN's board should consider what risks it is prepared to **tolerate** in the light of the organisation's strategy. Risk management comprises the systems and processes for dealing with the risks that the board is prepared to tolerate in order for LMN to fulfil its **strategic objectives**.

Develop a consistent framework for dealing with risk

A coherent risk management framework can help LMN compare risks with **obvious financial consequences** (poor cost control, loss of income due to bad debts) with risks whose financial consequences are less obvious (dissatisfied tenants). It also should provide guidelines that can be applied by staff operating across all areas of LMN's activities.

Develop risk response strategies

The risk management process should **identify and evaluate risks** (for example by the high-medium-low method described) and therefore provide the information necessary for management to decide what the best **response to risk** should be – bearing, reduction, elimination or transfer.

Importance of risk management

Improve financial position

The risk management framework can provide a means of judging the costs of **treating the risks** measured against the **benefits**. It can also help LMN's directors judge whether to take advantage of opportunities, for example property investment.

Minimise surprises and losses

By identifying risks in the **risk register**, the risk management process should reduce the occurrence of unexpected shocks. For example identifying property maintenance as a risk issue should encourage a programme of regular maintenance designed to deal with the risks associated with the types and ages of property.

Maintain reputation

As LMN is a charity, its reputation as a good corporate citizen is very important. Risk management should help it avoid risks to its reputation such as **poor treatment of tenants** or failing to comply with **regulatory requirements**.

Risk management and the internal control system

Internal control is action taken by management to achieve organisational objectives and goals. Internal control thus is bound up with the organisation's strategies, and is therefore also bound up with risk management that is dependent upon the organisation's strategies. Internal control is made up of two elements:

(i)   The **control environment**, the framework within which controls operate and within which attitudes towards risk are an important elements. **Communication** between directors and employees is a key element of the control environment.

(ii)   **Internal controls**, which should be operated when their **benefits outweigh costs**; controls focused on dealing with the most significant risks will have obvious benefits. Because risks as here affect different areas of activity, controls of different types will be required; financial controls, although significant, will not be enough.

Given the risks LMN faces, key controls will include **debtor management, maintenance inspections and logs**, **financial appraisal of new investments** and **tenant satisfaction questionnaires**, as well as **accounting**, **compliance** and **cost limitation** controls.

(b)   **Audit committee's role in internal control**

Under corporate governance guidelines audit committees are responsible for creating a **climate of discipline and control**. To do this, they have to obtain assurance that internal control is working **effectively** and providing an **adequate response** to the **risks** faced.

Importance of management review

The management review provides the audit committee with evidence of whether the **control systems** appear to be effectively managing the most significant risks. It also gives the audit committee an indication of the **scope and quality** of management's monitoring of risk and internal control; does the report appear to be an **adequate review** given the risks faced. The review should provide **feedback** that the audit committee should confirm has led to improvements in the control systems.

Other sources of evidence

However management's review of internal control is only one source of evidence that the audit committee should use to gain assurance. The committee should also receive reports from **staff** undertaking important and high-risk activities such as property investment. They should also receive reports from **control functions** such as human resources or internal audit (if any). Feedback from external sources such as **external audit** or **regulatory visits** will also provide information.

(c)   (i)   **Review of internal controls**

The UK's Turnbull committee emphasises the importance of a regular review and an annual review of internal control as part of an organisation's strategy for **minimising risk, ensuring adherence to strategic objectives, fulfilling responsibilities to stakeholders** and **establishing accountability at its senior levels**.

Regular review

Regular review is an essential part of the strategy for minimising risks. The audit committee is likely to have responsibility for this review, and as best practice recommends at least **three audit committee meetings a year**; this is thus how often the review should take place. Its findings should be communicated to the board.

The review should cover the following areas.

(1)   **Risk evaluation**

Whether LMN is **identifying** and **evaluating** all key risks, financial and non-financial. This is a very significant task given the variety of risks faced, and also the need to devote limited resources to the most important risks.

(2)   **Management response**

Whether **responses and management** of risks are **appropriate**; for example what level of risks should LMN bear without taking any steps (just low likelihood, small consequences risks or any others).

(3)   **Control effectiveness**

The **effectiveness of internal controls** in countering the risks. The board should consider how much controls could be expected to **reduce the incidence** of risks, any evidence that controls have **not been operating effectively** and how **weaknesses are being resolved**. The board would consider evidence such as incidence of bad debts, records of property occupation and complaints from tenants.

Annual review

The annual review of internal control should be more wide-ranging than the regular review, taking into account the **strategic objectives of the charity** and undertaken by the **whole board** rather than just the audit committee. It should examine controls and risk management systems in all major areas, covering in particular:

(1)   **Changes in risks**

The **changes** since the last assessment **in risks faced**, and the charity's ability to **respond to changes in its environment**. For example the board would consider any changes in the charity's credit ratings, also longer-term trends such as changes in the incidence of low income earners.

(2)   **Monitoring**

The **scope and quality of management's monitoring of risk and control**, also whether internal audit is required. In particular the review should consider whether the **scope and frequency of the regular review** should be increased.

(3)   **Reports to board**

The **extent and frequency of reports** to the board; should reports on high incidence, high likelihood risks be made more regularly.

(4)   **Significant aspects**

Significant controls, failings and weaknesses that may materially impact on the financial statements, for example problems over its property portfolio management.

(5)   **Communication to shareholders**

Communication to stakeholders of **risk objectives, targets** and **measures** taken to counter risks.

(ii)   **Disclosures in the annual report**

The report on compliance is a key part of the annual report by which LMN demonstrates its **compliance with regulations** and how it has **fulfilled the differing requirements of its stakeholders**.

Responsibility

The board should also **acknowledge its accountability** for LMN's system of control and **reviewing its effectiveness**.

Risk management

The Turnbull report recommends that as a minimum the board should disclose what has been done to **manage risk** and how the board has **reviewed the effectiveness of the risk management process**. The board should explain the limits of the process (it aims at risk management rather than risk elimination) and disclose any **material problems or weaknesses** that have been found.

ACCA Professional Level

Paper P1

Governance, Risk and Ethics

Mock Examination 2

Question Paper
Time allowed: 3 hours 15 minutes
This paper is divided into two sections: Section 1   This ONE question is compulsory and must be attempted Section 2   TWO questions only to be attempted
Do NOT open this question paper until instructed by the supervisor. Do NOT record any of your answers on the question paper. This question paper must not be removed from the examination hall.

Section A – This question is compulsory and must be attempted

Question 1

Pacific Goods is a large retail company, selling a wide range of goods from small household items such as cleaning materials to garden tools and a limited range of gifts and chocolates. The company was founded in the 1800's and now trades in 23 countries with more than 250 stores. The company's image has in the past been one of being 'cheap and cheerful' – that is staff have been seen historically as always happy to assist customers, although the goods themselves are moderately priced.

Although the company is not a listed company, it has a number of shareholders with significant holdings who are not actively involved in running the business. Most of the shareholders are descendants of the original founders of the company.

In terms of corporate governance, Pacific Goods also maintains an appointment committee and an audit committee. Each committee comprises two executive directors and one non-executive director. Mr Beckett, the Chairman of Pacific Goods and a major shareholder, has always maintained that it is important to follow the principles of corporate governance rather than follow rigorous regulations. The fact that Pacific Goods is not a quoted company confirms his belief that it is the 'spirit' of corporate governance only that needs to be followed. He has argued that it is to Pacific Goods' credit that it seeks to apply the spirit of governance guidance. However as much governance guidance is specifically targeted at listed companies and designed to satisfy the major institutional shareholders who have invested in those companies, it is not really relevant to Pacific Goods' ways of doing business.

The country in which Pacific Goods' Head Office is based follows a principles-based approach to corporate governance, with most of the guidelines being based on the OECD principles of corporate governance. Other local companies, with trading interests in America, have however chosen to adhere to the Sarbanes-Oxley legislation, and this is regarded as acceptable by the company's local stock exchange.

Over the past three years, Mr Carson (the CEO) has attempted to take Pacific Goods more 'up-market'. Ranges of cheap goods were discontinued and more expensive items placed on sale. A new company logo and corporate slogan were implemented in an attempt to re-brand the company. The board of Pacific Goods provided Mr Carson with unanimous support. The directors believed that Pacific Goods would be able to benefit from being able to open stores in upmarket shopping developments. One director commented: 'We should move away from the local malls and into the exclusive ends of large retail developments.' The directors however ignored warnings from some store managers concerning the demographic profile of their customers and how the move would adversely affect that profile.

The risk committee was also concerned that this strategy was not fully evaluated and raised the issue of whether the company was too committed to a speculative course of action and whether the changes to what had previously been successful policies were justified. However, the committee was not provided with the time or information to make an effective evaluation of most of the decisions associated with the strategy. Generally the committee only saw the papers the board saw and discussed the decisions once the board had already made them. The committee comprises one non-executive director and three store managers.

To complement the new image, Mr Carson required store managers to provide detailed monthly reports on achievement of profit and budget variances and insisted on downsizing the number of shop staff to achieve an enhanced level of profit. Remaining staff were also required to work longer hours with only minimal pay increases on an annual basis. Store managers were also to refer a range of decisions (although the exact list was never published) to the newly appointed human resources director, the son of Mr Carson. Mr Carson junior was 24 years old when appointed and had just graduated from business school. Mr Carson junior had not previously been in paid employment, apart from working in Pacific Goods' head office in a couple of summer vacations from business school. The appointment of Mr Carson jnr was made without the involvement of the appointments committee. Mr Carson senior justified his son's appointment, stating that he had all the necessary skills to assist store managers in their difficult task of managing budgets and people. Mr Carson senior commented that his son had all the qualities needed to 'shake things up at the stores.' Some of the other directors had their doubts about the appointment, but

BPP
LEARNING MEDIA

kept quiet as they knew Mr Carson senior rated his son's abilities highly and they did not wish to upset Mr Carson senior.

Unfortunately, the store managers (rather than the board's optimism) were proved correct and the move upmarket was disastrous. Sales at Pacific Goods have fallen by around 25% in the last two years. 40 stores have closed, including upmarket stores that had been opened in large retail developments. One of the reasons for the failure of the upmarket stores according to the trade press has been customer perception of a poor level of service, As a result of these problems, Mr Carson (senior and junior) resigned their positions. The remaining board members are attempting to 'rescue' the company. Mr Beckett collapsed from a heart attack at about the same time and is now convalescing; he does not expect to work for at least six months.

In response to the problems facing the company, the appointment committee has taken the unusual step of appointing Mr Staite to be the company's chairman and CEO. Mr Staite has had significant previous experience in re-focusing corporate strategy; it is the appointment committee's belief that this is the most effective way of ensuring Pacific Goods survives as a going concern over the next few years.

At a recent shareholder meeting, a number of the external shareholders expressed concern about the corporate governance arrangements that the company had been operating, saying that the basis of corporate governance appeared to be very vague and that they needed to enforce some definite rules on the directors. One of the non-executive directors on the board has also indicated that he will not seek re-election next year. He has accused the rest of the board of 'paying lip service to corporate governance best practice, in order to make Pacific Goods appear to be a good corporate citizen.'

Required

(a)   Prepare a memorandum for the board explaining what is meant by the term 'control environment' and criticising the control environment within Pacific Goods.   **(17 marks)**
                                                                                    (including 4 professional marks)

(b)   Explain to the external shareholders the principles-based approach to corporate governance, and construct a case for using this approach. Advise the external shareholders on whether a principles-based approach is appropriate for Pacific Goods.   **(13 marks)**

(c)   Define strategic and operational risk. Identify and describe the strategic and operational risks facing Pacific Goods.   **(13 marks)**

(d)   Identify the ethical and corporate governance issues resulting from Mr Staite's position on the board of Pacific Goods and recommend how the issues can be resolved.   **(7 marks)**

                                                                                                (Total = 50 marks)

Section B – TWO questions ONLY to be attempted

Question 2

Mary Hobbes joined the board of Rosh and Company, a large retailer, as finance director earlier this year. Whilst she was glad to have finally been given the chance to become finance director after several years as a financial accountant, she also quickly realised that the new appointment would offer her a lot of challenges. In the first board meeting, she realised that not only was she the only woman but she was also the youngest by many years.

Rosh was established almost 100 years ago. Members of the Rosh family have occupied senior board positions since the outset and even after the company's flotation 20 years ago a member of the Rosh family has either been executive chairman or chief executive. The current longstanding chairman, Timothy Rosh, has already prepared his slightly younger brother, Geoffrey (also a longstanding member of the board) to succeed him in two years' time when he plans to retire. The Rosh family, who still own 40% of the shares, consider it their right to occupy the most senior positions in the company so have never been very active in external recruitment. They only appointed Mary because they felt they needed a qualified accountant on the board to deal with changes in international financial reporting standards.

Several former executive members have been recruited as non-executives immediately after they retired from full-time service. A recent death, however, has reduced the number of non-executive directors to two. These sit alongside an executive board of seven that, apart from Mary, have all been in their posts for over ten years.

Mary noted that board meetings very rarely contain any significant discussion of strategy and never involve any debate or disagreement. When she asked why this was, she was told that the directors had all known each other for so long that they knew how each other thought. All of the other directors came from similar backgrounds, she was told, and had worked for the company for so long that they all knew what was 'best' for the company in any given situation.

Mary observed that notes on strategy were not presented at board meetings and she asked Timothy Rosh whether the existing board was fully equipped to formulate strategy in the changing world of retailing. She did not receive a reply.

Required

(a) Explain 'agency' in the context of corporate governance and criticise the governance arrangements of Rosh and Company. **(12 marks)**

(b) Explain the roles of a nomination committee and assess the potential usefulness of a nominations committee to the board of Rosh and Company. **(8 marks)**

(c) Define 'retirement by rotation' and explain its importance in the context of Rosh and Company. **(5 marks)**

(Total = 25 marks)

Question 3

At a recent conference on corporate social responsibility, one speaker (Professor Cheung) argued that professional codes of ethics for accountants were not as useful as some have claimed because: 'they assume professional accountants to be rules-driven, when in fact most professionals are more driven by principles that guide and underpin all aspects of professional behaviour, including professional ethics.'

When quizzed from the audience about his views on the usefulness of professional codes of ethics, Professor Cheung suggested that the costs of writing, implementing, disseminating and monitoring ethical codes outweighed their usefulness. He said that as long as professional accountants personally observe the highest values of probity and integrity then there is no need for detailed codes of ethics.

Required

(a) Critically evaluate Professor Cheung's views on codes of professional ethics. Use examples of ethical codes, where appropriate, to illustrate your answer. **(12 marks)**

(b) With reference to Professor Cheung's comments, explain what is meant by 'integrity' and assess its importance as an underlying principle in corporate governance. **(7 marks)**

(c) Explain and contrast a deontological with a consequentialist based approach to business ethics. **(6 marks)**

(Total = 25 marks)

Question 4

During the global economic recession that began in mid 2008, many companies found it difficult to gain enough credit in the form of short-term loans from their banks and other lenders. In some cases, this caused working capital problems as short-term cash flow deficits could not be funded.

Ultra-Uber Limited (UU), a large manufacturer based in an economically depressed region, had traditionally operated a voluntary supplier payment policy in which it was announced that all trade payables would be paid at or before 20 days and there would be no late payment. This was operated despite the normal payment terms being 30 days. The company gave the reason for this as 'a desire to publicly demonstrate our social responsibility and support our valued suppliers, most of whom, like UU, also provide employment in this region'. In the 20 years the policy had been in place, the UU website proudly boasted that it had never been broken. Brian Mills, the chief executive often mentioned this as the basis of the company's social responsibility. 'Rather than trying to delay our payments to suppliers,' he often said, 'we support them and their cash flow. It's the right thing to do.' Most of the other directors, however, especially the finance director, think that the voluntary supplier payment policy is a mistake. Some say that it is a means of Brian Mills exercising his own ethical beliefs in a way that is not supported by others at UU Limited.

When UU itself came under severe cash flow pressure in the summer of 2009 as a result of its bank's failure to extend credit, the finance director told Brian Mills that UU's liquidity problems would be greatly relieved if they took an average of 30 rather than the 20 days to pay suppliers.

> In addition, the manufacturing director said that he could offer another reason why the short-term liquidity at UU was a problem. He said that the credit control department was poor, taking approximately 50 days to receive payment from each customer. He also said that his own inventory control could be improved and he said he would look into that. It was pointed out to the manufacturing director that cost of goods sold was 65% of turnover and this proportion was continuously rising, driving down gross and profit margins. Due to poor inventory controls, excessively high levels of inventory were held in store at all stages of production. The long-serving sales manager wanted to keep high levels of finished goods so that customers could buy from existing inventory and the manufacturing director wanted to keep high levels of raw materials and work-in-progress to give him minimum response times when a new order came in.

One of the non-executive directors (NEDs) of UU Limited, Bob Ndumo, said that he could not work out why UU was in such a situation as no other company in which he was a NED was having liquidity problems. Bob Ndumo held a number of other NED positions but these were mainly in service-based companies.

Required

(a)   Define 'liquidity risk' and explain why it might be a significant risk to UU Limited.   **(5 marks)**

(b)   Define 'risk embeddedness' and explain the methods by which risk awareness and management can be embedded in organisations.   **(7 marks)**

(c)   Examine the obstacles to embedding liquidity risk management at UU Limited.   **(8 marks)**

(d)   Criticise the voluntary supplier payment policy as a means of demonstrating UU's social responsibility.   **(5 marks)**

(Total = 25 marks)

Answers

DO NOT TURN THIS PAGE UNTIL YOU HAVE
COMPLETED THE MOCK EXAM

Answers

A plan of attack

We've already established that you've been told to do it 101 times, so it is of course superfluous to tell you for the 102nd time to **take a good look at the paper before diving in to answer questions.**

First things first

Remember that the best way to use the 15 minutes of reading time in your exam is firstly to **look through the paper** in detail, working out **which questions to do** and the **order** in which to attempt them. Then spend the remaining time analysing the requirements of **Question 1** and highlighting the key issues in the question.

The next step

You may be thinking that this paper is a lot more straightforward than the first mock exam; however, having sailed through the first mock, you may think this paper is actually rather difficult.

Option 1 (Don't like this paper)

If you are challenged by this paper, it is still best to **do the compulsory question first**. You will feel better once you've got it out of the way. Honest.

- There are a lot of application marks in **Question 1**. Having read the requirements carefully, mark against each paragraph the part of the question to which it relates. Use this as the basis of your plan as hopefully the material in the scenario will jog your memory about the corporate governance theory that you need to discuss.

- The scenario in **Question 2** is quite a big help for generating ideas. It is a practical question, so you will not need to use a lot of theory to answer it, just focus on the information you're given.

- By contrast **Question 3** does not have much information in its scenario. If you are not comfortable with ethics, you will probably avoid this question, but it will help if you can quote some real-life examples from ethical codes.

- If you have sat F9 recently, that will be a big help with **Question 4**. (b) is quite a general part, and if you can remember the main elements of the control environment, that will be helpful in (c). If you are not sure what to put for (d), bear in mind that it is only worth 5 marks, fewer than the other question parts.

Option 2 (This paper's alright)

Are you **sure** it is? If you are then that's encouraging. You'll feel even happier when you've got the compulsory question out the way, so why not **do Question 1 first**.

- Although **Question 1** appears to require some fairly basic knowledge, you won't get all that many marks for it. Make sure therefore by marking the question that you identify the relevant issues in the scenario for each part of the question and that you maximise your score by including them within your answer.

- There is potentially lots of information in the scenario that you can use in your answer to **Question 2**. However read the question and scenario carefully to make sure that you cover all the elements that your answer has to contain. Check when you've completed your plan that your answer is complete and answers both requirements in each subsection.

- If you find ethics interesting, you might well answer **Question 3**. There are marks available for theoretical knowledge and also for any examples you can quote from real-life ethical codes.

- If you can remember what you learnt about working capital management in F9, that will be a big help in **Question 4**. If you also have good knowledge of the main elements of the internal environment, that will also assist you significantly in (b) and (c).

Once more

You must must must **allocate your time** according to the marks for the question in total, and for the parts of the questions. And you must must must also **follow the requirements exactly** and indicate which questions you're answering **clearly**.

Finished with fifteen minutes to spare?

Looks like you slipped up on the time allocation. However if you have, make sure you don't waste the last few minutes; go back to **any parts of questions that you didn't finish** because you ran out of time.

Forget about it!

Forget about what? Excellent, you already have.

Question 1

Marking scheme

		Marks
(a)	Up to 3 marks for definition of control environment	3
	Up to 2 marks for each issue covered in company's control environment	12
	Up to 4 professional marks for the form of the answer (memo in which Content is laid out in an orderly and informative manner)	4
		Max 17
(b)	Up to 3 marks for explanation of principles-based approach	3
	Up to 2 marks for each advantage identified	8
	Up to 2 marks for each point about application of approach to company	4
		Max 13
(c)	Up to 3 marks for definitions of strategic and operational risk	3
	Up to 2 marks for each risk described	12
		Max 13
(d)	Up to 3 marks for identification of issues	3
	Up to 4 marks for alternative solutions suggested	4
		Max 7
		50

(a)

Memo

To: Board
From: Consultant
Date: 5 May 20X8
Subject: Control environment in Pacific Goods

You have asked me to give my views on whether there are underlying causes that help or hinder the operation of controls at Pacific Goods. I therefore will explain the significance of the control environment, and comment on the control environment at the company.

Control environment

The **control environment** is the **overall attitude**, **awareness and actions** of directors and management regarding internal controls and their importance in the entity. The control environment encompasses the **management style**, **corporate culture and values** shared by all employees. It provides the **background** against which the various other controls are operated.

Control environment Pacific Goods – overview

While there appear to be the **correct structures** in place to **identify and implement control systems**, such as the risk committee, the structures do not appear to be effective. Specific matters that need to be addressed are noted below.

Risk identification

The risk committee appears to be ineffective because it **lacks clear strategies** for either identifying or dealing with those risks that have been identified. For example, the strategy of attempting to move Pacific Goods 'upmarket' was not fully considered, and the **possibility of failure** was **not considered** by the board.

Company culture

Pacific Goods' standard of customer service has been good. The fact that staff were prepared to assist customers provided a **good company reputation** and **repeat business**. However, the new emphasis on **profitability and cutting of expenses** (including the number of staff in each store) will have **adversely affected the company's image** and **contributed to falling sales**. Similarly, basing store manager performance entirely on **profit** rather than a range of indicators has meant a cultural emphasis on profit, again decreasing the good customer service ethic.

Reporting requirements

The **requirement to send monthly reports on profitability** with detailed comments on variances further implies a change in the company's culture. The detailed review implies a **lack of trust in the store managers**, which will also **decrease the motivation** of those managers. Staff **motivation will also have fallen** as they see an **increased focus on selling** rather than customer service, to say nothing of **redundancies** further decreasing motivation.

Consequences of poor appointment

The appointment of Mr Carson junior may have been premature. While business school will provide some skills, the director **lacked the real world experience and therefore credibility** within the role. It was unlikely that store managers would trust Mr Carson junior with the effect that they may not have deferred decisions to him and neglected to implement his advice.

Authority levels

The **lack of clear explanation of what decisions** would be made by Mr Carson junior was also not helpful. Store managers would have been in the situation of being **accountable for their budgets**, but **not having the authority** to make the decisions they need to manage those budgets effectively. Not only will this have further decreased their motivation, but also it will have **decreased the store manager's credibility** with shop staff as the managers would have been seen to lack the authority to run the store.

Appointment committee

There are two specific weaknesses within the control environment at Pacific Goods in relation to corporate governance. Firstly, the appointment committee can be **over-ridden by the board of directors**. The appointment of Mr Carson junior clearly shows this. There is the risk that inappropriate staff/directors will be appointed into the company, increasing the risk that their duties will not be carried out appropriately.

Risk committee

Secondly, the **risk committee appears to be ineffective** regarding the identification or evaluation of risks. This is due partly to lack of information provision, but also to lack of sufficient senior staff on the committee. Even if a full evaluation of the change in company image had taken place, it is unlikely that one non-executive director could sufficiently influence the rest of the board.

Conclusion

As a matter of urgency, the board needs to address a number of issues to improve the control environment in Pacific Goods. These include taking steps to enhance the profile and the terms of reference of key board committees. At an operational level, store managers' authority needs to be clarified and customer service levels assessed as well as cost control.

(b) **Principles-based approach to corporate governance**

The principles based approach focuses on **objectives of corporate governance** rather than **enforcing the mechanisms** by which those objectives should be achieved. The idea is that principles are easier to integrate into strategic planning systems than detailed rules and regulations.

Advantages of principles-based approach

Difficulty of applying rules

The principles-based approach is particularly useful where **rules cannot easily be applied**. For example, it is relatively straightforward to define rules for internal control systems, but not for areas such as organisational culture or maintaining relationships with stakeholders. Similarly, principles can be **applied across different legal jurisdictions** rather than being based on the legal regulations of one country.

Comply or explain basis

Principles-based approaches are also normally in force in corporate governance terms **on a comply or explain basis**. The extent to which a principle has or has not been applied can therefore be clearly explained, rather than simply stating that a rule has not been followed.

Ease of implementation

The approach is also **easier and cheaper to implement**. Being able to state principles removes the need for detailed or complicated legislation to attempt to cover every possible eventuality and is therefore cheaper from the legislative point-of-view. The law making body of each jurisdiction does not have to spend large amounts of time (and money) producing detailed legislation. From the point of view of companies, the benefit is less 'red-tape' or form filling.

Flexibility for companies

Using principles allows **each entity to decide how to implement those principles**, without having to follow detailed rules or guidelines that may simply not be applicable to that entity.

Investors' decision-making

The principles-based approach means that **emphasis is placed on investors** to decide what a company is doing, rather than the company providing lots of data about rules being followed, but no overall impression of the success or otherwise of the company.

Appropriateness for Pacific Goods

It is unclear whether the principles-based approach is applicable for Pacific Goods. Clearly, the benefits of the approach should apply to the company in terms of being able to **implement procedures appropriate** for the company, particularly in softer areas such as stakeholder communication and employee management.

Lack of commitment

However, the risk of this approach, as identified in Pacific Goods, is that the company may either choose **which principles to apply** from the longer list, or apply those principles in de-minimis form rather than being serious about corporate governance. For example, Pacific Goods does have an appointment committee and risk committee, but the members of those committees **do not have sufficient power to carry out their duties** correctly. Having only one non-executive director on each committee for example means an 'uphill' battle in persuading the board into a course of action and leaves the executives with the easy option of vetoing any suggestions.

Use of rules-based approach

Taking the alternative, a rules-based approach may be more appropriate for Pacific Goods as **compliance** with a set of rules would have to be stated. In other words, the extent of compliance would not be left up to

the company; the **extent would be inherent within the rules or regulations**. Taking this approach would mean, for example, that the appointment committee had the 'correct' numbers of non-executive directors. Obviously areas such as internal controls would still be difficult but at least 'lip-service' could not be paid.

Advice

Overall, a principles-based approach would be appropriate if the directors **actually were happy to follow the appropriate corporate governance guidelines**. Without that compliance, a rules based approach may be preferred, at least in the short term.

(c) **Strategic risks**

Strategic risks are risks that relate to the **fundamental and key decisions** that the directors take about the future of the organisation.

Company strategy

The main strategic risk relates to the **change in company strategy** at Pacific Goods. The directors have in effect risked the entire business in the attempt to move the company 'upmarket'. A strategy change in this way is notoriously difficult (for example even after the attempt to move 'upmarket' Skoda cars are still considered cheap and unreliable even though the company has won reliability awards). As the scenario appears to indicate, it has not worked.

Company culture

There has also been a significant change in company culture. There have been two key changes in this area; firstly the additional requirements placed on store managers and secondly the overall philosophy of customer service being reversed. The new emphasis on profit may succeed although there has been **considerable damage to morale** with respect to redundancies and treatment of store managers.

Liquidity risk

There is some liquidity risk relating to the falling sales, although **no financial information** is **available** to identify any effect on cash flow. However, a fall in volume may indicate that overheads **take a higher proportion of expenses**. In the longer term, Pacific Goods may have **cash flow problems** as falling inflows are insufficient to pay for fixed cash outflows.

Legal risk

There is the possibly of **legal risk** in relation to pay and working hours of staff. Most jurisdictions have **legislation on minimum wage and maximum working hours** and Pacific Goods may be in breach of these. There is specific concern regarding extension of working hours with minimal pay increase as the hourly rate payable is likely to fall, and this fall could be below the minimum wage. Breach of legislation would result in adverse publicity for Pacific Goods.

Operational risks

Operational risks relate to matters that can go wrong on a **day-to-day basis** while the organisation is carrying out its business.

For Pacific Goods, operational risks focus mainly on the business of ensuring that the correct goods are available for sale in its shops at the correct time. Given the focus on profit and downsizing, specific risks in the supply chain include late or **inappropriate orders to re-stock products** (mistakes made in reading inventory levels). In addition, **inappropriate orders could be placed** (store managers not being aware of the product ranges that could appeal to slightly more upmarket customers). **Products could also not be placed** on shelves quickly enough (insufficient staff for restocking).

In other words, overworked staff may cause an increased number of manual errors.

(d) **Issues arising**

Mr Staite is currently the **chairman and CEO of Pacific Goods**. Codes of corporate governance indicate that the roles of chairman and CEO should be taken by different people to avoid excessive power being vested in one individual.

In Pacific Goods, there is a risk that Mr Staite could **abuse his power** on the board, either to further his own interests in Pacific Goods, or to adversely affect the strategy of Pacific Goods without proper discussion at board level. Mr Staite will effectively dominate the board meeting.

Alternative options

There are two options available to Mr Staite.

Firstly, he can **resign from being either the chairman or the CEO** as soon as the appointment committee can identify and appoint a suitable replacement.

Secondly, he can **continue to be chairman and CEO to see out the crisis** at Pacific Goods. This course of action is allowed by codes of corporate governance in the short term only and has been used occasionally. For example, in the early 2000's, Marks & Spencer appointed a chairman/CEO in an attempt to revive the company.

Recommendations

Given Pacific Goods' current problems and Mr Staite's experience in alleviating similar problems in other companies, then it appears reasonable that he can **continue as chairman/CEO at least in the short term**. However, the appointment committee should be seeking suitable candidates to be CEO within a timescale of say 18 months from now.

This action allows Mr Staite to **attempt to see Pacific Goods through the current crisis**, while at the same time identifying the corporate governance requirement of keeping the roles separate wherever possible.

Question 2

Text references. Chapters 1 and 3.

Top tips. This is the sort of situation that will occur frequently in this exam, a board with a mix of corporate governance problems, some obvious, some not.

(a) emphasises the importance of working systematically through a scenario to ensure that you pick up all the examples that will support your answer. You need to use most of the information in the scenario. Note that criticise is a level 3 verb, so that as well as identifying problems, you also need to show why they are problems. (a) emphasises how governance should ensure board accountability; most of the problems discussed in (a) will ultimately result in less accountability.

Note that the role of the nomination committee isn't just to supervise the recruitment process whenever the main board believes the company needs a new director. Recruitment should flow naturally out of the nomination committee's ongoing review of the membership of the board. The second part of (b) is basically asking you to say that a nomination committee would benefit the board because . . .

(c) shows that retirement by rotation is not just a legal requirement, but a key means of ensuring accountability to shareholders. Make sure that you revise retirement by rotation if you didn't know what it was. It does not mean doing different jobs in the same organisation or succession planning.

Easy marks. The role of the nomination committee and retirement by rotation (revision from F4) should have generated easy marks.

Examiner's comments. A lot of students made the most of the many opportunities they had in (a) to criticise the current situation. Answers to (b) were more mixed, with some students confusing the work of the nomination committee with the work of the HR department. Some students appeared not to know the meaning of retirement by rotation in (c).

Marks

(a) 1 mark for each relevant point made — Max 4
1 mark for identification of each criticism — Max 5
1 mark for brief discussion of each criticism — Max 5

Max 12

(b) 1 mark for each relevant role of the nominations committee — Max 5
1 mark for each relevant point on the usefulness of a nominations committee to Rosh — Max 4

Max 8

(c) 1 mark for each relevant point made for definition — Max 2
1 mark for each relevant point made on importance — Max 3
1 mark for each relevant point made on applying to Rosh — Max 2

Max 5

25

(a) **Agency**

Corporate governance codes seek to provide mechanisms for **shareholders** (principals) to enforce accountability on their **agents** (the directors). Here the key shareholder-principals are the shareholders who are not family members who hold 60% of the voting shares.

Reports enforce accountability by, for example, recommending regular contact between directors and significant shareholders and emphasising the **importance of true and fair financial reporting**, so that shareholders can have the information necessary to judge directors' stewardship.

Shortcomings in governance arrangements

Recruitment of directors

The board does **not appear to recruit directors systematically**. The appointment of Mary Hobbes appears to be an attempt to correct a glaring lack of financial accounting experience on the board. However even that appointment appears flawed. It seems to be largely for reasons of ensuring accounting compliance rather than considering the wider contribution a finance director should make, for example assessing the financial aspects of strategic decisions.

Diversity of directors

As a consequence of the poor recruitment procedures, the board lacks a breadth of experience. In particular the non-executive directors should, but do not, bring insights gained from **occupying senior positions in other organisations**. Some governance reports, for example the King report in South Africa, state diversity and varied demographic contribute significantly to board effectiveness; if so Rosh's board is lacking, since Mary is the only woman, and the rest of the board are all elderly.

Number of non-executive directors

Governance reports state that boards should contain a **balance of executive and non-executive directors**, so that non-executive directors are able to make a strong contribution. The UK Corporate Governance Code recommends that at **least half** the directors should be **independent non-executive directors**. Two non-executive directors out of a board of nine does not fulfil this requirement.

Lack of independence of non-executive directors

The UK Corporate Governance Code highlights service on the board of **greater than nine years** as normally indicating non-executive directors are **not independent**, and Rosh's board therefore does not have any independent non-executive directors. The fact that they have worked as **executives in Rosh** within the last five years also indicates a lack of independence. Governance reports highlight the role of independent non-

executive directors in **scrutinising the board's activities** and **serving on key committees** including the audit and remuneration committees (which Rosh does not appear to have).

Discussion of issues

Governance reports stress the importance of board meetings covering key issues for the future of the business. The Cadbury report recommends that the board should have a formal schedule of matters reserved for its decision, including **major strategic issues**. Failure to do this means that Rosh is not being directed properly. The board is unlikely to be taking proper account of changing circumstances and risks in retailing, and hence failing to set the right objectives and to manage risks effectively.

(b)   **Roles of nomination committee**

Review of the board

When undertaking a **regular review of the current board** as well as making new board appointments, the nomination committee needs to consider the composition and strength of the current board. This involves assessing the balance between executives and non-executives, the board's skills, knowledge and experience and the need for continuity and succession planning. The nomination committee should also consider the desirable **size** of the board and number of non-executives, and the **diversity** of backgrounds of board members.

Appointments to board

The nomination committee should **oversee the process for board appointments** and make recommendations on appointment to the main board.

Leadership arrangements

The committee should also consider the adequacy of future leadership arrangements in the company. This needs to include **succession planning** and whether the company should **recruit externally** to fill leading positions.

Role of non-executive directors

The committee should examine the **role of non-executive directors** and consider whether they are spending enough time on their duties.

Usefulness to Rosh and Company

Compliance with governance codes

An active nomination committee should ensure the board fulfils the requirements of codes such as the UK Corporate Governance Code that there should be a **formal, rigorous and transparent procedure** for the appointment of new directors. At present the board appears not to be complying.

Balance of board

A systematic review by the nomination committee should **highlight for the board** areas where the board is still lacking in terms of **skills and experience**, and also consider the **contribution and independence** of non-executive directors.

Strength of board

The nomination committee should also assess whether the board is strong enough in terms of numbers and roles undertaken to **exercise effective control** over Rosh, and to recommend to the directors whether **further executive roles need to be created**.

Succession arrangements

A nomination committee made up of independent non-executive directors should be able to **assess objectively** whether it would be best for the company if Geoffrey Rosh should become chairman, or whether another director or an outsider should succeed.

(c)   **Retirement by rotation**

Retirement by rotation means that every year a certain number of directors retire from the board, and have to offer themselves for **re-election** if they wish to continue to serve. The directors retiring include directors who have been appointed during the year and then directors who have **served the longest on the board**. In most companies this means that directors serve for a **maximum of three years** before being required to retire. The chief executive may be exempt from these requirements.

Importance for Rosh

Shareholder rights

Retirement by rotation is important for Rosh because it gives shareholders who are **not members of the family** their main chance to **judge the contribution of individual directors** and deny them re-election if they have performed inadequately. It is an important mechanism to **ensure director accountability**.

Evolution of board

Compulsory retirement of directors forces directors and shareholders to consider the need for the board to **change over time**. This does not appear to have been considered at Rosh, with the result that board recruitment has stagnated. The fact that only some directors retire each year means that if board changes are felt to be necessary, they can happen gradually enough to ensure **some stability**.

Costs of contract termination

By limiting the length of service period, the **compensation paid to directors for loss of office** under their service contracts will also be limited. Contracts may well expire at the time the director is required to retire and if then the director is not re-elected, no compensation will be payable.

Question 3

Text references. Chapters 9 and 10.

Top tips. (a) is a good example of how the examiner may use the requirement to evaluate. Remember the definition in the front pages of evaluation meaning to determine the value of in the light of the arguments for and against. The word 'critically' reinforces the need to look at the pros and cons.

In (a) you should get a certain amount of mileage from using Professor Cheung's arguments in the question. Partly the disadvantages of codes is that accountants pay too much attention to the examples and not enough to understanding the basic principles. The impact of regional differences is interesting; you will remember that they impact upon individuals' ethical outlook, so how can codes respond. The arguments against the opinion bring out what codes can achieve, particularly minimum standards of behaviour.

(b) emphasises the key concept of integrity. The definition and the importance of integrity represent knowledge you must have; the examiner has laid a lot of stress on it.

(c) just asks for a definition of these two viewpoints. You may be asked in other questions to apply them to a situation where a deontological (absolute) perspective suggests one course of action, a consequentialist (teleological) perspective another.

Easy marks. (b) is the type of question that should represent easy marks; you need to be able to define key concepts and briefly explain their significance.

		Marks
(a)	Award 1 mark for each valid point made supporting codes of professional ethics	6
	Award 1 mark for each valid point made on limitations of codes of professional ethics	6
	Up to 2 marks for using an actual code of ethics by way of example	2
		Max 12
(b)	Definition of integrity – 1 mark for each relevant point	4
	Importance of integrity – 1 mark for each relevant point	4
		Max 7
(c)	Explanation of deontology – 1 mark for each valid point	4
	Explanation of consequentialism – 1 mark for each valid point	4
		Max 6
		25

(a) **In favour of Professor Cheung's views**

Stress on probity and integrity

Professor Cheung emphasises the **key principles** that should be at the heart of accountants' ethical thinking; arguably professional codes, with their **identification of many different situations** lack this focus.

Treatment as rules

Even if ethical codes stress that they are based on principles, evidence suggests that some treat them as a set of rules to be **complied with and 'box-ticked'**. In particular the examples codes give can be treated as actions to be taken in situations with different sets of circumstances where they may not be appropriate.

Situations outside the codes

Giving a lot of specific examples in codes may give the impression that ethical considerations are **primarily important** only when accountants are facing decisions illustrated in the codes. They may **downplay the importance of acting ethically** when facing decisions that are not clearly covered in the codes.

Limited values of codes

International codes, such as IFAC or ACCA, can **never fully encompass regional differences and variations** and thus are maybe of limited value. Focusing on the key principles of integrity and probity, which in all jurisdictions it is agreed accountants should possess, is a simple solution.

In addition the value of international codes may be limited by their not being legally enforceable around the world (although ACCA can **enforce sanctions** against members for serious breaches).

Against Professor Cheung's views

Building confidence in professions

Codes represent a clear statement that **professionals** are expected to act in the public interest, and act as a **benchmark** against which behaviour can be judged. They thus should enhance public confidence in the professions.

Fundamental principles

Both ACCA and IFAC's codes clearly state that they are based on **fundamental principles**, not a rulebook. These fundamental principles include integrity, also objectivity, professional competence, confidentiality and professional behaviour. Guidance is then in terms of **threats to adherence with these fundamental**

principles. They emphasise the importance of professionals considering ethical issues actively and seeking to comply, rather than only being concerned with avoiding what is forbidden.

Minimum standards

The codes state that the ethical principles are **minimum standards** that can be **applied internationally**; local differences are not significant.

Need for application

Although clearly accountants should be following principles of probity and integrity, accountants facing ethical decisions may have **difficulty applying these concepts**. More detailed guidance, based on fundamental principles and with examples, should **assist ethical decision-making**.

Examples

Codes stress that the examples given are **not universal guides for action**. Although accountants may appear to be in very similar situations to those described in the examples, they should exercise their own ethical judgement actively rather than simply following the examples.

Prohibitions

Although a code may be based on principles, it can include explicit prohibitions if principles are not felt to be adequate.

(b) ### Definition of integrity

Integrity is a **strong attachment to morality**. It implies **sticking to principles** no matter what the pressures are to deviate from them. For accountants it implies **probity, professionalism and straightforward dealings in relationships** with all the different people in business life. Trust is vital in relationships and **belief in the integrity of others** is the basis of trust. It also implies qualities beyond a mechanical adherence to accounting standard and law; the post-conventional, highest level of Kohlberg's morality.

Integrity in corporate governance

As corporate governance codes cannot cover every situation, **maintenance of good corporate governance** will sometimes depend on judgements not backed by codes; in these instances integrity is particularly important.

As integrity is partly about proper dealing in relationships, it also underpins the principles of **fair and equitable dealings with shareholders** in corporate governance, particularly in relation to directors exercising an **agency relationship** in respect of shareholders. Good corporate governance is also about **maintaining market confidence** that the company is being run honestly; firm belief that directors have integrity will promote confidence in the company.

(c) ### Deontological

Deontology is concerned with the **application of universal ethical principles** in order to arrive at rules of conduct. It lays down in advance conditions by which actions may be judged. The criteria for judgement are separate from the facts of the situation, and are determined on the basis of **consistency**, **universal application** and **human dignity**.

Consequentialist

The consequentialist approach to ethics is to make moral judgements about ethical decisions on the **basis of their outcomes**. Right or wrong then becomes a question of **benefit or harm**. One example of a consequentialist approach is **utilitarianism** – the principle that the chosen course of action is likely to result in the greatest good.

Contrast between deontological and consequentialist approaches

The main contrast between the two approaches is that the deontological approach takes **no account of consequences**; the same ethical decision will be made in all situations no matter what the differing outcomes of the decision might be in each situation. Consequentialist ethics by contrast **depend on the consequences**.

Question 4

Marking scheme

			Marks
(a)	Definition of liquidity risk	2	
	1 mark for each explanation of manufacturing vulnerability to liquidity risk	Max 3	
			5
(b)	2 marks for definition of risk embeddedness	2	
	1 mark for each method of risk embeddedness	Max 5	
			7
(c)	2 marks for each obstacle identified and examined. 1 mark for identification only	Max 8	
(d)	2 marks for each criticism made	Max 5	
			25

(a) **Liquidity risk**

Liquidity risk is the risk that an organisation is **unable to meet its day-to-day cash flow needs** and is **unable to settle or renew its short-term liabilities**. It is related to its **working capital**. Therefore significant influences over liquidity risk are the levels of inventory, receivables, cash and payables and how these are managed.

UU's position

UU has significant liquidity risk, because of its lengthy **cash operating cycle** – the period from ordering goods from suppliers to receiving monies from customers. As a manufacturing company, it has more significant working capital (particularly more inventory) than the service businesses that Bob Ndumo directs. There are problems in each area of working capital.

Suppliers

UU appears to have some leeway to **lengthen its payment period to suppliers** whilst still remaining within its credit limits. However any lengthening may give suppliers the impression that UU is in financial trouble, particularly as it has publicised its previous policy prominently. Suppliers may impose shorter credit periods than UU has had before, because UU is perceived to be of higher risk. Also if UU's inventory holding policies are to improve by, for example, the introduction of just-in-time ordering, then this will require the co-operation of suppliers.

Customers

The failure to enforce the debtor payment clearly has a significant impact upon UU's liquidity. Fifty days would be regarded as an **excessively generous period** by many companies. The problem UU may face is that attempts to enforce a tighter policy may result in a **loss of customer goodwill**. It could also **threaten the liquidity of customers**. As short-term finance is difficult to obtain from lenders, some customers may be using the **lengthening credit period from UU** as an informal source of short-term finance. Loss of customers will result in falling revenues.

Inventory

UU is a manufacturer and hence inventory pressure will always be an issue. Here excessive inventory is another reason for the lengthy cash cycle, with amounts held **appearing to be too high**. Again however customer pressures appear to explain the high levels. Finished goods levels are high so that products are available for **customers to buy on demand**, reducing the risk of customers purchasing from competitors if UU does not have products available. The raw material levels are being kept high to minimise production time and **hence also minimise the time between customer order and receipt of goods**.

(b) **Embedding risk**

Embedding risk means ensuring that risk **awareness and management** are innate elements of the **systems and culture** of an organisation. It means that **systems** should be **designed and operated** according to the **risk management objectives** of the organisation. It means ensuring that staff are thinking about **risk issues, the severity and frequency of risks**, as an **integral part of their work**. Staff should know that taking unnecessary risks will not only lead to disciplinary action, but be regarded as unacceptable by their fellow employees.

Methods of embedding risk

Management example and communication

Managers must set a good example and show that they will not tolerate recklessness. They should **discuss risk and associated risk responses** in regular communication with employees. **Risk management policies, standards and procedures** should be made **readily available to employees**.

Staff commitment

Staff should **acknowledge their commitment** to managing risks appropriately. **Signing a risk management code** would be a way of doing this. Risk management should be a part of everybody's **job description,** to ensure that staff's responsibilities are clearly defined.

Induction and training

Staff need regular **training** to increase their **awareness of major risk issues**. Risk awareness also needs to be built into the **induction process** so that staff are aware from when they start of the importance attached to risk management.

Information systems

Information systems need to make available **data about risks** and **performance indicators** that demonstrate to directors and managers how well risks are being managed. **Exception reporting** is an important element. This means the **immediate reporting** of certain risks if they rise above a certain level, and also having **channels available for staff to report poor risk management** directly to the board.

Assessment and remuneration

Staff assessment and the **remuneration packages** of staff need to be influenced by how staff handle risk management issues. In some instances staff will have to take risks as part of their jobs. The assessment procedures should consider whether they have handled risk appropriately – examining whether they have been too cautious as well as too aggressive.

(c) **Attitudes of operational managers towards liquidity risk**

Operational managers appear to **underestimate or ignore the consequences of liquidity risk**. Both the manufacturing director and the sales manager appear to give sole priority to meeting customers' requirements at all costs. They ignore the need to take some action to **reduce liquidity risk** and balance this action against the need to keep customers happy. It would appear that liquidity risk management is not a major performance objective of senior operational managers.

Complex organisational structure

The way **responsibilities are allocated** may hinder a unified approach to liquidity management. Inevitably, given the complexity of UU's operations, different senior managers are responsible for control of different elements of working capital. However they all seem concerned with their own areas, and insufficiently focused on the wider corporate objective of maintaining liquidity.

Lax control environment

The **control environment over the sales department** appears to be **poor**. No reason has been advanced why credit periods are so lengthy. Whilst credit control staff may be taking account of the need to keep customers happy, the manufacturing director appears to imply that the long credit periods are due to laxness by credit control staff and poor enforcement of targets.

In addition the manufacturing director does not seem to have taken much action to limit the **decline in profit margins**, suggesting that targets and performance assessment of senior management may also be lax.

Attitude of Brian Mills

Brian Mills is **failing to give a lead in treating liquidity management** as important. He is prioritising the non-financial objective of demonstrating corporate social responsibility over the financial objective of proper management of working capital. Not only will this influence the attitudes of staff, but it may be difficult to change the policy as it is being promoted by the chief executive.

(d) **Personal policy**

The policy has been **driven by Brian Mills** and does not enjoy the support of the other directors. The policy cannot be regarded as a long-term commitment and part of the company's **strategic positioning**, as it appears likely to change when there is a change of Chief Executive.

Costs and benefits of policy

The finance director has highlighted that the policy is **very costly** to UU. As far as the impact on the wider economy is concerned, it is debatable whether UU's policy is **making much difference**. Its suppliers will set credit periods for their own commercial reasons, and perhaps the main thing they require is the certainty that UU will pay within those periods rather than at some artificially early date.

Impact on reputation

How significant **damage to UU's reputation** would be if payment policy changed is **debatable**. As far as wide publicity is concerned, UU may be unlikely to suffer much damage if it merely reverts to paying within credit periods. The fact that one group of stakeholders (not perhaps the most vulnerable group) is being treated favourably may mean that UU does not gain much publicity benefit from its policy. Focusing social responsibility on different stakeholders or charitable causes, also examining more closely the environmental impact of its activities, may result in greater amounts of positive publicity and genuinely be more socially responsible.

ACCA Professional Level

Paper P1

Governance, Risk and Ethics

Mock Examination 3

September/December 2016

Question Paper		
Time allowed: 3 hours 15 minutes		
This paper is divided into two sections:		
Section A	This ONE question is compulsory and must be attempted	
Section B	TWO questions only to be attempted	
Do NOT open this question paper until instructed by the supervisor.		
Do NOT record any of your answers on the question paper.		
This question paper must not be removed from the examination hall.		

Section A – This ONE question is compulsory and MUST be attempted

Question 1

Xuland is a developing country. Certain bodies which monitor different governments consider Xuland to have problems with corruption. Xuland authorities are tolerant of breaches in corporate governance compliance among its listed companies. It is common for police officers to request, and receive, corrupt payments from members of society. There is also corruption among public servants, in educational establishments and in many companies.

In the senior levels of business, there is a network of interconnections between business directors and senior members of the government. The prime minister is known to be a reclusive figure and a law prevents the media or public gatherings from voicing any criticism of him or the government. The newspaper media is largely owned and controlled by the government, which means that published criticism of the government is very rarely seen by people in Xuland. Where it is in evidence, the state often takes drastic action to remove such people or to dissuade them from making public criticisms.

Bob Tong is the chief executive of the country's largest business (Xuland Oil). Xuland Oil had been owned by the government until five years ago. It is now listed on the Xuland stock exchange and has secondary listings in other, more developed countries, where the shares have become attractive to investors. This is because Xuland Oil is a monopoly supplier of energy in Xuland and therefore enjoys a home market without competition. Accordingly, it is believed to make strong profits in Xuland. It also exports energy (oil and gas) outside Xuland to neighbouring countries by pipeline, and to other countries by liquefying the gas and shipping it in very large container ships.

Chief executive Bob Tong is believed to receive a substantial fixed salary. However, he also receives 'rewards' from private sector companies for awarding them large support contracts such as for the supply of oil rigs, ships and other important non-current assets. He considers this a way of making money for his retirement. The culture in Xuland means that he is very rarely criticised in public for his behaviour. There is a listing rule about the separation of the roles of CEO and chairman but it is rarely enforced and Mr Tong is also the executive chairman of Xuland Oil. He considers it important that he occupies both roles to prevent his activities from being too closely scrutinised.

Alice Tuesday, a business journalist from outside Xuland, reported that the figure noted in Xuland Oil's remuneration report was clearly not the true figure of what Mr Tong actually received from his leadership of the company. This was because it failed to report the bribes he received from supply contracts.

A major international policy-making body is considering asking all oil and gas companies to produce a stand-alone environmental report each year, reporting in detail on the company's environmental footprint. This is because of a number of recent, high profile cases, in which the poor environmental performance of oil and gas companies has been questioned. A prominent intergovernmental body believes that oil and gas companies will be helping their own reputations by joining the scheme to produce high quality environmental reports each year.

The initiative proposes that each environmental report should contain a meaningful discussion of how each company is attempting to mitigate the worst effects of its environmental impacts. It has been suggested that this report should include figures on all aspects of a company's environmental impacts and also the changes from year-to-year so that stakeholders can monitor how each oil and gas company is performing over the longer term. Some companies, including Xuland Oil, are resisting this initiative, because the board believes that people in Xuland do not care much about the environment. The company's internal audit function has offered to advise on establishing internal controls, in order to assure the company that the information fed into the environmental report has integrity and is accurate.

Xuland Oil has been criticised in international media for acting as an arm of Xuland foreign policy. This has meant, for example, that countries which are not favoured by the Xuland government are charged higher prices for oil imports. Some of the shareholders have been angry about this, as they see their investment as a way of making reliable long-term returns and most shareholders care nothing about Xuland foreign policy. They believe that Xuland Oil should get on with producing returns and ignore the pressure by the Xuland government to be a part of Xuland foreign policy. The pressure for Mr Tong and the company board to enact foreign policy is thought to be linked to the intimate relations among the elites in Xuland society. Many government ministers and senior business figures went to the same universities and remain close friends outside their working lives.

The journalist, Alice Tuesday, has been investigating the problems at Xuland Oil for some years and has widely reported the corruption in Xuland society. She pointed out that many of the jobs in the Xuland public sector tended to be concentrated among one of the several ethnic groups in Xuland and this, she believed, was anti-meritocratic and did not serve the country's best interests. It was she who exposed Mr Tong for taking bribes on supply contracts. She has also recently accused the prime minister of taking money from public accounts for his own use. She said that Xuland Oil needs to decide if it is a business organisation or a part of the Xuland state, and to notify its shareholders accordingly. Mr Tong is a close personal friend of the prime minister and other senior government ministers. He is also a strong supporter of the government and its policies.

Alice Tuesday's view is that Xuland is structurally corrupt and needs a thorough review of its culture. As a developing country, Alice Tuesday says that it will not become a developed country until it tackles its problem with corruption, including corruption in the police and in the public services. She recently wrote that, 'if Xuland tolerates corruption, it is choosing poverty over development, and this a terrible shame for the decent, hard-working families in Xuland, who deserve a better future. Xuland has been appallingly-led for many years, and the ruling class has badly let down the people of Xuland.'

Required

(a)   Explain why, in the case of Xuland Oil, the shareholders would benefit if the roles of chief executive and chairman were split and an effective non-executive chairman was appointed.   **(8 marks)**

(b)   The bribes which Mr Tong accepted means that the remuneration report does not contain a complete picture of his annual income.

   Required

   (i)   Discuss the importance of completeness in a remuneration report and explain how the inaccuracy of information on the remuneration of executive directors creates a potential agency problem. **(8 marks)**

   (ii)   Explain why most shareholders would support a link between rewards and performance, and why this link is important to shareholders.   **(6 marks)**

(c)   Xuland Oil's overseas investors have encouraged the company to adopt the compulsory environmental reporting in order to ensure that all environmental risks are considered.

   Required

   Explain the importance of effective internal controls and internal audit in underpinning the proposed compulsory environmental reporting requirement.   **(8 marks)**

(d)   Alice Tuesday intends to write an article for international media to discuss several important issues with the governance of Xuland Oil. Draft this article, to include the following content.

   Required

   (i)   Explain the meaning of 'corruption' and discuss the barriers to improving the corrupt practices in Xuland.   **(8 marks)**

   (ii)   Propose measures which might be put in place to defeat corruption in Xuland.   **(8 marks)**

   Professional marks will be awarded in part (d) for flow, persuasiveness, tone and format of the answer.

          (4 marks)

          (Total = 50 marks)

Section B – TWO questions ONLY to be attempted

Question 2

Stefan Krank had been the most successful fund manager at Fortune Investments for the past five years. During this time he had earned a large salary, which was supplemented by considerable annual bonuses from the many profitable investment portfolios he had managed for his wealthy private clients. Consequently, he and his family had become accustomed to a very lavish lifestyle, which was threatened when he started to have a run of bad luck on the markets.

Over the past few months he had been unable to deliver the predicted levels of returns for his clients, so he decided to resort to drastic measures. Initially he tried to recover the position by investing funds in high risk securities to generate higher returns, even though his clients had only ever agreed to medium risk levels for their investments. However, even this tactic failed to deliver sufficient profits and some investments actually lost considerable amounts of money. In desperation Krank's behaviour took a very disturbing turn when he started a fraudulent investment operation where he paid returns to his existing investors from new capital paid into the fund by new investors, rather than from profit earned. He enticed new investors into the scheme by offering them far higher returns than were available from other comparable investments, often in the form of short-term profits which were both abnormally high and unusually consistent. Unfortunately in order to maintain this deception of seemingly perpetual high returns, Krank required an ever-increasing flow of money from new investors which was clearly unsustainable. Over time returns became far more volatile simply because of the higher risk investments and reduced amounts of new investment capital becoming available.

James Reynolds, a wealthy client who wanted to extract value from a fund managed by Krank for his impending retirement, noticed that returns on his fund were showing increased volatility. He demanded an explanation from Krank, who responded by advising him that he must have looked at his fund on a bad day. He assured Mr Reynolds he always aimed to maximise returns on his clients' investments even if this meant bending the rules occasionally. He further claimed that Mr Reynold's fund would both grow in value and stabilise very soon. Mr Reynolds was unconvinced by Krank's weak and unsubstantiated explanation; so he referred the matter to Krank's manager.

Required

(a) Discuss the extent to which the main objectives of an internal control system were not achieved at Fortune Investments, and criticise how the behaviour of Stefan Krank resulted in a clear breach in his duty to his clients as their fund manager. **(12 marks)**

(b) Explain the importance of good quality information both for the effective management of funds, and their monitoring by investors. **(7 marks)**

Stefan Krank had told Mr Reynolds that 'he always aimed to maximise returns on his clients' investments even if this meant bending the rules occasionally' to achieve this.

Required

(c) Explain ethical relativism, and examine how Stefan Krank cannot justify his actions using relativist arguments. **(6 marks)**

(Total = 25 marks)

Question 3

Recent changes to environmental regulations have shifted the onus of responsibility onto companies to prove that their actions did not cause environmental harm, rather than requiring the regulators to prove where fault lies. The board of Oskal Petroleum decided to review its strategic position and how this regulatory change could impact on Oskal Petroleum. The directors concluded that the new regulations potentially exposed their business to considerable costs if they were required to deal with the aftermath of a spillage of any environmentally hazardous substance, such as oil. These costs would be above and beyond any fines or compensation orders which might flow from a related prosecution.

A major spillage from a competitor's oil rig off the African coast several years ago is still under investigation and so far it has resulted in hundreds of millions in related costs, which damaged the business significantly and caused a large and sustained drop in the share price.

Oskal Petroleum, although based in Europe, is a global business with onshore and offshore oil fields in four continents. It has always enjoyed good relations with the host governments in those countries where it has operations, but recently several governments have adopted a more interventionist approach to domestic environmental policy in the aftermath of the African oil disaster. Consequently, the finance director strongly advised the board to set aside an amount of cash equal to 10% of profits, to mitigate against the impact of any costs which might arise if an Oskal oil field suffered a major spillage. The finance director's proposal was approved alongside the decision to undertake a formal environmental risk assessment of all Oskal operational assets throughout the world, particularly in those countries where governments were taking a keen interest in influencing the environmental and social policies of businesses.

In a further attempt to pacify its active stakeholders, and show shareholders that they were taking environmental risks seriously, the board decided to fully adopt the integrated reporting framework. It planned to include the findings from the environmental risk assessment in the next annual report.

Required

(a)   Describe environmental risk, and evaluate the sources of environmental risk which are likely to be identified during Oskal's forthcoming assessment, and suggest ways the company could reduce their impact.

(9 marks)

(b)   Describe a framework which could be utilised by the board of Oskal for the management of risk.   (8 marks)

(c)   Explain the concept of integrated reporting <IR>, and explore how an integrated report covering the six capitals provides insights for the shareholders and other stakeholders of Oskal Petroleum.   (8 marks)

(Total = 25 marks)

Question 4

John Mathers, a qualified accountant and the finance director of the International construction company Parkstone, was recently jailed for 18 months as a result of being convicted of insider trading. Mathers profited from dealing in his company's shares around the time that a $50m government contract was awarded for the construction of 2,000 new social houses, which sent Parkstone's share price soaring in value.

Using a false name to avoid being detected, Mathers bought 100,000 Parkstone shares in small batches regularly during the three-month period before the lucrative deal was finalised, when the price was settled at around $5.40. He sold all of the shares the day after the government-financed building contract was announced when the share price had risen by 22%, thereby making a clear profit of around $120,000.

Mathers was jailed because he used his inside knowledge at Parkstone to personally profit, abusing his senior position in the company because he was privy to all the negotiations leading up the deal. The judge at his trial acknowledged that Mathers had shown genuine remorse for his crime, but the offence was so serious that it warranted a custodial sentence. He said that Mathers used his position as finance director to unlawfully profit from information about the forthcoming contract, and had shown a clear breach of the trust placed in him. He had been motivated by personal greed and knew at the time that his actions were illegal. The judge told him that insider trading was not a victimless crime, and his actions had had a very negative impact on overall public confidence in the integrity of the market.

A spokesman for Parkstone said that they were reassured that an independent investigation into the company's financial conduct surrounding the insider trading incident did not raise any wider governance concerns. He insisted that the despite the gross misconduct of one its directors, the company's internal controls were sufficiently robust to provide the information necessary for the authorities to achieve a successful prosecution of Mathers. It was also acknowledged that because Parkstone had won a building contract for the public sector, it would need to demonstrate that it was delivering value for money throughout the duration of the contract.

Required

(a)   Describe insider trading and how it can compromise directors' corporate responsibilities, and explain how the actions of John Mathers could have undermined general confidence in the stock market.   **(8 marks)**

(b)   Discuss how John Mathers' behaviour was a clear breach of the IESBA [IFAC] code of ethics which, as a professional accountant, he should have strictly followed.   **(10 marks)**

(c)   Explain how Parkstone has a corporate social responsibility to act in the public interest because of the publicly funded building contract awarded, and evaluate how they are able to demonstrate that they are delivering value for money.   **(7 marks)**

(Total = 25 marks)

Answers

DO NOT TURN THIS PAGE UNTIL YOU HAVE
COMPLETED THE MOCK EXAM

A plan of attack

Yes we know you've heard it 102 times but, just in case for the 103rd time: **Take a good look at the paper before diving in to answer questions**.

First things first

Choose which questions to do and decide the **order** in which to attempt them. Then get stuck into analysing the requirements of **Question 1** and identifying the key issues in the scenario.

The next step

You may be thinking that this paper is OK compared with the previous two mocks. Alternatively you may like this paper a lot less than the other two.

Option 1 (Don't like it)

If you are challenged by this paper, it is still best to **do the compulsory question first.** You will feel better once you've got it out of the way. Honest.

- **Question 1** focuses on corruption, its effects and proposals to combat corrupt practices. Part (a) covers the role of the chief executive, chairman, and the effectiveness of non-executive directors. Part (b) deals with the remuneration report and the importance of accuracy, and also considers why shareholders wish to see a link between rewards and performance. In part (c) you are asked to explain the importance of internal control and internal audit with regard to environmental reporting. Part (d) requires the drafting of an article discussing important aspect of corporate governance, with an emphasis on corruption and measures to defeat it. A valuable four marks can be gained for presentation in part (d).

- **Question 2** examines internal controls and the information requirements of a fund management system. It also covers ethical relativism and justifying actions using relativist arguments.

- **Question 3** concerns environmental risk, its sources and a framework for managing risk. There is also a part on integrated reporting and the six capitals.

- **Question 4** is on the topic of insider trading and how this breaches codes of ethics. It also considers the corporate social responsibility of a company to act in the public interest.

Option 2 (It's a pleasant surprise)

Are you **sure** it is? If you are then that's encouraging. You'll feel even happier when you've got the compulsory question out of the way, so why not **do Question 1 first**. Your selection of questions from Section B will depend on which areas of the syllabus you feel more comfortable with, having considered the topics covered (see Option 1 analysis above).

Once, once more

You must allocate your time according to the marks for the question in total, and for the parts of the questions. And you must also **follow the requirements exactly**. It's easy to waffle on this exam if you don't follow the requirements strictly. If your answer contains irrelevant material, you will not be scoring marks efficiently and you will put yourself under **time pressure**. Also make sure you show **clearly** which question you're answering.

All finished and quarter of an hour to go?

Your time allocation must have been faulty. However make the most of the 15 minutes; go back to **any parts of questions that you didn't finish** because you ran out of time. Always write something rather than nothing if you possibly can and try not to leave questions unanswered.

Forget about it!

Just wipe it from your mind.

Question 1

			Marks
(a)		Up to 2 marks for each relevant point to a maximum of 8 marks.	8
(b)	(i)	Up to 4 marks on the importance of completeness in remuneration reports.	
		Up to 4 marks for explaining how inaccuracy of information in the remuneration report leads to an agency problem.	8
	(ii)	Up to 2 marks for each relevant point made, aligning the benefits of aligning executive remuneration with shareholder value.	6
(c)		2 marks for each relevant point on IC or IA at Xuland Oil.	8
(d)	(i)	2 marks for explanation of corruption.	
		2 marks for each relevant barrier. Related to Xuland.	8
	(ii)	2 marks for each relevant point on changing culture.	8
		Professional marks	4
			50

(a) An effective non-executive chairman would bring scrutiny to Mr Tong and his corrupt activities. Having to report to a chairman would mean that he would have to justify his behaviour if challenged by the chairman and this would make corruption less likely. The chairman usually needs to report in a chairman's letter to the shareholders on the state of the board and the company's governance, and in so doing, needs to be a trustworthy figure, capable of chairing an effective board, and holding other directors to account. An effective chairman could stop Mr Tong's corrupt payments by establishing a transparent tendering process and insisting that all supply contracts are subject to that process.

Mr Tong's behaviour is completely unacceptable and represents an ethical failure of leadership on his part. If others see Mr Tong receiving corrupt payments, the 'tone from the top' may mean that other managers lower down the organisation may also seek corrupt payments and this militates strongly against the efficiency of internal processes. It means that contracts are awarded on the size of the bribe and not on the basis of the value for money for shareholders. Companies and countries which tolerate corruption are self-selecting for themselves a lower efficiency and poorer value for money for shareholders (or taxpayers in the case of governments).

The shareholders are receiving poor value for money from Mr Tong's leadership because not only is he paid a 'substantial' reward, he also accepts corrupt payments for the award of contracts. This means that the tendering process is unlikely to be fair and transparent as he is likely to award contracts on the basis of how much of a bribe he will receive from the supplier. An effective chairman could ensure he gave his energies to pursuing value for money for the shareholders and not concentrating on his own corrupt forms of income.

An effective chairman could encourage the establishment of internal controls and an internal audit function for the monitoring of all activities related to the tendering and allocation of contracts. By making these functions report to a nonexecutive audit committee, the transparency and integrity of these processes can be assured and this is in the interests of shareholders because it ensures that all supply contracts are based on best value for money and not on the size of the bribe paid to Mr Tong.

(b) (i) **Importance of completeness of remuneration report**

Remuneration reports are important because they provide shareholders with information on how much the executive directors are paid and how their remuneration is configured. This is important so that shareholders know how they are motivated and how well their rewards are aligned to the interests of shareholders.

If there are payments (albeit illegal payments) missing from the remuneration report, then shareholders are not receiving accurate information on how Mr Tong is being rewarded. This, in turn, undermines the whole purpose of remuneration reporting as it is intended to convey important disclosure to shareholders. Missing payments means that shareholders are not being given the whole picture in the remuneration report and this represents a serious agency failure. The chairman of the remuneration committee (usually a senior non-executive director) should ensure that this information is fully accurate.

Agency issues with the incomplete remuneration report

Inaccuracy or a lack of completeness in a remuneration report means that the shareholders are not receiving a full picture of what Mr Tong earns. This undermines the purpose of remuneration reporting because shareholders do not know how Mr Tong is rewarded for performance and this means that shareholders, who collectively own the company, are receiving false information and this is a serious agency failure on the part of Xuland Oil.

The shareholders of Xuland are being lied to in the remuneration report and this is a serious lapse of trust on the part of Xuland Oil. As the collective owners of Xuland Oil, all material information should be disclosed to facilitate shareholder decision-making, but an incomplete remuneration report is a breach of this trust. The acceptance of bribes on his awarding of company contracts is such a serious breach of the trust placed in the CEO, that shareholders have a legal and ethical right to know bout this income, yet it is unaccountable in terms of the remuneration report.

The incompleteness of his income also means that shareholders are unable to assess Mr Tong's performance in terms of his leadership of the company. Shareholders may look at what the CEO is paid and assess that against the company's performance in that year to decide whether they are getting good value from the CEO. Without a full picture of his income and how he is rewarded to act in the shareholders' interest, shareholders are unable to see how his income is linked to company performance.

(ii) The agency problem is reduced when the interests of directors and shareholders are aligned. One way of doing this is to make the rewards of directors linked to the performance of the business they are managing. Shareholders tend to prefer this approach for several reasons.

It motivates the directors in that they make more income (usually in performance bonuses or share options) when the company does well. Typical measures upon which performance bonuses are based include return on equity or performance based on the nature of the company's operations such as sales, internal control compliance or other, context-specific measures. In each case, improvement is in line with the interests of shareholders in creating shareholder value.

It encourages directors to think about creating shareholder value, as it is this which provides directors with higher bonuses or the maximisation of the value of share options. This includes retaining talent, operating efficiently in resource markets and innovating to produce efficiencies and controlling internal activities. Any increase in organisational efficiency or effectiveness will serve the interests of shareholders and also potentially add to the bonus for the director and, accordingly, performance-related rewards serve the interests of both shareholders and directors.

It makes directors more accountable to shareholders. The issue of how directors remain strongly accountable to shareholders is one of the key challenges in corporate governance. By forcing directors to create shareholder value, the accountability link is strengthened as they are motivated to think in terms of maximising shareholder value. Directors are less likely to behave in ways which reduce shareholder value, and are more likely to think about how to maximise their own value to shareholders.

(c) The proposed new mandatory environmental reporting requirement will represent a challenge to many companies which do not currently produce an environmental report. Xuland Oil is currently resisting the requirement, but it is likely that because the shareholders are international in their distribution, they may not be able to resist the requirement over the longer term. Any reporting requirement, including environmental reporting, must have effective internal controls in place to ensure that the information reported is accurate, complete and in a state which can be employed and understood by shareholders and other interested stakeholders.

The requirements of the new reporting requirement contain some specific internal control issues.

The company will need internal controls to monitor and assure the collection of relevant metrics for the measurement of environmental measures. This will include measurements on resource consumption (eg water, energy) and emissions (eg of excess heat, pollutants). These will need to be accurately measured in order for Xuland Oil to be able to reports its progress each year against agreed measures in line with the reporting requirements.

The internal controls need to ensure that the metrics are measured in the same way each year to allow for year-to-year comparisons. Accordingly, standard forms of measurement will need to be established, which can be repeated consistently year-on-year in order to report consistently to interested readers. In this regard, agreed ways of measuring will need to be agreed, perhaps written up into a manual of agreed practice and enforced and audited by the internal audit department. There may be some need for environmental impact or resource usage targets to be set and variances between these targets and actual performance measured and investigated.

Because of the need to report on how environmental impact is being mitigated, it is important to have suitable 'good news' stories to report, and favourable trends in resource consumption and emissions. Internal controls can be employed to continually monitor certain measurements in order to ensure there is progress to report upon. It may be, for example, that water or energy use can be reduced by improving or redesigning internal processes which would be a good news story to report in subsequent years. The same argument could be applied to any of the company's emissions, such as of noxious emissions, polluted water or similar.

Internal audit can audit the processes used to gather and measure the environmental inputs and outputs. The need to audit this information assures the accuracy of the reporting. This is important in making the report trustworthy, and therefore, trusted by users. The integrity of reporting rests upon an internal process which assures the robustness of the measurement and reporting, and internal audit facilitates this.

(d)   (i)   Corruption, of which the offering and acceptance of bribes is an example, is a serious departure from the highest standards of integrity in the operation of an organisation. Mr Tong has shown himself to be corruptible in his pursuit of irregular payments in exchange for the offering of supply contracts. The effect of this is to reduce the efficiency of company operations and to undermine the confidence shown in Mr Tong by the shareholders of the company.

It is likely that Mr Tong and other senior officials in Xuland will resist any attempts to improve the situation for the following reasons:

First, there is a culture of offering and accepting corrupt payments in Xuland. The case scenario explains that there is corruption among police officers, among public servants and others. Once corrupt practices become normalised and embedded in a culture, and are seen to go unpunished, it is very hard to challenge them. If people grow up in a climate in which bribes are offered and accepted, they may begin to feel that this behaviour is normal and then it becomes a taken-for-granted part of the culture in Xuland. As with any cultural norm, it can be hard to challenge it in public.

Second, Mr Tong and others in senior positions in business can make a lot of money in what is seen in Xuland *society to be normal business activity*. Mr Tong does not seem to accept the argument that his personal enrichment is at the expense of shareholder value and so it seems unlikely that he will see the case for change. He may see his personal enrichment as a right, associated with his position as chief executive of Xuland Oil, and this is manifestly part of the problem: he has no right to additional money other than the pay allocated to him by the remunerations committee. So, it is a moral failure on his part if he sees his personal enrichment as a right.

Third, the senior members of society on Xuland are often highly interconnected, and there is a culture of making facilitation payments (bribes) for the award of public sector contracts and other capital investments. If contracts are offered to friends and allies among government supporters, new entrants to the provision of services are unlikely to be successful and this further concentrates power in the hands of a relatively small group of people in senior positions in government and industry.

(ii)   When it comes to defeating corruption in any society such as in Xuland, a complete change in culture is required in the country. This would involve a radical change in Xuland including among public servants, and a change in expectations, in the same way that some beliefs have been changed in some countries in line with changed values. There needs to be a recognition in Xuland that all forms

of corruption are wrong, and this would require a change on what are seen as ethical norms in the country.

The change in culture should include support for anybody challenging corruption, whether in the public sector or in public companies. Those willing to challenge corruption or the taking of bribes should be supported by senior management in whatever organisation they are working in. This would also help with the 'tone from the top' ensuring that corruption is not tolerated and that management is always supportive of those challenging corruption at any level.

It seems appropriate to open up public sector vacancies to all ethnic groups in Xuland and not to concentrate appointments to one ethnic group. By making appointments competitive from any ethnic group, diversity in the public sector will be encouraged and wider range of opinions will be given on matters of public policy. By encouraging diversity, it will be more difficult to condone corrupt behaviour and greater scrutiny will be present. By allowing and encouraging conversation and more intense inter-relationships in this way, all public sector activities will enjoy greater public scrutiny.

Legislation could be introduced, in which any form of corruption is outlawed. There would need to be high profile prosecutions of officials, and public servants, so that the intolerance of corruption is recognised by those able to offer and accept corrupt payments. If people are seen to be punished for corrupt practice, then this will help to facilitate the change necessary. This could be accompanied by a tone from the top of society (government ministers and business leaders), stating that government and business contracts are all awarded based on transparent and public tendering processes. If these tendering processes could be made available to the public (such as on government websites), it would create more confidence in the processes.

It could be explained in public places (such as the media) that it is unlikely that Xuland will develop into a developed country if it continues to tolerate large and small examples of corruption. Corruption creates inefficiencies in society and it is fundamentally undemocratic, and, in each case, an ethical failure. It also costs businesses and, in government corruption, taxpayers, a great deal of money in lost earnings as contracts are awarded based on the size of the bribe rather than value for money for the taxpayer or shareholder. It needs to be explained that corruption, as Alice Tuesday said, keeps people in poverty and excludes Xuland from becoming a fully developed country with all the benefits of that.

Question 2

Marking scheme

			Marks
(a)	Up to 2 marks for each internal control objective evaluated in relation to Fortune Investments.		
	1 mark only if the fact that objectives were not achieved is not included.	(Max = 10 marks)	
	Up to 2 marks for each criticism of Krank's behaviour.	(Max = 4 marks)	12
(b)	Up to 2 marks for each characteristic of good information for fund management.	(Max = 6 marks)	
	Up to 2 marks for each characteristic of good information for investor monitoring.	(Max = 4 marks	
	1 mark if the point lacks detail or application.		7
(c)	Up to 2 mark for explanation of ethical relativism.		
	Up to 2 marks for each aspect of Krank's behaviour examined.		
	Only 1 mark if not explained in terms of relativism.		6
			25

(a)   The main objectives of any internal control system are to manage the inherent risks faced by the organisation as far as is reasonably practicable. They comprise the following:

1.   Business activities should be conducted in an orderly and efficient manner, with internal procedures and practices strictly adhered to. It is apparent that Stefan Krank showed very little regard to both internal procedures and the wishes of his clients when he circumvented internal controls in order to deliver higher returns.

    However, by acting as he did, Krank put those funds which he managed at a far higher level of risk than that authorised by his clients, who were totally unaware of his unauthorised actions. The internal control system failed to ensure that he acted in line with client's instructions.

2.   The assets of a business need to be adequately safeguarded, a prime consideration for a business like Fortune Investments whose basic role is to manage funds on behalf of its wealthy clients. Unfortunately, the actions of Krank directly threatened the value of the funds he had under his control, with riskier investments actually resulting in lost value.

    By failing to safeguard his clients' funds, Krank's behaviour could have vicariously damaged the reputation and financial standing of Fortune Investments. This would have arisen if the funds he managed had incurred losses which the company were unable to cover.

3.   Fraudulent activities or material errors should be both detected and prevented by the internal control system. Significant errors and any fraud could be detected through management checks and by the audit of internal procedures; neither of which seem evident in the case of Fortune Investments.

    The fact that Krank had been the most successful fund manager for the company, delivering the best results for his clients possibly elevated him to a status which went unchecked, a clear weakness in the company's internal control system. It was only because James Reynolds escalated his concerns about his investment fund to Krank's manager that any action would have been instigated; and this was far too late.

4.   Accounting records must be both complete and accurately maintained. This could not have been the case at Fortune Investments because Krank tried to confuse Mr Reynolds with statements which revealed little resemblance to the reality of his investment fund. The company directors have obligations under corporate governance provisions and legal responsibilities to maintain accurate accounting information. Therefore as Krank failed to record the true value of clients' funds, they are at risk of charges of false accounting and the criminal consequences which might arise.

5.   Financial information must be prepared and available in a timely fashion. In the case of Fortune Investments, the information on the performance of individual investment funds must be available as and when the client requires it. To suggest that Mr Reynolds looked at his fund on a bad day which did not accurately represent its true performance infers that clients are reliant on Krank to furnish them with information at a time of his choosing. This arrangement is open to abuse and manipulation, as demonstrated by Krank.

Krank's behaviour

Stefan Krank's behaviour clearly breached the duty of care he owed to his clients. He was placed in a position of trust as their fund manager, which he abused in order to satisfy his own personal need to maintain his lifestyle by earning large bonuses. The clients unwittingly believed that their investments were being managed in a fund within their risk profile, when Krank was acting quite recklessly with their money.

Krank was employed by Fortune Investments to use his knowledge and skills to deliver high returns to their clients but within a controlled environment by following procedures and adhering to the expressed wishes of the investors. However, by disregarding company procedures, he failed to act in the best interest of his clients. This was compounded by the confused and wrong information which he gave to Mr Reynolds, further demonstrating a lack of care and diligence in the performance of his duties.

(b)   **Funds management**

Good quality information is necessary so that management can monitor business performance. In the case of Fortune Investments, this would have ensured that they were able to understand the level of risk the

business was being exposed to by the actions of Stefan Krank. They could then have taken necessary mitigating actions to reduce the risk to an acceptable level.

However, for this to be possible, the information used would require certain distinguishing characteristics:

1. It would need be accurate particularly because of the nature of the business under consideration. Complete knowledge of how individual funds are performing would allow senior managers to initiate appropriate procedures should they become suspicious about the performance of any individual fund manager. If the board had taken a more proactive stance and obtained accurate information about the funds which Krank managed, then the resultant losses and damage to clients' investments could have been avoided.

2. The information would have to be readily available in real time rather than being reliant on data compiled and submitted periodically by the fund managers. As the individual funds are invested on open capital markets, it should be possible to directly monitor their performance continuously, with alerts set up for any funds which appear to be performing outside agreed parameters. Fortune Investments should have invested in a management information system which enabled real time access to financial markets.

3. The board needs to maintain a comprehensive view of all clients' investments so that they can appraise how the business is performing holistically. Consequently investments information must be complete since any gaps would provide both a confusing and distorted picture which could possibly lead to the wrong decisions being taken.

Investor monitoring

Similarly individual investors, like James Reynolds, should be able to monitor constantly the performance of their funds so that they can be reassured that their investments are safe and delivering expected levels of returns in a risk managed way. This information would allow investors to decide whether to withdraw their money from the fund, maintain their fund as it is, or even invest further. However, such decisions are only possible if the information can be relied on for accuracy and be continuously available.

The current arrangements at Fortune Investments means that investors are overly reliant on their fund managers to supply them with information about the performance of their investments. This allows fund managers like Stefan Krank, acting as the investors' agent, to filter information ensuring that only positive results are reported and so deflecting any criticism of their own performance.

(c) **Ethical relativism**

Relativism adopts a pragmatic view by accepting that all circumstances are different, and therefore there is a need to apply different moral rules for varying situations and conditions. Indeed, relativists accept that there are numerous sets of moral rules and these can change over time because they are strongly influenced by prevailing cultures. However, the most striking feature of a proponent of ethical relativism is that they will determine what a correct action is by making reference to the conditions they face at that particular time rather than being guided by a pre-determined set of rules.

Stefan Krank's unethical behaviour

Stefan Krank's actions cannot be justified in ethical relativist terms, particularly because of his underlying motive of self-interest. However, by accepting that he 'always aimed to maximise returns on his clients' investments', it is reasonable to conclude that he assumed this pragmatic approach to investment decision making could be acceptable. However, he was aware that Fortune Investments attempted to impose a set of working practices on all fund managers to maintain control over their business, but these did not allow him to achieve his profit maximising objective. Therefore he elected to use his own initiative and skills to deliver strong returns on all funds by whatever means he thought appropriate, which proved to be successful for quite a long time. He was able to justify this to himself because his clients had been happy with the growth in their funds and his employer regarded him as its most successful fund manager, however, his actions clearly contravened company policy and were professionally unethical.

When the financial positions he held took a turn for the worse, he did not revert to a more risk averse approach but instead he undertook a highly dubious and illegal practice. The use of newly invested funds as a means of reporting profit on existing investments was both fraudulent and impossible to defend on any ethical grounds. Yet Krank believed he was doing the right thing and expected that eventually he would recover his position and return to normal levels of performance, so he believed his actions were justified. However, at the root of Krank's actions was his need to maintain his earnings at a level he and his family had enjoyed for several years, but in doing so he was harming those he was paid to serve and displaying a poor sense of morality and professional ethics.

Question 3

			Marks
(a)	Up to 2 marks for description of environmental risk.		
	Up to 2 marks for an evaluation of each source of environmental risk.	(Max = 4 marks)	
	Up to 2 marks for each risk reduction suggestion.	(Max = 4 marks)	
			9
(b)	Up to 2 mark for each descriptive element of a risk management framework.		
	[The suggested solution uses COSO]		
	Only 1 mark without reference to the Oskal situation.		8
(c)	Up to 4 marks for a detailed explanation of integrated reporting.		
	1 mark for each capital explained in context.	(Max = 6 marks)	
	½ mark if not related to Oskal Petroleum.		9
			25

(a) Environmental risk can be described as a loss or liability which arises from the effects of the natural environment on an organisation, or a loss or liability arising out of the environmental effects of the organisation's operations.

In the case of Oskal Petroleum, the principal risks will arise out of how its oil exploration, extraction and distribution processes could negatively impact [environmental footprint] on the natural environment in the vicinity. This risk would be exacerbated if the operations take place in a sensitive area, such as near a concentration of population or a designated area of significant importance for flora and fauna. A business consequence of environmental risk is that it may suffer significant costs and a loss of reputation if a problem arises.

Therefore during Oskal's forthcoming assessment it is essential that it identifies its sources of environmental risk.

Non-renewables

The core operations of Oskal will result in a steady depletion of non-renewable natural resources, namely oil. However, whilst there is a constant economic demand for oil derived products and services, Oskal has a justification for extracting oil from its onshore and offshore fields. In order to deflect criticism, it could aim to reduce its environmental footprint by implementing complementary measures to promote sustainable development in other areas. It could set a target to reduce the amount of fresh water consumed in its cooling systems; instead it could recycle water through its plant and machinery.

Unplanned spillages

Oil extraction may lead to spillages, most frequently caused by equipment failure, errors committed by employees and extreme environmental [weather] conditions. The environmental consequences of accidental discharges are especially severe when they occur near to shore, or in remote areas which cannot be cleaned up quickly. Oil spills may seriously impair the functioning of the marine ecosystem by: deterioration in the chemical composition of the water and its physical characteristics, resulting in deaths of living organisms as a result of oil products penetrating the surface layers of the skin and plumage, forced changes in migration routes, spawning and so on.

By undertaking carefully planned maintenance of all facilities, training employees to the highest standard and developing robust early warning systems, the likelihood and impact of any spillage will be significantly reduced.

Atmospheric emissions

Emissions of pollutants into the atmosphere are a common feature of operating oil fields. The most widespread source of such emissions is the burning of surplus quantities of hydrocarbons in the course of testing and exploiting wells. The burning of fossil fuel such as oil has been shown to make a significant contribution to climate change by emitting high quantities of greenhouse gases, which are known to damage the ozone layer and possibly leads to 'global warming'.

Although it would be clearly impossible for Oskal to operate as an oil company without some level of atmospheric emission, the overall effect could be reduced if the firm developed an environmental management system and considered its environmental impacts more holistically, offsetting its greenhouse gas emissions with improved recycling, waste management, etc.

Regulatory non-compliance

Due to the dangerous and environmentally damaging nature of the oil industry it is highly regulated, however, the regulations can vary significantly between countries and regions. So a firm like Oskal, with global operations, must have systems in place which ensure full compliance with all local and international regulations in all of its oilfields. Failure to do so could result in high financial penalties and the possible removal of operating licences, both of which would badly harm the business.

(b)   The board of Oskal must have a thorough understanding of all the key risks which affect the company, as well as an appreciation of what is being done to effectively manage them. The COSO Enterprise Risk Management (ERM) framework describes a way of linking a company's objectives to what it needs to do to actually achieve them, namely manage its risks.

ERM considers risk management in the context of business strategy, but applying it to every level of the organisation. Therefore everyone in the organisation has some responsibility for ERM, but the board is ultimately responsible and should assume ownership of risk management. ERM is primarily designed to identify potential events which, if they occur, could harm an organisation and to manage risk within its defined risk appetite. Consequently ERM should be able to provide reasonable assurance to the board of Oskal, and vicariously to its shareholders, that the business will achieve its strategic objectives.

ERM is an iterative process which comprises eight discrete stages:

Control environment

This is essentially the general tone from the top which the company adopts towards risk management, and so provides the basis for how risk is viewed and addressed. Emanating from the top of the organisation, the control environment is embedded in the company's culture and defines its risk appetite. Oskal will need to accept a level of risk commensurate with the level of returns expected from its shareholders, however, the board must also bear in mind the nature of the risks inherent to its industry.

Objective setting

The company's risk appetite must be aligned to its business strategy, which is achieved by the setting of suitable risk-adjusted objectives. The objectives must be agreed before management is able to identify any potential events which may affect their achievement. Oskal is likely to set challenging objectives to generate profitable returns for its shareholders, but within its risk tolerance boundary.

Event identification

These are the internal and external events, sometimes triggered by uncontrollable sources, which can ultimately affect the company's ability to achieve its objectives. Some of the events may present the business with positive opportunities whereas other present risks. In the case of Oskal, this could include an extreme weather event causing a fracture to an oil pipeline.

Risk assessment

Risks are analysed, considering likelihood and impact, as a basis for determining how they should be managed. Since likelihood can be measured in terms of probabilities and impact in terms of its financial consequences, it is possible to quantify the risk assessed and then prioritise relative importance to the operations at Oskal.

Risk response

Although not an automated process, management can then select an appropriate response to the individual risks assessed. Responses include avoiding the risk altogether, reducing it to an acceptable level, transferring it to a third party or accepting the risk if it falls within the pre-determined appetite. This will be key to Oskal as they will not wish to jeopardise the business by an inappropriate response to a potentially damaging risk.

Control activities

The company then devises policies and procedures, which are implemented to help ensure the risk responses are effectively carried out. At Oskal, this will include the standard operating procedures for its oil rigs to ensure that health and safety remain a prime consideration and environmental spillages are kept to a minimum.

Information and communication

Relevant risk information must be communicated in a manner which is readily understood, and in a timeframe which enables people throughout the company to carry out their responsibilities. In Oskal, it is essential that managers have information on the performance of all aspects of the business so that they can detect any unforeseen deviations and take appropriate mitigating action to avoid the consequences of the risk being realised.

Monitoring

Finally the whole process of ERM is monitored and modified as necessary. Like any system, it requires periodic update to reflect the changing operational environment, regulatory framework and the specific risks faced by Oskal.

[**Note:** *Other appropriate risk management frameworks could be used to structure an answer to this requirement*]

(c) **Integrated reporting**

Integrated reporting <IR> is a more concise communication of an organisation's strategy, governance and performance. It demonstrates the links between the organisation's financial performance and its wider social, environmental and economic context. Additionally, it illustrates how organisations create value from their activities over the short, medium and long term. The main purpose of <IR> is to enable more effective board level decision making, improve the quality of information available to investors, and encourage more integrated thinking and business practices.

The use of <IR> at Oskal will encourage the preparation of a report which shows its performance against strategy, explains the various 'capitals' used and affected, and gives a longer term view of the organisation and enable its stakeholders, like host governments, to make a more informed assessment of the organisation and its prospects.

<IR> capitals

All organisations depend on various forms of capital for their success. These 'capitals' store value which eventually become the inputs to the company's business model. The capitals will increase, decrease or transform through the various activities undertaken by the organisation. Therefore it is important that a company like Oskal is able to measure and monitor the use of its capitals, which can be incorporated into its annual report.

These capitals are classified under the following six headings under <IR>:

Financial capital is the pool of funds available to a company, including both debt and equity finance. The focus is on the source of funds, rather than its application which results in the acquisition of manufactured or other forms of capital. Oskal must be able to source sufficient financial resources to deliver its strategy and achieve its objectives, so by providing such information to its investors it will inspire greater confidence.

Manufactured capital is seen as human-created, production-oriented equipment and tools, with a distinction drawn between inventory and plant and equipment. These are the tangible assets which are employed by the company to create value. In Oskal, this would include the very expensive drilling and extraction equipment.

Intellectual capital is a key element in the company's future earning potential, with a tight link and contingency between investment in R&D, innovation, human resources and external relationships which can ultimately determine the company's sustainable competitive advantage. The intrinsic value in Oskal lies within its many oil reserves and it is essential that an accurate valuation appears on its statement of financial position, as any significant error could affect its share price. Oil companies usually have a considerable stock of intellectual capital and have large R&D budgets.

Human capital is the individual capabilities, knowledge, skills and experience of the company's employees and managers, as they are relevant to the task at hand. Oskal is operating in a knowledge-based industry and is highly dependent on the ingenuity of its employees to create and maintain its business value. Therefore reporting information on human capital will give a very valuable insight for the users of annual reports.

Social and relationship capital in a business context include community acceptance, government relations and customer loyalty. It is only by building relationships that a company can retain its social licence to operate. This is particularly pertinent for Oskal, which must maintain a licence to operate in each country, which is granted by the host governments. So investing in developing a sound business relationship with government authorities will ultimately help it to continue in business.

Natural capital includes naturally occurring resources, such as oil, which can be used by businesses to provide a return. The extraction of oil is the core business of Oskal, so providing detail about the levels of extraction compared to previous periods, and by area, will give stakeholders a very useful insight into the operation of the company. Oil companies also need to report on their 'environmental footprint' and the impact they have on the wider natural capital such as on the quality of water, causing damage to land and the sub-terrain, or to the atmosphere.

Question 4

			Marks
(a)	Up to 2 marks for a description of the insider trading/dealing. Up to 2 marks for a description of how directors' responsibilities are compromised by insider trading. 2 marks for every point explaining how Mathers' actions could impact on investor confidence in the stock market.	(Max = 4 marks)	8
(b)	Up to 2 marks for each principle discussed in the context of the insider trading described. Maximum of 1 mark if the point raised did not specifically refer to the actions of John Mathers and only a maximum of ½ mark available for identifying or listing each of the fundamental principles.		10
(c)	Up to 2 marks for an explanation of public accountability in this situation. 1 mark if point not related to the scenario . Up to 2 marks for a description of public interest issues at Parkstone. 1 mark if point not related to the scenario. 1 mark for each value for money criterion evaluated.		7
			25

(a)   **Insider trading**

Insider trading can be described as the illegal purchase of shares by someone who is in possession of useful inside information specific and precise about a company's performance and business prospects, and would affect the share price if made public. Clearly John Mathers abused his position as finance director at Parkstone to personally profit from the knowledge he had of an impending major contract which would be viewed positively by the financial markets. The sensitive inside information used by Mathers in this crime had not been made public at that time, yet he knew that when it was made public it would have a significant positive effect on the company's share price.

Directors' responsibilities

As a member of the board of Parkstone, Mathers had a duty of care to indemnify the company against any losses caused by any negligent behaviour. He held a fiduciary position in relation to the company, where he was required to act in good faith and in the best interest of both the company and its shareholders. In fact as a director, he had a duty not to make a personal profit from the company's business activities; so by failing to fully disclose his interests he was negligent in his duties.

As the company's finance director, Mathers would have both expressed and implied authority to deal in all financial matters which pertain to the ongoing success of the company, acting as an agent for the shareholders and promoting the success of the company. It is apparent that the insider trading perpetrated by Mathers compromised his core duties and responsibilities as a director of a public company in general, and as its finance director in particular. Apart from breaking the law, there were clear violations of corporate governance provisions which define the role of directors and safeguard the interests of shareholders and other stakeholders.

Confidence in the market

When news broke that Mathers had misused inside information to gain an advantage for himself, it would have caused a general loss of confidence in the integrity of the market, with the effect that investors would be reluctant to invest as much in the market going forward. For Parkstone, if it gains a reputation of insiders misusing sensitive and confidential corporate information for their own purposes, it will see its share price fall and the required cost of capital [returns to shareholders] rise significantly.

In the stock market more generally, if insider trading is viewed as more systemic, the loss in confidence among shareholders may result in them withdrawing their investments. This in turn will drive up the cost of capital for all companies by way of a compensating risk premium, possibly damaging the prosperity of the whole domestic economy. It is possible that if the equity finance required for corporate investments cannot be raised, it leads to market failure and, in the worst case scenario, to a crash of the whole stock market system. Therefore insider trading can have severely damaging consequences if it is not eliminated at source.

(b)   As a professionally qualified accountant, John Mathers was duty bound to comply with the following five fundamental principles which underpin the code of ethics issued by his professional body:

Professional behaviour

Accountants must comply with all relevant laws and regulations and shall avoid any action which may discredit the profession. It is clear from the statement made by the judge in court that Mathers knew that by insider trading he was breaking the law, so when he was caught it would have come as no surprise that he was liable for prosecution by the authorities. The publicity arising from his crime would have identified his professional status as a qualified accountant, and so indirectly brought the accountancy profession into disrepute.

Integrity

Integrity requires accountants to be straightforward and honest in all their professional and business relationships. Integrity also implies fair dealing and truthfulness, two characteristics which Mathers clearly failed to display. He was in effect found guilty of misleading his colleagues, possibly providing them with false statements about his real intentions and actions. The fact that he used a false name to cover his tracks when purchasing shares illegally clearly illustrates his profound lack of integrity.

Professional competence and due care

All accountants have a continuing duty to maintain their professional knowledge and skill at a level required to ensure that employers receive competent professional service, and at the same time they must act diligently in accordance with applicable technical and professional standards when providing professional services. The behaviour of John Mathers, although not suggesting a lack of knowledge and skill, was misplaced. He did not act with due care in the interests of Parkstone, but instead proceeded to damage the reputation and standing of the company in the market.

Confidentiality

Accountants must respect the confidentiality of information acquired as a result of professional and business relationships, and shall not disclose any such information to third parties without proper and specific authority or unless there is a legal or professional right or duty to disclose. Similarly, confidential information acquired as a result of professional and business relationships shall not be used to the personal advantage of members or third parties. The $120k profit earned by Mathers from insider trading was only possible because he used confidential business information for his own elicit purposes, and so represented a breach of professional confidentiality.

Objectivity

Accountants should not allow any bias, conflicts of interest or the undue influence of others to compromise their professional or business judgement. Mathers was placed in a position of trust as the finance director of a listed company and he had a fiduciary duty to act in the best interests of its shareholders. However, by using his insider knowledge of the forthcoming contract, he abused this trust placed in him, instead he acted in his own self-interest with greed as his primary motive.

(c) **Public accountability**

The board of Parkstone has a duty and obligation to ensure that the building works covered by the terms of the government contract are satisfactorily performed and completed within the agreed timescale and within budget, otherwise the company may face a consequential penalty for failure. However, as the contract is publicly financed, it assigns additional obligations on the company and its board, as they have effectively been entrusted with limited public resources.

The board is accountable for both the financial and social outcomes of the works undertaken to those who have assigned such responsibilities to it, in this case the government authority who awarded the contract. In effect the board must ensure that public money is spent properly.

Public interest

Public interest is concerned with delivering benefit for the general public at large, as opposed to solely serving the interests of a company and its shareholders. This view holds that society as a whole has a stake in publicly funded ventures, such as the Parkstone building contract, and therefore warrants protection by the government.

The insider trading at Parkstone has no direct impact on the contract which was awarded. However, it may subsequently affect the ability of the company to deliver the building works as specified, for example, if shareholders withdraw their investments due to a loss of confidence in the company and its management. Therefore it is essential that the board of Parkstone is able to demonstrate that they have used public money only for the purposes intended, and the contract has achieved value for money.

Value for money

Parkstone should be able to confirm and report to the government authority that they are delivering value for money using the following criteria:

Economy

This entails obtaining suitable quality inputs at the lowest price available. Parkstone would have been awarded the contract following a competitive tendering exercise, so provided they stay within budget it will be an economic use of public money.

Efficiency

This involves delivering the required works to an appropriate standard at minimum cost, time and effort. In effect the government will get an acceptable return on the public money invested in the social housing, and Parkstone will be able to deliver a profit to its shareholders.

Effectiveness

This criterion is primarily concerned with delivering desired pre-determined objectives. So provided Parkstone is able to build the 2,000 social houses to the standard in the particular specification covered by the contract, and within agreed timescales, it will have been an effective use of public money.

Review Form – Paper P1 Governance, Risk and Ethics (02/17)

Name: _____   Address: _____

_____

_____

How have you used this Kit?
(Tick one box only)

☐ Home study (book only)

☐ On a course: college _____

☐ With 'correspondence' package

☐ Other _____

Why did you decide to purchase this Kit?
(Tick one box only)

☐ Have used the complementary Study Text

☐ Have used other BPP products in the past

☐ Recommendation by friend/colleague

☐ Recommendation by a lecturer at college

☐ Saw advertising

☐ Other _____

During the past six months do you recall seeing/receiving any of the following?
(Tick as many boxes as are relevant)

☐ Our advertisement in *Student Accountant*

☐ Our advertisement in *Pass*

☐ Our advertisement in *PQ*

☐ Our brochure with a letter through the post

☐ Our website www.bpp.com

Which (if any) aspects of our advertising do you find useful?
(Tick as many boxes as are relevant)

☐ Prices and publication dates of new editions

☐ Information on product content

☐ Facility to order books off-the-page

☐ None of the above

Which BPP products have you used?

Study Text	☐	*Passcards*	☐	*Home Study Package*	☐
Kit	☑	*i-Pass*	☐		

Your ratings, comments and suggestions would be appreciated on the following areas.

	Very useful	Useful	Not useful
Passing P1			
Questions			
Top Tips etc in answers			
Content and structure of answers			
Mock exam answers			

Overall opinion of this Kit	Excellent	☐	Good	☐	Adequate	☐	Poor	☐

Do you intend to continue using BPP products?   Yes ☐   No ☐

The BPP author of this edition can be emailed at: accaqueries@bpp.com

Please return this form to: Head of ACCA & FIA Programmes, BPP Learning Media Ltd, FREEPOST, London, W12 8AA

Review Form (continued)

TELL US WHAT YOU THINK

Please note any further comments and suggestions/errors below.